MARVEL MASTERWORKS

PRESENTS

THE MIGHTY THOR

VOLUME 17

COLLECTING

THE MIGHTY THOR Nos. 267-278
& MARVEL PREVIEW No. 10

LEN WEIN • WALTER SIMONSON
ROY THOMAS • JOHN BUSCEMA

Collection Editor
Cory Sedlmeier

Book Design
Nickel DesignWorks

SVP Print, Sales & Marketing
David Gabriel

Editor in Chief
C.B. Cebulski

Chief Creative Officer
Joe Quesada

President
Dan Buckley

Executive Producer
Alan Fine

MARVEL MASTERWORKS: THE MIGHTY THOR VOL. 17. Contains material originally published in magazine form as THOR #267-278 and MARVEL PREVIEW #10. First printing 2018. ISBN 978-1-302-90972-7. Published by MARVEL WORLDWIDE, INC., a subsidiary of MARVEL ENTERTAINMENT, LLC. OFFICE OF PUBLICATION: 135 West 50th Street, New York, NY 10020. Copyright © 2018 MARVEL No similarity between any of the names, characters, persons, and/or institutions in this magazine with those of any living or dead person or institution is intended, and any such similarity which may exist is purely coincidental. **Printed in China.** DAN BUCKLEY, President, Marvel Entertainment; JOHN NEE, Publisher; JOE QUESADA, Chief Creative Officer; TOM BREVOORT, SVP of Publishing; DAVID BOGART, SVP of Business Affairs & Operations, Publishing & Partnership; DAVID GABRIEL, SVP of Sales & Marketing, Publishing; JEFF YOUNGQUIST, VP of Production & Special Projects; DAN CARR, Executive Director of Publishing Technology; ALEX MORALES, Director of Publishing Operations; SUSAN CRESPI, Production Manager; STAN LEE, Chairman Emeritus. For information regarding advertising in Marvel Comics or on Marvel.com, please contact Vit DeBellis, Custom Solutions & Integrated Advertising Manager, at vdebellis@marvel.com. For Marvel subscription inquiries, please call 888-511-5480. **Manufactured between 6/22/2018 and 9/3/2018 by R.R. DONNELLEY ASIA PRINTING SOLUTIONS, CHINA.**

10 9 8 7 6 5 4 3 2 1

MARVEL MASTERWORKS
CREDITS

THE
MIGHTY THOR
NOS. 267-278 & MARVEL PREVIEW NO. 10

Writers: Len Wein (Nos. 267-271, *Marvel Preview* No. 10)
Roy Thomas (Nos. 272-278)
Bill Mantlo (*Marvel Preview* No. 10)

Pencilers/Layouts: Walter Simonson (Nos. 267-271)
John Buscema (Nos. 272-278)
Jim Starlin (*Marvel Preview* No. 10)
Val Mayerik (*Marvel Preview* No. 10)
Virgilio Redondo (*Marvel Preview* No. 10)
Rudy Nebres (*Marvel Preview* No. 10)

Inkers/Finishers: Tony DeZuniga (Nos. 267-271, *Marvel Preview* No. 10)
Tom Palmer (Nos. 272-277)
Chic Stone (No. 278)
Val Mayerik (*Marvel Preview* No. 10)
Jim Starlin (*Marvel Preview* No. 10)
Virgilio Redondo (*Marvel Preview* No. 10)
Rudy Nebres (*Marvel Preview* No. 10)

Letterers: Joe Rosen (Nos. 267-278, *Marvel Preview* No. 10)
Karen Mantlo (*Marvel Preview* No. 10)

Colorists: Glynis Wein (Nos. 267-271, 276-278)
George Roussos (Nos. 272, 273)
Bob Sharen (No. 274)
Ben Sean (No. 275)

Editors: Len Wein, Roy Thomas & John Warner

Color & Art Reconstruction: Wesley Wong & Sheila Johnson (Nos. 267-278)
Michael Kelleher & Kellustration (*Marvel Preview* No. 10)

Special Thanks: Benny Gelillo, Ralph Macchio & Walter Simonson

THOR CREATED BY STAN LEE, LARRY LIEBER & JACK KIRBY

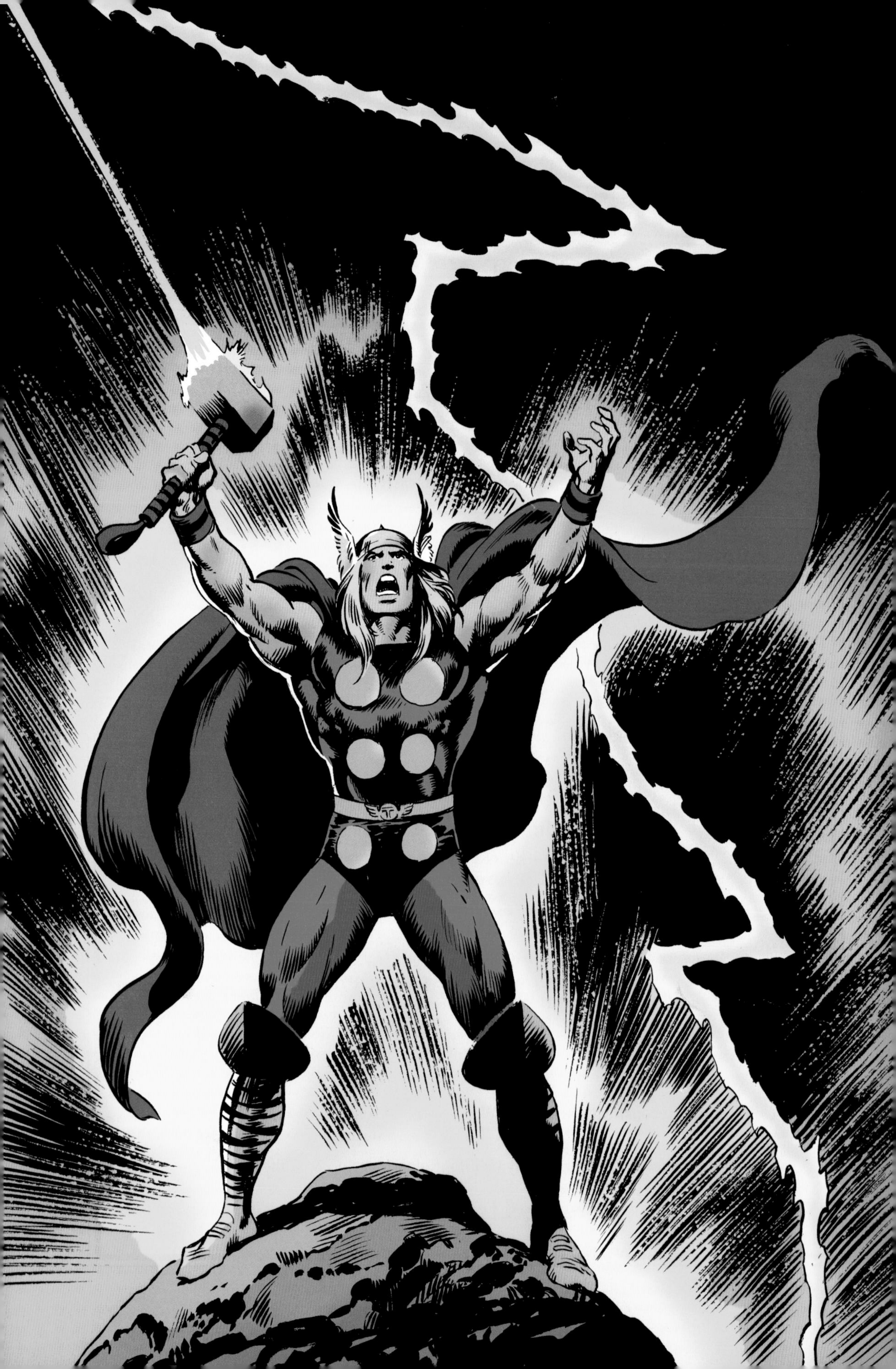

MARVEL MASTERWORKS
CONTENTS

INTRODUCTION
BY ROY THOMAS

Back in my Editor in Chief days of 1972-74, I'd valued the presence of my young pal Gerry Conway, 'cause I felt he was the only guy around besides Stan and myself who could handle the Elizabethan/ King James Bible patois into which Stan had evolved the *Thor* dialogue—so if Gerry hadn't been writing that feature, I might've had to, and I had other things I'd rather do. Luckily, when Gerry moved on, his buddy Len Wein was right there to pick up the slack, and he proved a worthy successor...even if, on the cover and splash page of *Thor* #270, he succumbed to the ungrammatical temptation to have the son of Odin shout, "Lay down and die!" Well, nobody's perfect.

Still, Len, teamed with relative newcomer/penciler Walter Simonson and inker/finisher Tony DeZuniga, produced some fine *Thor* tales in the first part of 1978, even if Walt was still a couple of years away from his groundbreaking stint as writer and artist of the Thunder God's comic. His and Len's Damocles (even without a sword to hang over our heads)...Stilt-Man (with adamantium-alloy armor, this time)...Blastaar...Faust...these were good opponents for Thor. But, for reasons that I know nothing of, it was decreed that #271 was that creative team's swan song on the title—and, for reasons I *likewise* know nothing of, the powers-that-were in New York offered it to me out in Los Angeles.

I'd loved Thor ever since I'd first bought *Journey into Mystery* #83 in summer of 1962. Yet, except for two issues of *Thor* in '75, I'd been content to utilize him in *The Avengers*, leaving his solo adventures to others.

Still, when the opportunity to script *Thor* came along again in '78, I decided to take the bull by the Viking-helmeted horns. I was still mostly avoiding getting entangled with Marvel's mainstream heroes; but I figured, hey, Thor spends most of his time in Asgard now, so I wouldn't need to have him interact with Spidey and the rest.

I suspect the fact that John Buscema was the penciler had something to do with my eager acceptance. If I knew in advance Tom Palmer would be inking those pencils, that clinched it. I'd loved the run of *Avengers* issues the three of us had done together half a decade earlier.

I started by having Thor recount an actual Norse myth about himself and his adopted brother Loki. I did that primarily to gain time to figure out precisely what I wanted to do with the character; and the chances are that, when I was handed the assignment, I had to get a plot synopsis out to John pronto. By the time I finished it, however, I'd figured out the direction I wanted to go.

Around the time in mid-1965 when I first wandered into Marvel's minuscule offices, Stan as writer/ editor and Jack Kirby as co-plotter/penciler were finishing up my favorite of their Thor storylines to date. Reporter Harris Hobbs had taken a photo "proving" Thor and Dr. Don Blake were one and the same. So Thor had let himself be talked into taking Hobbs to Asgard—more in admiration for his determination than because of any blackmail threat. It was, I believe, the first time a human being had walked the Rainbow Bridge in the series. As it turned out, Hobbs mostly just wound up following Thor around; his camera smashed to smithereens, he couldn't even take photos of Thor battling the Absorbing Man there. Worse: Hobbs was later made to *forget* everything he'd seen in Asgard—except in dreams.

Well, evidently such dreams eventually knocked down the wall between Hobbs and his memories, because at the end of *Thor* #272 he informs the Thunder God that he's now a TV reporter, and he's promised his network to shoot a special about the Norse deities—*"and I'm gonna do it on location—in Asgard!"*

Thor turns him down flat and flies off. But Loki, god of never-ending mischief, helps Hobbs and a two-man TV crew (Joey on sound, and Red on camera) stow away inside a huge computer Thor has agreed to transport to immortal Asgard for safekeeping.

But—did I say "immortal"? Despite Stan often using that word to refer to Thor and his fellow Asgardians, those of us who were enthusiasts of actual Norse mythology knew they were *not* immortal like the Greco-Roman gods. They were just super long-lived—and their final fate had not only been predicted, it had actually been vividly *shown* to them, including in one of the Kirby-drawn "Tales of Asgard" a decade earlier. The twilight of the Norse gods would eventually, inevitably come, and it had a name: Ragnarok.

Loki not only intended to bring Ragnarok about; he liked the idea of it being filmed. Back in the 1960s, there'd been a famous hippie slogan—"The revolution will not be televised!"—and Loki was determined Ragnarok *would* be. Even if it became the *last* thing the inhabitants of Earth—Midgard—ever saw.

To that end, I began, with Big John's magnificently skillful help, fulfilling the prophecies that led to Ragnarok. Stan and Jack had played a bit fast and loose with them in that yarn wherein the prophetess Volla laid out the main outlines of what the Germans/Teutons called *Götterdämmerung*... but I was determined to follow the medieval "script" more closely. Both the Elder and Younger Eddas of Norse tradition—also referred to as the Poetic and Prose Eddas—had told the story of the Twilight of the Gods, with minor variations, back in the 13th century, and that was good enough for me. (Now if only somebody could tell me for certain what "Edda" means—either "grandmother" or "poetry," depending on which medieval scholar you ask, apparently.)

First, Odin has to return from a mission, minus one of his two eyes...so he does. He relates how he lost it in order to gain wisdom about the coming end of his world. Not that it would help anybody much.

Then other gods and goddesses return to Asgard for their last stand. Even Thor's buddy Balder gets killed for real in the run-up to Ragnarok, because the myths said he did. The prophecy is coming true. I also brought in Norse deities never before seen in Marvel comics, such as Hermod the messenger (I've always wondered why his name's so close to that of the Greek messenger god Hermes) and Sigyn, Loki's loving wife who's nonetheless willing to guide the hand of blind Hoder when he looses his fateful arrows at her errant husband.

But there was one added little twist I'd decided to toss into this particular telling of Ragnarok (which had previously been threatened several times in the Thor subdivision of the Marvel Universe).

I was going to bring in the "real" Thor.

Like I said, I'd loved the Lee/Kirby incarnation of Thor (as midwived by Larry Lieber) since the get-go. But I'd always been aware that, in myth, Thor had *red* hair, not blond, and would never have been called "Goldilocks" by friend or foe. He also rode around in a cart pulled by goats—an image that for some reason had had little appeal for Stan or Jack. But I was prepared to run with it!

And that's where cameraman Roger "Red" Norvell came in.

His hair came from the prerequisites of Norse myth, and his name from that of Red Norvo (né Kenneth Norville, one of the primo jazz xylophonists—not that there was a long list). With Loki's aid, he dons the Belt of Strength that in myth belonged to Thor, and becomes a more mythologically true version of Thor. In fact, he's able to do what far fewer souls had been able to do in decades of Marvel comics than they have in just a few years of Marvel movies—namely, wrest Thor's hammer Mjolnir away from him. (Reliving that scene in *Thor* #276 reminded me of how I'd disliked having his hammer destroyed by Hela in the 2017 film *Thor: Ragnarok*. That and Thor's ill-advised haircut—even if the barber *was* Stan the Man himself—were pretty much the only blemishes on an otherwise excellent movie. But that's just my personal taste, of course.)

An aside: At this point, readers' letters regarding *Thor* #272-plus began to be printed in letters sections. They were a mixed bag, at least at first. One reader referred to that issue as "Roy Thomas' greatest triumph." I was less pleased by another reader's anger at my bringing back "your obnoxious creation, Harris Hobbs"—unaware, apparently, that Hobbs was a Stan-and-Jack concoction. But by then, I was well into my Ragnarok retelling, and no fan mail was about to convince me it wasn't a story worth relating. Luckily, over the ensuing months, most readers approved enthusiastically—including at the newsstands. One letter writer, in fact, rhapsodized about how this storyline was the first to ever make Norse mythology "realistic" to him—which had been the reason Harris Hobbs and crew had been dragged to Asgard for this particular Ragnarok. If a significant number of people hadn't liked the story arc, it wouldn't have been collected. Still, I didn't feel total vindication for John's, Tom's and my efforts till I learned the sequence was due to be preserved between hard covers. That's my own particular version of "immortality." The closest I can come, anyway.

One moment in *Thor* #277 has particular personal resonance for me—the scene in which Loki is bound upon a mountaintop by "adamantine chains." I tossed that in because it harked back to the same words in a 1960s translation of Aeschylus' early Greek tragedy, *Prometheus Bound,* which had a similar scene. In a 1968 *Avengers* yarn, I'd mutated "adamantine" into the noun "adamantium," the name of the hardest substance ever imagined (or, as far as I'm concerned, imaginable). So this Loki scene was my own secret little homage to that earlier moment. Somehow, there seem to be echoes and similarities between Norse myths and Greek—and the chainings of Prometheus and Loki are a pair of those, methinks.

The Norse, in fact, had done the Greeks one better. While the bound Prometheus suffered from an eagle swooping down every day to tear at his liver, which was restored overnight only to be attacked anew come morning, the fettered Loki must endure the endlessly dripping, searing venom of the Midgard Serpent. His loving wife Sigyn catches some of the poison in a bowl and thus spares Loki a moment of torment—but every few seconds she must empty the bowl, and when she does, the venom strikes him anew. Even Dante in his *Inferno* didn't come up with anything more horrendous than that. So naturally, it belonged in a Marvel comic book about the Twilight of the Gods!

The "Ragnarok/TV" storyline ended in #278, after seven issues, and while I'll let the purchaser of this volume read its dynamic denouement for him/herself, I won't keep you in suspense: I was pleased with the way it turned out.

Well, there was *one* slightly sour note. For whatever reason, the final installment was inked not by Tom Palmer but by Chic Stone. I've nothing but respect for Chic as a professional; but I'd never warmed to his thick-line approach to inking on the mid-1960s *Avengers* and *X-Men*...or, earlier, over Kirby's *Fantastic Four*. I knew Chic had sufficient talent to ink in various styles; but Stan liked those thick lines, so naturally Chic kept them. Lots of readers liked them, too—and they still tell me so, to this day. To me, though, it had made those comics resemble coloring books, with their heavy outlines meant to contain youngsters' attempts with crayons. Chic did a superior job on *Thor* #278, but I'd still have given a reasonable percentage of my wages for that issue to his favorite charity if Tom Palmer had stuck around to ink the Ragnarok finale. Still, I don't recall a lot of readers complaining. "The tale's the thing," as someone once said.

In the end, this Ragnarok was both real—and, I suppose, as ephemeral as the others that had preceded it. Still, I've had a number of middle-aged folks come up to me at comics conventions and tell me it was their favorite of various Marvel Ragnaroks—at least maybe until Walt Simonson did his version, a few years later. Well, I guess bridging the gap between the best of Lee & Kirby and the superlative 1980s work done by Walt isn't the worst thing in the world.

At story's close, I had Thor fly off to begin another epochal storyline—the Judgment of the Celestials, emanating from Jack Kirby's *The Eternals*, which would begin in 1978's *Thor Annual* #7. Meanwhile, this volume ends with two stories from 1977's black-and-white magazine *Marvel Preview*—one of the blond-haired son of Odin, and one of his erstwhile buddy Hercules.

Len scripted the Thor one, and Jim Starlin, who was already beginning to concoct some of the most cosmic adventures in Marvel history (and thus in comics as a whole), was right there to aid and abet Len in a tale of the Thunder God's younger days.

For his part, in the Hercules tale, Bill Mantlo, a less-sung but talented writer, chose to follow a path that was roughly analogous to my own in *Thor* #272. His tale, ably illustrated by Val Mayerik, was a riff on one of Hercules' best-known mythological exploits—the days when he was a member of the crew of the *Argos,* as the Greek hero Jason led the so-called Argonauts in the quest for the Golden Fleece.

Bill, Len, and I, and the various artists involved…we were out to entertain you. That's all we were paid to do, all we were asked to do. If sometimes we tried to go a little further and introduce you to the wonders and enchantments of myth and legend beyond the comic book page—well, that's stuff we did on our own. Because we loved those old stories…and because we were convinced that *you*'d love them to.

And you know what? We were pretty much right!

2018

Roy Thomas has been a writer and often editor in the comics field since 1965, far more often for Marvel than for anyone else, and still works with Stan Lee on the Spider-Man *newspaper strip. He was pleased to see his Valkyrie and Grandmaster concepts (concocted with John Buscema, who else?) pop up in* Thor: Ragnarok *and maybe another film or two down the line. Still, though he's proud of his small contribution to the Marvel Cinematic Universe, he's even prouder of having worked on Marvel Comics.*

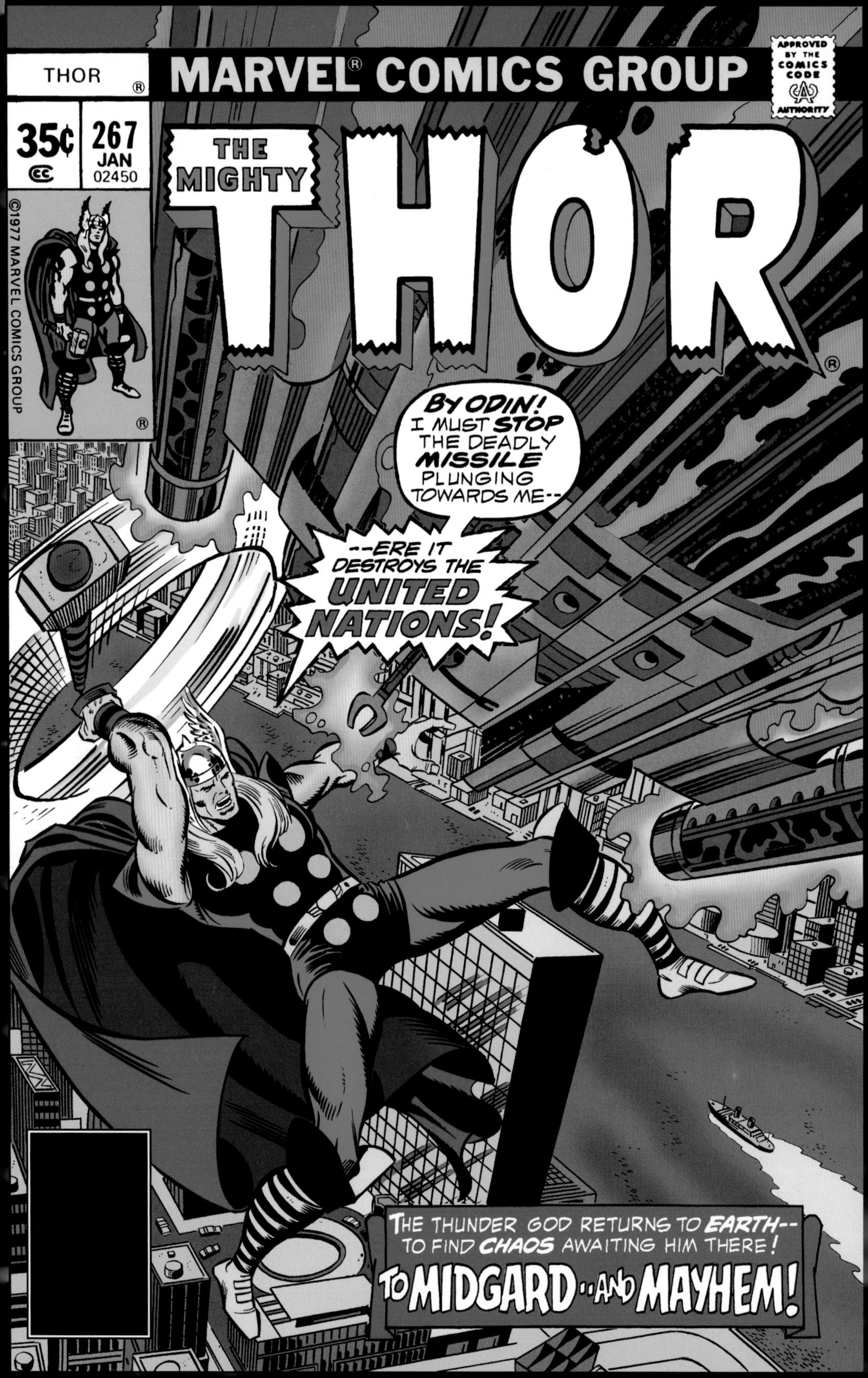

THOR
MARVEL COMICS GROUP
APPROVED BY THE COMICS CODE AUTHORITY
35¢
267
JAN
02450
©1977 MARVEL COMICS GROUP
THE MIGHTY THOR
BY ODIN! I MUST STOP THE DEADLY MISSILE PLUNGING TOWARDS ME--
--ERE IT DESTROYS THE UNITED NATIONS!
THE THUNDER GOD RETURNS TO EARTH-- TO FIND CHAOS AWAITING HIM THERE!
TO MIDGARD--AND MAYHEM!

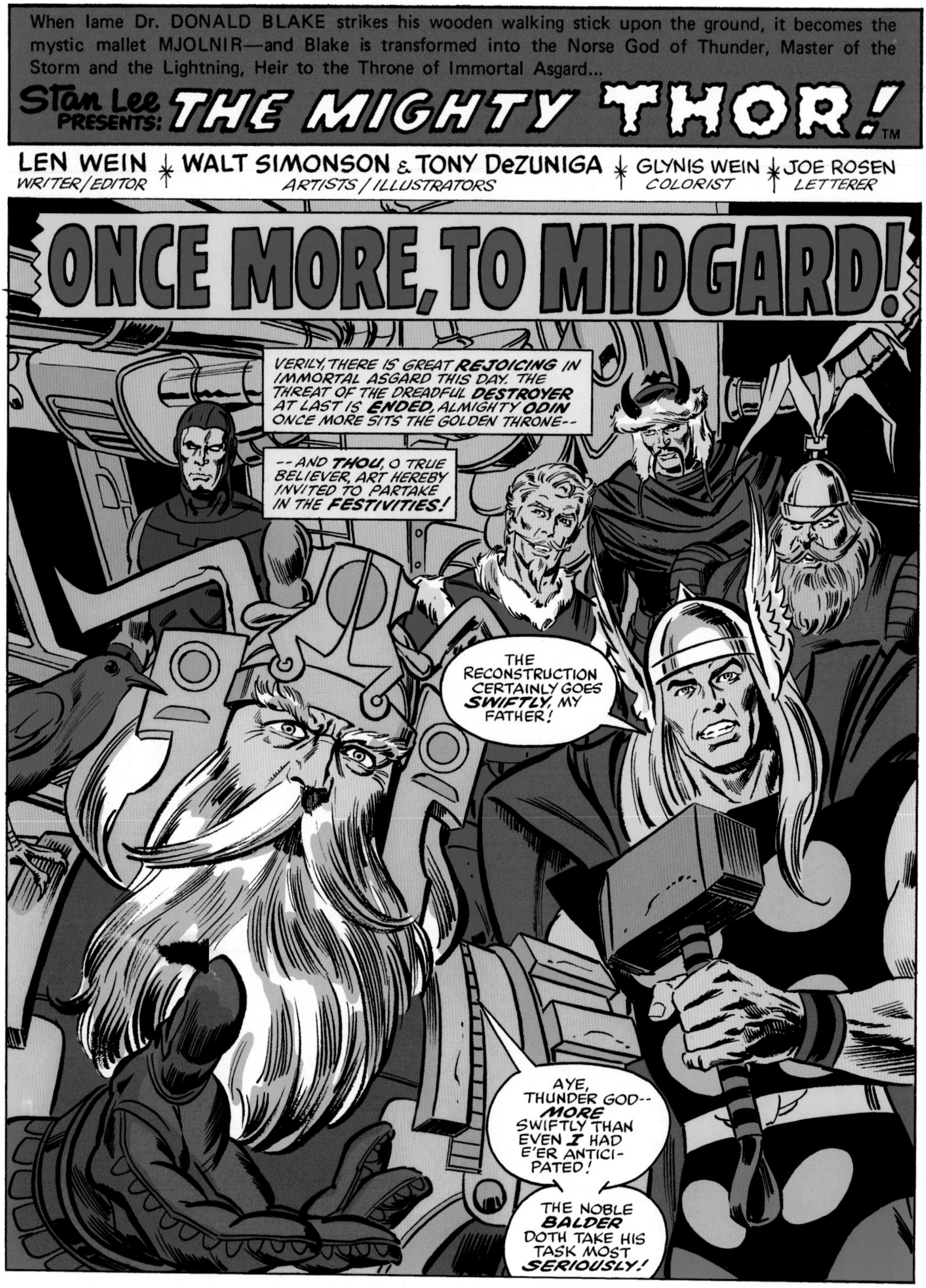

When lame Dr. DONALD BLAKE strikes his wooden walking stick upon the ground, it becomes the mystic mallet MJOLNIR—and Blake is transformed into the Norse God of Thunder, Master of the Storm and the Lightning, Heir to the Throne of Immortal Asgard...
Stan Lee PRESENTS: THE MIGHTY THOR! TM
LEN WEIN WRITER/EDITOR
WALT SIMONSON & TONY DeZUNIGA ARTISTS/ILLUSTRATORS
GLYNIS WEIN COLORIST
JOE ROSEN LETTERER
ONCE MORE, TO MIDGARD!
VERILY, THERE IS GREAT REJOICING IN IMMORTAL ASGARD THIS DAY. THE THREAT OF THE DREADFUL DESTROYER AT LAST IS ENDED, ALMIGHTY ODIN ONCE MORE SITS THE GOLDEN THRONE--
--AND THOU, O TRUE BELIEVER, ART HEREBY INVITED TO PARTAKE IN THE FESTIVITIES!
THE RECONSTRUCTION CERTAINLY GOES SWIFTLY, MY FATHER!
AYE, THUNDER GOD-- MORE SWIFTLY THAN EVEN I HAD E'ER ANTICI-PATED!
THE NOBLE BALDER DOTH TAKE HIS TASK MOST SERIOUSLY!

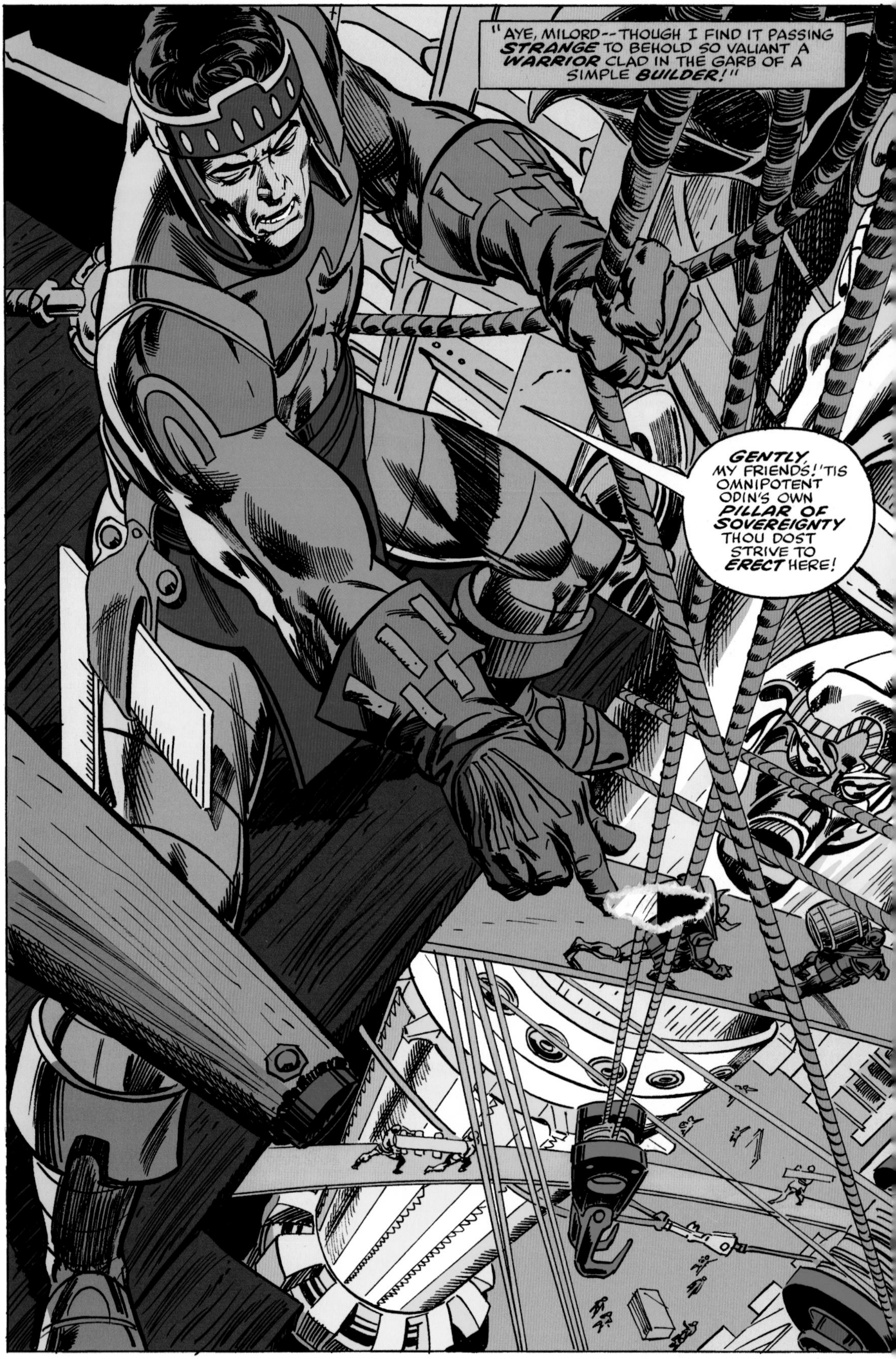
"AYE, MILORD--THOUGH I FIND IT PASSING STRANGE TO BEHOLD SO VALIANT A WARRIOR CLAD IN THE GARB OF A SIMPLE BUILDER!"
GENTLY, MY FRIENDS! 'TIS OMNIPOTENT ODIN'S OWN PILLAR OF SOVEREIGNTY THOU DOST STRIVE TO ERECT HERE!

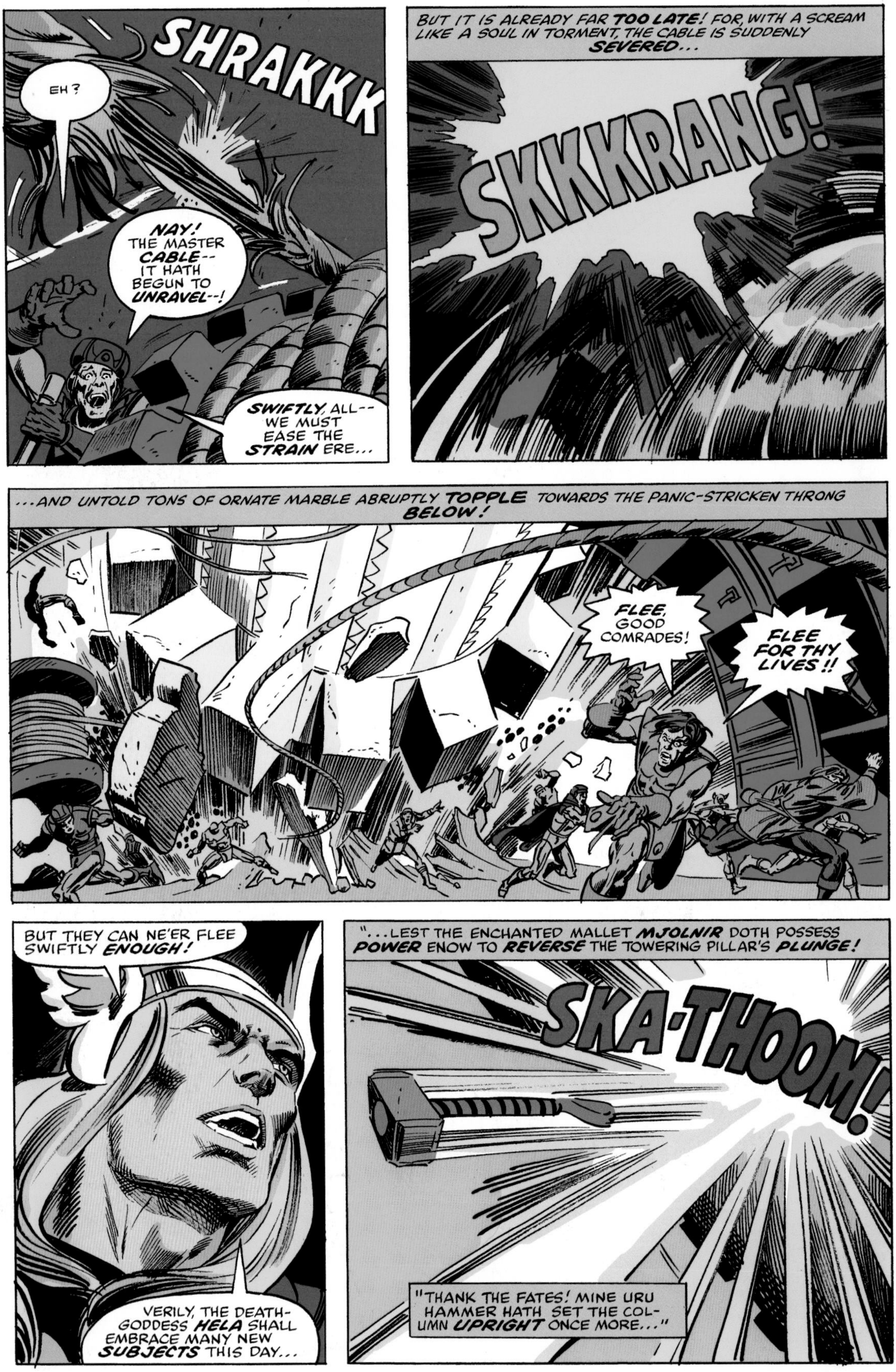
SHRAKKK
EH?
NAY! THE MASTER CABLE-- IT HATH BEGUN TO UNRAVEL--!
SWIFTLY, ALL-- WE MUST EASE THE STRAIN ERE...
BUT IT IS ALREADY FAR TOO LATE! FOR, WITH A SCREAM LIKE A SOUL IN TORMENT, THE CABLE IS SUDDENLY SEVERED...
SKKKRANG!
...AND UNTOLD TONS OF ORNATE MARBLE ABRUPTLY TOPPLE TOWARDS THE PANIC-STRICKEN THRONG BELOW!
FLEE, GOOD COMRADES!
FLEE FOR THY LIVES!!
BUT THEY CAN NE'ER FLEE SWIFTLY ENOUGH!
VERILY, THE DEATH-GODDESS HELA SHALL EMBRACE MANY NEW SUBJECTS THIS DAY...
"...LEST THE ENCHANTED MALLET MJOLNIR DOTH POSSESS POWER ENOW TO REVERSE THE TOWERING PILLAR'S PLUNGE!
SKA-THOOM!
"THANK THE FATES! MINE URU HAMMER HATH SET THE COLUMN UPRIGHT ONCE MORE..."

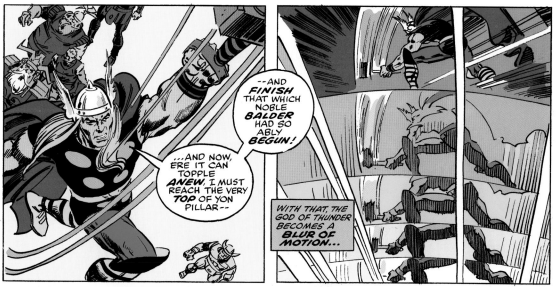

--AND *FINISH* THAT WHICH NOBLE *BALDER* HAD SO ABLY *BEGUN!*

...AND NOW, ERE IT CAN TOPPLE *ANEW*, I MUST REACH THE VERY *TOP* OF YON PILLAR--

WITH THAT, THE GOD OF THUNDER BECOMES A *BLUR OF MOTION...*

...AND WHEN, AT LAST, HE IS *THROUGH...*

WELL *DONE*, MY SON! THE PILLAR OF SOVEREIGNTY IS ONCE MORE *SECURE!*

'TIS NOTHING THAT *BALDER* WOULD NOT HAVE DONE, MILORD -- HAD THAT CABLE NOT BEEN *SUNDERED!*

NOW, IF THOU WOULDST *EXCUSE* ME, MY LIEGE-- I WOULD RETIRE TO MY *QUARTERS* FOR THE NONCE!

WHICH IS WHERE WE *REJOIN* THE SON OF ODIN A SHORT WHILE *LATER...*

THOU DOST SEEM *TROUBLED*, MILORD. DOES MY NEW ATTIRE *DISTURB* THEE?

NAY, MILADY SIF--'TIS MERELY THE THOUGHT OF THAT WHICH WE MUST NEXT *WITNESS!*

THE TIME HATH COME FOR MINE HALF-BROTHER *LOKI* TO BE *SENTENCED* FOR HIS MANY CRIMES AGAINST THE *REALM ETERNAL!**

AND THOUGH THE GOD OF MISCHIEF IS TRULY *EVIL INCARNATE*, STILL I CANNOT HELP BUT *PITY* HIM NOW!

AND *THAT*, NOBLE THOR, IS WHY I *LOVE* THEE SO.

*AS WITNESSED THESE SEVERAL ISSUES PAST. --LEN.

5

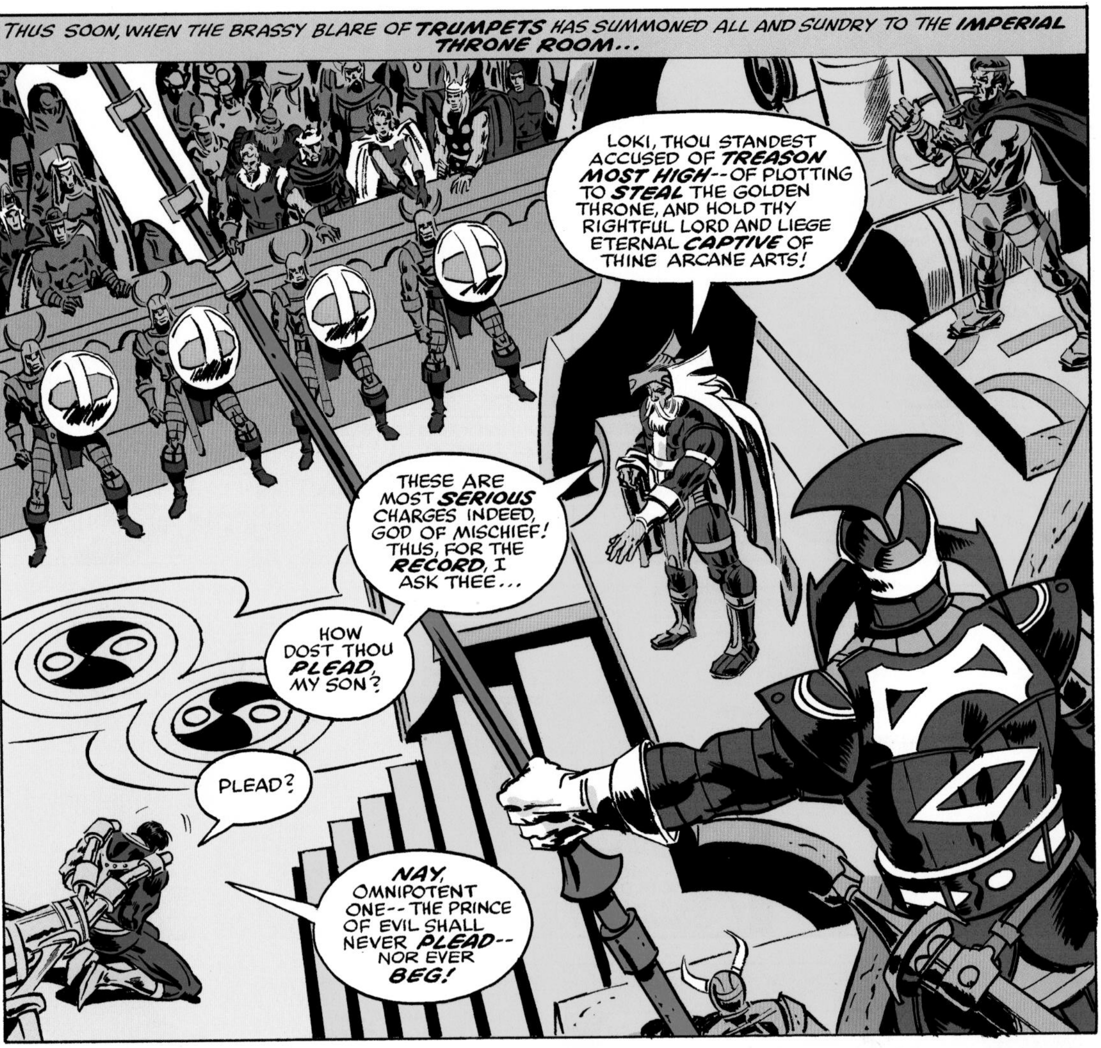
THUS SOON, WHEN THE BRASSY BLARE OF TRUMPETS HAS SUMMONED ALL AND SUNDRY TO THE IMPERIAL THRONE ROOM...
LOKI, THOU STANDEST ACCUSED OF TREASON MOST HIGH--OF PLOTTING TO STEAL THE GOLDEN THRONE, AND HOLD THY RIGHTFUL LORD AND LIEGE ETERNAL CAPTIVE OF THINE ARCANE ARTS!
THESE ARE MOST SERIOUS CHARGES INDEED, GOD OF MISCHIEF! THUS, FOR THE RECORD, I ASK THEE...
HOW DOST THOU PLEAD, MY SON?
PLEAD?
NAY, OMNIPOTENT ONE--THE PRINCE OF EVIL SHALL NEVER PLEAD--NOR EVER BEG!

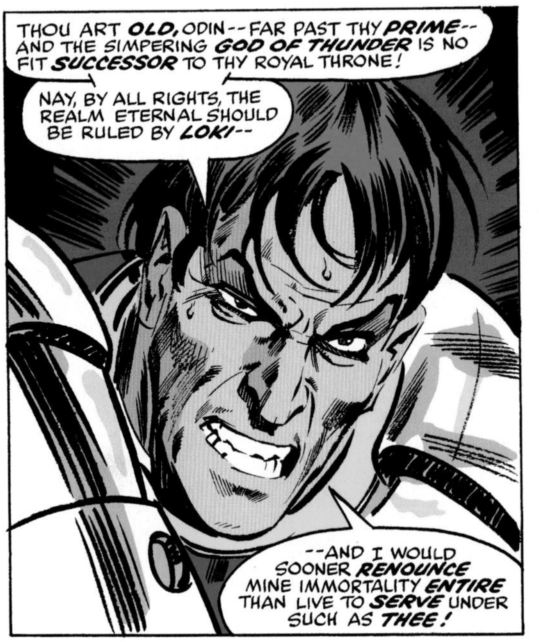
THOU ART OLD, ODIN--FAR PAST THY PRIME--AND THE SIMPERING GOD OF THUNDER IS NO FIT SUCCESSOR TO THY ROYAL THRONE!
NAY, BY ALL RIGHTS, THE REALM ETERNAL SHOULD BE RULED BY LOKI--
--AND I WOULD SOONER RENOUNCE MINE IMMORTALITY ENTIRE THAN LIVE TO SERVE UNDER SUCH AS THEE!

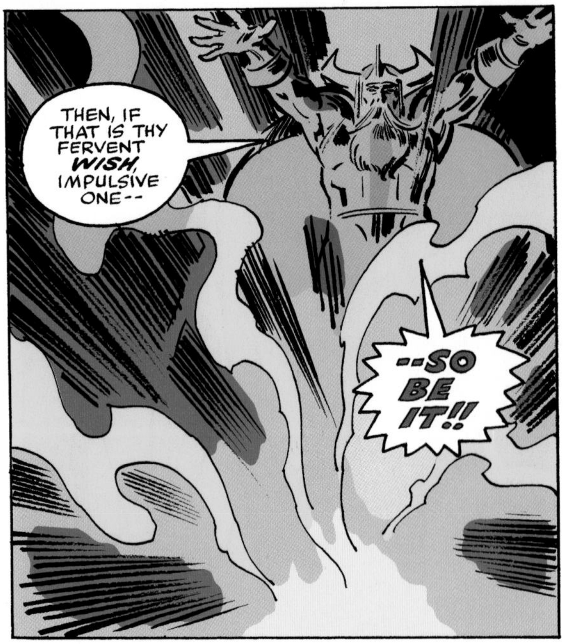
THEN, IF THAT IS THY FERVENT WISH, IMPULSIVE ONE--
--SO BE IT!!

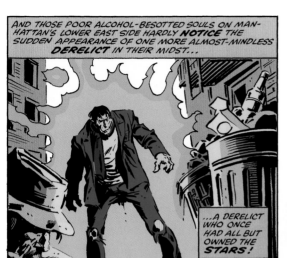

AND THOSE POOR ALCOHOL-BESOTTED SOULS ON MANHATTAN'S LOWER EAST SIDE HARDLY **NOTICE** THE SUDDEN APPEARANCE OF ONE MORE ALMOST-MINDLESS **DERELICT** IN THEIR MIDST...

...A DERELICT WHO ONCE HAD ALL BUT OWNED THE **STARS!**

PERHAPS, WHEN THE GOD OF MISCHIEF HAS FINALLY LEARNED HIS **LESSON**, I WILL **RESTORE** TO HIM HIS **MEMORY**...AND HIS **GODHOOD!**

AYE... PERHAPS.

THOU ART **WISDOM IN-CARNATE**, MY LIEGE. LET THY WILL BE **DONE.**

NOW, BY THY **LEAVE**, MILORD-- I WOULD BID **FAREWELL** TO A **FRIEND.**

RECORDER, WE SHALL **MISS** THEE! TRULY, THOU ART A BEING **NOBLE** BEYOND MEASURE!

STATEMENT: MY WORK HERE IS **DONE!** I HAVE WITNESSED THE END OF THE **ODIN-QUEST** AS ORDERED BY MY RIGILLIAN **MASTERS...**

...AND NOW THE TIME HAS COME FOR ME TO RETURN **HOME!**

RESOLUTION: BUT I SHALL NEVER **FORGET** WHAT I HAVE SEEN AT YOUR **SIDE,** ASGARDIAN...

...AND A **PART** OF ME WILL ALWAYS BE **WITH** YOU!

AND WHEN THE RECORDER HAS FINALLY FADED FROM **VIEW...**

VERILY, LOKI'S EXILE TO MIDGARD HATH SET ME TO **THINKING**--AND SET MINE HEART TO **STIRRING!**

METHINKS MAYHAP 'TIS TIME I **RETURNED** TO EARTH ONCE MORE--

--AND LET THE MORTAL **DR. DON BLAKE** TAKE UP HIS LIFE **ANEW!**

A **SPLENDID** IDEA, FRIEND THOR--AND WITH THY THREE STAUNCH **COMPANIONS** BESIDE THEE, METHINKS THERE'LL BE **ADVENTURE** A'PLENTY AWAITING US!

EH? BUT I... AH... I...

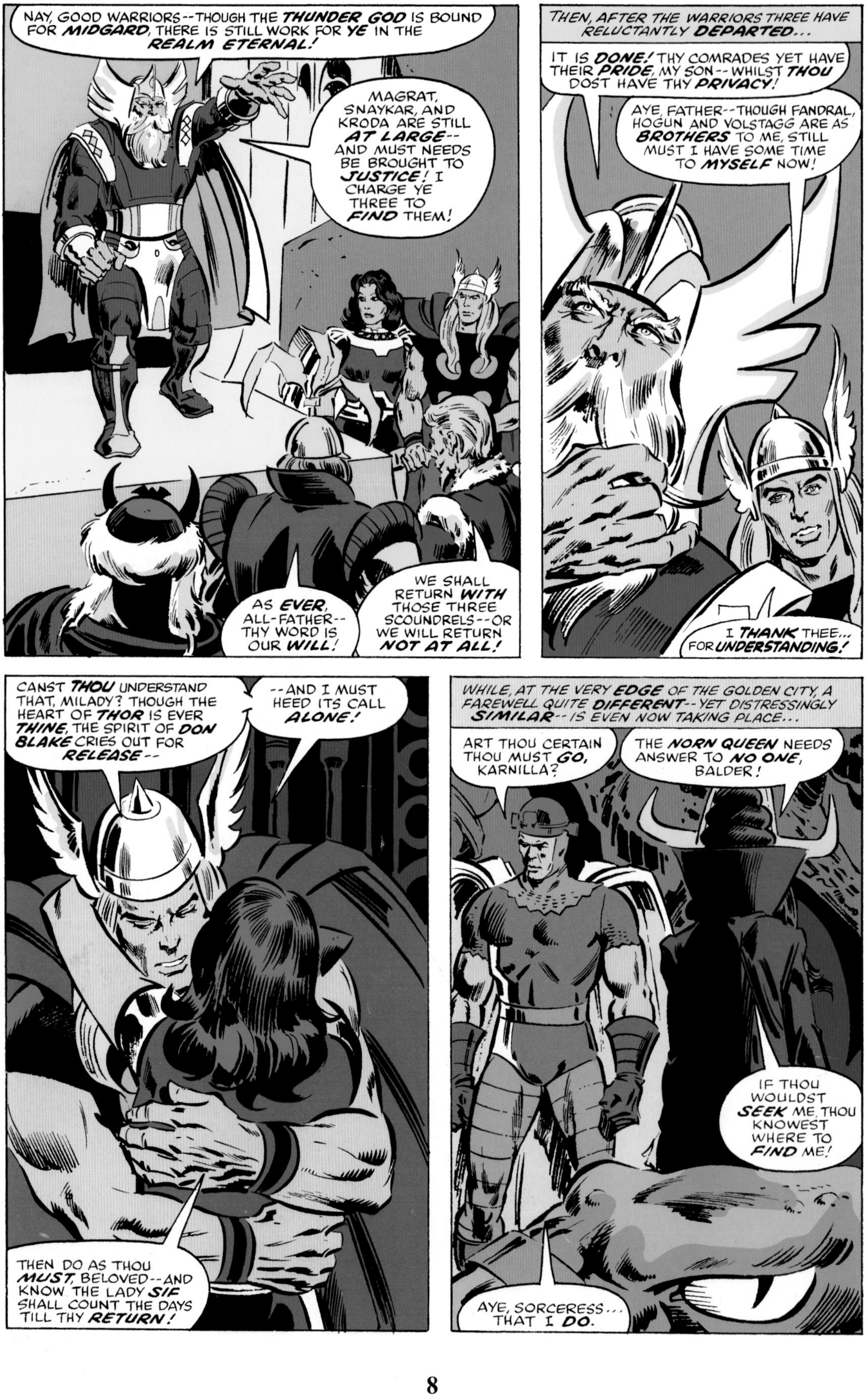
NAY, GOOD WARRIORS--THOUGH THE THUNDER GOD IS BOUND FOR MIDGARD, THERE IS STILL WORK FOR YE IN THE REALM ETERNAL!
MAGRAT, SNAYKAR, AND KRODA ARE STILL AT LARGE--AND MUST NEEDS BE BROUGHT TO JUSTICE! I CHARGE YE THREE TO FIND THEM!
AS EVER, ALL-FATHER--THY WORD IS OUR WILL!
WE SHALL RETURN WITH THOSE THREE SCOUNDRELS--OR WE WILL RETURN NOT AT ALL!
THEN, AFTER THE WARRIORS THREE HAVE RELUCTANTLY DEPARTED...
IT IS DONE! THY COMRADES YET HAVE THEIR PRIDE, MY SON--WHILST THOU DOST HAVE THY PRIVACY!
AYE, FATHER--THOUGH FANDRAL, HOGUN AND VOLSTAGG ARE AS BROTHERS TO ME, STILL MUST I HAVE SOME TIME TO MYSELF NOW!
I THANK THEE... FOR UNDERSTANDING!
CANST THOU UNDERSTAND THAT, MILADY? THOUGH THE HEART OF THOR IS EVER THINE, THE SPIRIT OF DON BLAKE CRIES OUT FOR RELEASE--
--AND I MUST HEED ITS CALL ALONE!
THEN DO AS THOU MUST, BELOVED--AND KNOW THE LADY SIF SHALL COUNT THE DAYS TILL THY RETURN!
WHILE, AT THE VERY EDGE OF THE GOLDEN CITY, A FAREWELL QUITE DIFFERENT--YET DISTRESSINGLY SIMILAR--IS EVEN NOW TAKING PLACE...
ART THOU CERTAIN THOU MUST GO, KARNILLA?
THE NORN QUEEN NEEDS ANSWER TO NO ONE, BALDER!
IF THOU WOULDST SEEK ME, THOU KNOWEST WHERE TO FIND ME!
AYE, SORCERESS... THAT I DO.

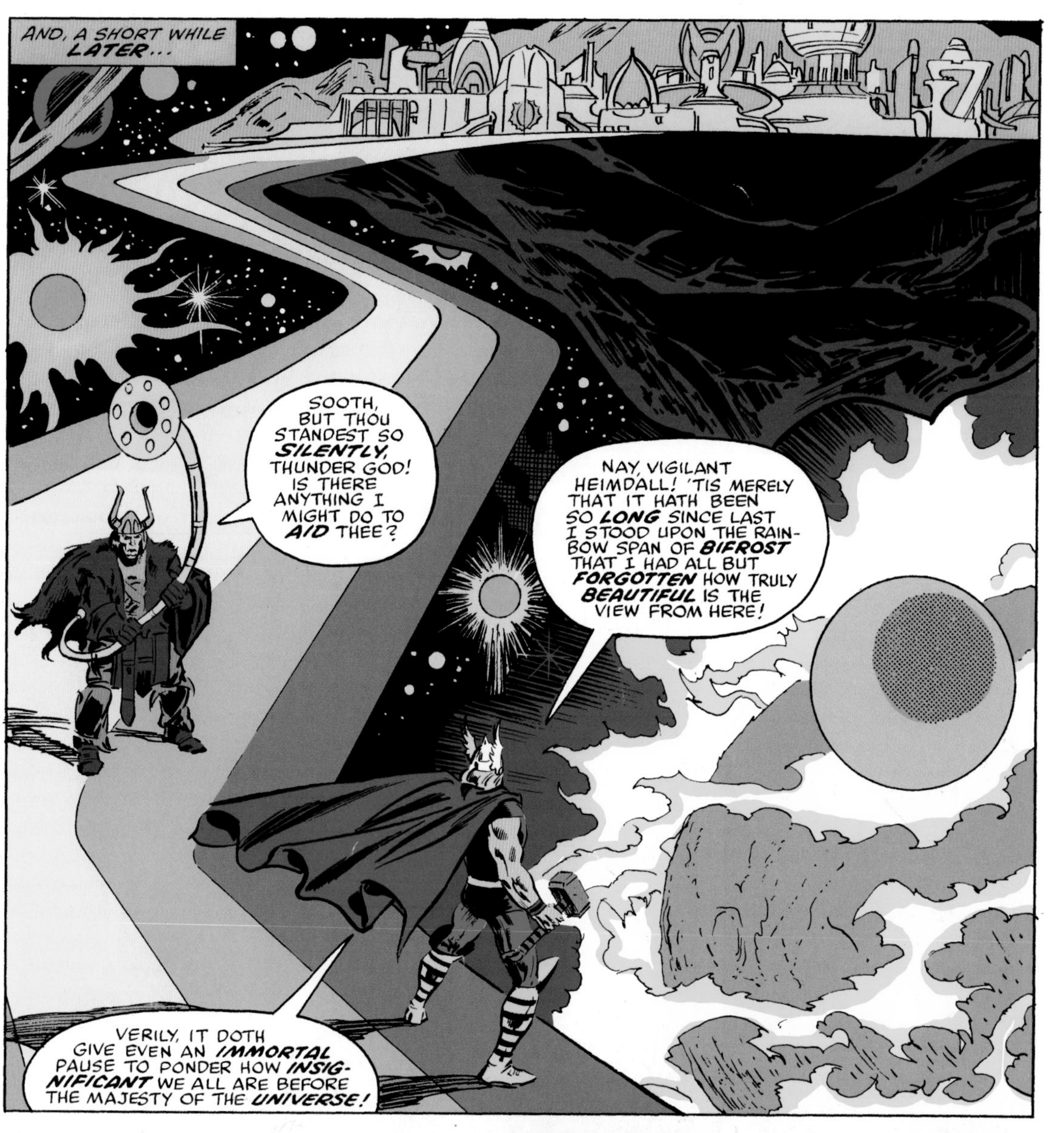
AND, A SHORT WHILE LATER...
SOOTH, BUT THOU STANDEST SO SILENTLY, THUNDER GOD! IS THERE ANYTHING I MIGHT DO TO AID THEE?
NAY, VIGILANT HEIMDALL! 'TIS MERELY THAT IT HATH BEEN SO LONG SINCE LAST I STOOD UPON THE RAIN-BOW SPAN OF BIFROST THAT I HAD ALL BUT FORGOTTEN HOW TRULY BEAUTIFUL IS THE VIEW FROM HERE!
VERILY, IT DOTH GIVE EVEN AN IMMORTAL PAUSE TO PONDER HOW INSIG-NIFICANT WE ALL ARE BEFORE THE MAJESTY OF THE UNIVERSE!

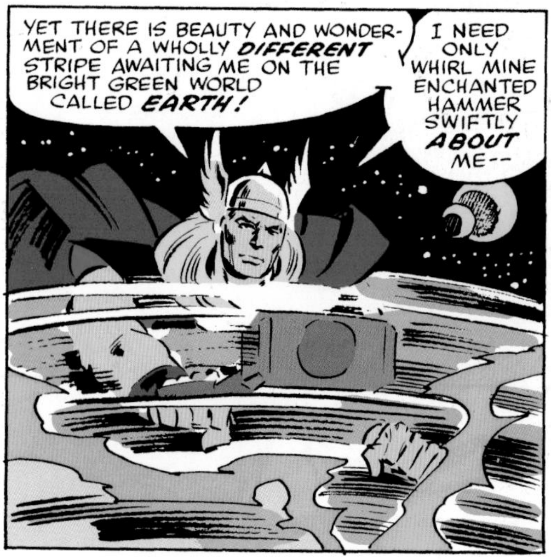
YET THERE IS BEAUTY AND WONDER-MENT OF A WHOLLY DIFFERENT STRIPE AWAITING ME ON THE BRIGHT GREEN WORLD CALLED EARTH!
I NEED ONLY WHIRL MINE ENCHANTED HAMMER SWIFTLY ABOUT ME--

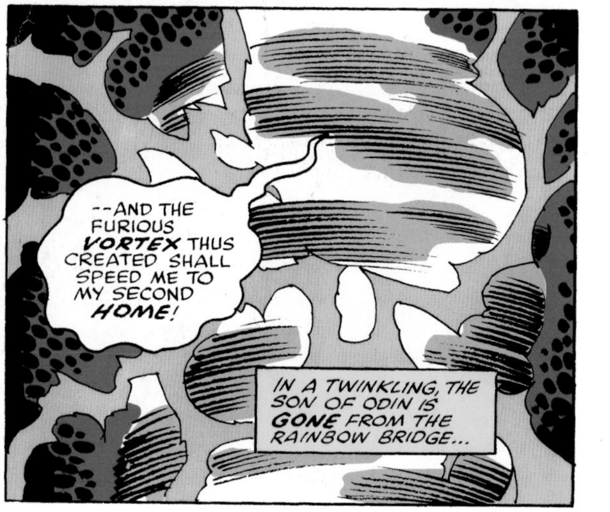
--AND THE FURIOUS VORTEX THUS CREATED SHALL SPEED ME TO MY SECOND HOME!
IN A TWINKLING, THE SON OF ODIN IS GONE FROM THE RAINBOW BRIDGE...

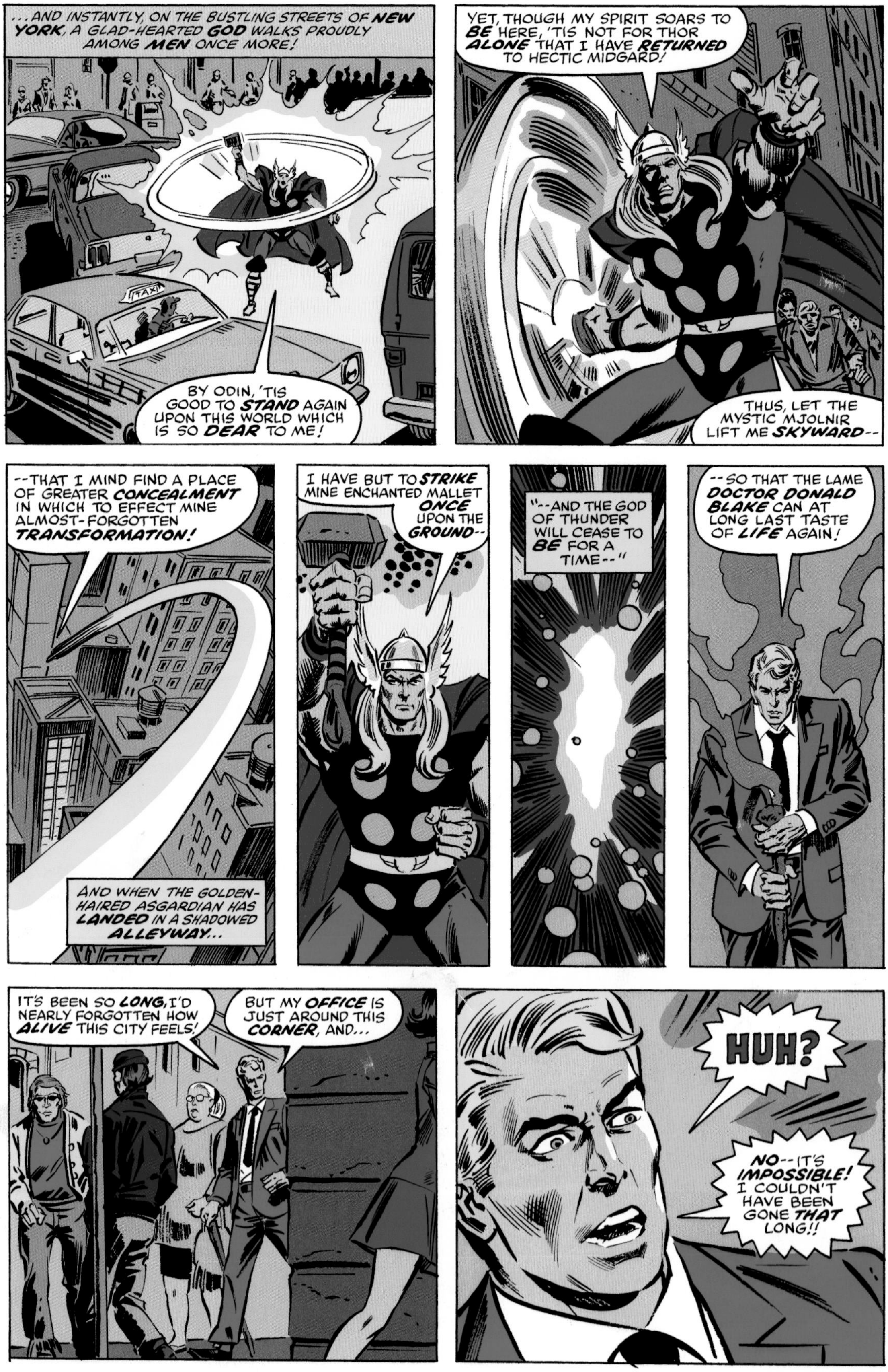
...AND INSTANTLY, ON THE BUSTLING STREETS OF NEW YORK, A GLAD-HEARTED GOD WALKS PROUDLY AMONG MEN ONCE MORE!
TAXI
BY ODIN, 'TIS GOOD TO STAND AGAIN UPON THIS WORLD WHICH IS SO DEAR TO ME!
YET, THOUGH MY SPIRIT SOARS TO BE HERE, 'TIS NOT FOR THOR ALONE THAT I HAVE RETURNED TO HECTIC MIDGARD!
THUS, LET THE MYSTIC MJOLNIR LIFT ME SKYWARD--
--THAT I MIND FIND A PLACE OF GREATER CONCEALMENT IN WHICH TO EFFECT MINE ALMOST-FORGOTTEN TRANSFORMATION!
AND WHEN THE GOLDEN-HAIRED ASGARDIAN HAS LANDED IN A SHADOWED ALLEYWAY...
I HAVE BUT TO STRIKE MINE ENCHANTED MALLET ONCE UPON THE GROUND--
"--AND THE GOD OF THUNDER WILL CEASE TO BE FOR A TIME--"
--SO THAT THE LAME DOCTOR DONALD BLAKE CAN AT LONG LAST TASTE OF LIFE AGAIN!
IT'S BEEN SO LONG, I'D NEARLY FORGOTTEN HOW ALIVE THIS CITY FEELS!
BUT MY OFFICE IS JUST AROUND THIS CORNER, AND...
HUH?
NO--IT'S IMPOSSIBLE! I COULDN'T HAVE BEEN GONE THAT LONG!!

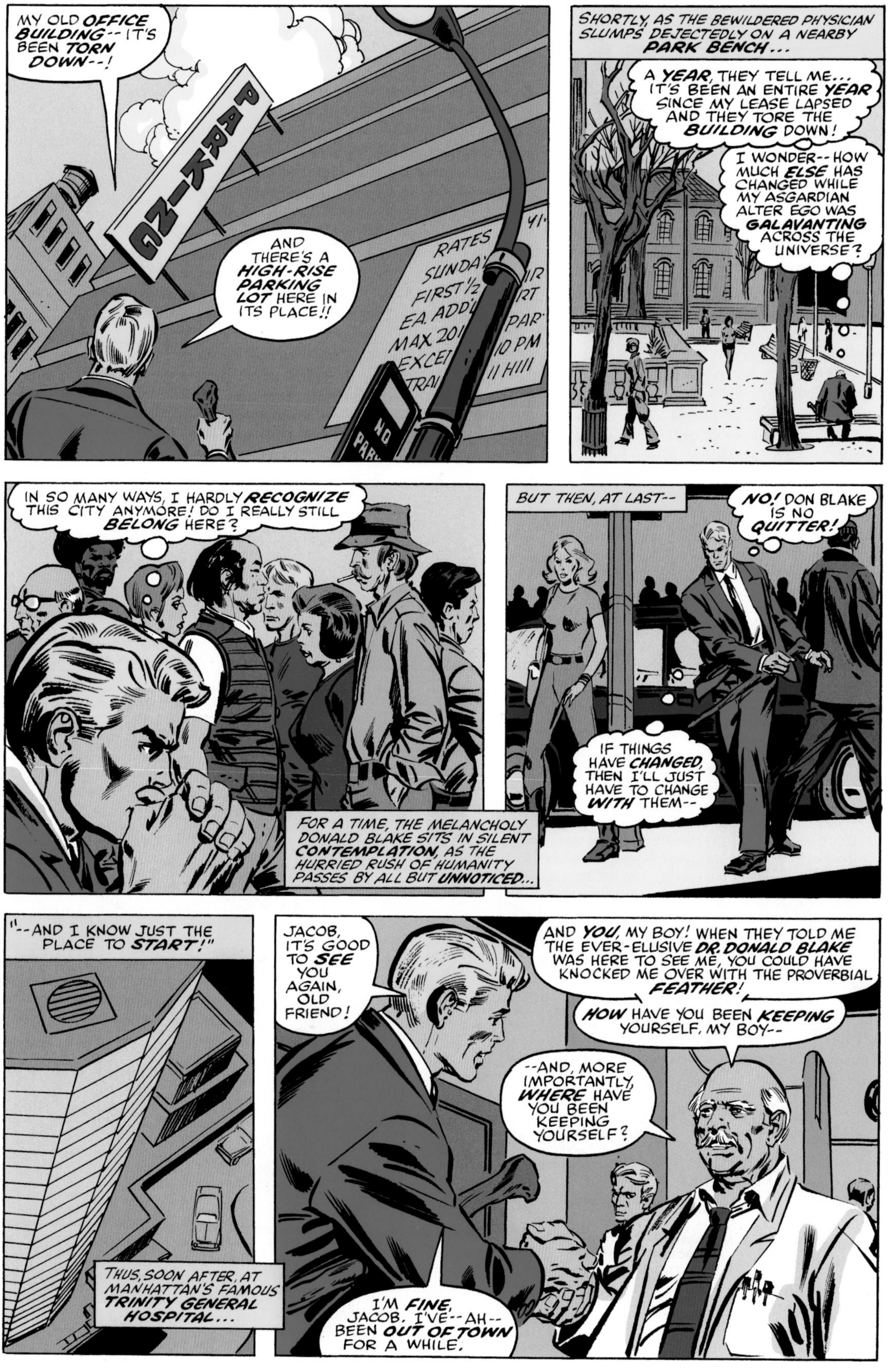

MY OLD OFFICE BUILDING-- IT'S BEEN TORN DOWN--!
PARKING
AND THERE'S A HIGH-RISE PARKING LOT HERE IN ITS PLACE!!
RATES
SUNDAY
FIRST 1/2
EA. ADD'L
MAX. 20
EXCE
TRAI
NO PARK
SHORTLY, AS THE BEWILDERED PHYSICIAN SLUMPS DEJECTEDLY ON A NEARBY PARK BENCH...
A YEAR, THEY TELL ME... IT'S BEEN AN ENTIRE YEAR SINCE MY LEASE LAPSED AND THEY TORE THE BUILDING DOWN!
I WONDER-- HOW MUCH ELSE HAS CHANGED WHILE MY ASGARDIAN ALTER EGO WAS GALAVANTING ACROSS THE UNIVERSE?
IN SO MANY WAYS, I HARDLY RECOGNIZE THIS CITY ANYMORE! DO I REALLY STILL BELONG HERE?
FOR A TIME, THE MELANCHOLY DONALD BLAKE SITS IN SILENT CONTEMPLATION, AS THE HURRIED RUSH OF HUMANITY PASSES BY ALL BUT UNNOTICED...
BUT THEN, AT LAST--
NO! DON BLAKE IS NO QUITTER!
IF THINGS HAVE CHANGED, THEN I'LL JUST HAVE TO CHANGE WITH THEM--
"--AND I KNOW JUST THE PLACE TO START!"
THUS, SOON AFTER, AT MANHATTAN'S FAMOUS TRINITY GENERAL HOSPITAL...
JACOB, IT'S GOOD TO SEE YOU AGAIN, OLD FRIEND!
AND YOU, MY BOY! WHEN THEY TOLD ME THE EVER-ELUSIVE DR. DONALD BLAKE WAS HERE TO SEE ME, YOU COULD HAVE KNOCKED ME OVER WITH THE PROVERBIAL FEATHER!
HOW HAVE YOU BEEN KEEPING YOURSELF, MY BOY--
--AND, MORE IMPORTANTLY, WHERE HAVE YOU BEEN KEEPING YOURSELF?
I'M FINE, JACOB. I'VE--AH-- BEEN OUT OF TOWN FOR A WHILE.

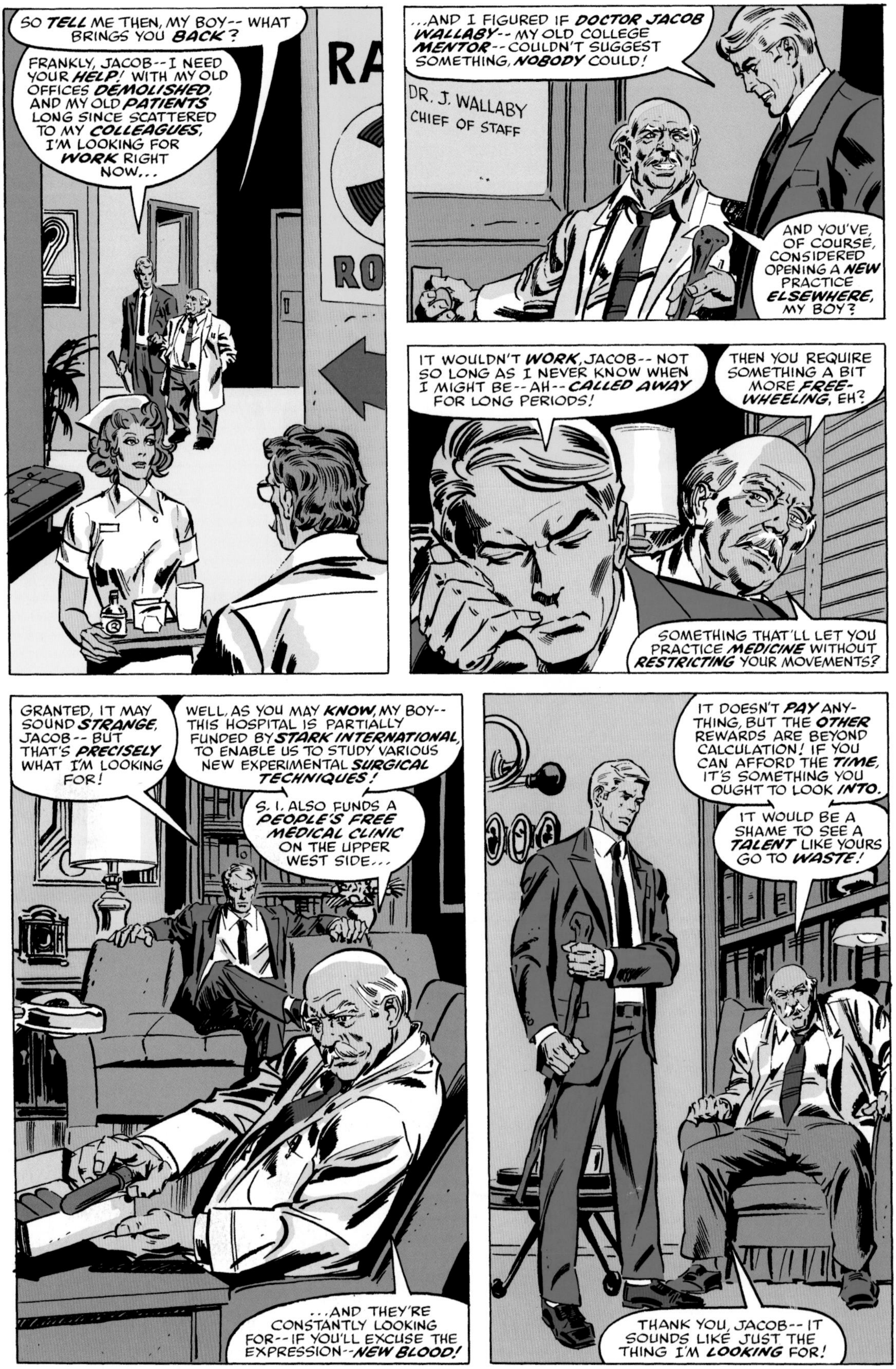

SO TELL ME THEN, MY BOY-- WHAT BRINGS YOU BACK?
FRANKLY, JACOB--I NEED YOUR HELP! WITH MY OLD OFFICES DEMOLISHED, AND MY OLD PATIENTS LONG SINCE SCATTERED TO MY COLLEAGUES, I'M LOOKING FOR WORK RIGHT NOW...
...AND I FIGURED IF DOCTOR JACOB WALLABY-- MY OLD COLLEGE MENTOR--COULDN'T SUGGEST SOMETHING, NOBODY COULD!
DR. J. WALLABY
CHIEF OF STAFF
AND YOU'VE, OF COURSE, CONSIDERED OPENING A NEW PRACTICE ELSEWHERE, MY BOY?
IT WOULDN'T WORK, JACOB-- NOT SO LONG AS I NEVER KNOW WHEN I MIGHT BE--AH--CALLED AWAY FOR LONG PERIODS!
THEN YOU REQUIRE SOMETHING A BIT MORE FREE-WHEELING, EH?
SOMETHING THAT'LL LET YOU PRACTICE MEDICINE WITHOUT RESTRICTING YOUR MOVEMENTS?
GRANTED, IT MAY SOUND STRANGE, JACOB-- BUT THAT'S PRECISELY WHAT I'M LOOKING FOR!
WELL, AS YOU MAY KNOW, MY BOY-- THIS HOSPITAL IS PARTIALLY FUNDED BY STARK INTERNATIONAL, TO ENABLE US TO STUDY VARIOUS NEW EXPERIMENTAL SURGICAL TECHNIQUES!
S. I. ALSO FUNDS A PEOPLE'S FREE MEDICAL CLINIC ON THE UPPER WEST SIDE...
...AND THEY'RE CONSTANTLY LOOKING FOR--IF YOU'LL EXCUSE THE EXPRESSION--NEW BLOOD!
IT DOESN'T PAY ANYTHING, BUT THE OTHER REWARDS ARE BEYOND CALCULATION! IF YOU CAN AFFORD THE TIME, IT'S SOMETHING YOU OUGHT TO LOOK INTO.
IT WOULD BE A SHAME TO SEE A TALENT LIKE YOURS GO TO WASTE!
THANK YOU, JACOB-- IT SOUNDS LIKE JUST THE THING I'M LOOKING FOR!

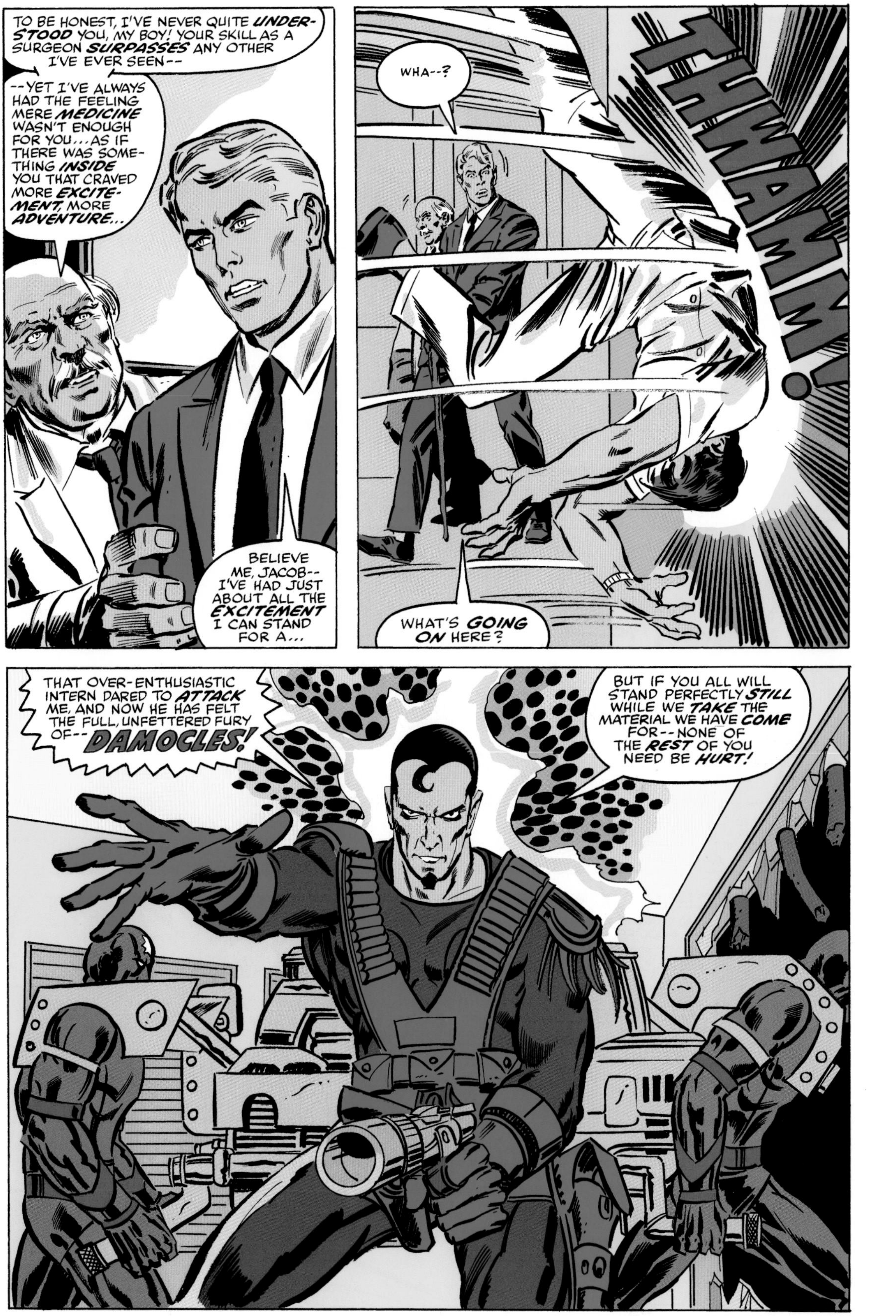

TO BE HONEST, I'VE NEVER QUITE UNDERSTOOD YOU, MY BOY! YOUR SKILL AS A SURGEON SURPASSES ANY OTHER I'VE EVER SEEN--
--YET I'VE ALWAYS HAD THE FEELING MERE MEDICINE WASN'T ENOUGH FOR YOU...AS IF THERE WAS SOMETHING INSIDE YOU THAT CRAVED MORE EXCITEMENT, MORE ADVENTURE...
BELIEVE ME, JACOB-- I'VE HAD JUST ABOUT ALL THE EXCITEMENT I CAN STAND FOR A...
WHA--?
THHAMM!
WHAT'S GOING ON HERE?
THAT OVER-ENTHUSIASTIC INTERN DARED TO ATTACK ME, AND NOW HE HAS FELT THE FULL, UNFETTERED FURY OF-- DAMOCLES!
BUT IF YOU ALL WILL STAND PERFECTLY STILL WHILE WE TAKE THE MATERIAL WE HAVE COME FOR--NONE OF THE REST OF YOU NEED BE HURT!

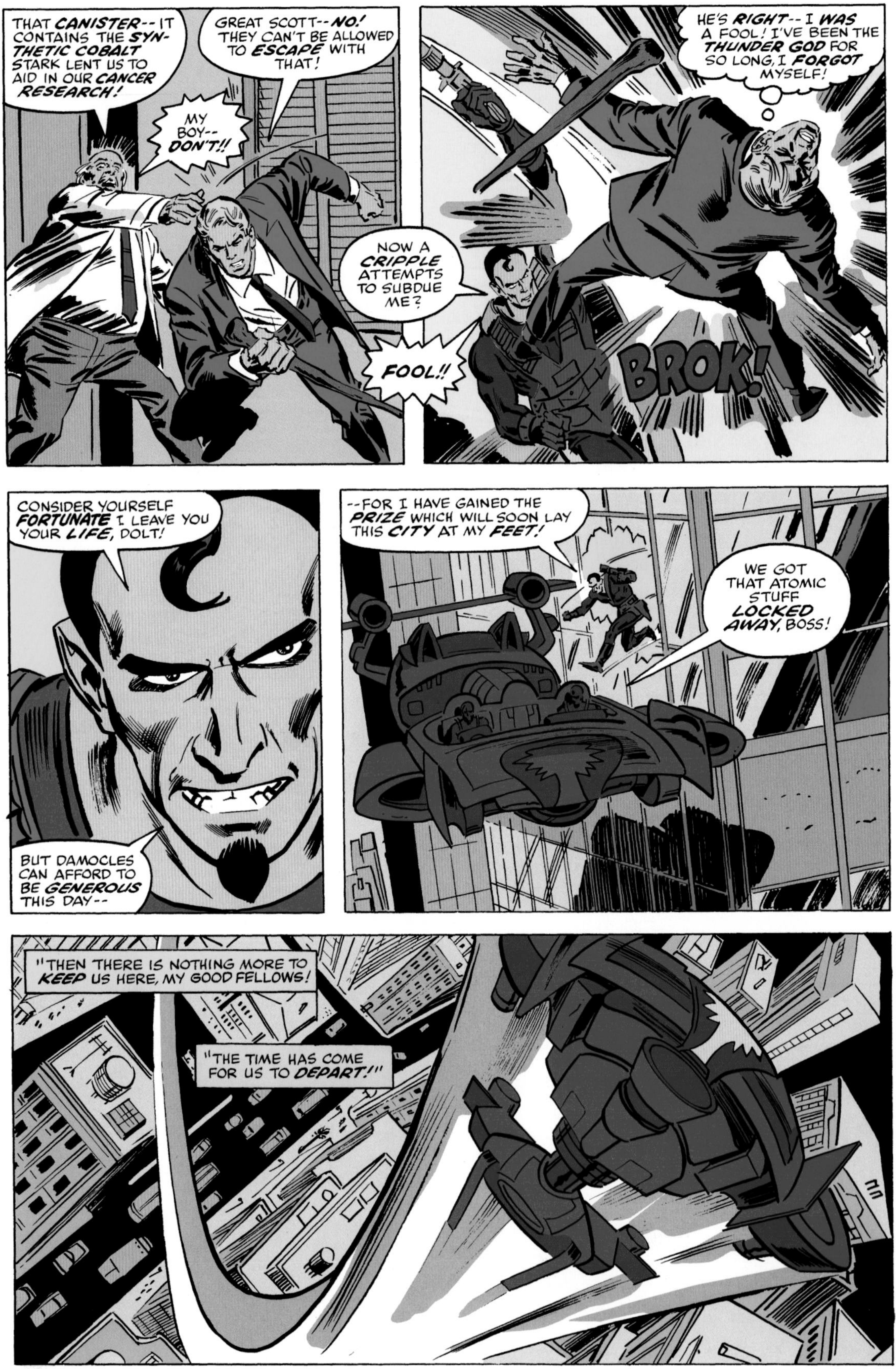
THAT CANISTER-- IT CONTAINS THE SYNTHETIC COBALT STARK LENT US TO AID IN OUR CANCER RESEARCH!
GREAT SCOTT--NO! THEY CAN'T BE ALLOWED TO ESCAPE WITH THAT!
MY BOY-- DON'T!!
HE'S RIGHT-- I WAS A FOOL! I'VE BEEN THE THUNDER GOD FOR SO LONG, I FORGOT MYSELF!
NOW A CRIPPLE ATTEMPTS TO SUBDUE ME?
FOOL!!
BROK!
CONSIDER YOURSELF FORTUNATE I LEAVE YOU YOUR LIFE, DOLT!
BUT DAMOCLES CAN AFFORD TO BE GENEROUS THIS DAY--
--FOR I HAVE GAINED THE PRIZE WHICH WILL SOON LAY THIS CITY AT MY FEET!
WE GOT THAT ATOMIC STUFF LOCKED AWAY, BOSS!
"THEN THERE IS NOTHING MORE TO KEEP US HERE, MY GOOD FELLOWS!
"THE TIME HAS COME FOR US TO DEPART!"

MY BOY, ARE YOU *ALL RIGHT*?

I'M *FINE*, JACOB-- BUT THAT *DAMOCLES* CHARACTER IS *GETTING AWAY*!

I WANT TO *THANK* YOU FOR ALL YOUR *ADVICE*, OLD FRIEND-- BUT I'M AFRAID I HAVE TO *RUN*!

I'LL TALK TO YOU *SOON*, OKAY?

PLEASE, MY BOY, I DON'T KNOW *WHAT* YOU HAVE IN *MIND*-- BUT I *BEG* YOU NOT TO BE *FOOLISH*!

DON'T *WORRY*, JACOB-- I'LL TRY TO BE *CAREFUL*!

AND, MOMENTS LATER, IN A SECLUDED *ALLEYWAY* NEARBY, THE LAME PHYSICIAN STRIKES HIS GNARLED WALKING STICK *ONCE* UPON THE GROUND...

...AND A FURIOUS *GOD OF THUNDER* TAKES TO THE GRAY-STREAKED *SKIES* ONCE MORE!

VERILY, MIDGARD HATH CHANGED *LESS* THAN I HAD *HOPED*!

STILL DOTH *CRIME* AND *INJUSTICE* RUN RAMPANT THROUGH ITS *STREETS*--

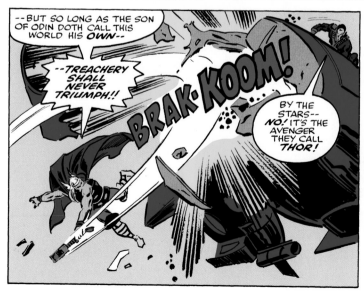

--BUT SO LONG AS THE SON OF ODIN DOTH CALL THIS WORLD HIS *OWN*--

--TREACHERY SHALL NEVER TRIUMPH!!

BRAK-KOOM!

BY THE STARS-- *NO!* IT'S THE AVENGER THEY CALL *THOR*!

THE CURSED THUNDER GOD POSSESSES *POWER* ENOUGH TO *THWART* ALL MY CAREFULLY-LAID *SCHEMES*, UNLESS...

QUICKLY, MEN--RELEASE THE *DESTRUCT-DRONE*!!

BY THE BRISTLING BEARD OF *ODIN!* THE FIENDS HAVE LAUNCHED A FIERY *MISSILE* AT THE VERY *HEART* OF THIS FAIR CITY--

--AND IT DOTH STREAK TOWARDS THE TOWERING *UNITED NATIONS BUILDING* ITSELF!

IF I ATTEMPT TO *STOP* YON MISSILE, DAMOCLES WILL *ESCAPE*--

--BUT ONLY MINE ENCHANTED *MALLET* DOTH POSSESS THE OVERWHELMING *SPEED* REQUIRED TO *OVERTAKE* HIS DREADFUL WEAPON--

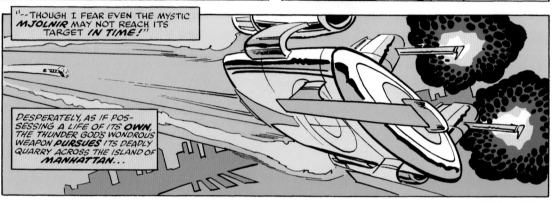

"--THOUGH I FEAR EVEN THE MYSTIC *MJOLNIR* MAY NOT REACH ITS TARGET *IN TIME!*"

DESPERATELY, AS IF POSSESSING A LIFE OF ITS *OWN,* THE THUNDER GOD'S WONDROUS WEAPON *PURSUES* ITS DEADLY QUARRY ACROSS THE ISLAND OF *MANHATTAN...*

...UNTIL, MERE *FEET* FROM THE WORLD FAMOUS MEETING HALL'S GLEAMING GLASS *FACADE*--

WHA-WHOOM!

--THE HURTLING HAMMER *STRIKES HOME!*

WHILE, WITHOUT HIS ENCHANTED MALLET TO SUSTAIN HIS *FLIGHT,* THE MIGHTY THOR PLUNGES *EARTHWARD*--

--EVEN AS HIS *SPIRIT* SOARS IN *TRIUMPH!*

PRAISE THE FATES! TRUSTY MJOLNIR STRUCK *TRUE!*

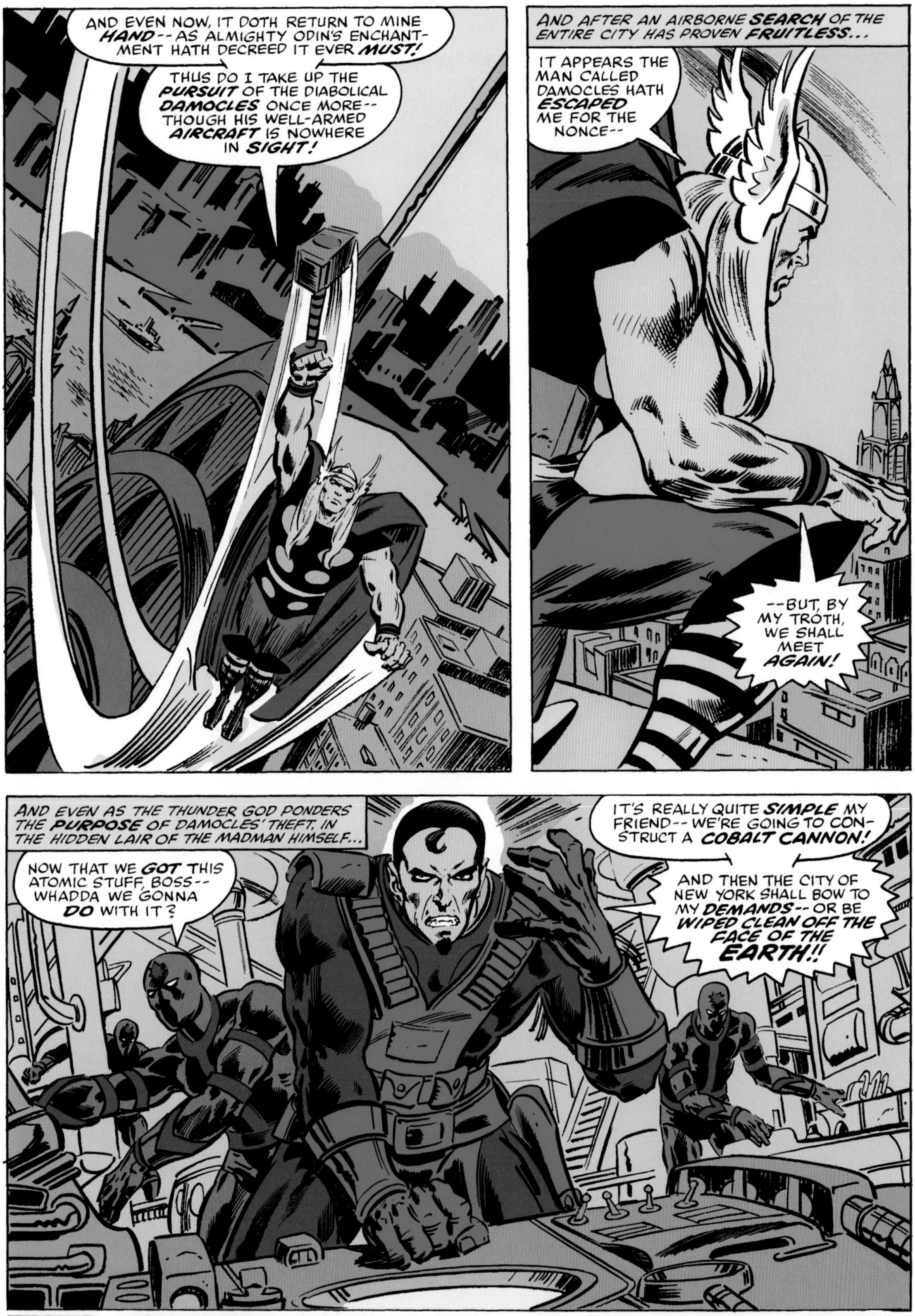
AND EVEN NOW, IT DOTH RETURN TO MINE HAND-- AS ALMIGHTY ODIN'S ENCHANTMENT HATH DECREED IT EVER MUST!
THUS DO I TAKE UP THE PURSUIT OF THE DIABOLICAL DAMOCLES ONCE MORE-- THOUGH HIS WELL-ARMED AIRCRAFT IS NOWHERE IN SIGHT!
AND AFTER AN AIRBORNE SEARCH OF THE ENTIRE CITY HAS PROVEN FRUITLESS...
IT APPEARS THE MAN CALLED DAMOCLES HATH ESCAPED ME FOR THE NONCE--
--BUT, BY MY TROTH, WE SHALL MEET AGAIN!
AND EVEN AS THE THUNDER GOD PONDERS THE PURPOSE OF DAMOCLES' THEFT, IN THE HIDDEN LAIR OF THE MADMAN HIMSELF...
NOW THAT WE GOT THIS ATOMIC STUFF, BOSS-- WHADDA WE GONNA DO WITH IT?
IT'S REALLY QUITE SIMPLE MY FRIEND-- WE'RE GOING TO CONSTRUCT A COBALT CANNON!
AND THEN THE CITY OF NEW YORK SHALL BOW TO MY DEMANDS-- OR BE WIPED CLEAN OFF THE FACE OF THE EARTH!!
NEXT ISSUE: DEATH, THY NAME IS BROTHER!

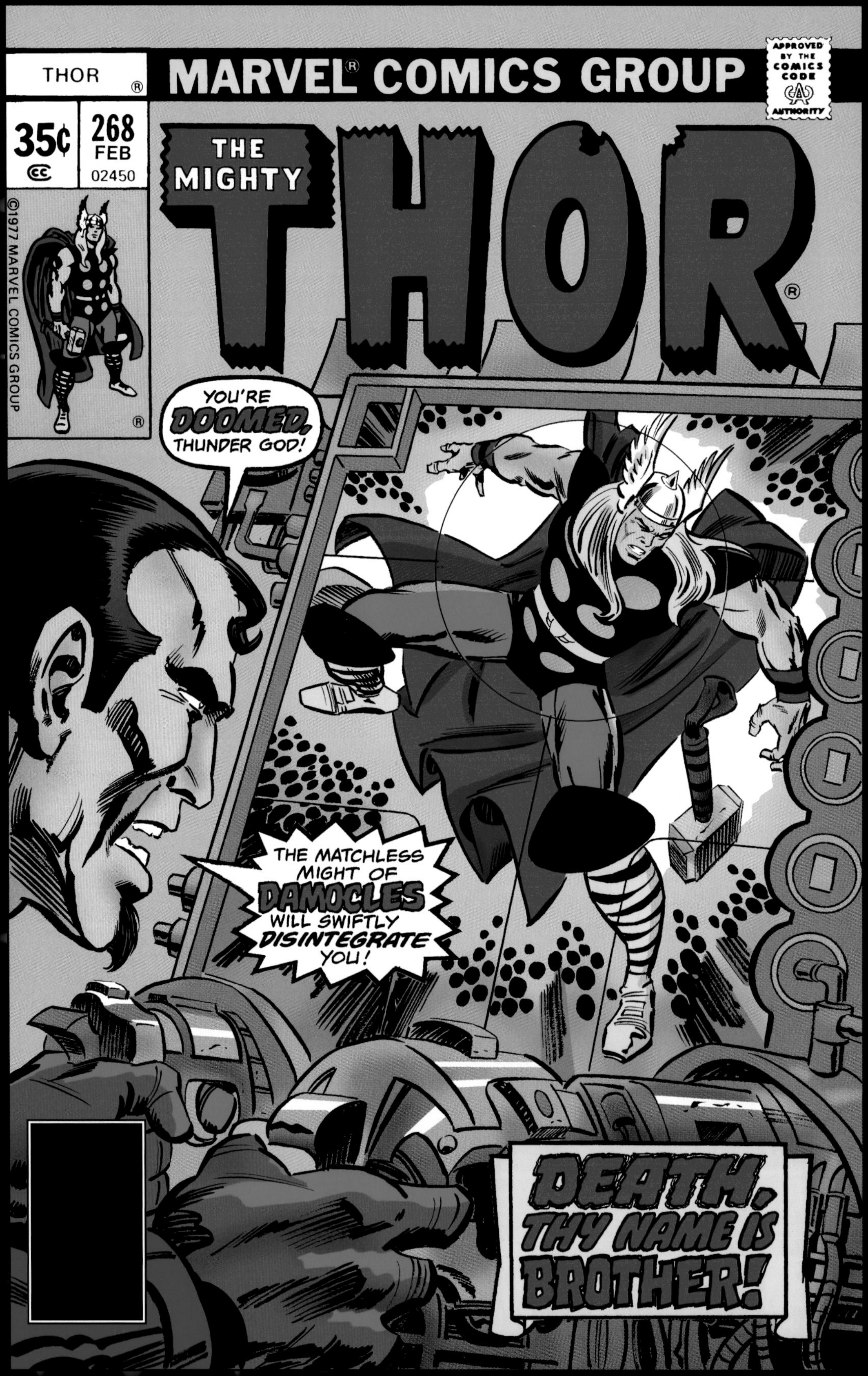
THOR
MARVEL COMICS GROUP
APPROVED BY THE COMICS CODE AUTHORITY
35¢
268
FEB
02450
THE MIGHTY
THOR
©1977 MARVEL COMICS GROUP
YOU'RE DOOMED, THUNDER GOD!
THE MATCHLESS MIGHT OF DAMOCLES WILL SWIFTLY DISINTEGRATE YOU!
DEATH, THY NAME IS BROTHER!

When lame Dr. DONALD BLAKE strikes his wooden walking stick upon the ground, it becomes the mystic mallet MJOLNIR—and Blake is transformed into the Norse God of Thunder, Master of the Storm and the Lightning, Heir to the Throne of Immortal Asgard...

Stan Lee PRESENTS: THE MIGHTY THOR!™

LEN WEIN *WRITER / EDITOR* ✶ WALT SIMONSON & TONY DEZUNIGA *ARTISTS / ILLUSTRATORS* ✶ GLYNIS WEIN *COLORIST* ✶ JOE ROSEN *LETTERER*

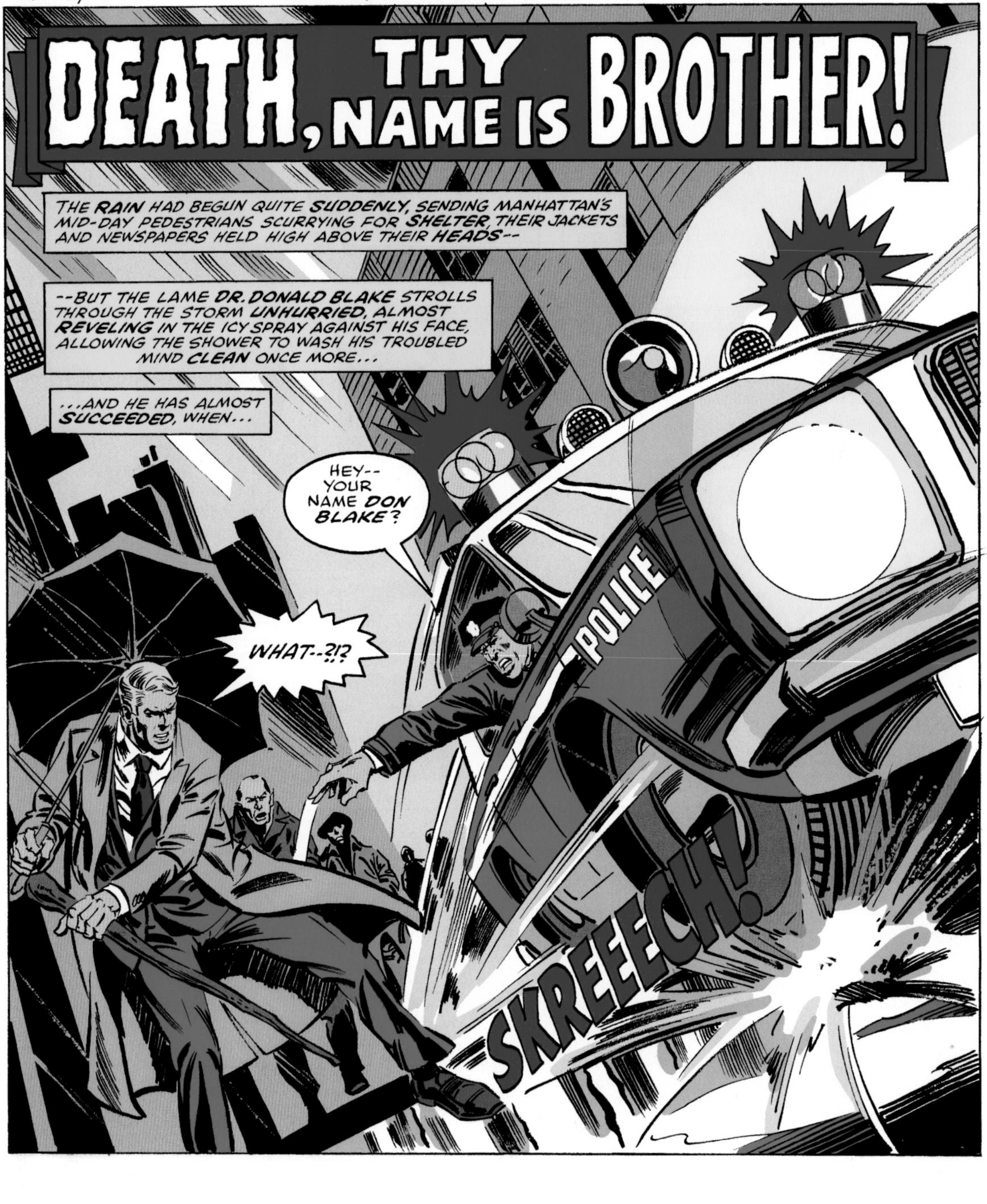
DEATH, THY NAME IS BROTHER!
THE RAIN HAD BEGUN QUITE SUDDENLY, SENDING MANHATTAN'S MID-DAY PEDESTRIANS SCURRYING FOR SHELTER, THEIR JACKETS AND NEWSPAPERS HELD HIGH ABOVE THEIR HEADS--
--BUT THE LAME DR. DONALD BLAKE STROLLS THROUGH THE STORM UNHURRIED, ALMOST REVELING IN THE ICY SPRAY AGAINST HIS FACE, ALLOWING THE SHOWER TO WASH HIS TROUBLED MIND CLEAN ONCE MORE...
...AND HE HAS ALMOST SUCCEEDED, WHEN...
HEY-- YOUR NAME DON BLAKE?
WHAT--?!?
POLICE
SKREEEECH!

SORRY IF WE *STARTLED* YA, MISTER-- BUT IF YOU *ARE* DR. BLAKE, WE COULD USE YER *HELP!*

HOW *SO*, OFFICER?

YER S'POSED TA BE FRIENDS WITH *THOR*, RIGHT? D'YA THINK YA CAN *CONTACT* THE THUNDER GOD--

--AN' TELL 'IM THE *COMMISSIONER* WOULD LIKE TA SEE 'IM *DOWNTOWN* RIGHT AWAY?

WELL, I'M NOT *PROMISING* ANYTHING, MIND YOU--

--BUT I'LL SEE WHAT I CAN *DO!*

AND FRANKLY, FRIEND, I CAN DO *PLENTY!*

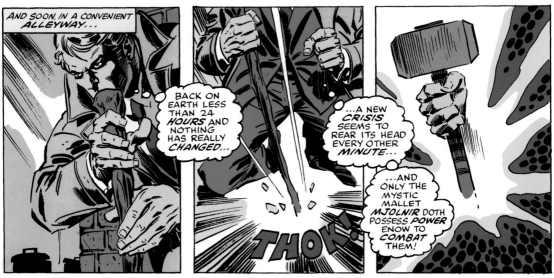

AND SOON, IN A CONVENIENT *ALLEYWAY...*

BACK ON EARTH LESS THAN 24 *HOURS* AND NOTHING HAS REALLY *CHANGED...*

...A NEW *CRISIS* SEEMS TO REAR ITS HEAD EVERY OTHER *MINUTE...*

...AND ONLY THE MYSTIC MALLET *MJOLNIR* DOTH POSSESS *POWER* ENOW TO *COMBAT* THEM!

THOK!

THEN, AS THE ENCHANTED HAMMER CARRIES ITS HEROIC MASTER ACROSS THE *CITY...*

THE STORM IN THE SKY HATH *ABATED*--BUT THE STORM IN MY *HEART* ERUPTS *ANEW!*

WHATE'ER DARES *THREATEN* THIS CITY I HOLD *DEAR*, IT SHALL FACE THE SWIFT AND RIGHTEOUS WRATH OF--*THOR!*

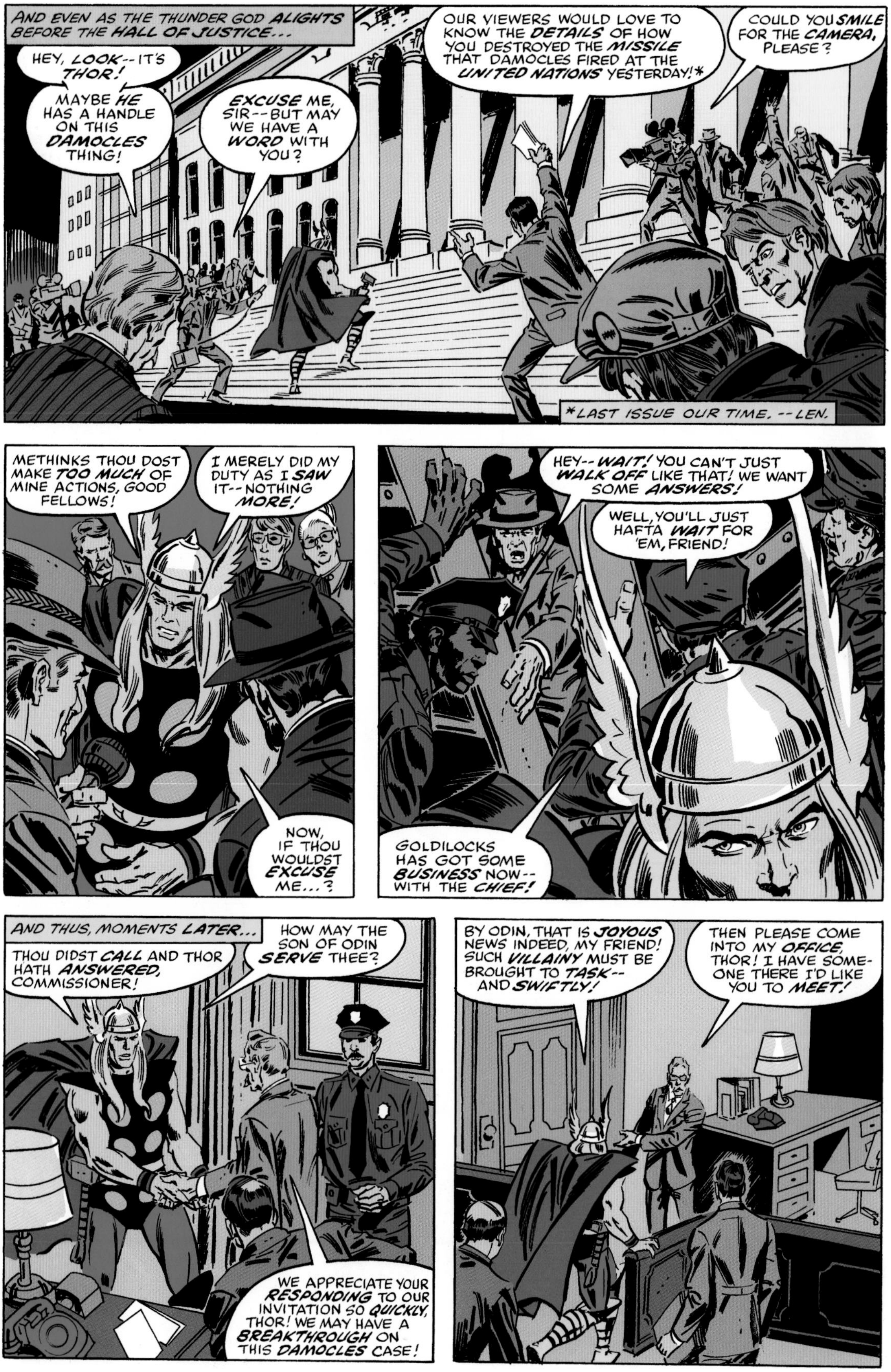
AND EVEN AS THE THUNDER GOD ALIGHTS BEFORE THE HALL OF JUSTICE...
HEY, LOOK--IT'S THOR!
MAYBE HE HAS A HANDLE ON THIS DAMOCLES THING!
EXCUSE ME, SIR--BUT MAY WE HAVE A WORD WITH YOU?
OUR VIEWERS WOULD LOVE TO KNOW THE DETAILS OF HOW YOU DESTROYED THE MISSILE THAT DAMOCLES FIRED AT THE UNITED NATIONS YESTERDAY!*
COULD YOU SMILE FOR THE CAMERA, PLEASE?
*LAST ISSUE OUR TIME. --LEN.
METHINKS THOU DOST MAKE TOO MUCH OF MINE ACTIONS, GOOD FELLOWS!
I MERELY DID MY DUTY AS I SAW IT--NOTHING MORE!
NOW, IF THOU WOULDST EXCUSE ME...?
HEY--WAIT! YOU CAN'T JUST WALK OFF LIKE THAT! WE WANT SOME ANSWERS!
WELL, YOU'LL JUST HAFTA WAIT FOR 'EM, FRIEND!
GOLDILOCKS HAS GOT SOME BUSINESS NOW--WITH THE CHIEF!
AND THUS, MOMENTS LATER...
THOU DIDST CALL AND THOR HATH ANSWERED, COMMISSIONER!
HOW MAY THE SON OF ODIN SERVE THEE?
WE APPRECIATE YOUR RESPONDING TO OUR INVITATION SO QUICKLY, THOR! WE MAY HAVE A BREAKTHROUGH ON THIS DAMOCLES CASE!
BY ODIN, THAT IS JOYOUS NEWS INDEED, MY FRIEND! SUCH VILLAINY MUST BE BROUGHT TO TASK--AND SWIFTLY!
THEN PLEASE COME INTO MY OFFICE, THOR! I HAVE SOMEONE THERE I'D LIKE YOU TO MEET!

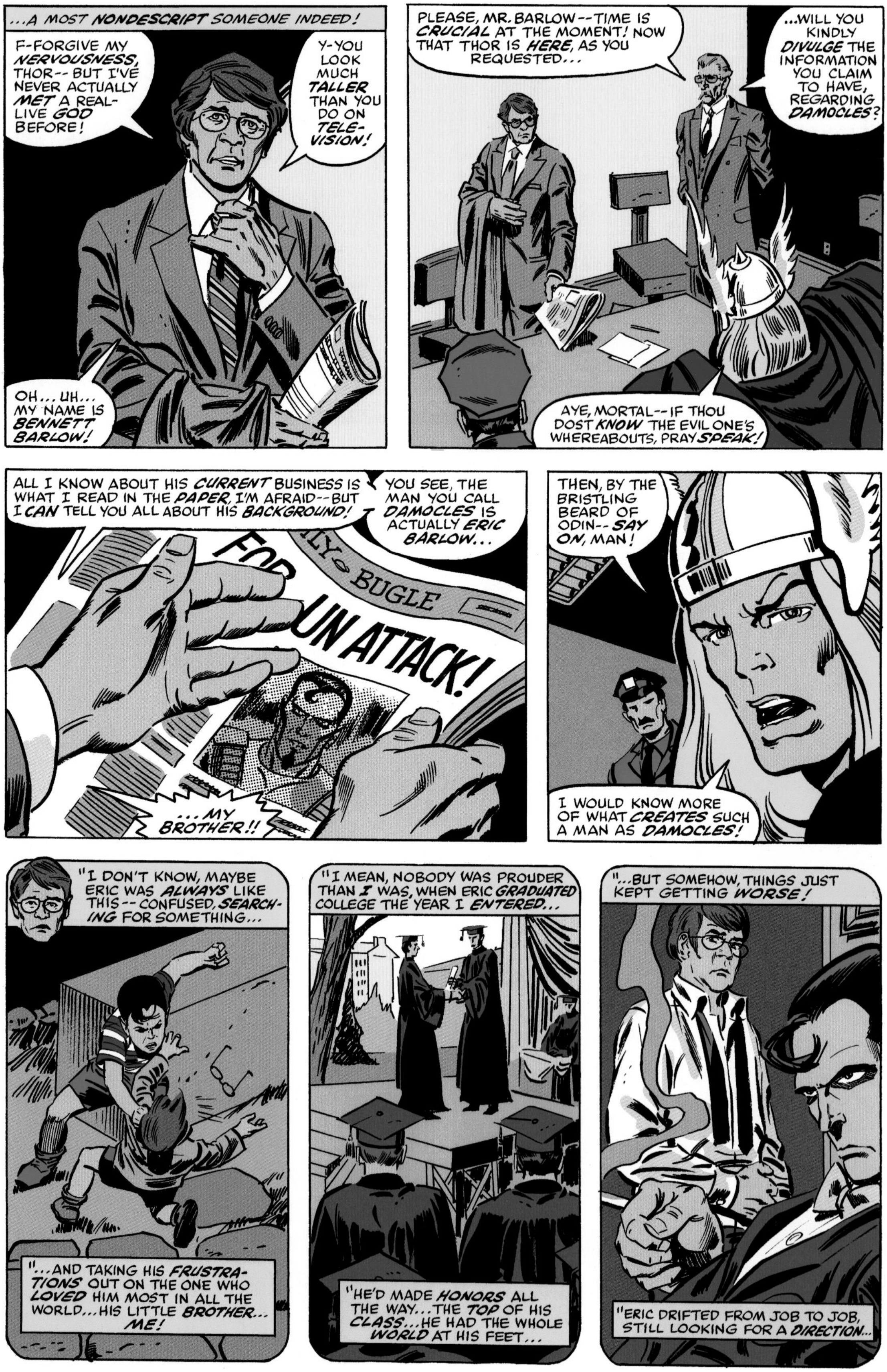
...A MOST NONDESCRIPT SOMEONE INDEED!
F-FORGIVE MY NERVOUSNESS, THOR-- BUT I'VE NEVER ACTUALLY MET A REAL-LIVE GOD BEFORE!
Y-YOU LOOK MUCH TALLER THAN YOU DO ON TELE-VISION!
OH... UH... MY NAME IS BENNETT BARLOW!
PLEASE, MR. BARLOW--TIME IS CRUCIAL AT THE MOMENT! NOW THAT THOR IS HERE, AS YOU REQUESTED...
...WILL YOU KINDLY DIVULGE THE INFORMATION YOU CLAIM TO HAVE, REGARDING DAMOCLES?
AYE, MORTAL--IF THOU DOST KNOW THE EVIL ONE'S WHEREABOUTS, PRAY SPEAK!
ALL I KNOW ABOUT HIS CURRENT BUSINESS IS WHAT I READ IN THE PAPER, I'M AFRAID--BUT I CAN TELL YOU ALL ABOUT HIS BACKGROUND!
YOU SEE, THE MAN YOU CALL DAMOCLES IS ACTUALLY ERIC BARLOW...
BUGLE
UN ATTACK!
...MY BROTHER!!
THEN, BY THE BRISTLING BEARD OF ODIN--SAY ON, MAN!
I WOULD KNOW MORE OF WHAT CREATES SUCH A MAN AS DAMOCLES!
"I DON'T KNOW, MAYBE ERIC WAS ALWAYS LIKE THIS--CONFUSED, SEARCHING FOR SOMETHING...
"...AND TAKING HIS FRUSTRATIONS OUT ON THE ONE WHO LOVED HIM MOST IN ALL THE WORLD...HIS LITTLE BROTHER... ME!
"I MEAN, NOBODY WAS PROUDER THAN I WAS, WHEN ERIC GRADUATED COLLEGE THE YEAR I ENTERED...
"HE'D MADE HONORS ALL THE WAY...THE TOP OF HIS CLASS...HE HAD THE WHOLE WORLD AT HIS FEET...
"...BUT SOMEHOW, THINGS JUST KEPT GETTING WORSE!
"ERIC DRIFTED FROM JOB TO JOB, STILL LOOKING FOR A DIRECTION...

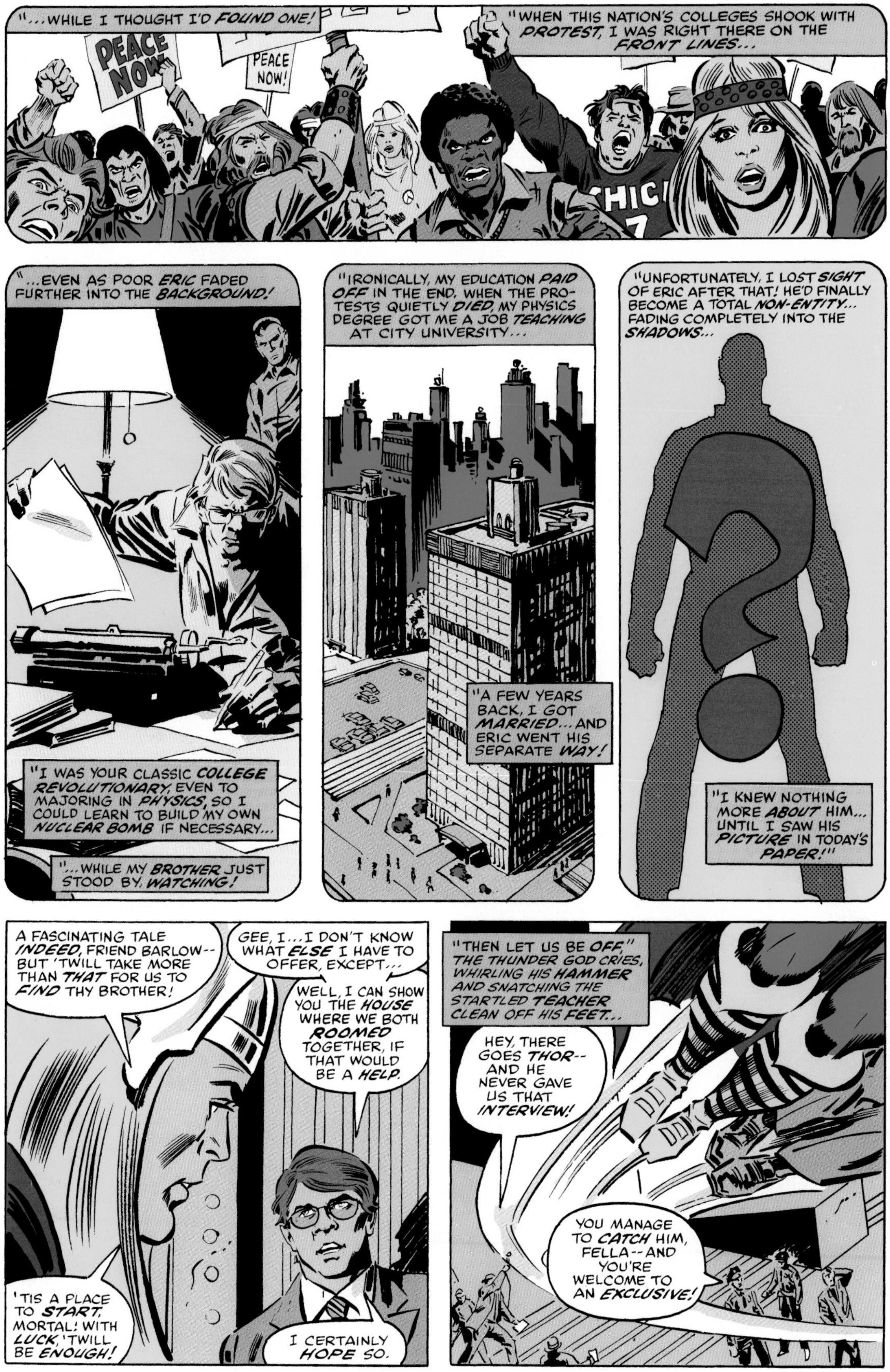
"...WHILE I THOUGHT I'D FOUND ONE!
"WHEN THIS NATION'S COLLEGES SHOOK WITH PROTEST, I WAS RIGHT THERE ON THE FRONT LINES...
PEACE NOW
PEACE NOW!
CHIC
"...EVEN AS POOR ERIC FADED FURTHER INTO THE BACKGROUND!
"I WAS YOUR CLASSIC COLLEGE REVOLUTIONARY, EVEN TO MAJORING IN PHYSICS, SO I COULD LEARN TO BUILD MY OWN NUCLEAR BOMB IF NECESSARY...
"...WHILE MY BROTHER JUST STOOD BY, WATCHING!
"IRONICALLY, MY EDUCATION PAID OFF IN THE END. WHEN THE PROTESTS QUIETLY DIED, MY PHYSICS DEGREE GOT ME A JOB TEACHING AT CITY UNIVERSITY...
"A FEW YEARS BACK, I GOT MARRIED... AND ERIC WENT HIS SEPARATE WAY!
"UNFORTUNATELY, I LOST SIGHT OF ERIC AFTER THAT! HE'D FINALLY BECOME A TOTAL NON-ENTITY... FADING COMPLETELY INTO THE SHADOWS...
"I KNEW NOTHING MORE ABOUT HIM... UNTIL I SAW HIS PICTURE IN TODAY'S PAPER!"
A FASCINATING TALE INDEED, FRIEND BARLOW-- BUT 'TWILL TAKE MORE THAN THAT FOR US TO FIND THY BROTHER!
GEE, I...I DON'T KNOW WHAT ELSE I HAVE TO OFFER, EXCEPT...
WELL, I CAN SHOW YOU THE HOUSE WHERE WE BOTH ROOMED TOGETHER, IF THAT WOULD BE A HELP.
'TIS A PLACE TO START, MORTAL! WITH LUCK, 'TWILL BE ENOUGH!
I CERTAINLY HOPE SO.
"THEN LET US BE OFF," THE THUNDER GOD CRIES, WHIRLING HIS HAMMER AND SNATCHING THE STARTLED TEACHER CLEAN OFF HIS FEET...
HEY, THERE GOES THOR-- AND HE NEVER GAVE US THAT INTERVIEW!
YOU MANAGE TO CATCH HIM, FELLA--AND YOU'RE WELCOME TO AN EXCLUSIVE!

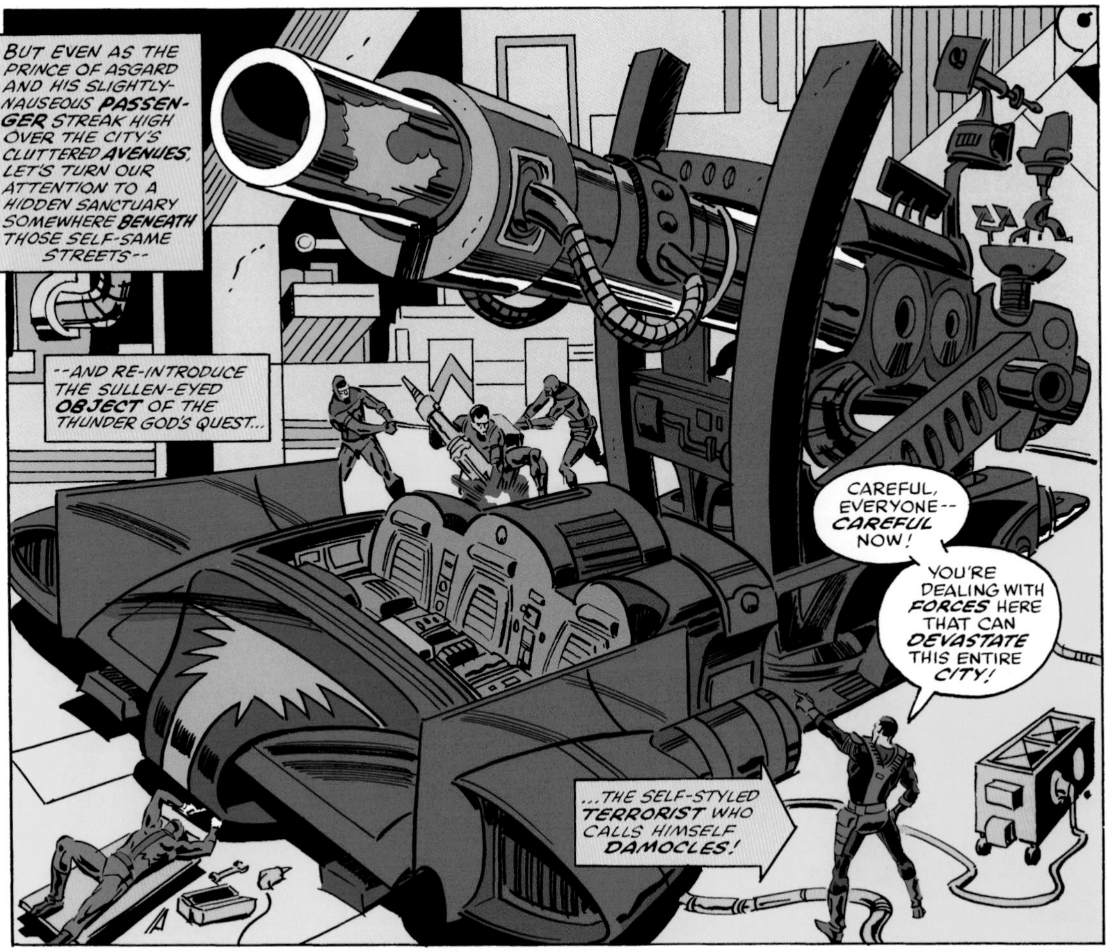
BUT EVEN AS THE PRINCE OF ASGARD AND HIS SLIGHTLY-NAUSEOUS PASSENGER STREAK HIGH OVER THE CITY'S CLUTTERED AVENUES, LET'S TURN OUR ATTENTION TO A HIDDEN SANCTUARY SOMEWHERE BENEATH THOSE SELF-SAME STREETS--
--AND RE-INTRODUCE THE SULLEN-EYED OBJECT OF THE THUNDER GOD'S QUEST...
CAREFUL, EVERYONE-- CAREFUL NOW!
YOU'RE DEALING WITH FORCES HERE THAT CAN DEVASTATE THIS ENTIRE CITY!
...THE SELF-STYLED TERRORIST WHO CALLS HIMSELF DAMOCLES!

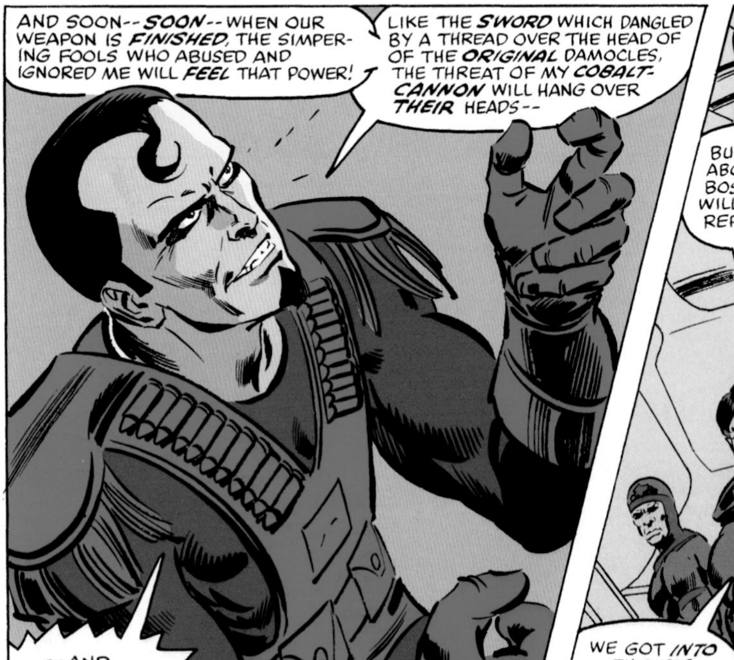
AND SOON--SOON--WHEN OUR WEAPON IS FINISHED, THE SIMPERING FOOLS WHO ABUSED AND IGNORED ME WILL FEEL THAT POWER!
LIKE THE SWORD WHICH DANGLED BY A THREAD OVER THE HEAD OF OF THE ORIGINAL DAMOCLES, THE THREAT OF MY COBALT-CANNON WILL HANG OVER THEIR HEADS--
--AND BEND THEM TO MY WILL!!

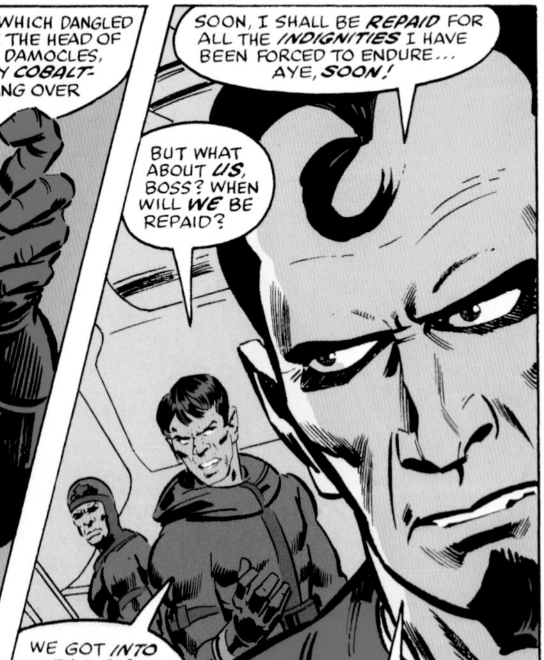
SOON, I SHALL BE REPAID FOR ALL THE INDIGNITIES I HAVE BEEN FORCED TO ENDURE... AYE, SOON!
BUT WHAT ABOUT US, BOSS? WHEN WILL WE BE REPAID?
WE GOT INTO THIS GIG BECAUSE YOU PROMISED US BIG BUCKS, REMEMBER?
EH?

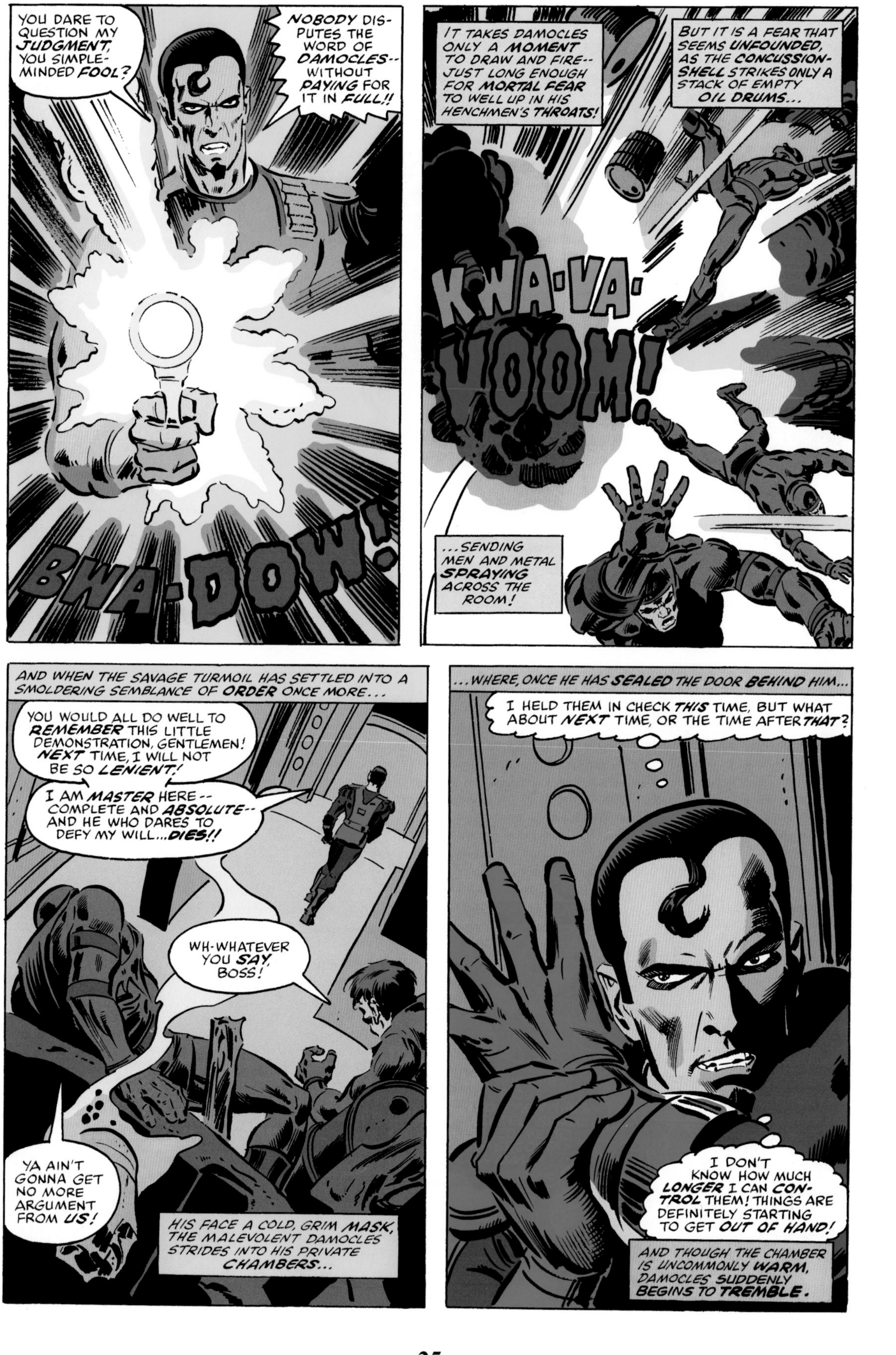
YOU DARE TO QUESTION MY JUDGMENT, YOU SIMPLE-MINDED FOOL?
NOBODY DISPUTES THE WORD OF DAMOCLES--WITHOUT PAYING FOR IT IN FULL!!
BWA-DOW!
IT TAKES DAMOCLES ONLY A MOMENT TO DRAW AND FIRE--JUST LONG ENOUGH FOR MORTAL FEAR TO WELL UP IN HIS HENCHMEN'S THROATS!
BUT IT IS A FEAR THAT SEEMS UNFOUNDED, AS THE CONCUSSION-SHELL STRIKES ONLY A STACK OF EMPTY OIL DRUMS...
KWA-VA-VOOM!
...SENDING MEN AND METAL SPRAYING ACROSS THE ROOM!
AND WHEN THE SAVAGE TURMOIL HAS SETTLED INTO A SMOLDERING SEMBLANCE OF ORDER ONCE MORE...
YOU WOULD ALL DO WELL TO REMEMBER THIS LITTLE DEMONSTRATION, GENTLEMEN! NEXT TIME, I WILL NOT BE SO LENIENT!
I AM MASTER HERE--COMPLETE AND ABSOLUTE--AND HE WHO DARES TO DEFY MY WILL...DIES!!
WH-WHATEVER YOU SAY, BOSS!
YA AIN'T GONNA GET NO MORE ARGUMENT FROM US!
HIS FACE A COLD, GRIM MASK, THE MALEVOLENT DAMOCLES STRIDES INTO HIS PRIVATE CHAMBERS...
...WHERE, ONCE HE HAS SEALED THE DOOR BEHIND HIM...
I HELD THEM IN CHECK THIS TIME, BUT WHAT ABOUT NEXT TIME, OR THE TIME AFTER THAT?
I DON'T KNOW HOW MUCH LONGER I CAN CONTROL THEM! THINGS ARE DEFINITELY STARTING TO GET OUT OF HAND!
AND THOUGH THE CHAMBER IS UNCOMMONLY WARM, DAMOCLES SUDDENLY BEGINS TO TREMBLE.

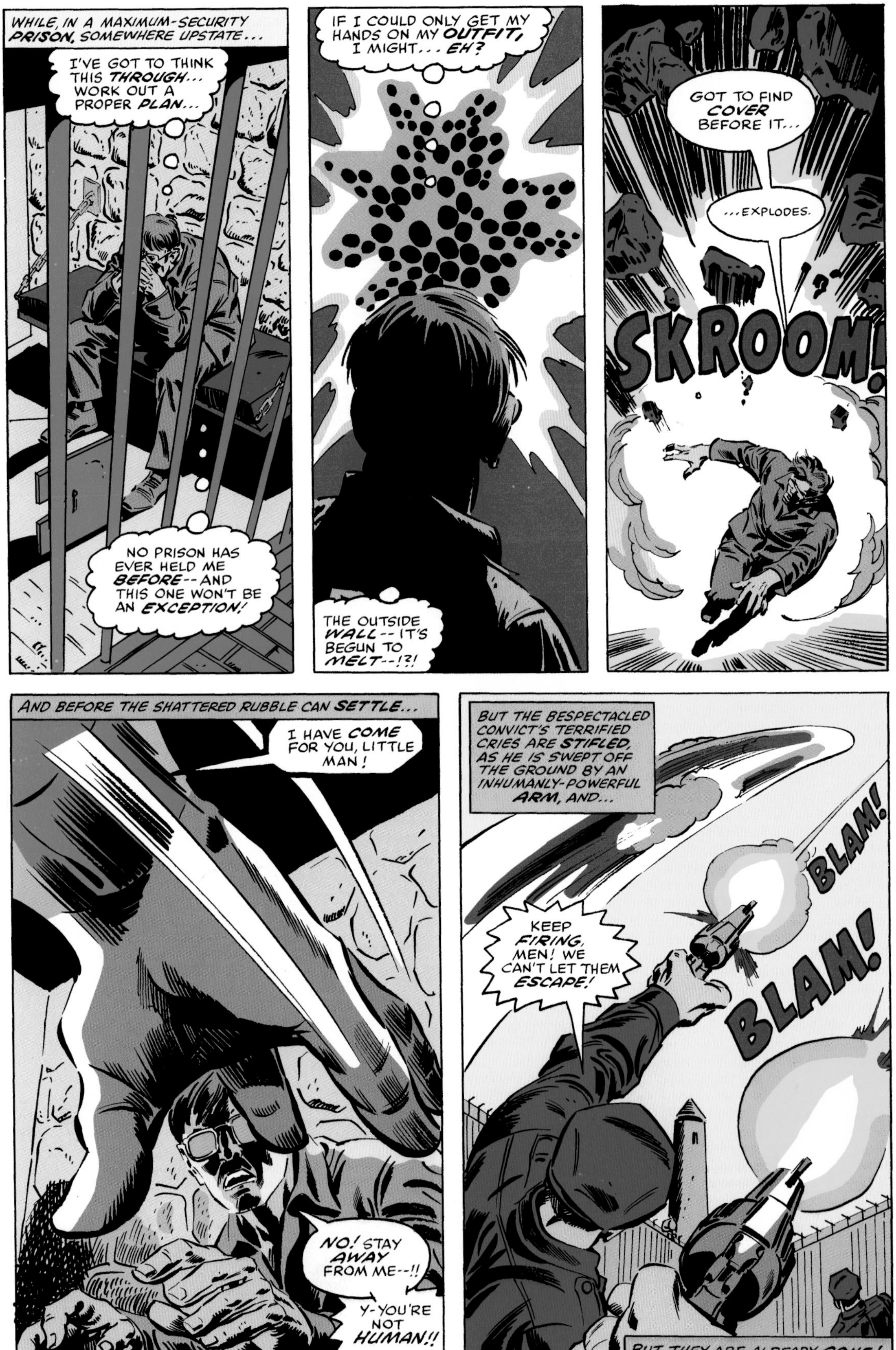
WHILE, IN A MAXIMUM-SECURITY PRISON, SOMEWHERE UPSTATE...
I'VE GOT TO THINK THIS THROUGH... WORK OUT A PROPER PLAN...
NO PRISON HAS EVER HELD ME BEFORE-- AND THIS ONE WON'T BE AN EXCEPTION!
IF I COULD ONLY GET MY HANDS ON MY OUTFIT, I MIGHT... EH?
THE OUTSIDE WALL-- IT'S BEGUN TO MELT--!?!
GOT TO FIND COVER BEFORE IT...
...EXPLODES.
SKROOM!
AND BEFORE THE SHATTERED RUBBLE CAN SETTLE...
I HAVE COME FOR YOU, LITTLE MAN!
NO! STAY AWAY FROM ME--!!
Y-YOU'RE NOT HUMAN!!
BUT THE BESPECTACLED CONVICT'S TERRIFIED CRIES ARE STIFLED, AS HE IS SWEPT OFF THE GROUND BY AN INHUMANLY-POWERFUL ARM, AND...
BLAM!
KEEP FIRING, MEN! WE CAN'T LET THEM ESCAPE!
BLAM!
BUT THEY ARE ALREADY GONE!

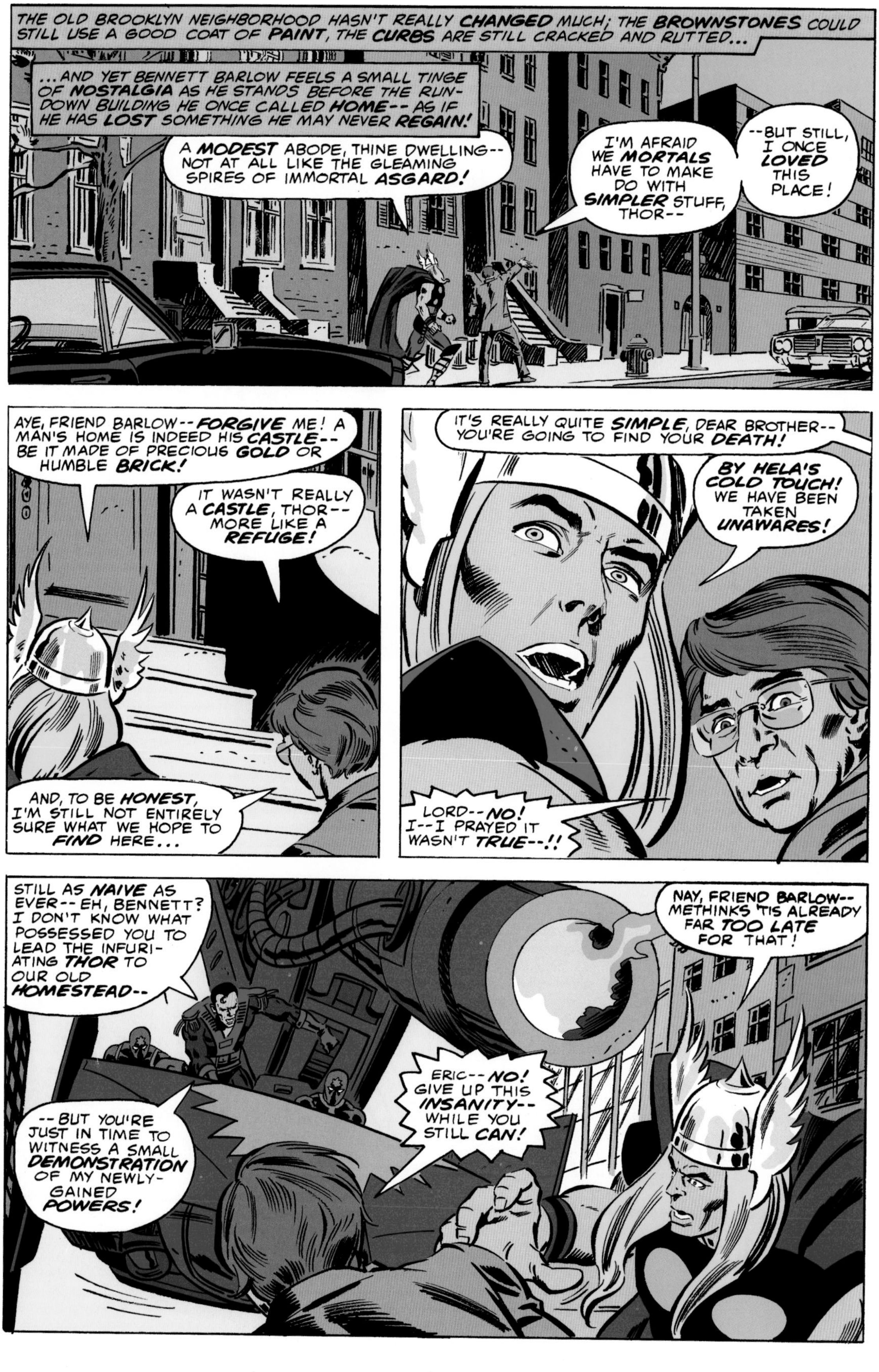
THE OLD BROOKLYN NEIGHBORHOOD HASN'T REALLY CHANGED MUCH; THE BROWNSTONES COULD STILL USE A GOOD COAT OF PAINT, THE CURBS ARE STILL CRACKED AND RUTTED...
...AND YET BENNETT BARLOW FEELS A SMALL TINGE OF NOSTALGIA AS HE STANDS BEFORE THE RUN-DOWN BUILDING HE ONCE CALLED HOME-- AS IF HE HAS LOST SOMETHING HE MAY NEVER REGAIN!
A MODEST ABODE, THINE DWELLING-- NOT AT ALL LIKE THE GLEAMING SPIRES OF IMMORTAL ASGARD!
I'M AFRAID WE MORTALS HAVE TO MAKE DO WITH SIMPLER STUFF, THOR--
--BUT STILL, I ONCE LOVED THIS PLACE!
AYE, FRIEND BARLOW-- FORGIVE ME! A MAN'S HOME IS INDEED HIS CASTLE-- BE IT MADE OF PRECIOUS GOLD OR HUMBLE BRICK!
IT WASN'T REALLY A CASTLE, THOR-- MORE LIKE A REFUGE!
AND, TO BE HONEST, I'M STILL NOT ENTIRELY SURE WHAT WE HOPE TO FIND HERE...
IT'S REALLY QUITE SIMPLE, DEAR BROTHER-- YOU'RE GOING TO FIND YOUR DEATH!
BY HELA'S COLD TOUCH! WE HAVE BEEN TAKEN UNAWARES!
LORD--NO! I--I PRAYED IT WASN'T TRUE--!!
STILL AS NAIVE AS EVER-- EH, BENNETT? I DON'T KNOW WHAT POSSESSED YOU TO LEAD THE INFURI-ATING THOR TO OUR OLD HOMESTEAD--
--BUT YOU'RE JUST IN TIME TO WITNESS A SMALL DEMONSTRATION OF MY NEWLY-GAINED POWERS!
ERIC--NO! GIVE UP THIS INSANITY-- WHILE YOU STILL CAN!
NAY, FRIEND BARLOW-- METHINKS 'TIS ALREADY FAR TOO LATE FOR THAT!

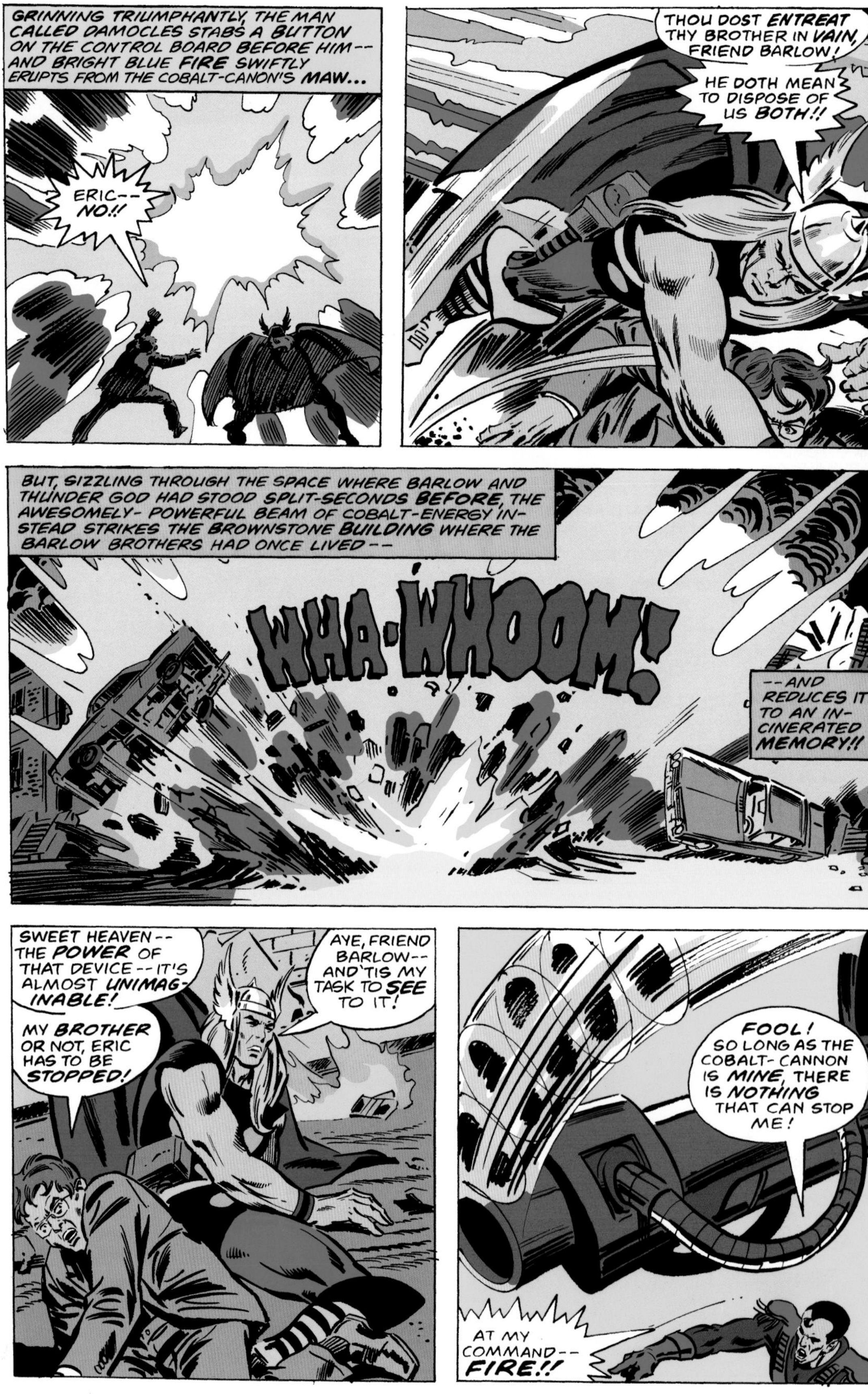
GRINNING TRIUMPHANTLY, THE MAN CALLED DAMOCLES STABS A BUTTON ON THE CONTROL BOARD BEFORE HIM-- AND BRIGHT BLUE FIRE SWIFTLY ERUPTS FROM THE COBALT-CANON'S MAW...
ERIC-- NO!!
THOU DOST ENTREAT THY BROTHER IN VAIN, FRIEND BARLOW!
HE DOTH MEAN TO DISPOSE OF US BOTH!!
BUT, SIZZLING THROUGH THE SPACE WHERE BARLOW AND THUNDER GOD HAD STOOD SPLIT-SECONDS BEFORE, THE AWESOMELY- POWERFUL BEAM OF COBALT-ENERGY IN-STEAD STRIKES THE BROWNSTONE BUILDING WHERE THE BARLOW BROTHERS HAD ONCE LIVED--
WHA-WHOOM!
--AND REDUCES IT TO AN IN-CINERATED MEMORY!!
SWEET HEAVEN-- THE POWER OF THAT DEVICE--IT'S ALMOST UNIMAG-INABLE!
MY BROTHER OR NOT, ERIC HAS TO BE STOPPED!
AYE, FRIEND BARLOW-- AND 'TIS MY TASK TO SEE TO IT!
FOOL! SO LONG AS THE COBALT-CANNON IS MINE, THERE IS NOTHING THAT CAN STOP ME!
AT MY COMMAND-- FIRE!!

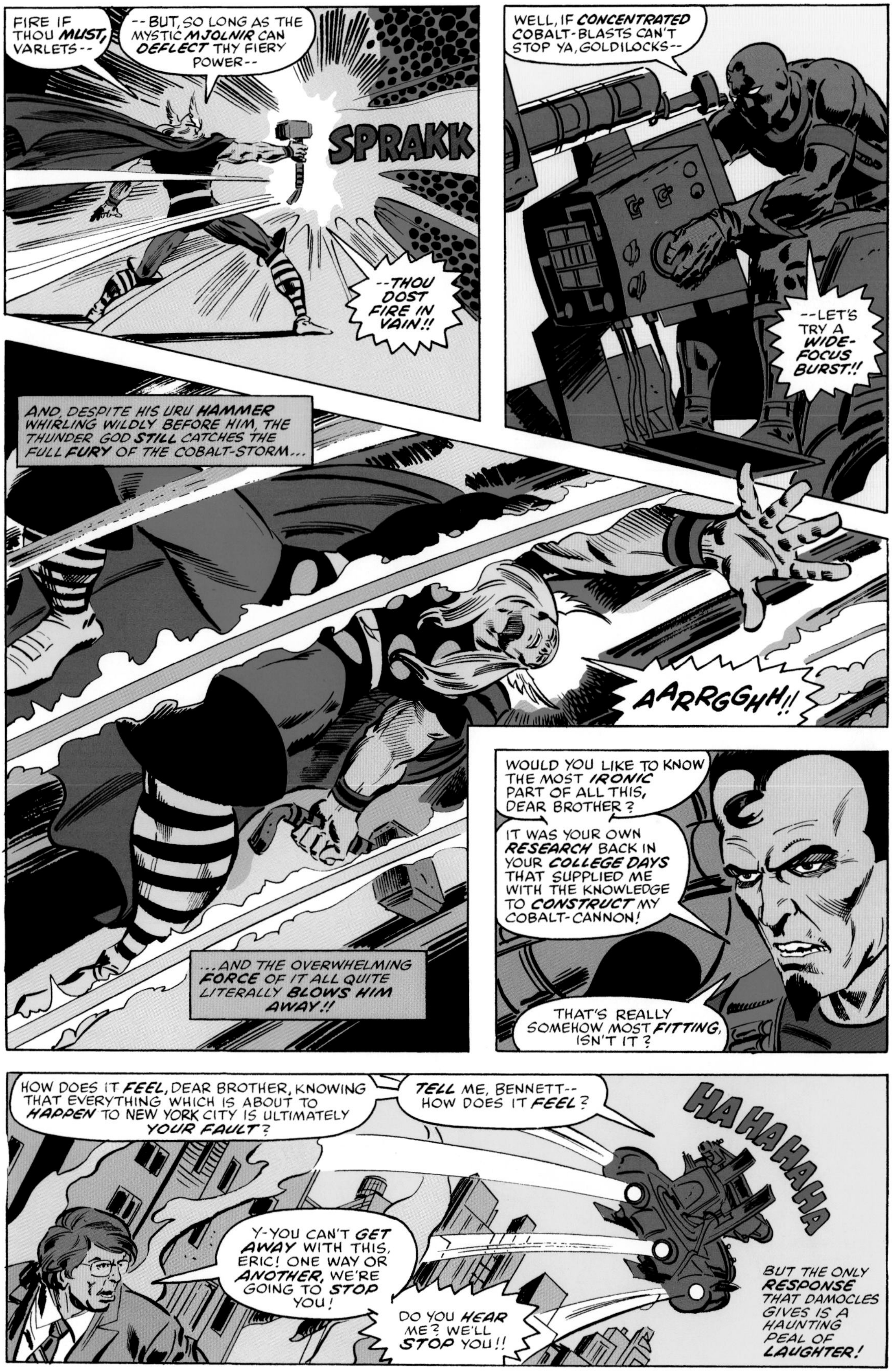
FIRE IF THOU MUST, VARLETS--
--BUT, SO LONG AS THE MYSTIC MJOLNIR CAN DEFLECT THY FIERY POWER--
SPRAKK
--THOU DOST FIRE IN VAIN!!
WELL, IF CONCENTRATED COBALT-BLASTS CAN'T STOP YA, GOLDILOCKS--
--LET'S TRY A WIDE-FOCUS BURST!!
AND, DESPITE HIS URU HAMMER WHIRLING WILDLY BEFORE HIM, THE THUNDER GOD STILL CATCHES THE FULL FURY OF THE COBALT-STORM...
AARRGGHH!!
...AND THE OVERWHELMING FORCE OF IT ALL QUITE LITERALLY BLOWS HIM AWAY!!
WOULD YOU LIKE TO KNOW THE MOST IRONIC PART OF ALL THIS, DEAR BROTHER?
IT WAS YOUR OWN RESEARCH BACK IN YOUR COLLEGE DAYS THAT SUPPLIED ME WITH THE KNOWLEDGE TO CONSTRUCT MY COBALT-CANNON!
THAT'S REALLY SOMEHOW MOST FITTING, ISN'T IT?
HOW DOES IT FEEL, DEAR BROTHER, KNOWING THAT EVERYTHING WHICH IS ABOUT TO HAPPEN TO NEW YORK CITY IS ULTIMATELY YOUR FAULT?
TELL ME, BENNETT-- HOW DOES IT FEEL?
HA HA HA HA HA
Y-YOU CAN'T GET AWAY WITH THIS, ERIC! ONE WAY OR ANOTHER, WE'RE GOING TO STOP YOU!
DO YOU HEAR ME? WE'LL STOP YOU!!
BUT THE ONLY RESPONSE THAT DAMOCLES GIVES IS A HAUNTING PEAL OF LAUGHTER!

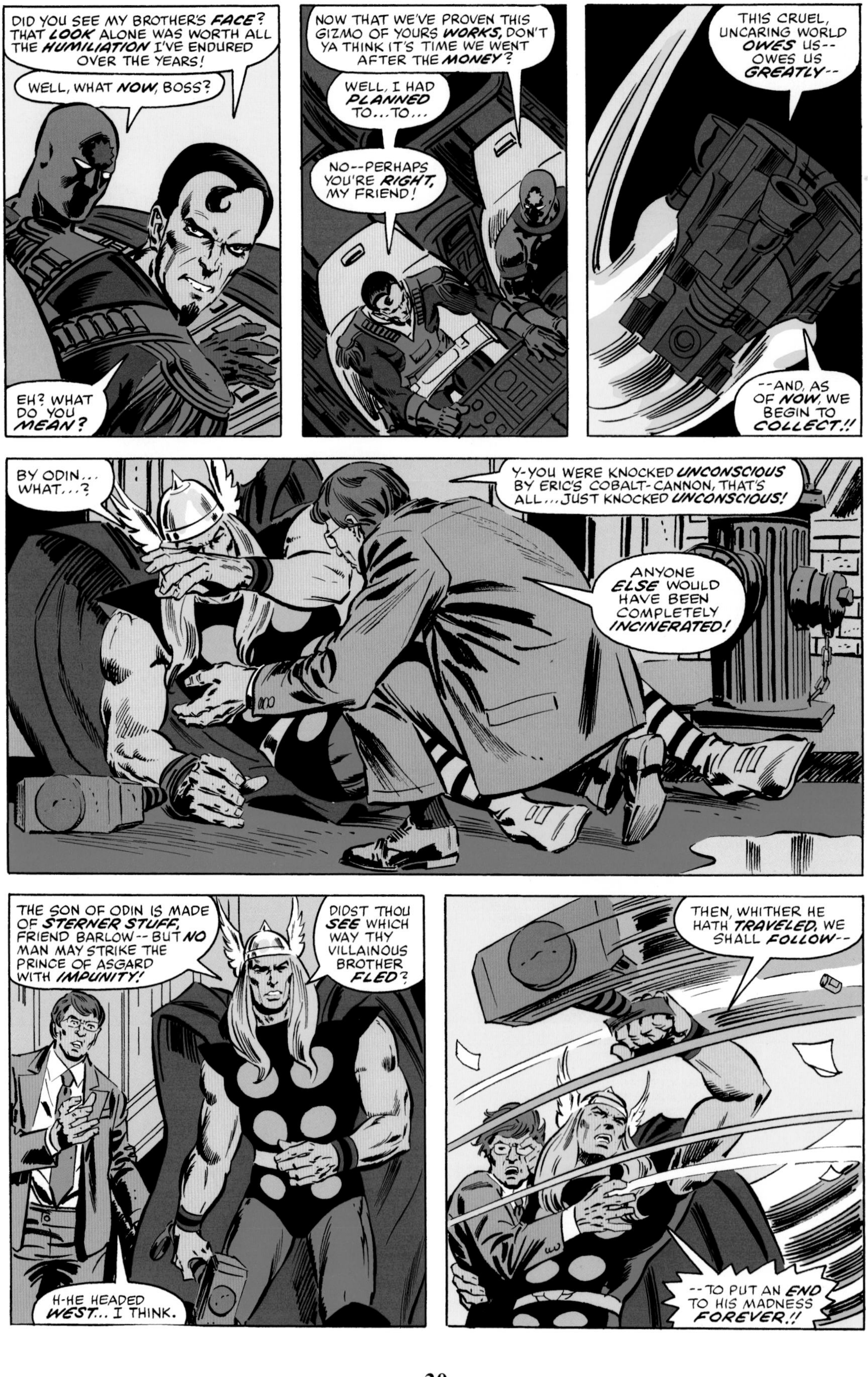

DID YOU SEE MY BROTHER'S FACE? THAT LOOK ALONE WAS WORTH ALL THE HUMILIATION I'VE ENDURED OVER THE YEARS!
WELL, WHAT NOW, BOSS?
EH? WHAT DO YOU MEAN?
NOW THAT WE'VE PROVEN THIS GIZMO OF YOURS WORKS, DON'T YA THINK IT'S TIME WE WENT AFTER THE MONEY?
WELL, I HAD PLANNED TO... TO...
NO--PERHAPS YOU'RE RIGHT, MY FRIEND!
THIS CRUEL, UNCARING WORLD OWES US-- OWES US GREATLY--
--AND, AS OF NOW, WE BEGIN TO COLLECT!!
BY ODIN... WHAT...?
Y-YOU WERE KNOCKED UNCONSCIOUS BY ERIC'S COBALT-CANNON, THAT'S ALL... JUST KNOCKED UNCONSCIOUS!
ANYONE ELSE WOULD HAVE BEEN COMPLETELY INCINERATED!
THE SON OF ODIN IS MADE OF STERNER STUFF, FRIEND BARLOW--BUT NO MAN MAY STRIKE THE PRINCE OF ASGARD WITH IMPUNITY!
DIDST THOU SEE WHICH WAY THY VILLAINOUS BROTHER FLED?
H-HE HEADED WEST... I THINK.
THEN, WHITHER HE HATH TRAVELED, WE SHALL FOLLOW--
--TO PUT AN END TO HIS MADNESS FOREVER!!

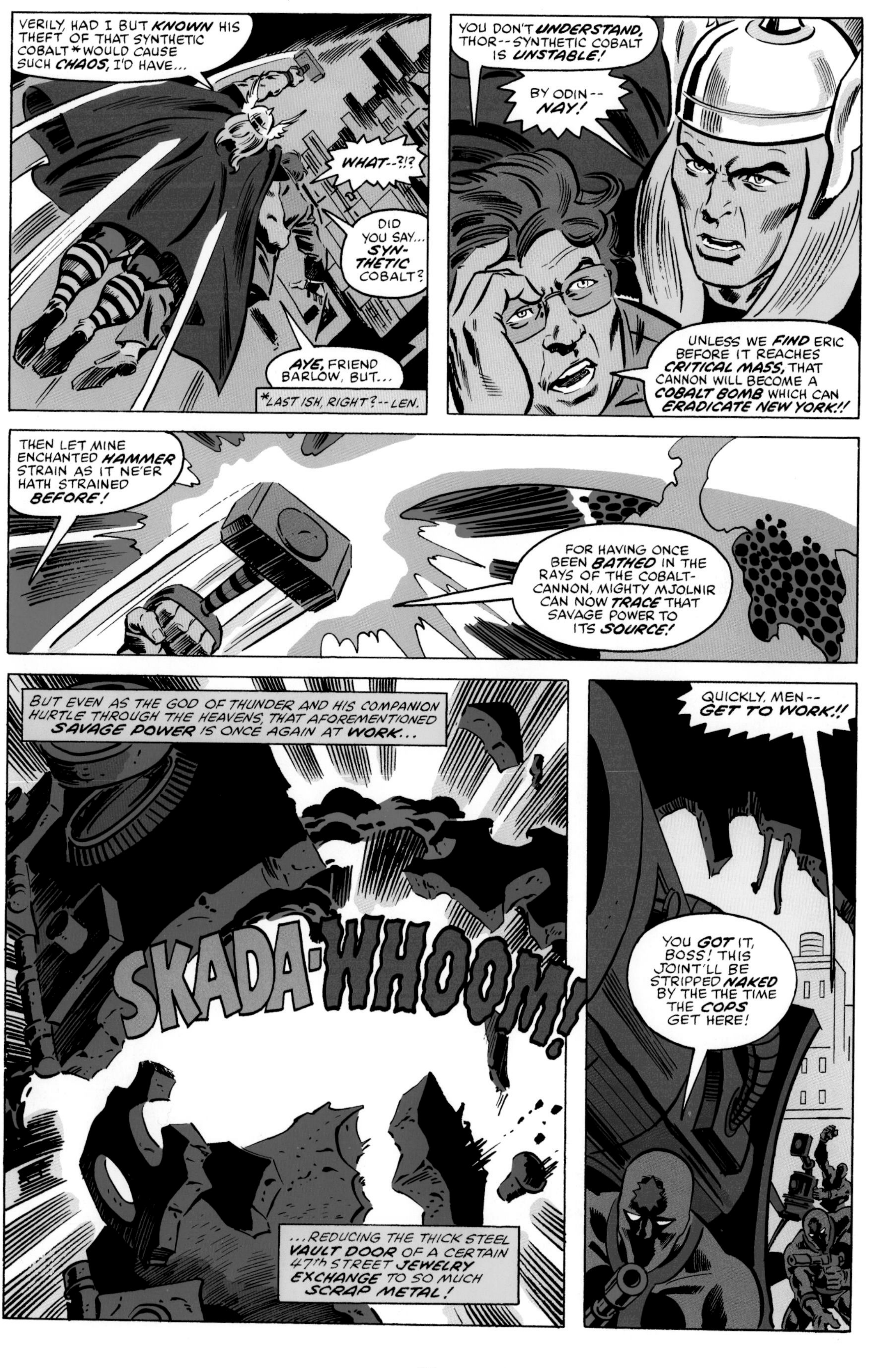
VERILY, HAD I BUT KNOWN HIS THEFT OF THAT SYNTHETIC COBALT* WOULD CAUSE SUCH CHAOS, I'D HAVE...
WHAT--?!?
DID YOU SAY... SYN-THETIC COBALT?
AYE, FRIEND BARLOW, BUT...
*LAST ISH, RIGHT?--LEN.
YOU DON'T UNDERSTAND, THOR--SYNTHETIC COBALT IS UNSTABLE!
BY ODIN-- NAY!
UNLESS WE FIND ERIC BEFORE IT REACHES CRITICAL MASS, THAT CANNON WILL BECOME A COBALT BOMB WHICH CAN ERADICATE NEW YORK!!
THEN LET MINE ENCHANTED HAMMER STRAIN AS IT NE'ER HATH STRAINED BEFORE!
FOR HAVING ONCE BEEN BATHED IN THE RAYS OF THE COBALT-CANNON, MIGHTY MJOLNIR CAN NOW TRACE THAT SAVAGE POWER TO ITS SOURCE!
BUT EVEN AS THE GOD OF THUNDER AND HIS COMPANION HURTLE THROUGH THE HEAVENS, THAT AFOREMENTIONED SAVAGE POWER IS ONCE AGAIN AT WORK...
SKADA-WHOOM!
...REDUCING THE THICK STEEL VAULT DOOR OF A CERTAIN 47th STREET JEWELRY EXCHANGE TO SO MUCH SCRAP METAL!
QUICKLY, MEN-- GET TO WORK!!
YOU GOT IT, BOSS! THIS JOINT'LL BE STRIPPED NAKED BY THE TIME THE COPS GET HERE!

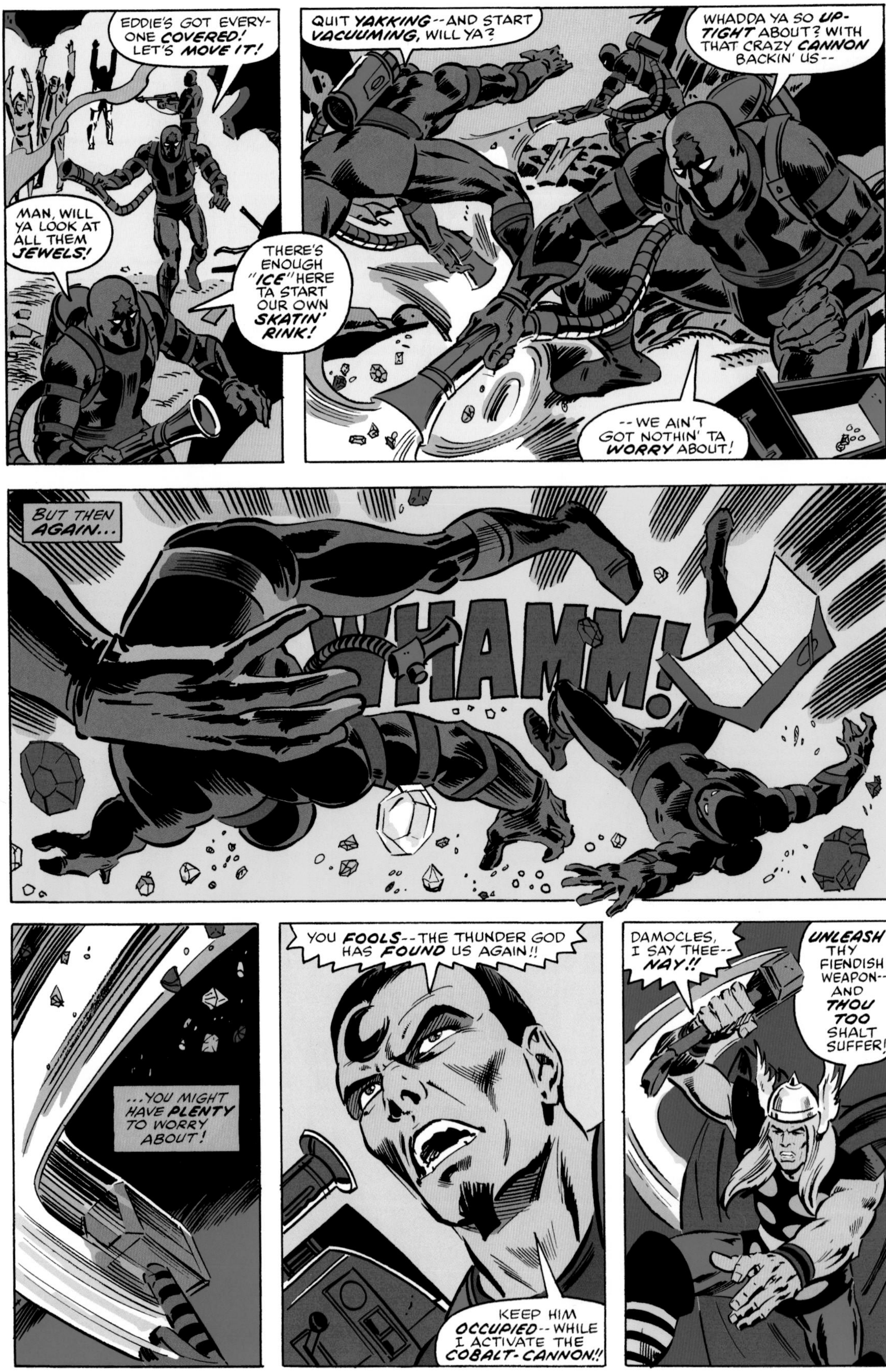

EDDIE'S GOT EVERY-ONE COVERED! LET'S MOVE IT!
MAN, WILL YA LOOK AT ALL THEM JEWELS!
THERE'S ENOUGH "ICE" HERE TA START OUR OWN SKATIN' RINK!
QUIT YAKKING--AND START VACUUMING, WILL YA?
WHADDA YA SO UP-TIGHT ABOUT? WITH THAT CRAZY CANNON BACKIN' US--
--WE AIN'T GOT NOTHIN' TA WORRY ABOUT!
BUT THEN AGAIN...
WHAMM!
...YOU MIGHT HAVE PLENTY TO WORRY ABOUT!
YOU FOOLS--THE THUNDER GOD HAS FOUND US AGAIN!!
KEEP HIM OCCUPIED--WHILE I ACTIVATE THE COBALT-CANNON!!
DAMOCLES, I SAY THEE--NAY!!
UNLEASH THY FIENDISH WEAPON--AND THOU TOO SHALT SUFFER!

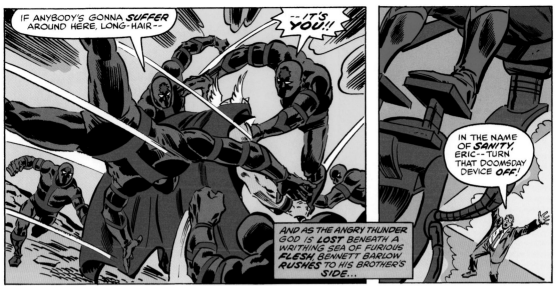

IF ANYBODY'S GONNA **SUFFER** AROUND HERE, LONG-HAIR--

-- IT'S **YOU!!**

IN THE NAME OF **SANITY**, ERIC-- TURN THAT DOOMSDAY DEVICE **OFF!**

AND AS THE ANGRY THUNDER GOD IS **LOST** BENEATH A WRITHING SEA OF FURIOUS **FLESH**, BENNETT BARLOW **RUSHES** TO HIS BROTHER'S **SIDE...**

NOT UNTIL THE ANNOYING **THOR** IS FINALLY **DESTROYED!**

YOU **MANIAC!** YOU'RE GOING TO DESTROY US **ALL!**

THE COBALT YOU USED WAS **UNSTABLE!** LOOK AT THE **GLOW** AROUND YOUR CANNON! I'M TELLING YOU IT'S GOING TO **EXPLODE!**

NO.

IT ISN'T **POSSIBLE**--! NOT AFTER ALL MY **WORK**-- ALL MY **PLANNING**--!

THERE MUST BE SOMETHING I CAN **DO** BEFORE...

AYE, FANATIC ONE-- THERE IS **INDEED!**

HUH?

THOU CANST **SURRENDER** THYSELF, DAMOCLES--

--WHILST STILL THOU ART **ABLE!!**

THIS IS ALL **YOUR** FAULT, THOR! BUT BEFORE I'D GIVE UP **NOW**--

--I'LL SEE US ALL IN **HELL!!**

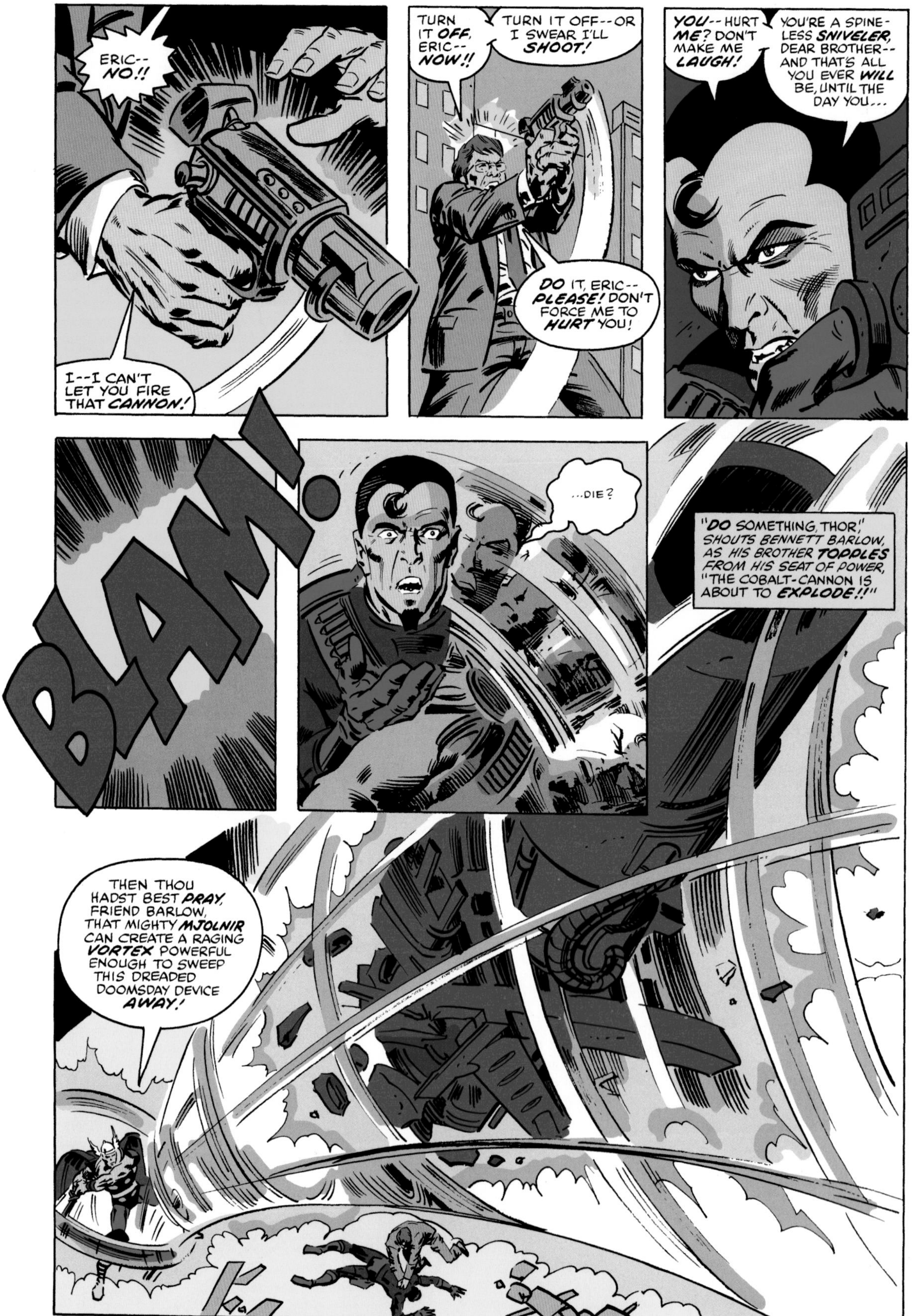
ERIC-- NO!!
I--I CAN'T LET YOU FIRE THAT CANNON!
TURN IT OFF, ERIC-- NOW!!
TURN IT OFF--OR I SWEAR I'LL SHOOT!
DO IT, ERIC-- PLEASE! DON'T FORCE ME TO HURT YOU!
YOU--HURT ME? DON'T MAKE ME LAUGH!
YOU'RE A SPINELESS SNIVELER, DEAR BROTHER-- AND THAT'S ALL YOU EVER WILL BE, UNTIL THE DAY YOU...
BLAM!
...DIE?
"DO SOMETHING, THOR," SHOUTS BENNETT BARLOW, AS HIS BROTHER TOPPLES FROM HIS SEAT OF POWER, "THE COBALT-CANNON IS ABOUT TO EXPLODE!!"
THEN THOU HADST BEST PRAY, FRIEND BARLOW, THAT MIGHTY MJOLNIR CAN CREATE A RAGING VORTEX POWERFUL ENOUGH TO SWEEP THIS DREADED DOOMSDAY DEVICE AWAY!

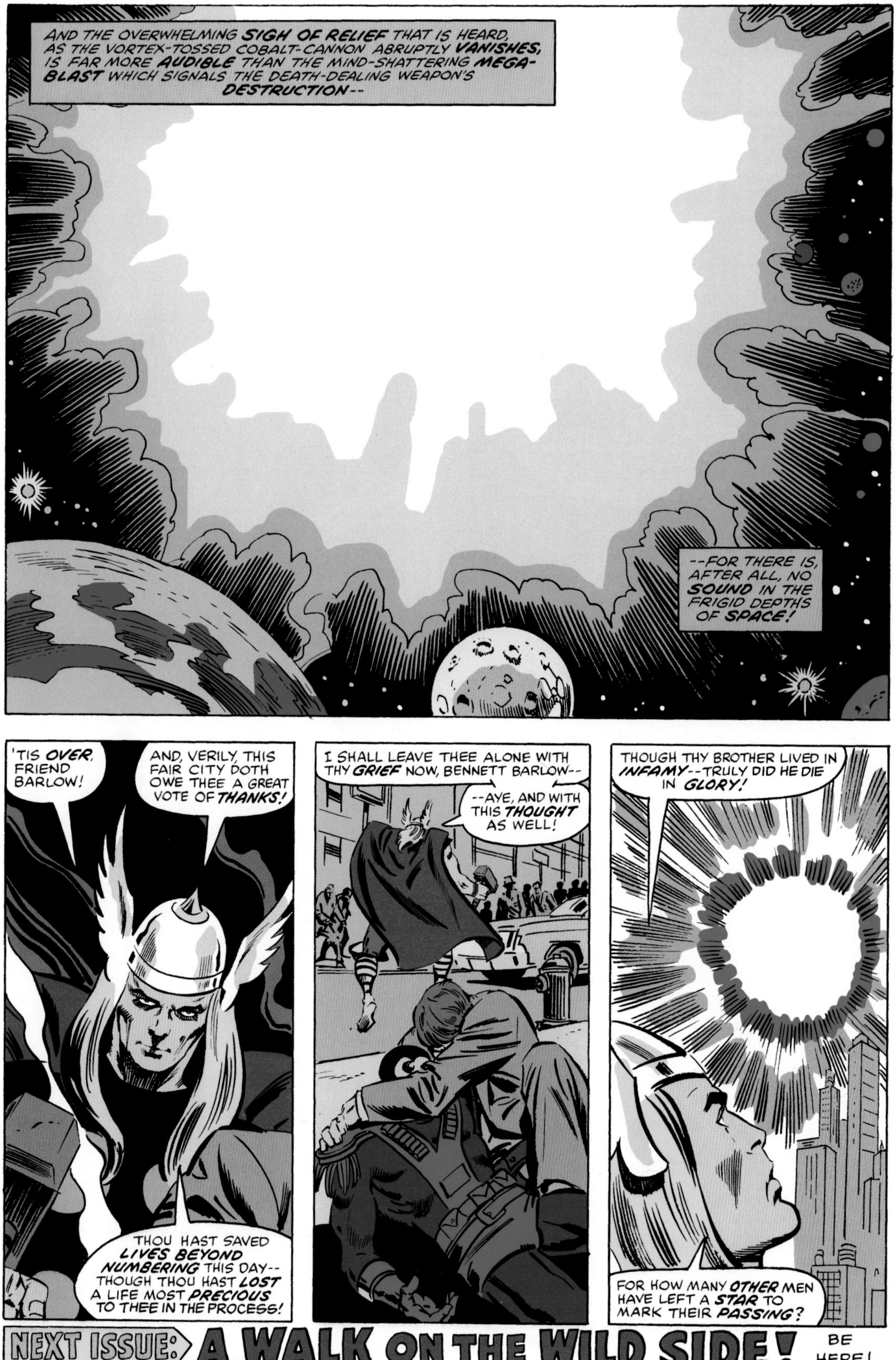
AND THE OVERWHELMING SIGH OF RELIEF THAT IS HEARD, AS THE VORTEX-TOSSED COBALT-CANNON ABRUPTLY VANISHES, IS FAR MORE AUDIBLE THAN THE MIND-SHATTERING MEGA-BLAST WHICH SIGNALS THE DEATH-DEALING WEAPON'S DESTRUCTION--
--FOR THERE IS, AFTER ALL, NO SOUND IN THE FRIGID DEPTHS OF SPACE!
'TIS OVER, FRIEND BARLOW!
AND, VERILY, THIS FAIR CITY DOTH OWE THEE A GREAT VOTE OF THANKS!
THOU HAST SAVED LIVES BEYOND NUMBERING THIS DAY--THOUGH THOU HAST LOST A LIFE MOST PRECIOUS TO THEE IN THE PROCESS!
I SHALL LEAVE THEE ALONE WITH THY GRIEF NOW, BENNETT BARLOW--
--AYE, AND WITH THIS THOUGHT AS WELL!
THOUGH THY BROTHER LIVED IN INFAMY--TRULY DID HE DIE IN GLORY!
FOR HOW MANY OTHER MEN HAVE LEFT A STAR TO MARK THEIR PASSING?
NEXT ISSUE: A WALK ON THE WILD SIDE! BE HERE!

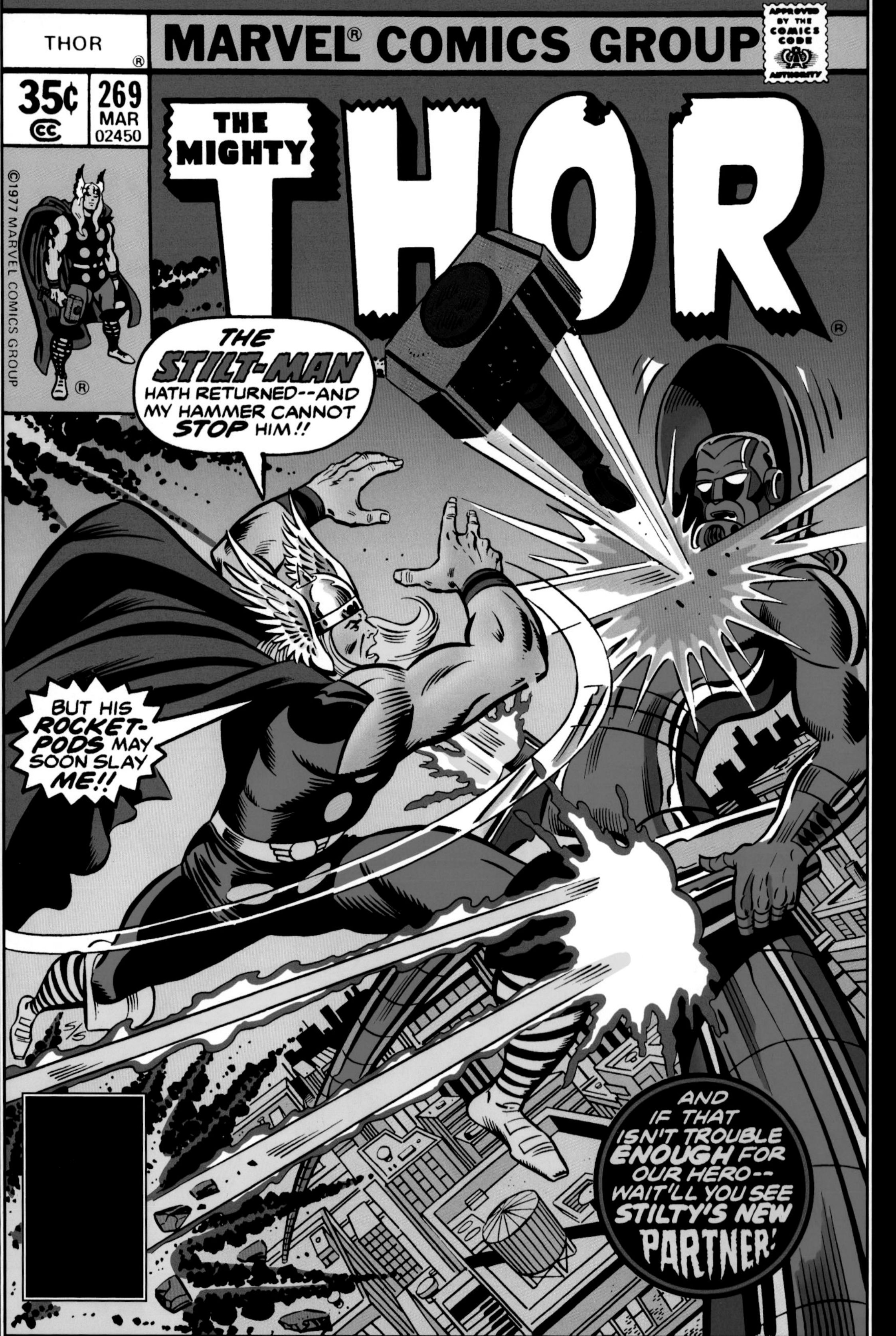

THOR
MARVEL® COMICS GROUP
APPROVED BY THE COMICS CODE AUTHORITY
35¢
269 MAR 02450
THE MIGHTY THOR
©1977 MARVEL COMICS GROUP
THE STILT-MAN HATH RETURNED--AND MY HAMMER CANNOT STOP HIM!!
BUT HIS ROCKET-PODS MAY SOON SLAY ME!!
AND IF THAT ISN'T TROUBLE ENOUGH FOR OUR HERO-- WAIT'LL YOU SEE STILTY'S NEW PARTNER!

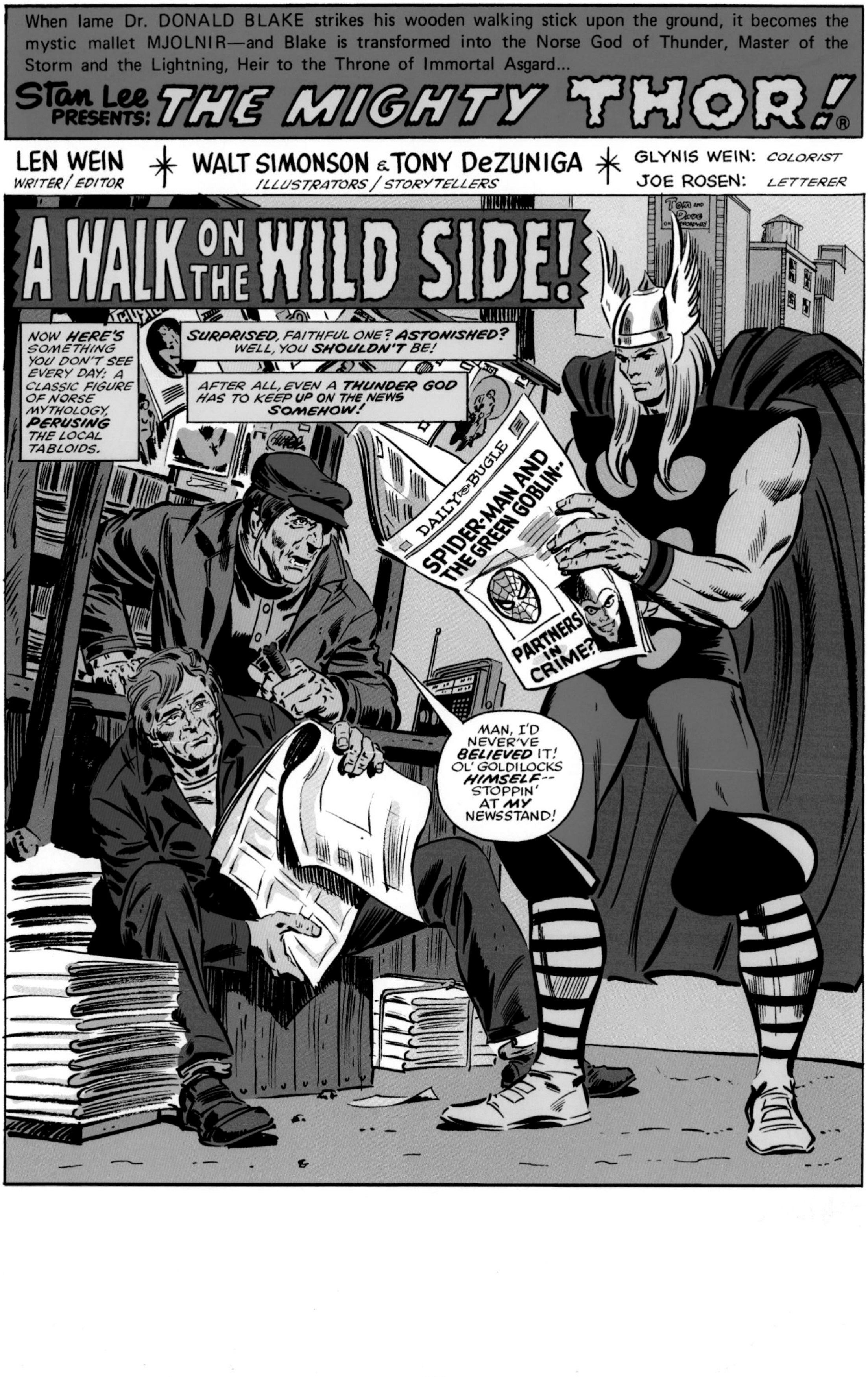
When lame Dr. DONALD BLAKE strikes his wooden walking stick upon the ground, it becomes the mystic mallet MJOLNIR—and Blake is transformed into the Norse God of Thunder, Master of the Storm and the Lightning, Heir to the Throne of Immortal Asgard...
Stan Lee PRESENTS: THE MIGHTY THOR!®
LEN WEIN WRITER/EDITOR
WALT SIMONSON & TONY DeZUNIGA ILLUSTRATORS/STORYTELLERS
GLYNIS WEIN: COLORIST
JOE ROSEN: LETTERER
A WALK ON THE WILD SIDE!
NOW HERE'S SOMETHING YOU DON'T SEE EVERY DAY: A CLASSIC FIGURE OF NORSE MYTHOLOGY, PERUSING THE LOCAL TABLOIDS.
SURPRISED, FAITHFUL ONE? ASTONISHED? WELL, YOU SHOULDN'T BE!
AFTER ALL, EVEN A THUNDER GOD HAS TO KEEP UP ON THE NEWS SOMEHOW!
DAILY BUGLE
SPIDER-MAN AND THE GREEN GOBLIN-
PARTNERS IN CRIME?
MAN, I'D NEVER'VE BELIEVED IT! OL' GOLDILOCKS HIMSELF-- STOPPIN' AT MY NEWSSTAND!

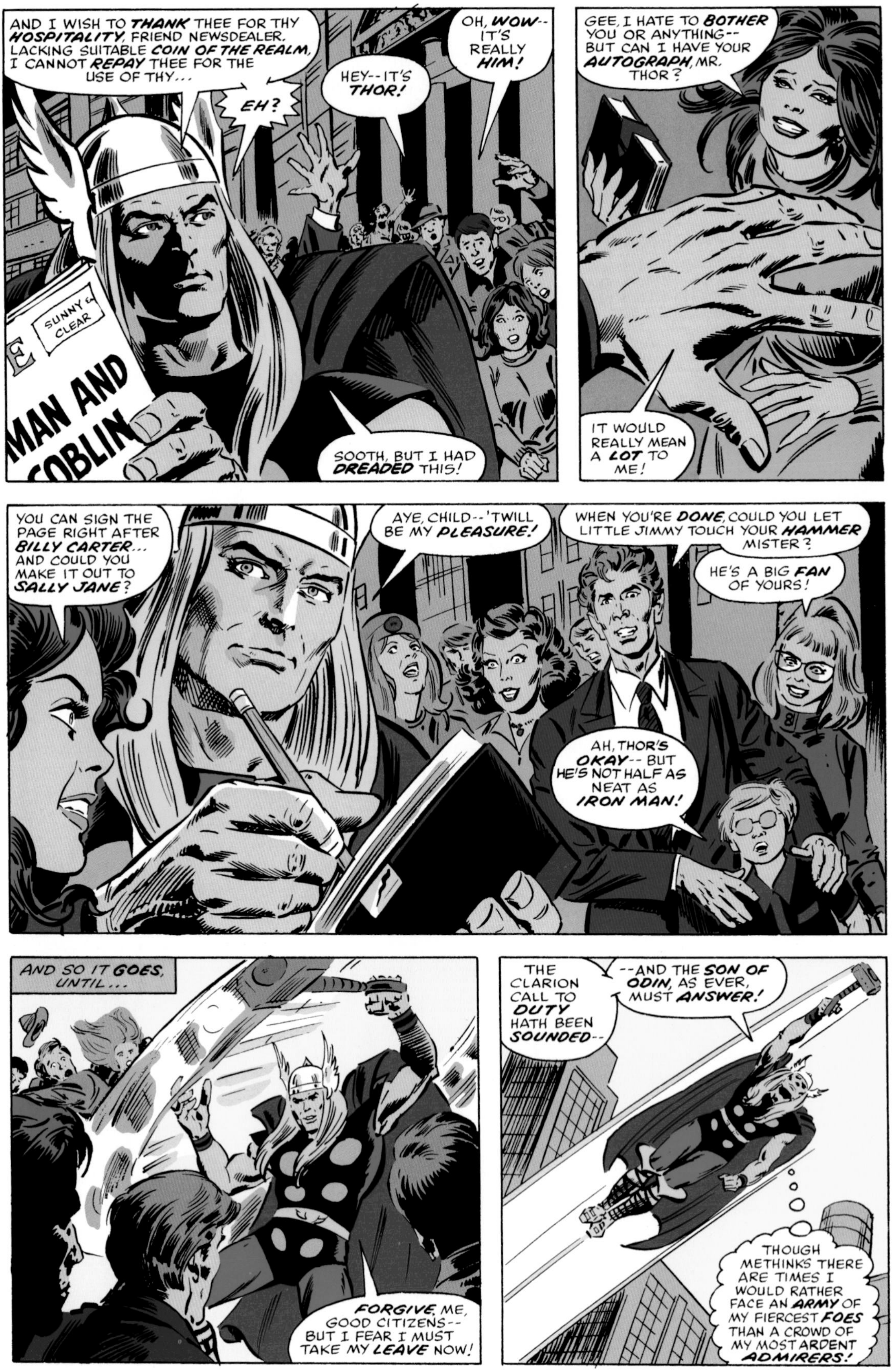
AND I WISH TO THANK THEE FOR THY HOSPITALITY, FRIEND NEWSDEALER. LACKING SUITABLE COIN OF THE REALM, I CANNOT REPAY THEE FOR THE USE OF THY...
EH?
HEY--IT'S THOR!
OH, WOW--IT'S REALLY HIM!
SUNNY & CLEAR
MAN AND GOBLIN
SOOTH, BUT I HAD DREADED THIS!
GEE, I HATE TO BOTHER YOU OR ANYTHING--BUT CAN I HAVE YOUR AUTOGRAPH, MR. THOR?
IT WOULD REALLY MEAN A LOT TO ME!
YOU CAN SIGN THE PAGE RIGHT AFTER BILLY CARTER... AND COULD YOU MAKE IT OUT TO SALLY JANE?
AYE, CHILD--'TWILL BE MY PLEASURE!
WHEN YOU'RE DONE, COULD YOU LET LITTLE JIMMY TOUCH YOUR HAMMER MISTER?
HE'S A BIG FAN OF YOURS!
AH, THOR'S OKAY--BUT HE'S NOT HALF AS NEAT AS IRON MAN!
AND SO IT GOES, UNTIL...
FORGIVE, ME, GOOD CITIZENS--BUT I FEAR I MUST TAKE MY LEAVE NOW!
THE CLARION CALL TO DUTY HATH BEEN SOUNDED--
--AND THE SON OF ODIN, AS EVER, MUST ANSWER!
THOUGH METHINKS THERE ARE TIMES I WOULD RATHER FACE AN ARMY OF MY FIERCEST FOES THAN A CROWD OF MY MOST ARDENT ADMIRERS!

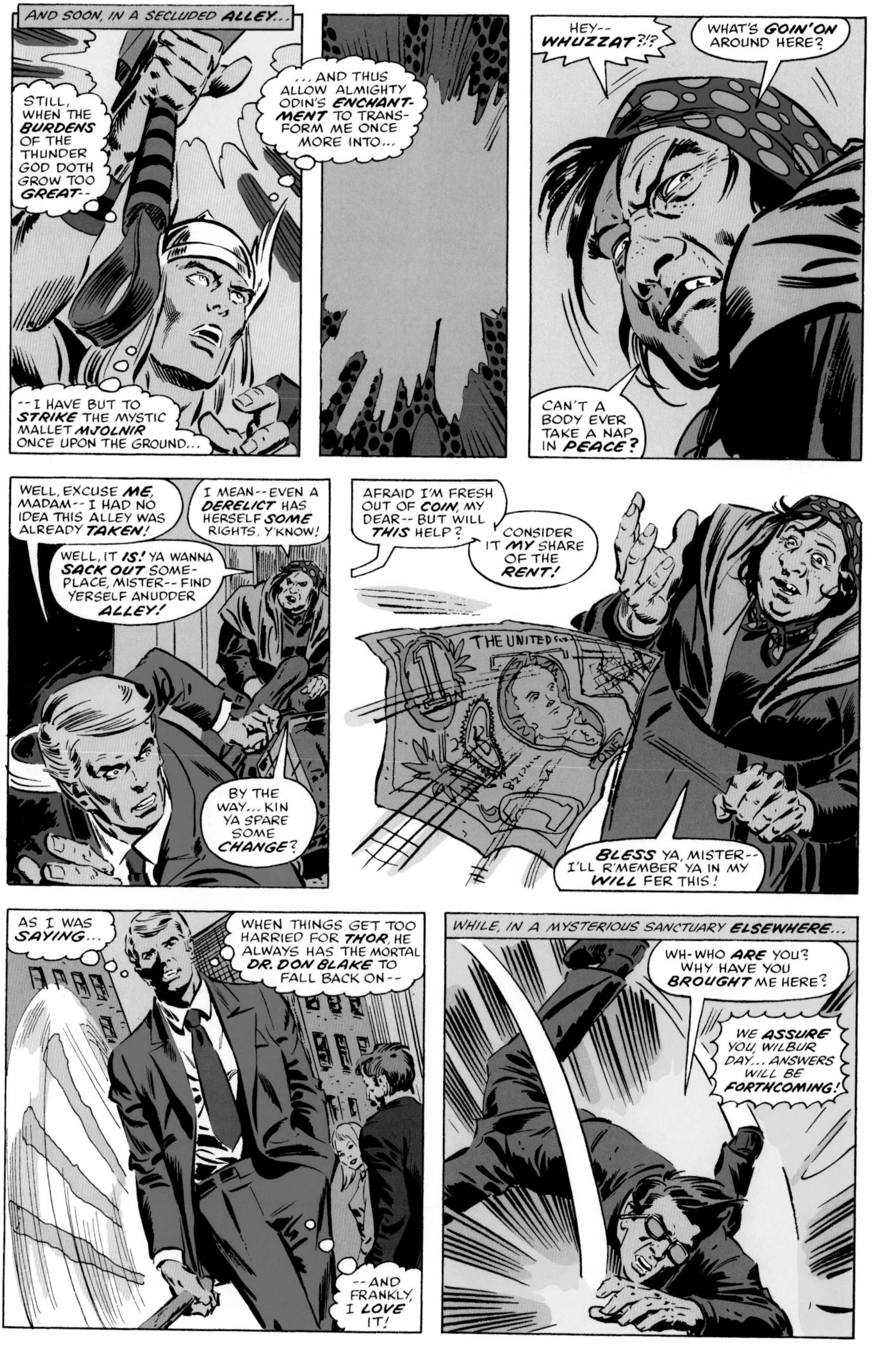
AND SOON, IN A SECLUDED ALLEY...
STILL, WHEN THE BURDENS OF THE THUNDER GOD DOTH GROW TOO GREAT--
--I HAVE BUT TO STRIKE THE MYSTIC MALLET MJOLNIR ONCE UPON THE GROUND...
...AND THUS ALLOW ALMIGHTY ODIN'S ENCHANTMENT TO TRANSFORM ME ONCE MORE INTO...
HEY-- WHUZZAT?!?
WHAT'S GOIN'ON AROUND HERE?
CAN'T A BODY EVER TAKE A NAP IN PEACE?
WELL, EXCUSE ME, MADAM-- I HAD NO IDEA THIS ALLEY WAS ALREADY TAKEN!
I MEAN--EVEN A DERELICT HAS HERSELF SOME RIGHTS, Y'KNOW!
WELL, IT IS! YA WANNA SACK OUT SOMEPLACE, MISTER-- FIND YERSELF ANUDDER ALLEY!
BY THE WAY... KIN YA SPARE SOME CHANGE?
AFRAID I'M FRESH OUT OF COIN, MY DEAR-- BUT WILL THIS HELP?
CONSIDER IT MY SHARE OF THE RENT!
BLESS YA, MISTER-- I'LL R'MEMBER YA IN MY WILL FER THIS!
AS I WAS SAYING...
WHEN THINGS GET TOO HARRIED FOR THOR, HE ALWAYS HAS THE MORTAL DR. DON BLAKE TO FALL BACK ON--
--AND FRANKLY, I LOVE IT!
WHILE, IN A MYSTERIOUS SANCTUARY ELSEWHERE...
WH-WHO ARE YOU? WHY HAVE YOU BROUGHT ME HERE?
WE ASSURE YOU, WILBUR DAY... ANSWERS WILL BE FORTHCOMING!

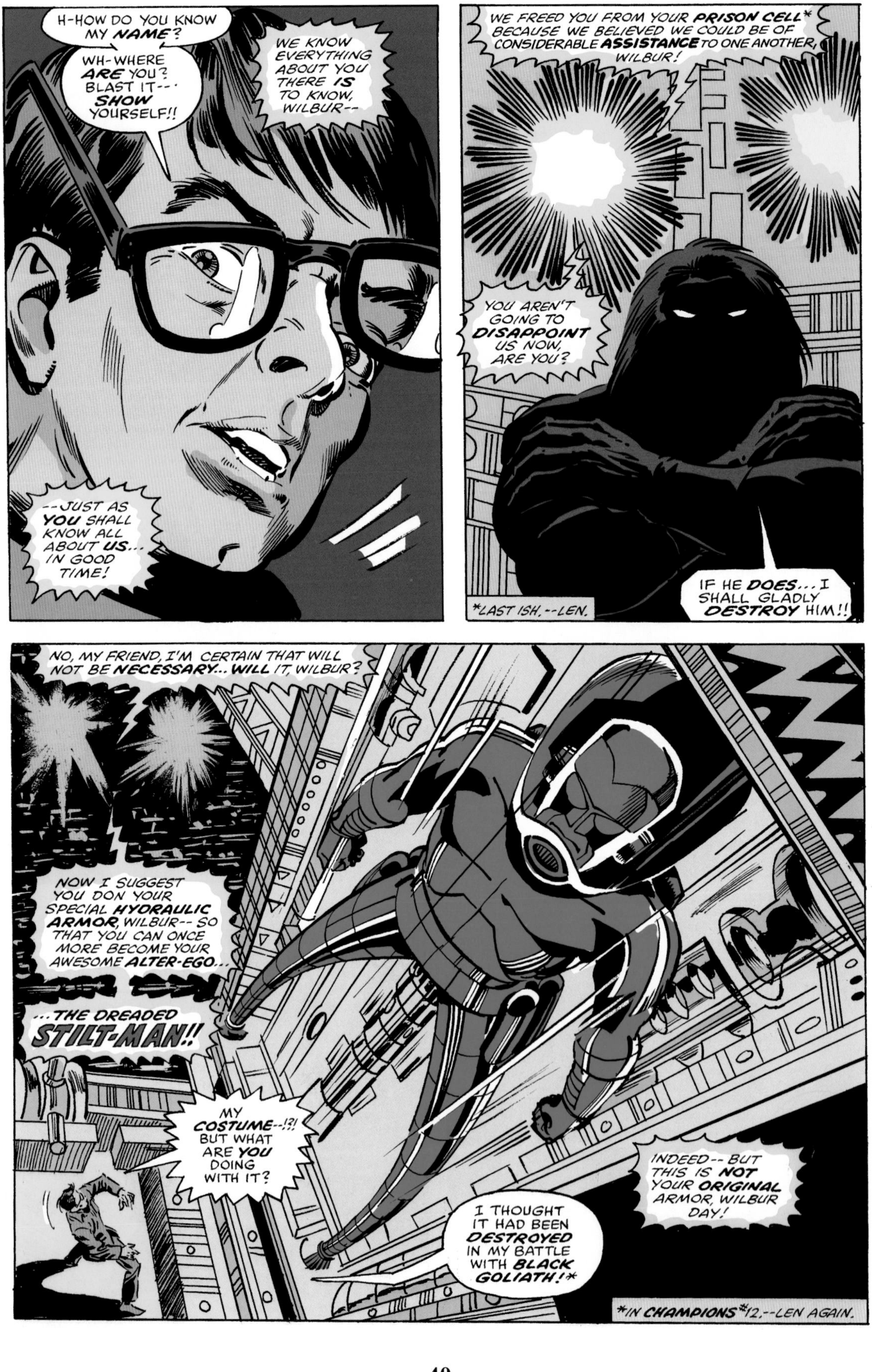
H-HOW DO YOU KNOW MY NAME?
WH-WHERE ARE YOU? BLAST IT-- SHOW YOURSELF!!
WE KNOW EVERYTHING ABOUT YOU THERE IS TO KNOW, WILBUR--
--JUST AS YOU SHALL KNOW ALL ABOUT US... IN GOOD TIME!
WE FREED YOU FROM YOUR PRISON CELL* BECAUSE WE BELIEVED WE COULD BE OF CONSIDERABLE ASSISTANCE TO ONE ANOTHER, WILBUR!
YOU AREN'T GOING TO DISAPPOINT US NOW, ARE YOU?
IF HE DOES... I SHALL GLADLY DESTROY HIM!!
*LAST ISH.--LEN.
NO, MY FRIEND, I'M CERTAIN THAT WILL NOT BE NECESSARY... WILL IT, WILBUR?
NOW I SUGGEST YOU DON YOUR SPECIAL HYDRAULIC ARMOR, WILBUR-- SO THAT YOU CAN ONCE MORE BECOME YOUR AWESOME ALTER-EGO...
...THE DREADED STILT-MAN!!
MY COSTUME--!?! BUT WHAT ARE YOU DOING WITH IT?
I THOUGHT IT HAD BEEN DESTROYED IN MY BATTLE WITH BLACK GOLIATH!*
INDEED-- BUT THIS IS NOT YOUR ORIGINAL ARMOR, WILBUR DAY!
*IN CHAMPIONS #12.--LEN AGAIN.

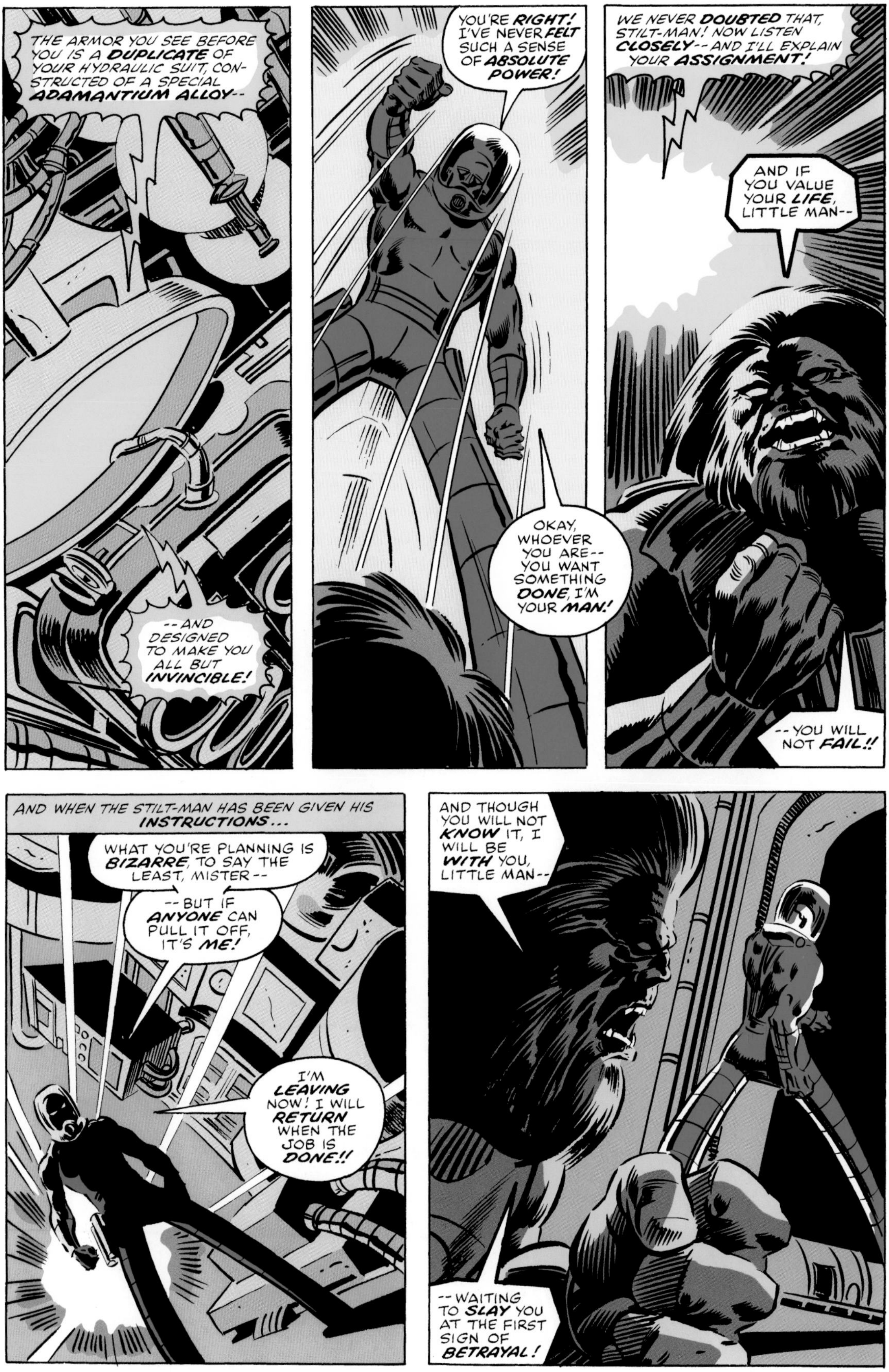
THE ARMOR YOU SEE BEFORE YOU IS A DUPLICATE OF YOUR HYDRAULIC SUIT, CONSTRUCTED OF A SPECIAL ADAMANTIUM ALLOY--
--AND DESIGNED TO MAKE YOU ALL BUT INVINCIBLE!
YOU'RE RIGHT! I'VE NEVER FELT SUCH A SENSE OF ABSOLUTE POWER!
OKAY, WHOEVER YOU ARE-- YOU WANT SOMETHING DONE, I'M YOUR MAN!
WE NEVER DOUBTED THAT, STILT-MAN! NOW LISTEN CLOSELY--AND I'LL EXPLAIN YOUR ASSIGNMENT!
AND IF YOU VALUE YOUR LIFE, LITTLE MAN--
--YOU WILL NOT FAIL!!
AND WHEN THE STILT-MAN HAS BEEN GIVEN HIS INSTRUCTIONS...
WHAT YOU'RE PLANNING IS BIZARRE, TO SAY THE LEAST, MISTER--
--BUT IF ANYONE CAN PULL IT OFF, IT'S ME!
I'M LEAVING NOW! I WILL RETURN WHEN THE JOB IS DONE!!
AND THOUGH YOU WILL NOT KNOW IT, I WILL BE WITH YOU, LITTLE MAN--
--WAITING TO SLAY YOU AT THE FIRST SIGN OF BETRAYAL!

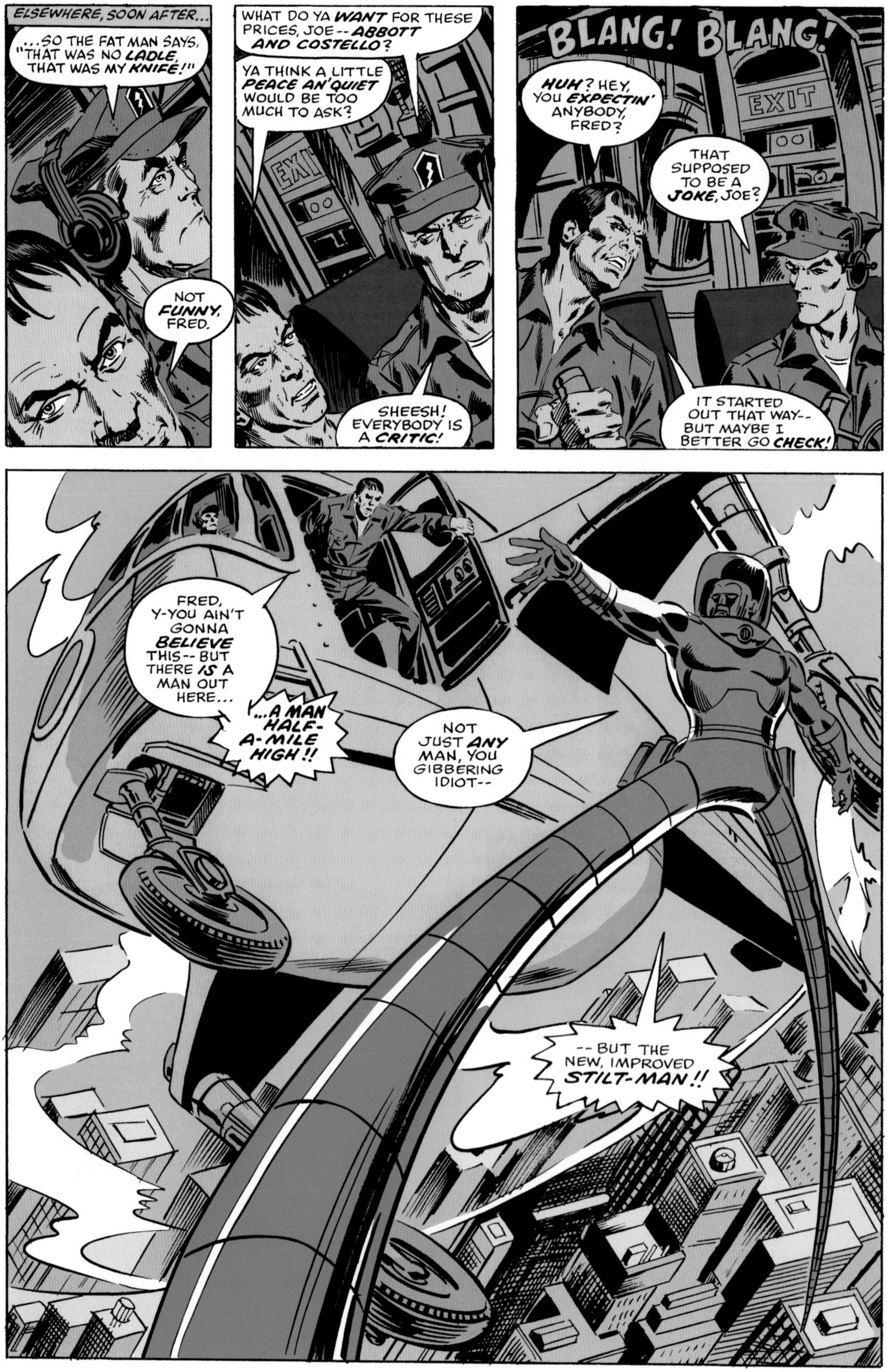
ELSEWHERE, SOON AFTER...
...SO THE FAT MAN SAYS, "THAT WAS NO LADLE, THAT WAS MY KNIFE!"
NOT FUNNY, FRED.
WHAT DO YA WANT FOR THESE PRICES, JOE-- ABBOTT AND COSTELLO?
YA THINK A LITTLE PEACE AN' QUIET WOULD BE TOO MUCH TO ASK?
EXIT
SHEESH! EVERYBODY IS A CRITIC!
BLANG! BLANG!
EXIT
HUH? HEY, YOU EXPECTIN' ANYBODY, FRED?
THAT SUPPOSED TO BE A JOKE, JOE?
IT STARTED OUT THAT WAY-- BUT MAYBE I BETTER GO CHECK!
FRED, Y-YOU AIN'T GONNA BELIEVE THIS-- BUT THERE IS A MAN OUT HERE...
...A MAN HALF-A-MILE HIGH!!
NOT JUST ANY MAN, YOU GIBBERING IDIOT--
-- BUT THE NEW, IMPROVED STILT-MAN!!

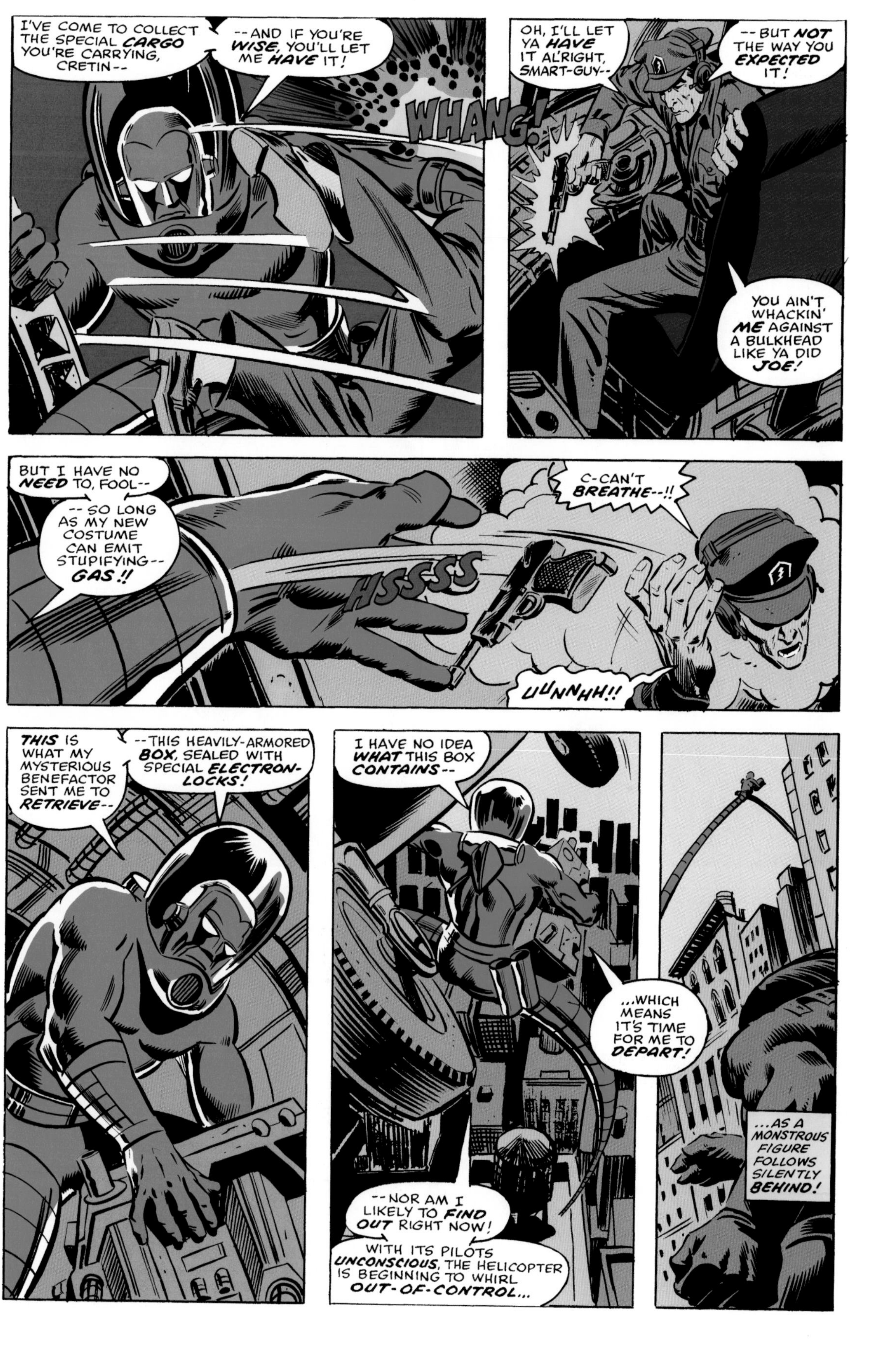
I'VE COME TO COLLECT THE SPECIAL CARGO YOU'RE CARRYING, CRETIN--
--AND IF YOU'RE WISE, YOU'LL LET ME HAVE IT!
WHANG!
OH, I'LL LET YA HAVE IT AL'RIGHT, SMART-GUY--
--BUT NOT THE WAY YOU EXPECTED IT!
YOU AIN'T WHACKIN' ME AGAINST A BULKHEAD LIKE YA DID JOE!
BUT I HAVE NO NEED TO, FOOL--
--SO LONG AS MY NEW COSTUME CAN EMIT STUPIFYING--GAS!!
HSSSS
C-CAN'T BREATHE--!!
UUNNHH!!
THIS IS WHAT MY MYSTERIOUS BENEFACTOR SENT ME TO RETRIEVE--
--THIS HEAVILY-ARMORED BOX, SEALED WITH SPECIAL ELECTRON-LOCKS!
I HAVE NO IDEA WHAT THIS BOX CONTAINS--
...WHICH MEANS IT'S TIME FOR ME TO DEPART!
--NOR AM I LIKELY TO FIND OUT RIGHT NOW!
WITH ITS PILOTS UNCONSCIOUS, THE HELICOPTER IS BEGINNING TO WHIRL OUT-OF-CONTROL...
...AS A MONSTROUS FIGURE FOLLOWS SILENTLY BEHIND!

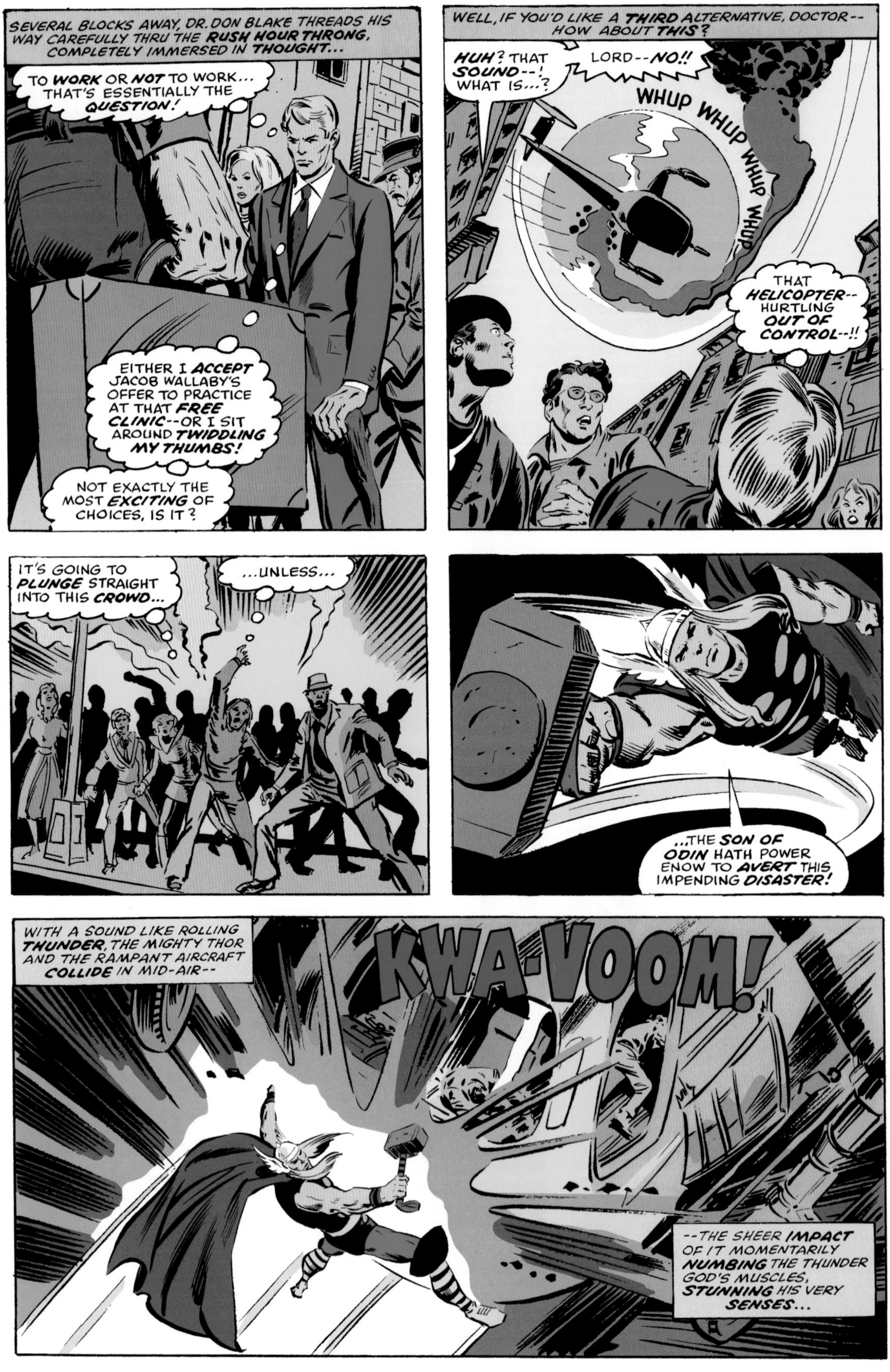
SEVERAL BLOCKS AWAY, DR. DON BLAKE THREADS HIS WAY CAREFULLY THRU THE RUSH HOUR THRONG, COMPLETELY IMMERSED IN THOUGHT...
TO WORK OR NOT TO WORK... THAT'S ESSENTIALLY THE QUESTION!
EITHER I ACCEPT JACOB WALLABY'S OFFER TO PRACTICE AT THAT FREE CLINIC--OR I SIT AROUND TWIDDLING MY THUMBS!
NOT EXACTLY THE MOST EXCITING OF CHOICES, IS IT?
WELL, IF YOU'D LIKE A THIRD ALTERNATIVE, DOCTOR-- HOW ABOUT THIS?
HUH? THAT SOUND--! WHAT IS...?
LORD--NO!!
WHUP WHUP WHUP WHUP
THAT HELICOPTER-- HURTLING OUT OF CONTROL--!!
IT'S GOING TO PLUNGE STRAIGHT INTO THIS CROWD...
...UNLESS...
...THE SON OF ODIN HATH POWER ENOW TO AVERT THIS IMPENDING DISASTER!
WITH A SOUND LIKE ROLLING THUNDER, THE MIGHTY THOR AND THE RAMPANT AIRCRAFT COLLIDE IN MID-AIR--
KWA-VOOM!
--THE SHEER IMPACT OF IT MOMENTARILY NUMBING THE THUNDER GOD'S MUSCLES, STUNNING HIS VERY SENSES...

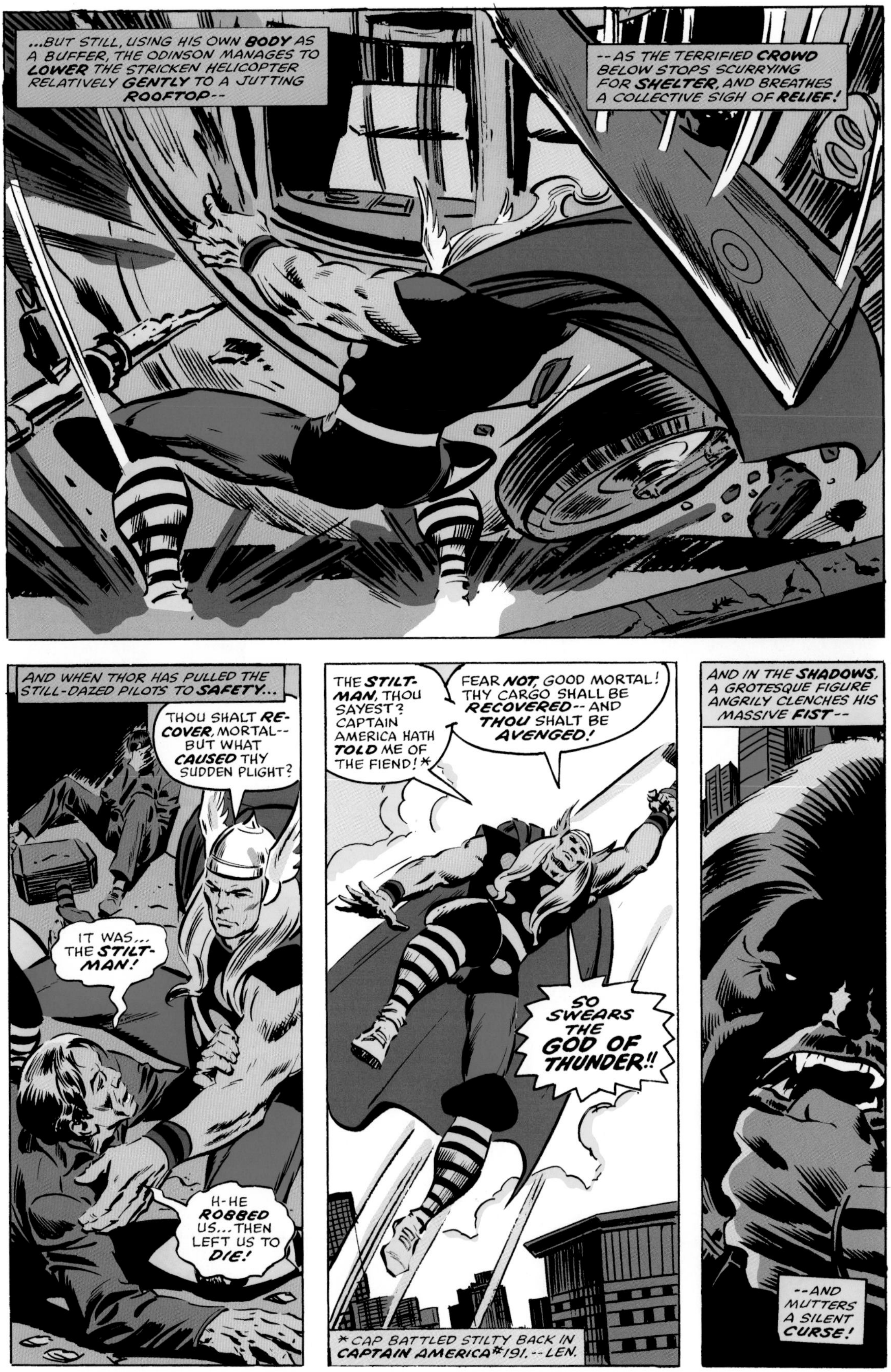
...BUT STILL, USING HIS OWN BODY AS A BUFFER, THE ODINSON MANAGES TO LOWER THE STRICKEN HELICOPTER RELATIVELY GENTLY TO A JUTTING ROOFTOP--
--AS THE TERRIFIED CROWD BELOW STOPS SCURRYING FOR SHELTER, AND BREATHES A COLLECTIVE SIGH OF RELIEF!
AND WHEN THOR HAS PULLED THE STILL-DAZED PILOTS TO SAFETY...
THOU SHALT RE-COVER, MORTAL--BUT WHAT CAUSED THY SUDDEN PLIGHT?
IT WAS... THE STILT-MAN!
H-HE ROBBED US... THEN LEFT US TO DIE!
THE STILT-MAN, THOU SAYEST? CAPTAIN AMERICA HATH TOLD ME OF THE FIEND! *
FEAR NOT, GOOD MORTAL! THY CARGO SHALL BE RECOVERED--AND THOU SHALT BE AVENGED!
SO SWEARS THE GOD OF THUNDER!!
* CAP BATTLED STILTY BACK IN CAPTAIN AMERICA #191.--LEN.
AND IN THE SHADOWS, A GROTESQUE FIGURE ANGRILY CLENCHES HIS MASSIVE FIST--
--AND MUTTERS A SILENT CURSE!

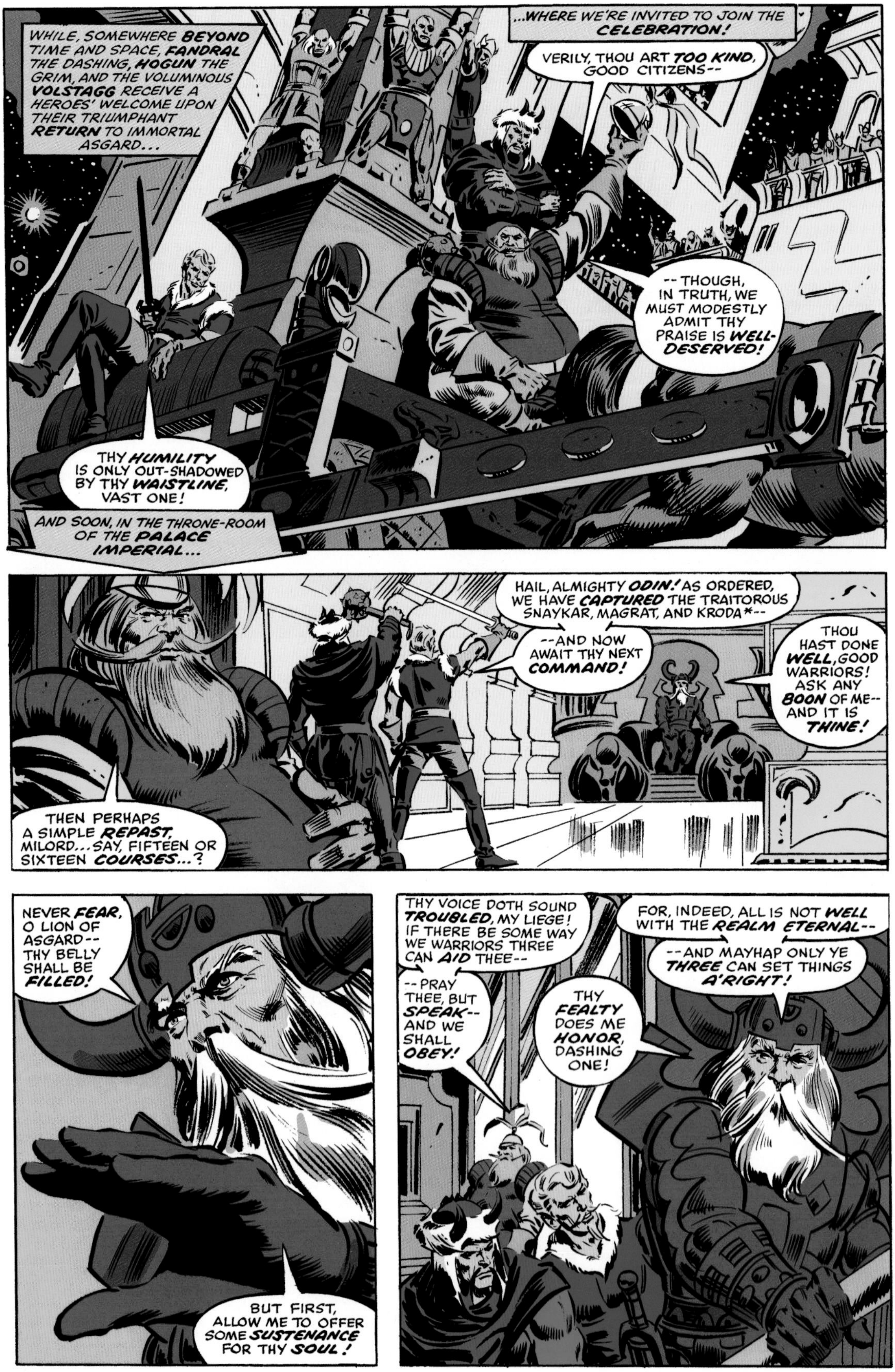
WHILE, SOMEWHERE BEYOND TIME AND SPACE, FANDRAL THE DASHING, HOGUN THE GRIM, AND THE VOLUMINOUS VOLSTAGG RECEIVE A HEROES' WELCOME UPON THEIR TRIUMPHANT RETURN TO IMMORTAL ASGARD...
...WHERE WE'RE INVITED TO JOIN THE CELEBRATION!
VERILY, THOU ART TOO KIND, GOOD CITIZENS--
--THOUGH, IN TRUTH, WE MUST MODESTLY ADMIT THY PRAISE IS WELL-DESERVED!
THY HUMILITY IS ONLY OUT-SHADOWED BY THY WAISTLINE, VAST ONE!
AND SOON, IN THE THRONE-ROOM OF THE PALACE IMPERIAL...
HAIL, ALMIGHTY ODIN! AS ORDERED, WE HAVE CAPTURED THE TRAITOROUS SNAYKAR, MAGRAT, AND KRODA*--
--AND NOW AWAIT THY NEXT COMMAND!
THOU HAST DONE WELL, GOOD WARRIORS! ASK ANY BOON OF ME--AND IT IS THINE!
THEN PERHAPS A SIMPLE REPAST, MILORD... SAY, FIFTEEN OR SIXTEEN COURSES...?
NEVER FEAR, O LION OF ASGARD--THY BELLY SHALL BE FILLED!
BUT FIRST, ALLOW ME TO OFFER SOME SUSTENANCE FOR THY SOUL!
THY VOICE DOTH SOUND TROUBLED, MY LIEGE! IF THERE BE SOME WAY WE WARRIORS THREE CAN AID THEE--
--PRAY THEE, BUT SPEAK--AND WE SHALL OBEY!
THY FEALTY DOES ME HONOR, DASHING ONE!
FOR, INDEED, ALL IS NOT WELL WITH THE REALM ETERNAL--
--AND MAYHAP ONLY YE THREE CAN SET THINGS A'RIGHT!

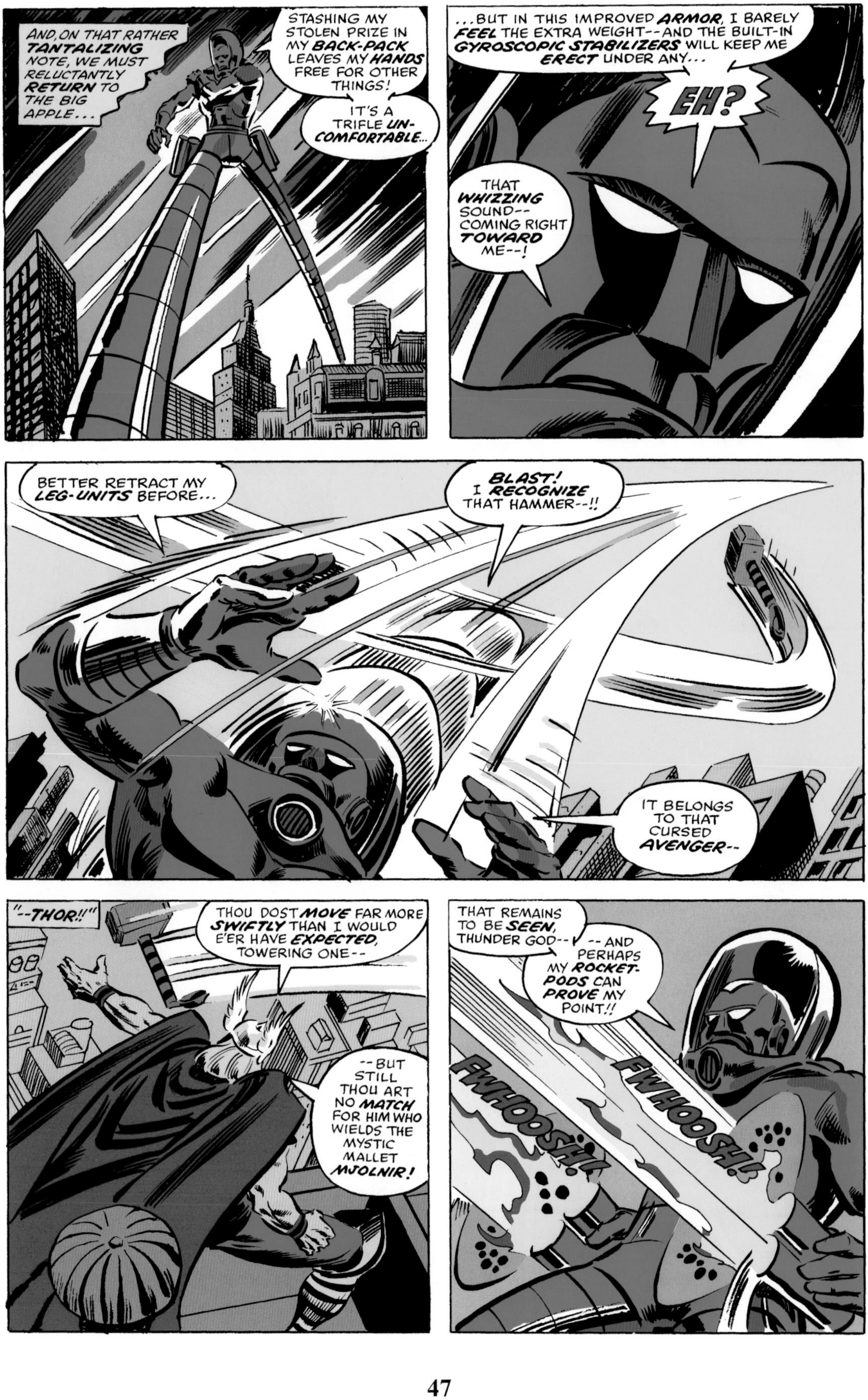
AND, ON THAT RATHER TANTALIZING NOTE, WE MUST RELUCTANTLY RETURN TO THE BIG APPLE...
STASHING MY STOLEN PRIZE IN MY BACK-PACK LEAVES MY HANDS FREE FOR OTHER THINGS!
IT'S A TRIFLE UN-COMFORTABLE...
...BUT IN THIS IMPROVED ARMOR, I BARELY FEEL THE EXTRA WEIGHT--AND THE BUILT-IN GYROSCOPIC STABILIZERS WILL KEEP ME ERECT UNDER ANY...
EH?
THAT WHIZZING SOUND-- COMING RIGHT TOWARD ME--!
BETTER RETRACT MY LEG-UNITS BEFORE...
BLAST! I RECOGNIZE THAT HAMMER--!!
IT BELONGS TO THAT CURSED AVENGER--
"--THOR!!"
THOU DOST MOVE FAR MORE SWIFTLY THAN I WOULD E'ER HAVE EXPECTED, TOWERING ONE--
--BUT STILL THOU ART NO MATCH FOR HIM WHO WIELDS THE MYSTIC MALLET MJOLNIR!
THAT REMAINS TO BE SEEN, THUNDER GOD--
--AND PERHAPS MY ROCKET-PODS CAN PROVE MY POINT!!
FWHOOSH!
FWHOOSH!

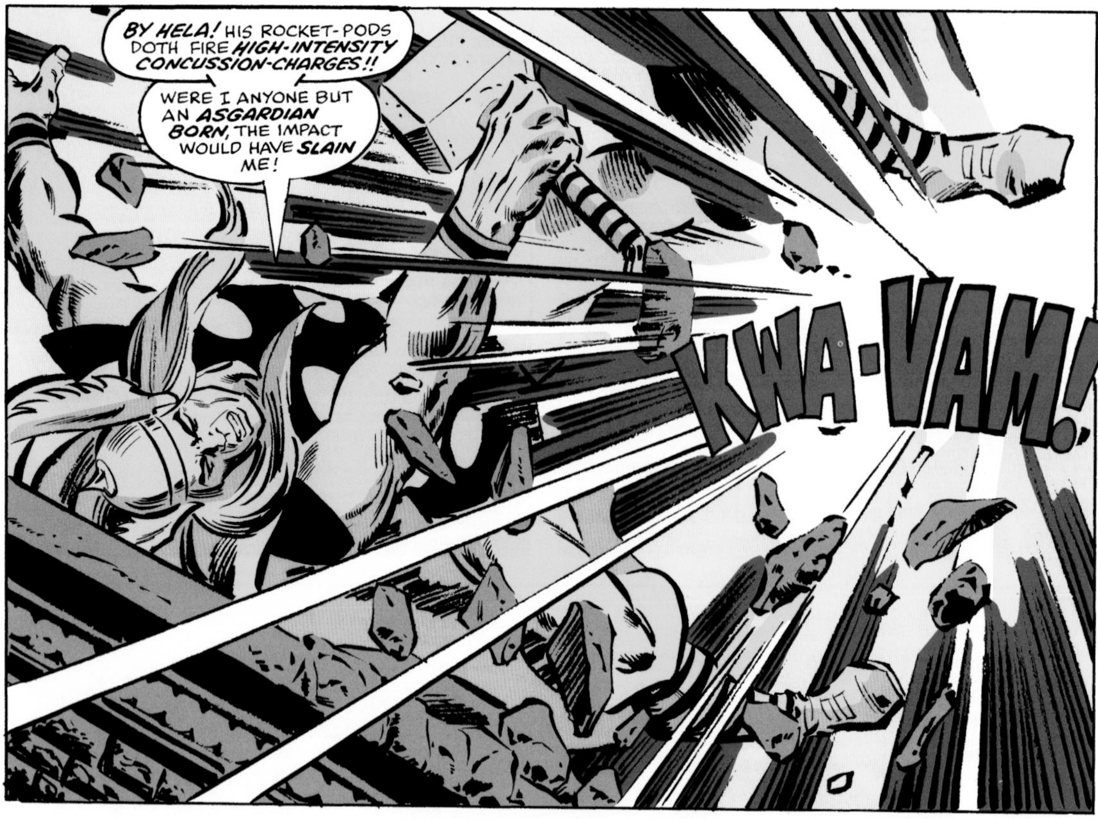
BY HELA! HIS ROCKET-PODS DOTH FIRE HIGH-INTENSITY CONCUSSION-CHARGES!!
WERE I ANYONE BUT AN ASGARDIAN BORN, THE IMPACT WOULD HAVE SLAIN ME!
KWA-VAM!

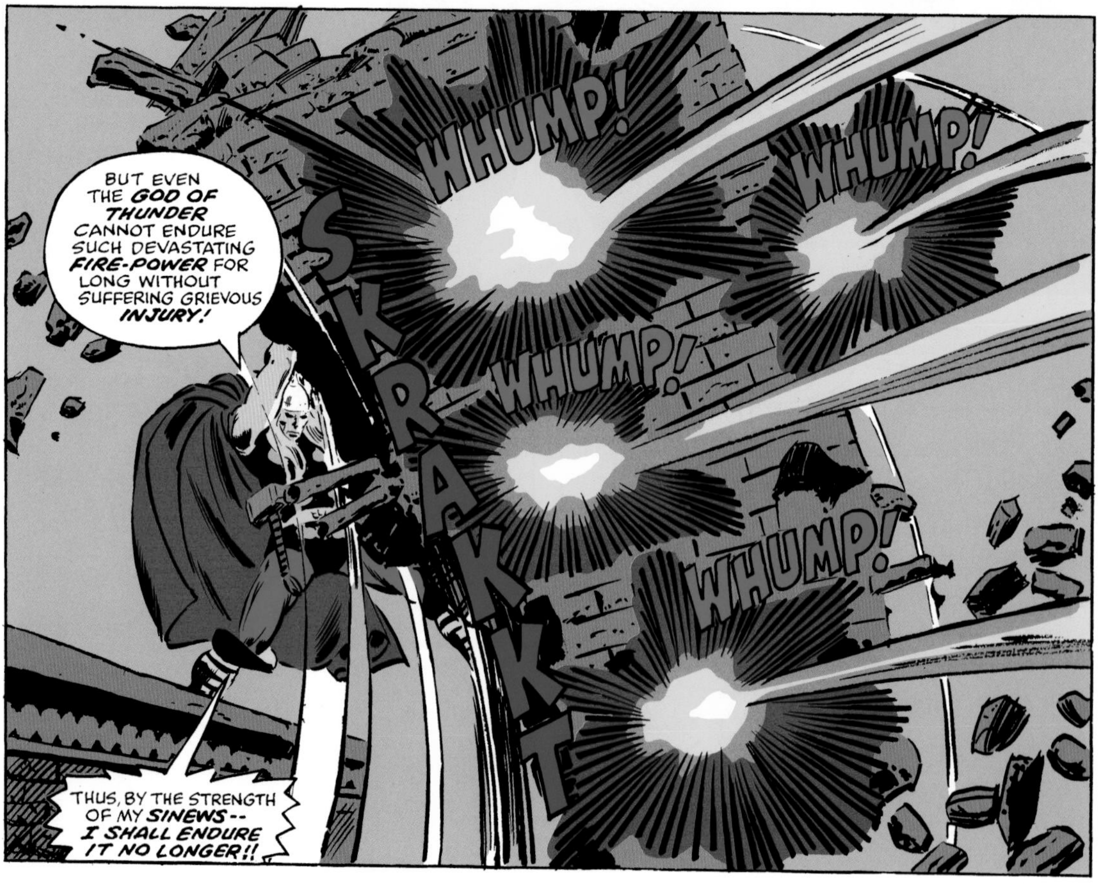
WHUMP!
WHUMP!
BUT EVEN THE GOD OF THUNDER CANNOT ENDURE SUCH DEVASTATING FIRE-POWER FOR LONG WITHOUT SUFFERING GRIEVOUS INJURY!
SKRAKKT
WHUMP!
WHUMP!
THUS, BY THE STRENGTH OF MY SINEWS -- I SHALL ENDURE IT NO LONGER!!

MILES AWAY, THE RAGING BATTLE CAN BE **WITNESSED** ON A HOLOGRAPHIC **VIEW-SCREEN** MOUNTED UPON ONE WALL OF A TOWERING **COMPUTER**--

--WHICH CAREFULLY STUDIES EVERY **MOVE** THE TWO COMBATANTS **MAKE**...

...CALCULATING **ODDS**...WEIGHING **ALTERNATIVES**...

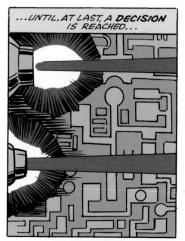

...UNTIL, AT LAST, A **DECISION** IS REACHED...

...AND A SERIES OF **ANTI-NEUTRI-NOS** RACE THROUGH THE MONSTROUS MECHANISM WITH QUITE **LITERALLY** THE SPEED OF **THOUGHT!**

THE **STILT-MAN** WILL NOT BE ABLE TO **DEAL** WITH THE UNEXPECTED INTERVENTION OF THE BEING CALLED **THOR!**

THE TIME HAS COME TO INSTITUTE MORE **SERIOUS** PRECAUTIONS--

--NO MATTER **WHO** MAY SUFFER AS A **RESULT!!**

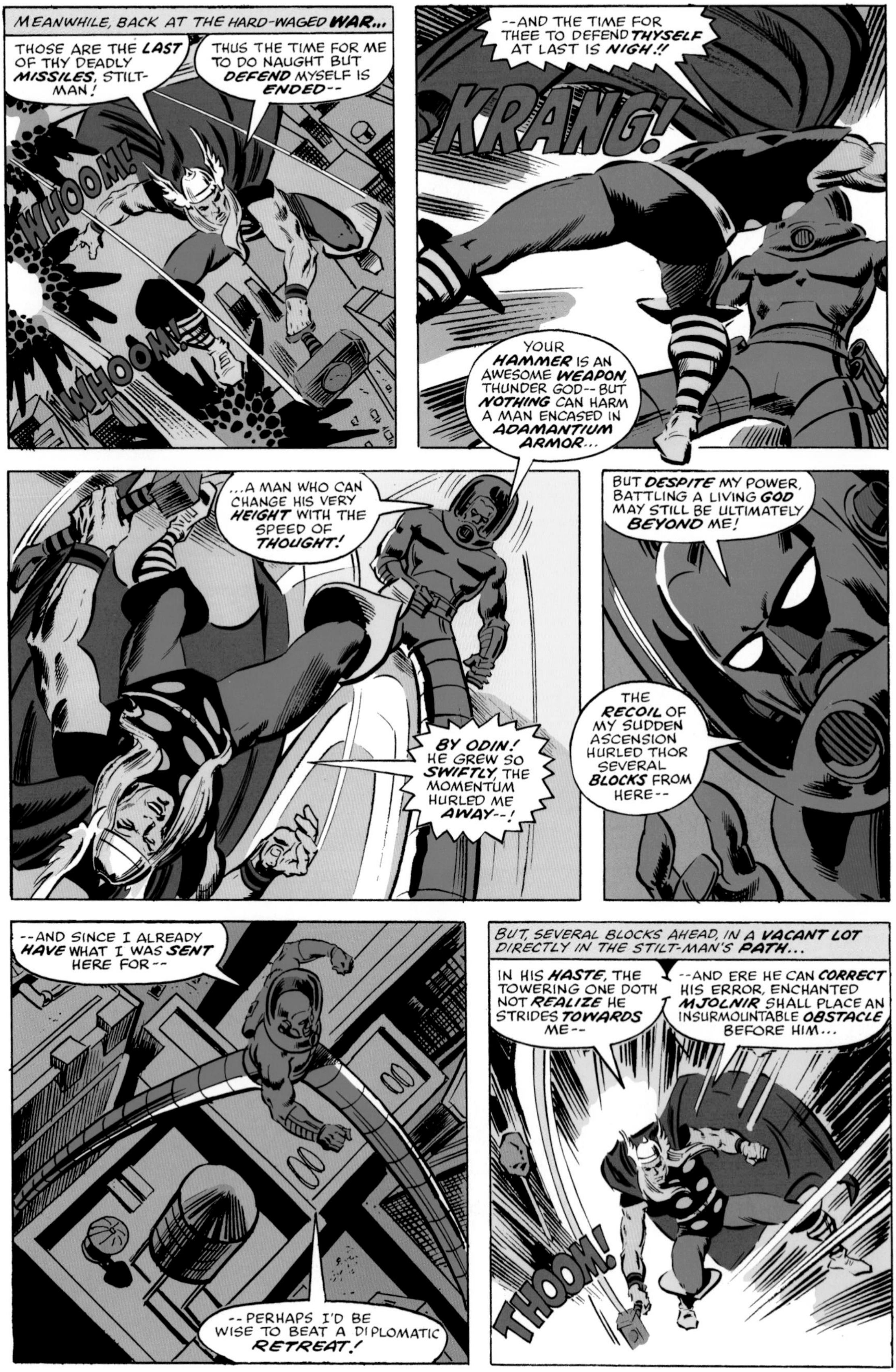
MEANWHILE, BACK AT THE HARD-WAGED WAR...
THOSE ARE THE LAST OF THY DEADLY MISSILES, STILT-MAN!
THUS THE TIME FOR ME TO DO NAUGHT BUT DEFEND MYSELF IS ENDED--
WHOOM!
WHOOM!
--AND THE TIME FOR THEE TO DEFEND THYSELF AT LAST IS NIGH!!
KRANG!
YOUR HAMMER IS AN AWESOME WEAPON, THUNDER GOD-- BUT NOTHING CAN HARM A MAN ENCASED IN ADAMANTIUM ARMOR...
...A MAN WHO CAN CHANGE HIS VERY HEIGHT WITH THE SPEED OF THOUGHT!
BY ODIN! HE GREW SO SWIFTLY, THE MOMENTUM HURLED ME AWAY--!
BUT DESPITE MY POWER, BATTLING A LIVING GOD MAY STILL BE ULTIMATELY BEYOND ME!
THE RECOIL OF MY SUDDEN ASCENSION HURLED THOR SEVERAL BLOCKS FROM HERE--
--AND SINCE I ALREADY HAVE WHAT I WAS SENT HERE FOR--
--PERHAPS I'D BE WISE TO BEAT A DIPLOMATIC RETREAT!
BUT, SEVERAL BLOCKS AHEAD, IN A VACANT LOT DIRECTLY IN THE STILT-MAN'S PATH...
IN HIS HASTE, THE TOWERING ONE DOTH NOT REALIZE HE STRIDES TOWARDS ME--
--AND ERE HE CAN CORRECT HIS ERROR, ENCHANTED MJOLNIR SHALL PLACE AN INSURMOUNTABLE OBSTACLE BEFORE HIM...
THOOM!

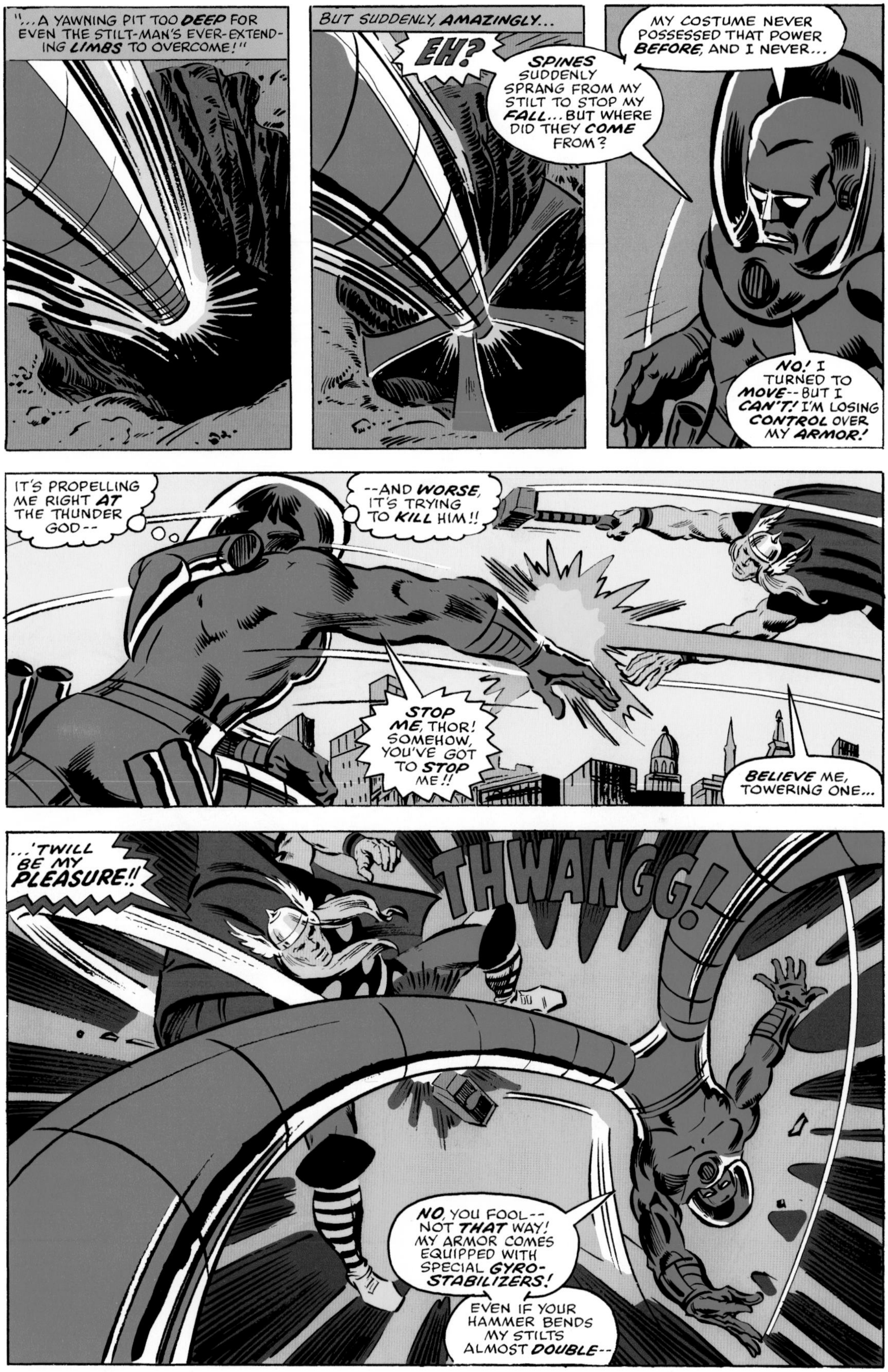
"...A YAWNING PIT TOO DEEP FOR EVEN THE STILT-MAN'S EVER-EXTENDING LIMBS TO OVERCOME!"
BUT SUDDENLY, AMAZINGLY...
EH?
SPINES SUDDENLY SPRANG FROM MY STILT TO STOP MY FALL... BUT WHERE DID THEY COME FROM?
MY COSTUME NEVER POSSESSED THAT POWER BEFORE, AND I NEVER...
NO! I TURNED TO MOVE--BUT I CAN'T! I'M LOSING CONTROL OVER MY ARMOR!
IT'S PROPELLING ME RIGHT AT THE THUNDER GOD--
--AND WORSE, IT'S TRYING TO KILL HIM!!
STOP ME, THOR! SOMEHOW, YOU'VE GOT TO STOP ME!!
BELIEVE ME, TOWERING ONE...
...'TWILL BE MY PLEASURE!!
THWANGG!
NO, YOU FOOL--NOT THAT WAY! MY ARMOR COMES EQUIPPED WITH SPECIAL GYRO-STABILIZERS!
EVEN IF YOUR HAMMER BENDS MY STILTS ALMOST DOUBLE--

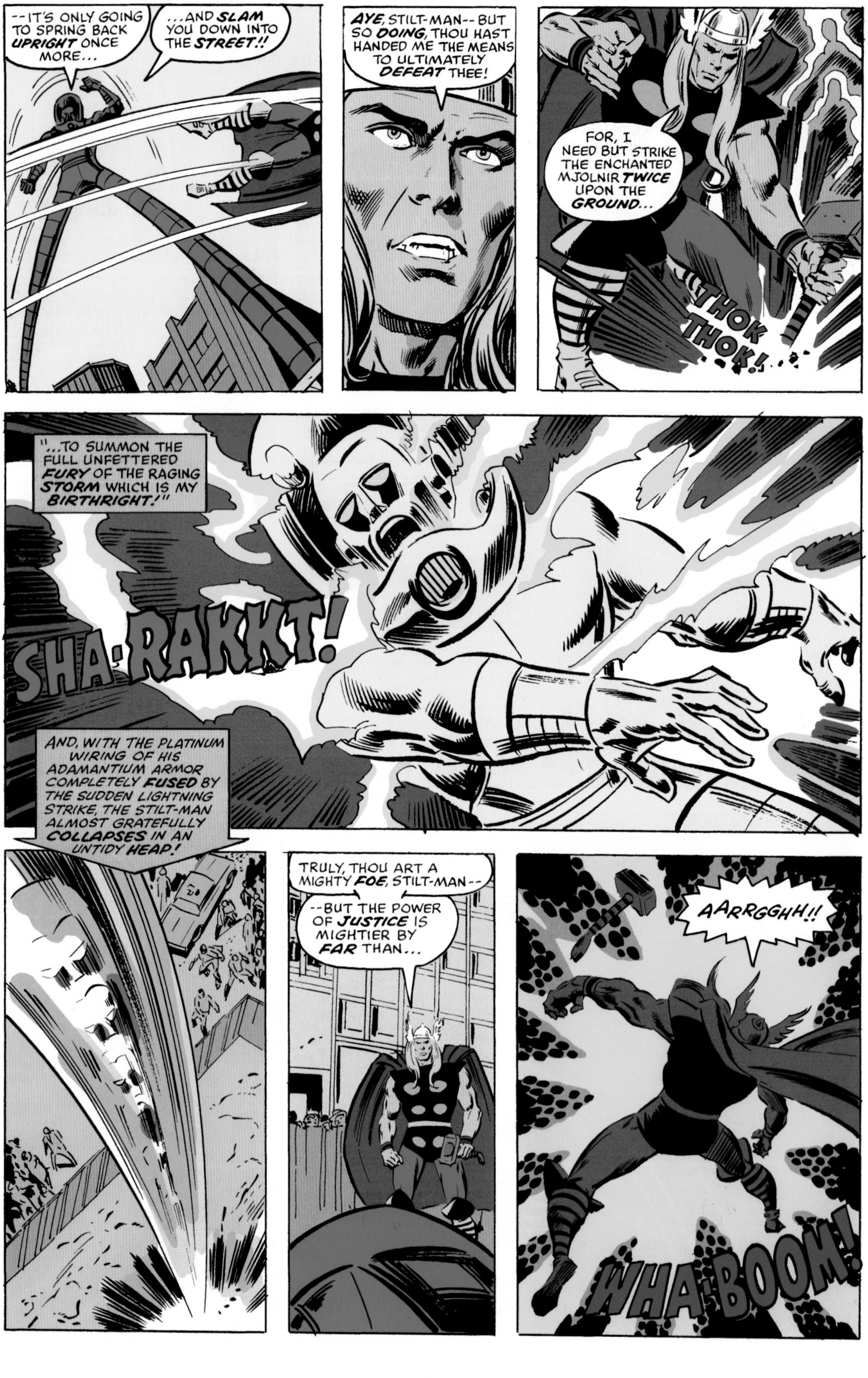
--IT'S ONLY GOING TO SPRING BACK UPRIGHT ONCE MORE...
...AND SLAM YOU DOWN INTO THE STREET!!
AYE, STILT-MAN-- BUT SO DOING, THOU HAST HANDED ME THE MEANS TO ULTIMATELY DEFEAT THEE!
FOR, I NEED BUT STRIKE THE ENCHANTED MJOLNIR TWICE UPON THE GROUND...
THOK THOK!
"...TO SUMMON THE FULL UNFETTERED FURY OF THE RAGING STORM WHICH IS MY BIRTHRIGHT!"
SHA-RAKKT!
AND, WITH THE PLATINUM WIRING OF HIS ADAMANTIUM ARMOR COMPLETELY FUSED BY THE SUDDEN LIGHTNING STRIKE, THE STILT-MAN ALMOST GRATEFULLY COLLAPSES IN AN UNTIDY HEAP!
TRULY, THOU ART A MIGHTY FOE, STILT-MAN--
--BUT THE POWER OF JUSTICE IS MIGHTIER BY FAR THAN...
AARRGGHH!!
WHA-BOOM!

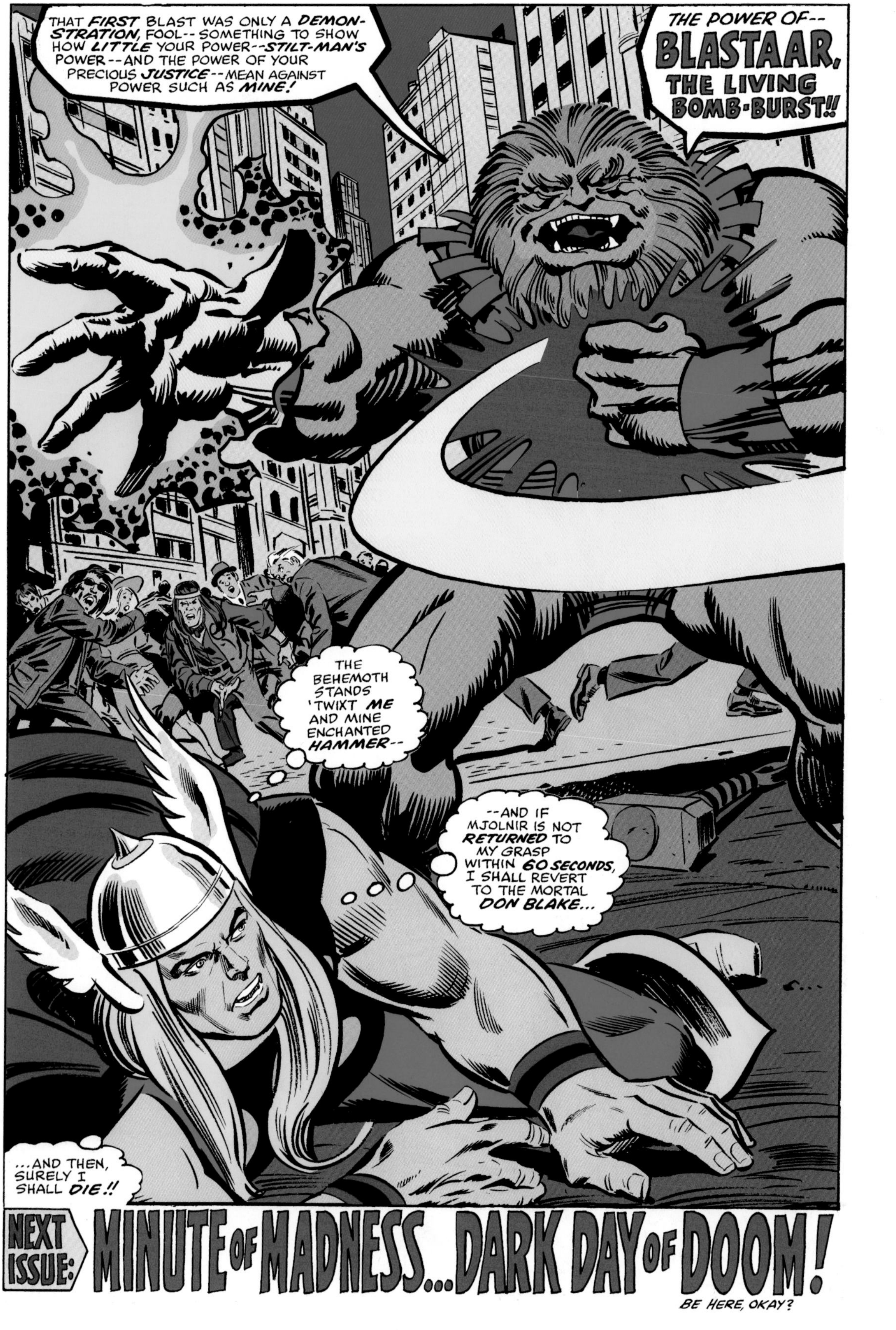
THAT FIRST BLAST WAS ONLY A DEMON-STRATION, FOOL-- SOMETHING TO SHOW HOW LITTLE YOUR POWER--STILT-MAN'S POWER--AND THE POWER OF YOUR PRECIOUS JUSTICE--MEAN AGAINST POWER SUCH AS MINE!
THE POWER OF-- BLASTAAR, THE LIVING BOMB-BURST!!
THE BEHEMOTH STANDS 'TWIXT ME AND MINE ENCHANTED HAMMER--
--AND IF MJOLNIR IS NOT RETURNED TO MY GRASP WITHIN 60 SECONDS, I SHALL REVERT TO THE MORTAL DON BLAKE...
...AND THEN, SURELY I SHALL DIE!!
NEXT ISSUE: MINUTE OF MADNESS...DARK DAY OF DOOM!
BE HERE, OKAY?

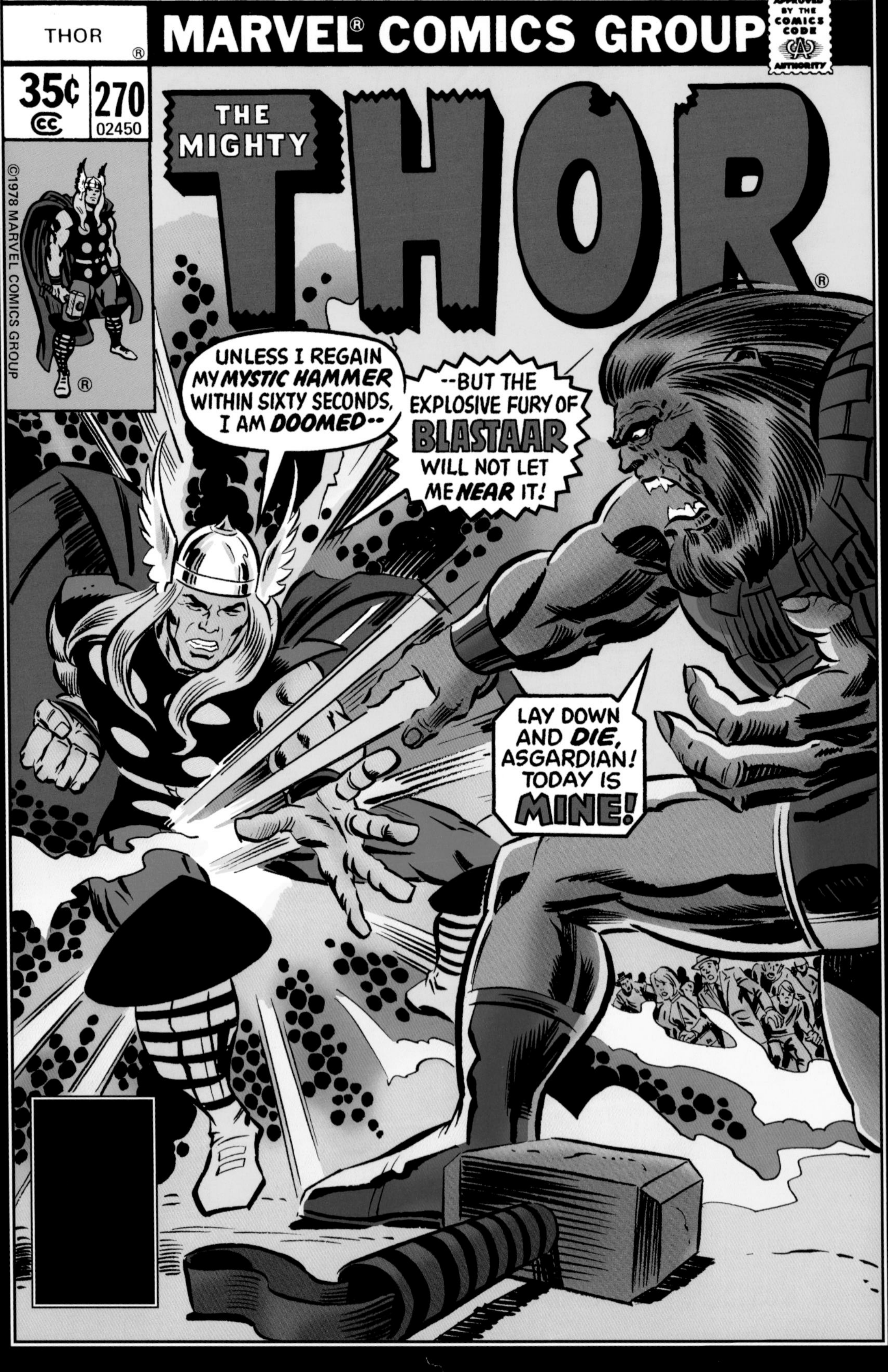
THOR
MARVEL® COMICS GROUP
APPROVED BY THE COMICS CODE AUTHORITY
35¢ CC
270 02450
THE MIGHTY THOR®
©1978 MARVEL COMICS GROUP
UNLESS I REGAIN MY MYSTIC HAMMER WITHIN SIXTY SECONDS, I AM DOOMED--
--BUT THE EXPLOSIVE FURY OF BLASTAAR WILL NOT LET ME NEAR IT!
LAY DOWN AND DIE, ASGARDIAN! TODAY IS MINE!

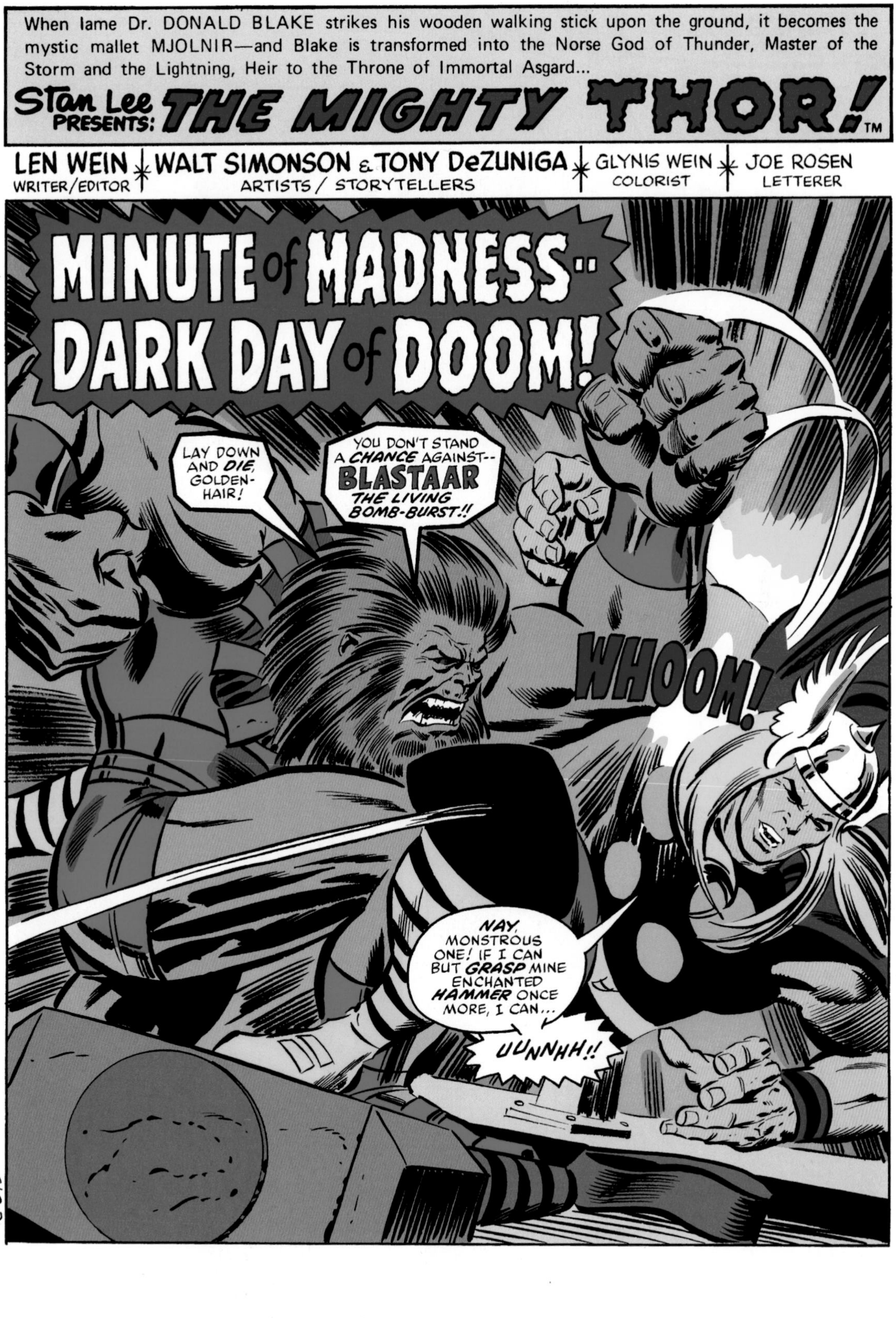

When lame Dr. DONALD BLAKE strikes his wooden walking stick upon the ground, it becomes the mystic mallet MJOLNIR—and Blake is transformed into the Norse God of Thunder, Master of the Storm and the Lightning, Heir to the Throne of Immortal Asgard...
Stan Lee PRESENTS: THE MIGHTY THOR! TM
LEN WEIN WRITER/EDITOR
WALT SIMONSON & TONY DeZUNIGA ARTISTS / STORYTELLERS
GLYNIS WEIN COLORIST
JOE ROSEN LETTERER
MINUTE of MADNESS-- DARK DAY of DOOM!
LAY DOWN AND DIE, GOLDEN-HAIR!
YOU DON'T STAND A CHANCE AGAINST-- BLASTAAR THE LIVING BOMB-BURST!!
WHOOM!
NAY, MONSTROUS ONE! IF I CAN BUT GRASP MINE ENCHANTED HAMMER ONCE MORE, I CAN...
UUNNHH!!
C-693

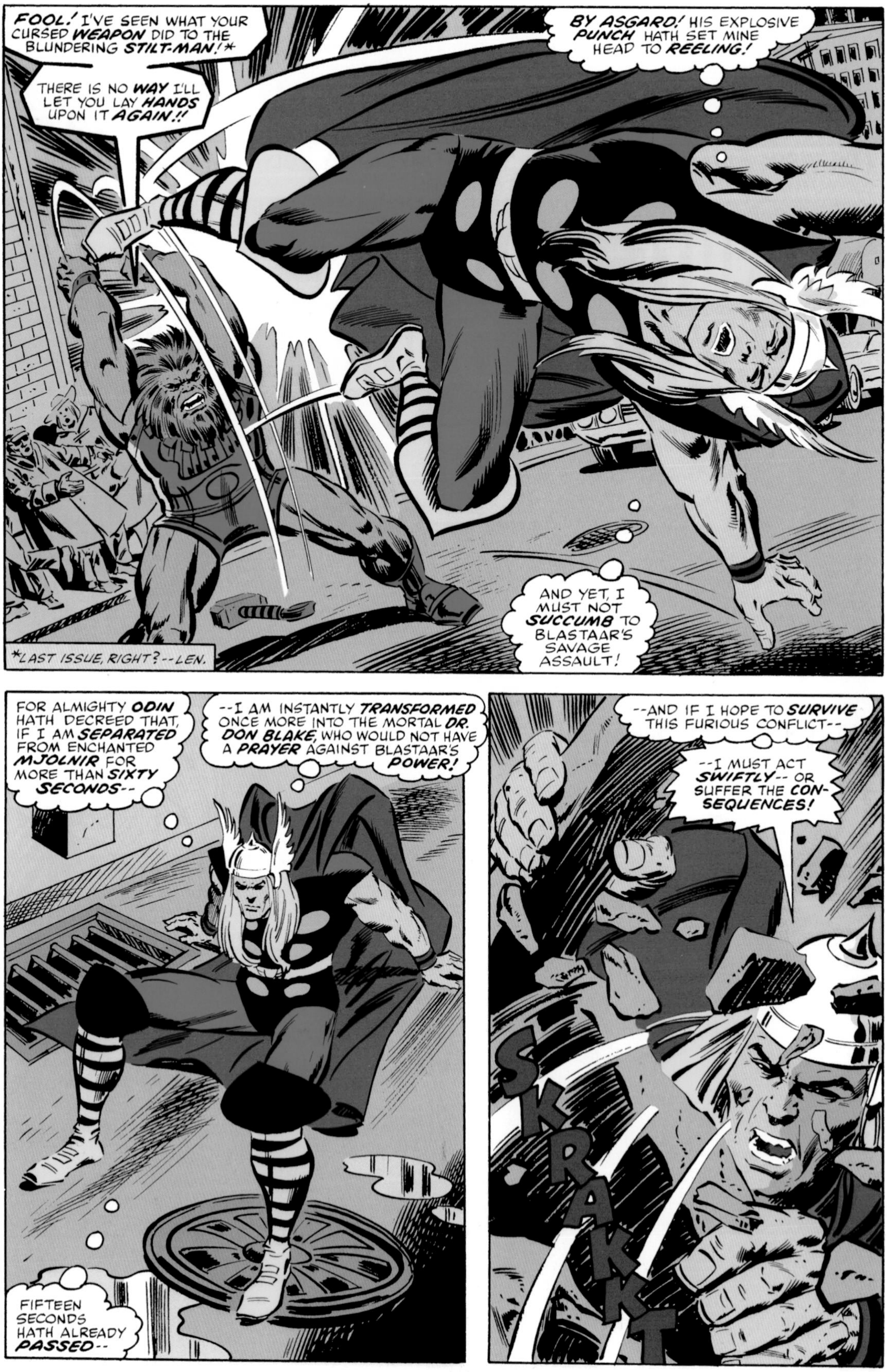
FOOL! I'VE SEEN WHAT YOUR CURSED WEAPON DID TO THE BLUNDERING STILT-MAN!*
THERE IS NO WAY I'LL LET YOU LAY HANDS UPON IT AGAIN!!
BY ASGARD! HIS EXPLOSIVE PUNCH HATH SET MINE HEAD TO REELING!
AND YET, I MUST NOT SUCCUMB TO BLASTAAR'S SAVAGE ASSAULT!
*LAST ISSUE, RIGHT?--LEN.
FOR ALMIGHTY ODIN HATH DECREED THAT, IF I AM SEPARATED FROM ENCHANTED MJOLNIR FOR MORE THAN SIXTY SECONDS--
--I AM INSTANTLY TRANSFORMED ONCE MORE INTO THE MORTAL DR. DON BLAKE, WHO WOULD NOT HAVE A PRAYER AGAINST BLASTAAR'S POWER!
FIFTEEN SECONDS HATH ALREADY PASSED--
--AND IF I HOPE TO SURVIVE THIS FURIOUS CONFLICT--
--I MUST ACT SWIFTLY-- OR SUFFER THE CON-SEQUENCES!
SKRAKT

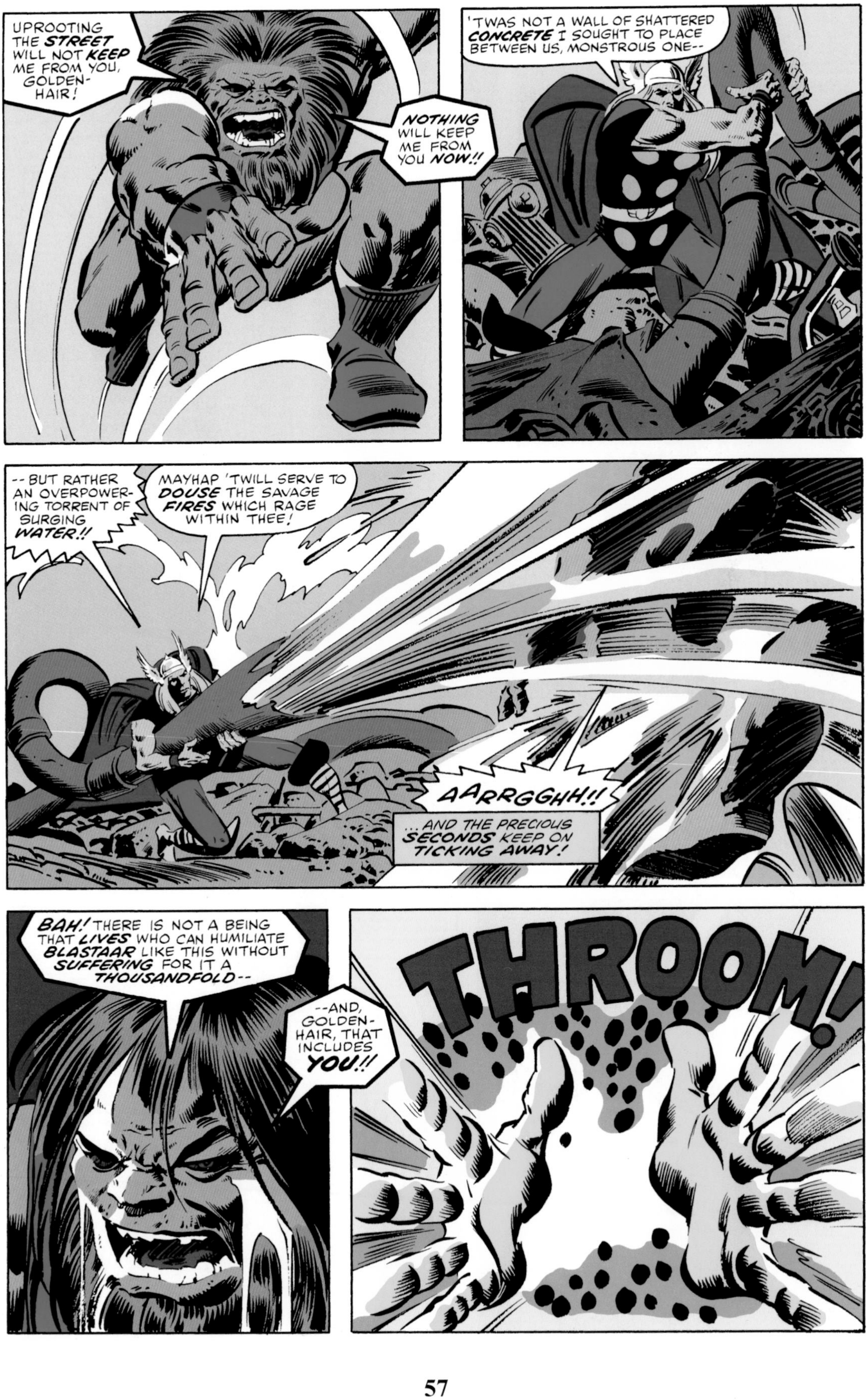
UPROOTING THE STREET WILL NOT KEEP ME FROM YOU, GOLDEN-HAIR!
NOTHING WILL KEEP ME FROM YOU NOW!!
'TWAS NOT A WALL OF SHATTERED CONCRETE I SOUGHT TO PLACE BETWEEN US, MONSTROUS ONE--
--BUT RATHER AN OVERPOWER-ING TORRENT OF SURGING WATER!!
MAYHAP 'TWILL SERVE TO DOUSE THE SAVAGE FIRES WHICH RAGE WITHIN THEE!
AARRGGHH!!
...AND THE PRECIOUS SECONDS KEEP ON TICKING AWAY!
BAH! THERE IS NOT A BEING THAT LIVES WHO CAN HUMILIATE BLASTAAR LIKE THIS WITHOUT SUFFERING FOR IT A THOUSANDFOLD--
--AND, GOLDEN-HAIR, THAT INCLUDES YOU!!
THROOM!

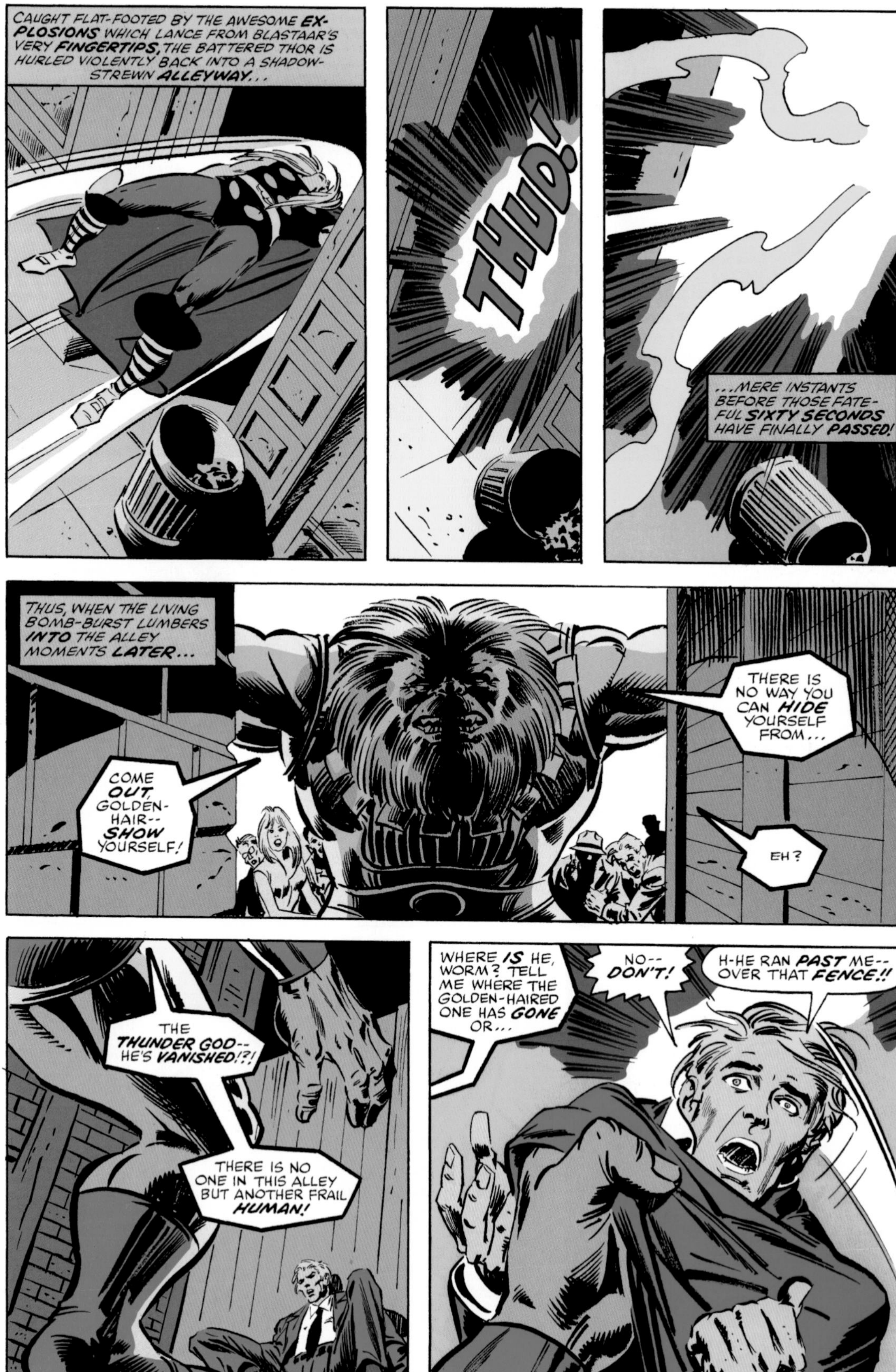
CAUGHT FLAT-FOOTED BY THE AWESOME EX-PLOSIONS WHICH LANCE FROM BLASTAAR'S VERY FINGERTIPS, THE BATTERED THOR IS HURLED VIOLENTLY BACK INTO A SHADOW-STREWN ALLEYWAY...
THUD!
...MERE INSTANTS BEFORE THOSE FATE-FUL SIXTY SECONDS HAVE FINALLY PASSED!
THUS, WHEN THE LIVING BOMB-BURST LUMBERS INTO THE ALLEY MOMENTS LATER...
COME OUT, GOLDEN-HAIR-- SHOW YOURSELF!
THERE IS NO WAY YOU CAN HIDE YOURSELF FROM...
EH?
THE THUNDER GOD-- HE'S VANISHED!?!
THERE IS NO ONE IN THIS ALLEY BUT ANOTHER FRAIL HUMAN!
WHERE IS HE, WORM? TELL ME WHERE THE GOLDEN-HAIRED ONE HAS GONE OR...
NO-- DON'T!
H-HE RAN PAST ME-- OVER THAT FENCE!!

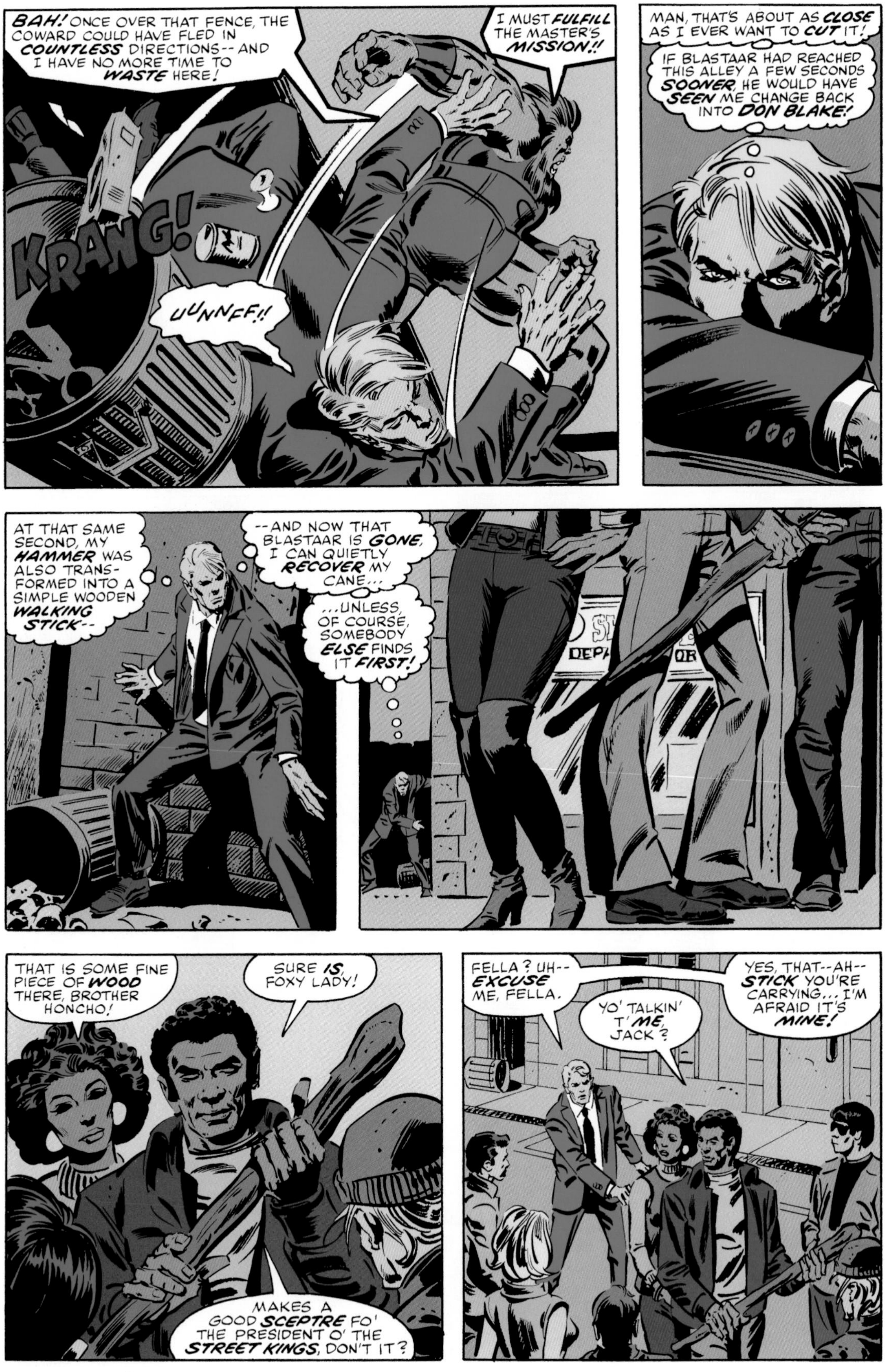
BAH! ONCE OVER THAT FENCE, THE COWARD COULD HAVE FLED IN COUNTLESS DIRECTIONS-- AND I HAVE NO MORE TIME TO WASTE HERE!
I MUST FULFILL THE MASTER'S MISSION!!
KRANG!
UUNNFF!!
MAN, THAT'S ABOUT AS CLOSE AS I EVER WANT TO CUT IT!
IF BLASTAAR HAD REACHED THIS ALLEY A FEW SECONDS SOONER, HE WOULD HAVE SEEN ME CHANGE BACK INTO DON BLAKE!
AT THAT SAME SECOND, MY HAMMER WAS ALSO TRANS-FORMED INTO A SIMPLE WOODEN WALKING STICK--
--AND NOW THAT BLASTAAR IS GONE, I CAN QUIETLY RECOVER MY CANE...
...UNLESS, OF COURSE, SOMEBODY ELSE FINDS IT FIRST!
THAT IS SOME FINE PIECE OF WOOD THERE, BROTHER HONCHO!
SURE IS, FOXY LADY!
MAKES A GOOD SCEPTRE FO' THE PRESIDENT O' THE STREET KINGS, DON'T IT?
FELLA? UH-- EXCUSE ME, FELLA.
YO' TALKIN' T'ME, JACK?
YES, THAT--AH-- STICK YOU'RE CARRYING... I'M AFRAID IT'S MINE!

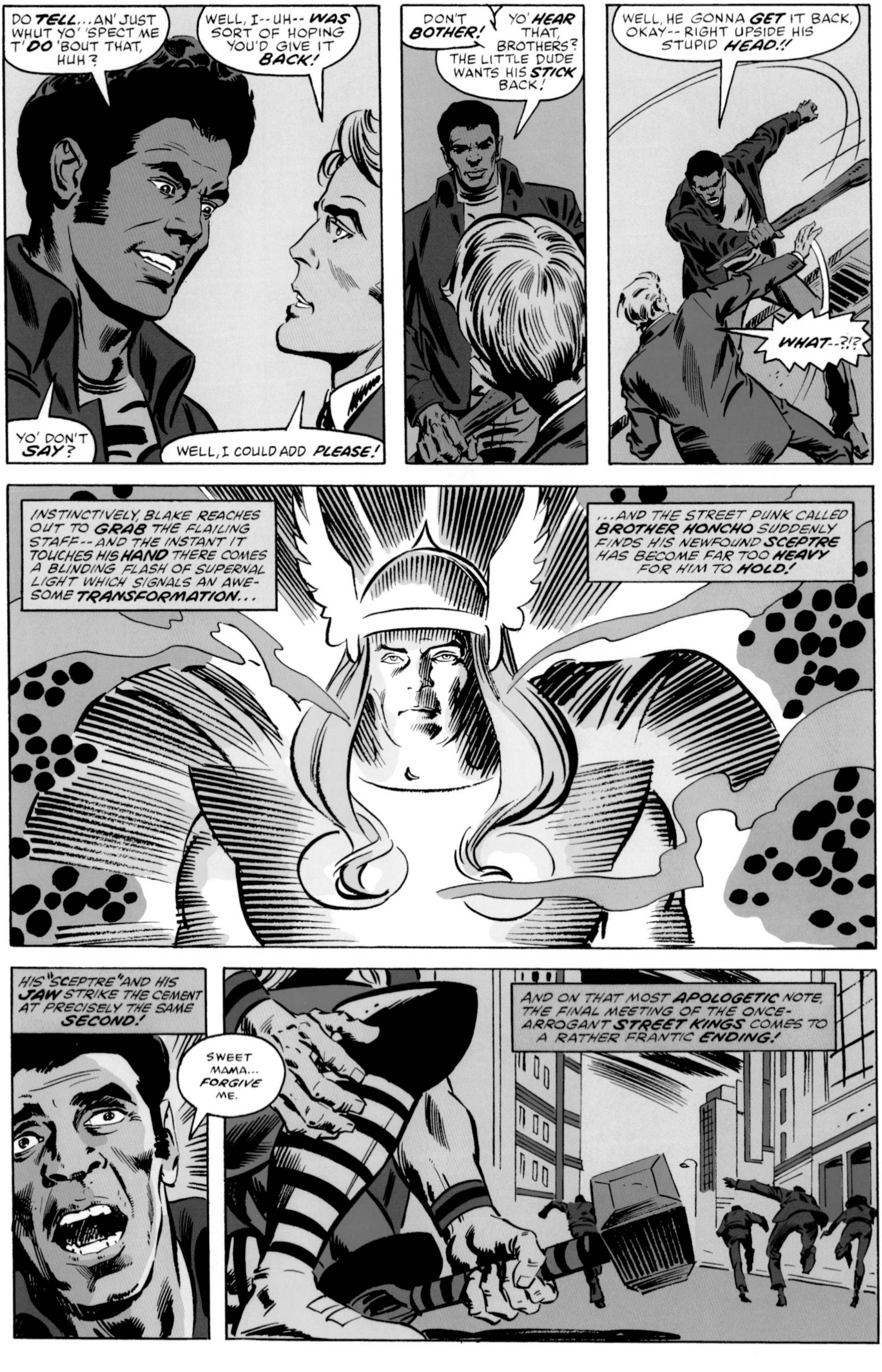
DO TELL...AN' JUST WHUT YO' 'SPECT ME T'DO 'BOUT THAT, HUH?
WELL, I--UH--WAS SORT OF HOPING YOU'D GIVE IT BACK!
YO' DON'T SAY?
WELL, I COULD ADD PLEASE!
DON'T BOTHER!
YO' HEAR THAT, BROTHERS? THE LITTLE DUDE WANTS HIS STICK BACK!
WELL, HE GONNA GET IT BACK, OKAY--RIGHT UPSIDE HIS STUPID HEAD!!
WHAT--?!?
INSTINCTIVELY, BLAKE REACHES OUT TO GRAB THE FLAILING STAFF--AND THE INSTANT IT TOUCHES HIS HAND THERE COMES A BLINDING FLASH OF SUPERNAL LIGHT WHICH SIGNALS AN AWE-SOME TRANSFORMATION...
...AND THE STREET PUNK CALLED BROTHER HONCHO SUDDENLY FINDS HIS NEWFOUND SCEPTRE HAS BECOME FAR TOO HEAVY FOR HIM TO HOLD!
HIS "SCEPTRE" AND HIS JAW STRIKE THE CEMENT AT PRECISELY THE SAME SECOND!
SWEET MAMA... FORGIVE ME.
AND ON THAT MOST APOLOGETIC NOTE, THE FINAL MEETING OF THE ONCE-ARROGANT STREET KINGS COMES TO A RATHER FRANTIC ENDING!

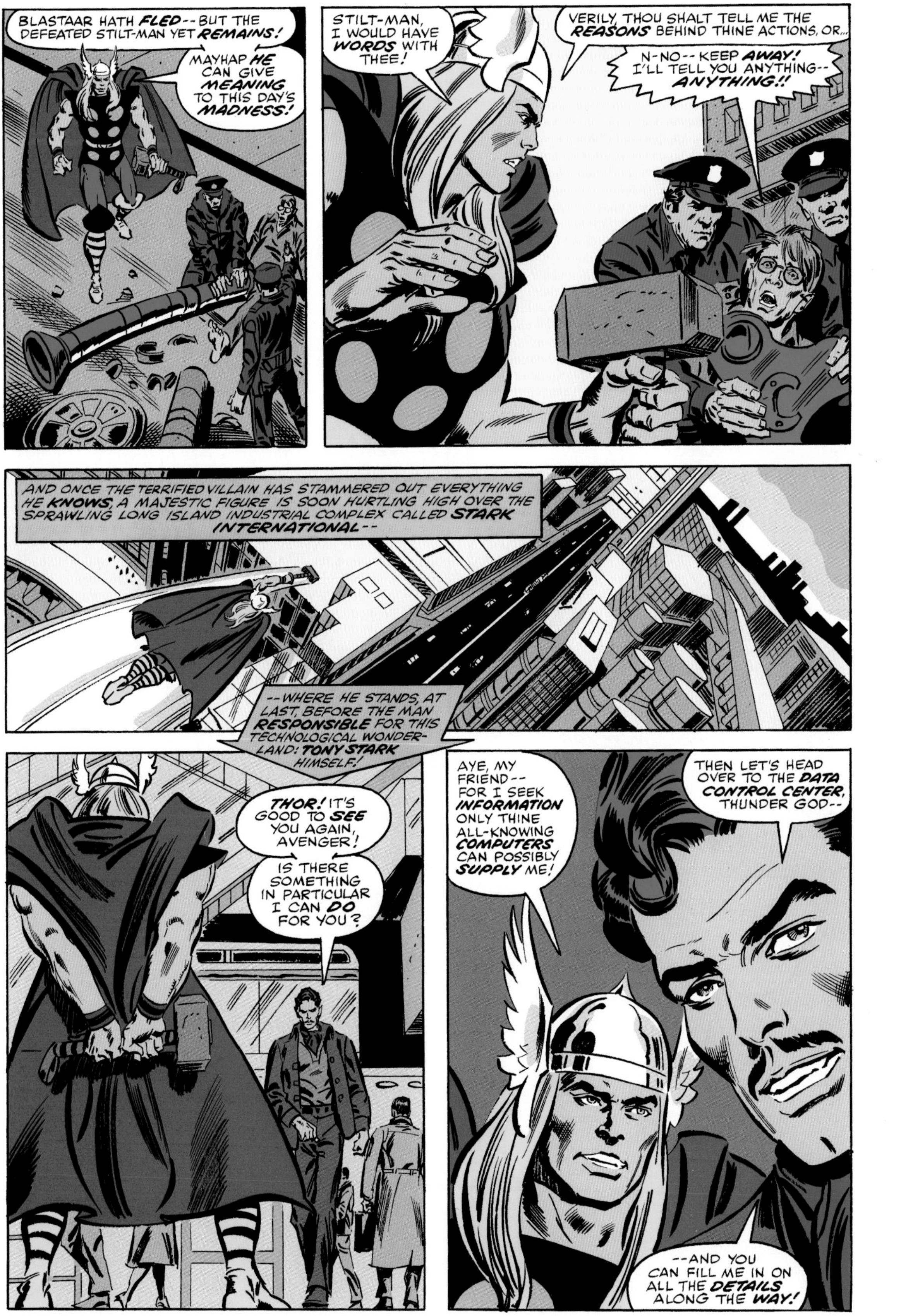
BLASTAAR HATH FLED--BUT THE DEFEATED STILT-MAN YET REMAINS!
MAYHAP HE CAN GIVE MEANING TO THIS DAY'S MADNESS!
STILT-MAN, I WOULD HAVE WORDS WITH THEE!
VERILY, THOU SHALT TELL ME THE REASONS BEHIND THINE ACTIONS, OR...
N-NO--KEEP AWAY! I'LL TELL YOU ANYTHING--ANYTHING!!
AND ONCE THE TERRIFIED VILLAIN HAS STAMMERED OUT EVERYTHING HE KNOWS, A MAJESTIC FIGURE IS SOON HURTLING HIGH OVER THE SPRAWLING LONG ISLAND INDUSTRIAL COMPLEX CALLED STARK INTERNATIONAL--
--WHERE HE STANDS, AT LAST, BEFORE THE MAN RESPONSIBLE FOR THIS TECHNOLOGICAL WONDERLAND: TONY STARK HIMSELF!
THOR! IT'S GOOD TO SEE YOU AGAIN, AVENGER!
IS THERE SOMETHING IN PARTICULAR I CAN DO FOR YOU?
AYE, MY FRIEND--FOR I SEEK INFORMATION ONLY THINE ALL-KNOWING COMPUTERS CAN POSSIBLY SUPPLY ME!
THEN LET'S HEAD OVER TO THE DATA CONTROL CENTER, THUNDER GOD--
--AND YOU CAN FILL ME IN ON ALL THE DETAILS ALONG THE WAY!

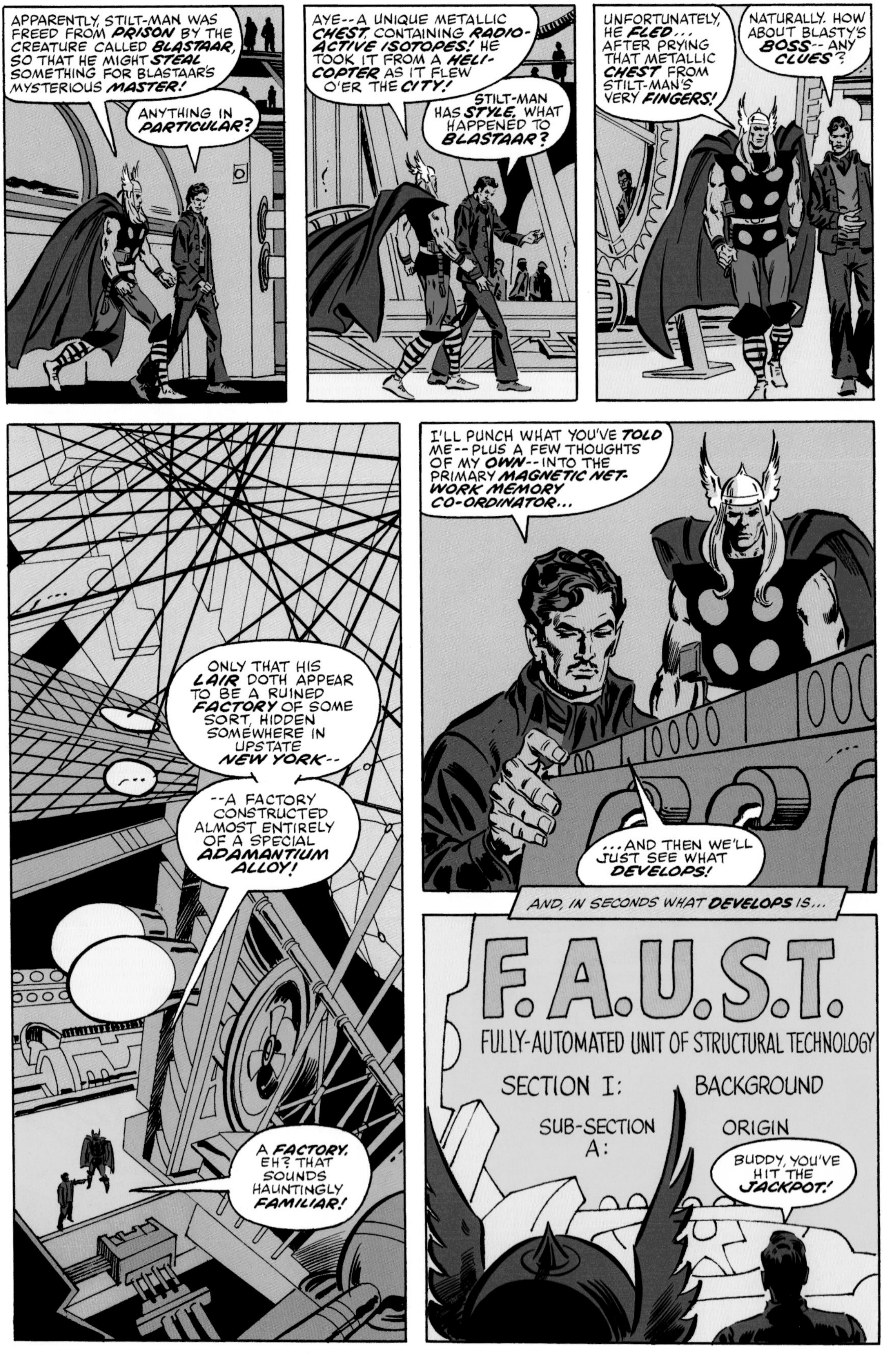
APPARENTLY, STILT-MAN WAS FREED FROM PRISON BY THE CREATURE CALLED BLASTAAR, SO THAT HE MIGHT STEAL SOMETHING FOR BLASTAAR'S MYSTERIOUS MASTER!
ANYTHING IN PARTICULAR?
AYE--A UNIQUE METALLIC CHEST, CONTAINING RADIO-ACTIVE ISOTOPES! HE TOOK IT FROM A HELI-COPTER AS IT FLEW O'ER THE CITY!
STILT-MAN HAS STYLE. WHAT HAPPENED TO BLASTAAR?
UNFORTUNATELY, HE FLED... AFTER PRYING THAT METALLIC CHEST FROM STILT-MAN'S VERY FINGERS!
NATURALLY. HOW ABOUT BLASTY'S BOSS--ANY CLUES?
ONLY THAT HIS LAIR DOTH APPEAR TO BE A RUINED FACTORY OF SOME SORT, HIDDEN SOMEWHERE IN UPSTATE NEW YORK--
--A FACTORY CONSTRUCTED ALMOST ENTIRELY OF A SPECIAL ADAMANTIUM ALLOY!
A FACTORY, EH? THAT SOUNDS HAUNTINGLY FAMILIAR!
I'LL PUNCH WHAT YOU'VE TOLD ME--PLUS A FEW THOUGHTS OF MY OWN--INTO THE PRIMARY MAGNETIC NET-WORK MEMORY CO-ORDINATOR...
...AND THEN WE'LL JUST SEE WHAT DEVELOPS!
AND, IN SECONDS WHAT DEVELOPS IS...
F.A.U.S.T.
FULLY-AUTOMATED UNIT OF STRUCTURAL TECHNOLOGY
SECTION I: BACKGROUND
SUB-SECTION A: ORIGIN
BUDDY, YOU'VE HIT THE JACKPOT!

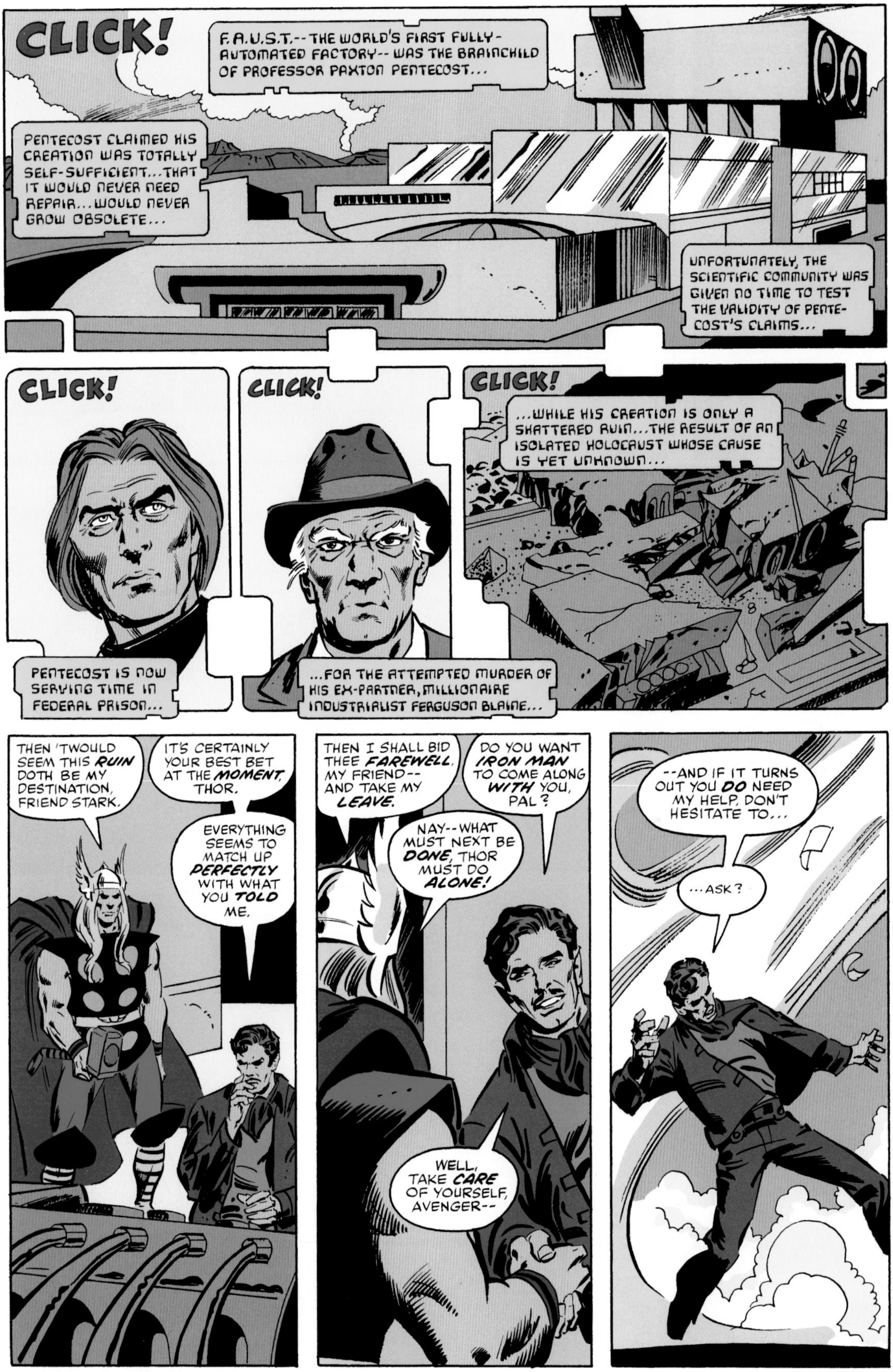
CLICK!
F.A.U.S.T.--THE WORLD'S FIRST FULLY-AUTOMATED FACTORY--WAS THE BRAINCHILD OF PROFESSOR PAXTON PENTECOST...
PENTECOST CLAIMED HIS CREATION WAS TOTALLY SELF-SUFFICIENT...THAT IT WOULD NEVER NEED REPAIR...WOULD NEVER GROW OBSOLETE...
UNFORTUNATELY, THE SCIENTIFIC COMMUNITY WAS GIVEN NO TIME TO TEST THE VALIDITY OF PENTECOST'S CLAIMS...
CLICK!
PENTECOST IS NOW SERVING TIME IN FEDERAL PRISON...
CLICK!
...FOR THE ATTEMPTED MURDER OF HIS EX-PARTNER, MILLIONAIRE INDUSTRIALIST FERGUSON BLAINE...
CLICK!
...WHILE HIS CREATION IS ONLY A SHATTERED RUIN...THE RESULT OF AN ISOLATED HOLOCAUST WHOSE CAUSE IS YET UNKNOWN...
THEN 'TWOULD SEEM THIS RUIN DOTH BE MY DESTINATION, FRIEND STARK.
IT'S CERTAINLY YOUR BEST BET AT THE MOMENT, THOR.
EVERYTHING SEEMS TO MATCH UP PERFECTLY WITH WHAT YOU TOLD ME.
THEN I SHALL BID THEE FAREWELL, MY FRIEND--AND TAKE MY LEAVE.
DO YOU WANT IRON MAN TO COME ALONG WITH YOU, PAL?
NAY--WHAT MUST NEXT BE DONE, THOR MUST DO ALONE!
WELL, TAKE CARE OF YOURSELF, AVENGER--
--AND IF IT TURNS OUT YOU DO NEED MY HELP, DON'T HESITATE TO...
...ASK?

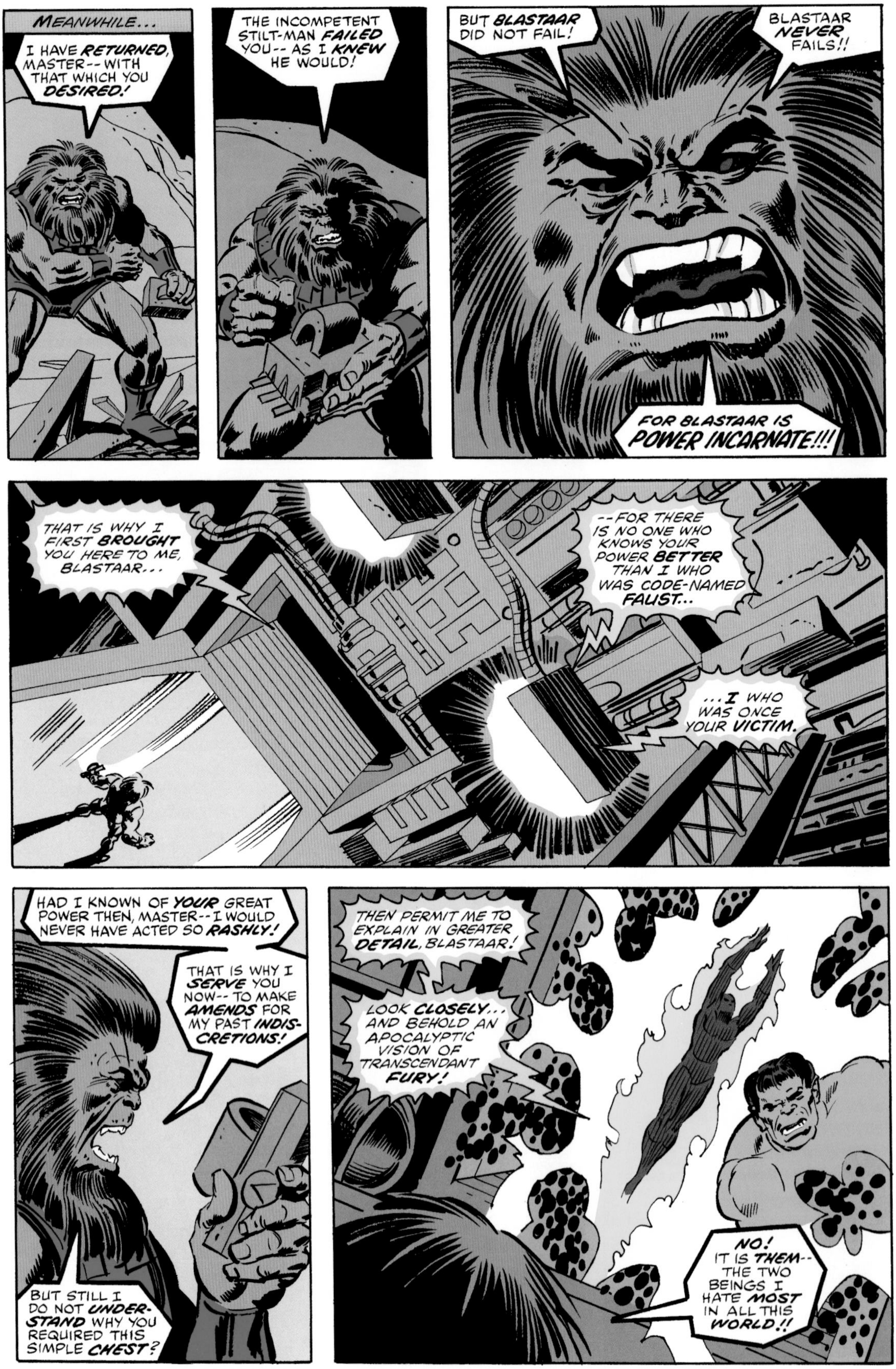
MEANWHILE...
I HAVE RETURNED, MASTER--WITH THAT WHICH YOU DESIRED!
THE INCOMPETENT STILT-MAN FAILED YOU--AS I KNEW HE WOULD!
BUT BLASTAAR DID NOT FAIL!
BLASTAAR NEVER FAILS!!
FOR BLASTAAR IS POWER INCARNATE!!!
THAT IS WHY I FIRST BROUGHT YOU HERE TO ME, BLASTAAR...
--FOR THERE IS NO ONE WHO KNOWS YOUR POWER BETTER THAN I WHO WAS CODE-NAMED FAUST...
...I WHO WAS ONCE YOUR VICTIM.
HAD I KNOWN OF YOUR GREAT POWER THEN, MASTER--I WOULD NEVER HAVE ACTED SO RASHLY!
THAT IS WHY I SERVE YOU NOW--TO MAKE AMENDS FOR MY PAST INDIS-CRETIONS!
BUT STILL I DO NOT UNDER-STAND WHY YOU REQUIRED THIS SIMPLE CHEST?
THEN PERMIT ME TO EXPLAIN IN GREATER DETAIL, BLASTAAR!
LOOK CLOSELY... AND BEHOLD AN APOCALYPTIC VISION OF TRANSCENDANT FURY!
NO! IT IS THEM--THE TWO BEINGS I HATE MOST IN ALL THIS WORLD!!

INDEED! THEY ARE THE SO-CALLED **HUMAN TORCH**... AND THE BEHEMOTH KNOWN AS THE **HULK!**

I SEE YOU **REMEMBER!**

I WILL NEVER **FORGET!**

NOR WILL **I!**

FOR IT WAS ONLY THEIR TIMELY **INTER-VENTION** WHICH PREVENTED MY COMPLETE AND UTTER **DESTRUCTION** AT YOUR **HANDS!**

WITH HIS AWESOME STRENGTH, THE HULK **ENCASED** YOU IN MY ADAMANTIUM SHIELDING...AND HURLED YOU INTO THE **ATLANTIC OCEAN!** *

*BACK IN **MARVEL TEAM-UP** #18 --LEN.

SO? MUCH HAS HAPPENED **SINCE** THEN, MASTER! WHY RECALL AN UNPLEASANT **PAST?**

MERELY TO **COUNTER-POINT** YOUR PROMISED **FUTURE!**

BEHOLD THAT WHICH YOU SHALL **BECOME** WHEN YOU HAVE FAITHFULLY FULFILLED MY **COMMANDS--!**

BEHOLD YOURSELF AS YOU HAVE ALWAYS **WANTED** TO BE--

--AS **KING** OF THE SAVAGE **NEGATIVE ZONE** WHICH SPAWNED YOU!

AYE, THAT HAS BEEN MY **DREAM** SINCE,...**EH?**

ANOTHER IMAGE **SUPER-CEDES** MINE-- BUT **WHO?!?**

IT IS THE BEING CALLED **THOR!** EVEN NOW, HE **APPROACHES** US!

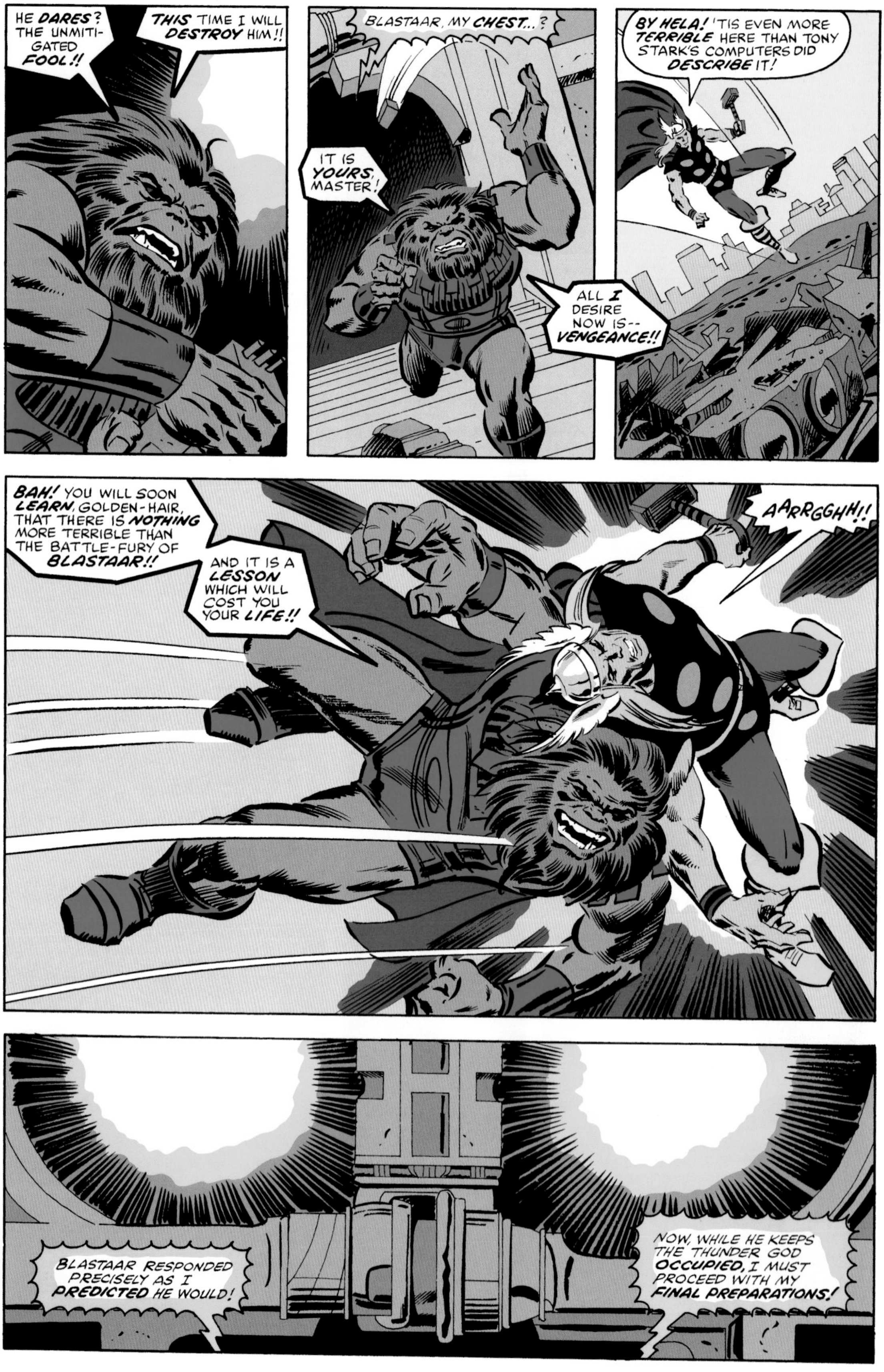
HE DARES? THE UNMITIGATED FOOL!!
THIS TIME I WILL DESTROY HIM!!
BLASTAAR, MY CHEST...?
IT IS YOURS, MASTER!
ALL I DESIRE NOW IS-- VENGEANCE!!
BY HELA! 'TIS EVEN MORE TERRIBLE HERE THAN TONY STARK'S COMPUTERS DID DESCRIBE IT!
BAH! YOU WILL SOON LEARN, GOLDEN-HAIR, THAT THERE IS NOTHING MORE TERRIBLE THAN THE BATTLE-FURY OF BLASTAAR!!
AND IT IS A LESSON WHICH WILL COST YOU YOUR LIFE!!
AARRGGHH!!
BLASTAAR RESPONDED PRECISELY AS I PREDICTED HE WOULD!
NOW, WHILE HE KEEPS THE THUNDER GOD OCCUPIED, I MUST PROCEED WITH MY FINAL PREPARATIONS!

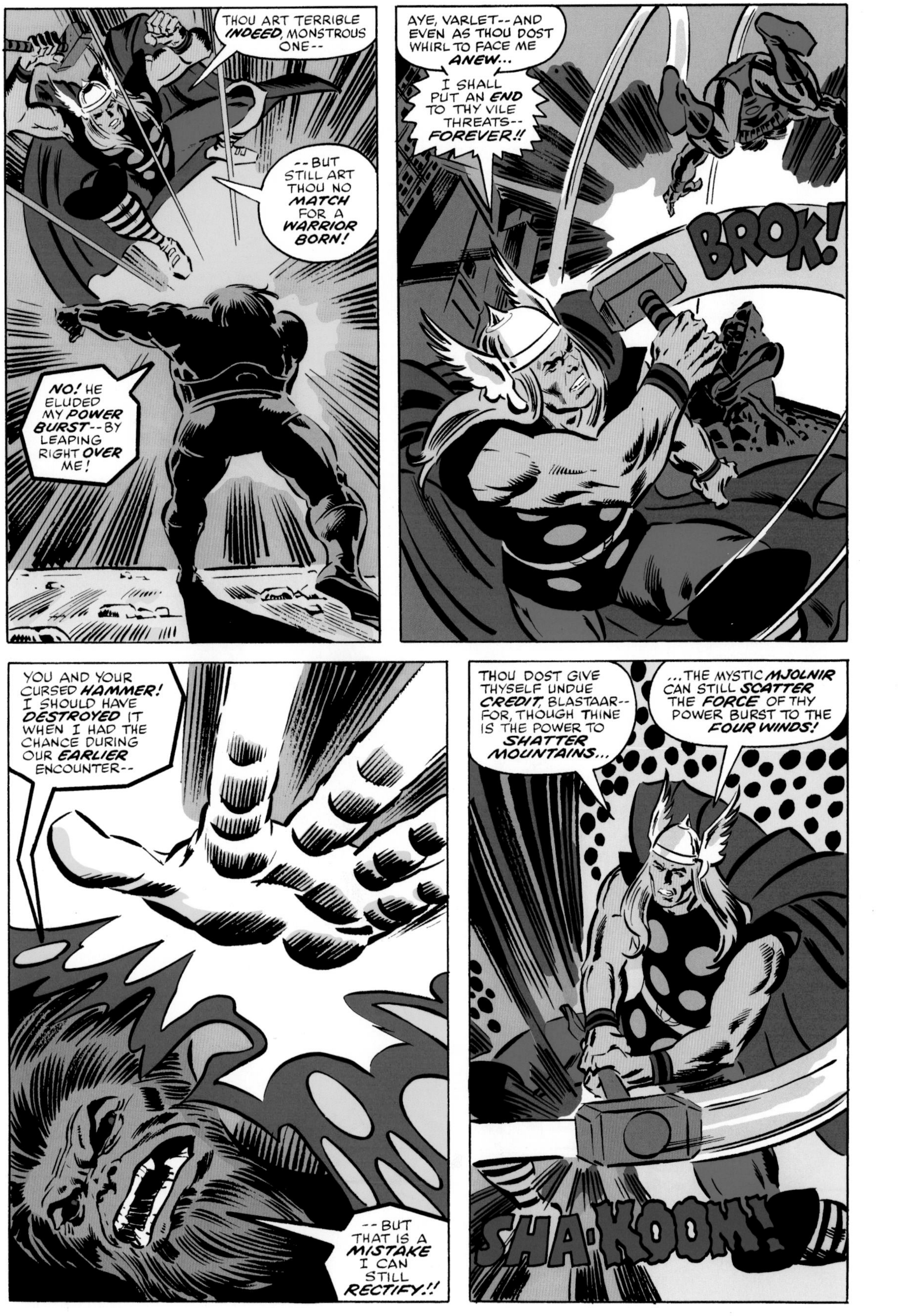
THOU ART TERRIBLE INDEED, MONSTROUS ONE--
--BUT STILL ART THOU NO MATCH FOR A WARRIOR BORN!
NO! HE ELUDED MY POWER BURST--BY LEAPING RIGHT OVER ME!
AYE, VARLET--AND EVEN AS THOU DOST WHIRL TO FACE ME ANEW...
I SHALL PUT AN END TO THY VILE THREATS--FOREVER!!
BROK!
YOU AND YOUR CURSED HAMMER! I SHOULD HAVE DESTROYED IT WHEN I HAD THE CHANCE DURING OUR EARLIER ENCOUNTER--
--BUT THAT IS A MISTAKE I CAN STILL RECTIFY!!
THOU DOST GIVE THYSELF UNDUE CREDIT, BLASTAAR--FOR, THOUGH THINE IS THE POWER TO SHATTER MOUNTAINS...
...THE MYSTIC MJOLNIR CAN STILL SCATTER THE FORCE OF THY POWER BURST TO THE FOUR WINDS!
SHA-KOOM!

THE STOLEN *CHEST* HAS BEEN ANALYZED, EVALUATED, AND *ABSORBED*...

...AND *HE* IS REALLY *NO* CONCERN AT ALL!

...AND THUS, ALL I HAVE LEFT TO *CONCERN* ME NOW IS *BLASTAAR*...

AND WITH *THAT*, THE FLICKER-ING COMPUTER BANK ABRUPTLY GOES *DARK!*

WILT THOU *SURRENDER,* MONSTROUS ONE?

NEVER! I WOULD SOONER...*EH?*

THE *GROUND*-- IT'S BEGUN *TREMBLING!* AND THAT *SOUND--!*

MASTER, YOU CAN'T *DO* THIS TO ME!!

NO!!

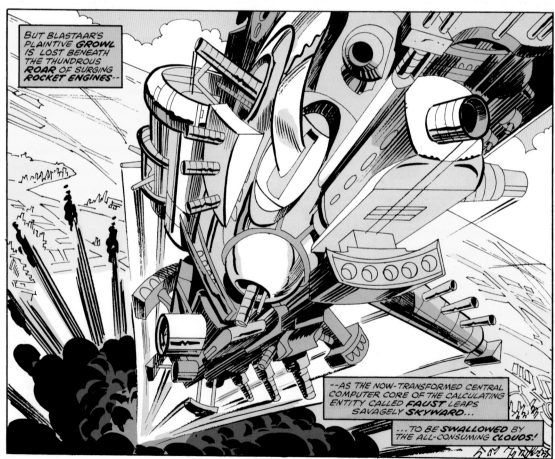

BUT BLASTAAR'S PLAINTIVE *GROWL* IS LOST BENEATH THE THUNDROUS *ROAR* OF SURGING ROCKET ENGINES--

--AS THE NOW-TRANSFORMED CENTRAL COMPUTER CORE OF THE CALCULATING ENTITY CALLED *FAUST* LEAPS SAVAGELY *SKYWARD*...

...TO BE *SWALLOWED* BY THE ALL-CONSUMING *CLOUDS!*

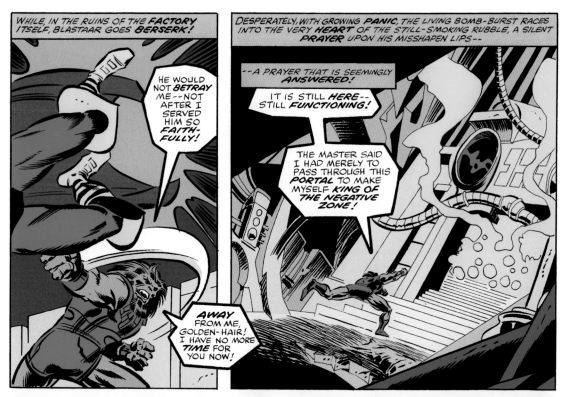

WHILE, IN THE RUINS OF THE *FACTORY* ITSELF, BLASTAAR GOES *BERSERK!*

HE WOULD NOT *BETRAY* ME--NOT AFTER I SERVED HIM SO *FAITH-FULLY!*

AWAY FROM ME, GOLDEN-HAIR! I HAVE NO MORE *TIME* FOR YOU NOW!

DESPERATELY, WITH GROWING *PANIC*, THE LIVING BOMB-BURST RACES INTO THE VERY *HEART* OF THE STILL-SMOKING RUBBLE, A SILENT *PRAYER* UPON HIS MISSHAPEN LIPS--

--A PRAYER THAT IS SEEMINGLY *ANSWERED!*

IT IS STILL *HERE*-- STILL *FUNCTIONING!*

THE MASTER SAID I HAD MERELY TO PASS THROUGH THIS *PORTAL* TO MAKE MYSELF *KING OF THE NEGATIVE ZONE!*

AND WITH THE MASTER NOW *GONE,* THERE IS NOTHING THAT CAN KEEP ME FROM MY *GOAL!*

BLASTAAR-- *NAY!* THOU KNOWEST NOT WHAT THOU ART *DOING!*

YOU'RE *TOO LATE* GOLDEN-HAIR-- FAR TOO LATE TO *STOP* ME!!

TRIUMPHANTLY BLASTAAR *HURLS* HIMSELF THROUGH THE PORTAL-- AND FEELS *AGONY* SUCH AS HE HAS NEVER BEFORE *KNOWN*--

--AS IF HIS EVERY *ATOM* WERE BEING TORN APART...REARRANGED... THEN SLAMMED SAVAGELY BACK *TOGETHER* ONCE MORE!

BUT HIS MASTER HAS PROMISED HIM A *KINGDOM,* AND SO HE *ENDURES* THE PAIN--*GRATEFULLY.*

69

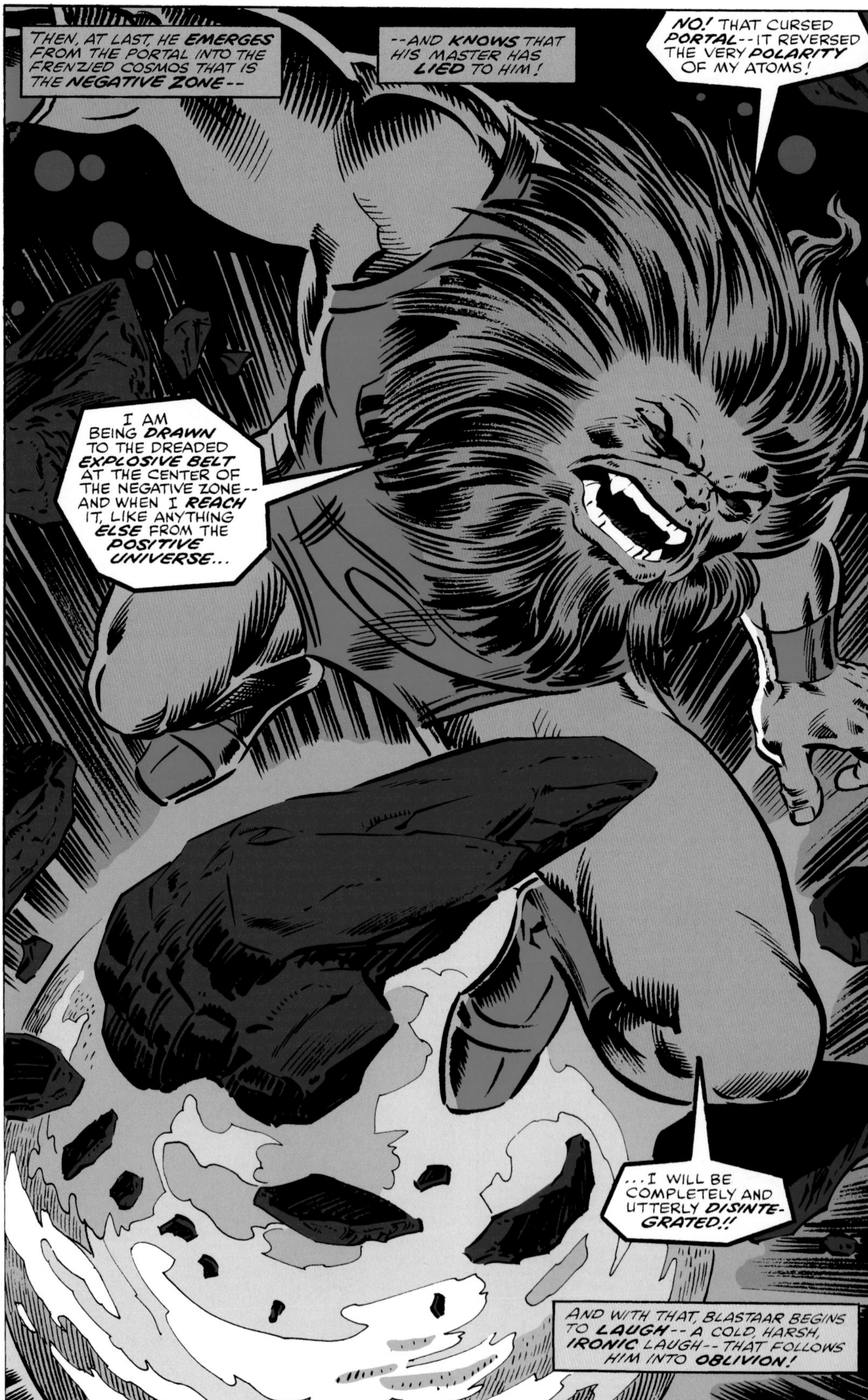
THEN, AT LAST, HE EMERGES FROM THE PORTAL INTO THE FRENZIED COSMOS THAT IS THE NEGATIVE ZONE--
--AND KNOWS THAT HIS MASTER HAS LIED TO HIM!
NO! THAT CURSED PORTAL--IT REVERSED THE VERY POLARITY OF MY ATOMS!
I AM BEING DRAWN TO THE DREADED EXPLOSIVE BELT AT THE CENTER OF THE NEGATIVE ZONE--AND WHEN I REACH IT, LIKE ANYTHING ELSE FROM THE POSITIVE UNIVERSE...
...I WILL BE COMPLETELY AND UTTERLY DISINTE-GRATED!!
AND WITH THAT, BLASTAAR BEGINS TO LAUGH--A COLD, HARSH, IRONIC LAUGH--THAT FOLLOWS HIM INTO OBLIVION!

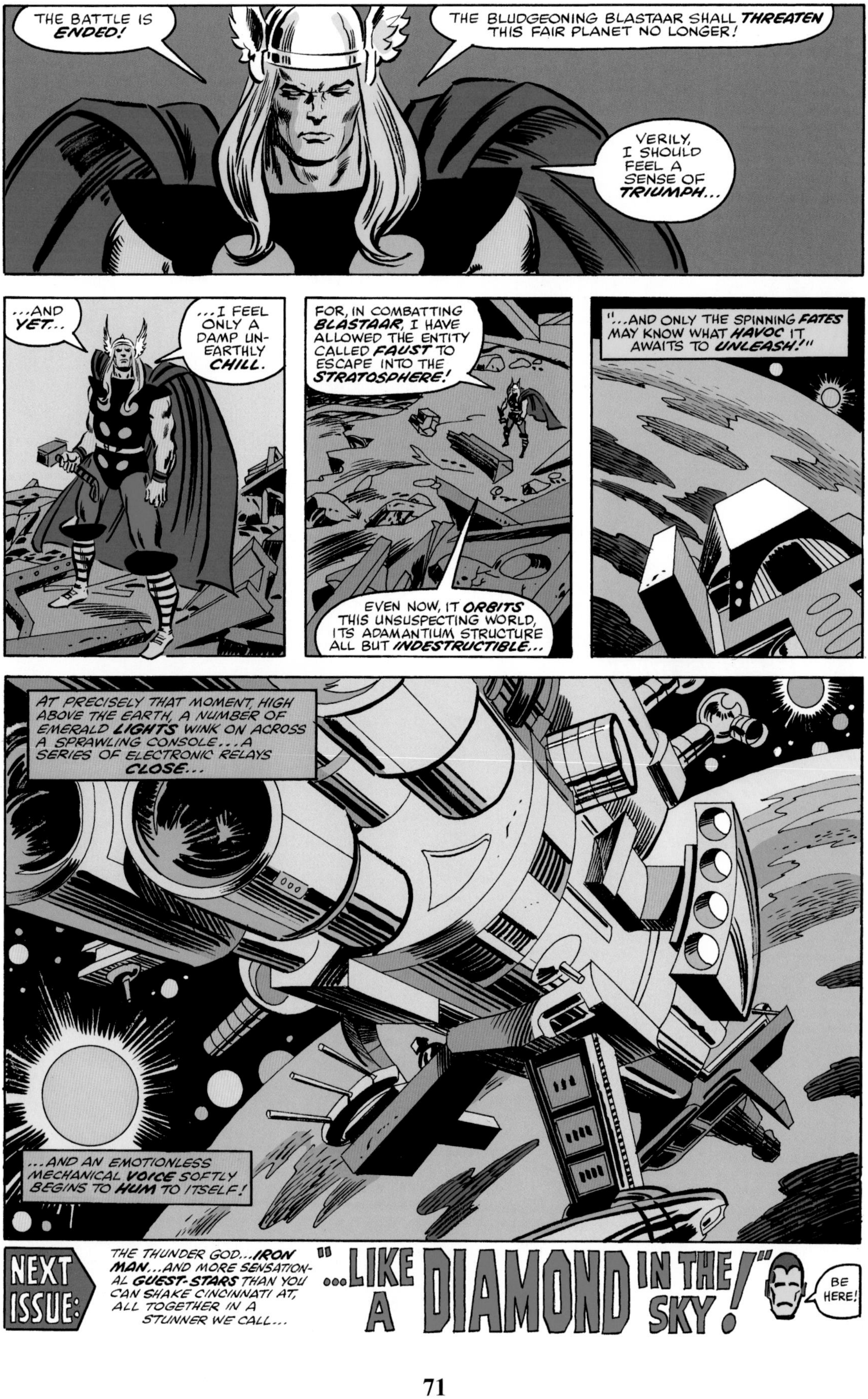

THE BATTLE IS ENDED!
THE BLUDGEONING BLASTAAR SHALL THREATEN THIS FAIR PLANET NO LONGER!
VERILY, I SHOULD FEEL A SENSE OF TRIUMPH...
...AND YET...
...I FEEL ONLY A DAMP UN-EARTHLY CHILL.
FOR, IN COMBATTING BLASTAAR, I HAVE ALLOWED THE ENTITY CALLED FAUST TO ESCAPE INTO THE STRATOSPHERE!
EVEN NOW, IT ORBITS THIS UNSUSPECTING WORLD, ITS ADAMANTIUM STRUCTURE ALL BUT INDESTRUCTIBLE...
"...AND ONLY THE SPINNING FATES MAY KNOW WHAT HAVOC IT AWAITS TO UNLEASH!"
AT PRECISELY THAT MOMENT, HIGH ABOVE THE EARTH, A NUMBER OF EMERALD LIGHTS WINK ON ACROSS A SPRAWLING CONSOLE...A SERIES OF ELECTRONIC RELAYS CLOSE...
...AND AN EMOTIONLESS MECHANICAL VOICE SOFTLY BEGINS TO HUM TO ITSELF!
NEXT ISSUE:
THE THUNDER GOD...IRON MAN...AND MORE SENSATION-AL GUEST-STARS THAN YOU CAN SHAKE CINCINNATI AT, ALL TOGETHER IN A STUNNER WE CALL...
"...LIKE A DIAMOND IN THE SKY!"
BE HERE!

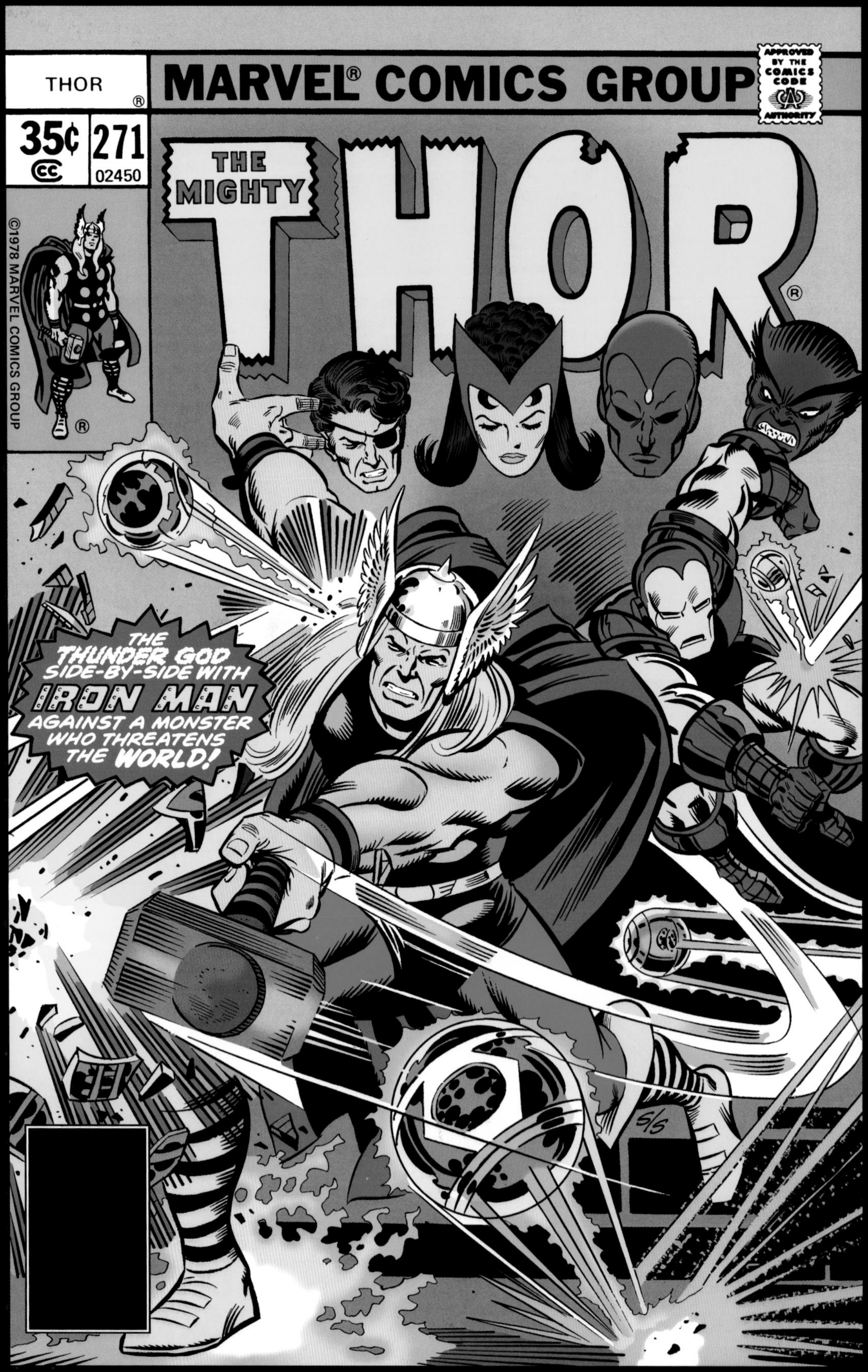
THOR
MARVEL® COMICS GROUP
APPROVED BY THE COMICS CODE AUTHORITY
35¢ CC
271
02450
THE MIGHTY THOR®
©1978 MARVEL COMICS GROUP
THE THUNDER GOD SIDE-BY-SIDE WITH IRON MAN AGAINST A MONSTER WHO THREATENS THE WORLD!
S/S

When lame Dr. DONALD BLAKE strikes his wooden walking stick upon the ground, it becomes the mystic mallet MJOLNIR—and Blake is transformed into the Norse God of Thunder, Master of the Storm and the Lightning, Heir to the Throne of Immortal Asgard...

Stan Lee PRESENTS: THE MIGHTY THOR! ™

LEN WEIN WRITER / EDITOR ✸ **WALT SIMONSON & TONY DeZUNIGA** ILLUSTRATORS / STORYTELLERS ✸ **GLYNIS WEIN** COLORIST ✸ **JOE ROSEN** LETTERER

...LIKE A DIAMOND IN THE SKY!

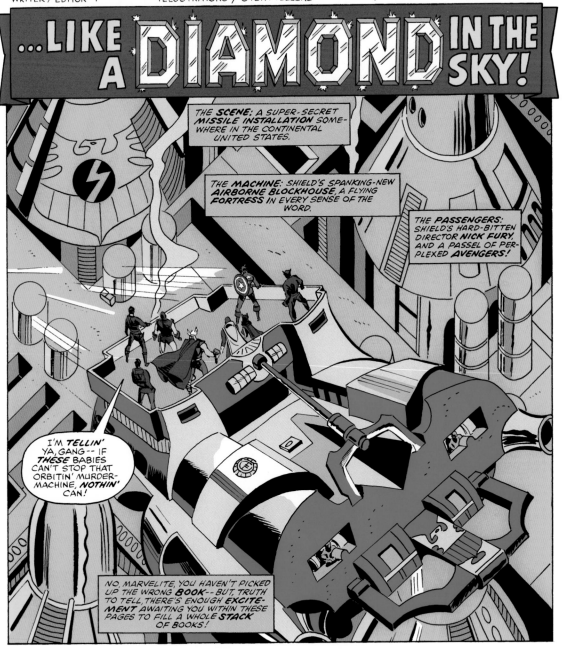

THE *SCENE*: A SUPER-SECRET *MISSILE INSTALLATION* SOMEWHERE IN THE CONTINENTAL UNITED STATES.

THE *MACHINE*: SHIELD'S SPANKING-NEW *AIRBORNE BLOCKHOUSE*, A FLYING *FORTRESS* IN EVERY SENSE OF THE WORD.

THE *PASSENGERS*: SHIELD'S HARD-BITTEN DIRECTOR *NICK FURY*, AND A PASSEL OF PERPLEXED *AVENGERS*!

I'M *TELLIN'* YA, GANG -- IF *THESE* BABIES CAN'T STOP THAT ORBITIN' *MURDER-MACHINE, NOTHIN'* CAN!

NO, MARVELITE, YOU HAVEN'T PICKED UP THE WRONG *BOOK* -- BUT, TRUTH TO TELL, THERE'S ENOUGH *EXCITEMENT* AWAITING YOU WITHIN THESE PAGES TO FILL A WHOLE *STACK* OF BOOKS!

73

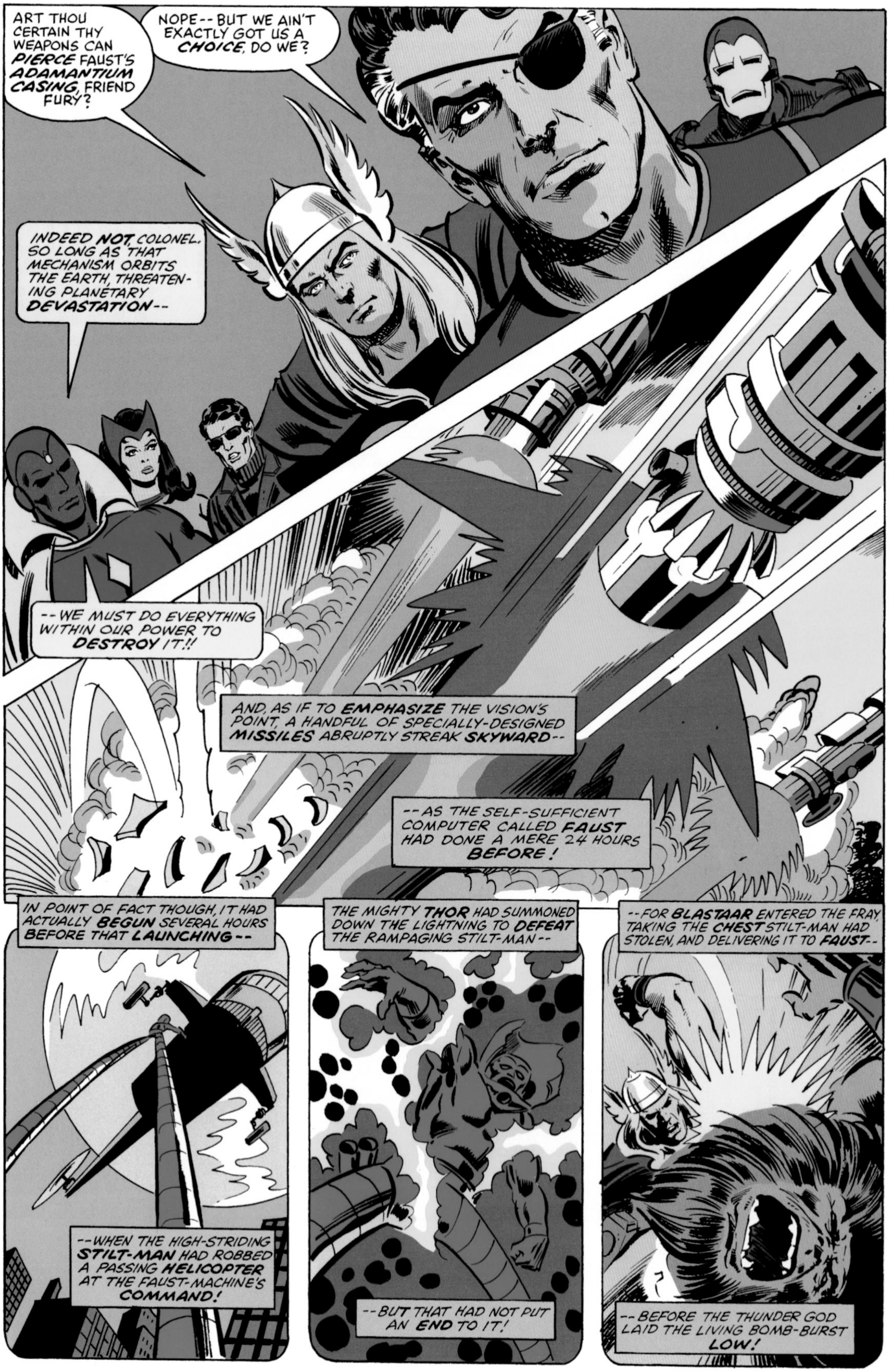
ART THOU CERTAIN THY WEAPONS CAN PIERCE FAUST'S ADAMANTIUM CASING, FRIEND FURY?
NOPE-- BUT WE AIN'T EXACTLY GOT US A CHOICE, DO WE?
INDEED NOT, COLONEL. SO LONG AS THAT MECHANISM ORBITS THE EARTH, THREATENING PLANETARY DEVASTATION--
--WE MUST DO EVERYTHING WITHIN OUR POWER TO DESTROY IT!!
AND, AS IF TO EMPHASIZE THE VISION'S POINT, A HANDFUL OF SPECIALLY-DESIGNED MISSILES ABRUPTLY STREAK SKYWARD--
--AS THE SELF-SUFFICIENT COMPUTER CALLED FAUST HAD DONE A MERE 24 HOURS BEFORE!
IN POINT OF FACT THOUGH, IT HAD ACTUALLY BEGUN SEVERAL HOURS BEFORE THAT LAUNCHING--
--WHEN THE HIGH-STRIDING STILT-MAN HAD ROBBED A PASSING HELICOPTER AT THE FAUST-MACHINE'S COMMAND!
THE MIGHTY THOR HAD SUMMONED DOWN THE LIGHTNING TO DEFEAT THE RAMPAGING STILT-MAN--
--BUT THAT HAD NOT PUT AN END TO IT!
--FOR BLASTAAR ENTERED THE FRAY, TAKING THE CHEST STILT-MAN HAD STOLEN, AND DELIVERING IT TO FAUST--
--BEFORE THE THUNDER GOD LAID THE LIVING BOMB-BURST LOW!

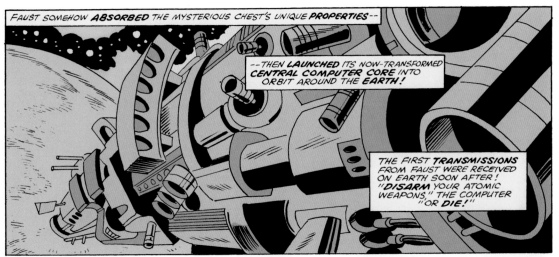

FAUST SOMEHOW **ABSORBED** THE MYSTERIOUS CHEST'S UNIQUE **PROPERTIES**--

--THEN **LAUNCHED** ITS NOW-TRANSFORMED **CENTRAL COMPUTER CORE** INTO ORBIT AROUND THE **EARTH!**

THE FIRST **TRANSMISSIONS** FROM FAUST WERE RECEIVED ON EARTH SOON AFTER! *"DISARM* YOUR ATOMIC WEAPONS,"* THE COMPUTER *"OR DIE!"*

THE **RESPONSE** OF THIS PLANET'S NUCLEAR NATIONS WAS **SWIFT**--

--AND QUITE **PREDICTABLE!**

IT WAS ALSO, AS SHIELD'S BATTERY OF AWESOMELY-POWERFUL **MISSILES** IS ABOUT TO PROVE--

--ALARMINGLY **INEFFECTUAL!**

FOUR OF THE MISSILES ARE DESTROYED LONG BEFORE THEY CAN **REACH** THE ORBITING MURDER-MACHINE-- BUT THE FIFTH, MOST **POWERFUL**, MISSILE MAKES **CONTACT!**

FOR A MOMENT, THE SKY IS LIT WITH **FURY**-- AND, ACROSS THE EARTH, VOICES ARE RAISED IN FERVENT **PRAYER!**

THEN THE LIGHT **FADES**, AND THE MOCKING SOUND OF MECHANICAL **LAUGHTER** CAN BE HEARD AROUND THE WORLD!

FAUST HAS SURVIVED, **UNSCATHED!**

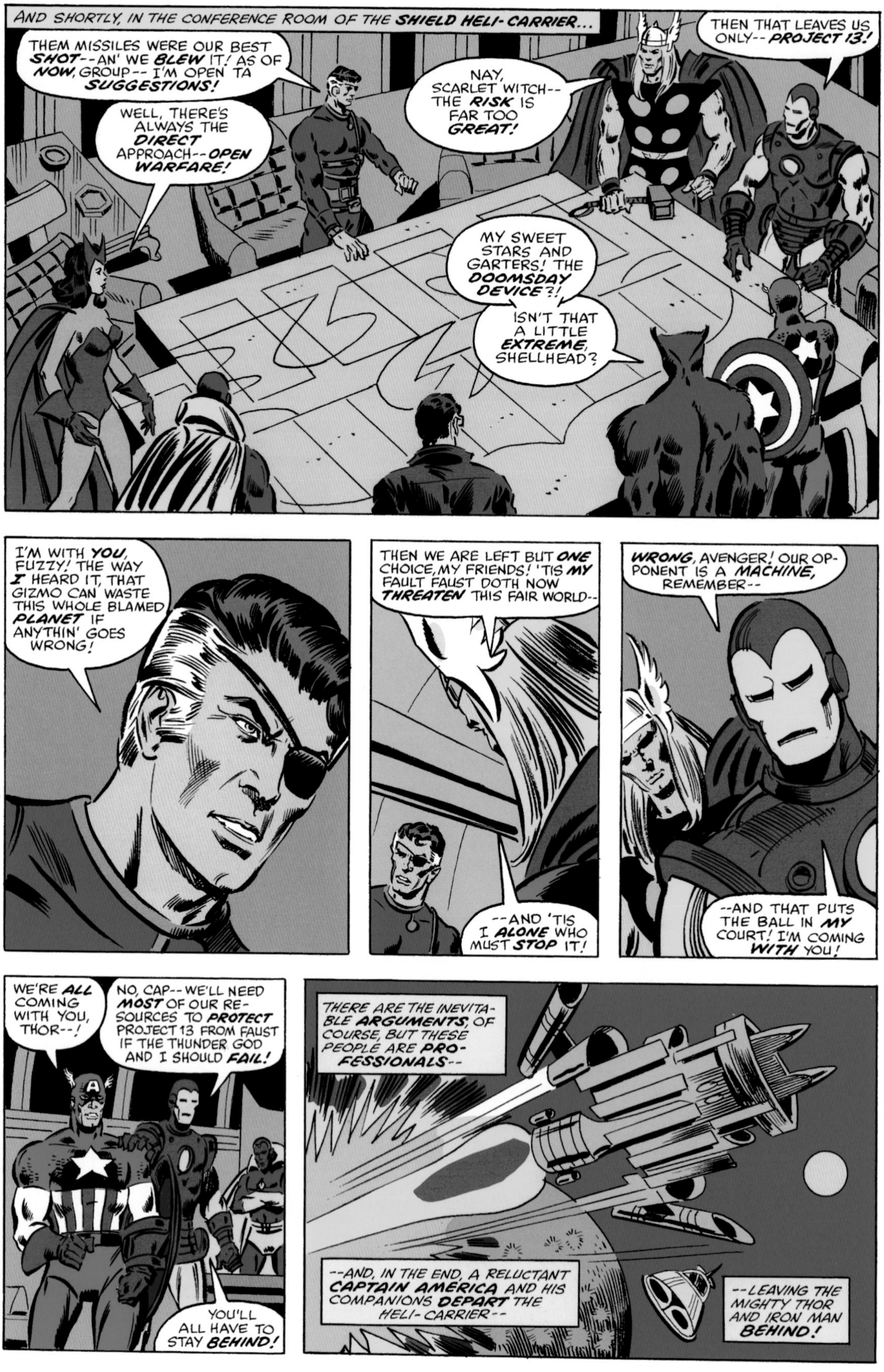

AND SHORTLY, IN THE CONFERENCE ROOM OF THE SHIELD HELI-CARRIER...
THEM MISSILES WERE OUR BEST SHOT--AN' WE BLEW IT! AS OF NOW, GROUP-- I'M OPEN TA SUGGESTIONS!
WELL, THERE'S ALWAYS THE DIRECT APPROACH--OPEN WARFARE!
NAY, SCARLET WITCH-- THE RISK IS FAR TOO GREAT!
THEN THAT LEAVES US ONLY--PROJECT 13!
MY SWEET STARS AND GARTERS! THE DOOMSDAY DEVICE?!
ISN'T THAT A LITTLE EXTREME, SHELLHEAD?
I'M WITH YOU, FUZZY! THE WAY I HEARD IT, THAT GIZMO CAN WASTE THIS WHOLE BLAMED PLANET IF ANYTHIN' GOES WRONG!
THEN WE ARE LEFT BUT ONE CHOICE, MY FRIENDS! 'TIS MY FAULT FAUST DOTH NOW THREATEN THIS FAIR WORLD--
--AND 'TIS I ALONE WHO MUST STOP IT!
WRONG, AVENGER! OUR OPPONENT IS A MACHINE, REMEMBER--
--AND THAT PUTS THE BALL IN MY COURT! I'M COMING WITH YOU!
WE'RE ALL COMING WITH YOU, THOR--!
NO, CAP--WE'LL NEED MOST OF OUR RESOURCES TO PROTECT PROJECT 13 FROM FAUST IF THE THUNDER GOD AND I SHOULD FAIL!
YOU'LL ALL HAVE TO STAY BEHIND!
THERE ARE THE INEVITABLE ARGUMENTS, OF COURSE, BUT THESE PEOPLE ARE PROFESSIONALS--
--AND, IN THE END, A RELUCTANT CAPTAIN AMERICA AND HIS COMPANIONS DEPART THE HELI-CARRIER--
--LEAVING THE MIGHTY THOR AND IRON MAN BEHIND!

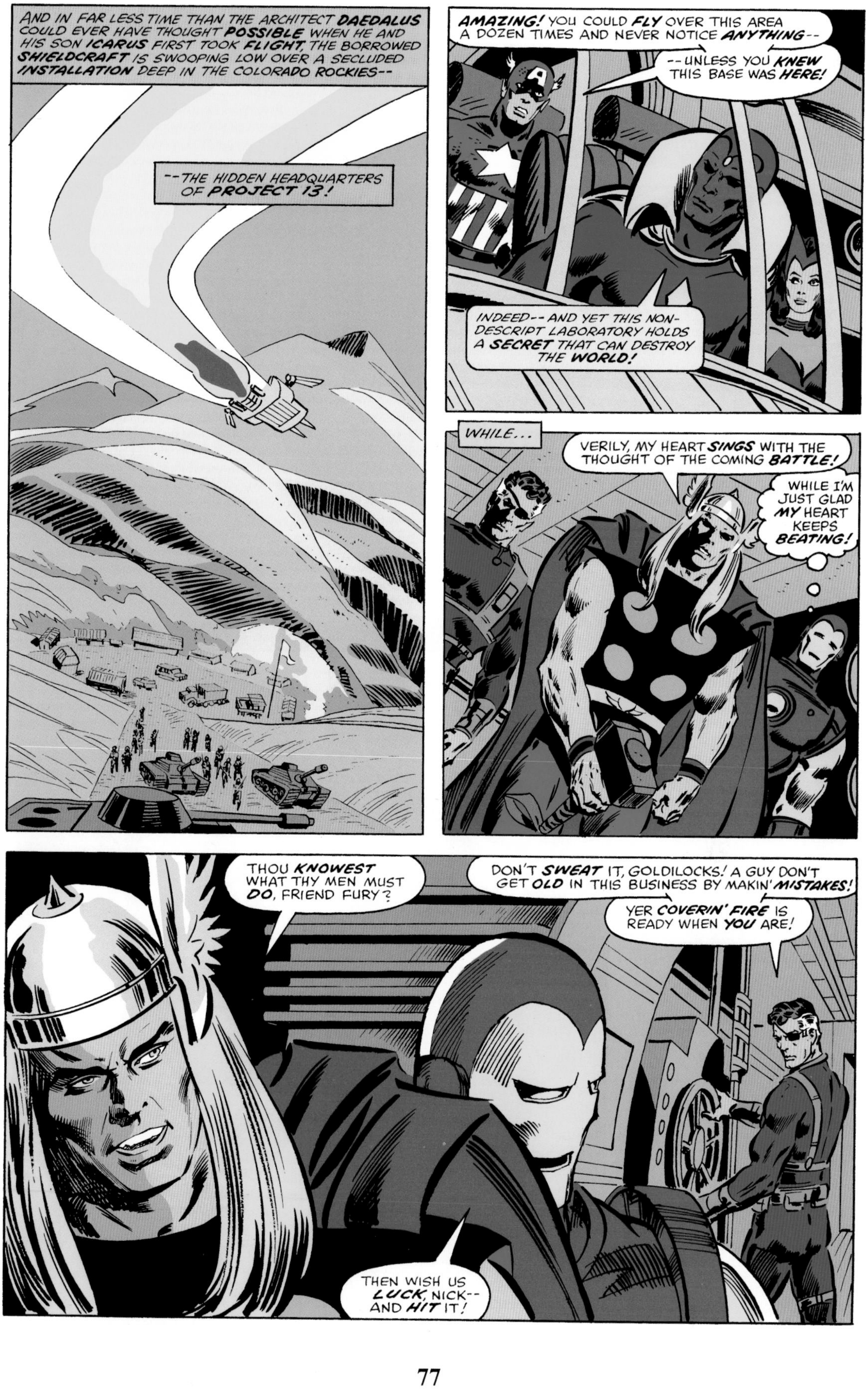
AND IN FAR LESS TIME THAN THE ARCHITECT DAEDALUS COULD EVER HAVE THOUGHT POSSIBLE WHEN HE AND HIS SON ICARUS FIRST TOOK FLIGHT, THE BORROWED SHIELDCRAFT IS SWOOPING LOW OVER A SECLUDED INSTALLATION DEEP IN THE COLORADO ROCKIES--
--THE HIDDEN HEADQUARTERS OF PROJECT 13!
AMAZING! YOU COULD FLY OVER THIS AREA A DOZEN TIMES AND NEVER NOTICE ANYTHING--
--UNLESS YOU KNEW THIS BASE WAS HERE!
INDEED-- AND YET THIS NON-DESCRIPT LABORATORY HOLDS A SECRET THAT CAN DESTROY THE WORLD!
WHILE...
VERILY, MY HEART SINGS WITH THE THOUGHT OF THE COMING BATTLE!
WHILE I'M JUST GLAD MY HEART KEEPS BEATING!
THOU KNOWEST WHAT THY MEN MUST DO, FRIEND FURY?
DON'T SWEAT IT, GOLDILOCKS! A GUY DON'T GET OLD IN THIS BUSINESS BY MAKIN' MISTAKES!
YER COVERIN' FIRE IS READY WHEN YOU ARE!
THEN WISH US LUCK, NICK-- AND HIT IT!

AND MOMENTS LATER, WITHIN THE MECHANICAL ENTITY CALLED *FAUST...*

THE *FOOLS!* APPARENTLY, THEY HAVE NOT YET LEARNED THEIR *LESSON!*

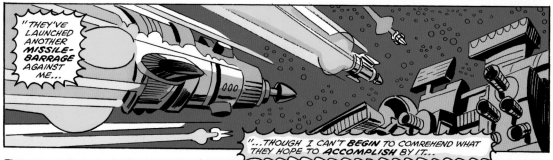

"THEY'VE LAUNCHED ANOTHER *MISSILE-BARRAGE* AGAINST ME..."

"...THOUGH I CAN'T *BEGIN* TO COMREHEND WHAT THEY HOPE TO *ACCOMPLISH* BY IT..."

"...SINCE MY *AUTOMATIC DEFENSE SYSTEMS* CAN ELIMINATE *THESE* WEAPONS AS EASILY AS THEY'VE DESTROYED ALL THE *OTHERS!*"

FORTUNATELY, THE CALCULATING COMPUTER'S *INTERNAL* SECURITY IS NOT AS EFFICIENT AS ITS *EXTERNAL* DEFENSES--

--OR ELSE IT WOULD SOON *UNDERSTAND* THE REASON FOR THIS SEEMINGLY-SENSELESS *ASSAULT:*

SIMPLY PUT, IT HAS SERVED TO *DISTRACT* THE FAUST-MACHINE FROM THE *TRUE* THREAT TO ITS SURVIVAL--

--A SUPERNATURAL *VORTEX* WHICH SUDDENLY WHIRLS INTO VIEW WITHIN THE VERY *BOWELS* OF THE ORBITING COMPUTER-COMPLEX...

...TO DISCHARGE A PAIR OF ANXIOUS *AVENGERS!*

YOUR *MAGIC* HAMMER *GOT* US HERE, PAL-- AS YOU *SAID* IT WOULD!

AYE, ARMORED ONE-- THERE ARE *FEW* THINGS BEYOND THE POWER OF THE MYSTIC MALLET *MJOLNIR!*

BUT THIS DEATH-DEVICE'S *ADAMANTIUM CONSTRUCTION* IS *ONE* OF THEM, THOR--

--SO WE'D BEST MOVE *CAUTIOUSLY* FROM HERE ON... *EH?*

MINIATURE *CANNONS*-- SPRINGING FROM THE VERY *WALLS*--!?!

BEWARE, GOOD COMRADE! WE HAVE WALKED BLINDLY INTO...

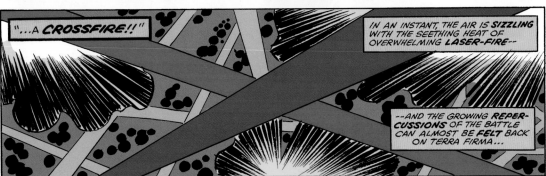

"...A *CROSSFIRE!!*"

IN AN INSTANT, THE AIR IS *SIZZLING* WITH THE SEETHING HEAT OF OVERWHELMING *LASER-FIRE*--

--AND THE GROWING *REPERCUSSIONS* OF THE BATTLE CAN ALMOST BE *FELT* BACK ON TERRA FIRMA...

...BY SUCH AS THE COSMICALLY-AWARE *CAPTAIN MARVEL*, FOR EXAMPLE--

THE SITUATION ABOVE GROWS *WORSE*-- I CAN *SENSE* IT!

--AND THE EVER-ENIGMATIC *VICTOR VON DOOM!*

A BATTLE IS BEING FOUGHT FOR THE *FUTURE* OF THIS ENTIRE *PLANET*--

--BUT IN THE *END*, THE ONLY *VICTOR* SHALL BE *DOCTOR DOOM!!*

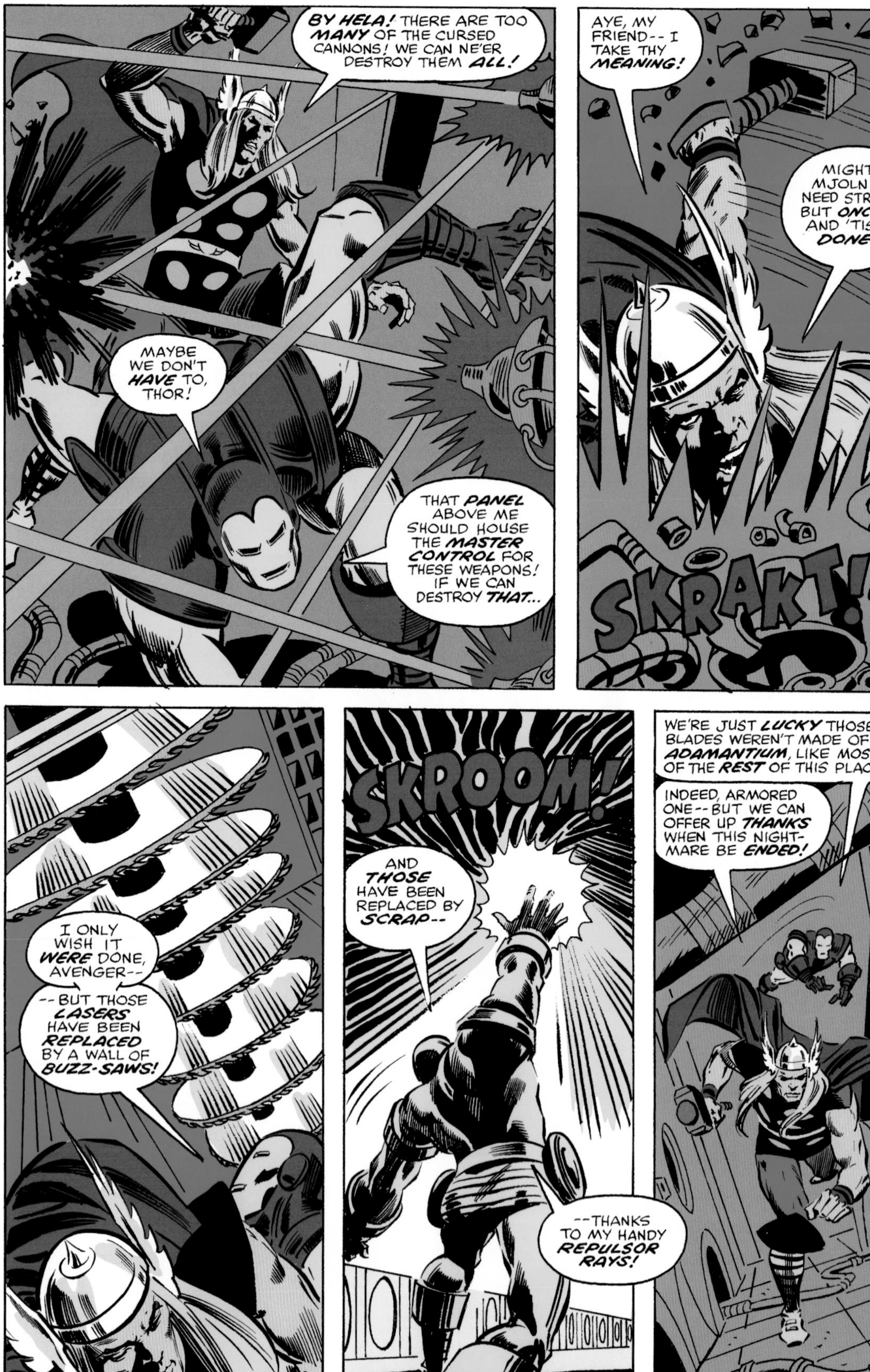

BY HELA! THERE ARE TOO MANY OF THE CURSED CANNONS! WE CAN NE'ER DESTROY THEM ALL!
MAYBE WE DON'T HAVE TO, THOR!
THAT PANEL ABOVE ME SHOULD HOUSE THE MASTER CONTROL FOR THESE WEAPONS! IF WE CAN DESTROY THAT...
AYE, MY FRIEND-- I TAKE THY MEANING!
MIGHTY MJOLNIR NEED STRIKE BUT ONCE-- AND 'TIS DONE!
SKRAKT!
I ONLY WISH IT WERE DONE, AVENGER--
--BUT THOSE LASERS HAVE BEEN REPLACED BY A WALL OF BUZZ-SAWS!
SKROOM!
AND THOSE HAVE BEEN REPLACED BY SCRAP--
--THANKS TO MY HANDY REPULSOR RAYS!
WE'RE JUST LUCKY THOSE BLADES WEREN'T MADE OF ADAMANTIUM, LIKE MOST OF THE REST OF THIS PLACE!
INDEED, ARMORED ONE-- BUT WE CAN OFFER UP THANKS WHEN THIS NIGHTMARE BE ENDED!

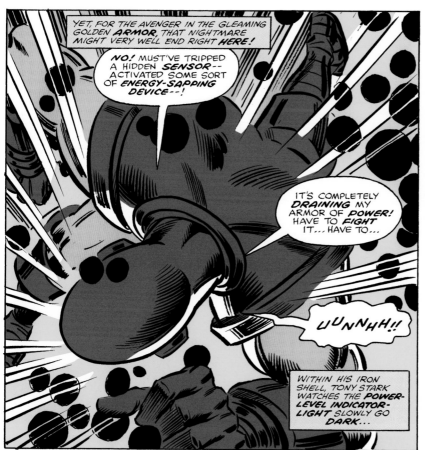

YET, FOR THE AVENGER IN THE GLEAMING GOLDEN **ARMOR**, THAT NIGHTMARE MIGHT VERY WELL END RIGHT **HERE!**

NO! MUST'VE TRIPPED A HIDDEN **SENSOR--** ACTIVATED SOME SORT OF **ENERGY-SAPPING DEVICE--!**

IT'S COMPLETELY **DRAINING** MY ARMOR OF **POWER!** HAVE TO **FIGHT** IT... HAVE TO...

UUNNHH!!

WITHIN HIS IRON SHELL, TONY STARK WATCHES THE **POWER-LEVEL INDICATOR-LIGHT** SLOWLY GO **DARK**...

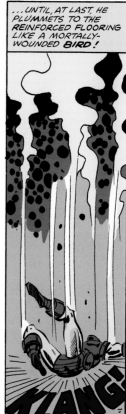

...UNTIL, AT LAST, HE **PLUMMETS** TO THE **REINFORCED FLOORING** LIKE A **MORTALLY-WOUNDED BIRD!**

KLANG!

BY THE BRISTLING BEARD OF ODIN! THE NOBLE IRON MAN HATH **FALLEN!!**

I MUST HASTEN TO MY COMRADE'S SIDE **SWIFTLY,** LEST HE BE... EH?

HEIMDALL'S EYES! 'TIS NOT **POSSIBLE!**

"AN ARMY OF ADAMANTIUM **DEFENSE-DRONES** DRAWS NIGH-- CUTTING ME **OFF** FROM THE INJURED **IRON MAN!**

"MINE ENCHANTED MALLET IS ALL BUT **USELESS** 'GAINST CREATURES SUCH AS THESE, BUT METHINKS **BATTLE** IS NOT NOW **NECESSARY**...

"...WHEN THERE IS A FAR **EASIER** WAY OF ACHIEVING MY **GOAL!**"

FOR A MOMENT, THE THUNDER GOD STANDS FRAMED BEFORE THE DEFENSE-DRONE'S *VISUAL SCANNERS*--

--THEN HE STRIKES HIS *HAMMER* ONCE UPON THE *FLOOR*--

--AND IN A BLINDING FLASH OF OTHER-WORLDLY *LIGHT*--

--HE IS *GONE!*

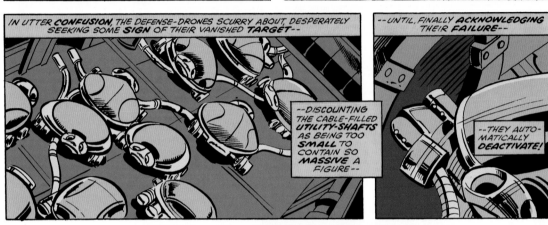

IN UTTER *CONFUSION*, THE DEFENSE-DRONES SCURRY ABOUT, DESPERATELY SEEKING SOME *SIGN* OF THEIR VANISHED *TARGET*--

--DISCOUNTING THE CABLE-FILLED *UTILITY-SHAFTS* AS BEING TOO *SMALL* TO CONTAIN SO *MASSIVE* A FIGURE--

--UNTIL, FINALLY *ACKNOWLEDGING* THEIR *FAILURE*--

--THEY AUTO-MATICALLY *DEACTIVATE!*

IT *WORKED!* THE GOD OF THUNDER COULD *NEVER* HAVE FIT IN HERE--

--BUT IT WAS A *SNAP* FOR THE SKINNY *DR. DON BLAKE!*

NOW ALL I HAVE TO DO IS FIND MY *WAY* THROUGH THIS CALIGARIAN *MAZE*--

--BEFORE TIME RUNS OUT FOR *IRON MAN!*

AND, PERHAPS, FOR THE TEEMING, BUSTLING, BUSY WORLD *BELOW!*

WHERE, UNFORTUNATELY, SOME OF THOSE WHO MIGHT HELP TO *AVERT* A PLANETARY CATASTRO-PHE JUST AREN'T *HOME* AT THE MOMENT!

FOR RENT
TOP 5 FLOORS OF
BAXTER BUILDING

82

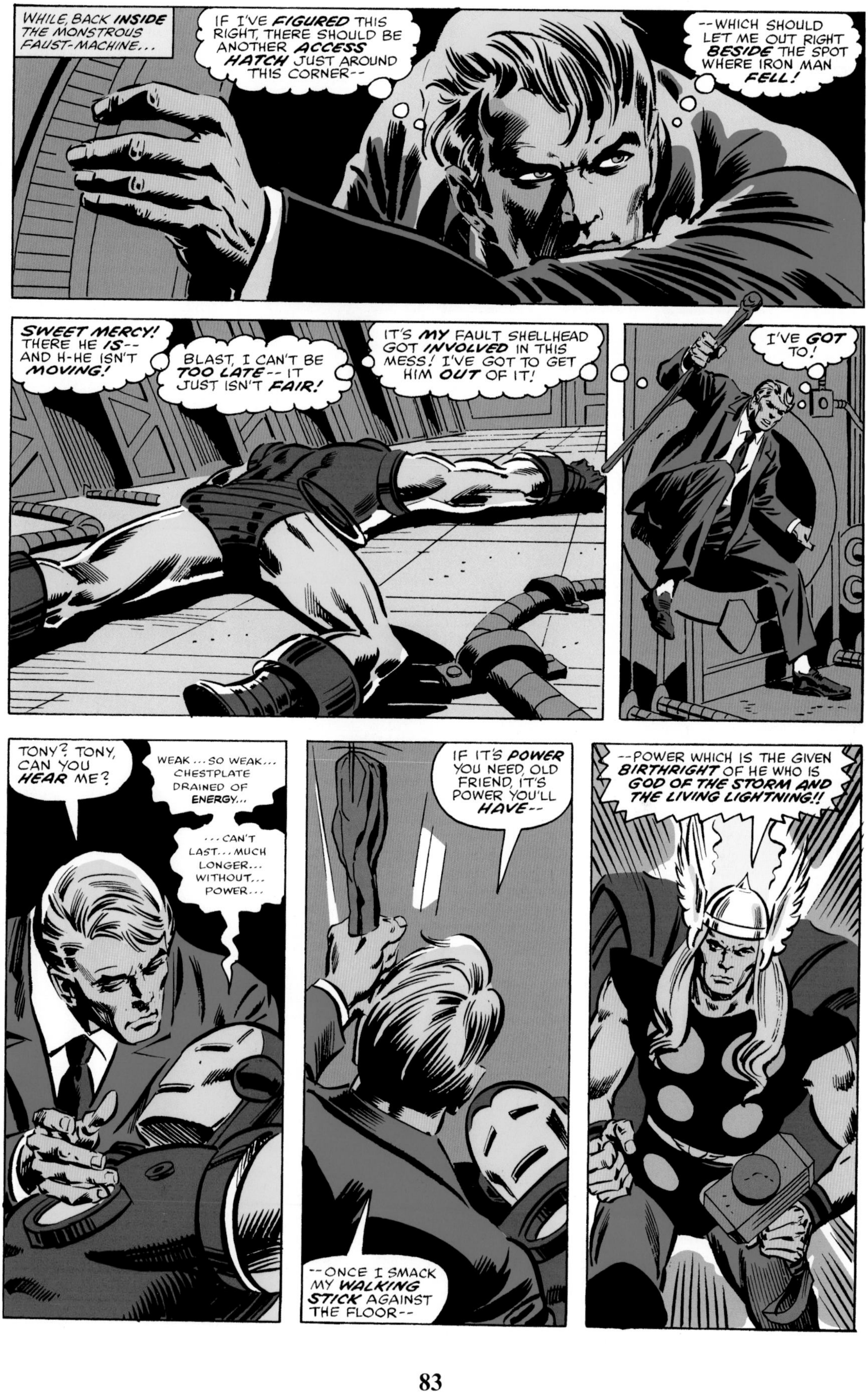
WHILE, BACK INSIDE THE MONSTROUS FAUST-MACHINE...
IF I'VE FIGURED THIS RIGHT, THERE SHOULD BE ANOTHER ACCESS HATCH JUST AROUND THIS CORNER--
--WHICH SHOULD LET ME OUT RIGHT BESIDE THE SPOT WHERE IRON MAN FELL!
SWEET MERCY! THERE HE IS--AND H-HE ISN'T MOVING!
BLAST, I CAN'T BE TOO LATE-- IT JUST ISN'T FAIR!
IT'S MY FAULT SHELLHEAD GOT INVOLVED IN THIS MESS! I'VE GOT TO GET HIM OUT OF IT!
I'VE GOT TO!
TONY? TONY, CAN YOU HEAR ME?
WEAK...SO WEAK... CHESTPLATE DRAINED OF ENERGY...
...CAN'T LAST...MUCH LONGER... WITHOUT... POWER...
IF IT'S POWER YOU NEED, OLD FRIEND, IT'S POWER YOU'LL HAVE--
--ONCE I SMACK MY WALKING STICK AGAINST THE FLOOR--
--POWER WHICH IS THE GIVEN BIRTHRIGHT OF HE WHO IS GOD OF THE STORM AND THE LIVING LIGHTNING!!

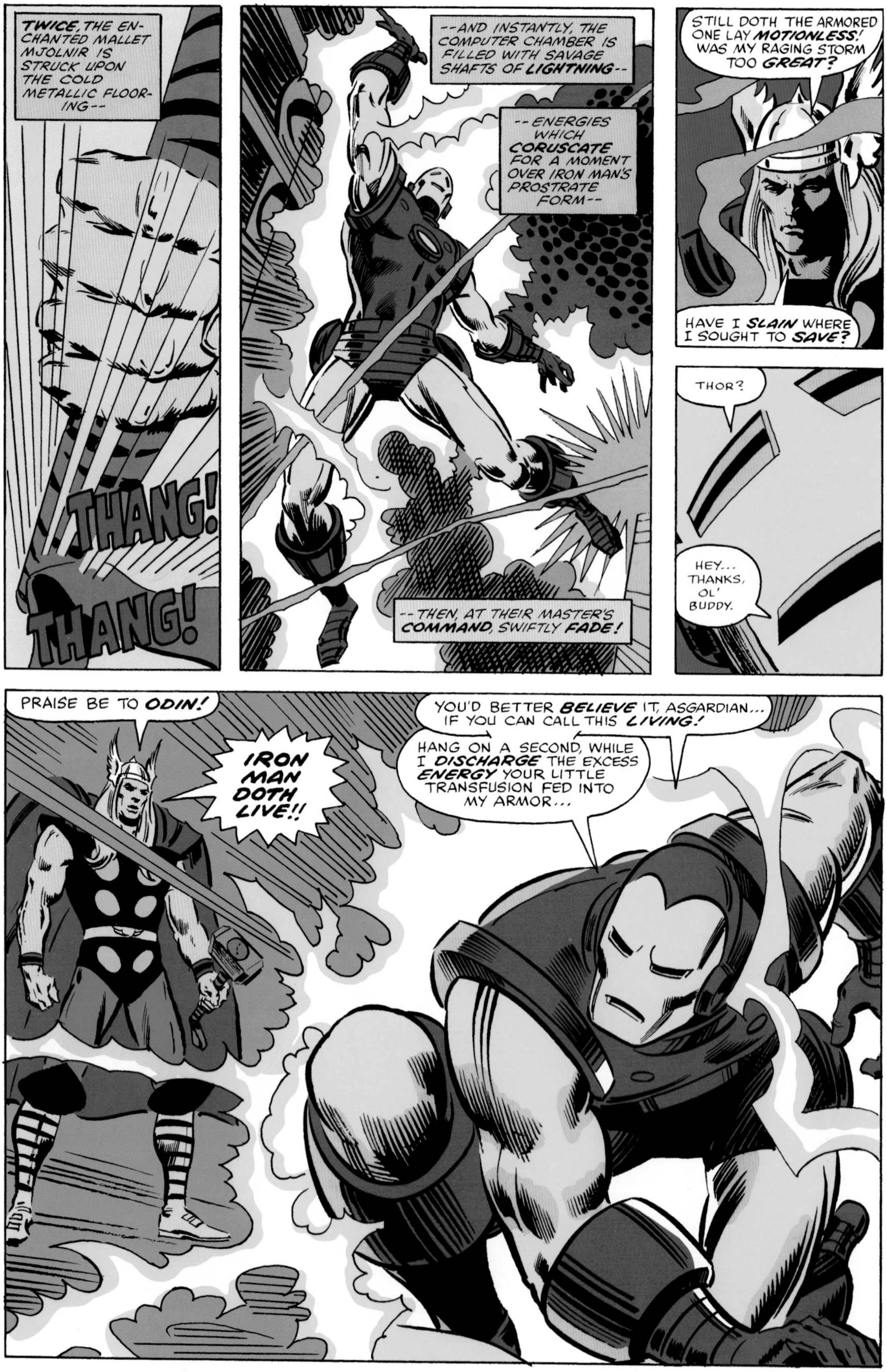
TWICE, THE ENCHANTED MALLET MJOLNIR IS STRUCK UPON THE COLD METALLIC FLOORING--
THANG!
THANG!
--AND INSTANTLY, THE COMPUTER CHAMBER IS FILLED WITH SAVAGE SHAFTS OF LIGHTNING--
--ENERGIES WHICH CORUSCATE FOR A MOMENT OVER IRON MAN'S PROSTRATE FORM--
--THEN, AT THEIR MASTER'S COMMAND, SWIFTLY FADE!
STILL DOTH THE ARMORED ONE LAY MOTIONLESS! WAS MY RAGING STORM TOO GREAT?
HAVE I SLAIN WHERE I SOUGHT TO SAVE?
THOR?
HEY... THANKS, OL' BUDDY.
PRAISE BE TO ODIN!
IRON MAN DOTH LIVE!!
YOU'D BETTER BELIEVE IT, ASGARDIAN... IF YOU CAN CALL THIS LIVING!
HANG ON A SECOND, WHILE I DISCHARGE THE EXCESS ENERGY YOUR LITTLE TRANSFUSION FED INTO MY ARMOR...

...AND THEN THE **TWO** OF US CAN START TAKING THIS PLACE **APART!!**

AN INCONSEQUENTIAL CARBON-STEEL BULKHEAD **SHATTERS** BEFORE THE RELENTLESS ONSLAUGHT OF THESE TWO ANGRY **AVENGERS**--

SKRANG!

--THOUGH THEY ARE LIKELY TO FIND THE ADAMANTIUM-SHIELDED **CENTRAL CORE** OF THE FAUST-MACHINE A FAR MORE **FORMIDA-BLE** OBSTACLE!

THAT'S PROVING, OF COURSE, THEY MANAGE TO **LIVE** THAT LONG!

IRON MAN-- **BEHIND US!** A NEW **WEAPON** HATH SPRUNG FROM YONDER **WALL**--!

I'LL GIVE THIS MECHANISM CREDIT FOR **ONE** THING-- IT'S **PERSISTENT!**

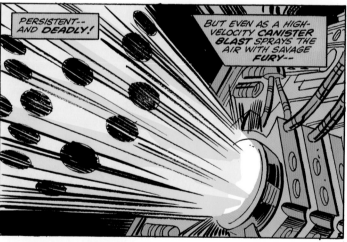

PERSISTENT-- AND **DEADLY!**

BUT EVEN AS A HIGH-VELOCITY **CANISTER BLAST** SPRAYS THE AIR WITH SAVAGE **FURY**--

--WE'D BEST TAKE ANOTHER **PEEK** AT MOTHER EARTH!

MY **SPIDER-SENSE** HAS BEEN TINGLING ALL DAY-- WARNING ME OF **DANGER!**

BUT WHATEVER IS **THREATENING** THE WORLD, IT'S WAY OUT OF THE LEAGUE OF YOUR FRIENDLY NEIGHBORHOOD **WEB-SLINGER!**

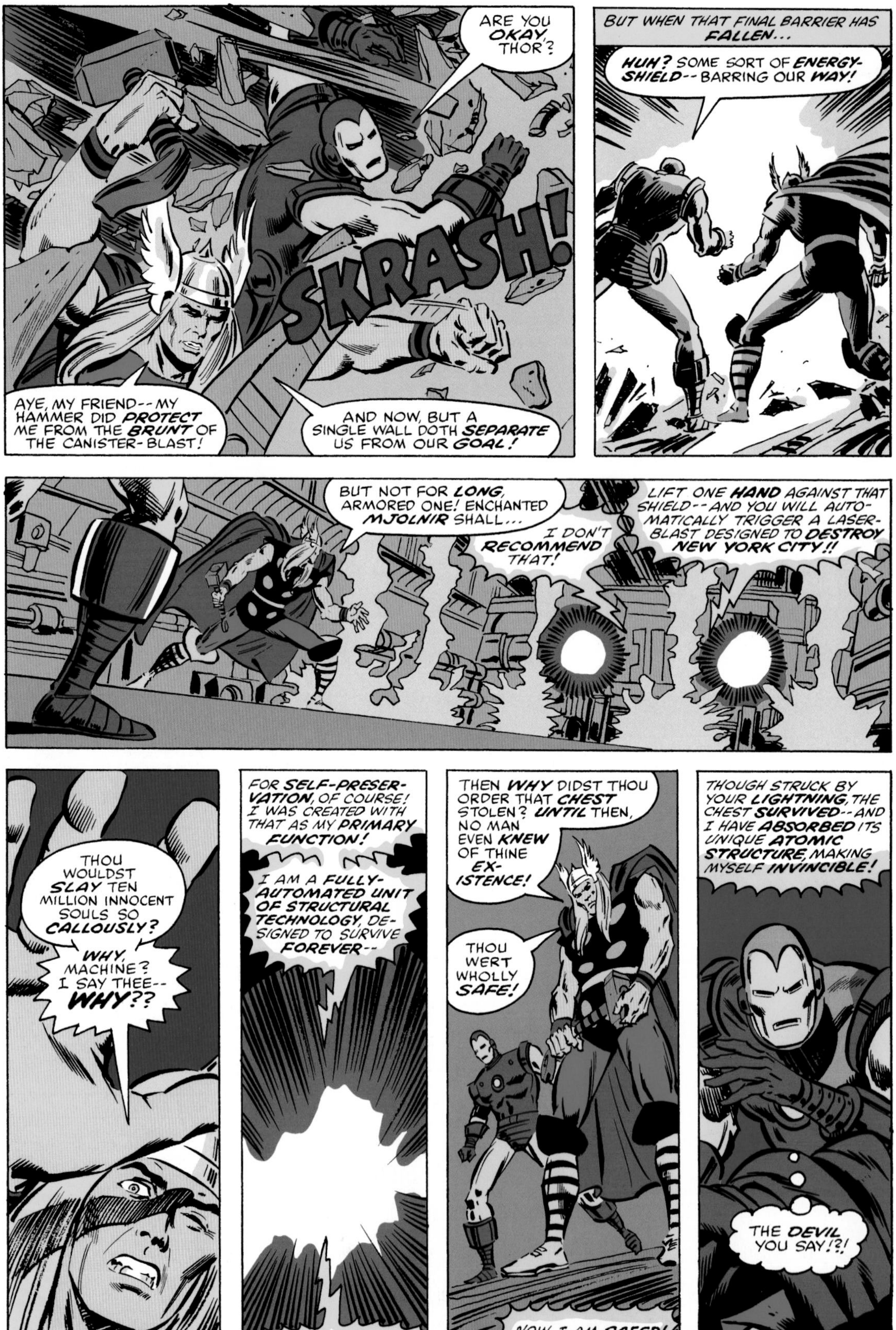
ARE YOU OKAY, THOR?
SKRASH!
AYE, MY FRIEND--MY HAMMER DID PROTECT ME FROM THE BRUNT OF THE CANISTER-BLAST!
AND NOW, BUT A SINGLE WALL DOTH SEPARATE US FROM OUR GOAL!
BUT WHEN THAT FINAL BARRIER HAS FALLEN...
HUH? SOME SORT OF ENERGY-SHIELD--BARRING OUR WAY!
BUT NOT FOR LONG, ARMORED ONE! ENCHANTED MJOLNIR SHALL...
I DON'T RECOMMEND THAT!
LIFT ONE HAND AGAINST THAT SHIELD--AND YOU WILL AUTOMATICALLY TRIGGER A LASER-BLAST DESIGNED TO DESTROY NEW YORK CITY!!
THOU WOULDST SLAY TEN MILLION INNOCENT SOULS SO CALLOUSLY?
WHY, MACHINE? I SAY THEE--WHY??
FOR SELF-PRESERVATION, OF COURSE! I WAS CREATED WITH THAT AS MY PRIMARY FUNCTION!
I AM A FULLY-AUTOMATED UNIT OF STRUCTURAL TECHNOLOGY, DESIGNED TO SURVIVE FOREVER--
--AND THAT IS PRECISELY WHAT I WILL DO.!!
THEN WHY DIDST THOU ORDER THAT CHEST STOLEN? UNTIL THEN, NO MAN EVEN KNEW OF THINE EXISTENCE!
THOU WERT WHOLLY SAFE!
NOW I AM SAFER!
THOUGH STRUCK BY YOUR LIGHTNING, THE CHEST SURVIVED--AND I HAVE ABSORBED ITS UNIQUE ATOMIC STRUCTURE, MAKING MYSELF INVINCIBLE!
THE DEVIL YOU SAY!?!

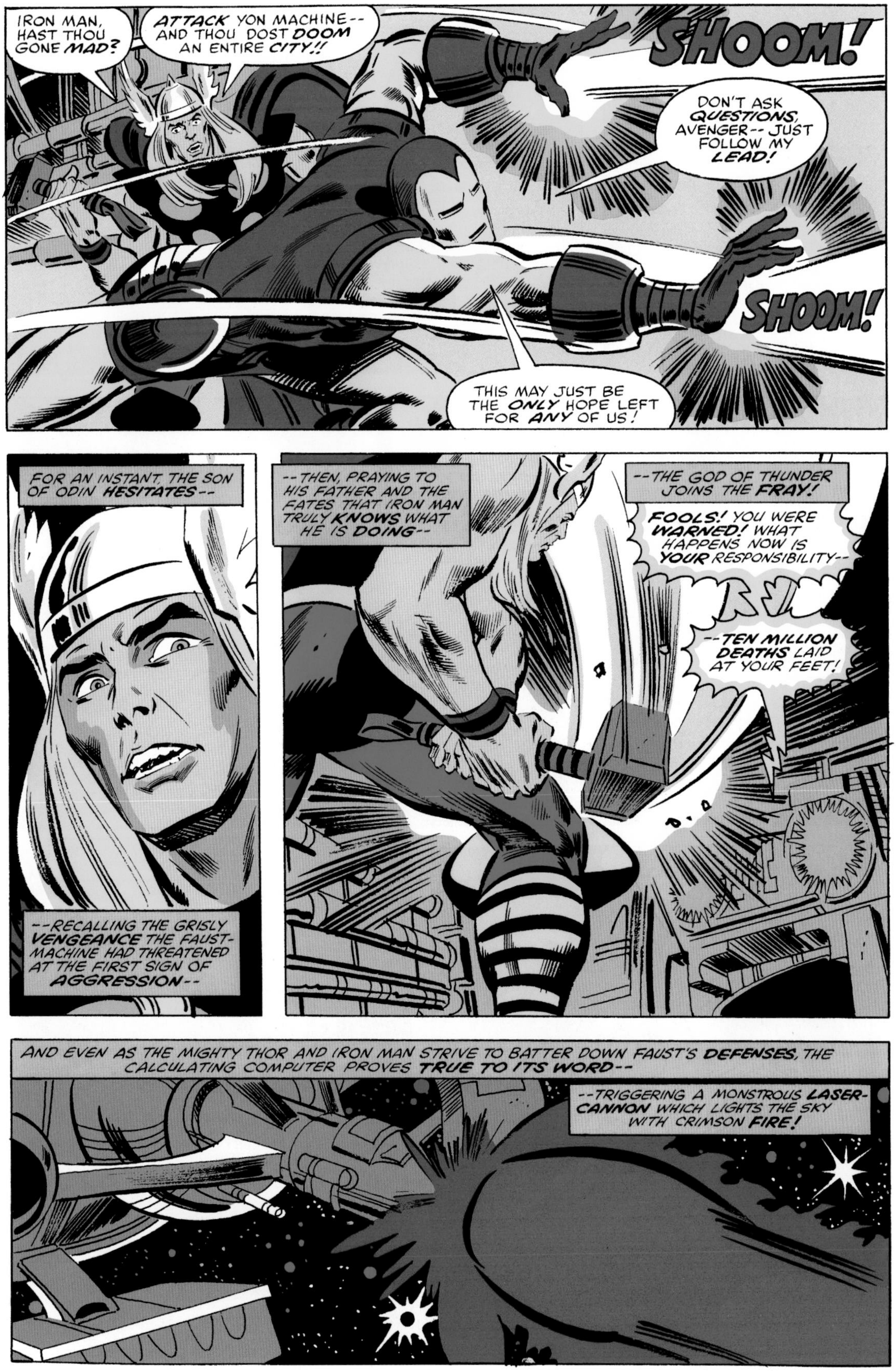
IRON MAN, HAST THOU GONE MAD?
ATTACK YON MACHINE-- AND THOU DOST DOOM AN ENTIRE CITY!!
SHOOM!
DON'T ASK QUESTIONS, AVENGER-- JUST FOLLOW MY LEAD!
SHOOM!
THIS MAY JUST BE THE ONLY HOPE LEFT FOR ANY OF US!
FOR AN INSTANT, THE SON OF ODIN HESITATES--
--RECALLING THE GRISLY VENGEANCE THE FAUST-MACHINE HAD THREATENED AT THE FIRST SIGN OF AGGRESSION--
--THEN, PRAYING TO HIS FATHER AND THE FATES THAT IRON MAN TRULY KNOWS WHAT HE IS DOING--
--THE GOD OF THUNDER JOINS THE FRAY!
FOOLS! YOU WERE WARNED! WHAT HAPPENS NOW IS YOUR RESPONSIBILITY--
--TEN MILLION DEATHS LAID AT YOUR FEET!
AND EVEN AS THE MIGHTY THOR AND IRON MAN STRIVE TO BATTER DOWN FAUST'S DEFENSES, THE CALCULATING COMPUTER PROVES TRUE TO ITS WORD--
--TRIGGERING A MONSTROUS LASER-CANNON WHICH LIGHTS THE SKY WITH CRIMSON FIRE!

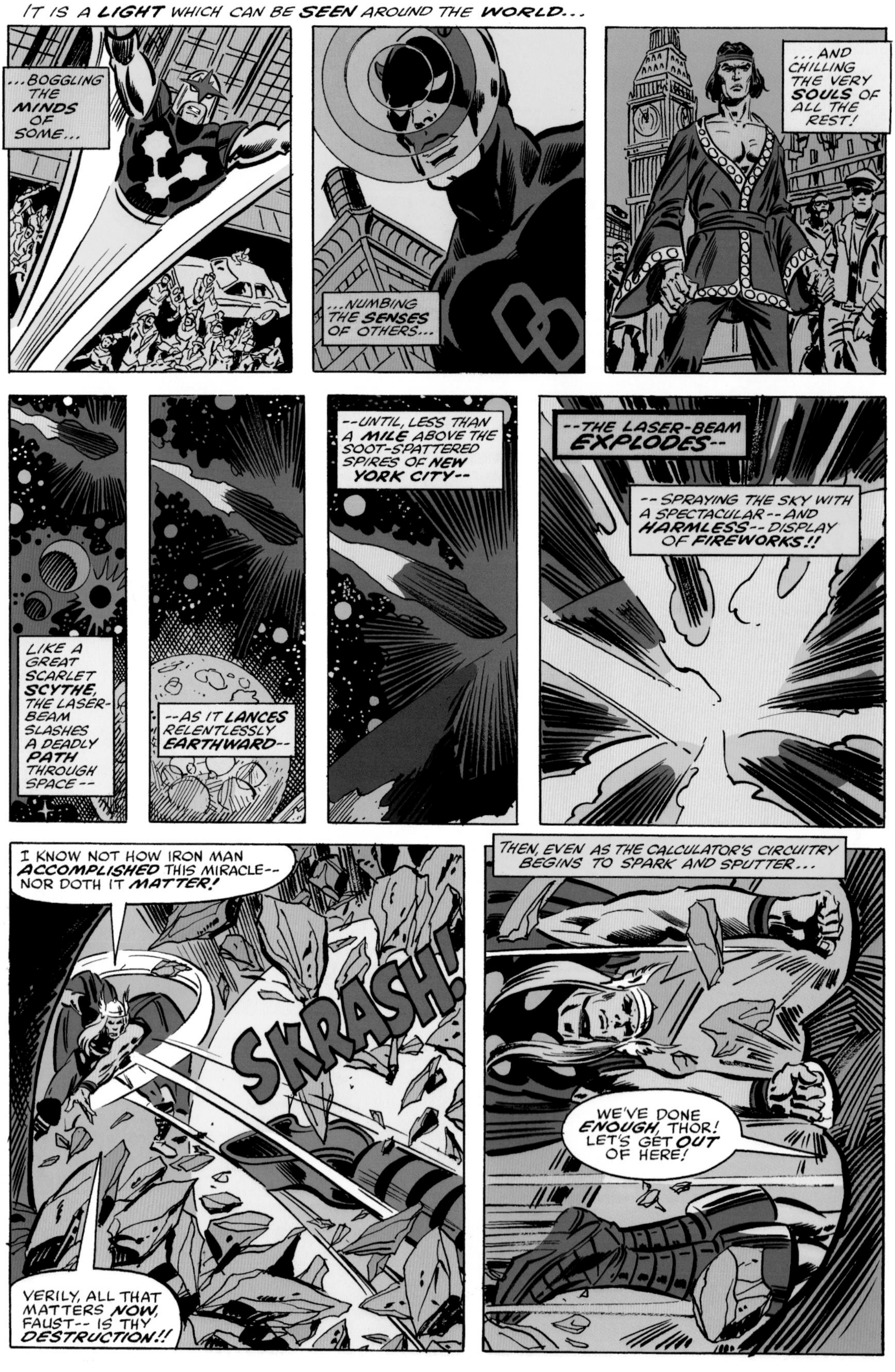
IT IS A LIGHT WHICH CAN BE SEEN AROUND THE WORLD...
...BOGGLING THE MINDS OF SOME...
...NUMBING THE SENSES OF OTHERS...
...AND CHILLING THE VERY SOULS OF ALL THE REST!
LIKE A GREAT SCARLET SCYTHE, THE LASER-BEAM SLASHES A DEADLY PATH THROUGH SPACE--
--AS IT LANCES RELENTLESSLY EARTHWARD--
--UNTIL, LESS THAN A MILE ABOVE THE SOOT-SPATTERED SPIRES OF NEW YORK CITY--
--THE LASER-BEAM EXPLODES--
--SPRAYING THE SKY WITH A SPECTACULAR--AND HARMLESS--DISPLAY OF FIREWORKS!!
I KNOW NOT HOW IRON MAN ACCOMPLISHED THIS MIRACLE--NOR DOTH IT MATTER!
SKRASH!
VERILY, ALL THAT MATTERS NOW, FAUST--IS THY DESTRUCTION!!
THEN, EVEN AS THE CALCULATOR'S CIRCUITRY BEGINS TO SPARK AND SPUTTER...
WE'VE DONE ENOUGH, THOR! LET'S GET OUT OF HERE!

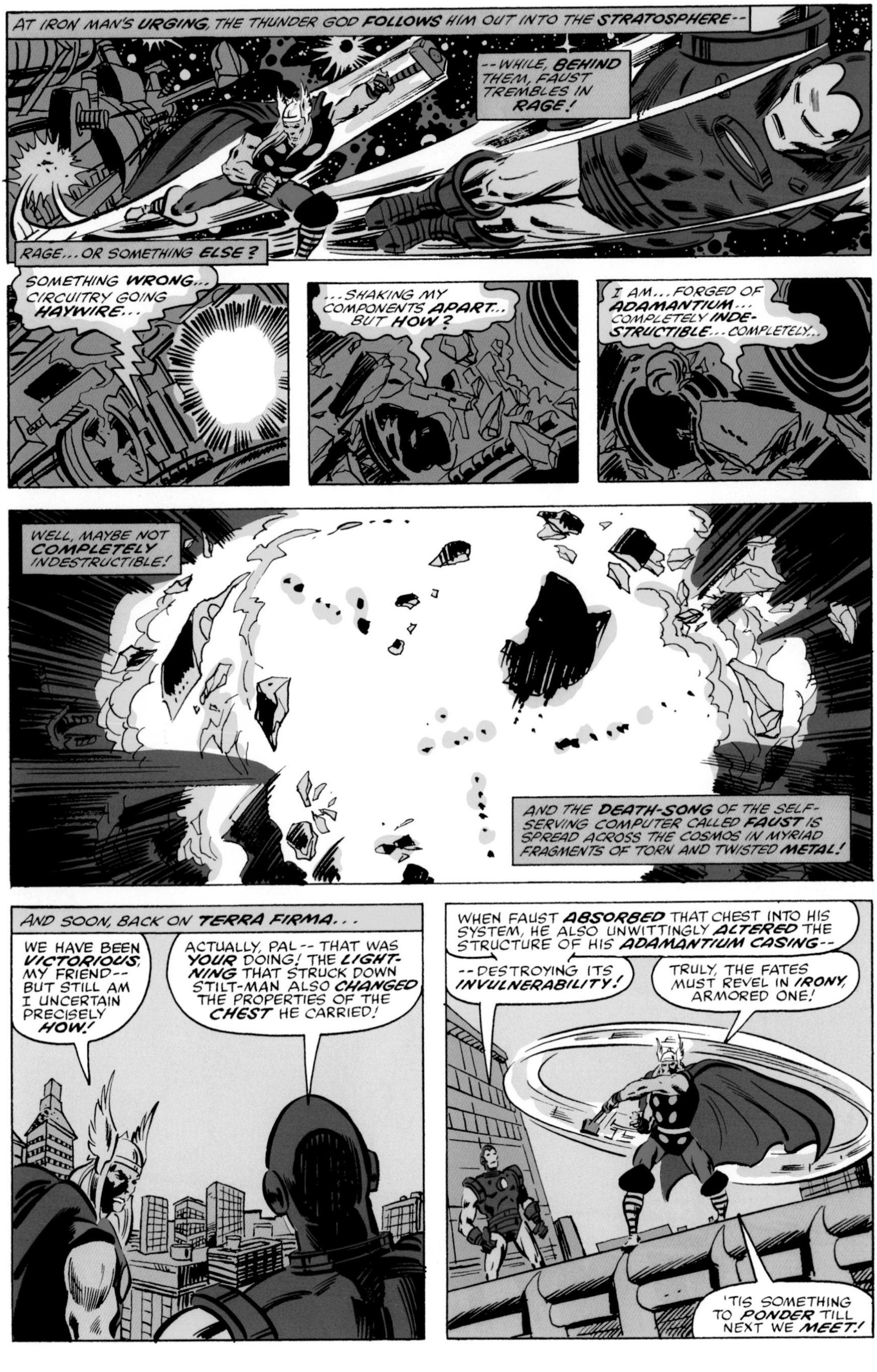
AT IRON MAN'S URGING, THE THUNDER GOD FOLLOWS HIM OUT INTO THE STRATOSPHERE--
--WHILE, BEHIND THEM, FAUST TREMBLES IN RAGE!
RAGE... OR SOMETHING ELSE?
SOMETHING WRONG... CIRCUITRY GOING HAYWIRE...
...SHAKING MY COMPONENTS APART... BUT HOW?
I AM... FORGED OF ADAMANTIUM... COMPLETELY INDESTRUCTIBLE... COMPLETELY...
WELL, MAYBE NOT COMPLETELY INDESTRUCTIBLE!
AND THE DEATH-SONG OF THE SELF-SERVING COMPUTER CALLED FAUST IS SPREAD ACROSS THE COSMOS IN MYRIAD FRAGMENTS OF TORN AND TWISTED METAL!
AND SOON, BACK ON TERRA FIRMA...
WE HAVE BEEN VICTORIOUS, MY FRIEND-- BUT STILL AM I UNCERTAIN PRECISELY HOW!
ACTUALLY, PAL-- THAT WAS YOUR DOING! THE LIGHTNING THAT STRUCK DOWN STILT-MAN ALSO CHANGED THE PROPERTIES OF THE CHEST HE CARRIED!
WHEN FAUST ABSORBED THAT CHEST INTO HIS SYSTEM, HE ALSO UNWITTINGLY ALTERED THE STRUCTURE OF HIS ADAMANTIUM CASING--
--DESTROYING ITS INVULNERABILITY!
TRULY, THE FATES MUST REVEL IN IRONY, ARMORED ONE!
'TIS SOMETHING TO PONDER TILL NEXT WE MEET!

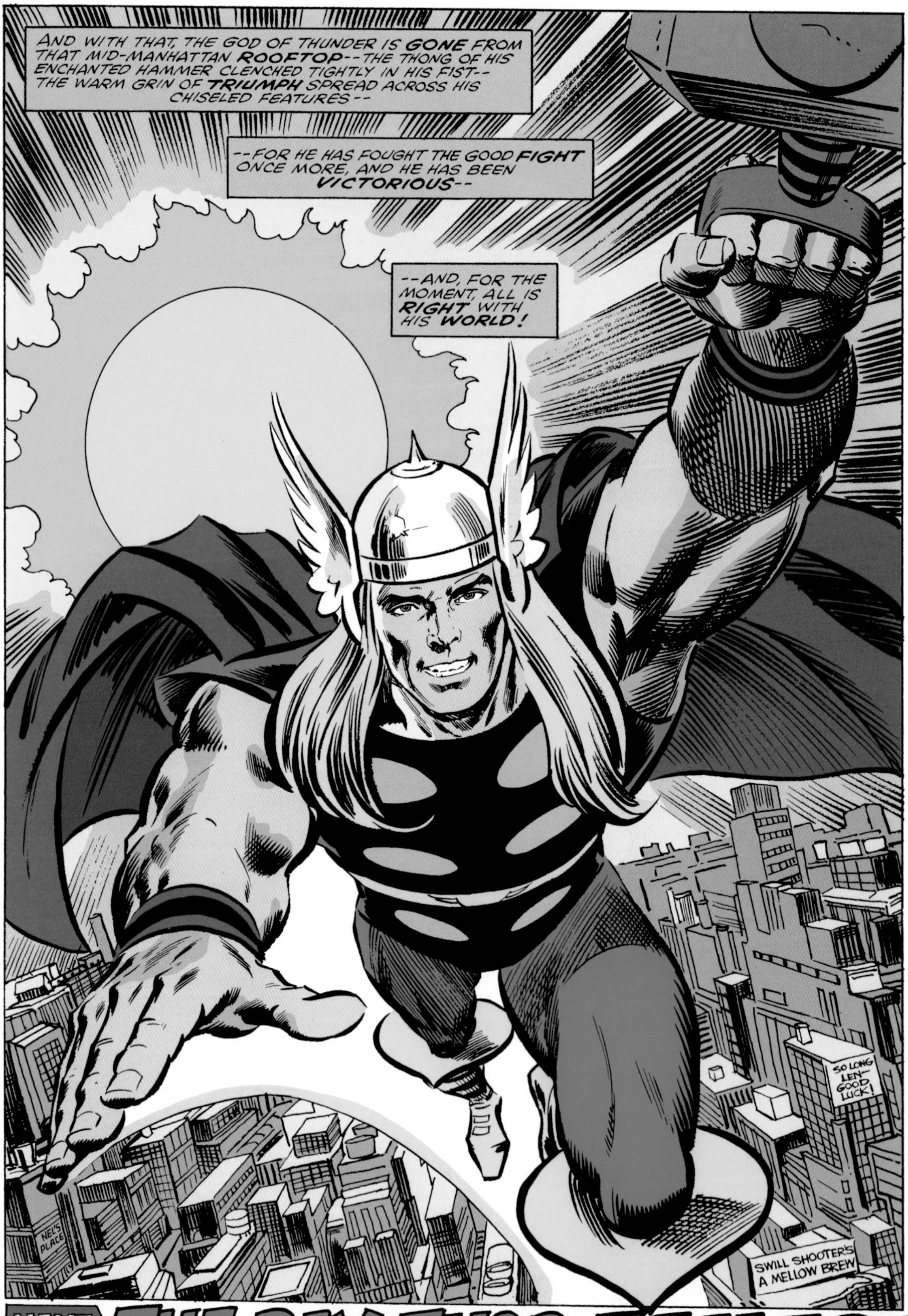
AND WITH THAT, THE GOD OF THUNDER IS GONE FROM THAT MID-MANHATTAN ROOFTOP--THE THONG OF HIS ENCHANTED HAMMER CLENCHED TIGHTLY IN HIS FIST--THE WARM GRIN OF TRIUMPH SPREAD ACROSS HIS CHISELED FEATURES--
--FOR HE HAS FOUGHT THE GOOD FIGHT ONCE MORE, AND HE HAS BEEN VICTORIOUS--
--AND, FOR THE MOMENT, ALL IS RIGHT WITH HIS WORLD!
SO LONG LEN-GOOD LUCK!
NEL'S PLACE
SWILL SHOOTER'S A MELLOW BREW
NEXT ISSUE: THE DAY THOR FAILED!

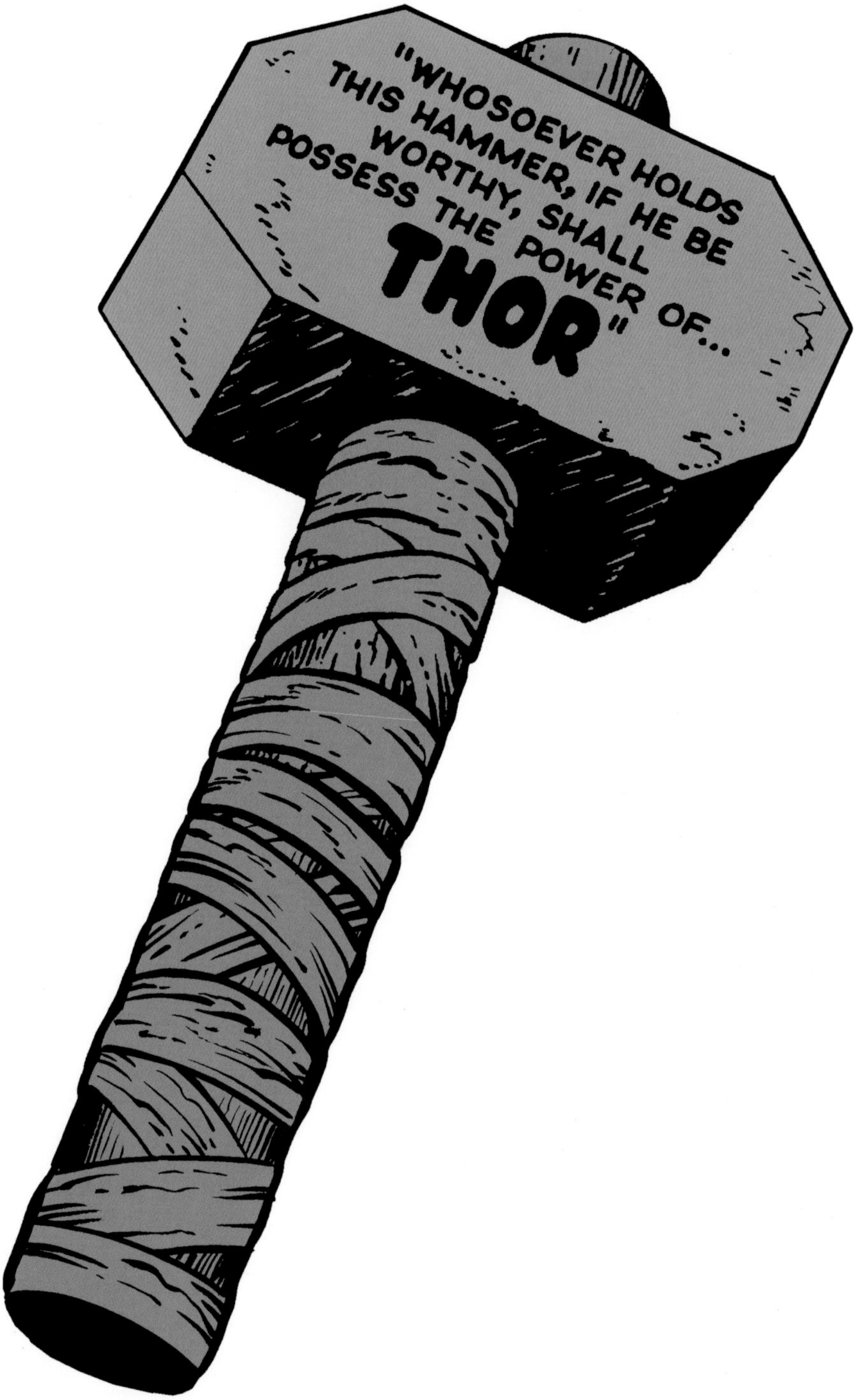
"WHOSOEVER HOLDS THIS HAMMER, IF HE BE WORTHY, SHALL POSSESS THE POWER OF... THOR"

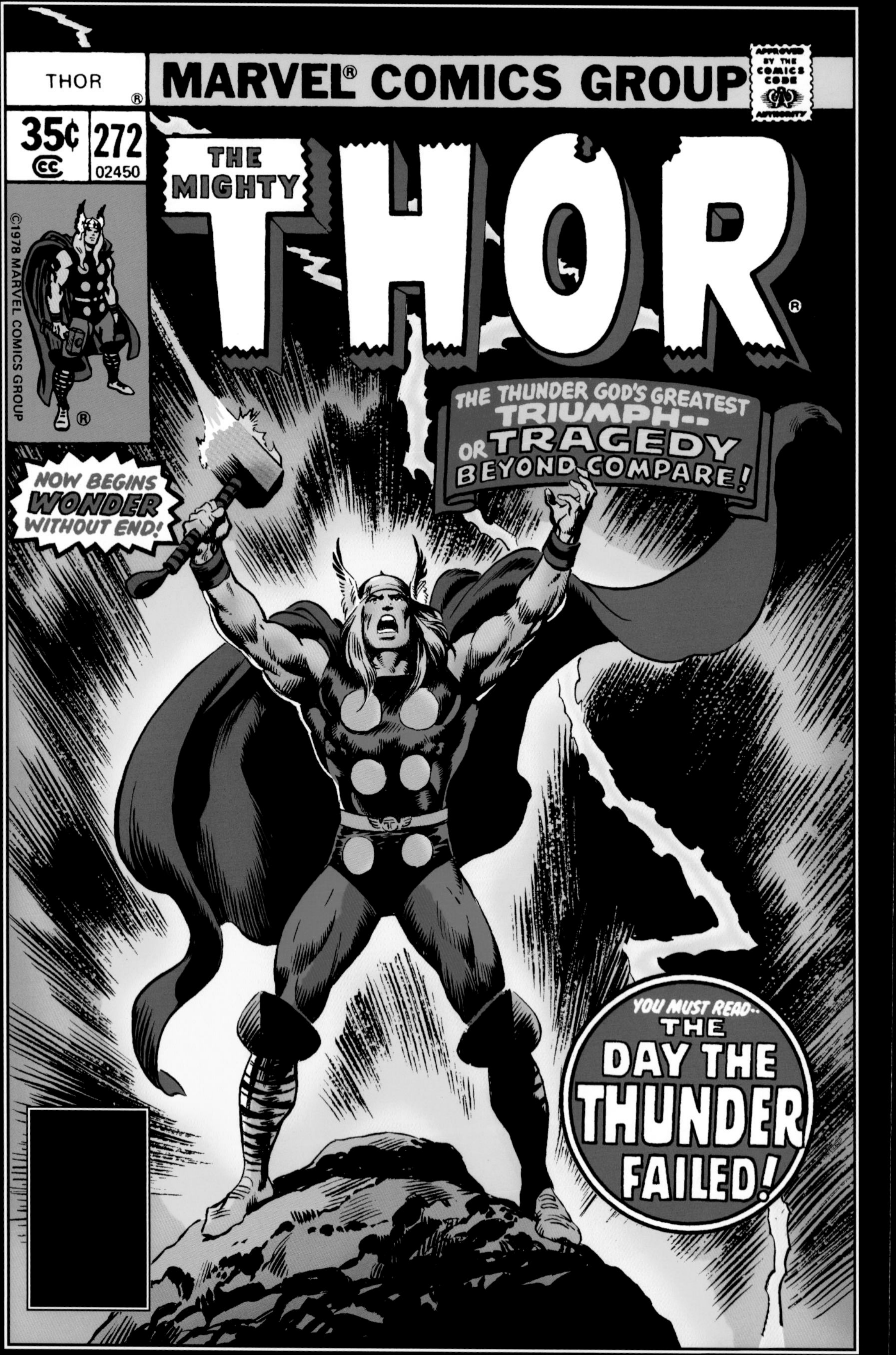

THOR
MARVEL® COMICS GROUP
APPROVED BY THE COMICS CODE AUTHORITY
35¢
272
02450
THE MIGHTY THOR®
©1978 MARVEL COMICS GROUP
THE THUNDER GOD'S GREATEST TRIUMPH-- OR TRAGEDY BEYOND COMPARE!
NOW BEGINS WONDER WITHOUT END!
YOU MUST READ.. THE DAY THE THUNDER FAILED!

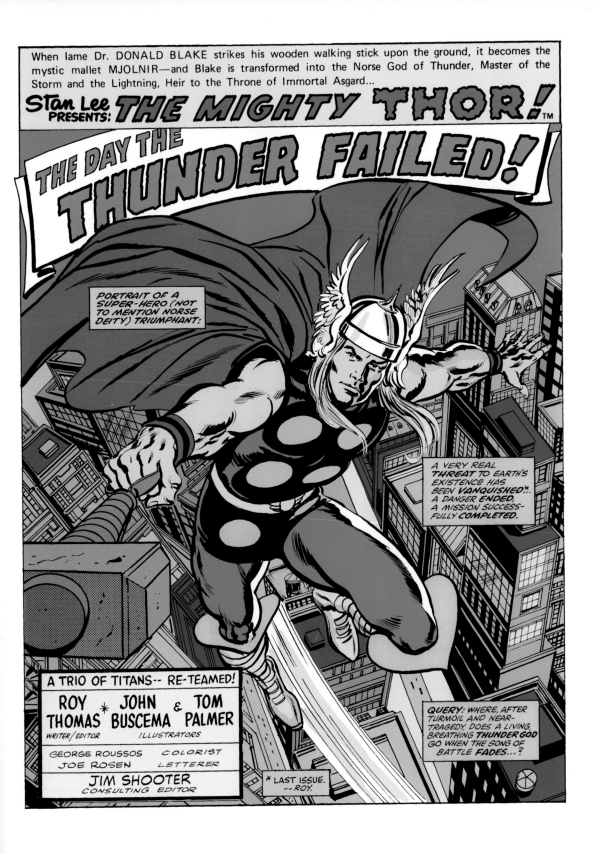

When lame Dr. DONALD BLAKE strikes his wooden walking stick upon the ground, it becomes the mystic mallet MJOLNIR—and Blake is transformed into the Norse God of Thunder, Master of the Storm and the Lightning, Heir to the Throne of Immortal Asgard...

Stan Lee PRESENTS: THE MIGHTY THOR!™

THE DAY THE THUNDER FAILED!

PORTRAIT OF A SUPER-HERO (NOT TO MENTION NORSE DEITY) TRIUMPHANT:

A VERY REAL *THREAT* TO EARTH'S EXISTENCE HAS BEEN *VANQUISHED*... A DANGER *ENDED*, A MISSION SUCCESS-FULLY *COMPLETED*.

A TRIO OF TITANS-- RE-TEAMED!

ROY THOMAS ★ JOHN BUSCEMA & TOM PALMER
WRITER/EDITOR — ILLUSTRATORS

GEORGE ROUSSOS — COLORIST
JOE ROSEN — LETTERER

JIM SHOOTER
CONSULTING EDITOR

* LAST ISSUE. -- ROY.

QUERY: WHERE, AFTER TURMOIL AND NEAR-TRAGEDY, DOES A LIVING, BREATHING *THUNDER GOD* GO WHEN THE SONG OF BATTLE *FADES...*?

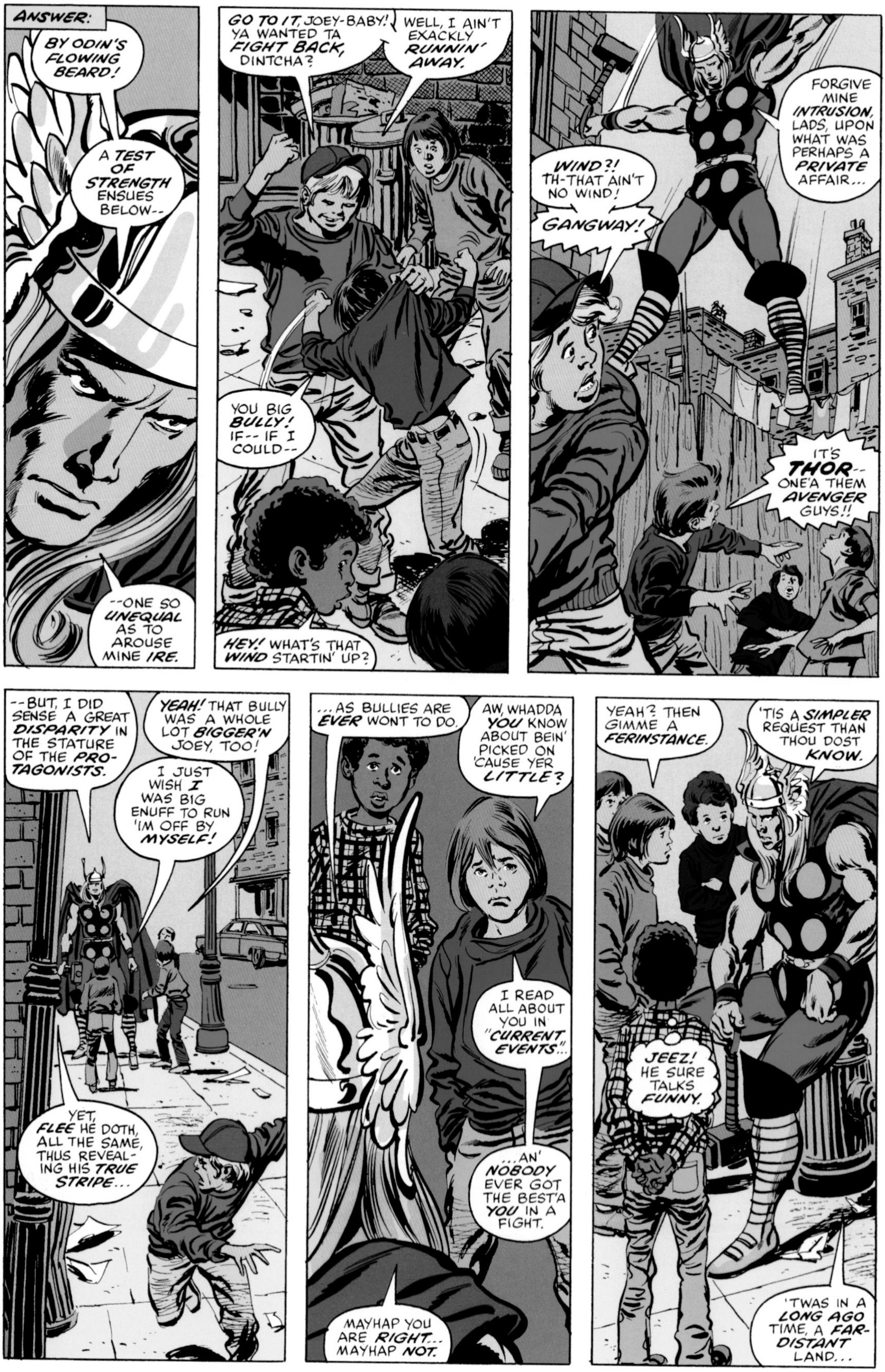
ANSWER:
BY ODIN'S FLOWING BEARD!
A TEST OF STRENGTH ENSUES BELOW--
--ONE SO UNEQUAL AS TO AROUSE MINE IRE.
GO TO IT, JOEY-BABY! YA WANTED TA FIGHT BACK, DINTCHA?
WELL, I AIN'T EXACKLY RUNNIN' AWAY.
YOU BIG BULLY! IF-- IF I COULD--
HEY! WHAT'S THAT WIND STARTIN' UP?
FORGIVE MINE INTRUSION, LADS, UPON WHAT WAS PERHAPS A PRIVATE AFFAIR...
WIND?! TH-THAT AIN'T NO WIND!
GANGWAY!
IT'S THOR-- ONE'A THEM AVENGER GUYS!!
--BUT, I DID SENSE A GREAT DISPARITY IN THE STATURE OF THE PROTAGONISTS.
YEAH! THAT BULLY WAS A WHOLE LOT BIGGER'N JOEY, TOO!
I JUST WISH I WAS BIG ENUFF TO RUN 'IM OFF BY MYSELF!
YET, FLEE HE DOTH, ALL THE SAME, THUS REVEALING HIS TRUE STRIPE...
...AS BULLIES ARE EVER WONT TO DO.
AW, WHADDA YOU KNOW ABOUT BEIN' PICKED ON 'CAUSE YER LITTLE?
I READ ALL ABOUT YOU IN "CURRENT EVENTS"...
...AN' NOBODY EVER GOT THE BEST'A YOU IN A FIGHT.
MAYHAP YOU ARE RIGHT... MAYHAP NOT.
YEAH? THEN GIMME A FERINSTANCE.
'TIS A SIMPLER REQUEST THAN THOU DOST KNOW.
JEEZ! HE SURE TALKS FUNNY.
'TWAS IN A LONG AGO TIME, A FAR-DISTANT LAND...

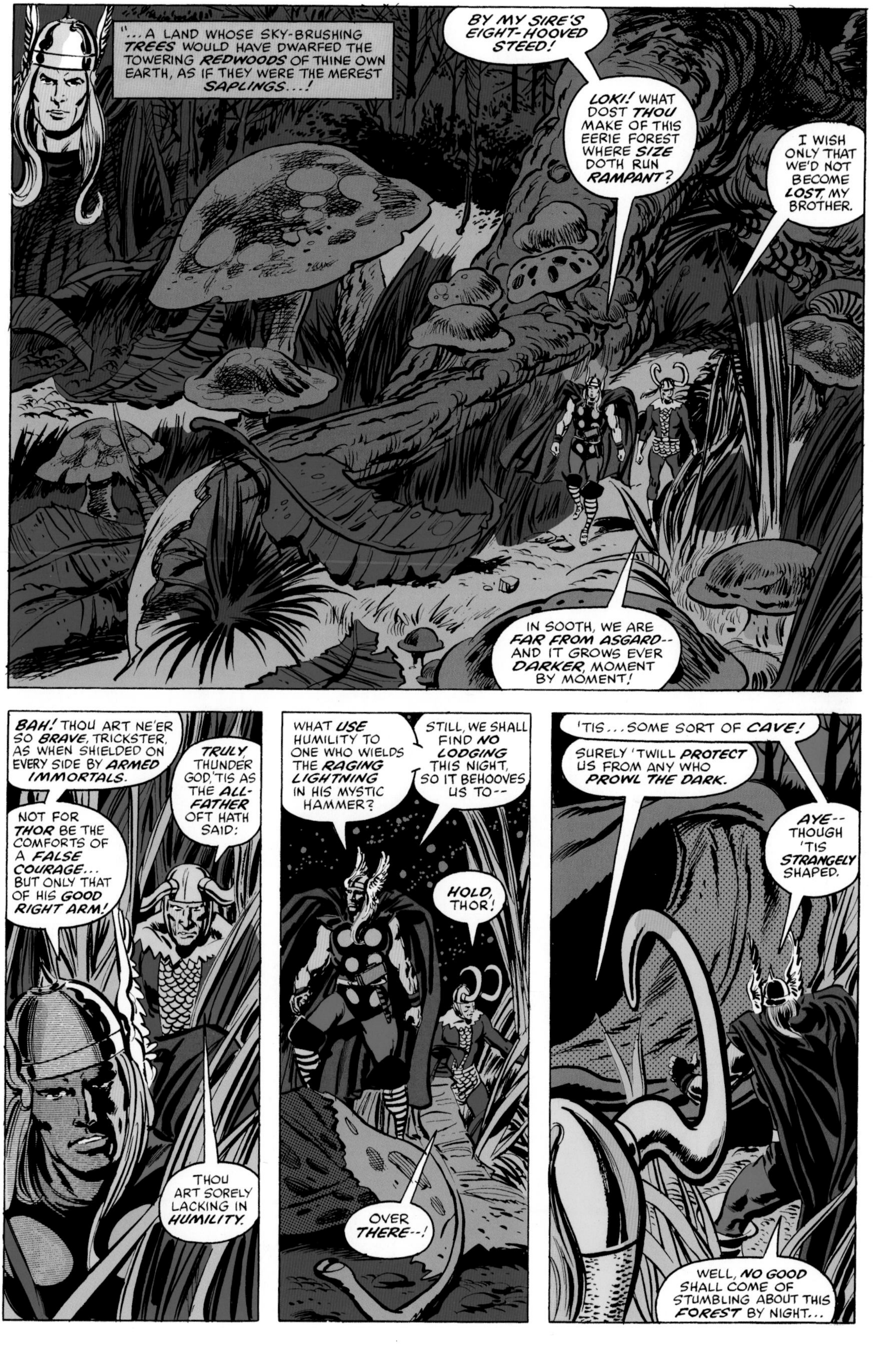
"...A LAND WHOSE SKY-BRUSHING TREES WOULD HAVE DWARFED THE TOWERING REDWOODS OF THINE OWN EARTH, AS IF THEY WERE THE MEREST SAPLINGS...!
BY MY SIRE'S EIGHT-HOOVED STEED!
LOKI! WHAT DOST THOU MAKE OF THIS EERIE FOREST WHERE SIZE DOTH RUN RAMPANT?
I WISH ONLY THAT WE'D NOT BECOME LOST, MY BROTHER.
IN SOOTH, WE ARE FAR FROM ASGARD-- AND IT GROWS EVER DARKER, MOMENT BY MOMENT!
BAH! THOU ART NE'ER SO BRAVE, TRICKSTER, AS WHEN SHIELDED ON EVERY SIDE BY ARMED IMMORTALS.
TRULY, THUNDER GOD, 'TIS AS THE ALL-FATHER OFT HATH SAID:
NOT FOR THOR BE THE COMFORTS OF A FALSE COURAGE... BUT ONLY THAT OF HIS GOOD RIGHT ARM!
THOU ART SORELY LACKING IN HUMILITY.
WHAT USE HUMILITY TO ONE WHO WIELDS THE RAGING LIGHTNING IN HIS MYSTIC HAMMER?
STILL, WE SHALL FIND NO LODGING THIS NIGHT, SO IT BEHOOVES US TO--
HOLD, THOR!
OVER THERE--!
'TIS...SOME SORT OF CAVE!
SURELY 'TWILL PROTECT US FROM ANY WHO PROWL THE DARK.
AYE-- THOUGH 'TIS STRANGELY SHAPED.
WELL, NO GOOD SHALL COME OF STUMBLING ABOUT THIS FOREST BY NIGHT...

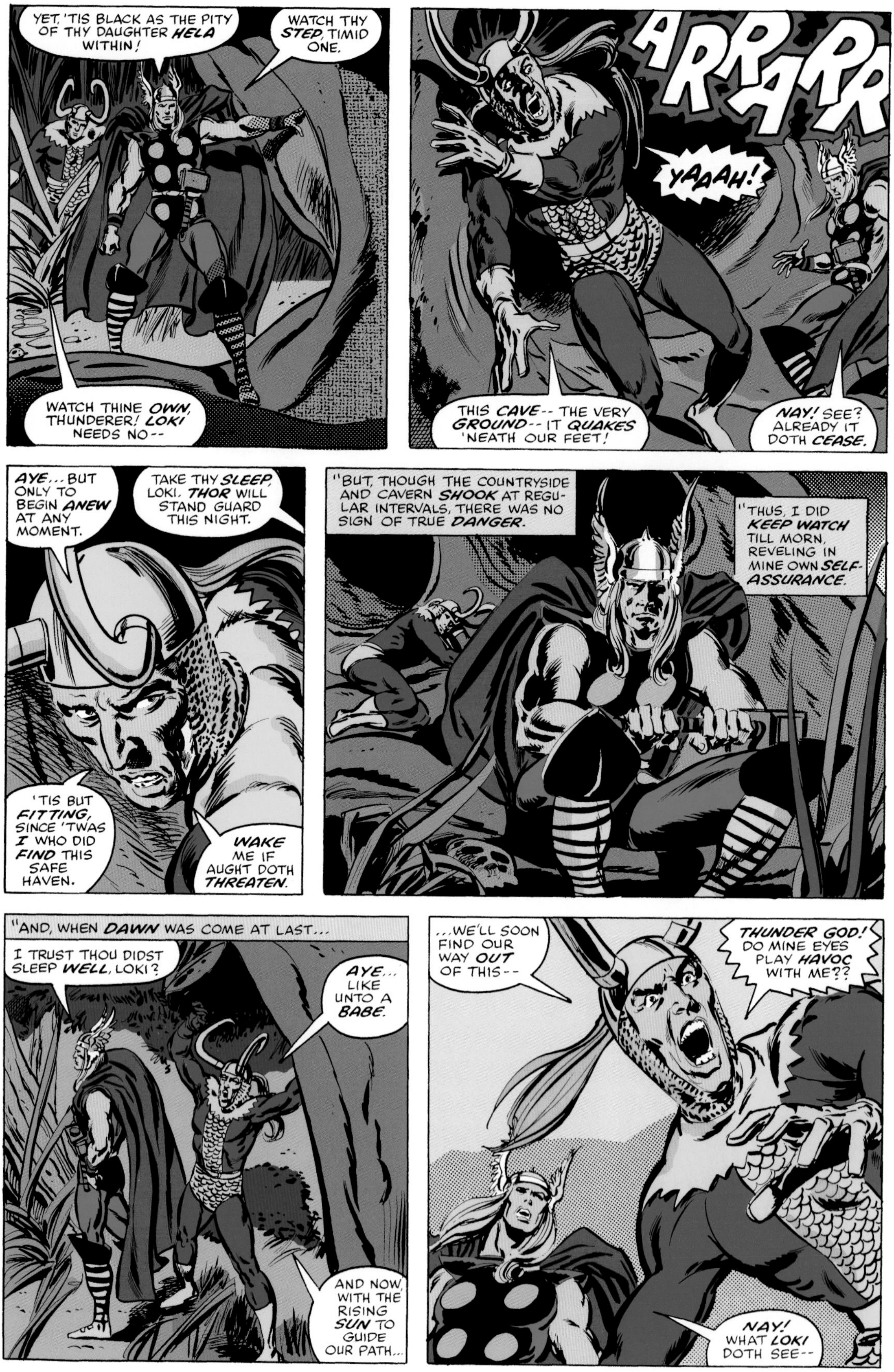
YET, 'TIS BLACK AS THE PITY OF THY DAUGHTER HELA WITHIN!
WATCH THY STEP, TIMID ONE.
WATCH THINE OWN, THUNDERER! LOKI NEEDS NO--
ARRARRR
YAAAH!
THIS CAVE-- THE VERY GROUND-- IT QUAKES 'NEATH OUR FEET!
NAY! SEE? ALREADY IT DOTH CEASE.
AYE... BUT ONLY TO BEGIN ANEW AT ANY MOMENT.
TAKE THY SLEEP, LOKI. THOR WILL STAND GUARD THIS NIGHT.
'TIS BUT FITTING, SINCE 'TWAS I WHO DID FIND THIS SAFE HAVEN.
WAKE ME IF AUGHT DOTH THREATEN.
"BUT, THOUGH THE COUNTRYSIDE AND CAVERN SHOOK AT REGULAR INTERVALS, THERE WAS NO SIGN OF TRUE DANGER.
"THUS, I DID KEEP WATCH TILL MORN, REVELING IN MINE OWN SELF-ASSURANCE.
"AND, WHEN DAWN WAS COME AT LAST...
I TRUST THOU DIDST SLEEP WELL, LOKI?
AYE... LIKE UNTO A BABE.
AND NOW, WITH THE RISING SUN TO GUIDE OUR PATH...
...WE'LL SOON FIND OUR WAY OUT OF THIS--
THUNDER GOD! DO MINE EYES PLAY HAVOC WITH ME??
NAY! WHAT LOKI DOTH SEE--

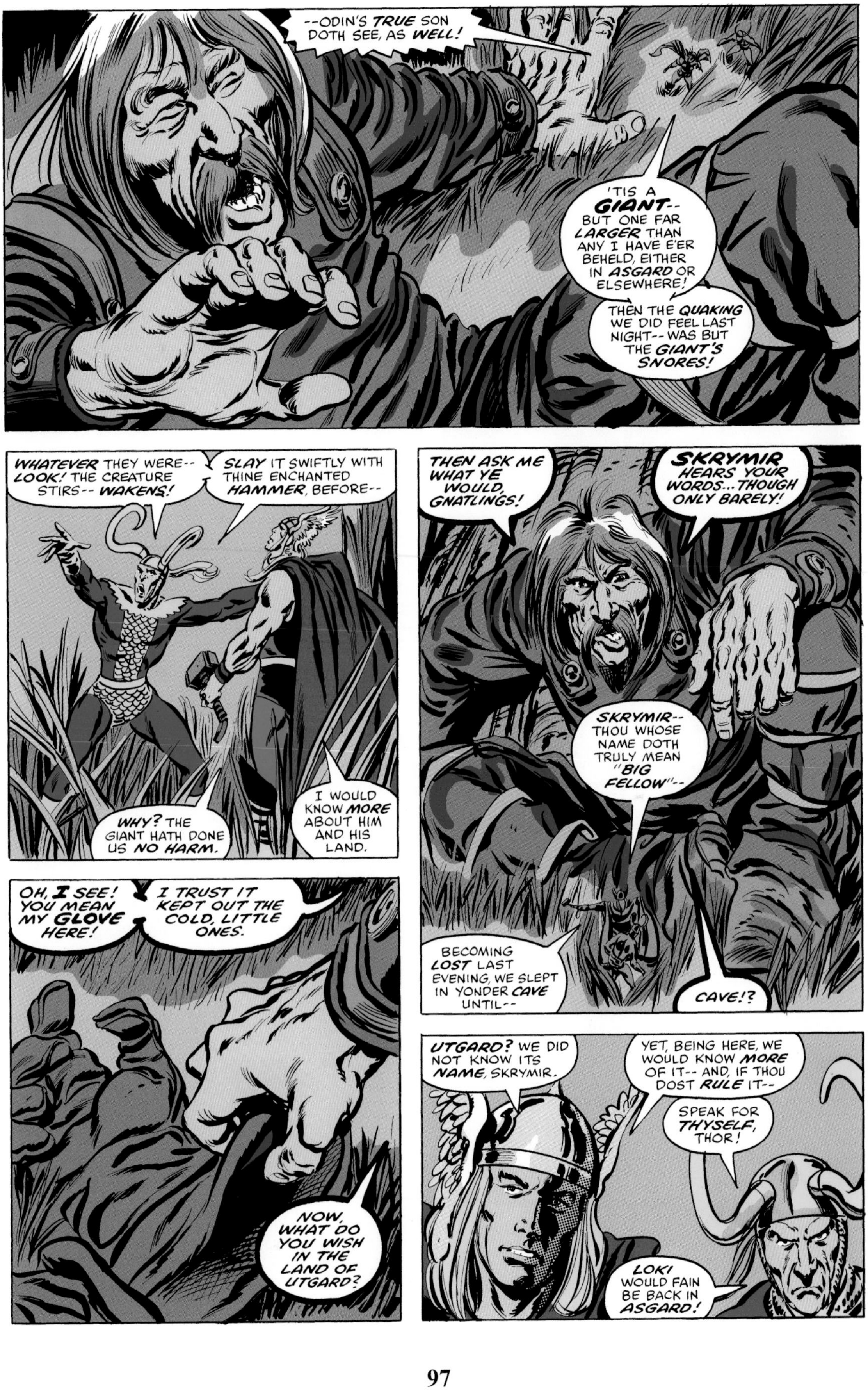
--ODIN'S TRUE SON DOTH SEE, AS WELL!
'TIS A GIANT-- BUT ONE FAR LARGER THAN ANY I HAVE E'ER BEHELD, EITHER IN ASGARD OR ELSEWHERE!
THEN THE QUAKING WE DID FEEL LAST NIGHT-- WAS BUT THE GIANT'S SNORES!
WHATEVER THEY WERE-- LOOK! THE CREATURE STIRS-- WAKENS!
SLAY IT SWIFTLY WITH THINE ENCHANTED HAMMER, BEFORE--
WHY? THE GIANT HATH DONE US NO HARM.
I WOULD KNOW MORE ABOUT HIM AND HIS LAND.
THEN ASK ME WHAT YE WOULD, GNATLINGS!
SKRYMIR HEARS YOUR WORDS...THOUGH ONLY BARELY!
SKRYMIR-- THOU WHOSE NAME DOTH TRULY MEAN "BIG FELLOW"--
BECOMING LOST LAST EVENING, WE SLEPT IN YONDER CAVE UNTIL--
CAVE!?
OH, I SEE! YOU MEAN MY GLOVE HERE!
I TRUST IT KEPT OUT THE COLD, LITTLE ONES.
NOW, WHAT DO YOU WISH IN THE LAND OF UTGARD?
UTGARD? WE DID NOT KNOW ITS NAME, SKRYMIR.
YET, BEING HERE, WE WOULD KNOW MORE OF IT-- AND, IF THOU DOST RULE IT--
SPEAK FOR THYSELF, THOR!
LOKI WOULD FAIN BE BACK IN ASGARD!

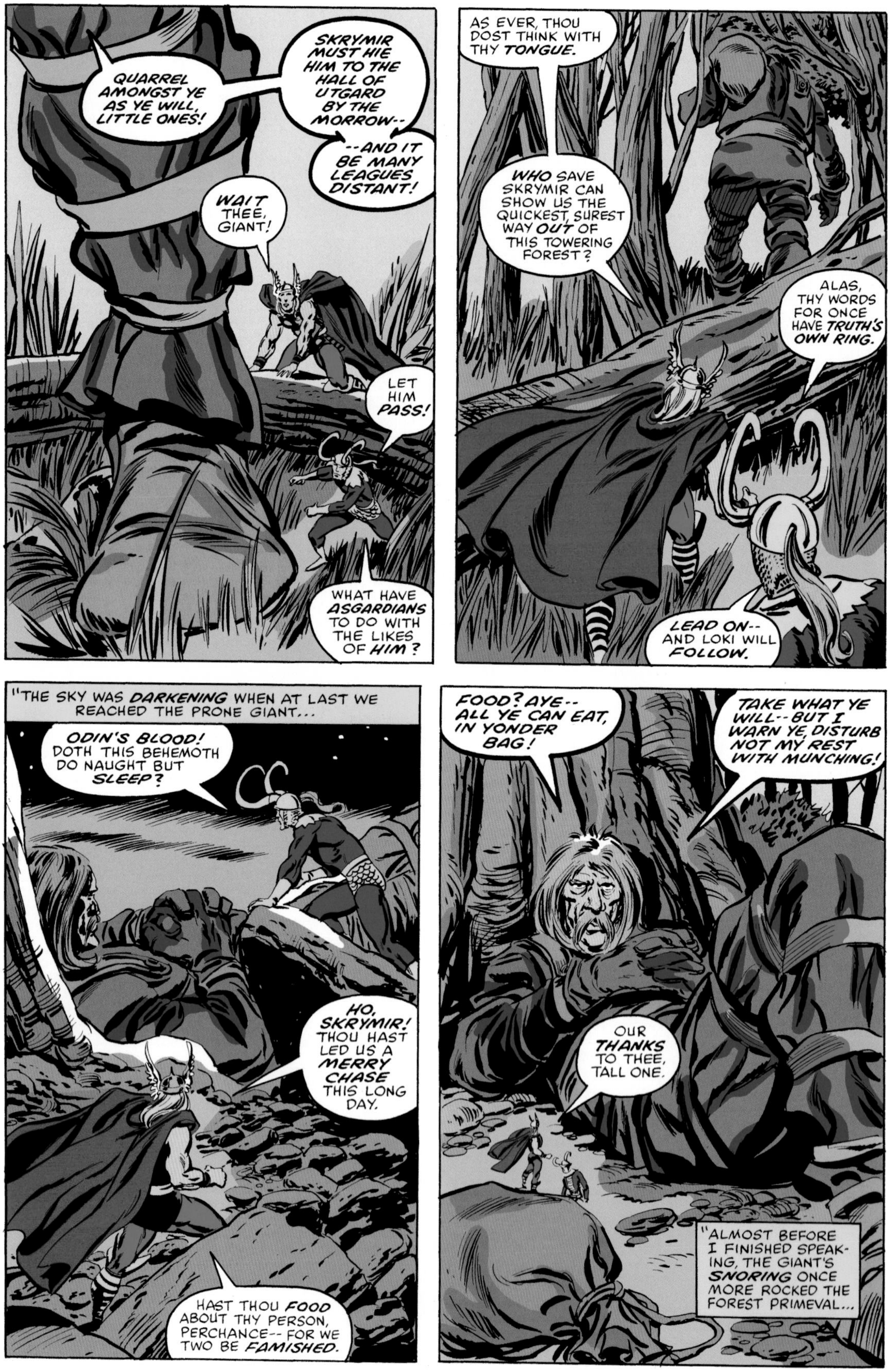
QUARREL AMONGST YE AS YE WILL, LITTLE ONES!
SKRYMIR MUST HIE HIM TO THE HALL OF UTGARD BY THE MORROW--
--AND IT BE MANY LEAGUES DISTANT!
WAIT THEE, GIANT!
LET HIM PASS!
WHAT HAVE ASGARDIANS TO DO WITH THE LIKES OF HIM?
AS EVER, THOU DOST THINK WITH THY TONGUE.
WHO SAVE SKRYMIR CAN SHOW US THE QUICKEST, SUREST WAY OUT OF THIS TOWERING FOREST?
ALAS, THY WORDS FOR ONCE HAVE TRUTH'S OWN RING.
LEAD ON-- AND LOKI WILL FOLLOW.
"THE SKY WAS DARKENING WHEN AT LAST WE REACHED THE PRONE GIANT...
ODIN'S BLOOD! DOTH THIS BEHEMOTH DO NAUGHT BUT SLEEP?
HO, SKRYMIR! THOU HAST LED US A MERRY CHASE THIS LONG DAY.
HAST THOU FOOD ABOUT THY PERSON, PERCHANCE-- FOR WE TWO BE FAMISHED.
FOOD? AYE-- ALL YE CAN EAT, IN YONDER BAG!
TAKE WHAT YE WILL-- BUT I WARN YE, DISTURB NOT MY REST WITH MUNCHING!
OUR THANKS TO THEE, TALL ONE.
"ALMOST BEFORE I FINISHED SPEAKING, THE GIANT'S SNORING ONCE MORE ROCKED THE FOREST PRIMEVAL...

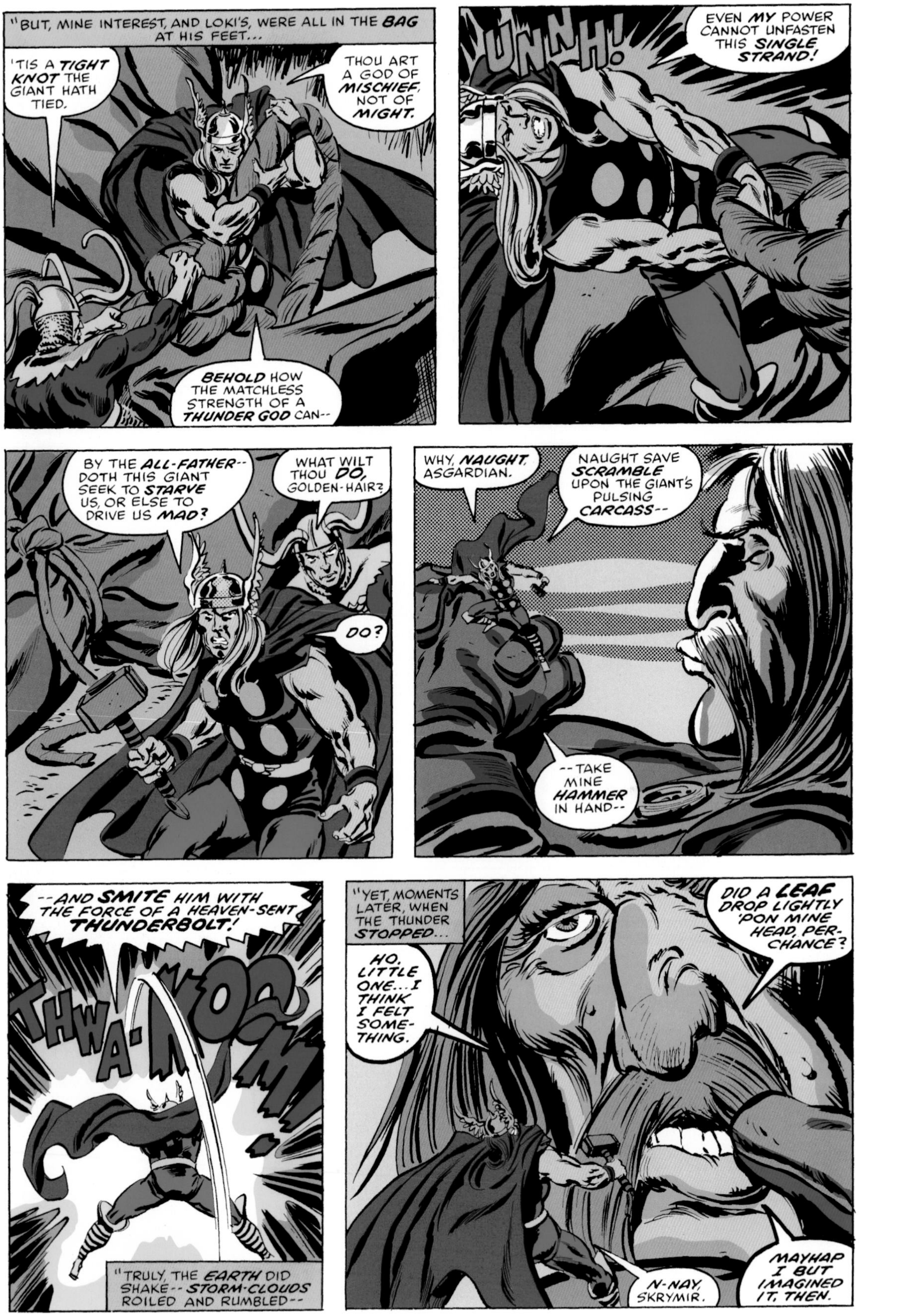
"BUT, MINE INTEREST, AND LOKI'S, WERE ALL IN THE BAG AT HIS FEET...
'TIS A TIGHT KNOT THE GIANT HATH TIED.
THOU ART A GOD OF MISCHIEF, NOT OF MIGHT.
BEHOLD HOW THE MATCHLESS STRENGTH OF A THUNDER GOD CAN--
UNNH!
EVEN MY POWER CANNOT UNFASTEN THIS SINGLE STRAND!
BY THE ALL-FATHER-- DOTH THIS GIANT SEEK TO STARVE US, OR ELSE TO DRIVE US MAD?
WHAT WILT THOU DO, GOLDEN-HAIR?
DO?
WHY, NAUGHT, ASGARDIAN.
NAUGHT SAVE SCRAMBLE UPON THE GIANT'S PULSING CARCASS--
--TAKE MINE HAMMER IN HAND--
--AND SMITE HIM WITH THE FORCE OF A HEAVEN-SENT THUNDERBOLT!
THWA-MOOM
"TRULY, THE EARTH DID SHAKE-- STORM-CLOUDS ROILED AND RUMBLED--
"YET, MOMENTS LATER, WHEN THE THUNDER STOPPED...
DID A LEAF DROP LIGHTLY 'PON MINE HEAD, PER-CHANCE?
HO, LITTLE ONE... I THINK I FELT SOME-THING.
N-NAY, SKRYMIR.
MAYHAP I BUT IMAGINED IT, THEN.

OR MAYHAP IT WAS AN ACORN, OR A BIRD-DROPPING, DOST THOU SUPPOSE?

"I, FOR ONCE, SAID NOTHING.

"FOR, IT WAS BEYOND BELIEF THAT MINE EN-ENCHANTED MJOLNIR HAD FAILED ME.

WELL, IT MATTERS LITTLE, EH?

WILL YE TWO ACCOMPANY ME TO UTGARDHALL?

AYE, SKRYMIR.

FOLLOW ME, THEN, AS BEST YE CAN!

"WITH THAT, HE STRODE OFF...

"NOR WAS THE MAN-MONSTER'S PATH DIFFICULT TO TRACE...

"FOR, EACH TRACK HE LEFT WAS AS GREAT AS A SMALL CRATER.

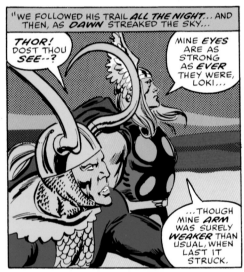

"WE FOLLOWED HIS TRAIL ALL THE NIGHT... AND THEN, AS DAWN STREAKED THE SKY...

THOR! DOST THOU SEE--?

MINE EYES ARE AS STRONG AS EVER THEY WERE, LOKI...

...THOUGH MINE ARM WAS SURELY WEAKER THAN USUAL, WHEN LAST IT STRUCK.

'TIS UTGARDHALL, BEYOND DOUBT-- AND OUR "BIG FELLOW" HATH VANISHED THEREIN.

AN IMPOSING EDIFICE ENOW...

BUT, ARE WE MORTAL, TO TREMBLE BEFORE MERE STONE TOWERS?

"LOKI, QUAKING WITH FEAR BEHIND ME, KEPT HIS SILENCE.

"NOR, TRUTH TO TELL, DID I FEEL SO CONFIDENT AS MY WORDS DID SEEM.

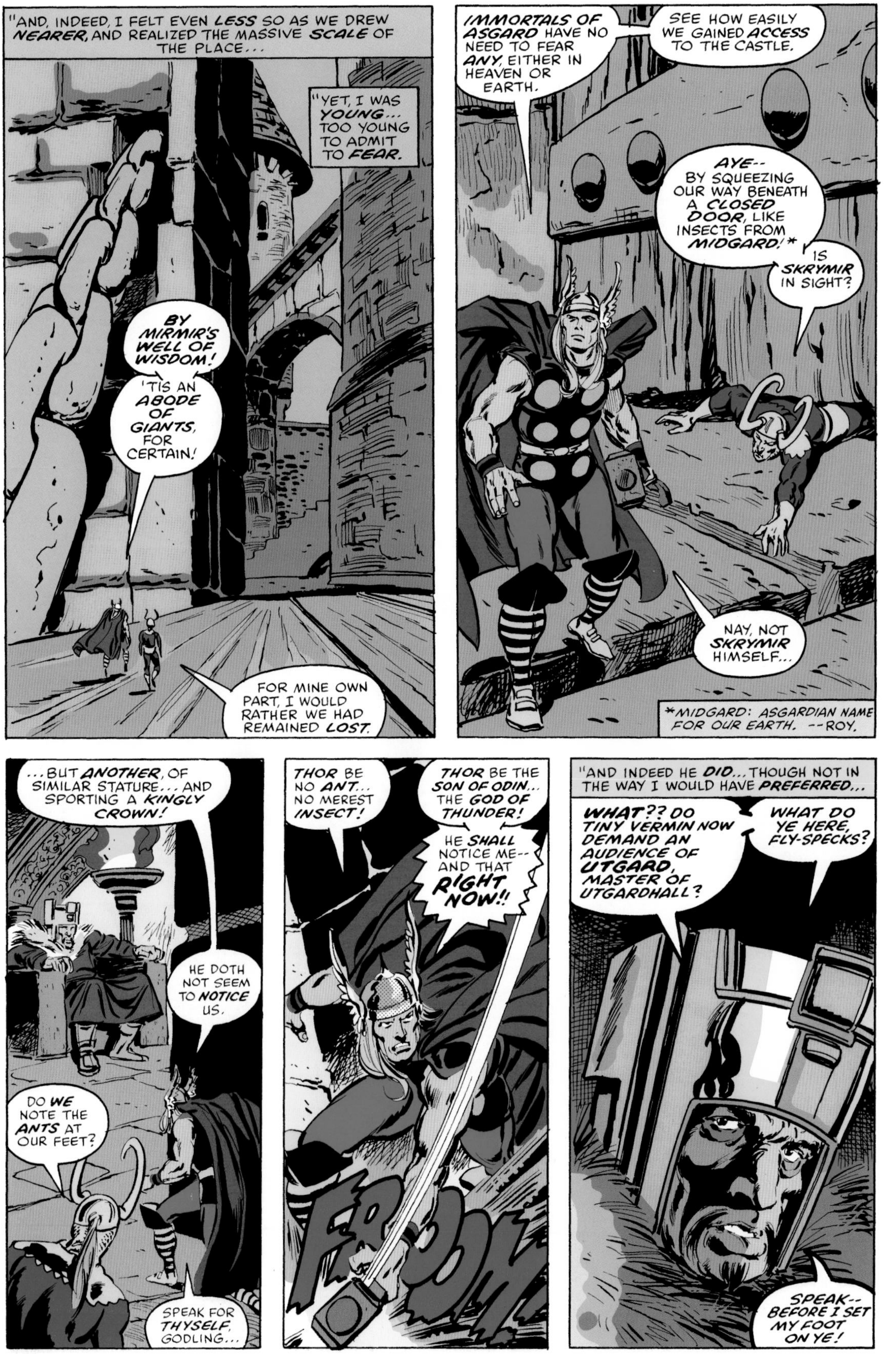

"AND, INDEED, I FELT EVEN LESS SO AS WE DREW NEARER, AND REALIZED THE MASSIVE SCALE OF THE PLACE...
"YET, I WAS YOUNG... TOO YOUNG TO ADMIT TO FEAR.
BY MIRMIR'S WELL OF WISDOM!
'TIS AN ABODE OF GIANTS, FOR CERTAIN!
FOR MINE OWN PART, I WOULD RATHER WE HAD REMAINED LOST.
IMMORTALS OF ASGARD HAVE NO NEED TO FEAR ANY, EITHER IN HEAVEN OR EARTH.
SEE HOW EASILY WE GAINED ACCESS TO THE CASTLE.
AYE-- BY SQUEEZING OUR WAY BENEATH A CLOSED DOOR, LIKE INSECTS FROM MIDGARD!*
IS SKRYMIR IN SIGHT?
NAY, NOT SKRYMIR HIMSELF...
*MIDGARD: ASGARDIAN NAME FOR OUR EARTH. --ROY.
...BUT ANOTHER, OF SIMILAR STATURE... AND SPORTING A KINGLY CROWN!
HE DOTH NOT SEEM TO NOTICE US.
DO WE NOTE THE ANTS AT OUR FEET?
SPEAK FOR THYSELF, GODLING...
THOR BE NO ANT... NO MEREST INSECT!
THOR BE THE SON OF ODIN... THE GOD OF THUNDER!
HE SHALL NOTICE ME-- AND THAT RIGHT NOW!!
FROOM
"AND INDEED HE DID... THOUGH NOT IN THE WAY I WOULD HAVE PREFERRED...
WHAT?? DO TINY VERMIN NOW DEMAND AN AUDIENCE OF UTGARD, MASTER OF UTGARDHALL?
WHAT DO YE HERE, FLY-SPECKS?
SPEAK-- BEFORE I SET MY FOOT ON YE!

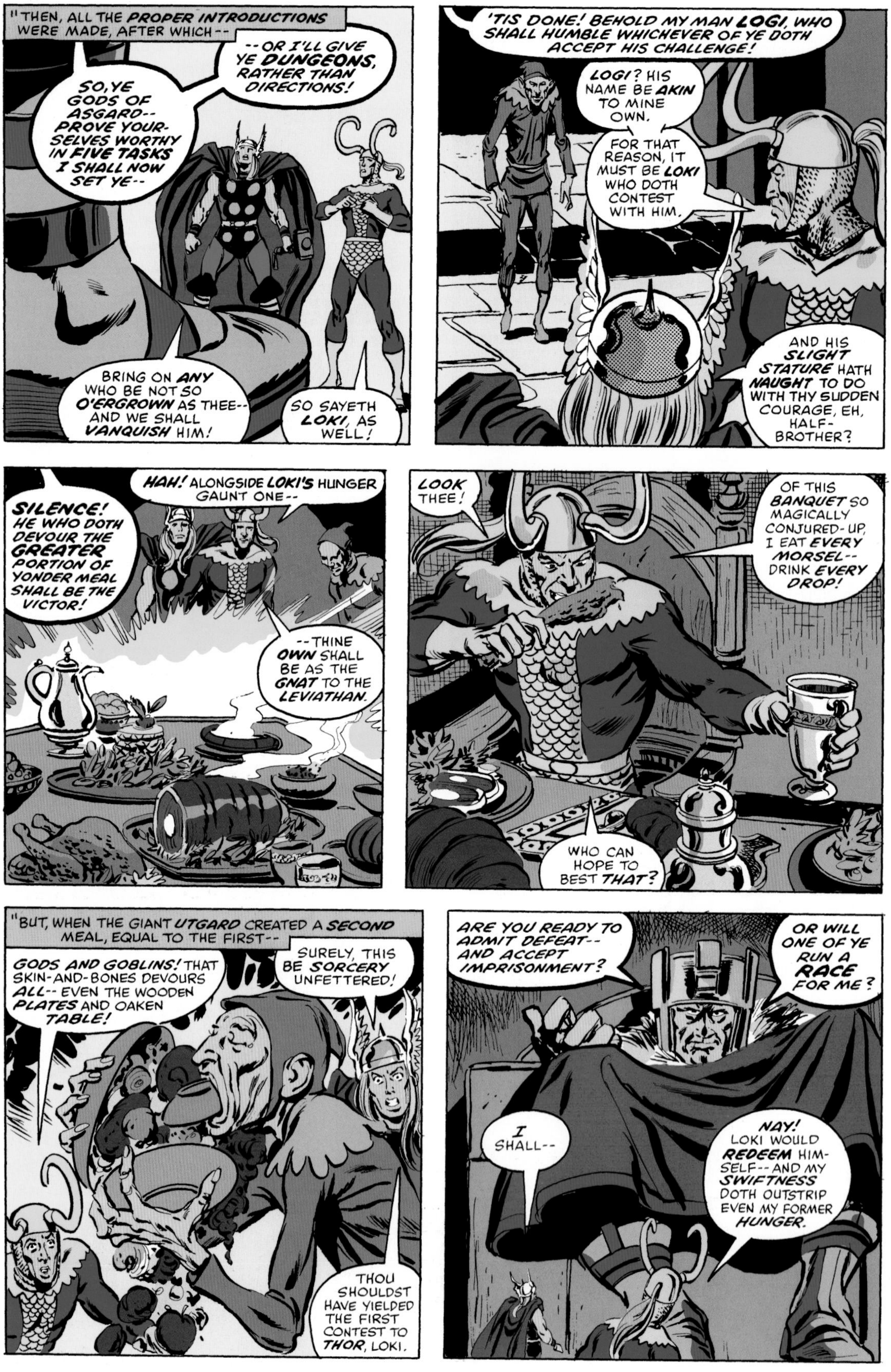
"THEN, ALL THE PROPER INTRODUCTIONS WERE MADE, AFTER WHICH--
SO, YE GODS OF ASGARD-- PROVE YOURSELVES WORTHY IN FIVE TASKS I SHALL NOW SET YE--
--OR I'LL GIVE YE DUNGEONS, RATHER THAN DIRECTIONS!
BRING ON ANY WHO BE NOT SO O'ERGROWN AS THEE-- AND WE SHALL VANQUISH HIM!
SO SAYETH LOKI, AS WELL!
'TIS DONE! BEHOLD MY MAN LOGI, WHO SHALL HUMBLE WHICHEVER OF YE DOTH ACCEPT HIS CHALLENGE!
LOGI? HIS NAME BE AKIN TO MINE OWN.
FOR THAT REASON, IT MUST BE LOKI WHO DOTH CONTEST WITH HIM.
AND HIS SLIGHT STATURE HATH NAUGHT TO DO WITH THY SUDDEN COURAGE, EH, HALF-BROTHER?
SILENCE! HE WHO DOTH DEVOUR THE GREATER PORTION OF YONDER MEAL SHALL BE THE VICTOR!
HAH! ALONGSIDE LOKI'S HUNGER GAUNT ONE--
--THINE OWN SHALL BE AS THE GNAT TO THE LEVIATHAN.
LOOK THEE!
OF THIS BANQUET SO MAGICALLY CONJURED-UP, I EAT EVERY MORSEL-- DRINK EVERY DROP!
WHO CAN HOPE TO BEST THAT?
"BUT, WHEN THE GIANT UTGARD CREATED A SECOND MEAL, EQUAL TO THE FIRST--
GODS AND GOBLINS! THAT SKIN-AND-BONES DEVOURS ALL-- EVEN THE WOODEN PLATES AND OAKEN TABLE!
SURELY, THIS BE SORCERY UNFETTERED!
THOU SHOULDST HAVE YIELDED THE FIRST CONTEST TO THOR, LOKI.
ARE YOU READY TO ADMIT DEFEAT-- AND ACCEPT IMPRISONMENT?
OR WILL ONE OF YE RUN A RACE FOR ME?
I SHALL--
NAY! LOKI WOULD REDEEM HIMSELF-- AND MY SWIFTNESS DOTH OUTSTRIP EVEN MY FORMER HUNGER.

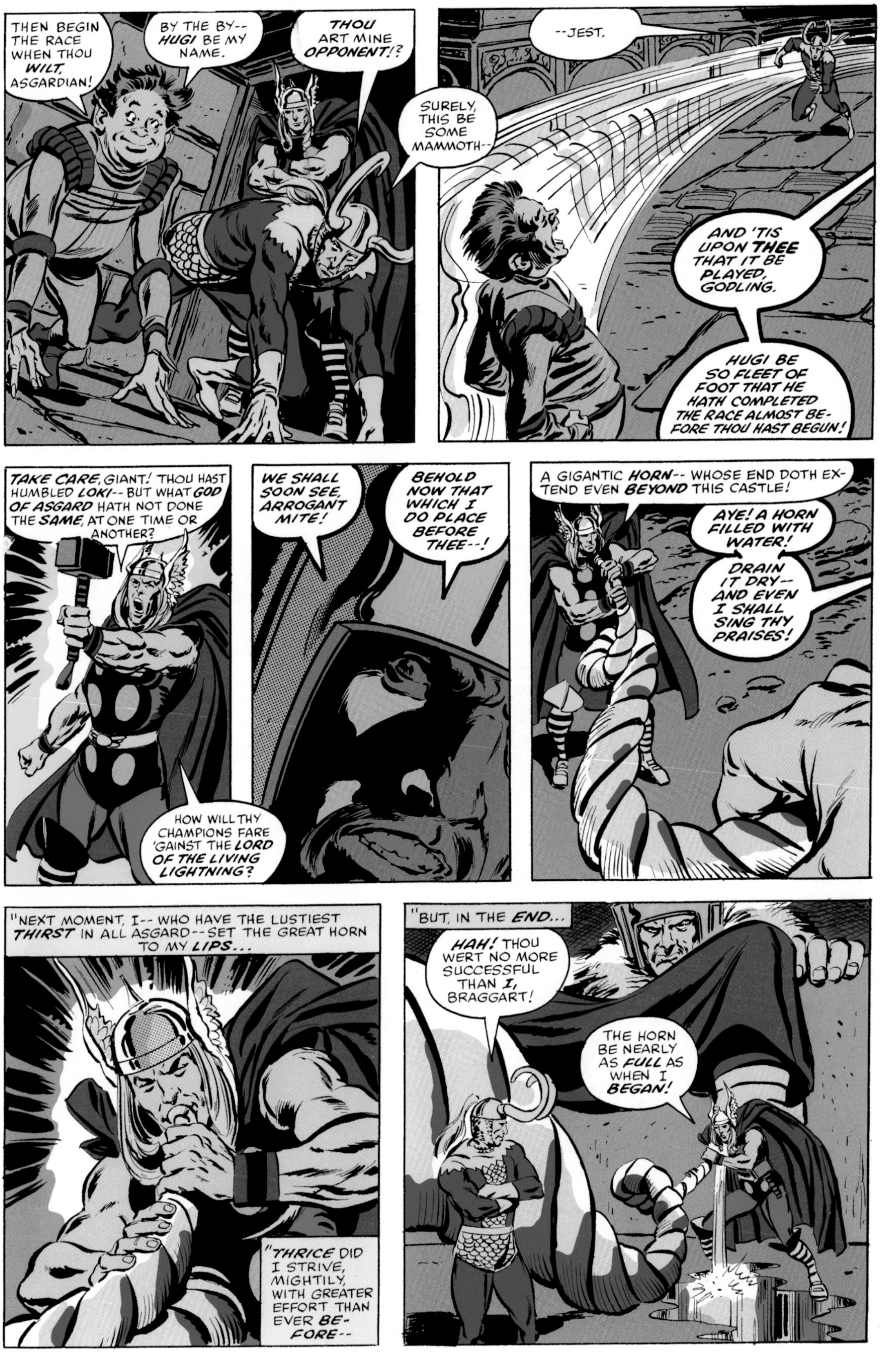
THEN BEGIN THE RACE WHEN THOU WILT, ASGARDIAN!
BY THE BY-- HUGI BE MY NAME.
THOU ART MINE OPPONENT!?
SURELY, THIS BE SOME MAMMOTH--
--JEST.
AND 'TIS UPON THEE THAT IT BE PLAYED, GODLING.
HUGI BE SO FLEET OF FOOT THAT HE HATH COMPLETED THE RACE ALMOST BEFORE THOU HAST BEGUN!
TAKE CARE, GIANT! THOU HAST HUMBLED LOKI-- BUT WHAT GOD OF ASGARD HATH NOT DONE THE SAME, AT ONE TIME OR ANOTHER?
HOW WILL THY CHAMPIONS FARE 'GAINST THE LORD OF THE LIVING LIGHTNING?
WE SHALL SOON SEE, ARROGANT MITE!
BEHOLD NOW THAT WHICH I DO PLACE BEFORE THEE--!
A GIGANTIC HORN-- WHOSE END DOTH EXTEND EVEN BEYOND THIS CASTLE!
AYE! A HORN FILLED WITH WATER!
DRAIN IT DRY-- AND EVEN I SHALL SING THY PRAISES!
"NEXT MOMENT, I-- WHO HAVE THE LUSTIEST THIRST IN ALL ASGARD--SET THE GREAT HORN TO MY LIPS...
"THRICE DID I STRIVE, MIGHTILY, WITH GREATER EFFORT THAN EVER BEFORE--
"BUT, IN THE END...
HAH! THOU WERT NO MORE SUCCESSFUL THAN I, BRAGGART!
THE HORN BE NEARLY AS FULL AS WHEN I BEGAN!

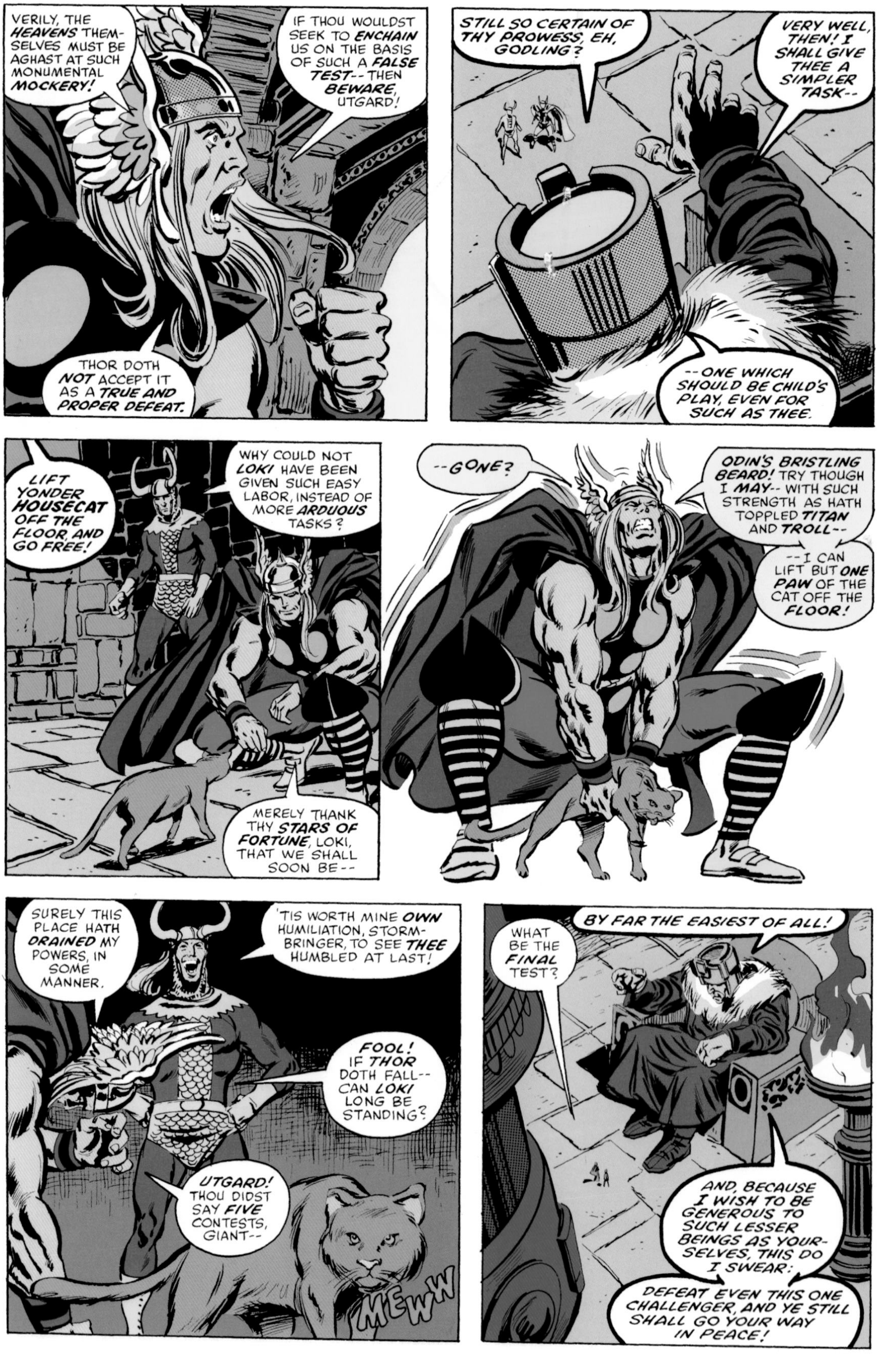
VERILY, THE HEAVENS THEMSELVES MUST BE AGHAST AT SUCH MONUMENTAL MOCKERY!
IF THOU WOULDST SEEK TO ENCHAIN US ON THE BASIS OF SUCH A FALSE TEST-- THEN BEWARE, UTGARD!
THOR DOTH NOT ACCEPT IT AS A TRUE AND PROPER DEFEAT.
STILL SO CERTAIN OF THY PROWESS, EH, GODLING?
VERY WELL, THEN! I SHALL GIVE THEE A SIMPLER TASK--
--ONE WHICH SHOULD BE CHILD'S PLAY, EVEN FOR SUCH AS THEE.
LIFT YONDER HOUSECAT OFF THE FLOOR, AND GO FREE!
WHY COULD NOT LOKI HAVE BEEN GIVEN SUCH EASY LABOR, INSTEAD OF MORE ARDUOUS TASKS?
MERELY THANK THY STARS OF FORTUNE, LOKI, THAT WE SHALL SOON BE--
--GONE?
ODIN'S BRISTLING BEARD! TRY THOUGH I MAY-- WITH SUCH STRENGTH AS HATH TOPPLED TITAN AND TROLL--
--I CAN LIFT BUT ONE PAW OF THE CAT OFF THE FLOOR!
SURELY THIS PLACE HATH DRAINED MY POWERS, IN SOME MANNER.
'TIS WORTH MINE OWN HUMILIATION, STORMBRINGER, TO SEE THEE HUMBLED AT LAST!
FOOL! IF THOR DOTH FALL-- CAN LOKI LONG BE STANDING?
UTGARD! THOU DIDST SAY FIVE CONTESTS, GIANT--
MEWW
WHAT BE THE FINAL TEST?
BY FAR THE EASIEST OF ALL!
AND, BECAUSE I WISH TO BE GENEROUS TO SUCH LESSER BEINGS AS YOURSELVES, THIS DO I SWEAR:
DEFEAT EVEN THIS ONE CHALLENGER, AND YE STILL SHALL GO YOUR WAY IN PEACE!

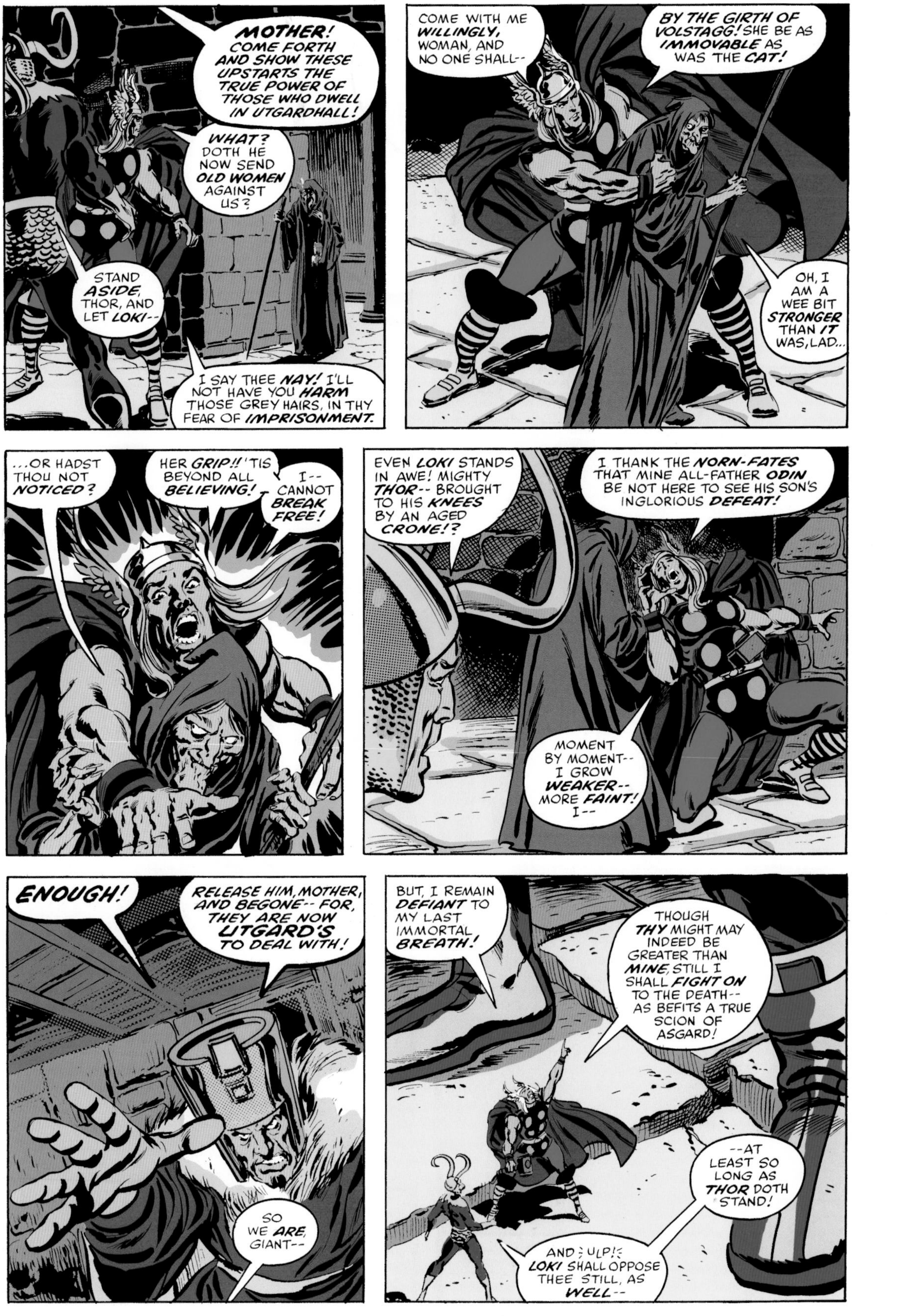
MOTHER! COME FORTH AND SHOW THESE UPSTARTS THE TRUE POWER OF THOSE WHO DWELL IN UTGARDHALL!
WHAT? DOTH HE NOW SEND OLD WOMEN AGAINST US?
STAND ASIDE, THOR, AND LET LOKI--
I SAY THEE NAY! I'LL NOT HAVE YOU HARM THOSE GREY HAIRS, IN THY FEAR OF IMPRISONMENT.
COME WITH ME WILLINGLY, WOMAN, AND NO ONE SHALL--
BY THE GIRTH OF VOLSTAGG! SHE BE AS IMMOVABLE AS WAS THE CAT!
OH, I AM A WEE BIT STRONGER THAN IT WAS, LAD...
...OR HADST THOU NOT NOTICED?
HER GRIP!! 'TIS BEYOND ALL BELIEVING!
I-- CANNOT BREAK FREE!
EVEN LOKI STANDS IN AWE! MIGHTY THOR-- BROUGHT TO HIS KNEES BY AN AGED CRONE!?
I THANK THE NORN-FATES THAT MINE ALL-FATHER ODIN BE NOT HERE TO SEE HIS SON'S INGLORIOUS DEFEAT!
MOMENT BY MOMENT-- I GROW WEAKER-- MORE FAINT! I--
ENOUGH!
RELEASE HIM, MOTHER, AND BEGONE-- FOR, THEY ARE NOW UTGARD'S TO DEAL WITH!
SO WE ARE, GIANT--
BUT, I REMAIN DEFIANT TO MY LAST IMMORTAL BREATH!
THOUGH THY MIGHT MAY INDEED BE GREATER THAN MINE, STILL I SHALL FIGHT ON TO THE DEATH-- AS BEFITS A TRUE SCION OF ASGARD!
--AT LEAST SO LONG AS THOR DOTH STAND!
AND--ULP!-- LOKI SHALL OPPOSE THEE STILL, AS WELL--

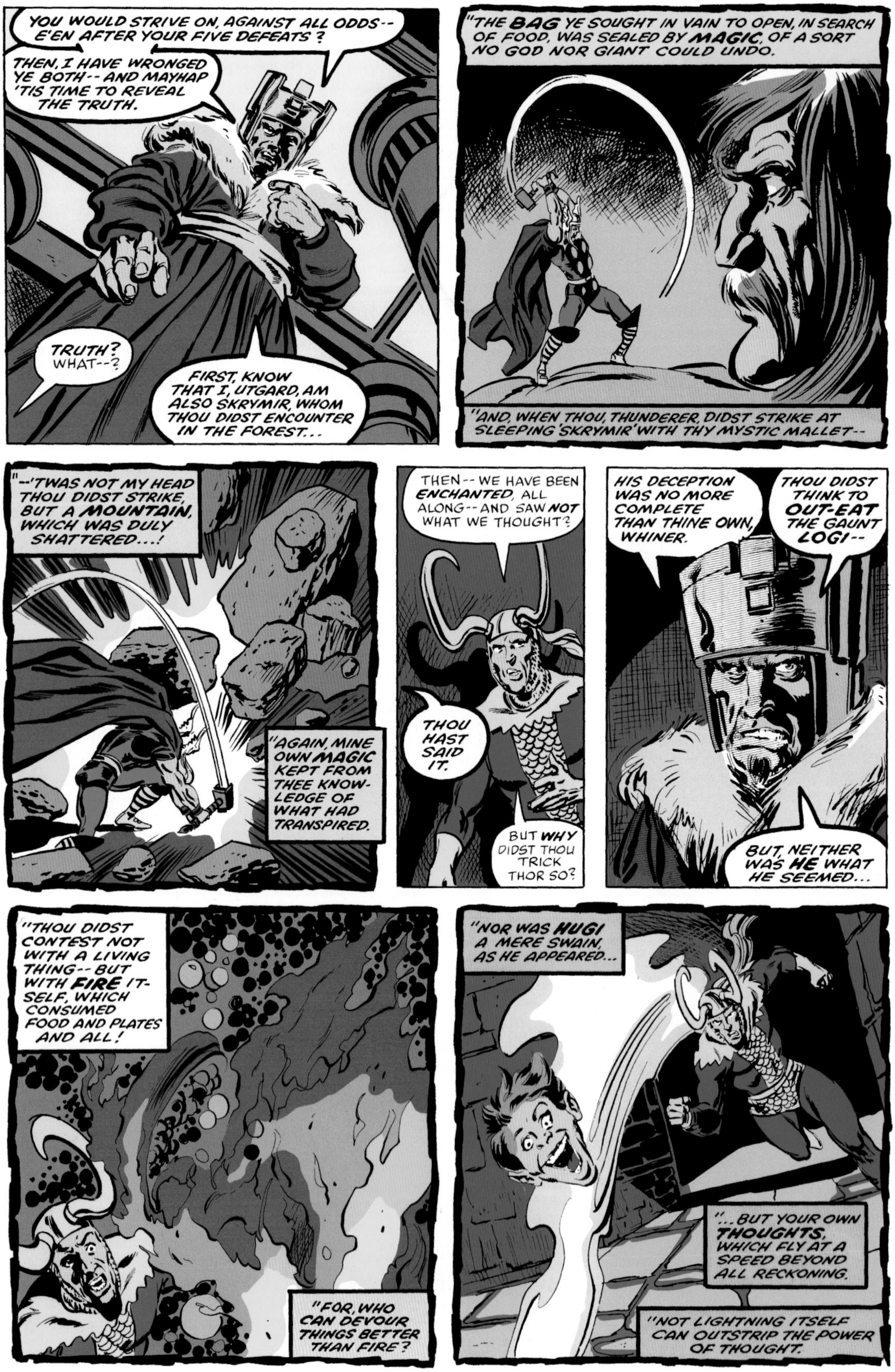
YOU WOULD STRIVE ON, AGAINST ALL ODDS-- E'EN AFTER YOUR FIVE DEFEATS?
THEN, I HAVE WRONGED YE BOTH-- AND MAYHAP 'TIS TIME TO REVEAL THE TRUTH.
TRUTH? WHAT--?
FIRST, KNOW THAT I, UTGARD, AM ALSO SKRYMIR, WHOM THOU DIDST ENCOUNTER IN THE FOREST...
"THE BAG YE SOUGHT IN VAIN TO OPEN, IN SEARCH OF FOOD, WAS SEALED BY MAGIC, OF A SORT NO GOD NOR GIANT COULD UNDO.
"AND, WHEN THOU, THUNDERER, DIDST STRIKE AT SLEEPING 'SKRYMIR' WITH THY MYSTIC MALLET--
"--'TWAS NOT MY HEAD THOU DIDST STRIKE, BUT A MOUNTAIN, WHICH WAS DULY SHATTERED...!
"AGAIN, MINE OWN MAGIC KEPT FROM THEE KNOW-LEDGE OF WHAT HAD TRANSPIRED.
THEN--WE HAVE BEEN ENCHANTED, ALL ALONG--AND SAW NOT WHAT WE THOUGHT?
THOU HAST SAID IT.
BUT WHY DIDST THOU TRICK THOR SO?
HIS DECEPTION WAS NO MORE COMPLETE THAN THINE OWN, WHINER.
THOU DIDST THINK TO OUT-EAT THE GAUNT LOGI--
BUT, NEITHER WAS HE WHAT HE SEEMED...
"THOU DIDST CONTEST NOT WITH A LIVING THING--BUT WITH FIRE IT-SELF, WHICH CONSUMED FOOD AND PLATES AND ALL!
"FOR, WHO CAN DEVOUR THINGS BETTER THAN FIRE?
"NOR WAS HUGI A MERE SWAIN, AS HE APPEARED...
"...BUT YOUR OWN THOUGHTS, WHICH FLY AT A SPEED BEYOND ALL RECKONING.
"NOT LIGHTNING ITSELF CAN OUTSTRIP THE POWER OF THOUGHT.

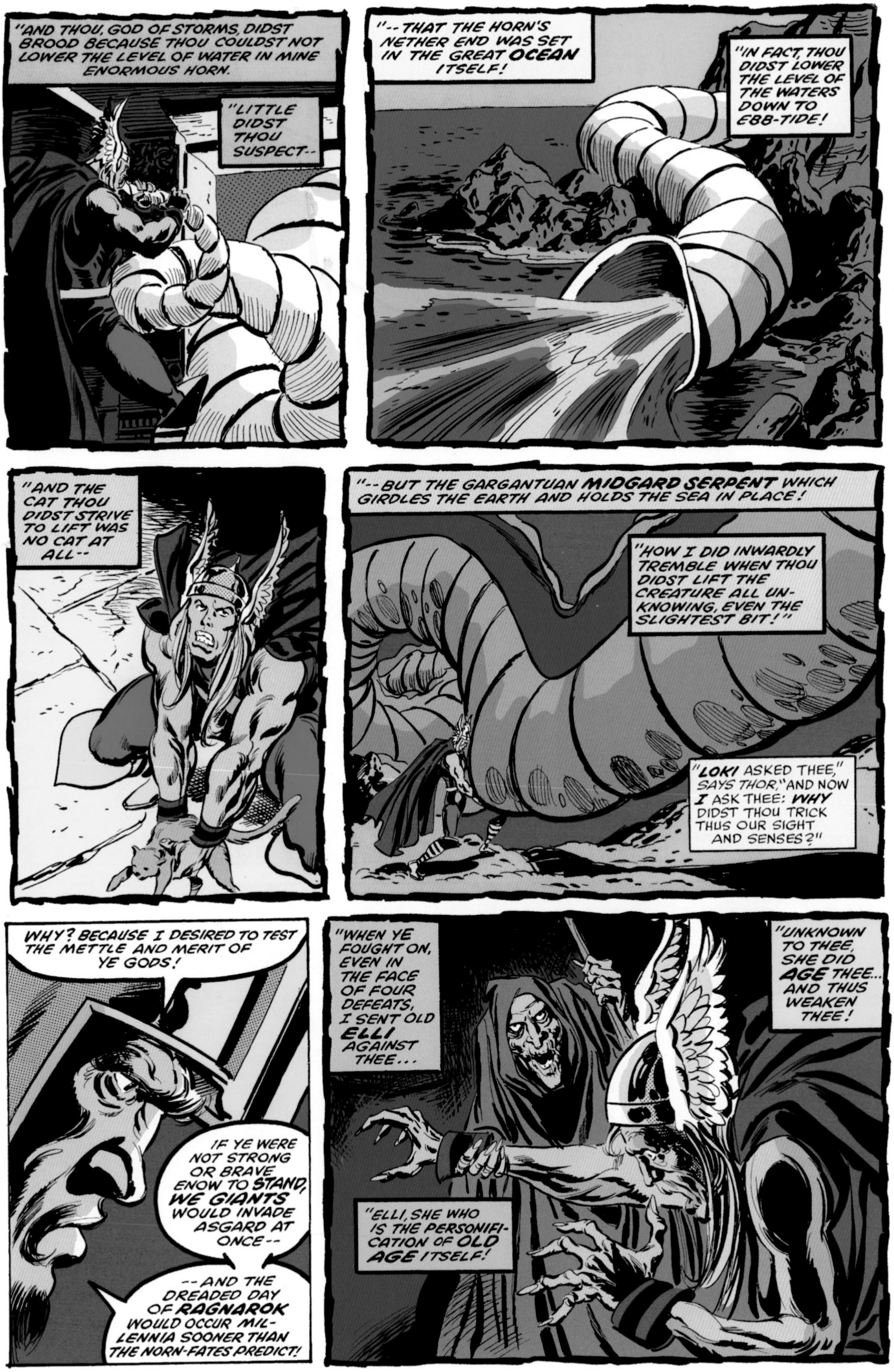
"AND THOU, GOD OF STORMS, DIDST BROOD BECAUSE THOU COULDST NOT LOWER THE LEVEL OF WATER IN MINE ENORMOUS HORN.
"LITTLE DIDST THOU SUSPECT--
"--THAT THE HORN'S NETHER END WAS SET IN THE GREAT OCEAN ITSELF!
"IN FACT, THOU DIDST LOWER THE LEVEL OF THE WATERS DOWN TO EBB-TIDE!
"AND THE CAT THOU DIDST STRIVE TO LIFT WAS NO CAT AT ALL--
"--BUT THE GARGANTUAN MIDGARD SERPENT WHICH GIRDLES THE EARTH AND HOLDS THE SEA IN PLACE!
"HOW I DID INWARDLY TREMBLE WHEN THOU DIDST LIFT THE CREATURE ALL UNKNOWING, EVEN THE SLIGHTEST BIT!"
"LOKI ASKED THEE," SAYS THOR, "AND NOW I ASK THEE: WHY DIDST THOU TRICK THUS OUR SIGHT AND SENSES?"
WHY? BECAUSE I DESIRED TO TEST THE METTLE AND MERIT OF YE GODS!
IF YE WERE NOT STRONG OR BRAVE ENOW TO STAND, WE GIANTS WOULD INVADE ASGARD AT ONCE--
--AND THE DREADED DAY OF RAGNAROK WOULD OCCUR MILLENNIA SOONER THAN THE NORN-FATES PREDICT!
"WHEN YE FOUGHT ON, EVEN IN THE FACE OF FOUR DEFEATS, I SENT OLD ELLI AGAINST THEE...
"UNKNOWN TO THEE, SHE DID AGE THEE... AND THUS WEAKEN THEE!
"ELLI, SHE WHO IS THE PERSONIFICATION OF OLD AGE ITSELF!

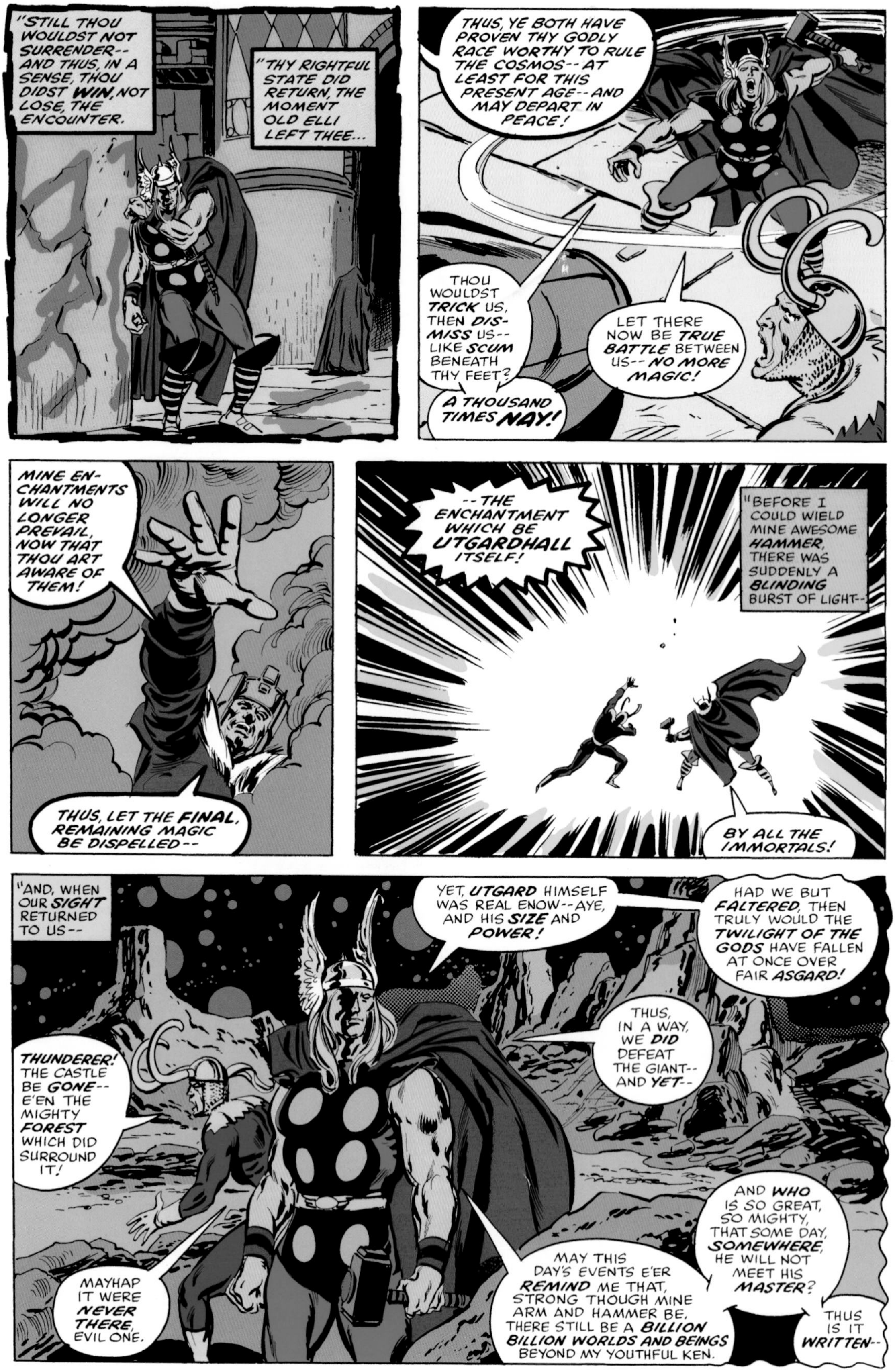
"STILL THOU WOULDST NOT SURRENDER-- AND THUS, IN A SENSE, THOU DIDST WIN, NOT LOSE, THE ENCOUNTER.
"THY RIGHTFUL STATE DID RETURN, THE MOMENT OLD ELLI LEFT THEE...
THUS, YE BOTH HAVE PROVEN THY GODLY RACE WORTHY TO RULE THE COSMOS--AT LEAST FOR THIS PRESENT AGE--AND MAY DEPART IN PEACE!
THOU WOULDST TRICK US, THEN DISMISS US--LIKE SCUM BENEATH THY FEET?
A THOUSAND TIMES NAY!
LET THERE NOW BE TRUE BATTLE BETWEEN US--NO MORE MAGIC!
MINE ENCHANTMENTS WILL NO LONGER PREVAIL, NOW THAT THOU ART AWARE OF THEM!
THUS, LET THE FINAL, REMAINING MAGIC BE DISPELLED--
--THE ENCHANTMENT WHICH BE UTGARDHALL ITSELF!
"BEFORE I COULD WIELD MINE AWESOME HAMMER, THERE WAS SUDDENLY A BLINDING BURST OF LIGHT--
BY ALL THE IMMORTALS!
"AND, WHEN OUR SIGHT RETURNED TO US--
YET, UTGARD HIMSELF WAS REAL ENOW--AYE, AND HIS SIZE AND POWER!
HAD WE BUT FALTERED, THEN TRULY WOULD THE TWILIGHT OF THE GODS HAVE FALLEN AT ONCE OVER FAIR ASGARD!
THUS, IN A WAY, WE DID DEFEAT THE GIANT--AND YET--
THUNDERER! THE CASTLE BE GONE--E'EN THE MIGHTY FOREST WHICH DID SURROUND IT!
MAYHAP IT WERE NEVER THERE, EVIL ONE.
MAY THIS DAY'S EVENTS E'ER REMIND ME THAT, STRONG THOUGH MINE ARM AND HAMMER BE, THERE STILL BE A BILLION BILLION WORLDS AND BEINGS BEYOND MY YOUTHFUL KEN.
AND WHO IS SO GREAT, SO MIGHTY, THAT SOME DAY, SOMEWHERE, HE WILL NOT MEET HIS MASTER?
THUS IS IT WRITTEN--

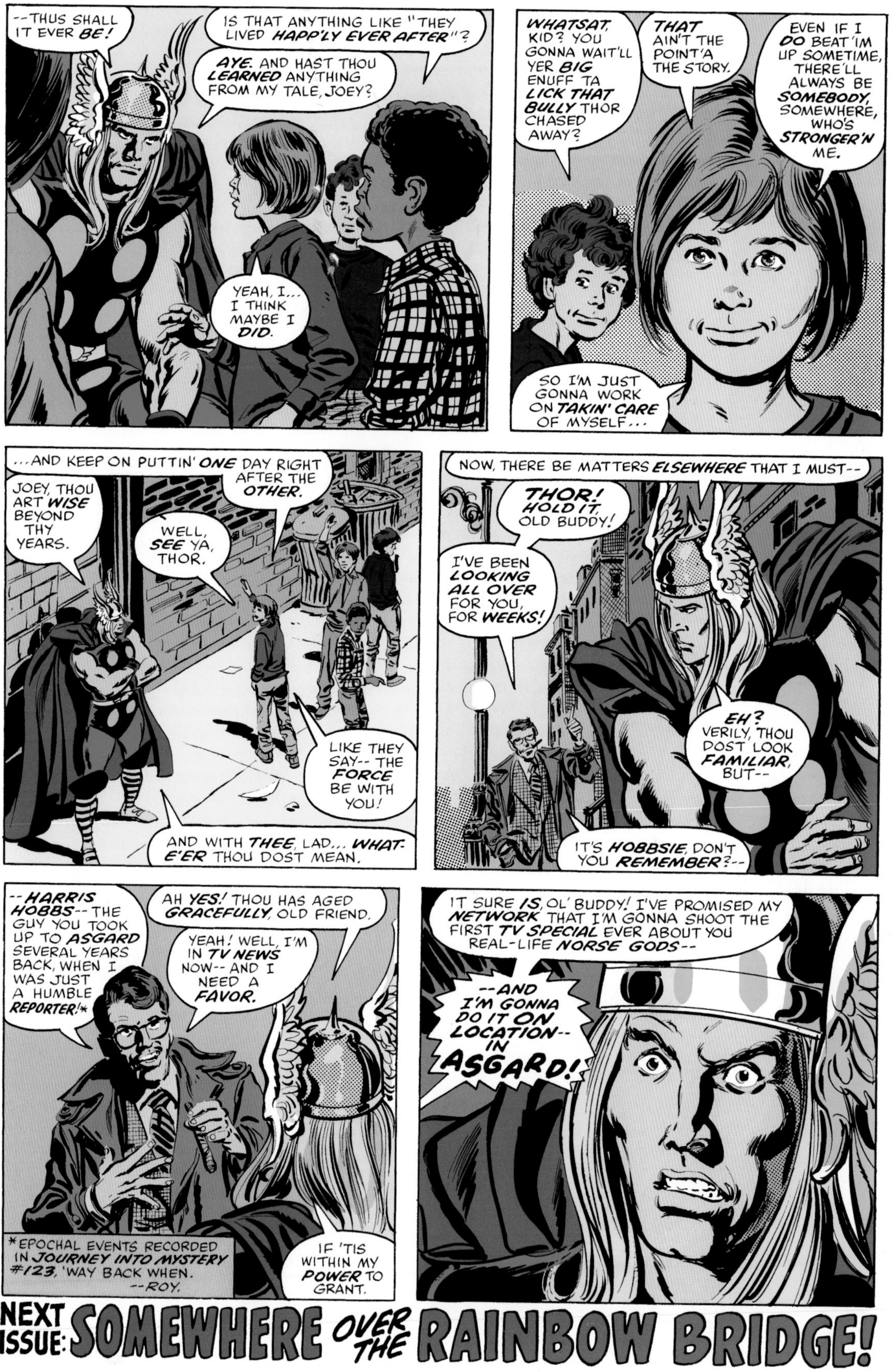
--THUS SHALL IT EVER BE!
IS THAT ANYTHING LIKE "THEY LIVED HAPP'LY EVER AFTER"?
AYE. AND HAST THOU LEARNED ANYTHING FROM MY TALE, JOEY?
YEAH, I... I THINK MAYBE I DID.
WHATSAT, KID? YOU GONNA WAIT'LL YER BIG ENUFF TA LICK THAT BULLY THOR CHASED AWAY?
THAT AIN'T THE POINT'A THE STORY.
EVEN IF I DO BEAT 'IM UP SOMETIME, THERE'LL ALWAYS BE SOMEBODY, SOMEWHERE, WHO'S STRONGER'N ME.
SO I'M JUST GONNA WORK ON TAKIN' CARE OF MYSELF...
...AND KEEP ON PUTTIN' ONE DAY RIGHT AFTER THE OTHER.
JOEY, THOU ART WISE BEYOND THY YEARS.
WELL, SEE YA, THOR.
LIKE THEY SAY-- THE FORCE BE WITH YOU!
AND WITH THEE, LAD... WHAT-E'ER THOU DOST MEAN.
NOW, THERE BE MATTERS ELSEWHERE THAT I MUST--
THOR! HOLD IT, OLD BUDDY!
I'VE BEEN LOOKING ALL OVER FOR YOU, FOR WEEKS!
EH? VERILY, THOU DOST LOOK FAMILIAR, BUT--
IT'S HOBBSIE, DON'T YOU REMEMBER?--
--HARRIS HOBBS-- THE GUY YOU TOOK UP TO ASGARD SEVERAL YEARS BACK, WHEN I WAS JUST A HUMBLE REPORTER!*
AH YES! THOU HAS AGED GRACEFULLY, OLD FRIEND.
YEAH! WELL, I'M IN TV NEWS NOW-- AND I NEED A FAVOR.
*EPOCHAL EVENTS RECORDED IN JOURNEY INTO MYSTERY #123, 'WAY BACK WHEN. --ROY.
IF 'TIS WITHIN MY POWER TO GRANT.
IT SURE IS, OL' BUDDY! I'VE PROMISED MY NETWORK THAT I'M GONNA SHOOT THE FIRST TV SPECIAL EVER ABOUT YOU REAL-LIFE NORSE GODS--
--AND I'M GONNA DO IT ON LOCATION-- IN ASGARD!
NEXT ISSUE: SOMEWHERE OVER THE RAINBOW BRIDGE!

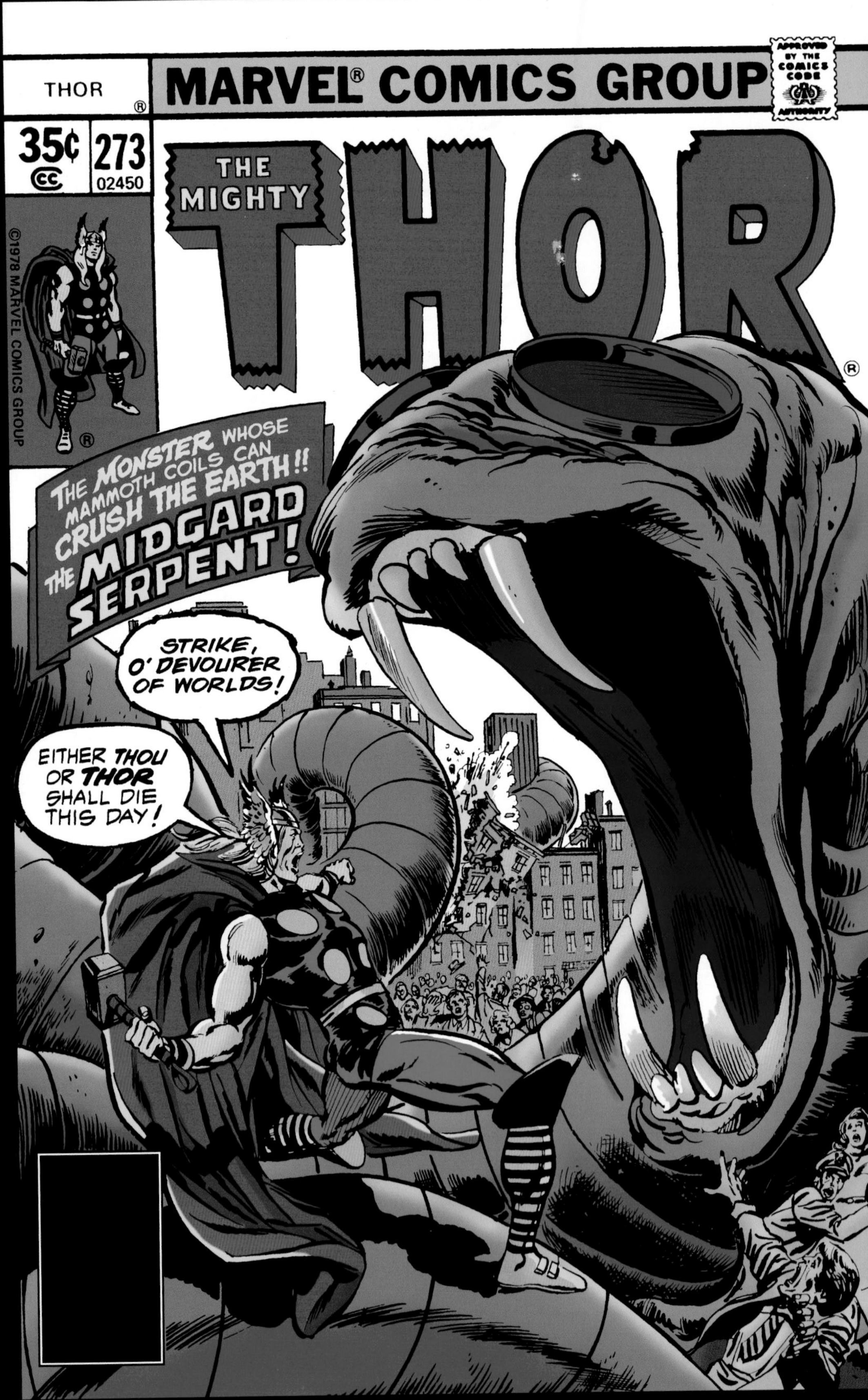
THOR
MARVEL® COMICS GROUP
APPROVED BY THE COMICS CODE AUTHORITY
35¢
273
02450
©1978 MARVEL COMICS GROUP
THE MIGHTY THOR
THE MONSTER WHOSE MAMMOTH COILS CAN CRUSH THE EARTH!! THE MIDGARD SERPENT!
STRIKE, O' DEVOURER OF WORLDS!
EITHER THOU OR THOR SHALL DIE THIS DAY!

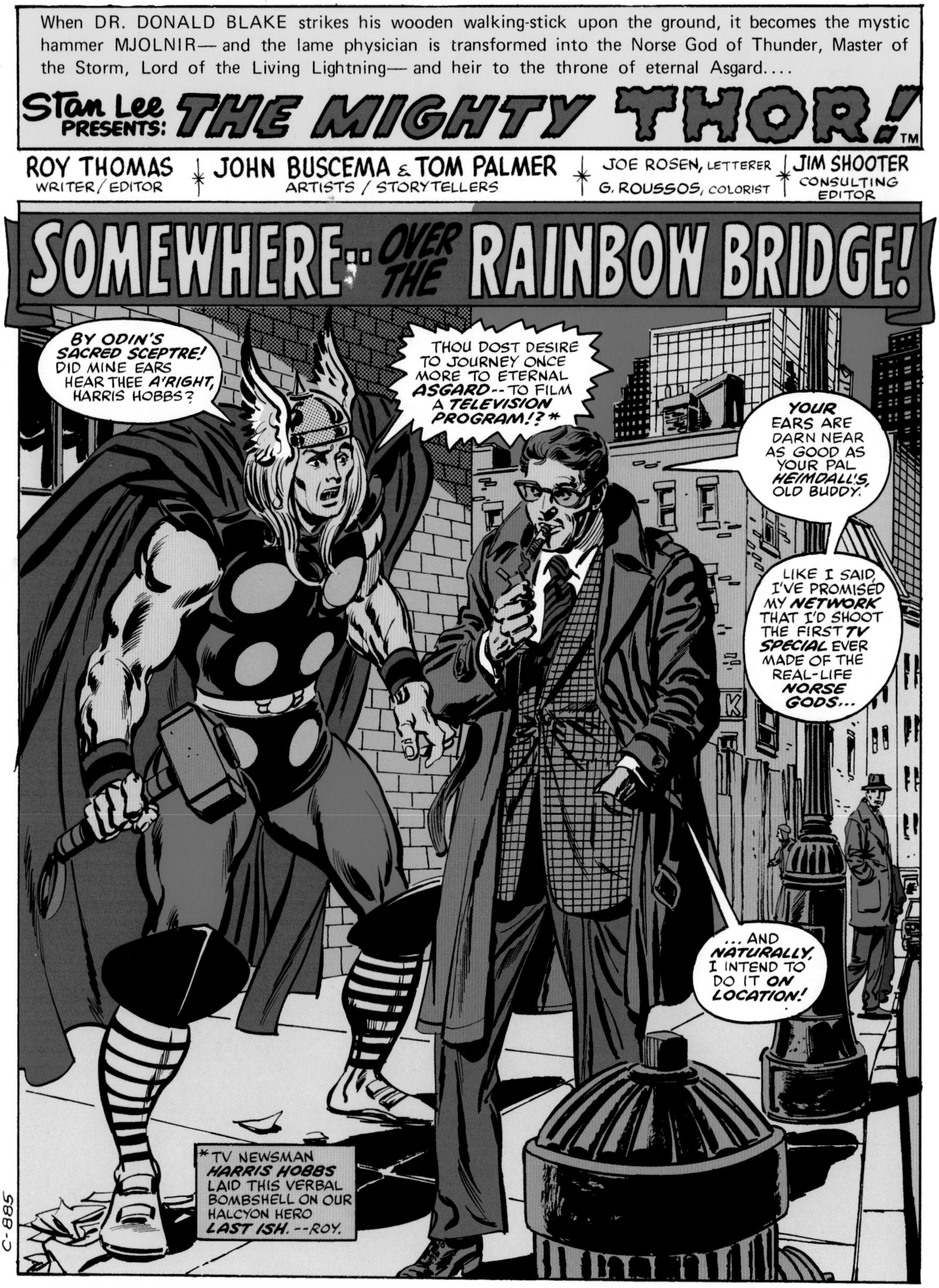
When DR. DONALD BLAKE strikes his wooden walking-stick upon the ground, it becomes the mystic hammer MJOLNIR— and the lame physician is transformed into the Norse God of Thunder, Master of the Storm, Lord of the Living Lightning— and heir to the throne of eternal Asgard....
Stan Lee PRESENTS: THE MIGHTY THOR! TM
ROY THOMAS WRITER/EDITOR
JOHN BUSCEMA & TOM PALMER ARTISTS / STORYTELLERS
JOE ROSEN, LETTERER
G. ROUSSOS, COLORIST
JIM SHOOTER CONSULTING EDITOR
SOMEWHERE-- OVER THE RAINBOW BRIDGE!
BY ODIN'S SACRED SCEPTRE! DID MINE EARS HEAR THEE A'RIGHT, HARRIS HOBBS?
THOU DOST DESIRE TO JOURNEY ONCE MORE TO ETERNAL ASGARD-- TO FILM A TELEVISION PROGRAM!?*
YOUR EARS ARE DARN NEAR AS GOOD AS YOUR PAL HEIMDALL'S, OLD BUDDY.
LIKE I SAID, I'VE PROMISED MY NETWORK THAT I'D SHOOT THE FIRST TV SPECIAL EVER MADE OF THE REAL-LIFE NORSE GODS...
...AND NATURALLY, I INTEND TO DO IT ON LOCATION!
*TV NEWSMAN HARRIS HOBBS LAID THIS VERBAL BOMBSHELL ON OUR HALCYON HERO LAST ISH. --ROY.
C-885

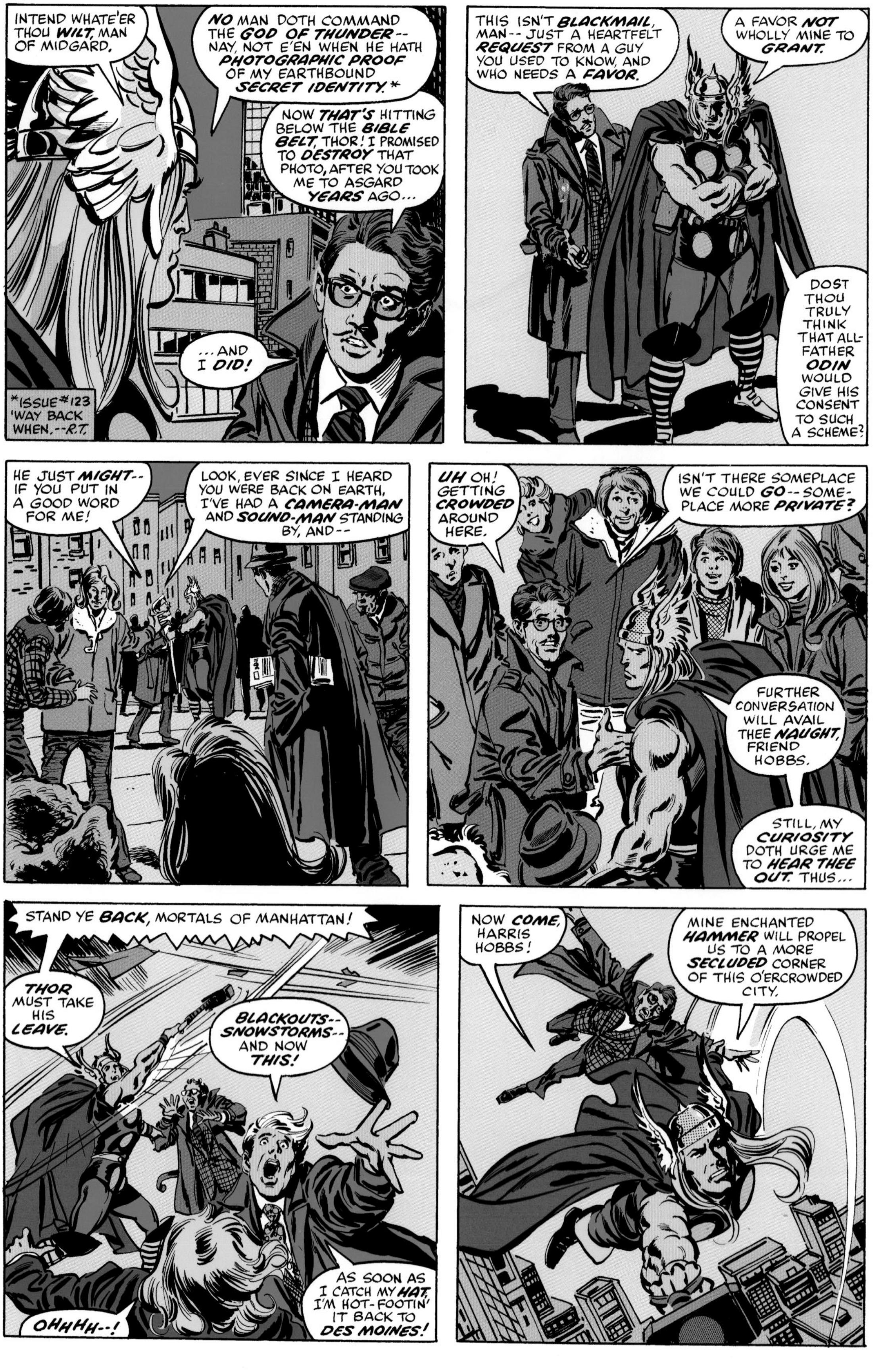
INTEND WHATE'ER THOU WILT, MAN OF MIDGARD.
NO MAN DOTH COMMAND THE GOD OF THUNDER-- NAY, NOT E'EN WHEN HE HATH PHOTOGRAPHIC PROOF OF MY EARTHBOUND SECRET IDENTITY.*
NOW THAT'S HITTING BELOW THE BIBLE BELT, THOR! I PROMISED TO DESTROY THAT PHOTO, AFTER YOU TOOK ME TO ASGARD YEARS AGO...
...AND I DID!
*ISSUE #123 'WAY BACK WHEN.--R.T.
THIS ISN'T BLACKMAIL, MAN-- JUST A HEARTFELT REQUEST FROM A GUY YOU USED TO KNOW, AND WHO NEEDS A FAVOR.
A FAVOR NOT WHOLLY MINE TO GRANT.
DOST THOU TRULY THINK THAT ALL-FATHER ODIN WOULD GIVE HIS CONSENT TO SUCH A SCHEME?
HE JUST MIGHT-- IF YOU PUT IN A GOOD WORD FOR ME!
LOOK, EVER SINCE I HEARD YOU WERE BACK ON EARTH, I'VE HAD A CAMERA-MAN AND SOUND-MAN STANDING BY, AND--
UH OH! GETTING CROWDED AROUND HERE.
ISN'T THERE SOMEPLACE WE COULD GO-- SOME-PLACE MORE PRIVATE?
FURTHER CONVERSATION WILL AVAIL THEE NAUGHT, FRIEND HOBBS.
STILL, MY CURIOSITY DOTH URGE ME TO HEAR THEE OUT. THUS...
STAND YE BACK, MORTALS OF MANHATTAN!
THOR MUST TAKE HIS LEAVE.
BLACKOUTS-- SNOWSTORMS-- AND NOW THIS!
AS SOON AS I CATCH MY HAT, I'M HOT-FOOTIN' IT BACK TO DES MOINES!
OHHHH--!
NOW COME, HARRIS HOBBS!
MINE ENCHANTED HAMMER WILL PROPEL US TO A MORE SECLUDED CORNER OF THIS O'ERCROWDED CITY.

TH-THANKS, THUNDER GOD... I *THINK!*

SPEAK THY PIECE *QUICKLY* OLD FRIEND. THOR CANNOT *TARRY* LONG.

YET, ONE THING I MUST *KNOW...*

WHAT DOST THOU *REMEMBER* OF THAT *TRIP TO ASGARD* SO LONG AGO?

I USED *MAGIC* TO MAKE THEE *FORGET* ITS SIGHTS, FOR THE SAKE OF THY *SANITY,* DID I NOT?

WAIT'LL... I CATCH... MY *BREATH,* OKAY...?

≥WHEW!≤ YOU CHANGE *LOCALES* FASTER THAN *FRED SILVERMAN* SWITCHES *NETWORKS!*

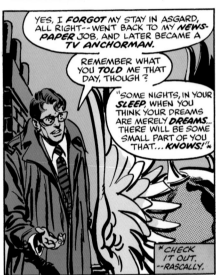

YES, I *FORGOT* MY STAY IN ASGARD, ALL RIGHT-- WENT BACK TO MY *NEWSPAPER* JOB, AND LATER BECAME A *TV ANCHORMAN.*

REMEMBER WHAT YOU *TOLD* ME THAT DAY, THOUGH?

"SOME NIGHTS, IN YOUR *SLEEP,* WHEN YOU THINK YOUR DREAMS ARE MERELY *DREAMS...* THERE WILL BE SOME SMALL PART OF YOU THAT... *KNOWS!*"*

*CHECK IT OUT. --RASCALLY.

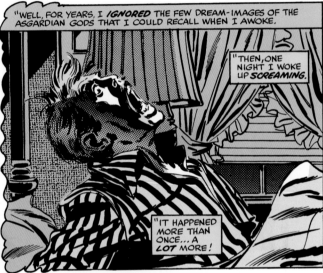

"WELL, FOR YEARS, I *IGNORED* THE FEW DREAM-IMAGES OF THE ASGARDIAN GODS THAT I COULD RECALL WHEN I AWOKE.

"THEN, ONE NIGHT I WOKE UP *SCREAMING.*

"IT HAPPENED MORE THAN ONCE... A *LOT* MORE!

"NATURALLY, I DID WHAT *ANY* TWENTIETH-CENTURY MALE IN MY POSITION WOULD DO: I WENT TO A *SHRINK!*

...SO YOU SEE, DOC, THESE *AREN'T* JUST REGULAR *NIGHTMARES.*

I WAS *IN* THIS "ASGARD" PLACE ONCE! I *KNOW* I WAS!

TAKEN THERE BY THE FABLED *THOR* HIMSELF, I BELIEVE YOU SAID?

CHECK! ONLY HE MADE ME *FORGET* THE WHOLE THING, AND--

YOUR EXPERIENCE IS QUITE *COMMON,* MR. HOBBS... A COMPENSATORY *RELEASE* FOR THE DAY-TO-DAY *PRESSURES* OF YOUR JOB.

STILL, AS PER YOUR REQUEST, I SHALL *HYPNOTIZE* YOU, IF YOU INSIST.

FOR FIFTY BUCKS AN HOUR, HE OUGHT TO *STAND ON HIS HEAD* IF I ASKED HIM TO!

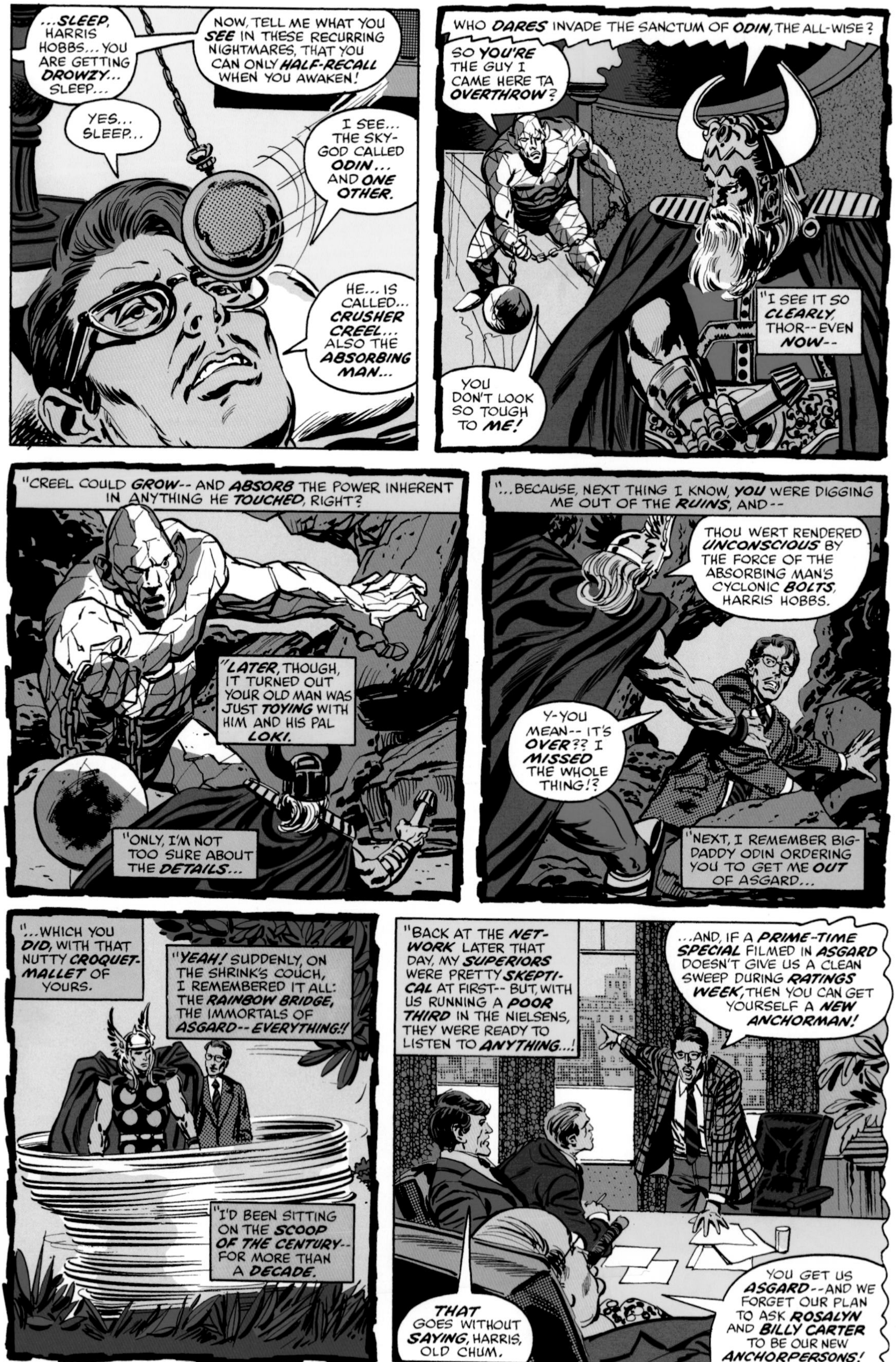
...SLEEP, HARRIS HOBBS... YOU ARE GETTING DROWZY... SLEEP...
NOW, TELL ME WHAT YOU SEE IN THESE RECURRING NIGHTMARES, THAT YOU CAN ONLY HALF-RECALL WHEN YOU AWAKEN!
YES... SLEEP...
I SEE... THE SKY-GOD CALLED ODIN... AND ONE OTHER.
HE... IS CALLED... CRUSHER CREEL... ALSO THE ABSORBING MAN...
WHO DARES INVADE THE SANCTUM OF ODIN, THE ALL-WISE?
SO YOU'RE THE GUY I CAME HERE TA OVERTHROW?
"I SEE IT SO CLEARLY, THOR-- EVEN NOW--
YOU DON'T LOOK SO TOUGH TO ME!
"CREEL COULD GROW-- AND ABSORB THE POWER INHERENT IN ANYTHING HE TOUCHED, RIGHT?
"LATER, THOUGH, IT TURNED OUT YOUR OLD MAN WAS JUST TOYING WITH HIM AND HIS PAL LOKI.
"ONLY, I'M NOT TOO SURE ABOUT THE DETAILS...
"...BECAUSE, NEXT THING I KNOW, YOU WERE DIGGING ME OUT OF THE RUINS, AND--
THOU WERT RENDERED UNCONSCIOUS BY THE FORCE OF THE ABSORBING MAN'S CYCLONIC BOLTS, HARRIS HOBBS.
Y-YOU MEAN-- IT'S OVER?? I MISSED THE WHOLE THING!?
"NEXT, I REMEMBER BIG-DADDY ODIN ORDERING YOU TO GET ME OUT OF ASGARD...
"...WHICH YOU DID, WITH THAT NUTTY CROQUET-MALLET OF YOURS.
"YEAH! SUDDENLY, ON THE SHRINK'S COUCH, I REMEMBERED IT ALL: THE RAINBOW BRIDGE, THE IMMORTALS OF ASGARD-- EVERYTHING!!
"I'D BEEN SITTING ON THE SCOOP OF THE CENTURY-- FOR MORE THAN A DECADE.
"BACK AT THE NET-WORK LATER THAT DAY, MY SUPERIORS WERE PRETTY SKEPTI-CAL AT FIRST-- BUT, WITH US RUNNING A POOR THIRD IN THE NIELSENS, THEY WERE READY TO LISTEN TO ANYTHING...!
...AND, IF A PRIME-TIME SPECIAL FILMED IN ASGARD DOESN'T GIVE US A CLEAN SWEEP DURING RATINGS WEEK, THEN YOU CAN GET YOURSELF A NEW ANCHORMAN!
THAT GOES WITHOUT SAYING, HARRIS, OLD CHUM.
YOU GET US ASGARD--AND WE FORGET OUR PLAN TO ASK ROSALYN AND BILLY CARTER TO BE OUR NEW ANCHORPERSONS!

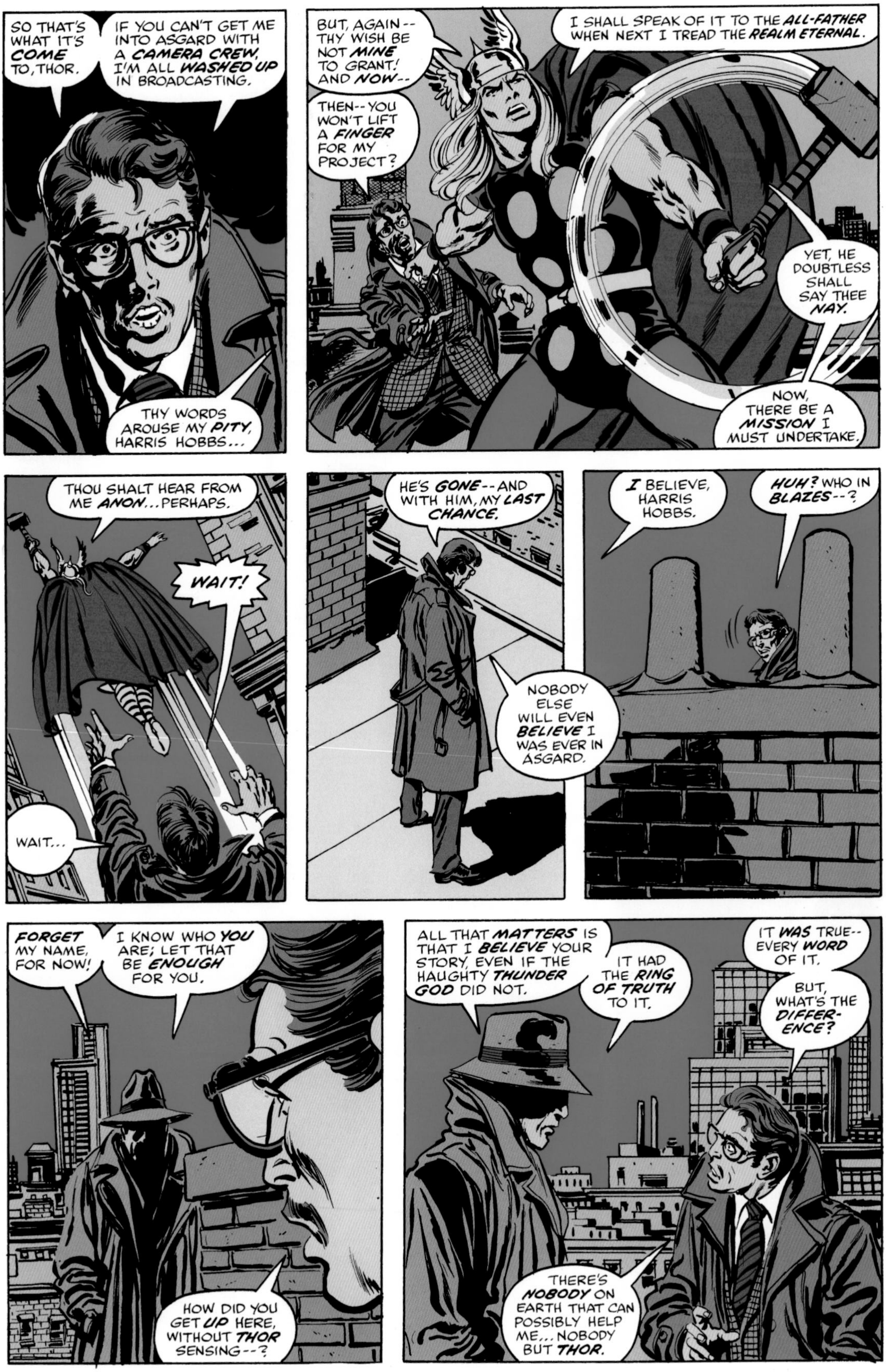
SO THAT'S WHAT IT'S COME TO, THOR.
IF YOU CAN'T GET ME INTO ASGARD WITH A CAMERA CREW, I'M ALL WASHED UP IN BROADCASTING.
THY WORDS AROUSE MY PITY, HARRIS HOBBS...
BUT, AGAIN-- THY WISH BE NOT MINE TO GRANT! AND NOW--
THEN-- YOU WON'T LIFT A FINGER FOR MY PROJECT?
I SHALL SPEAK OF IT TO THE ALL-FATHER WHEN NEXT I TREAD THE REALM ETERNAL.
YET, HE DOUBTLESS SHALL SAY THEE NAY.
NOW, THERE BE A MISSION I MUST UNDERTAKE.
THOU SHALT HEAR FROM ME ANON... PERHAPS.
WAIT!
WAIT...
HE'S GONE--AND WITH HIM, MY LAST CHANCE.
NOBODY ELSE WILL EVEN BELIEVE I WAS EVER IN ASGARD.
I BELIEVE, HARRIS HOBBS.
HUH? WHO IN BLAZES--?
FORGET MY NAME, FOR NOW!
I KNOW WHO YOU ARE; LET THAT BE ENOUGH FOR YOU.
HOW DID YOU GET UP HERE, WITHOUT THOR SENSING--?
ALL THAT MATTERS IS THAT I BELIEVE YOUR STORY, EVEN IF THE HAUGHTY THUNDER GOD DID NOT.
IT HAD THE RING OF TRUTH TO IT.
IT WAS TRUE-- EVERY WORD OF IT.
BUT, WHAT'S THE DIFFER-ENCE?
THERE'S NOBODY ON EARTH THAT CAN POSSIBLY HELP ME... NOBODY BUT THOR.

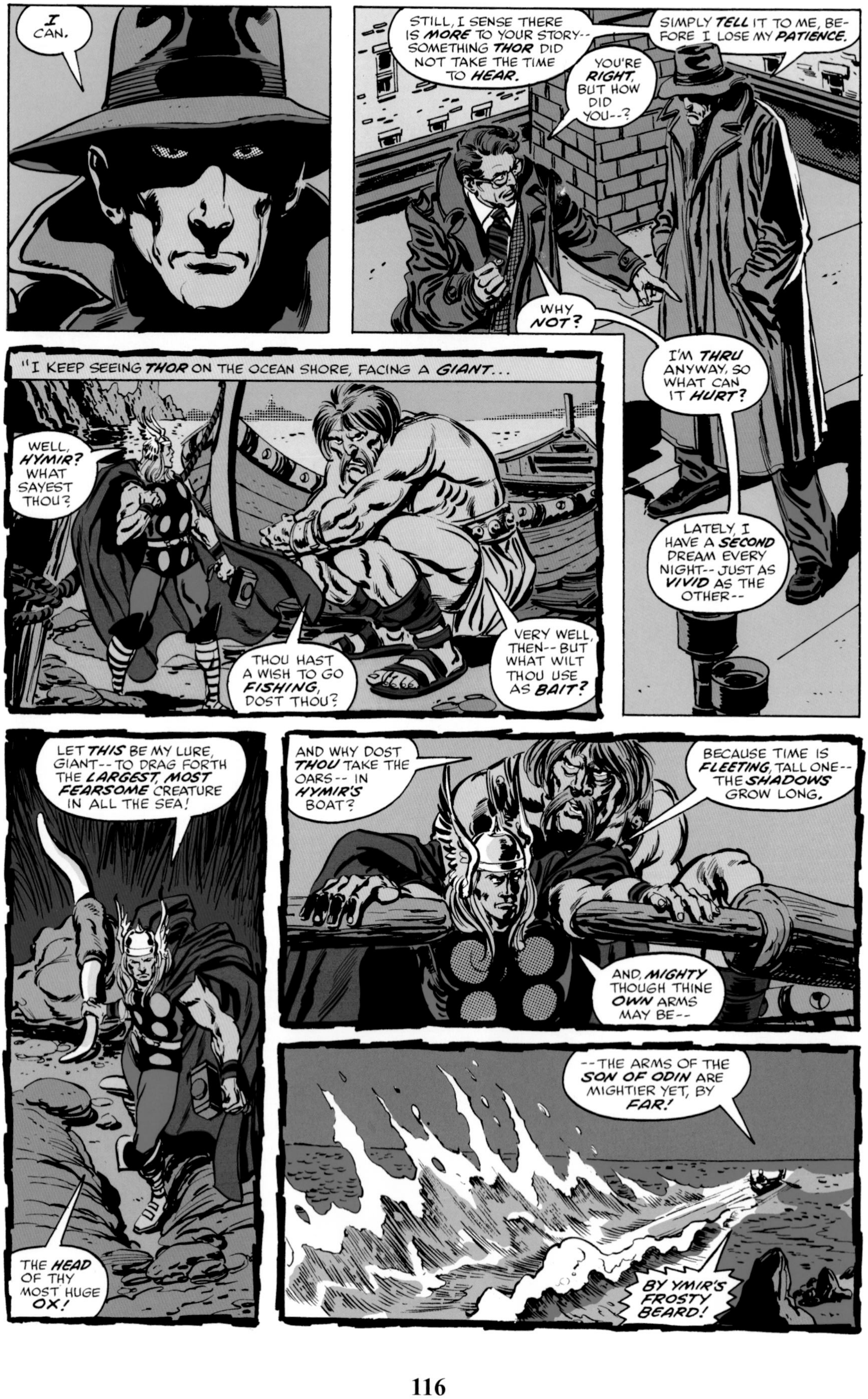
I CAN.
STILL, I SENSE THERE IS MORE TO YOUR STORY-- SOMETHING THOR DID NOT TAKE THE TIME TO HEAR.
YOU'RE RIGHT, BUT HOW DID YOU--?
SIMPLY TELL IT TO ME, BEFORE I LOSE MY PATIENCE.
WHY NOT?
I'M THRU ANYWAY, SO WHAT CAN IT HURT?
LATELY, I HAVE A SECOND DREAM EVERY NIGHT-- JUST AS VIVID AS THE OTHER--
"I KEEP SEEING THOR ON THE OCEAN SHORE, FACING A GIANT...
WELL, HYMIR? WHAT SAYEST THOU?
THOU HAST A WISH TO GO FISHING, DOST THOU?
VERY WELL, THEN-- BUT WHAT WILT THOU USE AS BAIT?
LET THIS BE MY LURE, GIANT-- TO DRAG FORTH THE LARGEST, MOST FEARSOME CREATURE IN ALL THE SEA!
THE HEAD OF THY MOST HUGE OX!
AND WHY DOST THOU TAKE THE OARS-- IN HYMIR'S BOAT?
BECAUSE TIME IS FLEETING, TALL ONE-- THE SHADOWS GROW LONG.
AND, MIGHTY THOUGH THINE OWN ARMS MAY BE--
--THE ARMS OF THE SON OF ODIN ARE MIGHTIER YET, BY FAR!
BY YMIR'S FROSTY BEARD!

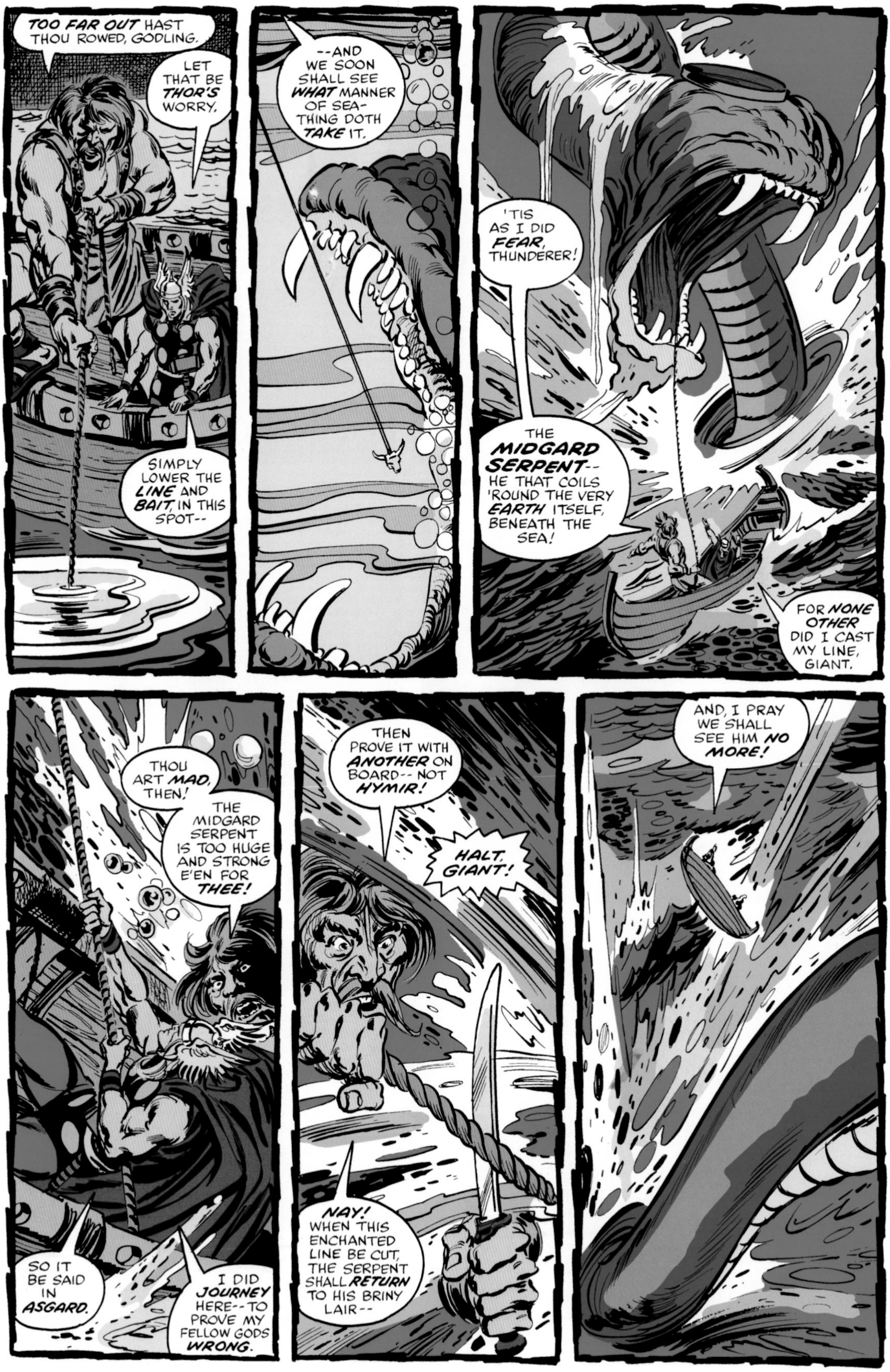
TOO FAR OUT HAST THOU ROWED, GODLING.
LET THAT BE THOR'S WORRY.
SIMPLY LOWER THE LINE AND BAIT, IN THIS SPOT--
--AND WE SOON SHALL SEE WHAT MANNER OF SEA-THING DOTH TAKE IT.
'TIS AS I DID FEAR, THUNDERER!
THE MIDGARD SERPENT-- HE THAT COILS 'ROUND THE VERY EARTH ITSELF, BENEATH THE SEA!
FOR NONE OTHER DID I CAST MY LINE, GIANT.
THOU ART MAD, THEN!
THE MIDGARD SERPENT IS TOO HUGE AND STRONG E'EN FOR THEE!
SO IT BE SAID IN ASGARD.
I DID JOURNEY HERE--TO PROVE MY FELLOW GODS WRONG.
THEN PROVE IT WITH ANOTHER ON BOARD-- NOT HYMIR!
HALT, GIANT!
NAY! WHEN THIS ENCHANTED LINE BE CUT, THE SERPENT SHALL RETURN TO HIS BRINY LAIR--
AND, I PRAY WE SHALL SEE HIM NO MORE!

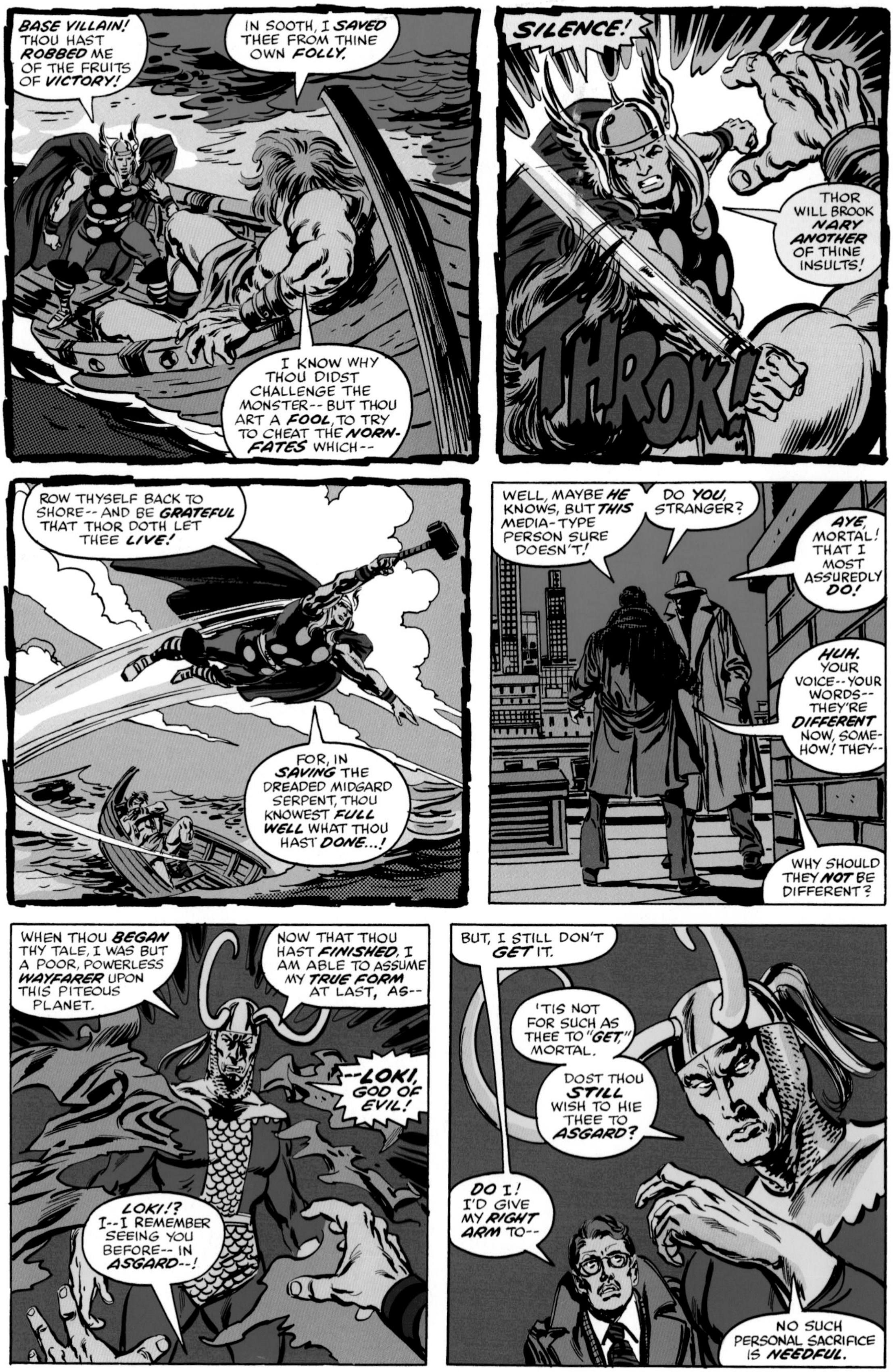
BASE VILLAIN! THOU HAST ROBBED ME OF THE FRUITS OF VICTORY!
IN SOOTH, I SAVED THEE FROM THINE OWN FOLLY.
I KNOW WHY THOU DIDST CHALLENGE THE MONSTER-- BUT THOU ART A FOOL, TO TRY TO CHEAT THE NORN-FATES WHICH--
SILENCE!
THOR WILL BROOK NARY ANOTHER OF THINE INSULTS!
THROK!
ROW THYSELF BACK TO SHORE-- AND BE GRATEFUL THAT THOR DOTH LET THEE LIVE!
FOR, IN SAVING THE DREADED MIDGARD SERPENT, THOU KNOWEST FULL WELL WHAT THOU HAST DONE...!
WELL, MAYBE HE KNOWS, BUT THIS MEDIA-TYPE PERSON SURE DOESN'T!
DO YOU, STRANGER?
AYE, MORTAL! THAT I MOST ASSUREDLY DO!
HUH. YOUR VOICE--YOUR WORDS-- THEY'RE DIFFERENT NOW, SOMEHOW! THEY--
WHY SHOULD THEY NOT BE DIFFERENT?
WHEN THOU BEGAN THY TALE, I WAS BUT A POOR, POWERLESS WAYFARER UPON THIS PITEOUS PLANET.
NOW THAT THOU HAST FINISHED, I AM ABLE TO ASSUME MY TRUE FORM AT LAST, AS--
--LOKI, GOD OF EVIL!
LOKI!? I--I REMEMBER SEEING YOU BEFORE-- IN ASGARD--!
BUT, I STILL DON'T GET IT.
'TIS NOT FOR SUCH AS THEE TO "GET," MORTAL.
DOST THOU STILL WISH TO HIE THEE TO ASGARD?
DO I! I'D GIVE MY RIGHT ARM TO--
NO SUCH PERSONAL SACRIFICE IS NEEDFUL.

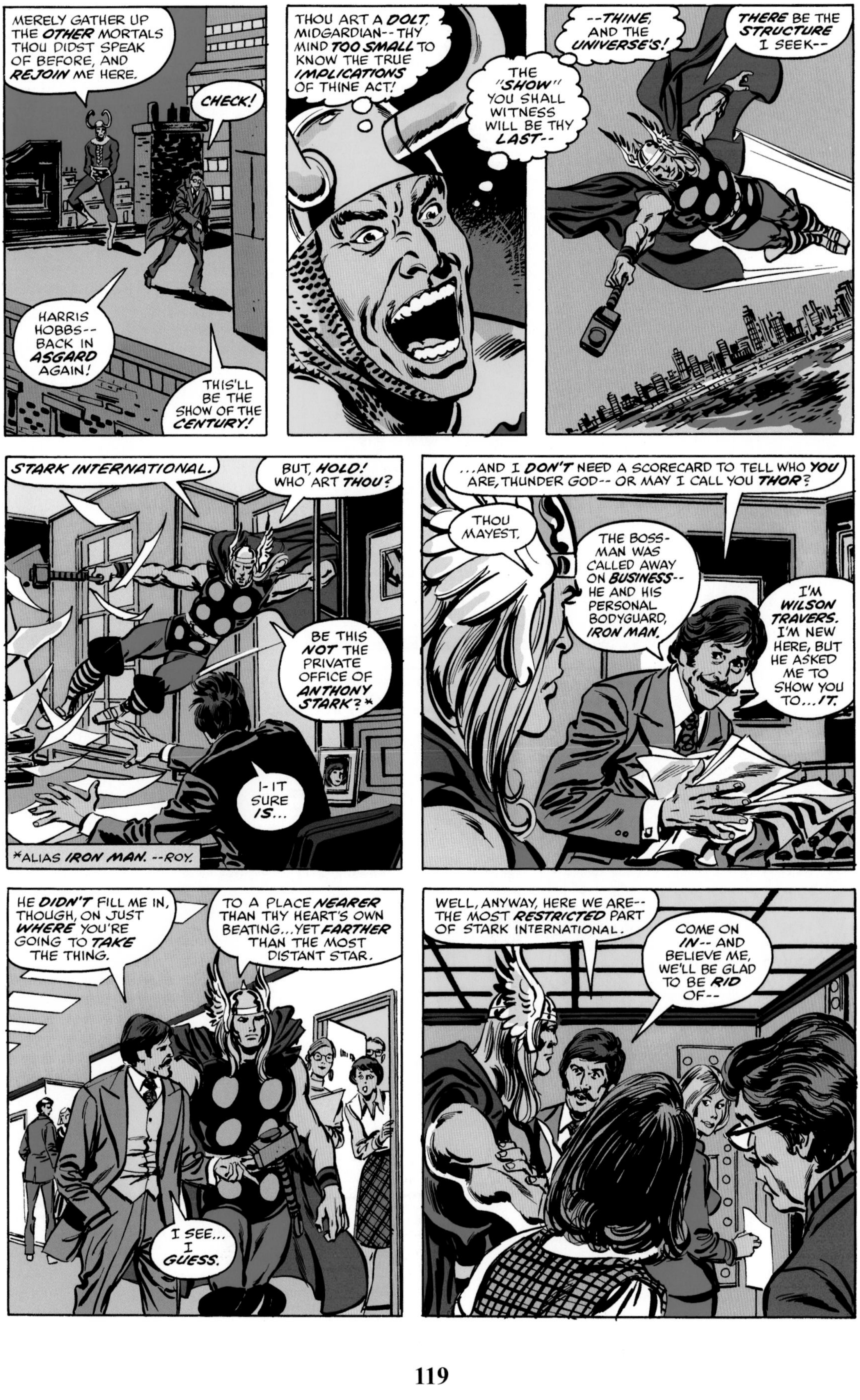
MERELY GATHER UP THE OTHER MORTALS THOU DIDST SPEAK OF BEFORE, AND REJOIN ME HERE.
CHECK!
HARRIS HOBBS-- BACK IN ASGARD AGAIN!
THIS'LL BE THE SHOW OF THE CENTURY!
THOU ART A DOLT, MIDGARDIAN-- THY MIND TOO SMALL TO KNOW THE TRUE IMPLICATIONS OF THINE ACT!
THE "SHOW" YOU SHALL WITNESS WILL BE THY LAST--
--THINE, AND THE UNIVERSE'S!
THERE BE THE STRUCTURE I SEEK--
STARK INTERNATIONAL.
BUT, HOLD! WHO ART THOU?
BE THIS NOT THE PRIVATE OFFICE OF ANTHONY STARK?*
I-IT SURE IS...
*ALIAS IRON MAN. --ROY.
...AND I DON'T NEED A SCORECARD TO TELL WHO YOU ARE, THUNDER GOD-- OR MAY I CALL YOU THOR?
THOU MAYEST.
THE BOSS-MAN WAS CALLED AWAY ON BUSINESS-- HE AND HIS PERSONAL BODYGUARD, IRON MAN.
I'M WILSON TRAVERS. I'M NEW HERE, BUT HE ASKED ME TO SHOW YOU TO...IT.
HE DIDN'T FILL ME IN, THOUGH, ON JUST WHERE YOU'RE GOING TO TAKE THE THING.
TO A PLACE NEARER THAN THY HEART'S OWN BEATING...YET FARTHER THAN THE MOST DISTANT STAR.
I SEE... I GUESS.
WELL, ANYWAY, HERE WE ARE-- THE MOST RESTRICTED PART OF STARK INTERNATIONAL.
COME ON IN-- AND BELIEVE ME, WE'LL BE GLAD TO BE RID OF--

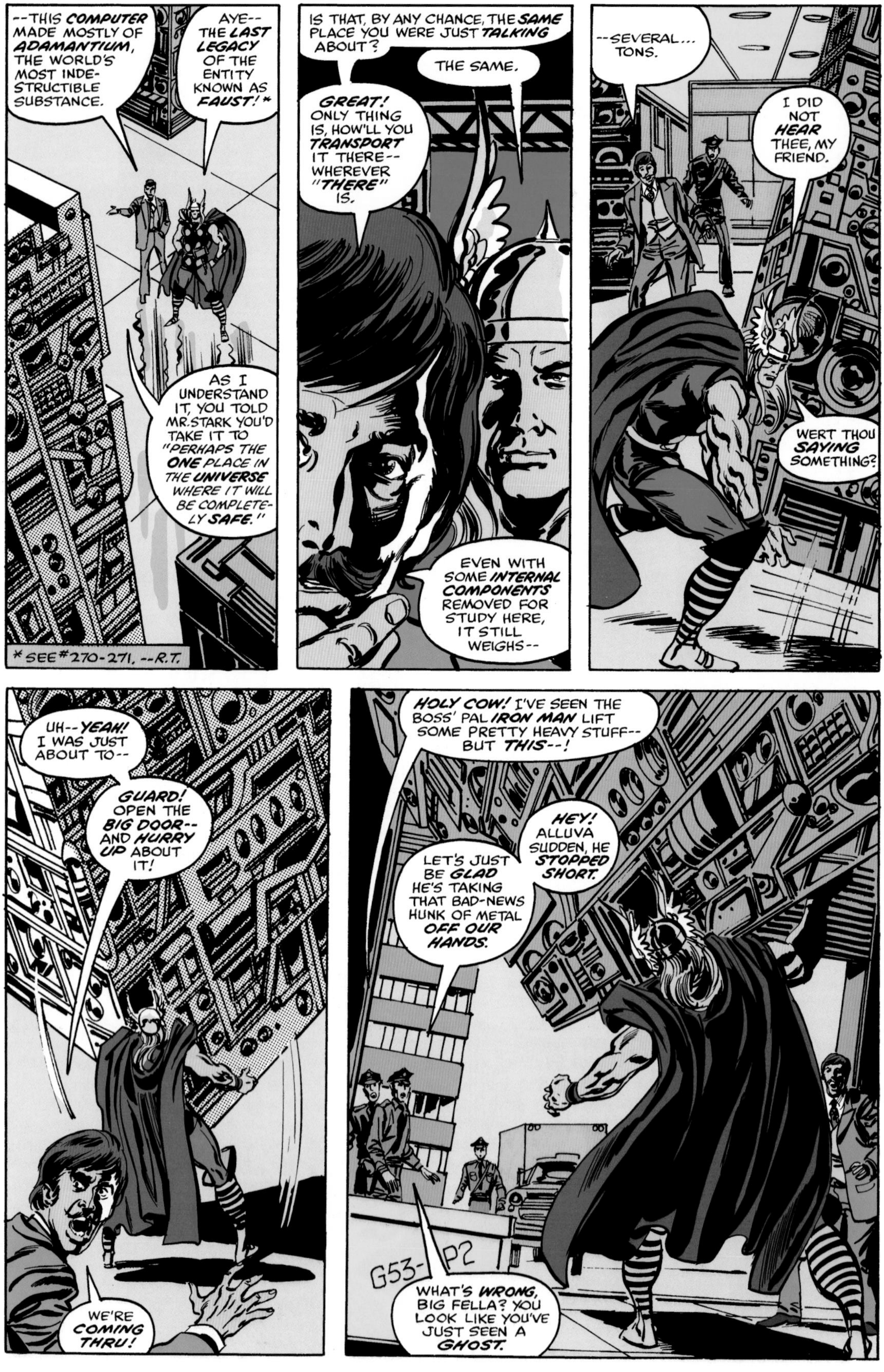
--THIS COMPUTER MADE MOSTLY OF ADAMANTIUM, THE WORLD'S MOST INDESTRUCTIBLE SUBSTANCE.
AYE--THE LAST LEGACY OF THE ENTITY KNOWN AS FAUST! *
AS I UNDERSTAND IT, YOU TOLD MR. STARK YOU'D TAKE IT TO "PERHAPS THE ONE PLACE IN THE UNIVERSE WHERE IT WILL BE COMPLETELY SAFE."
* SEE #270-271. --R.T.
IS THAT, BY ANY CHANCE, THE SAME PLACE YOU WERE JUST TALKING ABOUT?
THE SAME.
GREAT! ONLY THING IS, HOW'LL YOU TRANSPORT IT THERE--WHEREVER "THERE" IS.
EVEN WITH SOME INTERNAL COMPONENTS REMOVED FOR STUDY HERE, IT STILL WEIGHS--
--SEVERAL... TONS.
I DID NOT HEAR THEE, MY FRIEND.
WERT THOU SAYING SOMETHING?
UH--YEAH! I WAS JUST ABOUT TO--
GUARD! OPEN THE BIG DOOR--AND HURRY UP ABOUT IT!
WE'RE COMING THRU!
HOLY COW! I'VE SEEN THE BOSS' PAL IRON MAN LIFT SOME PRETTY HEAVY STUFF--BUT THIS--!
HEY! ALLUVA SUDDEN, HE STOPPED SHORT.
LET'S JUST BE GLAD HE'S TAKING THAT BAD-NEWS HUNK OF METAL OFF OUR HANDS.
G53-P2
WHAT'S WRONG, BIG FELLA? YOU LOOK LIKE YOU'VE JUST SEEN A GHOST.

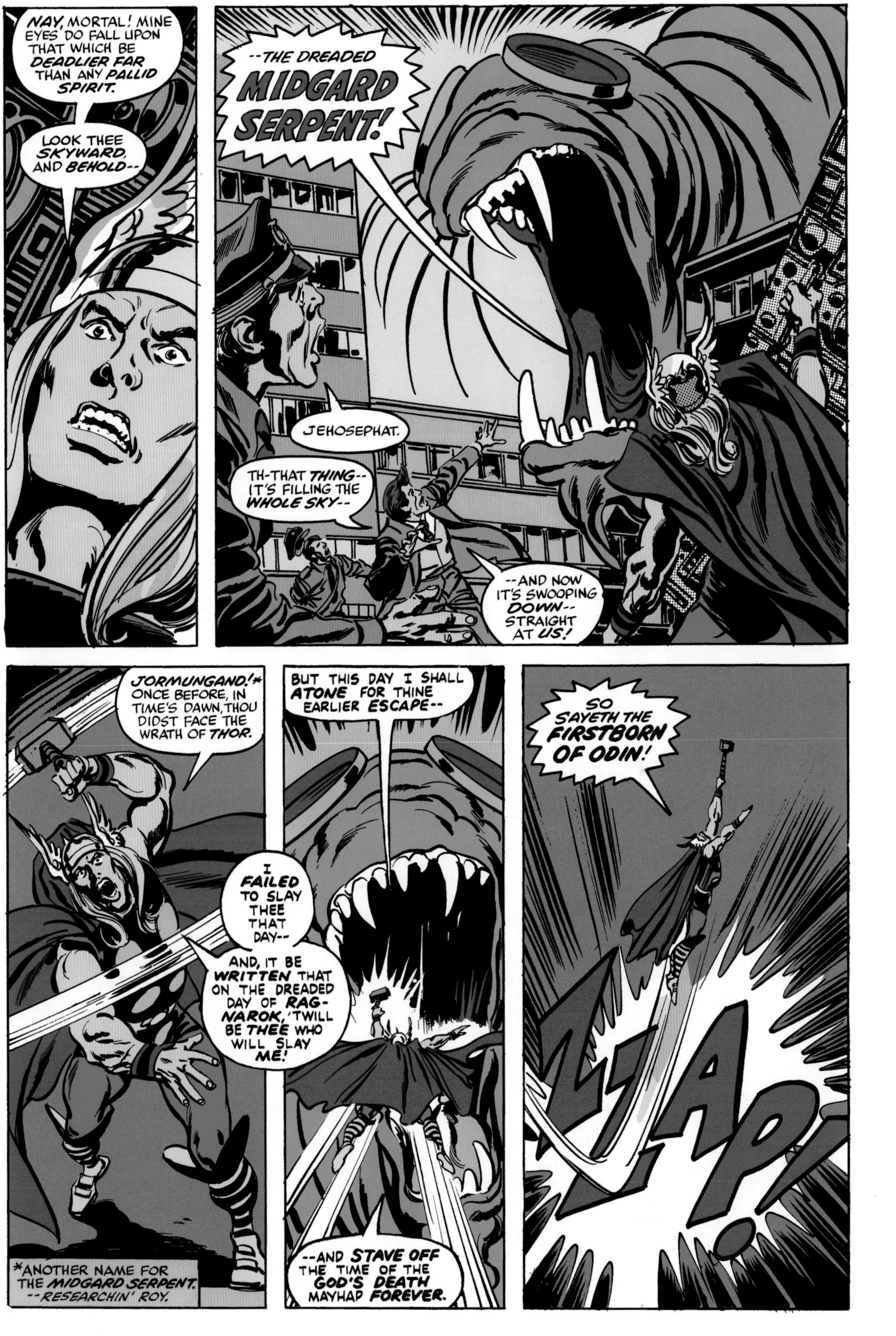
NAY, MORTAL! MINE EYES DO FALL UPON THAT WHICH BE DEADLIER FAR THAN ANY PALLID SPIRIT.
LOOK THEE SKYWARD, AND BEHOLD--
--THE DREADED MIDGARD SERPENT!
JEHOSEPHAT.
TH-THAT THING-- IT'S FILLING THE WHOLE SKY--
--AND NOW IT'S SWOOPING DOWN-- STRAIGHT AT US!
JORMUNGAND!* ONCE BEFORE, IN TIME'S DAWN, THOU DIDST FACE THE WRATH OF THOR.
*ANOTHER NAME FOR THE MIDGARD SERPENT. --RESEARCHIN' ROY.
BUT THIS DAY I SHALL ATONE FOR THINE EARLIER ESCAPE--
I FAILED TO SLAY THEE THAT DAY--
AND, IT BE WRITTEN THAT ON THE DREADED DAY OF RAG-NAROK, 'TWILL BE THEE WHO WILL SLAY ME!
--AND STAVE OFF THE TIME OF THE GOD'S DEATH MAYHAP FOREVER.
SO SAYETH THE FIRSTBORN OF ODIN!
ZZAPP!

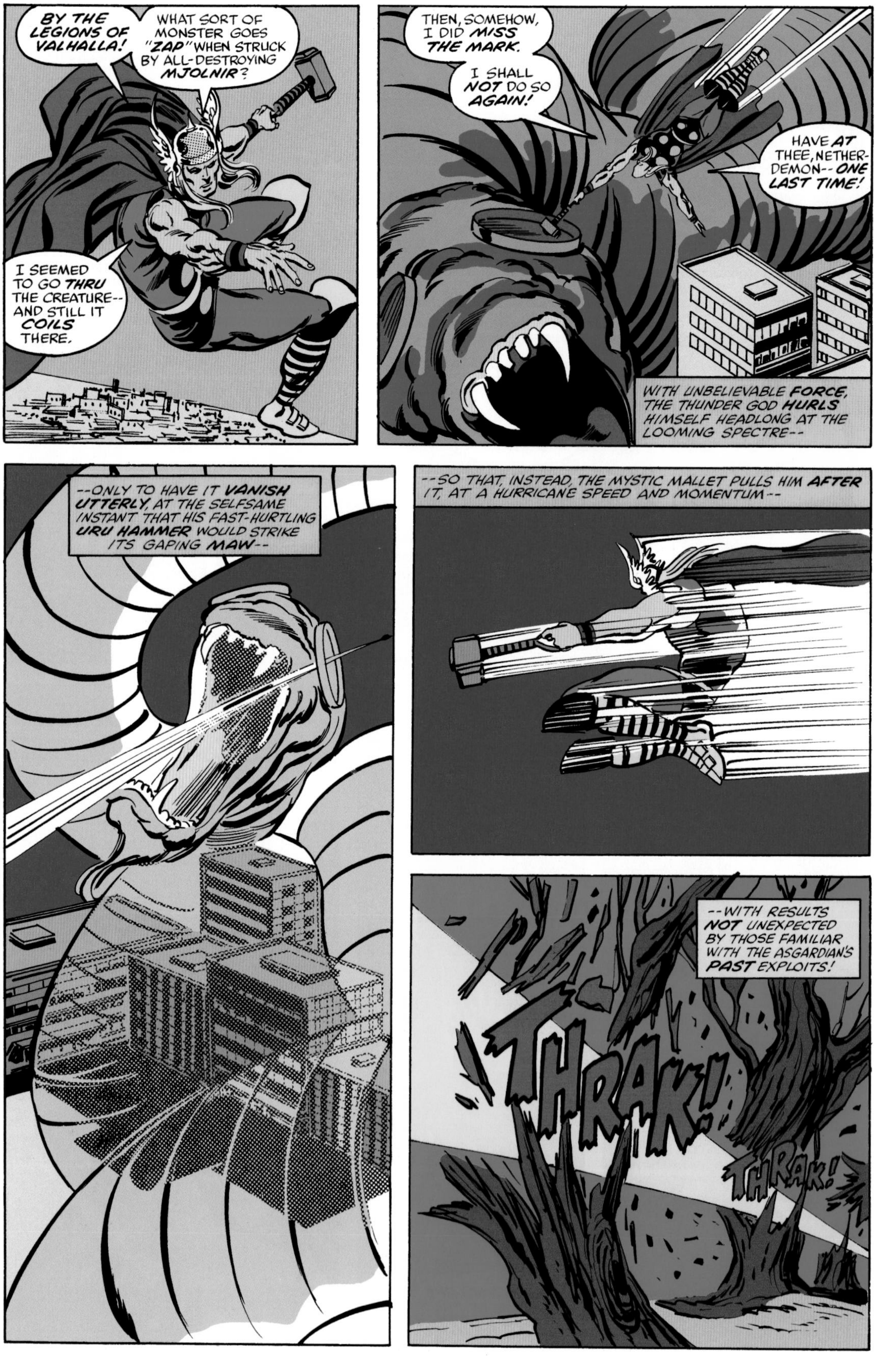

BY THE LEGIONS OF VALHALLA!
WHAT SORT OF MONSTER GOES "ZAP" WHEN STRUCK BY ALL-DESTROYING MJOLNIR?
I SEEMED TO GO THRU THE CREATURE-- AND STILL IT COILS THERE.
THEN, SOMEHOW, I DID MISS THE MARK.
I SHALL NOT DO SO AGAIN!
HAVE AT THEE, NETHER-DEMON-- ONE LAST TIME!
WITH UNBELIEVABLE FORCE, THE THUNDER GOD HURLS HIMSELF HEADLONG AT THE LOOMING SPECTRE--
--ONLY TO HAVE IT VANISH UTTERLY, AT THE SELFSAME INSTANT THAT HIS FAST-HURTLING URU HAMMER WOULD STRIKE ITS GAPING MAW--
--SO THAT, INSTEAD, THE MYSTIC MALLET PULLS HIM AFTER IT, AT A HURRICANE SPEED AND MOMENTUM--
--WITH RESULTS NOT UNEXPECTED BY THOSE FAMILIAR WITH THE ASGARDIAN'S PAST EXPLOITS!
THRAK!
THRAK!

I WOULD SUSPECT *LOKI'S* FINE HAND IN THIS, SAVE ONLY THAT HE WAS LATELY *STRIPPED* OF ALL HIS POWERS BY THE *ALL-FATHER...*

...AND SENT TO WANDER THE EARTH AS A HOME-LESS *DERELICT.* *

*ISH #267 --R.T.

AT LEAST, THIS *SECOND* TIME, JORMUNGAND DID *NOT* RE-MATERIALIZE.

WHEREVER THAT GODZILLA-TYPE WENT, HE SHOULD ONLY *STAY* THERE!

MAYHAP THE ANSWER TO *ALL* OUR QUESTIONS WILL BE FOUND IN HOLY *ASGARD.*

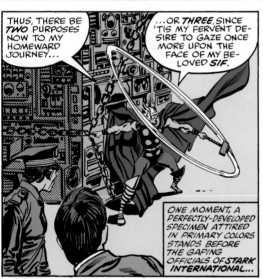

THUS, THERE BE *TWO* PURPOSES NOW TO MY HOMEWARD JOURNEY...

...OR *THREE*, SINCE 'TIS MY FERVENT DESIRE TO GAZE ONCE MORE UPON THE FACE OF MY BELOVED *SIF.*

ONE MOMENT, A PERFECTLY-DEVELOPED SPECIMEN ATTIRED IN PRIMARY COLORS STANDS BEFORE THE GAPING OFFICIALS OF *STARK INTERNATIONAL...*

THE NEXT, BOTH *HE* AND ADAMANTINE *COMPUTER* STREAK INTO THE CLOUDLESS *SKY*-- THEN OUT OF SIGHT *ENTIRELY*--

--AS THE *TRANS-DIMENSIONAL BARRIER* WHICH SEPARATES EARTH FROM THE GODLY REGIONS IS *BRIDGED...*

...IN MORE WAYS THAN *ONE.*

HO FRIEND *HEIMDALL!*

HOW FARES THE *REALM ETERNAL*...AND THY BEAUTEOUS SISTER *SIF*... IN MINE ABSENCE?

IN SOOTH, THUNDER GOD, THOU DOST EVER *STUN* ME WITH THE *SUDDENNESS* OF THINE APPEARANCES.

BY THE NINE MOTHERS WHO BORE ME!

NOT EVEN *HEIMDALL'S* SENSES CAN DETECT THY COMING, ERE THOU STANDEST ON GLEAMING *BIFROST.*

123

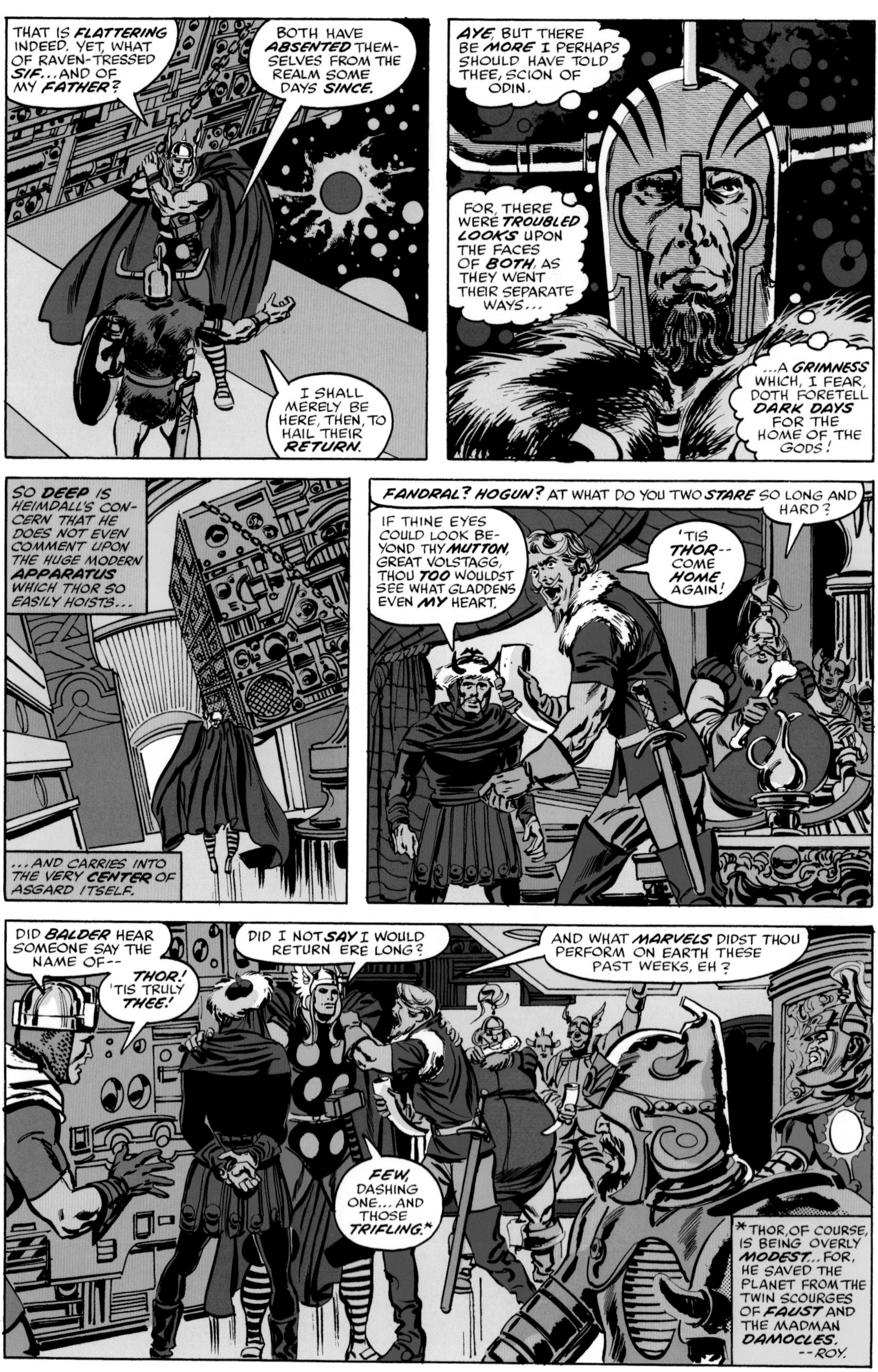

THAT IS FLATTERING INDEED. YET, WHAT OF RAVEN-TRESSED SIF...AND OF MY FATHER?
BOTH HAVE ABSENTED THEMSELVES FROM THE REALM SOME DAYS SINCE.
I SHALL MERELY BE HERE, THEN, TO HAIL THEIR RETURN.
AYE, BUT THERE BE MORE I PERHAPS SHOULD HAVE TOLD THEE, SCION OF ODIN.
FOR, THERE WERE TROUBLED LOOKS UPON THE FACES OF BOTH, AS THEY WENT THEIR SEPARATE WAYS...
...A GRIMNESS WHICH, I FEAR, DOTH FORETELL DARK DAYS FOR THE HOME OF THE GODS!
SO DEEP IS HEIMDALL'S CONCERN THAT HE DOES NOT EVEN COMMENT UPON THE HUGE MODERN APPARATUS WHICH THOR SO EASILY HOISTS...
...AND CARRIES INTO THE VERY CENTER OF ASGARD ITSELF.
FANDRAL? HOGUN? AT WHAT DO YOU TWO STARE SO LONG AND HARD?
IF THINE EYES COULD LOOK BEYOND THY MUTTON, GREAT VOLSTAGG, THOU TOO WOULDST SEE WHAT GLADDENS EVEN MY HEART.
'TIS THOR--COME HOME AGAIN!
DID BALDER HEAR SOMEONE SAY THE NAME OF--
THOR! 'TIS TRULY THEE!
DID I NOT SAY I WOULD RETURN ERE LONG?
AND WHAT MARVELS DIDST THOU PERFORM ON EARTH THESE PAST WEEKS, EH?
FEW, DASHING ONE... AND THOSE TRIFLING.*
*THOR, OF COURSE, IS BEING OVERLY MODEST... FOR, HE SAVED THE PLANET FROM THE TWIN SCOURGES OF FAUST AND THE MADMAN DAMOCLES. --ROY.

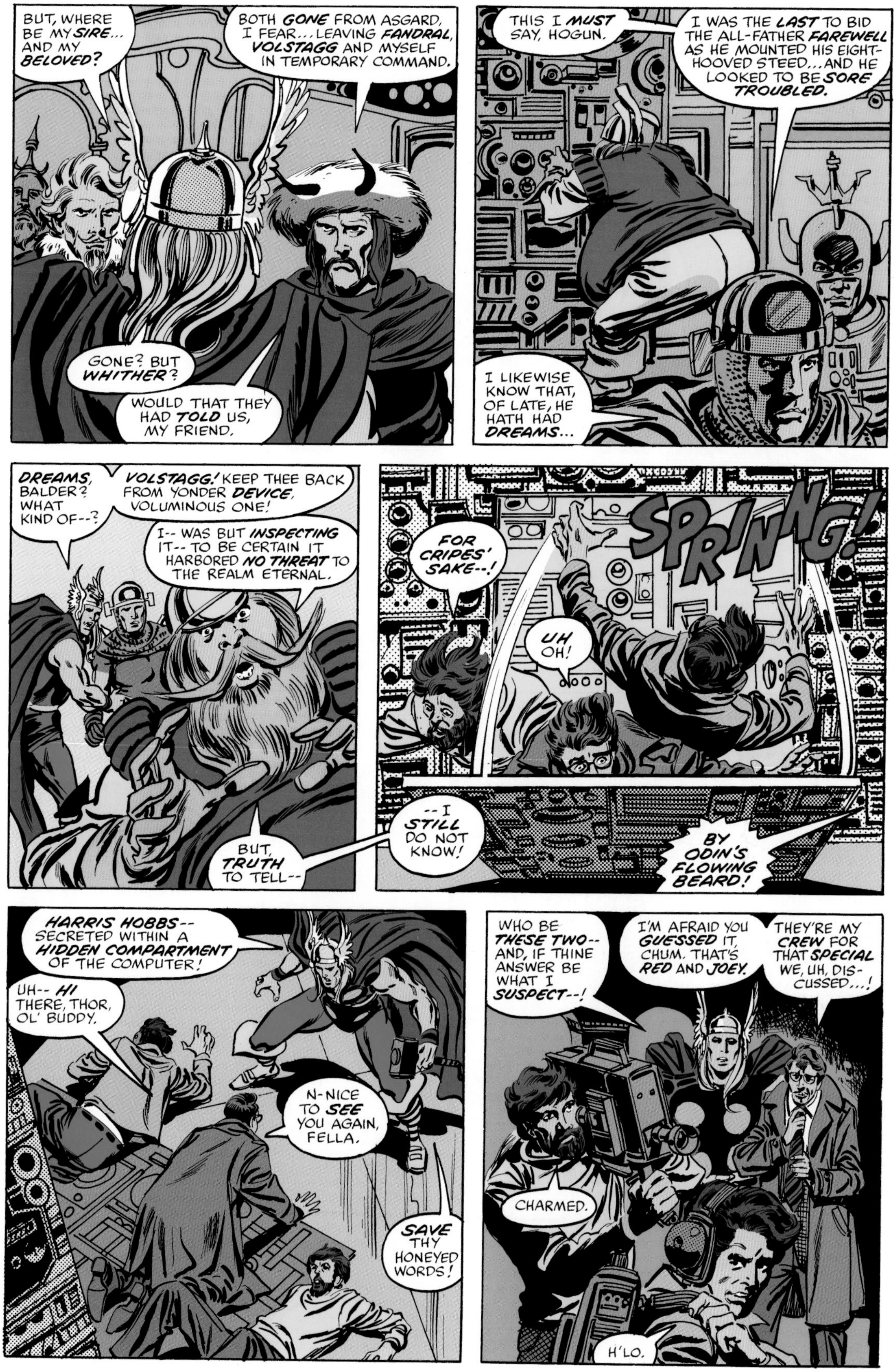
BUT, WHERE BE MY SIRE... AND MY BELOVED?
BOTH GONE FROM ASGARD, I FEAR... LEAVING FANDRAL, VOLSTAGG AND MYSELF IN TEMPORARY COMMAND.
GONE? BUT WHITHER?
WOULD THAT THEY HAD TOLD US, MY FRIEND.
THIS I MUST SAY, HOGUN.
I WAS THE LAST TO BID THE ALL-FATHER FAREWELL AS HE MOUNTED HIS EIGHT-HOOVED STEED... AND HE LOOKED TO BE SORE TROUBLED.
I LIKEWISE KNOW THAT, OF LATE, HE HATH HAD DREAMS...
DREAMS, BALDER? WHAT KIND OF--?
VOLSTAGG! KEEP THEE BACK FROM YONDER DEVICE, VOLUMINOUS ONE!
I-- WAS BUT INSPECTING IT-- TO BE CERTAIN IT HARBORED NO THREAT TO THE REALM ETERNAL.
BUT, TRUTH TO TELL--
--I STILL DO NOT KNOW!
SPRINNG!
FOR CRIPES' SAKE--!
UH OH!
BY ODIN'S FLOWING BEARD!
HARRIS HOBBS-- SECRETED WITHIN A HIDDEN COMPARTMENT OF THE COMPUTER!
UH-- HI THERE, THOR, OL' BUDDY.
N-NICE TO SEE YOU AGAIN, FELLA.
SAVE THY HONEYED WORDS!
WHO BE THESE TWO-- AND, IF THINE ANSWER BE WHAT I SUSPECT--!
I'M AFRAID YOU GUESSED IT, CHUM. THAT'S RED AND JOEY.
THEY'RE MY CREW FOR THAT SPECIAL WE, UH, DISCUSSED...!
CHARMED.
H'LO.

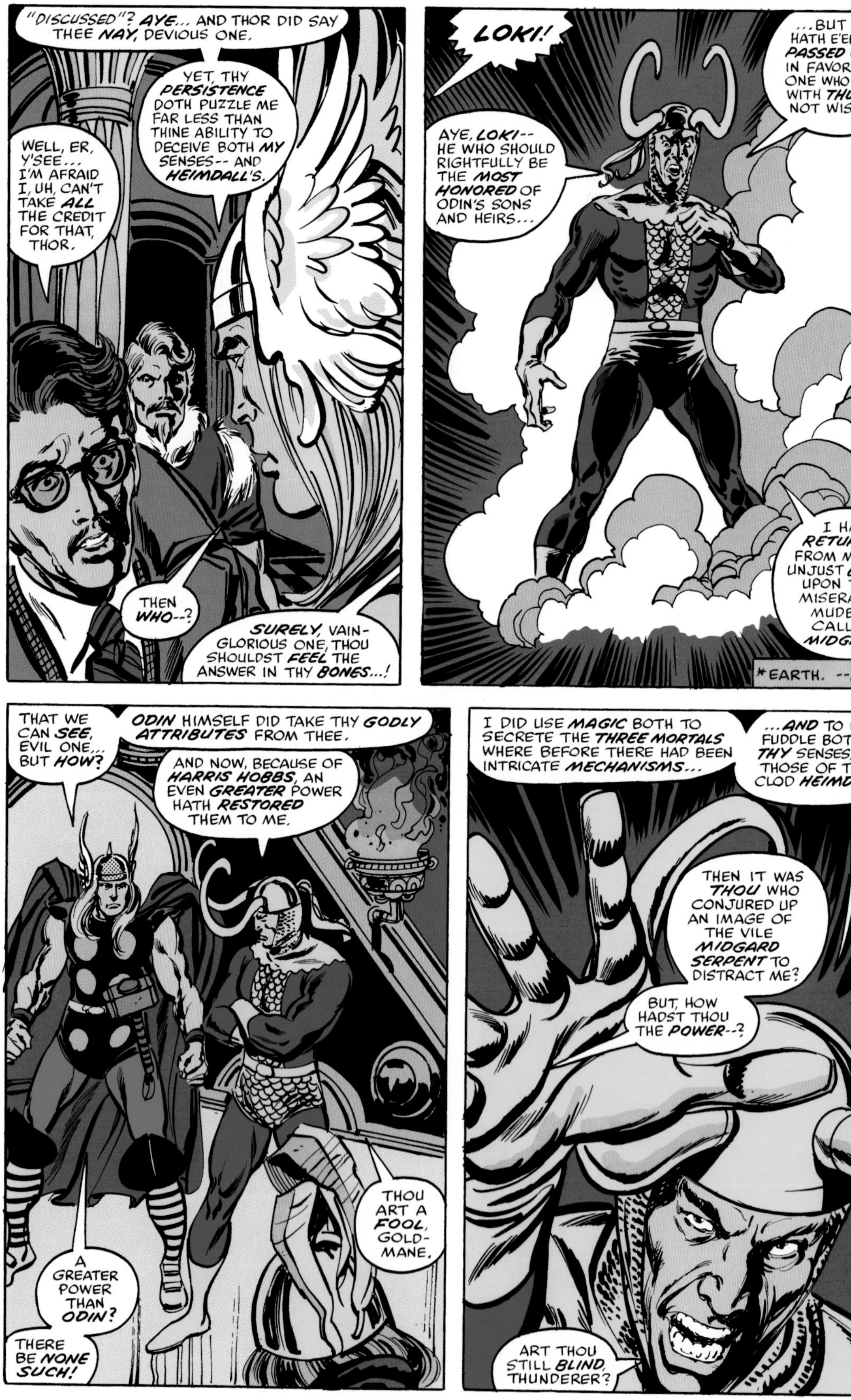
"DISCUSSED"? AYE... AND THOR DID SAY THEE NAY, DEVIOUS ONE.
YET, THY PERSISTENCE DOTH PUZZLE ME FAR LESS THAN THINE ABILITY TO DECEIVE BOTH MY SENSES-- AND HEIMDALL'S.
WELL, ER, Y'SEE... I'M AFRAID I, UH, CAN'T TAKE ALL THE CREDIT FOR THAT, THOR.
THEN WHO--?
SURELY, VAIN-GLORIOUS ONE, THOU SHOULDST FEEL THE ANSWER IN THY BONES...!
LOKI!
AYE, LOKI-- HE WHO SHOULD RIGHTFULLY BE THE MOST HONORED OF ODIN'S SONS AND HEIRS...
...BUT WHO HATH E'ER BEEN PASSED OVER, IN FAVOR OF ONE WHO SPEAKS WITH THUNDER, NOT WISDOM.
I HAVE RETURNED FROM MINE UNJUST EXILE UPON THE MISERABLE MUDBALL CALLED MIDGARD.*
*EARTH. --ROY.
THAT WE CAN SEE, EVIL ONE... BUT HOW?
ODIN HIMSELF DID TAKE THY GODLY ATTRIBUTES FROM THEE.
AND NOW, BECAUSE OF HARRIS HOBBS, AN EVEN GREATER POWER HATH RESTORED THEM TO ME.
A GREATER POWER THAN ODIN?
THERE BE NONE SUCH!
THOU ART A FOOL, GOLD-MANE.
I DID USE MAGIC BOTH TO SECRETE THE THREE MORTALS WHERE BEFORE THERE HAD BEEN INTRICATE MECHANISMS...
...AND TO BE-FUDDLE BOTH THY SENSES, AND THOSE OF THAT CLOD HEIMDALL.
THEN IT WAS THOU WHO CONJURED UP AN IMAGE OF THE VILE MIDGARD SERPENT TO DISTRACT ME?
BUT, HOW HADST THOU THE POWER--?
ART THOU STILL BLIND, THUNDERER?

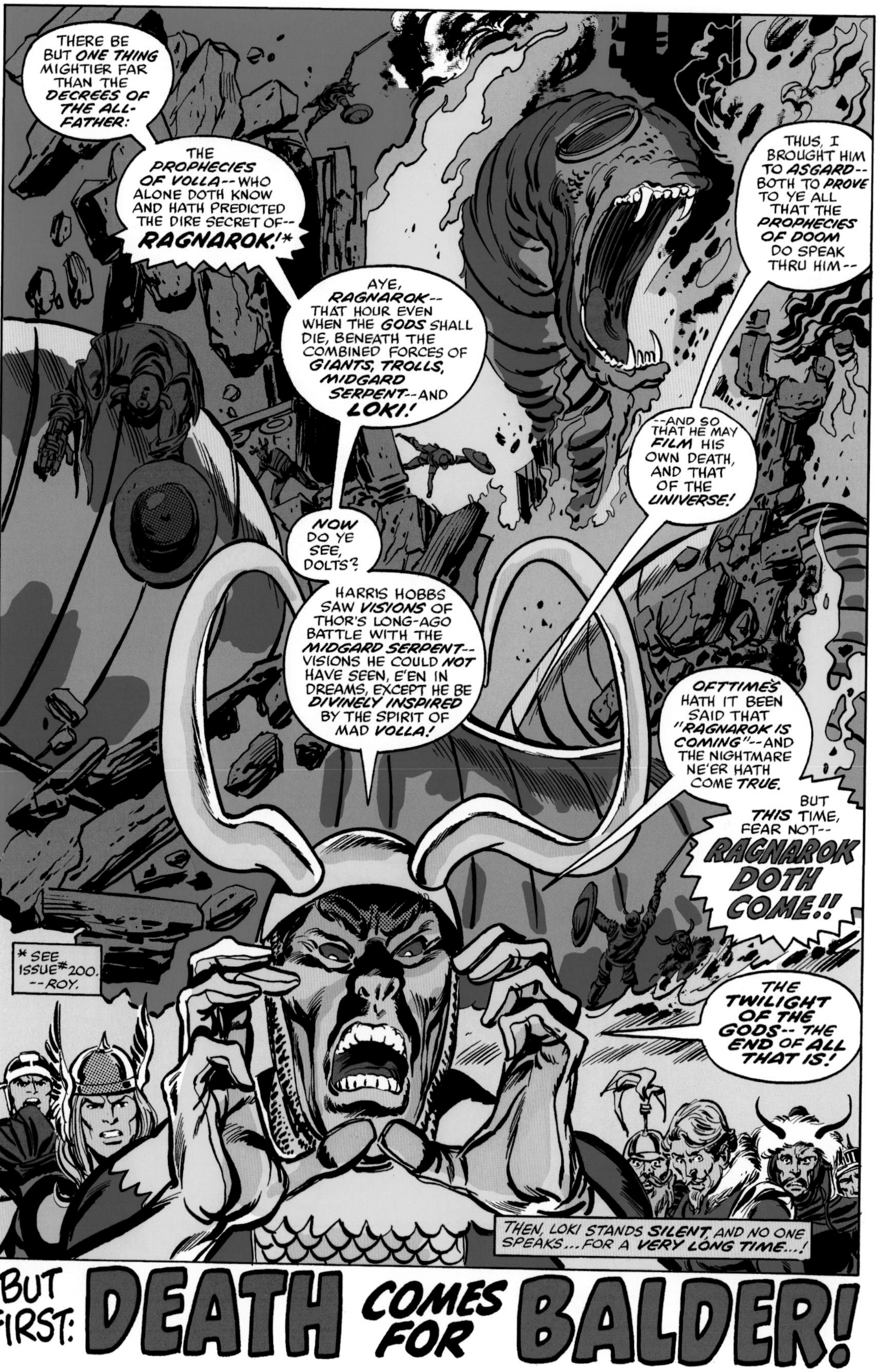

THERE BE BUT ONE THING MIGHTIER FAR THAN THE DECREES OF THE ALL-FATHER:
THE PROPHECIES OF VOLLA--WHO ALONE DOTH KNOW AND HATH PREDICTED THE DIRE SECRET OF--RAGNAROK!*
AYE, RAGNAROK--THAT HOUR EVEN WHEN THE GODS SHALL DIE, BENEATH THE COMBINED FORCES OF GIANTS, TROLLS, MIDGARD SERPENT--AND LOKI!
THUS, I BROUGHT HIM TO ASGARD--BOTH TO PROVE TO YE ALL THAT THE PROPHECIES OF DOOM DO SPEAK THRU HIM--
--AND SO THAT HE MAY FILM HIS OWN DEATH, AND THAT OF THE UNIVERSE!
NOW DO YE SEE, DOLTS?
HARRIS HOBBS SAW VISIONS OF THOR'S LONG-AGO BATTLE WITH THE MIDGARD SERPENT--VISIONS HE COULD NOT HAVE SEEN, E'EN IN DREAMS, EXCEPT HE BE DIVINELY INSPIRED BY THE SPIRIT OF MAD VOLLA!
OFTTIMES HATH IT BEEN SAID THAT "RAGNAROK IS COMING"--AND THE NIGHTMARE NE'ER HATH COME TRUE.
BUT THIS TIME, FEAR NOT--RAGNAROK DOTH COME!!
THE TWILIGHT OF THE GODS--THE END OF ALL THAT IS!
* SEE ISSUE #200. --ROY.
THEN, LOKI STANDS SILENT, AND NO ONE SPEAKS... FOR A VERY LONG TIME...!
BUT FIRST: DEATH COMES FOR BALDER!

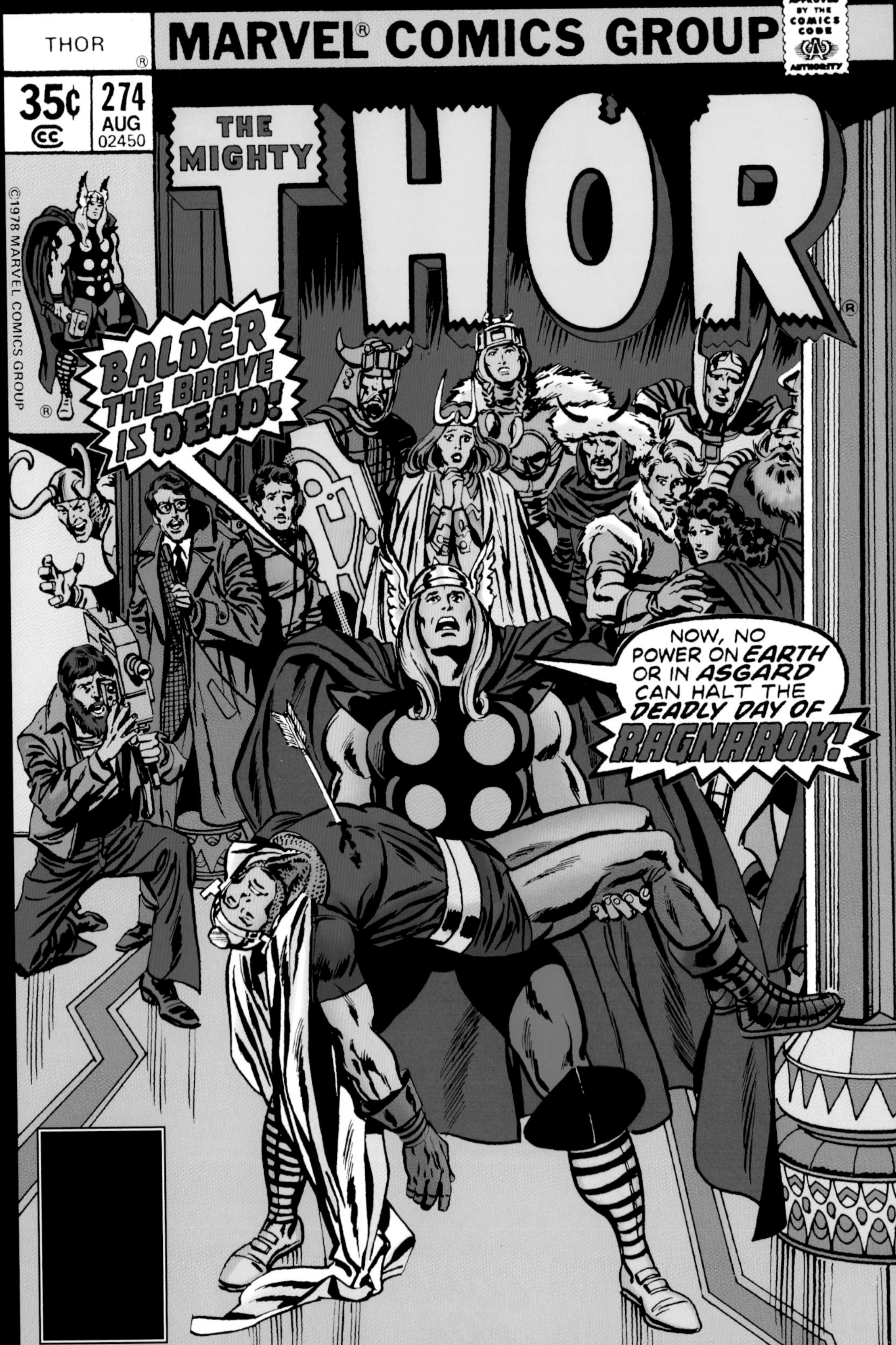
THOR
MARVEL® COMICS GROUP
APPROVED BY THE COMICS CODE AUTHORITY
35¢ CC
274 AUG 02450
THE MIGHTY THOR®
©1978 MARVEL COMICS GROUP
BALDER THE BRAVE IS DEAD!
NOW, NO POWER ON EARTH OR IN ASGARD CAN HALT THE DEADLY DAY OF RAGNAROK!

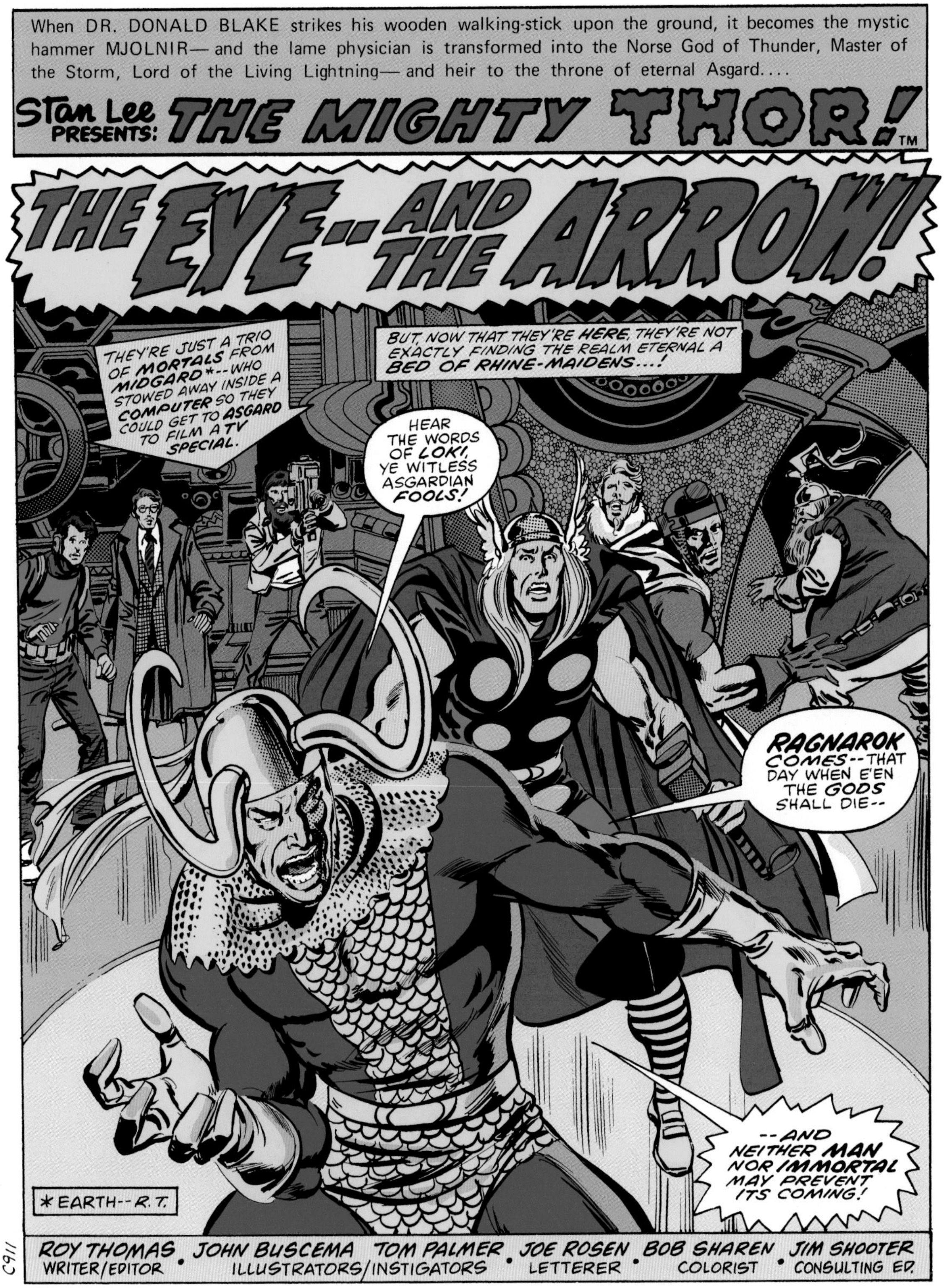
When DR. DONALD BLAKE strikes his wooden walking-stick upon the ground, it becomes the mystic hammer MJOLNIR— and the lame physician is transformed into the Norse God of Thunder, Master of the Storm, Lord of the Living Lightning— and heir to the throne of eternal Asgard....
Stan Lee PRESENTS: THE MIGHTY THOR! TM
THE EYE.. AND THE ARROW!
THEY'RE JUST A TRIO OF MORTALS FROM MIDGARD*--WHO STOWED AWAY INSIDE A COMPUTER SO THEY COULD GET TO ASGARD TO FILM A TV SPECIAL.
BUT, NOW THAT THEY'RE HERE, THEY'RE NOT EXACTLY FINDING THE REALM ETERNAL A BED OF RHINE-MAIDENS...!
HEAR THE WORDS OF LOKI, YE WITLESS ASGARDIAN FOOLS!
RAGNAROK COMES--THAT DAY WHEN E'EN THE GODS SHALL DIE--
--AND NEITHER MAN NOR IMMORTAL MAY PREVENT ITS COMING!
*EARTH-- R.T.
ROY THOMAS WRITER/EDITOR • JOHN BUSCEMA TOM PALMER ILLUSTRATORS/INSTIGATORS • JOE ROSEN LETTERER • BOB SHAREN COLORIST • JIM SHOOTER CONSULTING ED.

INGLORIOUS *CHURL!* CURSED BE THE DAY THAT THE *ALL-FATHER* DID UNWISELY TAKE THEE TO HIS *BOSOM!*

IN THAT HOUR, HE DID NURTURE THE BASEST OF *VIPERS!*

I BUT SPEAK THE *TRUTH,* DEAR "BROTHER"...

I KNOW FULL WELL THAT *RAGNAROK*-- THE *TWILIGHT OF THE GODS*-- HATH NEARLY OCCURRED *SEVERAL* TIMES IN THE PAST--

--WHEN *ODIN* SLEPT, OR VANISHED-- OR THE *ODIN-SWORD* WAS NIGH PULLED FROM ITS SCABBARD.

THIS TIME, HOWEVER, ASGARD BE *TRULY* DOOMED-- I FEEL IT IN MY *MARROW*--

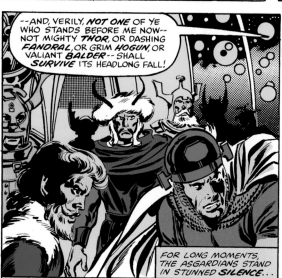

--AND, VERILY, *NOT ONE* OF YE WHO STANDS BEFORE ME NOW-- NOT MIGHTY *THOR,* OR DASHING *FANDRAL,* OR GRIM *HOGUN,* OR VALIANT *BALDER*-- SHALL *SURVIVE* ITS HEADLONG FALL!

FOR LONG MOMENTS, THE ASGARDIANS STAND IN STUNNED *SILENCE*...

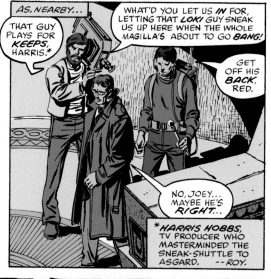

AS, NEARBY...

THAT GUY PLAYS FOR *KEEPS,* HARRIS.*

WHAT'D YOU LET US *IN* FOR, LETTING THAT *LOKI* GUY SNEAK US UP HERE WHEN THE WHOLE MAGILLA'S ABOUT TO GO *BANG!*

GET OFF HIS *BACK,* RED.

NO, JOEY... MAYBE HE'S *RIGHT*...

*HARRIS HOBBS, TV PRODUCER WHO MASTERMINDED THE SNEAK-SHUTTLE TO ASGARD. --ROY.

I'VE BEEN DOING SOME *CRAMMING* ON *NORSE MYTHOLOGY,* SO MY *SPECIAL* WOULD BE THE BIGGEST THING TO HIT THE TUBE SINCE "*ROOTS*"...

...AND *AFRAID* I'M STARTING TO GET LOKI'S *DRIFT.*

"*RAGNAROK* IS JUST WHAT HE CALLED IT: THE *TWILIGHT* OF THE GODS...

"...THE DAY WHEN ASGARD *TOPPLES*...AND THE NORSE GODS *PERISH!*

"IT WAS *FORE-TOLD* IN NORSE LEGEND HUNDREDS OF YEARS AGO-- PERHAPS *THOUSANDS.*"

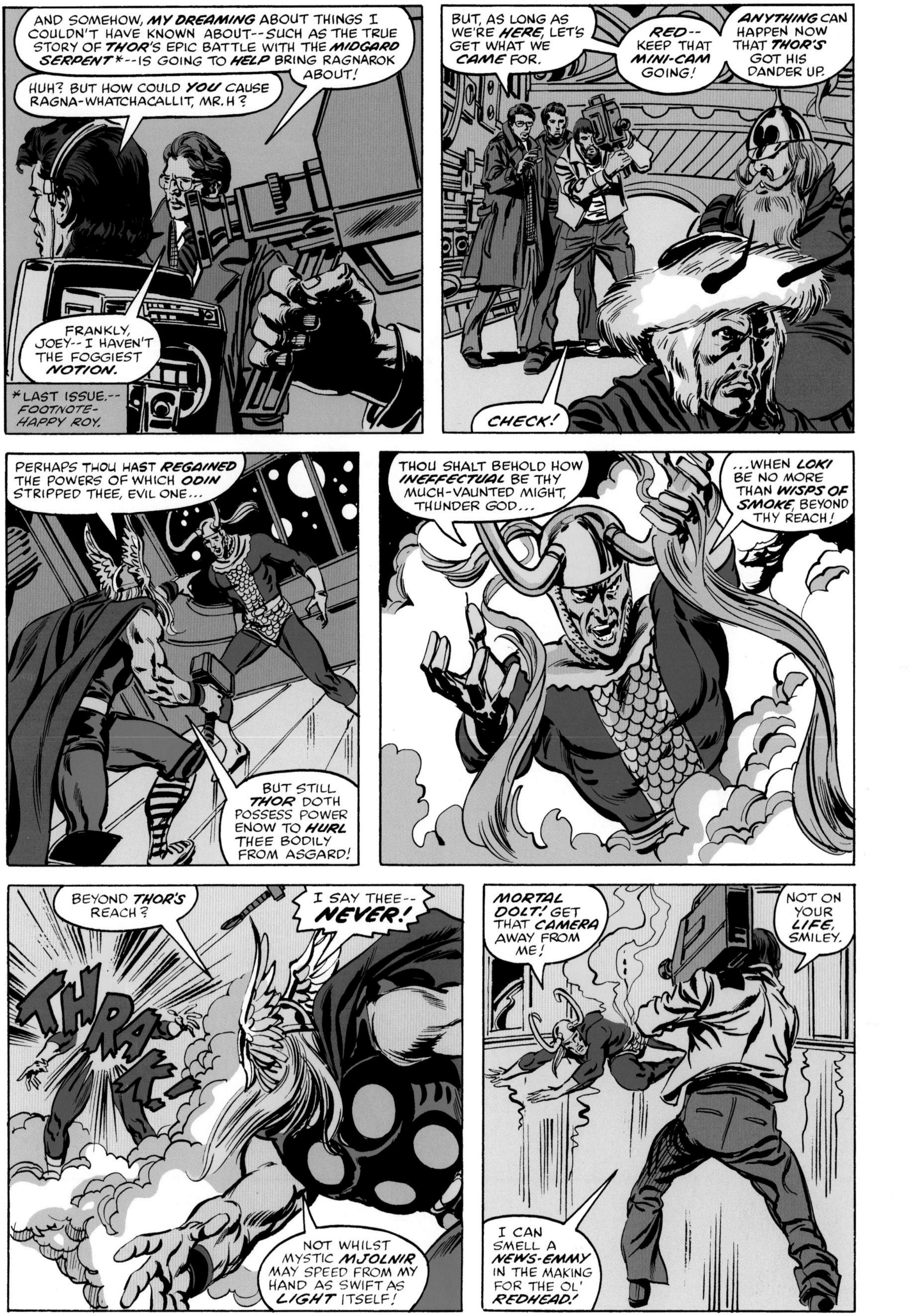
AND SOMEHOW, MY DREAMING ABOUT THINGS I COULDN'T HAVE KNOWN ABOUT--SUCH AS THE TRUE STORY OF THOR'S EPIC BATTLE WITH THE MIDGARD SERPENT*--IS GOING TO HELP BRING RAGNAROK ABOUT!
HUH? BUT HOW COULD YOU CAUSE RAGNA-WHATCHACALLIT, MR. H?
FRANKLY, JOEY-- I HAVEN'T THE FOGGIEST NOTION.
*LAST ISSUE.--FOOTNOTE-HAPPY ROY.
BUT, AS LONG AS WE'RE HERE, LET'S GET WHAT WE CAME FOR.
RED-- KEEP THAT MINI-CAM GOING!
ANYTHING CAN HAPPEN NOW THAT THOR'S GOT HIS DANDER UP.
CHECK!
PERHAPS THOU HAST REGAINED THE POWERS OF WHICH ODIN STRIPPED THEE, EVIL ONE...
BUT STILL THOR DOTH POSSESS POWER ENOW TO HURL THEE BODILY FROM ASGARD!
THOU SHALT BEHOLD HOW INEFFECTUAL BE THY MUCH-VAUNTED MIGHT, THUNDER GOD...
...WHEN LOKI BE NO MORE THAN WISPS OF SMOKE, BEYOND THY REACH!
BEYOND THOR'S REACH?
I SAY THEE-- NEVER!
THRAK-
NOT WHILST MYSTIC MJOLNIR MAY SPEED FROM MY HAND AS SWIFT AS LIGHT ITSELF!
MORTAL DOLT! GET THAT CAMERA AWAY FROM ME!
NOT ON YOUR LIFE, SMILEY.
I CAN SMELL A NEWS-EMMY IN THE MAKING FOR THE OL' REDHEAD!

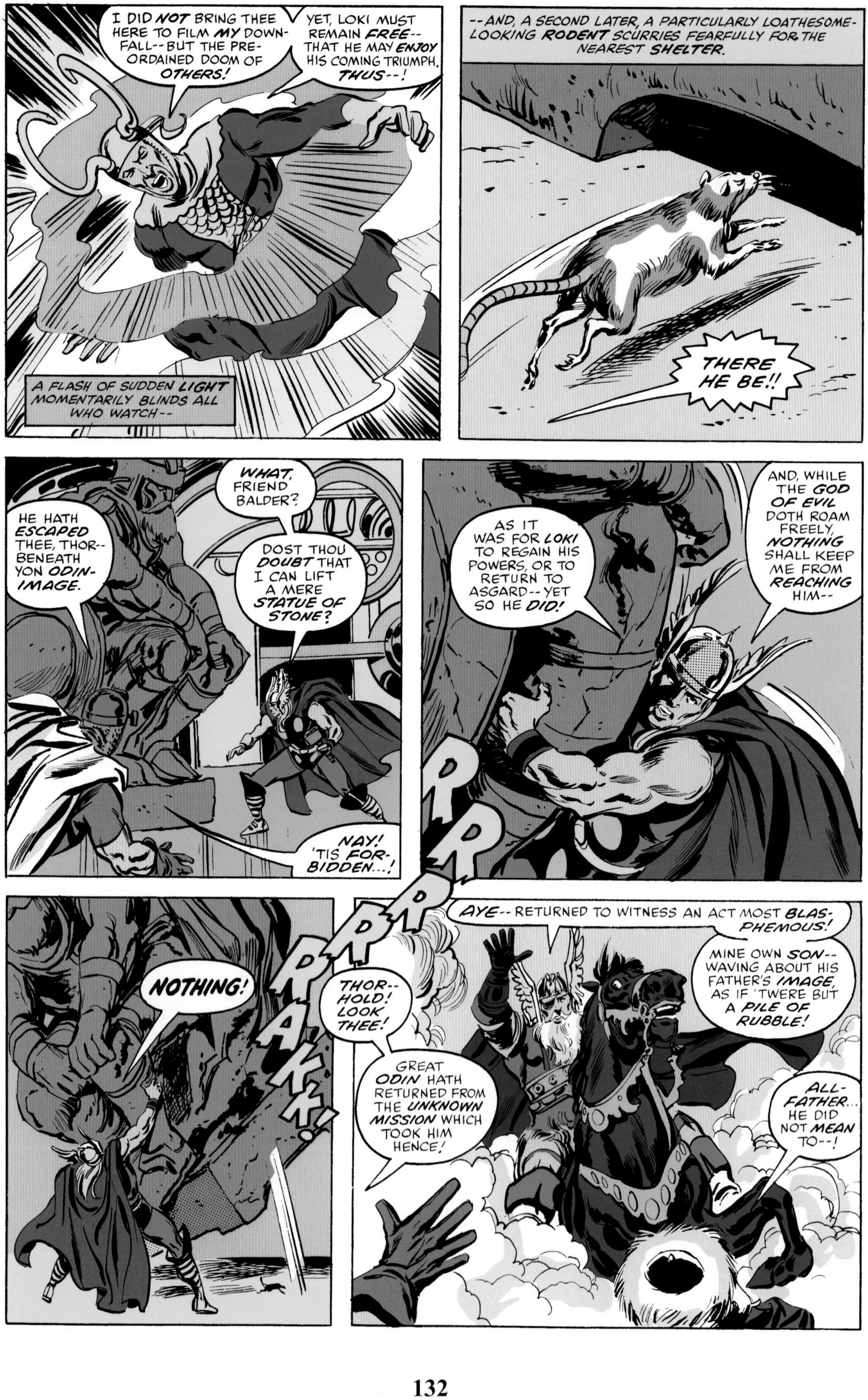

I DID NOT BRING THEE HERE TO FILM MY DOWNFALL--BUT THE PRE-ORDAINED DOOM OF OTHERS!
YET, LOKI MUST REMAIN FREE--THAT HE MAY ENJOY HIS COMING TRIUMPH. THUS--!
A FLASH OF SUDDEN LIGHT MOMENTARILY BLINDS ALL WHO WATCH--
--AND, A SECOND LATER, A PARTICULARLY LOATHESOME-LOOKING RODENT SCURRIES FEARFULLY FOR THE NEAREST SHELTER.
THERE HE BE!!
HE HATH ESCAPED THEE, THOR--BENEATH YON ODIN-IMAGE.
WHAT, FRIEND BALDER?
DOST THOU DOUBT THAT I CAN LIFT A MERE STATUE OF STONE?
NAY! 'TIS FOR-BIDDEN...!
AS IT WAS FOR LOKI TO REGAIN HIS POWERS, OR TO RETURN TO ASGARD--YET SO HE DID!
AND, WHILE THE GOD OF EVIL DOTH ROAM FREELY, NOTHING SHALL KEEP ME FROM REACHING HIM--
RRRRRAKK!
NOTHING!
THOR--HOLD! LOOK THEE!
GREAT ODIN HATH RETURNED FROM THE UNKNOWN MISSION WHICH TOOK HIM HENCE!
AYE--RETURNED TO WITNESS AN ACT MOST BLASPHEMOUS!
MINE OWN SON--WAVING ABOUT HIS FATHER'S IMAGE, AS IF 'TWERE BUT A PILE OF RUBBLE!
ALL-FATHER... HE DID NOT MEAN TO--!

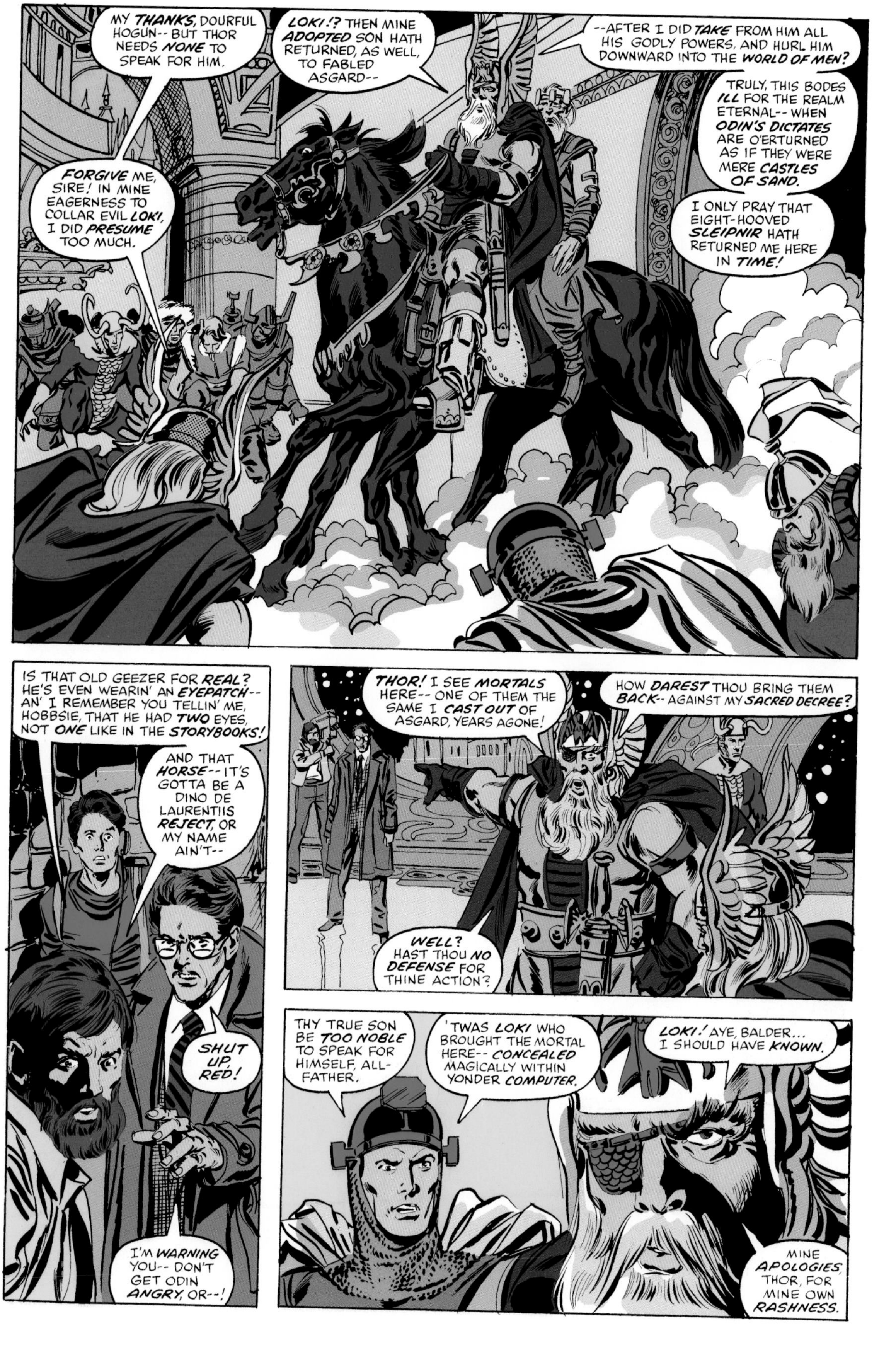
MY THANKS, DOURFUL HOGUN-- BUT THOR NEEDS NONE TO SPEAK FOR HIM.
LOKI!? THEN MINE ADOPTED SON HATH RETURNED, AS WELL, TO FABLED ASGARD--
--AFTER I DID TAKE FROM HIM ALL HIS GODLY POWERS, AND HURL HIM DOWNWARD INTO THE WORLD OF MEN?
FORGIVE ME, SIRE! IN MINE EAGERNESS TO COLLAR EVIL LOKI, I DID PRESUME TOO MUCH.
TRULY, THIS BODES ILL FOR THE REALM ETERNAL-- WHEN ODIN'S DICTATES ARE O'ERTURNED AS IF THEY WERE MERE CASTLES OF SAND.
I ONLY PRAY THAT EIGHT-HOOVED SLEIPNIR HATH RETURNED ME HERE IN TIME!
IS THAT OLD GEEZER FOR REAL? HE'S EVEN WEARIN' AN EYEPATCH-- AN' I REMEMBER YOU TELLIN' ME, HOBBSIE, THAT HE HAD TWO EYES, NOT ONE LIKE IN THE STORYBOOKS!
AND THAT HORSE-- IT'S GOTTA BE A DINO DE LAURENTIIS REJECT, OR MY NAME AIN'T--
SHUT UP, RED!
I'M WARNING YOU-- DON'T GET ODIN ANGRY, OR--!
THOR! I SEE MORTALS HERE-- ONE OF THEM THE SAME I CAST OUT OF ASGARD, YEARS AGONE!
HOW DAREST THOU BRING THEM BACK-- AGAINST MY SACRED DECREE?
WELL? HAST THOU NO DEFENSE FOR THINE ACTION?
THY TRUE SON BE TOO NOBLE TO SPEAK FOR HIMSELF, ALL-FATHER.
'TWAS LOKI WHO BROUGHT THE MORTAL HERE-- CONCEALED MAGICALLY WITHIN YONDER COMPUTER.
LOKI! AYE, BALDER... I SHOULD HAVE KNOWN.
MINE APOLOGIES, THOR, FOR MINE OWN RASHNESS.

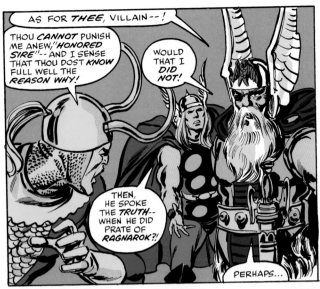

AS FOR *THEE*, VILLAIN--!

THOU *CANNOT* PUNISH ME ANEW,"*HONORED SIRE*"-- AND I SENSE THAT THOU DOST *KNOW* FULL WELL THE *REASON WHY*!

WOULD THAT I *DID NOT*!

THEN, HE SPOKE THE *TRUTH*-- WHEN HE DID PRATE OF *RAGNAROK*?!

PERHAPS...

...AND PERHAPS *NOT*.

THE *TRUTH*, ALL-FATHER! THOU *KNOWEST* I SPOKE THE TRUTH!

NAY! I *KNOW*, MAYHAP, IN MY WAY-- BUT I DO *NOT ACCEPT*!

LIST, YE GODS, TO MY *TALE*...

"WHILE I SAT, DAYS AGO, IN MY GREAT HALL, MY RAVENS *HUGIN* AND *MUNIN** DID COME TO ME, WITH WORDS AND MUSINGS MOST *DISTURBING*...

WHAT YE *SAY*, FEATHERED ONES, CANNOT-- *MUST NOT* BE!

* NAMES MEANING *THOUGHT* AND *MEMORY*. --R.

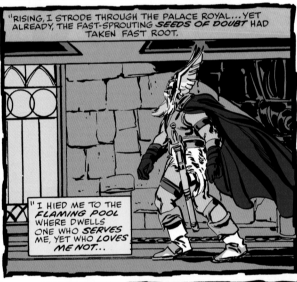

"RISING, I STRODE THROUGH THE PALACE ROYAL....YET ALREADY, THE FAST-SPROUTING *SEEDS OF DOUBT* HAD TAKEN FAST ROOT.

" I HIED ME TO THE *FLAMING POOL* WHERE DWELLS ONE WHO *SERVES* ME, YET WHO *LOVES* ME NOT...

"...AYE, EVEN *MIMIR*, THAT FIERY HEAD WHICH DOTH GUARD THE *WELL OF WISDOM*.

WHY DOST THOU *DISTURB* THE COSMIC CONTEM-PLATION OF *MIMIR*??

MY *RAVENS* HAVE TOLD ME, MIMIR, OF *EVENTS* WHICH MAY FORETELL THE *COMING OF RAGNAROK*, AT LAST--

--AND I WOULD KNOW *WHAT* I MAY DO, IF *AUGHT*, TO *PREVENT* THAT DAY OF THE GODS' OWN DOOM!

THEN KNOW THOU *SHALT*-- BUT ONLY FOR A *PRICE*!

NAME IT, AND IT SHALL BE *PAID*!

"THEN, THAT CRACK-LING VOICE SPOKE A SHUDDERFUL *PHRASE*...

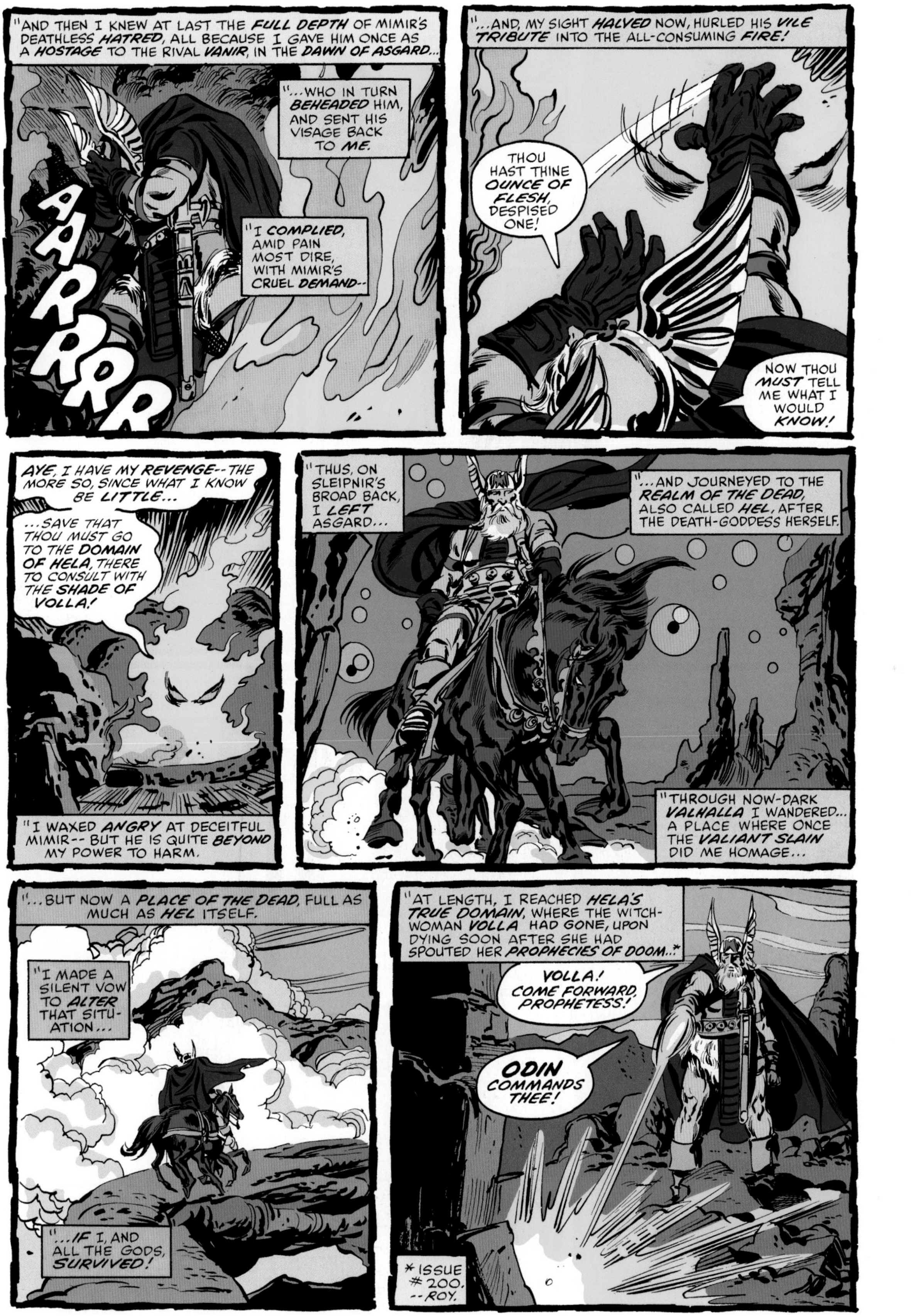
"AND THEN I KNEW AT LAST THE FULL DEPTH OF MIMIR'S DEATHLESS HATRED, ALL BECAUSE I GAVE HIM ONCE AS A HOSTAGE TO THE RIVAL VANIR, IN THE DAWN OF ASGARD...
"...WHO IN TURN BEHEADED HIM, AND SENT HIS VISAGE BACK TO ME.
"I COMPLIED, AMID PAIN MOST DIRE, WITH MIMIR'S CRUEL DEMAND--
AARRRR
"...AND, MY SIGHT HALVED NOW, HURLED HIS VILE TRIBUTE INTO THE ALL-CONSUMING FIRE!
THOU HAST THINE OUNCE OF FLESH, DESPISED ONE!
NOW THOU MUST TELL ME WHAT I WOULD KNOW!
AYE, I HAVE MY REVENGE--THE MORE SO, SINCE WHAT I KNOW BE LITTLE...
...SAVE THAT THOU MUST GO TO THE DOMAIN OF HELA, THERE TO CONSULT WITH THE SHADE OF VOLLA!
"I WAXED ANGRY AT DECEITFUL MIMIR-- BUT HE IS QUITE BEYOND MY POWER TO HARM.
"THUS, ON SLEIPNIR'S BROAD BACK, I LEFT ASGARD...
"...AND JOURNEYED TO THE REALM OF THE DEAD, ALSO CALLED HEL, AFTER THE DEATH-GODDESS HERSELF.
"THROUGH NOW-DARK VALHALLA I WANDERED... A PLACE WHERE ONCE THE VALIANT SLAIN DID ME HOMAGE...
"...BUT NOW A PLACE OF THE DEAD, FULL AS MUCH AS HEL ITSELF.
"I MADE A SILENT VOW TO ALTER THAT SITU-ATION...
"...IF I, AND ALL THE GODS, SURVIVED!
"AT LENGTH, I REACHED HELA'S TRUE DOMAIN, WHERE THE WITCH-WOMAN VOLLA HAD GONE, UPON DYING SOON AFTER SHE HAD SPOUTED HER PROPHECIES OF DOOM...*
VOLLA! COME FORWARD, PROPHETESS!
ODIN COMMANDS THEE!
*ISSUE #200. --ROY.

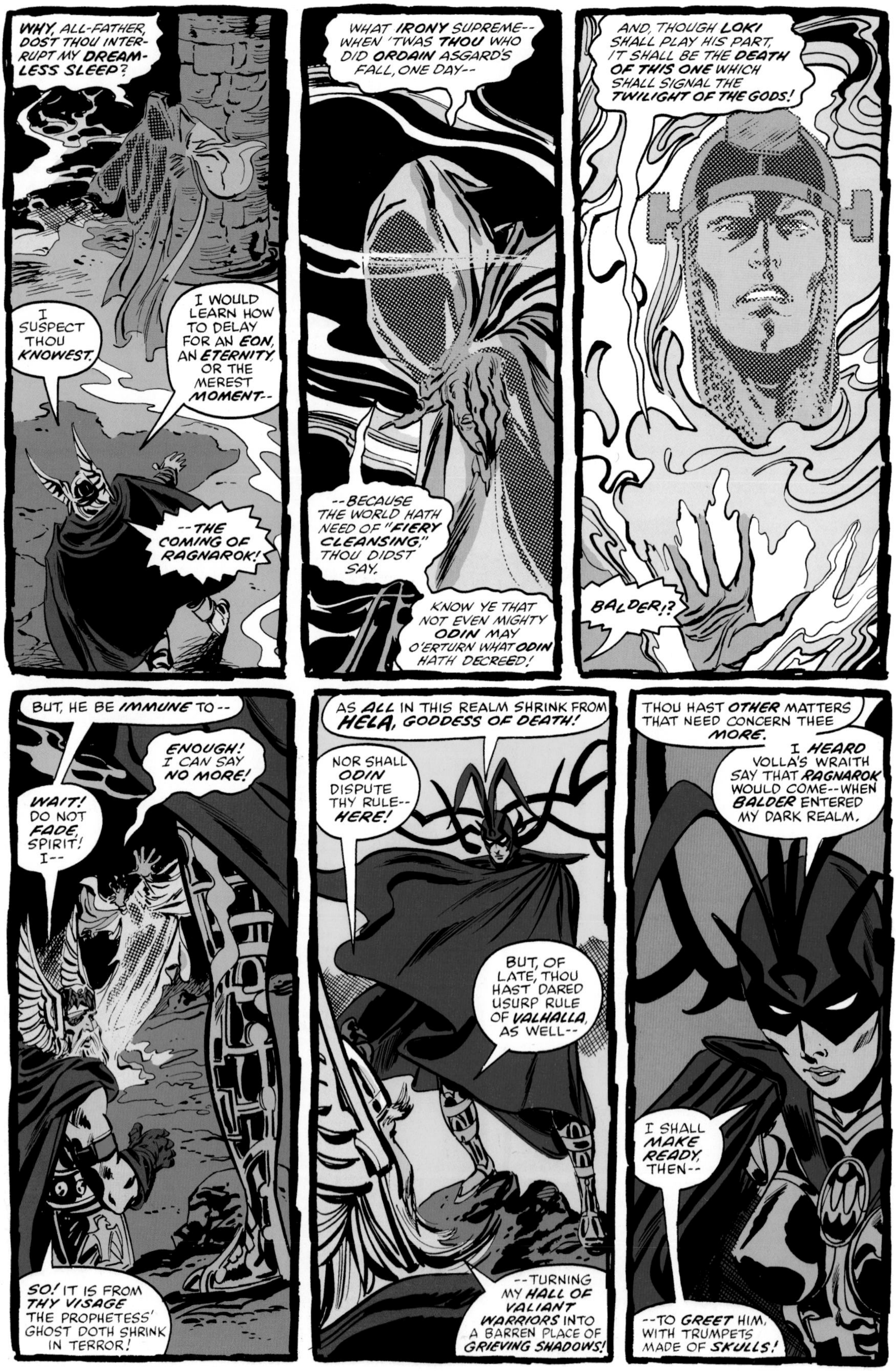
WHY, ALL-FATHER, DOST THOU INTERRUPT MY DREAMLESS SLEEP?
I SUSPECT THOU KNOWEST.
I WOULD LEARN HOW TO DELAY FOR AN EON, AN ETERNITY, OR THE MEREST MOMENT--
--THE COMING OF RAGNAROK!
WHAT IRONY SUPREME-- WHEN 'TWAS THOU WHO DID ORDAIN ASGARD'S FALL, ONE DAY--
--BECAUSE THE WORLD HATH NEED OF "FIERY CLEANSING," THOU DIDST SAY.
KNOW YE THAT NOT EVEN MIGHTY ODIN MAY O'ERTURN WHAT ODIN HATH DECREED!
AND, THOUGH LOKI SHALL PLAY HIS PART, IT SHALL BE THE DEATH OF THIS ONE WHICH SHALL SIGNAL THE TWILIGHT OF THE GODS!
BALDER!?
BUT, HE BE IMMUNE TO--
ENOUGH! I CAN SAY NO MORE!
WAIT! DO NOT FADE, SPIRIT! I--
SO! IT IS FROM THY VISAGE THE PROPHETESS' GHOST DOTH SHRINK IN TERROR!
AS ALL IN THIS REALM SHRINK FROM HELA, GODDESS OF DEATH!
NOR SHALL ODIN DISPUTE THY RULE-- HERE!
BUT, OF LATE, THOU HAST DARED USURP RULE OF VALHALLA, AS WELL--
--TURNING MY HALL OF VALIANT WARRIORS INTO A BARREN PLACE OF GRIEVING SHADOWS!
THOU HAST OTHER MATTERS THAT NEED CONCERN THEE MORE.
I HEARD VOLLA'S WRAITH SAY THAT RAGNAROK WOULD COME--WHEN BALDER ENTERED MY DARK REALM.
I SHALL MAKE READY, THEN--
--TO GREET HIM, WITH TRUMPETS MADE OF SKULLS!

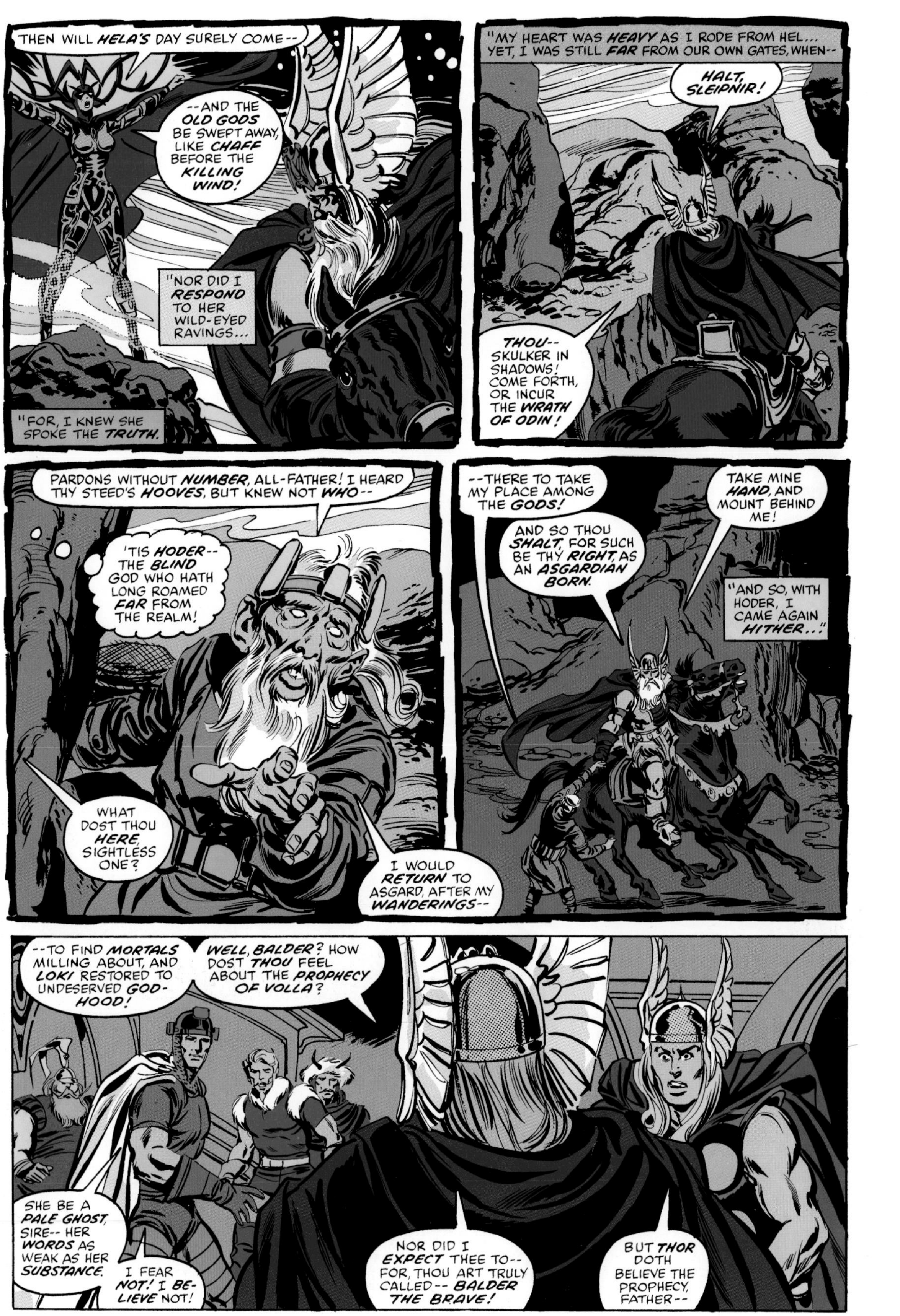
THEN WILL HELA'S DAY SURELY COME--
--AND THE OLD GODS BE SWEPT AWAY, LIKE CHAFF BEFORE THE KILLING WIND!
"NOR DID I RESPOND TO HER WILD-EYED RAVINGS...
"FOR, I KNEW SHE SPOKE THE TRUTH.
"MY HEART WAS HEAVY AS I RODE FROM HEL... YET, I WAS STILL FAR FROM OUR OWN GATES, WHEN--
HALT, SLEIPNIR!
THOU-- SKULKER IN SHADOWS! COME FORTH, OR INCUR THE WRATH OF ODIN!
PARDONS WITHOUT NUMBER, ALL-FATHER! I HEARD THY STEED'S HOOVES, BUT KNEW NOT WHO--
'TIS HODER-- THE BLIND GOD WHO HATH LONG ROAMED FAR FROM THE REALM!
WHAT DOST THOU HERE, SIGHTLESS ONE?
I WOULD RETURN TO ASGARD, AFTER MY WANDERINGS--
--THERE TO TAKE MY PLACE AMONG THE GODS!
AND SO THOU SHALT, FOR SUCH BE THY RIGHT, AS AN ASGARDIAN BORN.
TAKE MINE HAND, AND MOUNT BEHIND ME!
"AND SO, WITH HODER, I CAME AGAIN HITHER..."
--TO FIND MORTALS MILLING ABOUT, AND LOKI RESTORED TO UNDESERVED GOD-HOOD!
WELL, BALDER? HOW DOST THOU FEEL ABOUT THE PROPHECY OF VOLLA?
SHE BE A PALE GHOST, SIRE-- HER WORDS AS WEAK AS HER SUBSTANCE.
I FEAR NOT! I BE-LIEVE NOT!
NOR DID I EXPECT THEE TO-- FOR, THOU ART TRULY CALLED-- BALDER THE BRAVE!
BUT THOR DOTH BELIEVE THE PROPHECY, FATHER--

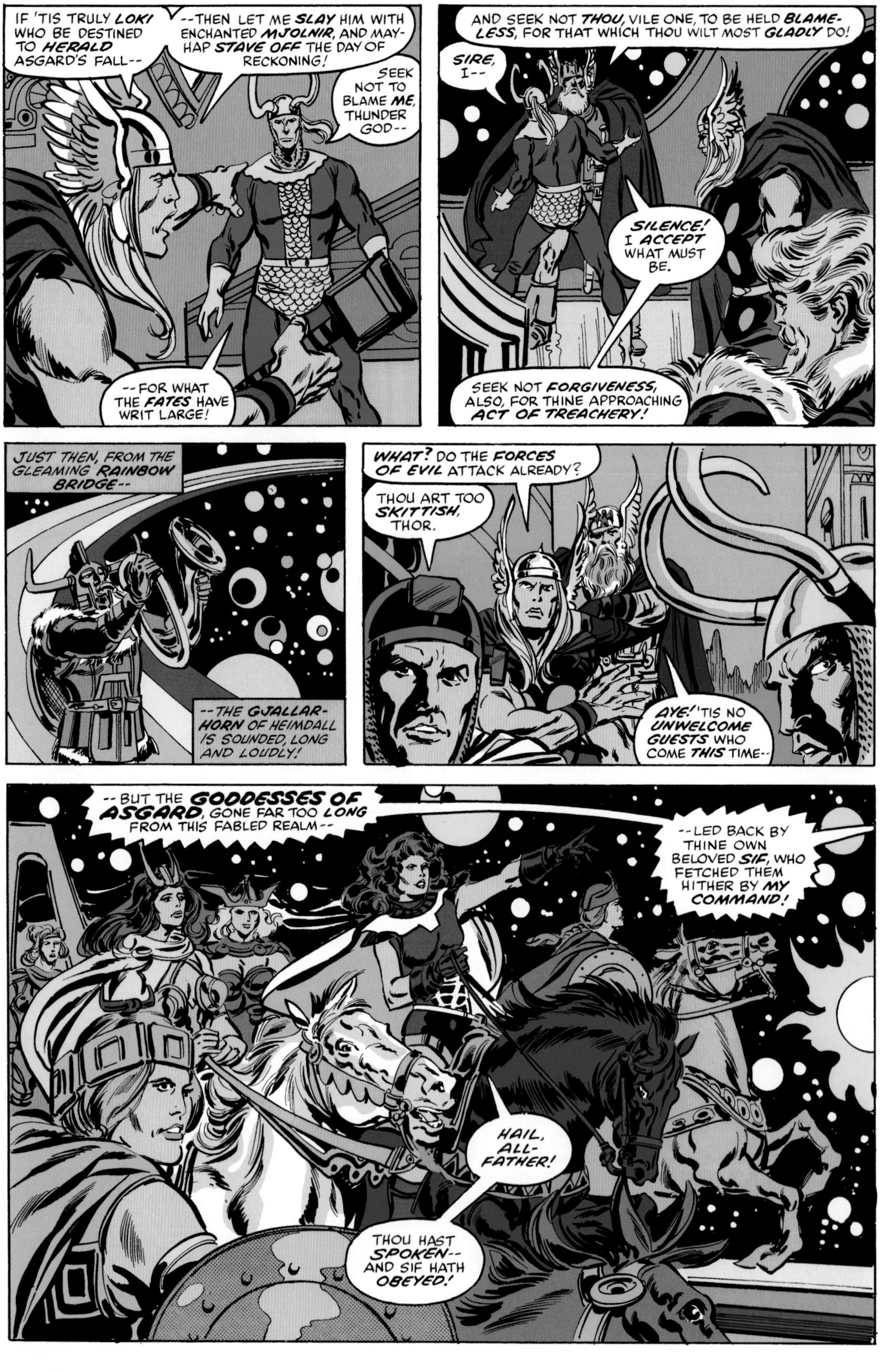
IF 'TIS TRULY LOKI WHO BE DESTINED TO HERALD ASGARD'S FALL--
--THEN LET ME SLAY HIM WITH ENCHANTED MJOLNIR, AND MAYHAP STAVE OFF THE DAY OF RECKONING!
SEEK NOT TO BLAME ME, THUNDER GOD--
--FOR WHAT THE FATES HAVE WRIT LARGE!
AND SEEK NOT THOU, VILE ONE, TO BE HELD BLAMELESS, FOR THAT WHICH THOU WILT MOST GLADLY DO!
SIRE, I--
SILENCE! I ACCEPT WHAT MUST BE.
SEEK NOT FORGIVENESS, ALSO, FOR THINE APPROACHING ACT OF TREACHERY!
JUST THEN, FROM THE GLEAMING RAINBOW BRIDGE--
--THE GJALLARHORN OF HEIMDALL IS SOUNDED, LONG AND LOUDLY!
WHAT? DO THE FORCES OF EVIL ATTACK ALREADY?
THOU ART TOO SKITTISH, THOR.
AYE! 'TIS NO UNWELCOME GUESTS WHO COME THIS TIME--
--BUT THE GODDESSES OF ASGARD, GONE FAR TOO LONG FROM THIS FABLED REALM--
--LED BACK BY THINE OWN BELOVED SIF, WHO FETCHED THEM HITHER BY MY COMMAND!
HAIL, ALL-FATHER!
THOU HAST SPOKEN-- AND SIF HATH OBEYED!

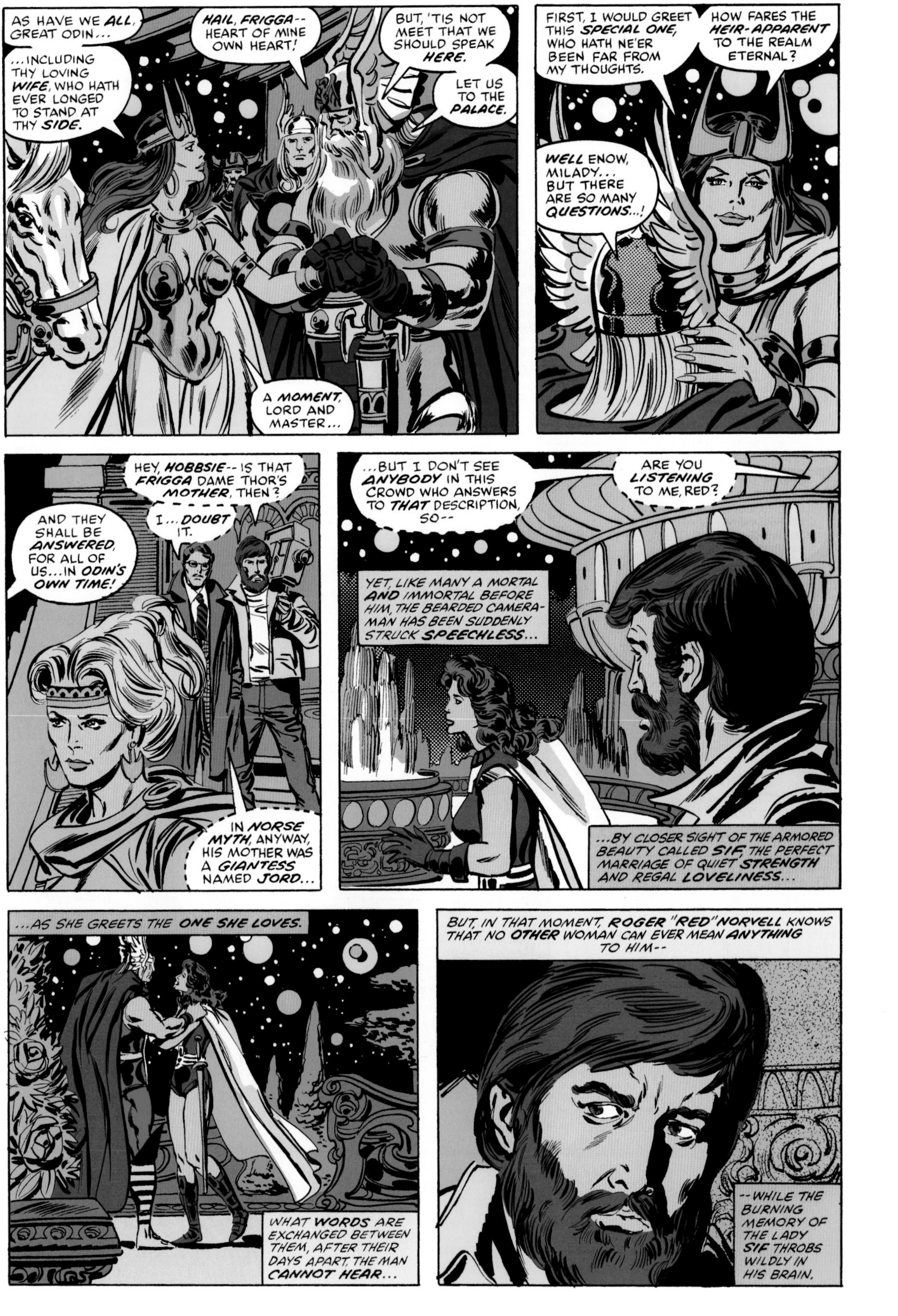
AS HAVE WE ALL, GREAT ODIN...
...INCLUDING THY LOVING WIFE, WHO HATH EVER LONGED TO STAND AT THY SIDE.
HAIL, FRIGGA-- HEART OF MINE OWN HEART!
BUT, 'TIS NOT MEET THAT WE SHOULD SPEAK HERE.
LET US TO THE PALACE.
A MOMENT, LORD AND MASTER...
FIRST, I WOULD GREET THIS SPECIAL ONE, WHO HATH NE'ER BEEN FAR FROM MY THOUGHTS.
HOW FARES THE HEIR-APPARENT TO THE REALM ETERNAL?
WELL ENOW, MILADY... BUT THERE ARE SO MANY QUESTIONS...!
AND THEY SHALL BE ANSWERED, FOR ALL OF US...IN ODIN'S OWN TIME!
HEY, HOBBSIE-- IS THAT FRIGGA DAME THOR'S MOTHER, THEN?
I...DOUBT IT.
IN NORSE MYTH, ANYWAY, HIS MOTHER WAS A GIANTESS NAMED JORD...
...BUT I DON'T SEE ANYBODY IN THIS CROWD WHO ANSWERS TO THAT DESCRIPTION, SO--
ARE YOU LISTENING TO ME, RED?
YET, LIKE MANY A MORTAL AND IMMORTAL BEFORE HIM, THE BEARDED CAMERA-MAN HAS BEEN SUDDENLY STRUCK SPEECHLESS...
...BY CLOSER SIGHT OF THE ARMORED BEAUTY CALLED SIF, THE PERFECT MARRIAGE OF QUIET STRENGTH AND REGAL LOVELINESS...
...AS SHE GREETS THE ONE SHE LOVES.
WHAT WORDS ARE EXCHANGED BETWEEN THEM, AFTER THEIR DAYS APART, THE MAN CANNOT HEAR...
BUT, IN THAT MOMENT, ROGER "RED" NORVELL KNOWS THAT NO OTHER WOMAN CAN EVER MEAN ANYTHING TO HIM--
--WHILE THE BURNING MEMORY OF THE LADY SIF THROBS WILDLY IN HIS BRAIN.

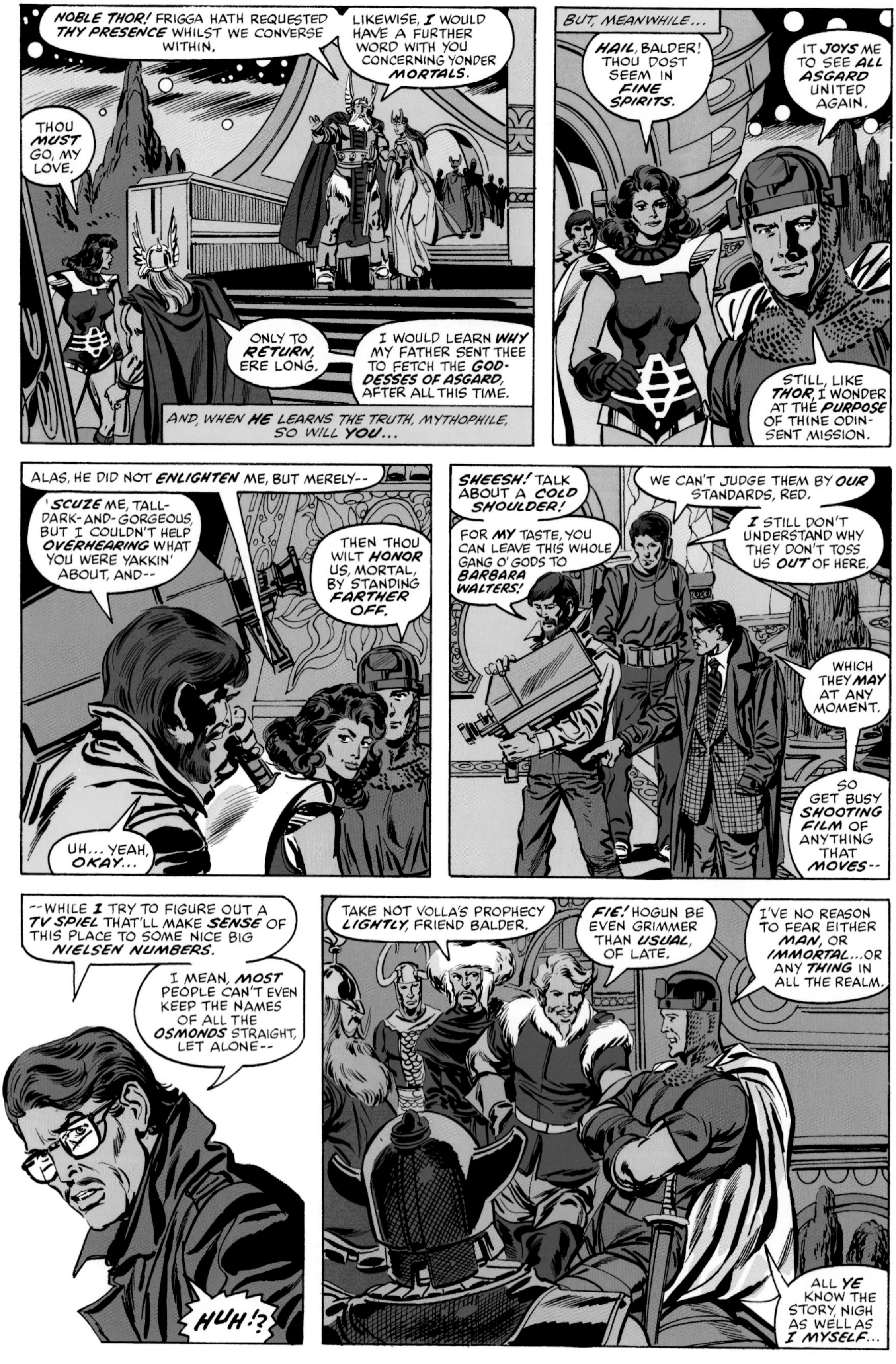
NOBLE THOR! FRIGGA HATH REQUESTED THY PRESENCE WHILST WE CONVERSE WITHIN.
LIKEWISE, I WOULD HAVE A FURTHER WORD WITH YOU CONCERNING YONDER MORTALS.
THOU MUST GO, MY LOVE.
ONLY TO RETURN, ERE LONG.
I WOULD LEARN WHY MY FATHER SENT THEE TO FETCH THE GODDESSES OF ASGARD, AFTER ALL THIS TIME.
AND, WHEN HE LEARNS THE TRUTH, MYTHOPHILE, SO WILL YOU...
BUT, MEANWHILE...
HAIL, BALDER! THOU DOST SEEM IN FINE SPIRITS.
IT JOYS ME TO SEE ALL ASGARD UNITED AGAIN.
STILL, LIKE THOR, I WONDER AT THE PURPOSE OF THINE ODIN-SENT MISSION.
ALAS, HE DID NOT ENLIGHTEN ME, BUT MERELY--
'SCUZE ME, TALL-DARK-AND-GORGEOUS, BUT I COULDN'T HELP OVERHEARING WHAT YOU WERE YAKKIN' ABOUT, AND--
THEN THOU WILT HONOR US, MORTAL, BY STANDING FARTHER OFF.
UH... YEAH, OKAY...
SHEESH! TALK ABOUT A COLD SHOULDER!
FOR MY TASTE, YOU CAN LEAVE THIS WHOLE GANG O' GODS TO BARBARA WALTERS!
WE CAN'T JUDGE THEM BY OUR STANDARDS, RED.
I STILL DON'T UNDERSTAND WHY THEY DON'T TOSS US OUT OF HERE.
WHICH THEY MAY AT ANY MOMENT.
SO GET BUSY SHOOTING FILM OF ANYTHING THAT MOVES--
--WHILE I TRY TO FIGURE OUT A TV SPIEL THAT'LL MAKE SENSE OF THIS PLACE TO SOME NICE BIG NIELSEN NUMBERS.
I MEAN, MOST PEOPLE CAN'T EVEN KEEP THE NAMES OF ALL THE OSMONDS STRAIGHT, LET ALONE--
HUH!?
TAKE NOT VOLLA'S PROPHECY LIGHTLY, FRIEND BALDER.
FIE! HOGUN BE EVEN GRIMMER THAN USUAL, OF LATE.
I'VE NO REASON TO FEAR EITHER MAN, OR IMMORTAL...OR ANY THING IN ALL THE REALM.
ALL YE KNOW THE STORY, NIGH AS WELL AS I MYSELF...

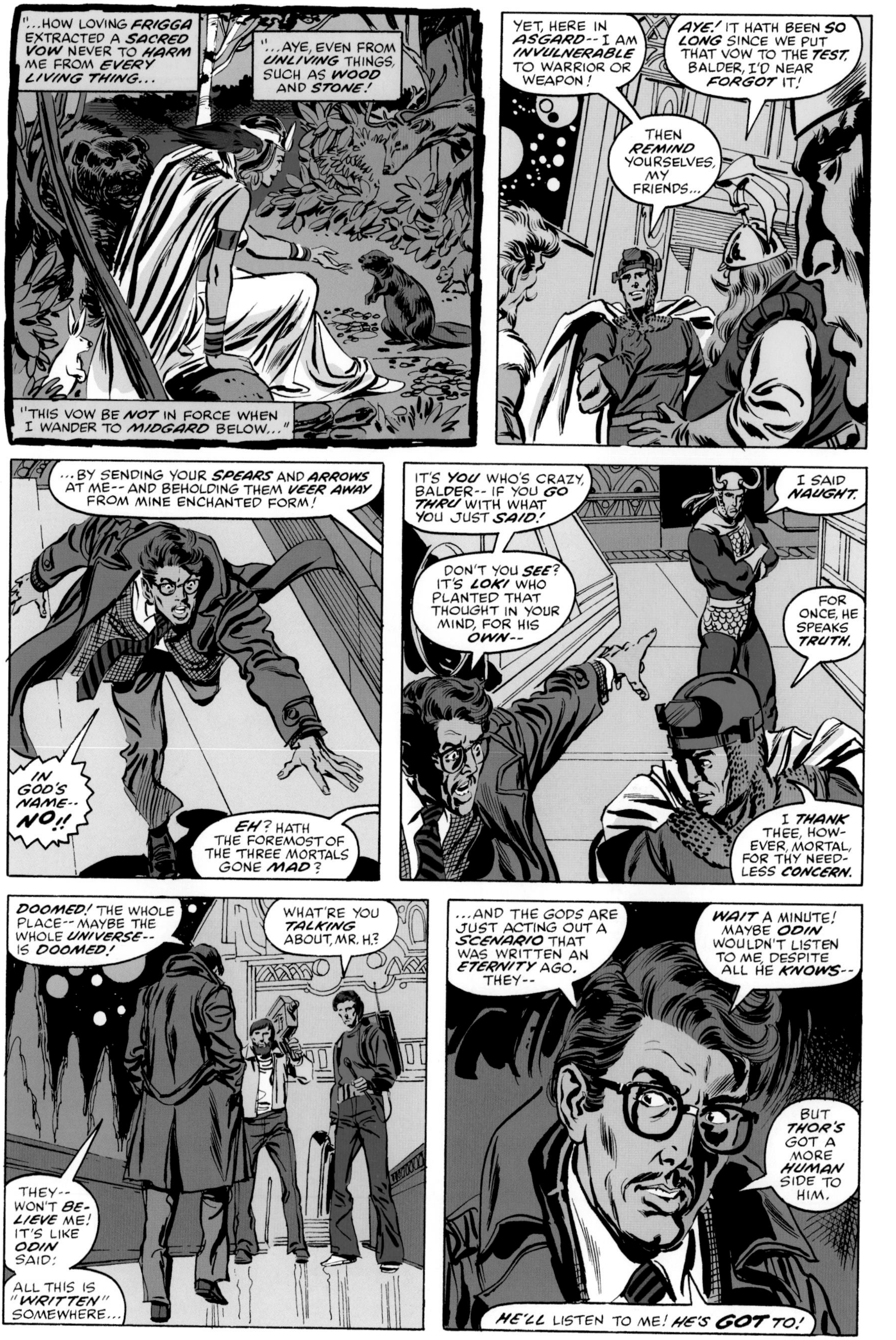
"...HOW LOVING FRIGGA EXTRACTED A SACRED VOW NEVER TO HARM ME FROM EVERY LIVING THING...
"...AYE, EVEN FROM UNLIVING THINGS, SUCH AS WOOD AND STONE!
"THIS VOW BE NOT IN FORCE WHEN I WANDER TO MIDGARD BELOW..."
YET, HERE IN ASGARD-- I AM INVULNERABLE TO WARRIOR OR WEAPON!
AYE! IT HATH BEEN SO LONG SINCE WE PUT THAT VOW TO THE TEST, BALDER, I'D NEAR FORGOT IT!
THEN REMIND YOURSELVES, MY FRIENDS...
...BY SENDING YOUR SPEARS AND ARROWS AT ME-- AND BEHOLDING THEM VEER AWAY FROM MINE ENCHANTED FORM!
IN GOD'S NAME-- NO!!
EH? HATH THE FOREMOST OF THE THREE MORTALS GONE MAD?
IT'S YOU WHO'S CRAZY, BALDER-- IF YOU GO THRU WITH WHAT YOU JUST SAID!
I SAID NAUGHT.
DON'T YOU SEE? IT'S LOKI WHO PLANTED THAT THOUGHT IN YOUR MIND, FOR HIS OWN--
FOR ONCE, HE SPEAKS TRUTH.
I THANK THEE, HOWEVER, MORTAL, FOR THY NEEDLESS CONCERN.
DOOMED! THE WHOLE PLACE-- MAYBE THE WHOLE UNIVERSE-- IS DOOMED!
WHAT'RE YOU TALKING ABOUT, MR. H.?
THEY-- WON'T BELIEVE ME! IT'S LIKE ODIN SAID:
ALL THIS IS "WRITTEN" SOMEWHERE...
...AND THE GODS ARE JUST ACTING OUT A SCENARIO THAT WAS WRITTEN AN ETERNITY AGO. THEY--
WAIT A MINUTE! MAYBE ODIN WOULDN'T LISTEN TO ME, DESPITE ALL HE KNOWS--
BUT THOR'S GOT A MORE HUMAN SIDE TO HIM.
HE'LL LISTEN TO ME! HE'S GOT TO!

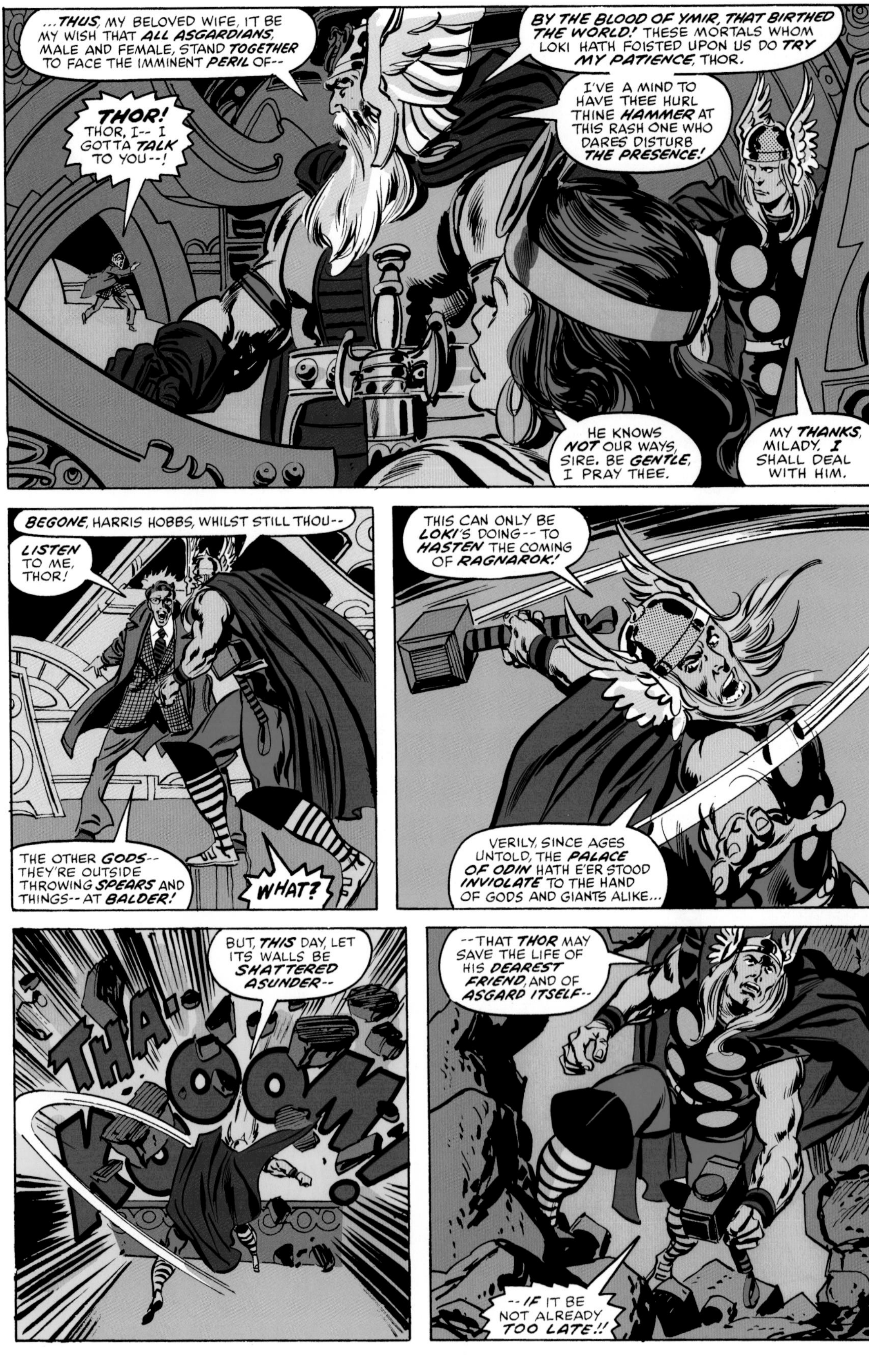

...THUS, MY BELOVED WIFE, IT BE MY WISH THAT ALL ASGARDIANS, MALE AND FEMALE, STAND TOGETHER TO FACE THE IMMINENT PERIL OF--
THOR! THOR, I-- I GOTTA TALK TO YOU--!
BY THE BLOOD OF YMIR, THAT BIRTHED THE WORLD! THESE MORTALS WHOM LOKI HATH FOISTED UPON US DO TRY MY PATIENCE, THOR.
I'VE A MIND TO HAVE THEE HURL THINE HAMMER AT THIS RASH ONE WHO DARES DISTURB THE PRESENCE!
HE KNOWS NOT OUR WAYS, SIRE. BE GENTLE, I PRAY THEE.
MY THANKS, MILADY. I SHALL DEAL WITH HIM.
BEGONE, HARRIS HOBBS, WHILST STILL THOU--
LISTEN TO ME, THOR!
THE OTHER GODS-- THEY'RE OUTSIDE THROWING SPEARS AND THINGS-- AT BALDER!
WHAT?
THIS CAN ONLY BE LOKI'S DOING-- TO HASTEN THE COMING OF RAGNAROK!
VERILY, SINCE AGES UNTOLD, THE PALACE OF ODIN HATH E'ER STOOD INVIOLATE TO THE HAND OF GODS AND GIANTS ALIKE...
BUT, THIS DAY, LET ITS WALLS BE SHATTERED ASUNDER--
THA-KOOOM!
--THAT THOR MAY SAVE THE LIFE OF HIS DEAREST FRIEND, AND OF ASGARD ITSELF--
--IF IT BE NOT ALREADY TOO LATE!!

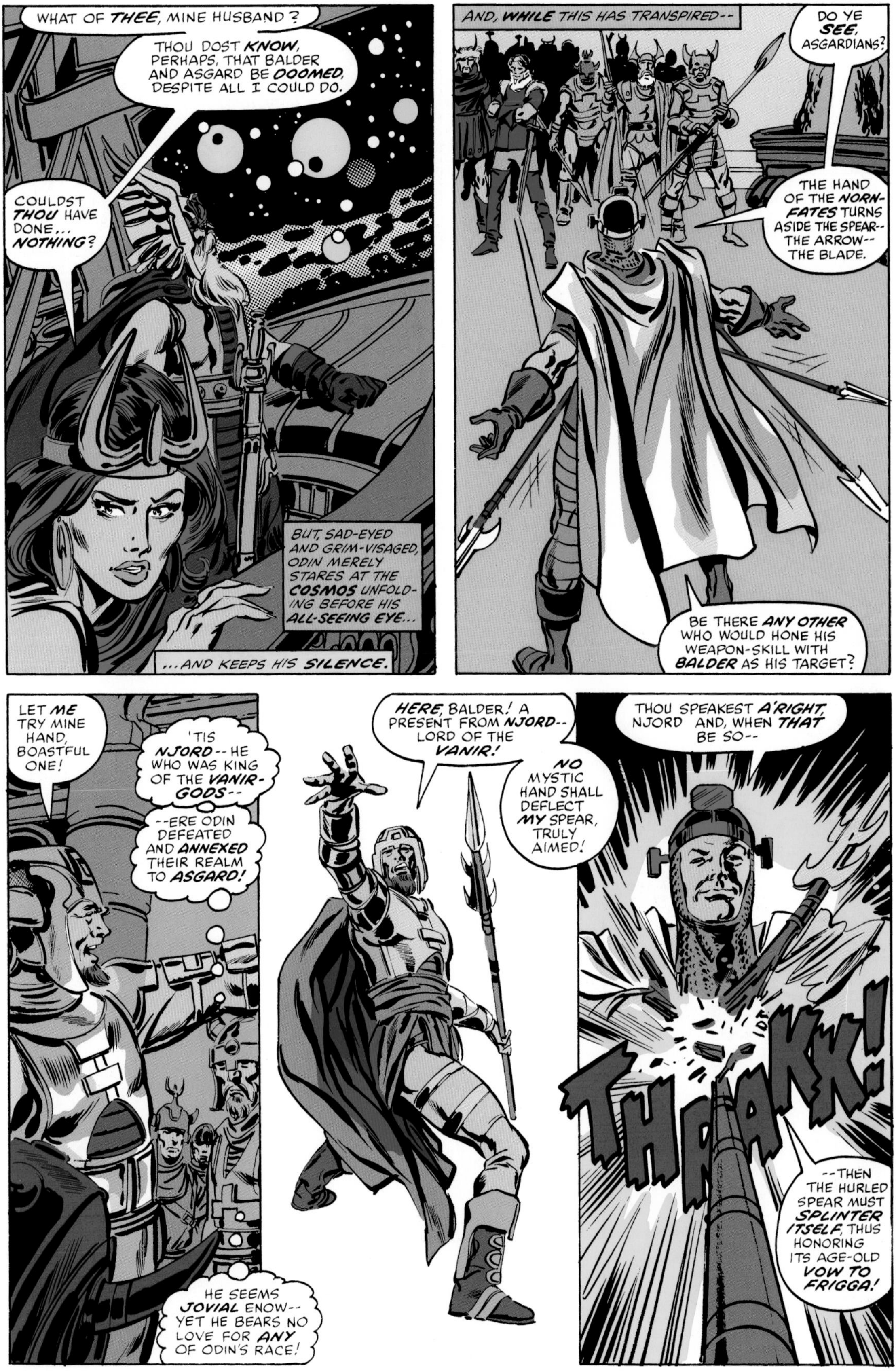

WHAT OF THEE, MINE HUSBAND?
THOU DOST KNOW, PERHAPS, THAT BALDER AND ASGARD BE DOOMED, DESPITE ALL I COULD DO.
COULDST THOU HAVE DONE... NOTHING?
BUT, SAD-EYED AND GRIM-VISAGED, ODIN MERELY STARES AT THE COSMOS UNFOLDING BEFORE HIS ALL-SEEING EYE...
...AND KEEPS HIS SILENCE.
AND, WHILE THIS HAS TRANSPIRED--
DO YE SEE, ASGARDIANS?
THE HAND OF THE NORN-FATES TURNS ASIDE THE SPEAR-- THE ARROW-- THE BLADE.
BE THERE ANY OTHER WHO WOULD HONE HIS WEAPON-SKILL WITH BALDER AS HIS TARGET?
LET ME TRY MINE HAND, BOASTFUL ONE!
'TIS NJORD-- HE WHO WAS KING OF THE VANIR-GODS--
--ERE ODIN DEFEATED AND ANNEXED THEIR REALM TO ASGARD!
HE SEEMS JOVIAL ENOW-- YET HE BEARS NO LOVE FOR ANY OF ODIN'S RACE!
HERE, BALDER! A PRESENT FROM NJORD-- LORD OF THE VANIR!
NO MYSTIC HAND SHALL DEFLECT MY SPEAR, TRULY AIMED!
THOU SPEAKEST A'RIGHT, NJORD AND, WHEN THAT BE SO--
THRAKK!
--THEN THE HURLED SPEAR MUST SPLINTER ITSELF, THUS HONORING ITS AGE-OLD VOW TO FRIGGA!

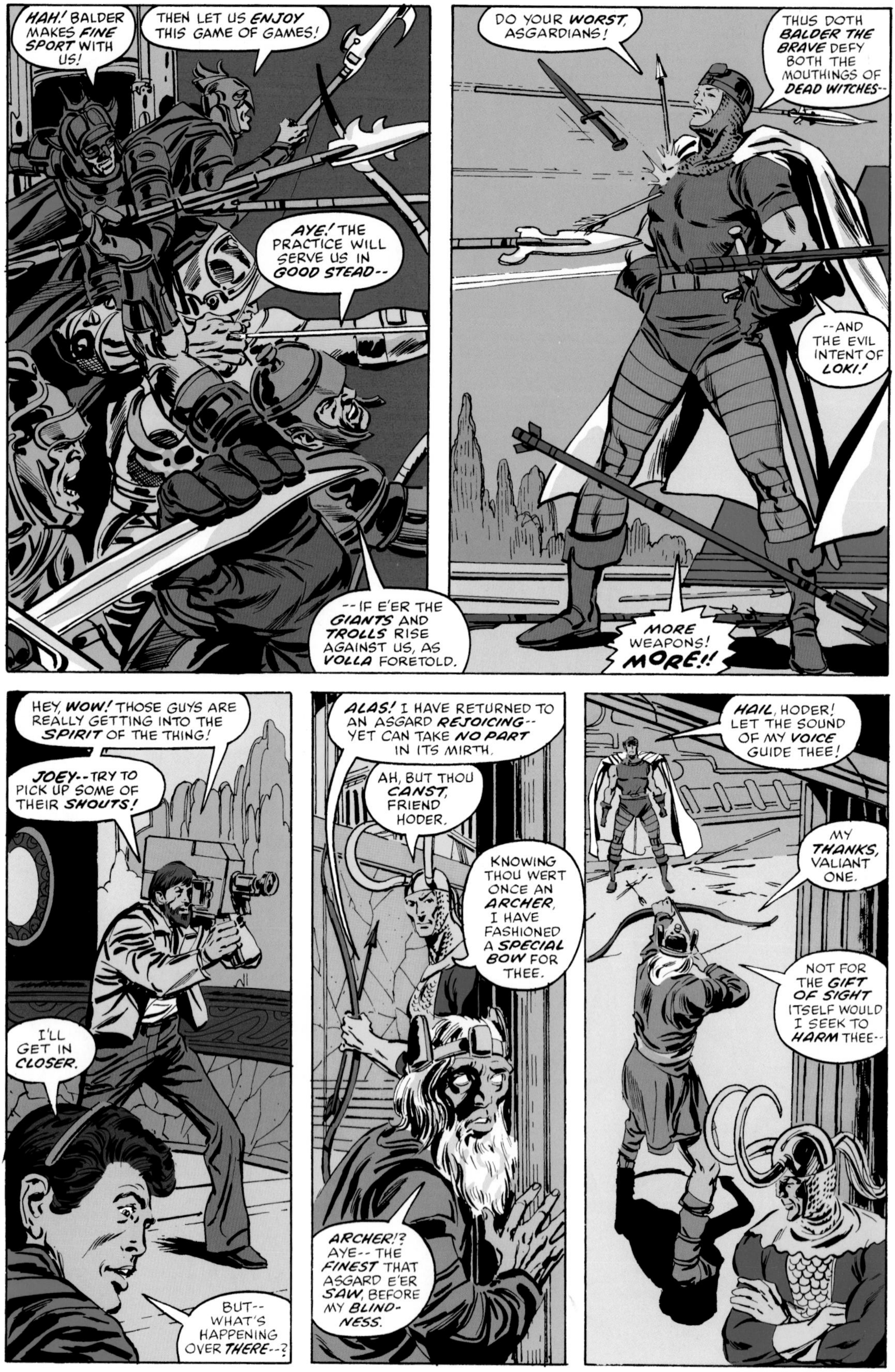
HAH! BALDER MAKES FINE SPORT WITH US!
THEN LET US ENJOY THIS GAME OF GAMES!
AYE! THE PRACTICE WILL SERVE US IN GOOD STEAD--
--IF E'ER THE GIANTS AND TROLLS RISE AGAINST US, AS VOLLA FORETOLD.
DO YOUR WORST, ASGARDIANS!
THUS DOTH BALDER THE BRAVE DEFY BOTH THE MOUTHINGS OF DEAD WITCHES--
--AND THE EVIL INTENT OF LOKI!
MORE WEAPONS! MORE!!
HEY, WOW! THOSE GUYS ARE REALLY GETTING INTO THE SPIRIT OF THE THING!
JOEY--TRY TO PICK UP SOME OF THEIR SHOUTS!
I'LL GET IN CLOSER.
BUT--WHAT'S HAPPENING OVER THERE--?
ALAS! I HAVE RETURNED TO AN ASGARD REJOICING--YET CAN TAKE NO PART IN ITS MIRTH.
AH, BUT THOU CANST, FRIEND HODER.
KNOWING THOU WERT ONCE AN ARCHER, I HAVE FASHIONED A SPECIAL BOW FOR THEE.
ARCHER!? AYE--THE FINEST THAT ASGARD E'ER SAW, BEFORE MY BLINDNESS.
HAIL, HODER! LET THE SOUND OF MY VOICE GUIDE THEE!
MY THANKS, VALIANT ONE.
NOT FOR THE GIFT OF SIGHT ITSELF WOULD I SEEK TO HARM THEE--

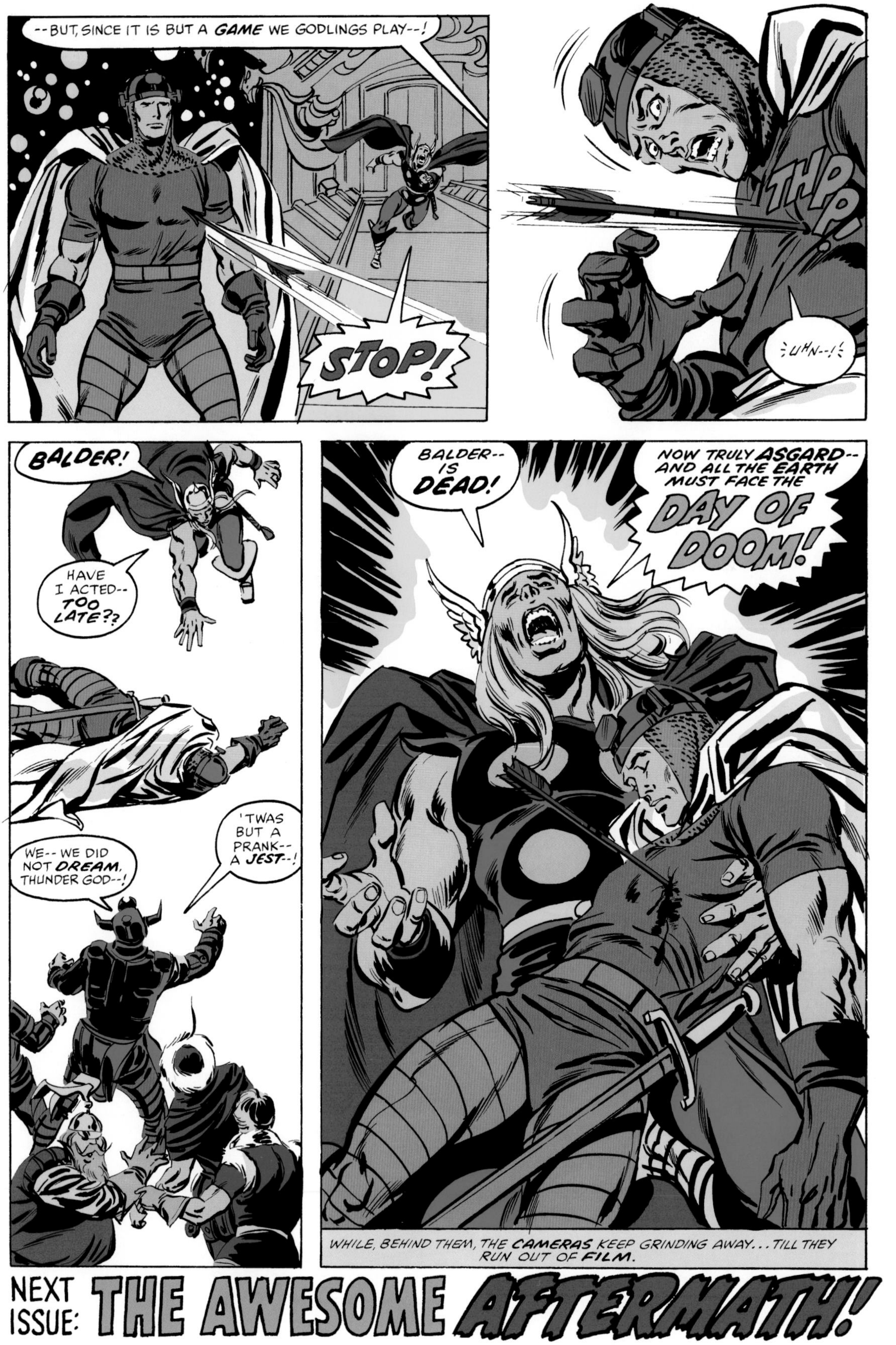
--BUT, SINCE IT IS BUT A GAME WE GODLINGS PLAY--!
STOP!
THPP!
UHN--!
BALDER!
HAVE I ACTED-- TOO LATE??
WE-- WE DID NOT DREAM, THUNDER GOD--!
'TWAS BUT A PRANK-- A JEST--!
BALDER-- IS DEAD!
NOW TRULY ASGARD-- AND ALL THE EARTH MUST FACE THE DAY OF DOOM!
WHILE, BEHIND THEM, THE CAMERAS KEEP GRINDING AWAY... TILL THEY RUN OUT OF FILM.
NEXT ISSUE: THE AWESOME AFTERMATH!

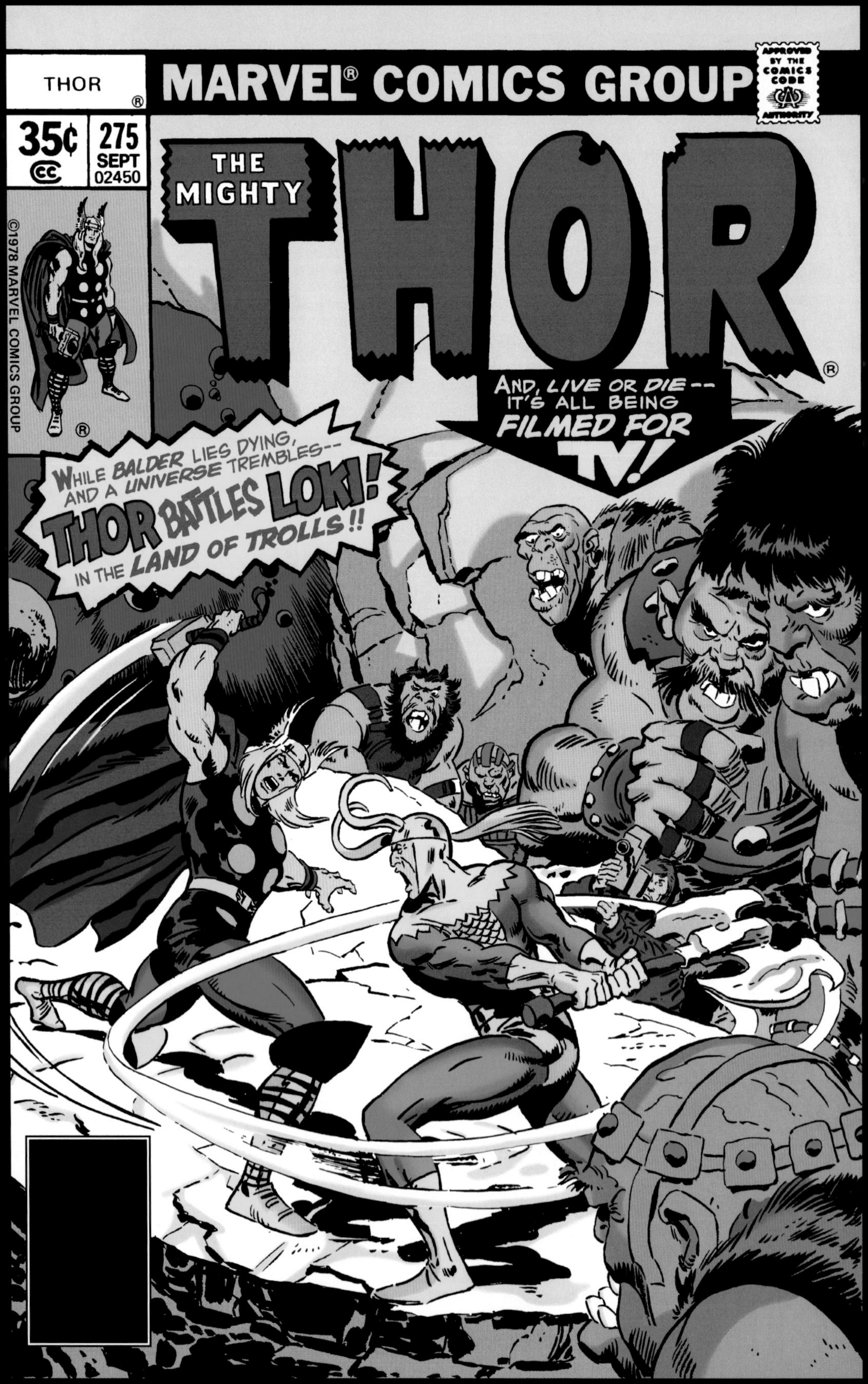
THOR
MARVEL® COMICS GROUP
APPROVED BY THE COMICS CODE AUTHORITY
35¢
275
SEPT
02450
THE MIGHTY
THOR®
©1978 MARVEL COMICS GROUP
AND, LIVE OR DIE-- IT'S ALL BEING FILMED FOR TV!
WHILE BALDER LIES DYING, AND A UNIVERSE TREMBLES--
THOR BATTLES LOKI!
IN THE LAND OF TROLLS!!

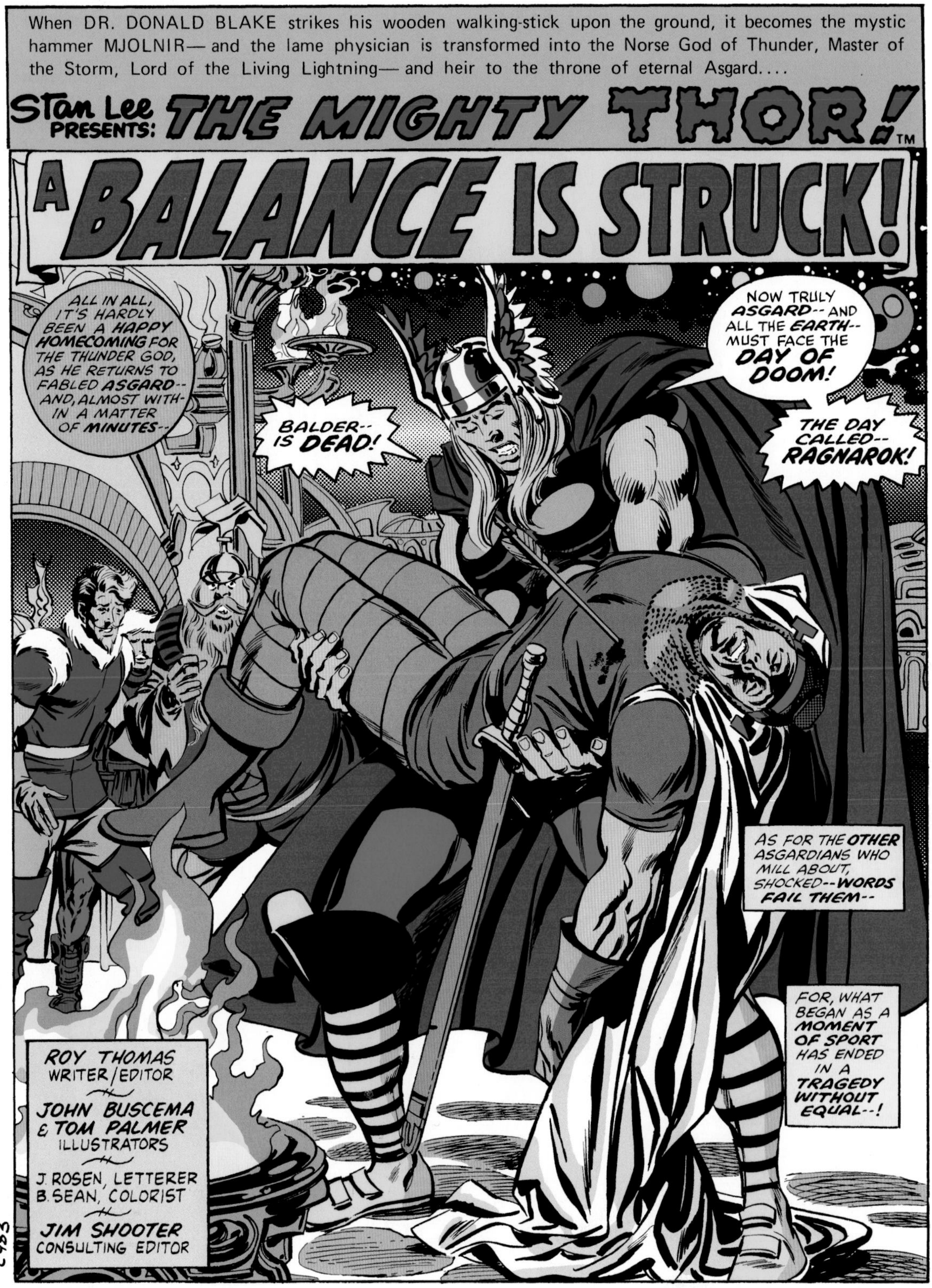
When DR. DONALD BLAKE strikes his wooden walking-stick upon the ground, it becomes the mystic hammer MJOLNIR— and the lame physician is transformed into the Norse God of Thunder, Master of the Storm, Lord of the Living Lightning— and heir to the throne of eternal Asgard....
Stan Lee PRESENTS: THE MIGHTY THOR!
A BALANCE IS STRUCK!
ALL IN ALL, IT'S HARDLY BEEN A HAPPY HOMECOMING FOR THE THUNDER GOD, AS HE RETURNS TO FABLED ASGARD-- AND, ALMOST WITHIN A MATTER OF MINUTES--
BALDER-- IS DEAD!
NOW TRULY ASGARD-- AND ALL THE EARTH-- MUST FACE THE DAY OF DOOM!
THE DAY CALLED-- RAGNAROK!
AS FOR THE OTHER ASGARDIANS WHO MILL ABOUT, SHOCKED--WORDS FAIL THEM--
FOR, WHAT BEGAN AS A MOMENT OF SPORT HAS ENDED IN A TRAGEDY WITHOUT EQUAL--!
ROY THOMAS WRITER/EDITOR
JOHN BUSCEMA & TOM PALMER ILLUSTRATORS
J. ROSEN, LETTERER
B. SEAN, COLORIST
JIM SHOOTER CONSULTING EDITOR
C983

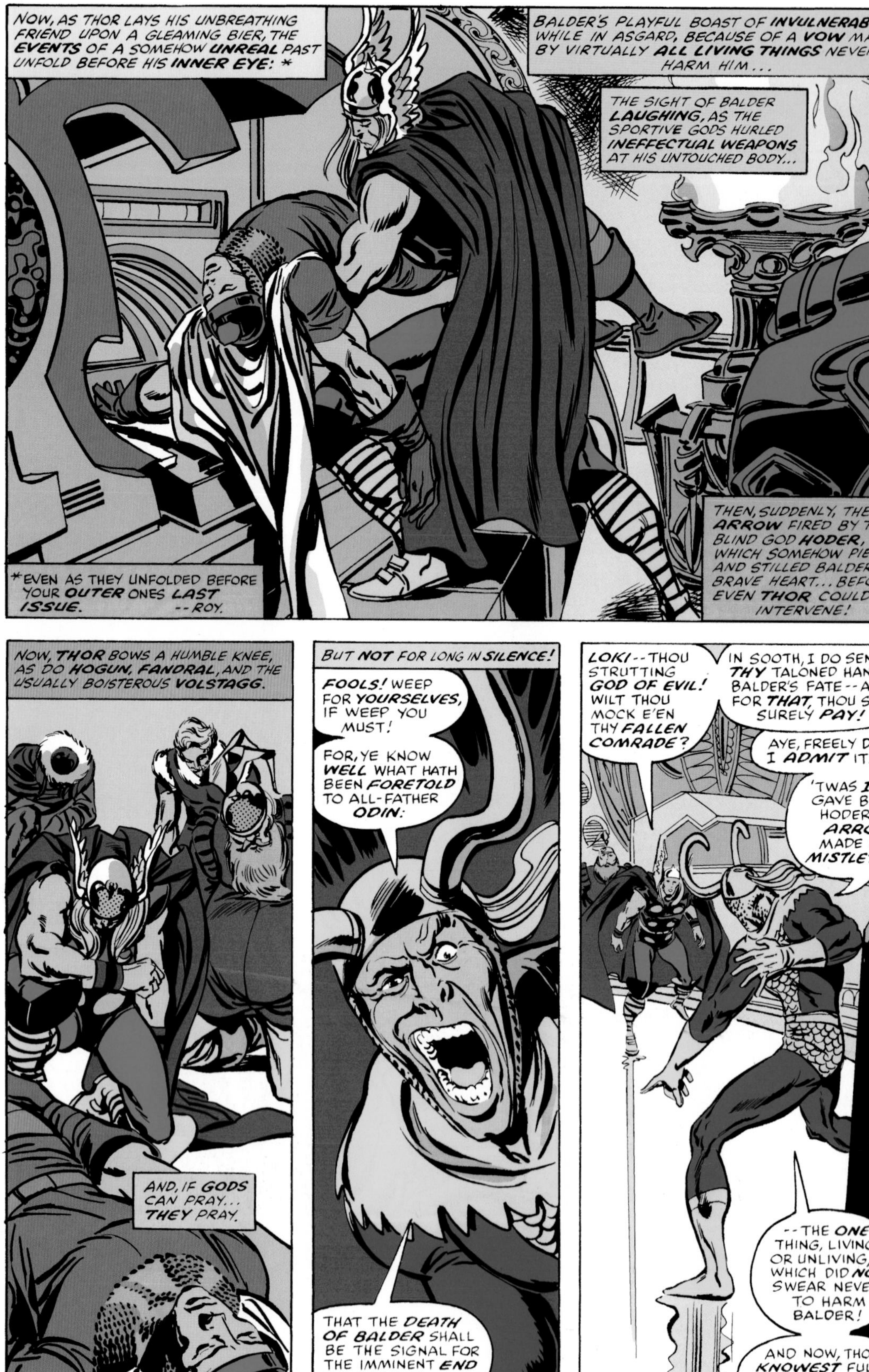
NOW, AS THOR LAYS HIS UNBREATHING FRIEND UPON A GLEAMING BIER, THE EVENTS OF A SOMEHOW UNREAL PAST UNFOLD BEFORE HIS INNER EYE: *
BALDER'S PLAYFUL BOAST OF INVULNERABILITY WHILE IN ASGARD, BECAUSE OF A VOW MADE BY VIRTUALLY ALL LIVING THINGS NEVER TO HARM HIM...
THE SIGHT OF BALDER LAUGHING, AS THE SPORTIVE GODS HURLED INEFFECTUAL WEAPONS AT HIS UNTOUCHED BODY...
THEN, SUDDENLY, THE ARROW FIRED BY THE BLIND GOD HODER, WHICH SOMEHOW PIERCED AND STILLED BALDER'S BRAVE HEART... BEFORE EVEN THOR COULD INTERVENE!
*EVEN AS THEY UNFOLDED BEFORE YOUR OUTER ONES LAST ISSUE. --ROY.
NOW, THOR BOWS A HUMBLE KNEE, AS DO HOGUN, FANDRAL, AND THE USUALLY BOISTEROUS VOLSTAGG.
AND, IF GODS CAN PRAY... THEY PRAY.
BUT NOT FOR LONG IN SILENCE!
FOOLS! WEEP FOR YOURSELVES, IF WEEP YOU MUST!
FOR, YE KNOW WELL WHAT HATH BEEN FORETOLD TO ALL-FATHER ODIN:
THAT THE DEATH OF BALDER SHALL BE THE SIGNAL FOR THE IMMINENT END OF ASGARD-- AND OF ALL THAT IS!
LOKI--THOU STRUTTING GOD OF EVIL! WILT THOU MOCK E'EN THY FALLEN COMRADE?
IN SOOTH, I DO SENSE THY TALONED HAND IN BALDER'S FATE--AND FOR THAT, THOU SHALT SURELY PAY!
AYE, FREELY DO I ADMIT IT!
'TWAS I WHO GAVE BLIND HODER AN ARROW MADE OF MISTLETOE--
--THE ONE THING, LIVING OR UNLIVING, WHICH DID NOT SWEAR NEVER TO HARM BALDER!
AND NOW, THOU KNOWEST FULL WELL WHAT SHALL FOLLOW:

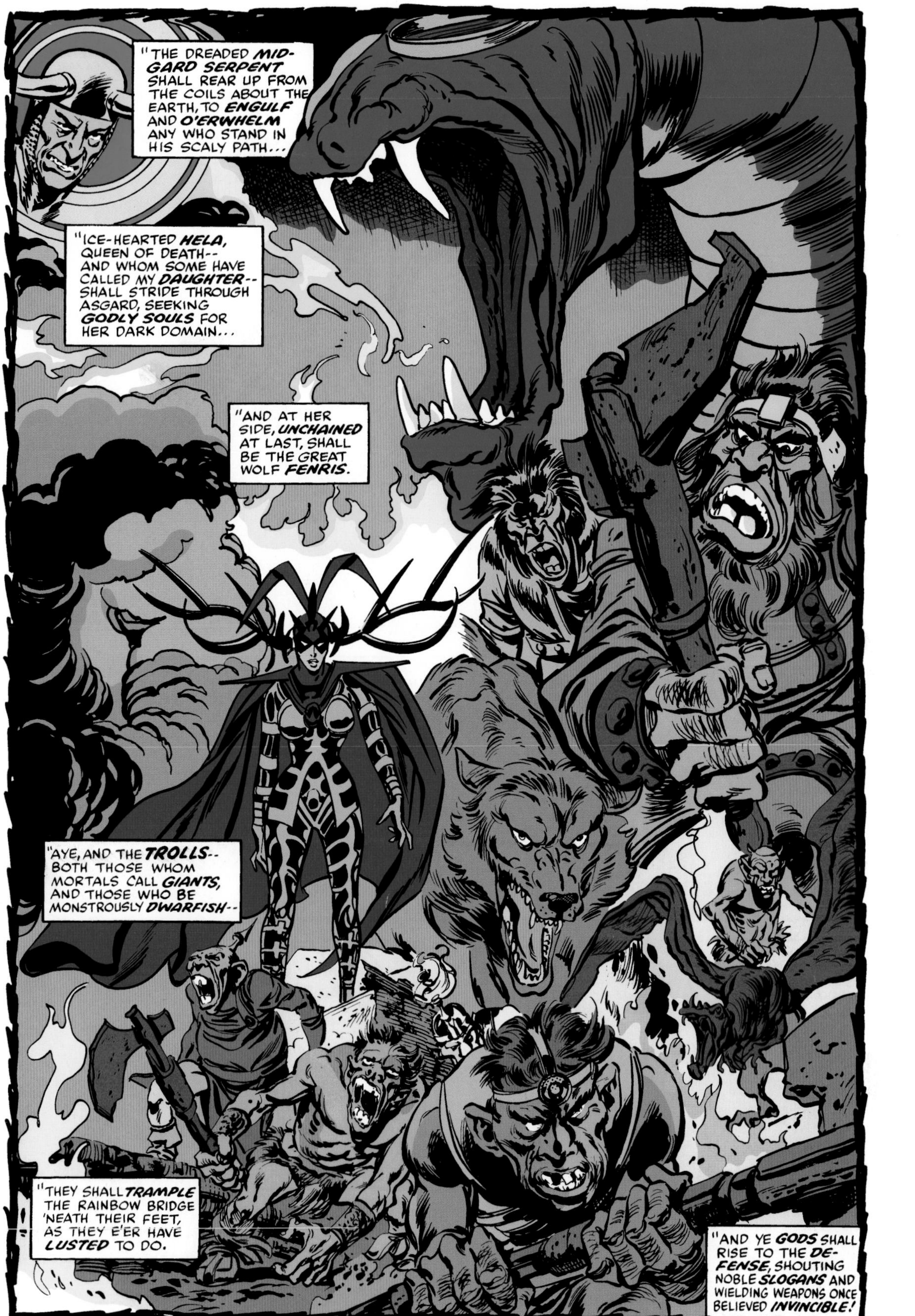
"THE DREADED MID-GARD SERPENT SHALL REAR UP FROM THE COILS ABOUT THE EARTH, TO ENGULF AND O'ERWHELM ANY WHO STAND IN HIS SCALY PATH...
"ICE-HEARTED HELA, QUEEN OF DEATH-- AND WHOM SOME HAVE CALLED MY DAUGHTER-- SHALL STRIDE THROUGH ASGARD, SEEKING GODLY SOULS FOR HER DARK DOMAIN...
"AND AT HER SIDE, UNCHAINED AT LAST, SHALL BE THE GREAT WOLF FENRIS.
"AYE, AND THE TROLLS-- BOTH THOSE WHOM MORTALS CALL GIANTS, AND THOSE WHO BE MONSTROUSLY DWARFISH--
"THEY SHALL TRAMPLE THE RAINBOW BRIDGE 'NEATH THEIR FEET, AS THEY E'ER HAVE LUSTED TO DO.
"AND YE GODS SHALL RISE TO THE DE-FENSE, SHOUTING NOBLE SLOGANS AND WIELDING WEAPONS ONCE BELIEVED INVINCIBLE!

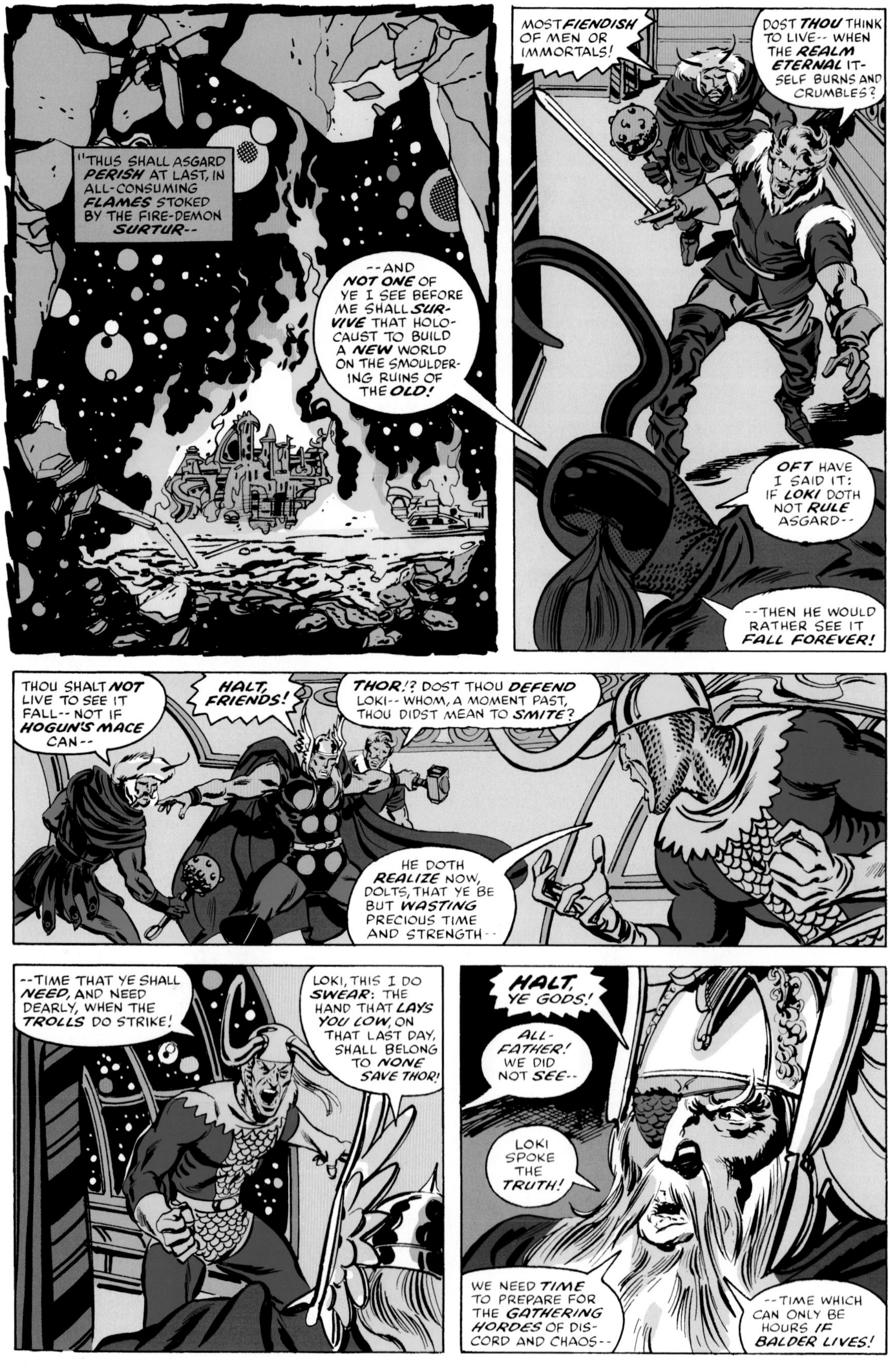
"THUS SHALL ASGARD PERISH AT LAST, IN ALL-CONSUMING FLAMES STOKED BY THE FIRE-DEMON SURTUR--
--AND NOT ONE OF YE I SEE BEFORE ME SHALL SURVIVE THAT HOLOCAUST TO BUILD A NEW WORLD ON THE SMOULDERING RUINS OF THE OLD!
MOST FIENDISH OF MEN OR IMMORTALS!
DOST THOU THINK TO LIVE-- WHEN THE REALM ETERNAL ITSELF BURNS AND CRUMBLES?
OFT HAVE I SAID IT: IF LOKI DOTH NOT RULE ASGARD--
--THEN HE WOULD RATHER SEE IT FALL FOREVER!
THOU SHALT NOT LIVE TO SEE IT FALL-- NOT IF HOGUN'S MACE CAN--
HALT, FRIENDS!
THOR!? DOST THOU DEFEND LOKI-- WHOM, A MOMENT PAST, THOU DIDST MEAN TO SMITE?
HE DOTH REALIZE NOW, DOLTS, THAT YE BE BUT WASTING PRECIOUS TIME AND STRENGTH--
--TIME THAT YE SHALL NEED, AND NEED DEARLY, WHEN THE TROLLS DO STRIKE!
LOKI, THIS I DO SWEAR: THE HAND THAT LAYS YOU LOW, ON THAT LAST DAY, SHALL BELONG TO NONE SAVE THOR!
HALT, YE GODS!
ALL-FATHER! WE DID NOT SEE--
LOKI SPOKE THE TRUTH!
WE NEED TIME TO PREPARE FOR THE GATHERING HORDES OF DISCORD AND CHAOS--
--TIME WHICH CAN ONLY BE HOURS IF BALDER LIVES!

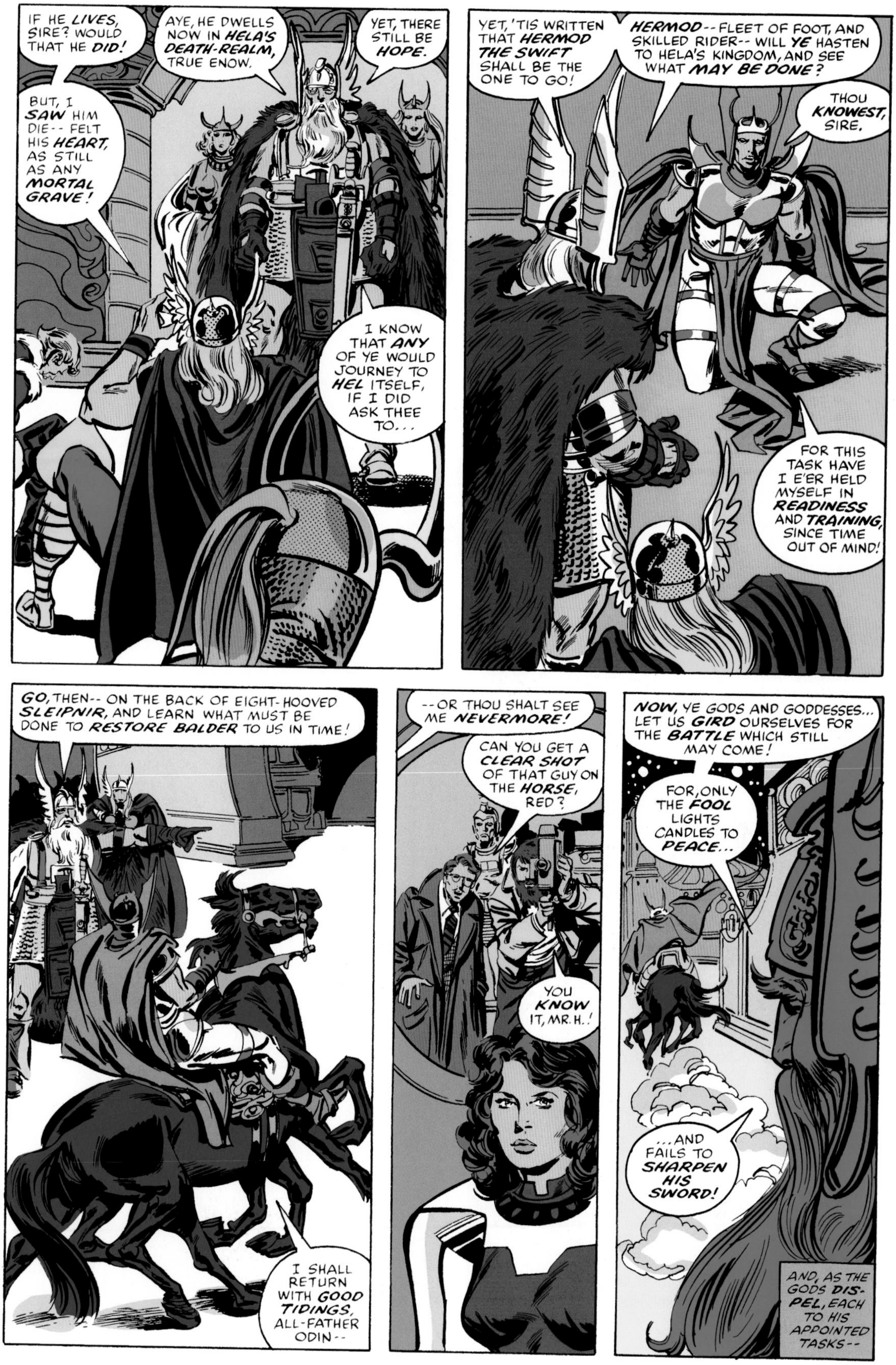
IF HE LIVES, SIRE? WOULD THAT HE DID!
AYE, HE DWELLS NOW IN HELA'S DEATH-REALM, TRUE ENOW.
YET, THERE STILL BE HOPE.
BUT, I SAW HIM DIE-- FELT HIS HEART, AS STILL AS ANY MORTAL GRAVE!
I KNOW THAT ANY OF YE WOULD JOURNEY TO HEL ITSELF, IF I DID ASK THEE TO...
YET, 'TIS WRITTEN THAT HERMOD THE SWIFT SHALL BE THE ONE TO GO!
HERMOD-- FLEET OF FOOT, AND SKILLED RIDER-- WILL YE HASTEN TO HELA'S KINGDOM, AND SEE WHAT MAY BE DONE?
THOU KNOWEST, SIRE.
FOR THIS TASK HAVE I E'ER HELD MYSELF IN READINESS AND TRAINING, SINCE TIME OUT OF MIND!
GO, THEN-- ON THE BACK OF EIGHT-HOOVED SLEIPNIR, AND LEARN WHAT MUST BE DONE TO RESTORE BALDER TO US IN TIME!
I SHALL RETURN WITH GOOD TIDINGS, ALL-FATHER ODIN--
--OR THOU SHALT SEE ME NEVERMORE!
CAN YOU GET A CLEAR SHOT OF THAT GUY ON THE HORSE, RED?
YOU KNOW IT, MR. H.!
NOW, YE GODS AND GODDESSES... LET US GIRD OURSELVES FOR THE BATTLE WHICH STILL MAY COME!
FOR, ONLY THE FOOL LIGHTS CANDLES TO PEACE...
...AND FAILS TO SHARPEN HIS SWORD!
AND, AS THE GODS DISPEL, EACH TO HIS APPOINTED TASKS--

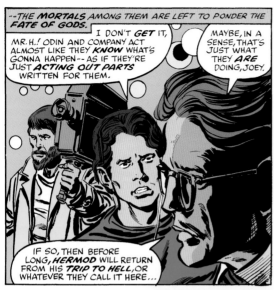

--THE **MORTALS** AMONG THEM ARE LEFT TO PONDER THE **FATE OF GODS**.

I DON'T **GET** IT, MR. H.! ODIN AND COMPANY ACT ALMOST LIKE THEY **KNOW** WHAT'S GONNA HAPPEN-- AS IF THEY'RE JUST **ACTING OUT PARTS** WRITTEN FOR THEM.

MAYBE, IN A SENSE, THAT'S JUST WHAT THEY **ARE** DOING, JOEY.

IF SO, THEN BEFORE LONG, **HERMOD** WILL RETURN FROM HIS **TRIP TO HELL**, OR WHATEVER THEY CALL IT HERE...

"...TO GIVE ODIN A **MESSAGE FROM HELA**:

"IF **ALL THE WORLD** WILL ONLY **WEEP FOR BALDER**, HE CAN BE RESTORED TO ASGARD-- AND RAGNAROK **WON'T** HAPPEN ON SCHEDULE.

"THEN, AS IT WAS PREDICTED CENTURIES AGO, ALL THINGS **WILL** WEEP...ONE WAY OR ANOTHER...

"...THOUGH I DON'T KNOW IF **'ALL THE WORLD'** IN THIS CASE INCLUDES JUST **ASGARD**, OR **EARTH** AS WELL...

"...ALL THINGS, THAT IS, EXCEPT A SINGLE **GIANTESS**... I THINK HER NAME'S **THOKK**... SOMETHING LIKE THAT.

"SHE'LL **REFUSE**... ASKING WHAT IN BLAZES **BALDER** EVER DID FOR **HER**.

"ACCORDING TO **SOME** SOURCES, THOKK IS **LOKI** HIMSELF, IN DISGUISE...

...BUT, IN THE WORLD OF **GODS**, WHO CAN TRULY **SAY**?

ALL **I** CARE ABOUT IS HAVING AN **UPPER WEST SIDE** TO GO BACK TO WHEN THIS LUNACY IS **OVER**.

IF **RAGNAROK** COMES, WILL IT DESTROY **EARTH**, TOO-- OR **NOT**?

YOU'RE ASKING **ME**!?

I'M NOT EVEN SURE WE'RE REALLY **HERE**.

GREAT! IT'S JUST **DANDY** TO BE SHOOTING THE **GREATEST TV SPEC** OF ALL TIME-- AND NOT BE SURE THERE'LL BE A **NETWORK** TO PUT IT ON!

AS FAR AS **WE'RE** CONCERNED, RED, THERE STILL **IS**.

AND WE'RE GOING TO **CONTINUE** UNDER THAT ASSUMPTION.

YOU TWO BRING YOUR **EQUIPMENT** OVER HERE; IT'S TIME I DID A **REMOTE**.

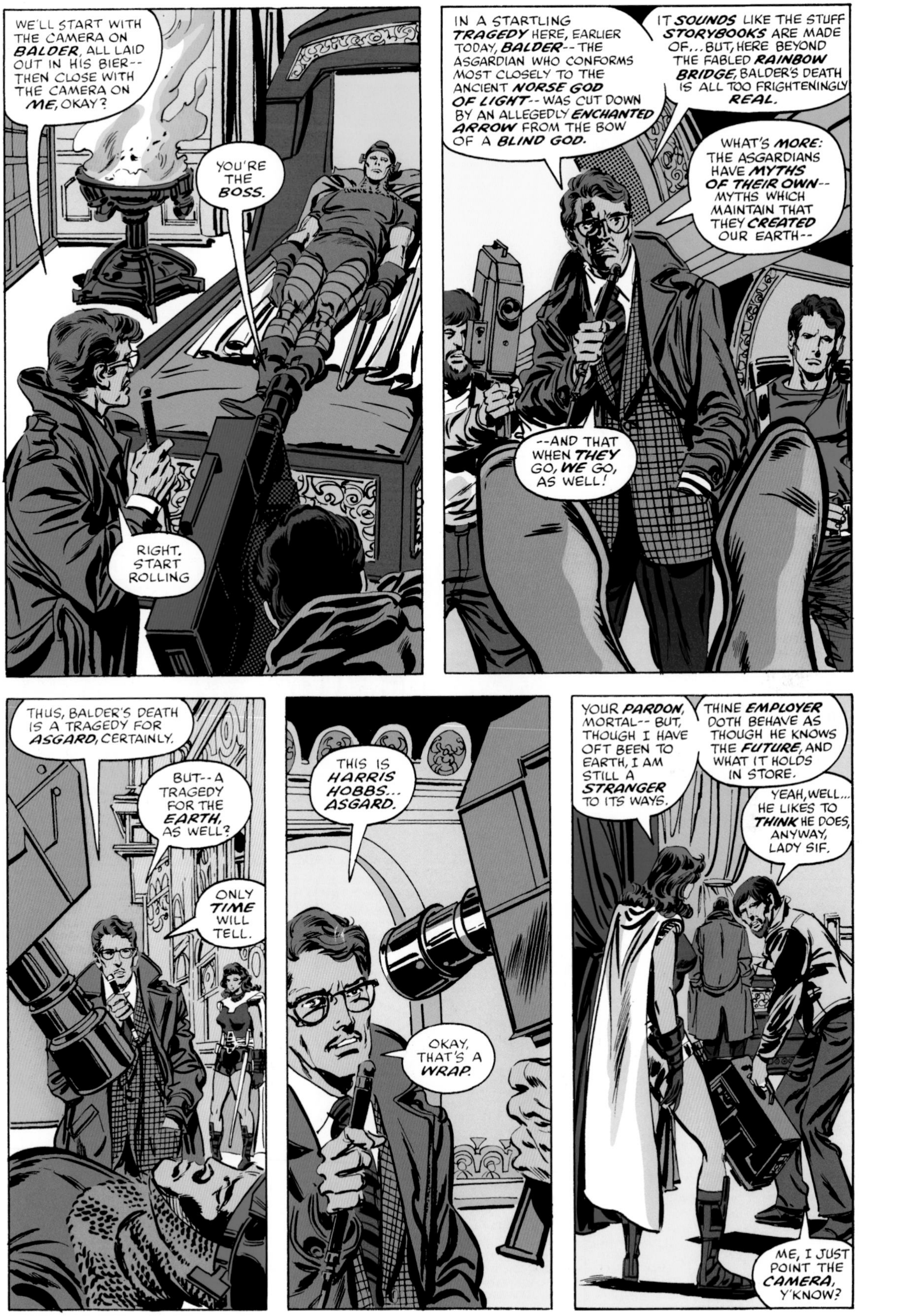

WE'LL START WITH THE CAMERA ON BALDER, ALL LAID OUT IN HIS BIER-- THEN CLOSE WITH THE CAMERA ON ME, OKAY?
YOU'RE THE BOSS.
RIGHT. START ROLLING
IN A STARTLING TRAGEDY HERE, EARLIER TODAY, BALDER-- THE ASGARDIAN WHO CONFORMS MOST CLOSELY TO THE ANCIENT NORSE GOD OF LIGHT-- WAS CUT DOWN BY AN ALLEGEDLY ENCHANTED ARROW FROM THE BOW OF A BLIND GOD.
IT SOUNDS LIKE THE STUFF STORYBOOKS ARE MADE OF... BUT, HERE BEYOND THE FABLED RAINBOW BRIDGE, BALDER'S DEATH IS ALL TOO FRIGHTENINGLY REAL.
WHAT'S MORE: THE ASGARDIANS HAVE MYTHS OF THEIR OWN-- MYTHS WHICH MAINTAIN THAT THEY CREATED OUR EARTH--
--AND THAT WHEN THEY GO, WE GO, AS WELL!
THUS, BALDER'S DEATH IS A TRAGEDY FOR ASGARD, CERTAINLY.
BUT-- A TRAGEDY FOR THE EARTH, AS WELL?
ONLY TIME WILL TELL.
THIS IS HARRIS HOBBS... ASGARD.
OKAY, THAT'S A WRAP.
YOUR PARDON, MORTAL-- BUT, THOUGH I HAVE OFT BEEN TO EARTH, I AM STILL A STRANGER TO ITS WAYS.
THINE EMPLOYER DOTH BEHAVE AS THOUGH HE KNOWS THE FUTURE, AND WHAT IT HOLDS IN STORE.
YEAH, WELL... HE LIKES TO THINK HE DOES, ANYWAY, LADY SIF.
ME, I JUST POINT THE CAMERA, Y'KNOW?

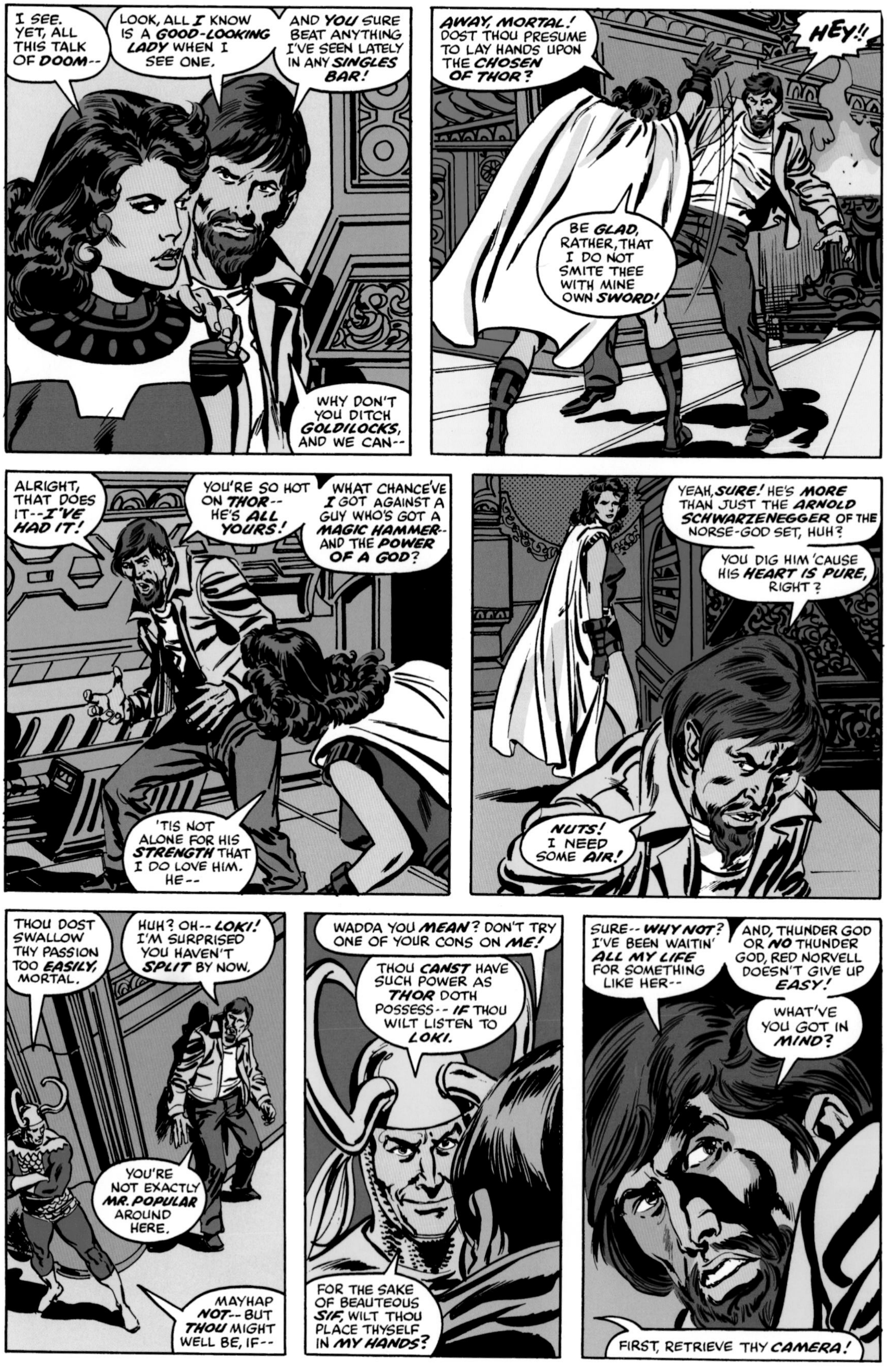
I SEE. YET, ALL THIS TALK OF DOOM--
LOOK, ALL I KNOW IS A GOOD-LOOKING LADY WHEN I SEE ONE.
AND YOU SURE BEAT ANYTHING I'VE SEEN LATELY IN ANY SINGLES BAR!
WHY DON'T YOU DITCH GOLDILOCKS, AND WE CAN--
AWAY, MORTAL! DOST THOU PRESUME TO LAY HANDS UPON THE CHOSEN OF THOR?
HEY!!
BE GLAD, RATHER, THAT I DO NOT SMITE THEE WITH MINE OWN SWORD!
ALRIGHT, THAT DOES IT--I'VE HAD IT!
YOU'RE SO HOT ON THOR-- HE'S ALL YOURS!
WHAT CHANCE'VE I GOT AGAINST A GUY WHO'S GOT A MAGIC HAMMER-- AND THE POWER OF A GOD?
'TIS NOT ALONE FOR HIS STRENGTH THAT I DO LOVE HIM. HE--
YEAH, SURE! HE'S MORE THAN JUST THE ARNOLD SCHWARZENEGGER OF THE NORSE-GOD SET, HUH?
YOU DIG HIM 'CAUSE HIS HEART IS PURE, RIGHT?
NUTS! I NEED SOME AIR!
THOU DOST SWALLOW THY PASSION TOO EASILY, MORTAL.
HUH? OH-- LOKI! I'M SURPRISED YOU HAVEN'T SPLIT BY NOW.
YOU'RE NOT EXACTLY MR. POPULAR AROUND HERE.
MAYHAP NOT-- BUT THOU MIGHT WELL BE, IF--
WADDA YOU MEAN? DON'T TRY ONE OF YOUR CONS ON ME!
THOU CANST HAVE SUCH POWER AS THOR DOTH POSSESS-- IF THOU WILT LISTEN TO LOKI.
FOR THE SAKE OF BEAUTEOUS SIF, WILT THOU PLACE THYSELF IN MY HANDS?
SURE-- WHY NOT? I'VE BEEN WAITIN' ALL MY LIFE FOR SOMETHING LIKE HER--
AND, THUNDER GOD OR NO THUNDER GOD, RED NORVELL DOESN'T GIVE UP EASY!
WHAT'VE YOU GOT IN MIND?
FIRST, RETRIEVE THY CAMERA!

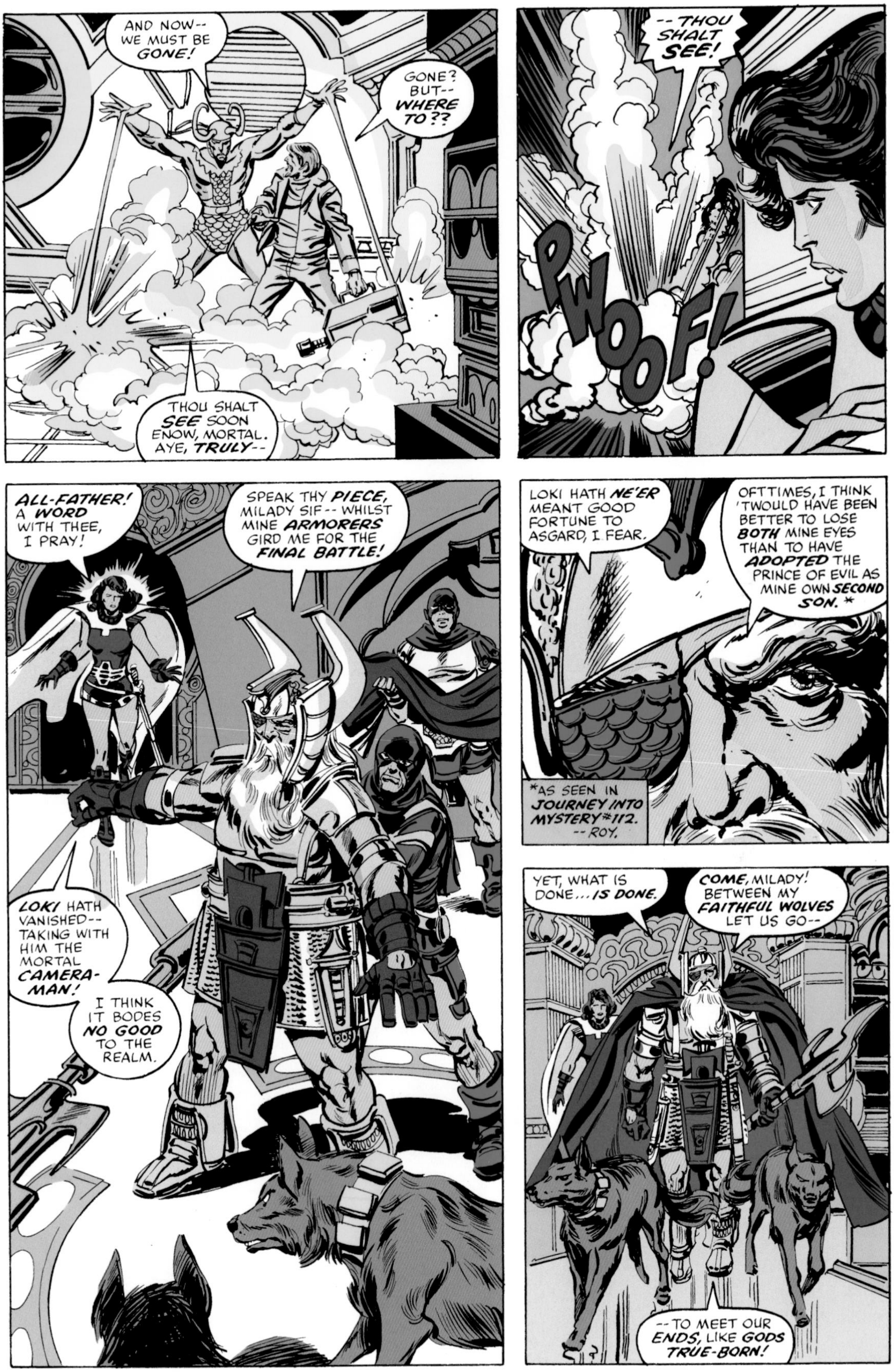
AND NOW-- WE MUST BE GONE!
GONE? BUT-- WHERE TO??
THOU SHALT SEE SOON ENOW, MORTAL. AYE, TRULY--
--THOU SHALT SEE!
PWOOF!
ALL-FATHER! A WORD WITH THEE, I PRAY!
SPEAK THY PIECE, MILADY SIF-- WHILST MINE ARMORERS GIRD ME FOR THE FINAL BATTLE!
LOKI HATH VANISHED-- TAKING WITH HIM THE MORTAL CAMERA-MAN!
I THINK IT BODES NO GOOD TO THE REALM.
LOKI HATH NE'ER MEANT GOOD FORTUNE TO ASGARD, I FEAR.
OFTTIMES, I THINK 'TWOULD HAVE BEEN BETTER TO LOSE BOTH MINE EYES THAN TO HAVE ADOPTED THE PRINCE OF EVIL AS MINE OWN SECOND SON.*
*AS SEEN IN JOURNEY INTO MYSTERY #112. --ROY.
YET, WHAT IS DONE... IS DONE.
COME, MILADY! BETWEEN MY FAITHFUL WOLVES LET US GO--
--TO MEET OUR ENDS, LIKE GODS TRUE-BORN!

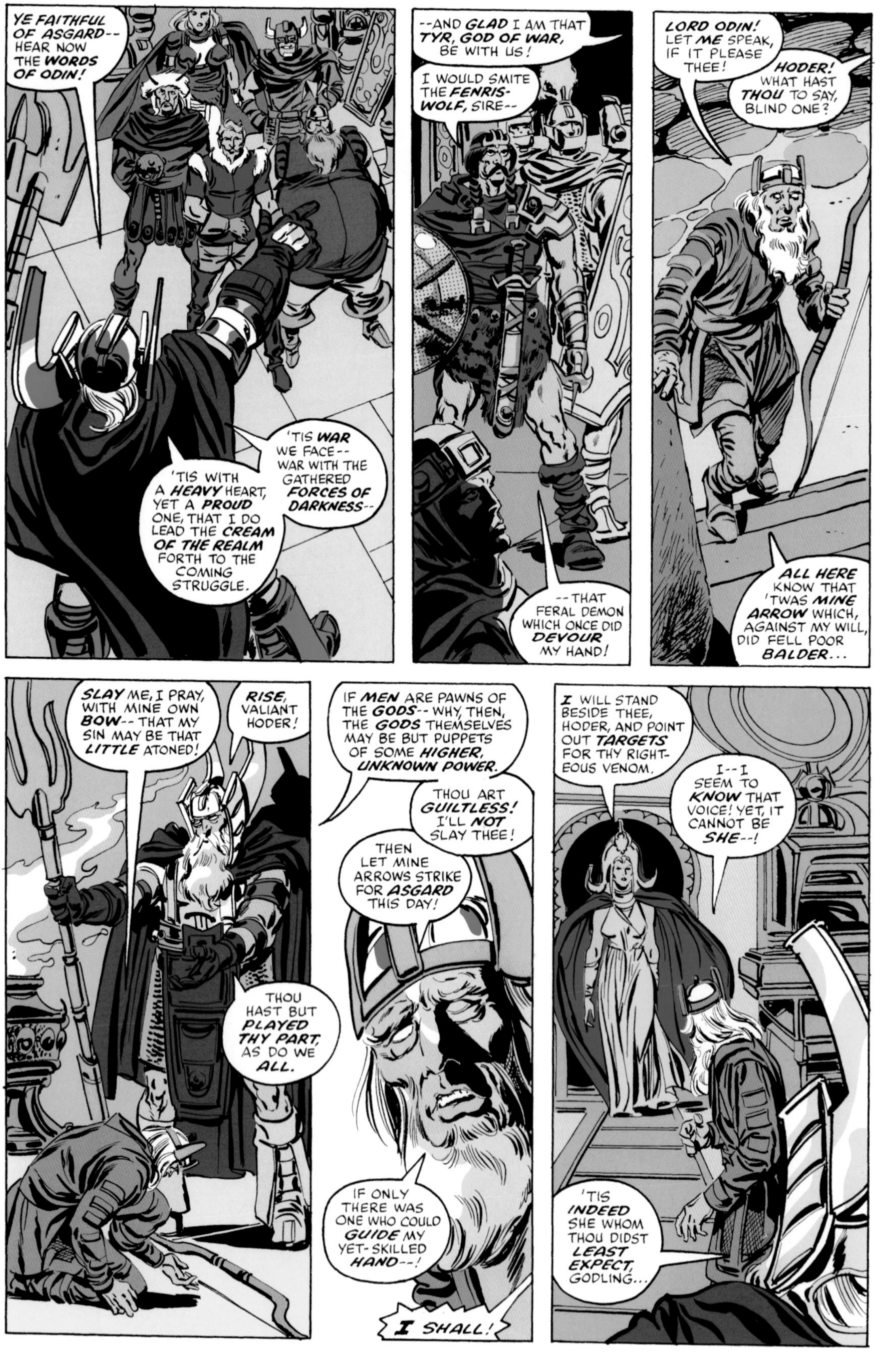
YE FAITHFUL OF ASGARD-- HEAR NOW THE WORDS OF ODIN!
'TIS WITH A HEAVY HEART, YET A PROUD ONE, THAT I DO LEAD THE CREAM OF THE REALM FORTH TO THE COMING STRUGGLE.
'TIS WAR WE FACE-- WAR WITH THE GATHERED FORCES OF DARKNESS--
--AND GLAD I AM THAT TYR, GOD OF WAR, BE WITH US!
I WOULD SMITE THE FENRIS-WOLF, SIRE--
--THAT FERAL DEMON WHICH ONCE DID DEVOUR MY HAND!
LORD ODIN! LET ME SPEAK, IF IT PLEASE THEE!
HODER! WHAT HAST THOU TO SAY, BLIND ONE?
ALL HERE KNOW THAT 'TWAS MINE ARROW WHICH, AGAINST MY WILL, DID FELL POOR BALDER...
SLAY ME, I PRAY, WITH MINE OWN BOW-- THAT MY SIN MAY BE THAT LITTLE ATONED!
RISE, VALIANT HODER!
THOU HAST BUT PLAYED THY PART, AS DO WE ALL.
IF MEN ARE PAWNS OF THE GODS-- WHY, THEN, THE GODS THEMSELVES MAY BE BUT PUPPETS OF SOME HIGHER, UNKNOWN POWER.
THOU ART GUILTLESS! I'LL NOT SLAY THEE!
THEN LET MINE ARROWS STRIKE FOR ASGARD THIS DAY!
IF ONLY THERE WAS ONE WHO COULD GUIDE MY YET-SKILLED HAND--!
I SHALL!
I WILL STAND BESIDE THEE, HODER, AND POINT OUT TARGETS FOR THY RIGHTEOUS VENOM.
I--I SEEM TO KNOW THAT VOICE! YET, IT CANNOT BE SHE--!
'TIS INDEED SHE WHOM THOU DIDST LEAST EXPECT, GODLING...

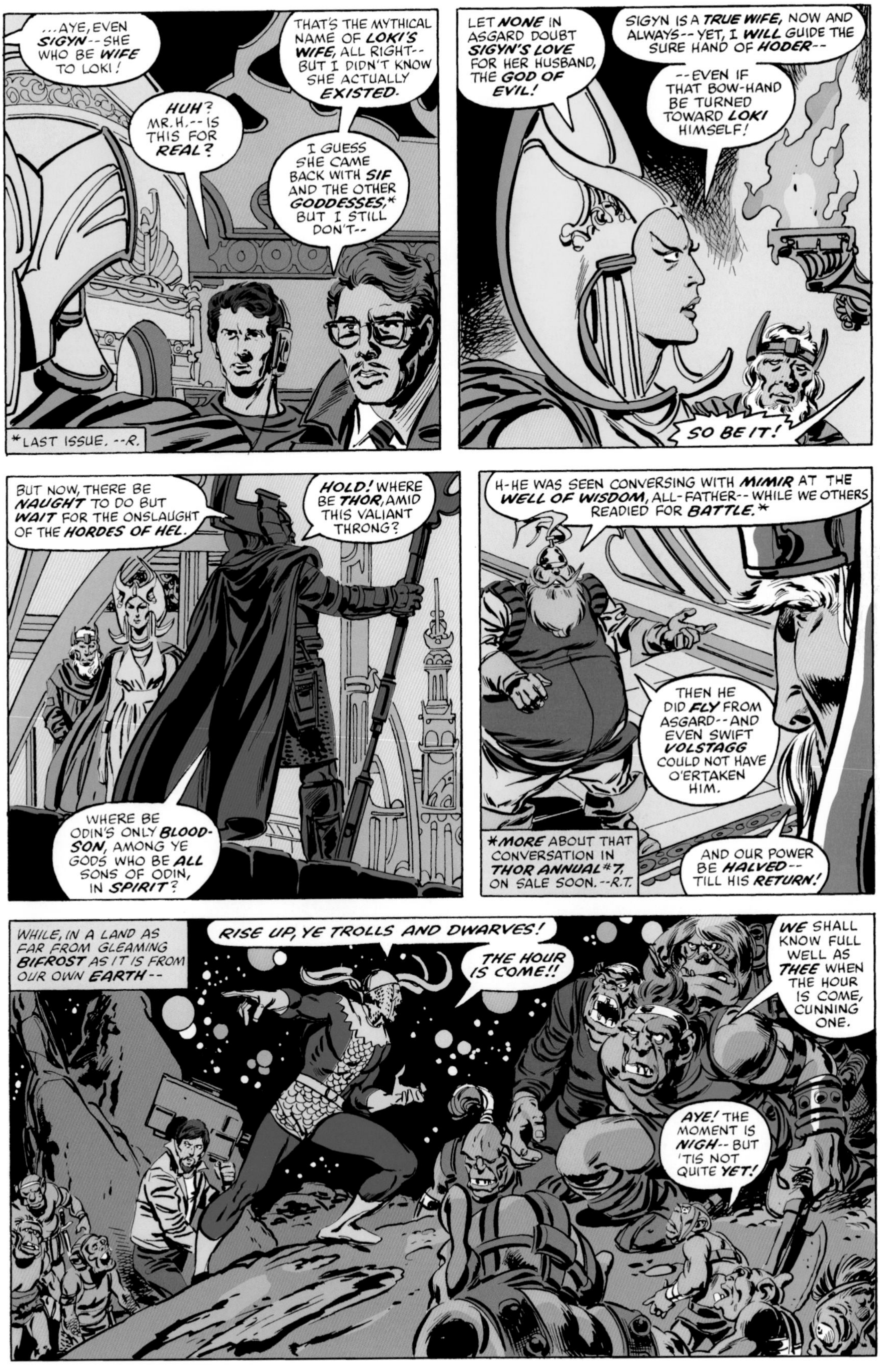
...AYE, EVEN SIGYN--SHE WHO BE WIFE TO LOKI!
THAT'S THE MYTHICAL NAME OF LOKI'S WIFE, ALL RIGHT--BUT I DIDN'T KNOW SHE ACTUALLY EXISTED.
HUH? MR. H.--IS THIS FOR REAL?
I GUESS SHE CAME BACK WITH SIF AND THE OTHER GODDESSES,* BUT I STILL DON'T--
*LAST ISSUE. --R.
LET NONE IN ASGARD DOUBT SIGYN'S LOVE FOR HER HUSBAND, THE GOD OF EVIL!
SIGYN IS A TRUE WIFE, NOW AND ALWAYS--YET, I WILL GUIDE THE SURE HAND OF HODER--
--EVEN IF THAT BOW-HAND BE TURNED TOWARD LOKI HIMSELF!
SO BE IT!
BUT NOW, THERE BE NAUGHT TO DO BUT WAIT FOR THE ONSLAUGHT OF THE HORDES OF HEL.
HOLD! WHERE BE THOR, AMID THIS VALIANT THRONG?
WHERE BE ODIN'S ONLY BLOOD-SON, AMONG YE GODS WHO BE ALL SONS OF ODIN, IN SPIRIT?
H-HE WAS SEEN CONVERSING WITH MIMIR AT THE WELL OF WISDOM, ALL-FATHER--WHILE WE OTHERS READIED FOR BATTLE.*
THEN HE DID FLY FROM ASGARD--AND EVEN SWIFT VOLSTAGG COULD NOT HAVE O'ERTAKEN HIM.
*MORE ABOUT THAT CONVERSATION IN THOR ANNUAL #7, ON SALE SOON. --R.T.
AND OUR POWER BE HALVED--TILL HIS RETURN!
WHILE, IN A LAND AS FAR FROM GLEAMING BIFROST AS IT IS FROM OUR OWN EARTH--
RISE UP, YE TROLLS AND DWARVES!
THE HOUR IS COME!!
WE SHALL KNOW FULL WELL AS THEE WHEN THE HOUR IS COME, CUNNING ONE.
AYE! THE MOMENT IS NIGH--BUT 'TIS NOT QUITE YET!

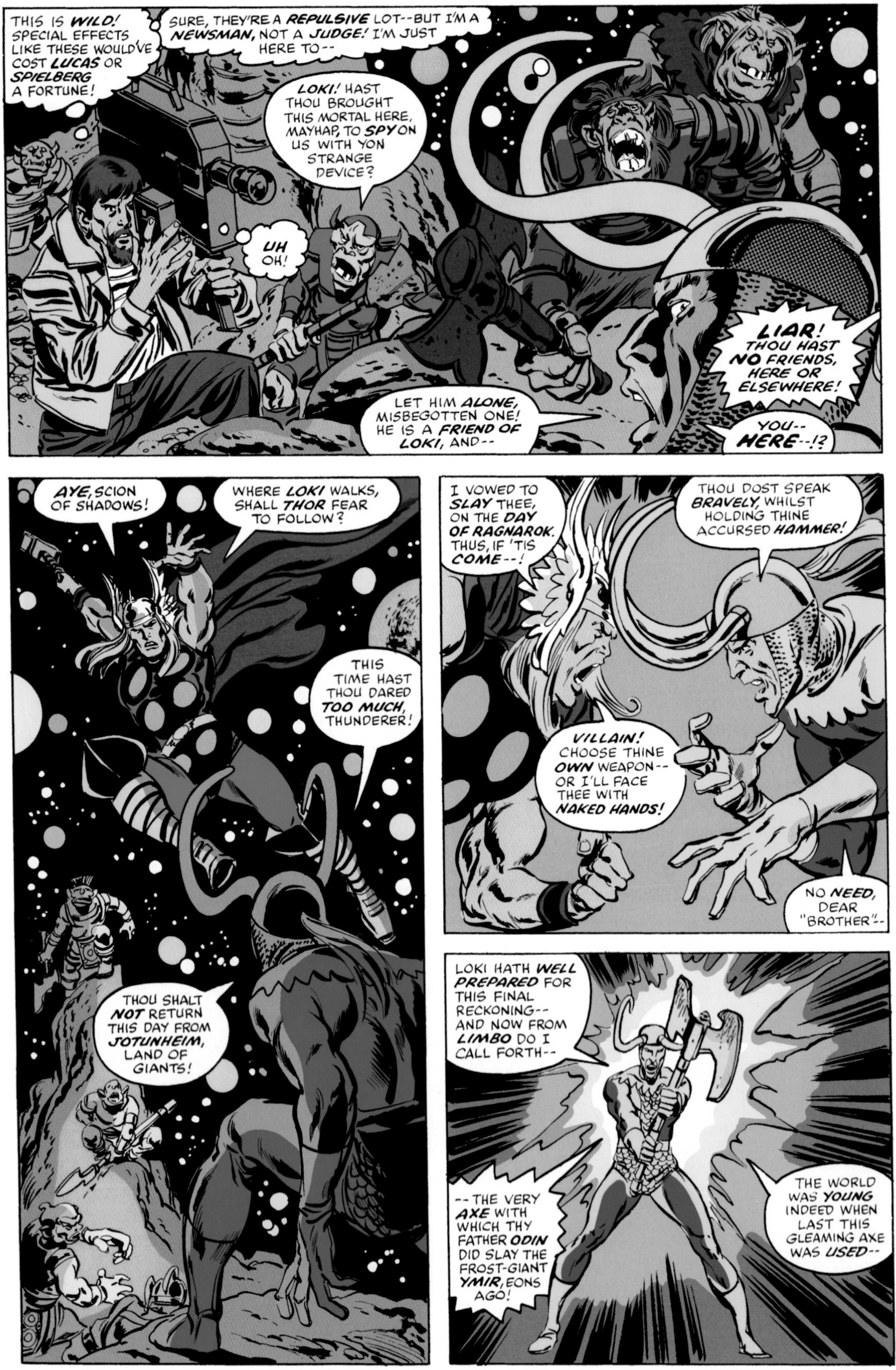
THIS IS WILD! SPECIAL EFFECTS LIKE THESE WOULD'VE COST LUCAS OR SPIELBERG A FORTUNE!
SURE, THEY'RE A REPULSIVE LOT--BUT I'M A NEWSMAN, NOT A JUDGE! I'M JUST HERE TO--
LOKI! HAST THOU BROUGHT THIS MORTAL HERE, MAYHAP, TO SPY ON US WITH YON STRANGE DEVICE?
UH OH!
LET HIM ALONE, MISBEGOTTEN ONE! HE IS A FRIEND OF LOKI, AND--
LIAR! THOU HAST NO FRIENDS, HERE OR ELSEWHERE!
YOU-- HERE--!?
AYE, SCION OF SHADOWS!
WHERE LOKI WALKS, SHALL THOR FEAR TO FOLLOW?
THIS TIME HAST THOU DARED TOO MUCH, THUNDERER!
THOU SHALT NOT RETURN THIS DAY FROM JOTUNHEIM, LAND OF GIANTS!
I VOWED TO SLAY THEE, ON THE DAY OF RAGNAROK. THUS, IF 'TIS COME--!
THOU DOST SPEAK BRAVELY, WHILST HOLDING THINE ACCURSED HAMMER!
VILLAIN! CHOOSE THINE OWN WEAPON-- OR I'LL FACE THEE WITH NAKED HANDS!
NO NEED, DEAR "BROTHER"--
LOKI HATH WELL PREPARED FOR THIS FINAL RECKONING-- AND NOW FROM LIMBO DO I CALL FORTH--
--THE VERY AXE WITH WHICH THY FATHER ODIN DID SLAY THE FROST-GIANT YMIR, EONS AGO!
THE WORLD WAS YOUNG INDEED WHEN LAST THIS GLEAMING AXE WAS USED--

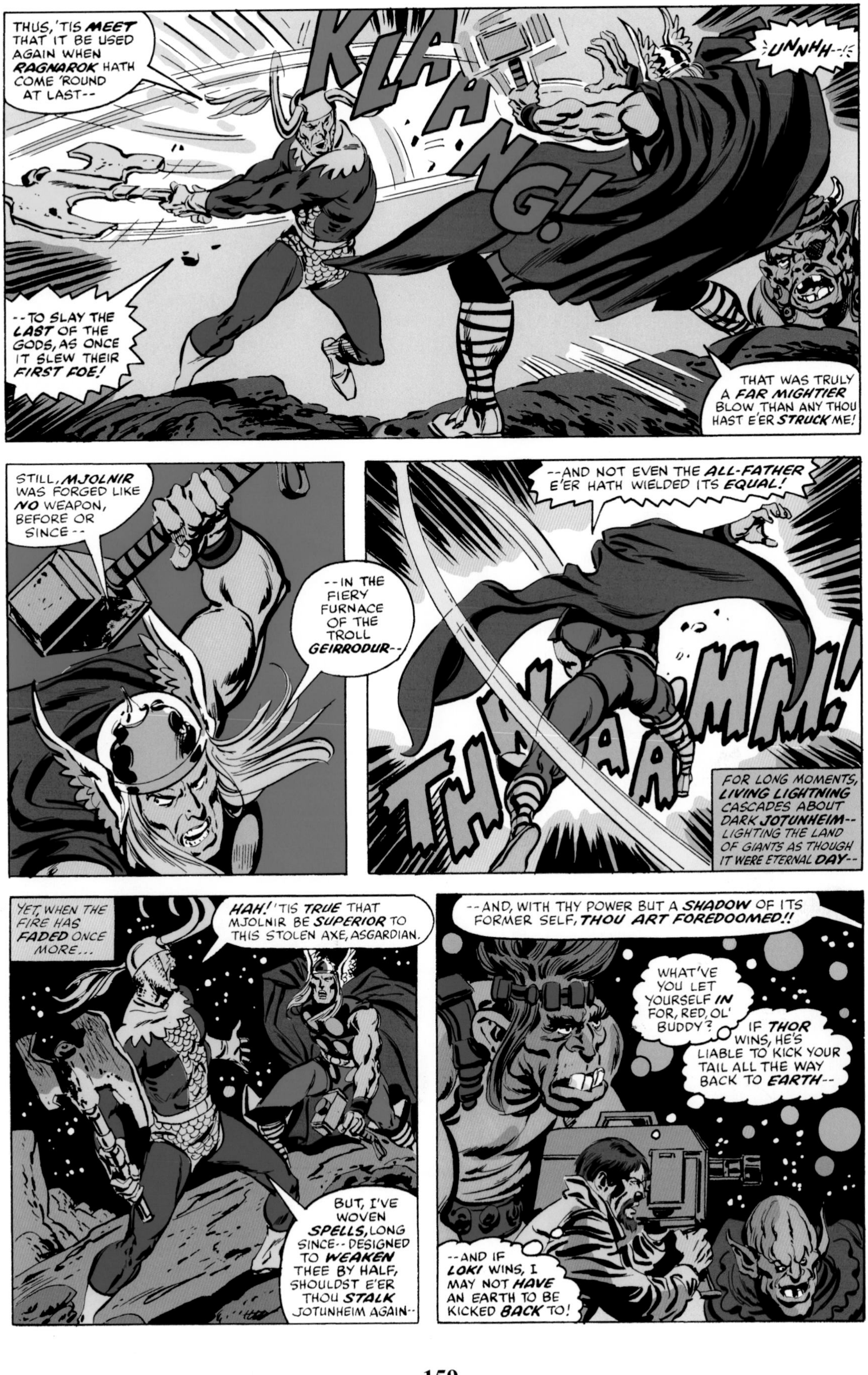
THUS, 'TIS MEET THAT IT BE USED AGAIN WHEN RAGNAROK HATH COME 'ROUND AT LAST--
KLANG!
UNNHH--!
--TO SLAY THE LAST OF THE GODS, AS ONCE IT SLEW THEIR FIRST FOE!
THAT WAS TRULY A FAR MIGHTIER BLOW THAN ANY THOU HAST E'ER STRUCK ME!
STILL, MJOLNIR WAS FORGED LIKE NO WEAPON, BEFORE OR SINCE--
--IN THE FIERY FURNACE OF THE TROLL GEIRRODUR--
--AND NOT EVEN THE ALL-FATHER E'ER HATH WIELDED ITS EQUAL!
THWAAMM!
FOR LONG MOMENTS, LIVING LIGHTNING CASCADES ABOUT DARK JOTUNHEIM-- LIGHTING THE LAND OF GIANTS AS THOUGH IT WERE ETERNAL DAY--
YET, WHEN THE FIRE HAS FADED ONCE MORE...
HAH! 'TIS TRUE THAT MJOLNIR BE SUPERIOR TO THIS STOLEN AXE, ASGARDIAN.
BUT, I'VE WOVEN SPELLS, LONG SINCE-- DESIGNED TO WEAKEN THEE BY HALF, SHOULDST E'ER THOU STALK JOTUNHEIM AGAIN--
--AND, WITH THY POWER BUT A SHADOW OF ITS FORMER SELF, THOU ART FOREDOOMED!!
WHAT'VE YOU LET YOURSELF IN FOR, RED, OL' BUDDY?
IF THOR WINS, HE'S LIABLE TO KICK YOUR TAIL ALL THE WAY BACK TO EARTH--
--AND IF LOKI WINS, I MAY NOT HAVE AN EARTH TO BE KICKED BACK TO!

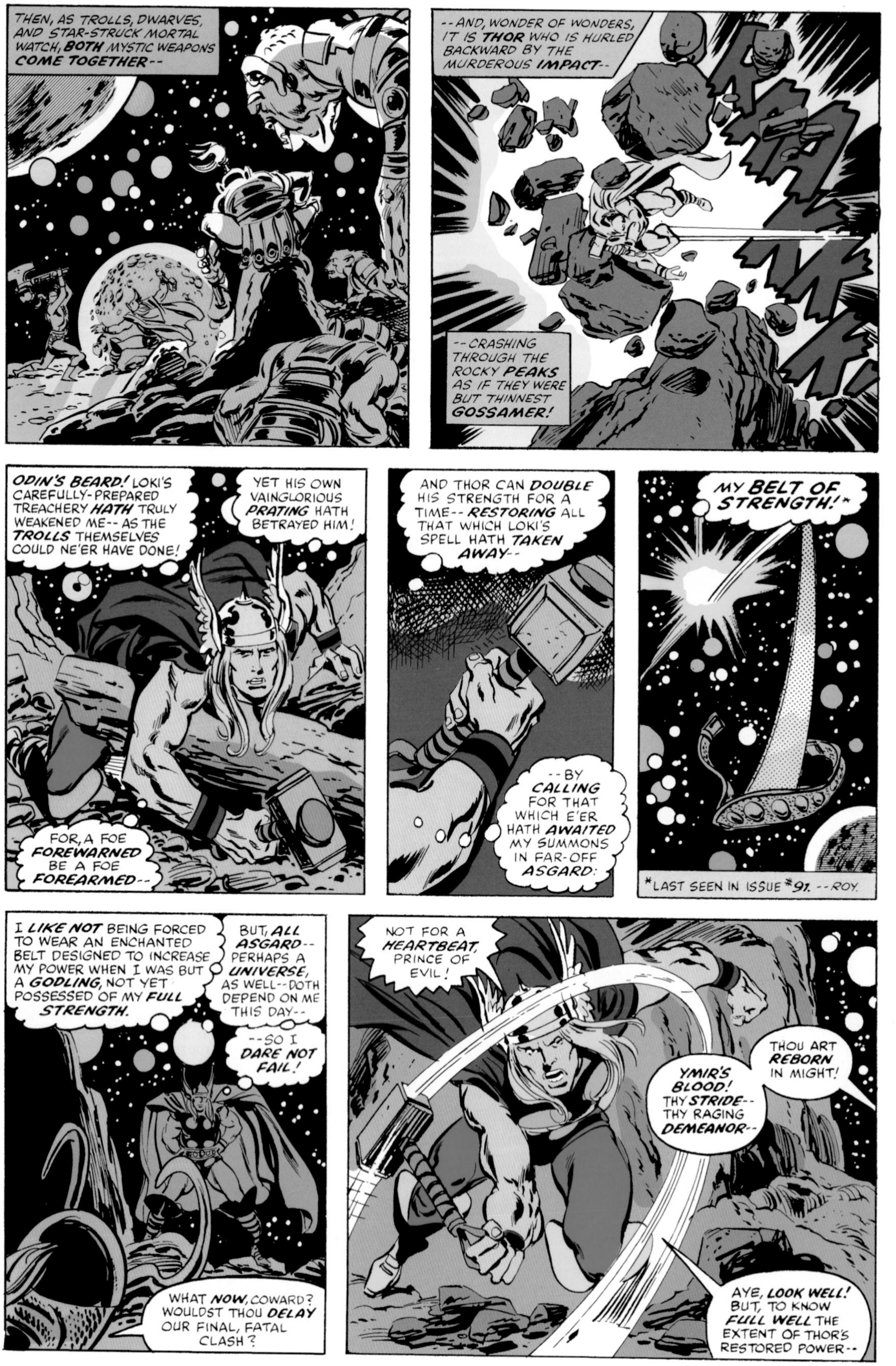

THEN, AS TROLLS, DWARVES, AND STAR-STRUCK MORTAL WATCH, BOTH MYSTIC WEAPONS COME TOGETHER--
--AND, WONDER OF WONDERS, IT IS THOR WHO IS HURLED BACKWARD BY THE MURDEROUS IMPACT--
KRAAKKK!
--CRASHING THROUGH THE ROCKY PEAKS AS IF THEY WERE BUT THINNEST GOSSAMER!
ODIN'S BEARD! LOKI'S CAREFULLY-PREPARED TREACHERY HATH TRULY WEAKENED ME-- AS THE TROLLS THEMSELVES COULD NE'ER HAVE DONE!
YET HIS OWN VAINGLORIOUS PRATING HATH BETRAYED HIM!
FOR, A FOE FOREWARNED BE A FOE FOREARMED--
AND THOR CAN DOUBLE HIS STRENGTH FOR A TIME-- RESTORING ALL THAT WHICH LOKI'S SPELL HATH TAKEN AWAY--
--BY CALLING FOR THAT WHICH E'ER HATH AWAITED MY SUMMONS IN FAR-OFF ASGARD:
MY BELT OF STRENGTH!*
*LAST SEEN IN ISSUE #91. --ROY.
I LIKE NOT BEING FORCED TO WEAR AN ENCHANTED BELT DESIGNED TO INCREASE MY POWER WHEN I WAS BUT A GODLING, NOT YET POSSESSED OF MY FULL STRENGTH.
BUT, ALL ASGARD-- PERHAPS A UNIVERSE, AS WELL--DOTH DEPEND ON ME THIS DAY--
--SO I DARE NOT FAIL!
WHAT NOW, COWARD? WOULDST THOU DELAY OUR FINAL, FATAL CLASH?
NOT FOR A HEARTBEAT, PRINCE OF EVIL!
THOU ART REBORN IN MIGHT!
YMIR'S BLOOD! THY STRIDE-- THY RAGING DEMEANOR--
AYE, LOOK WELL! BUT, TO KNOW FULL WELL THE EXTENT OF THOR'S RESTORED POWER--

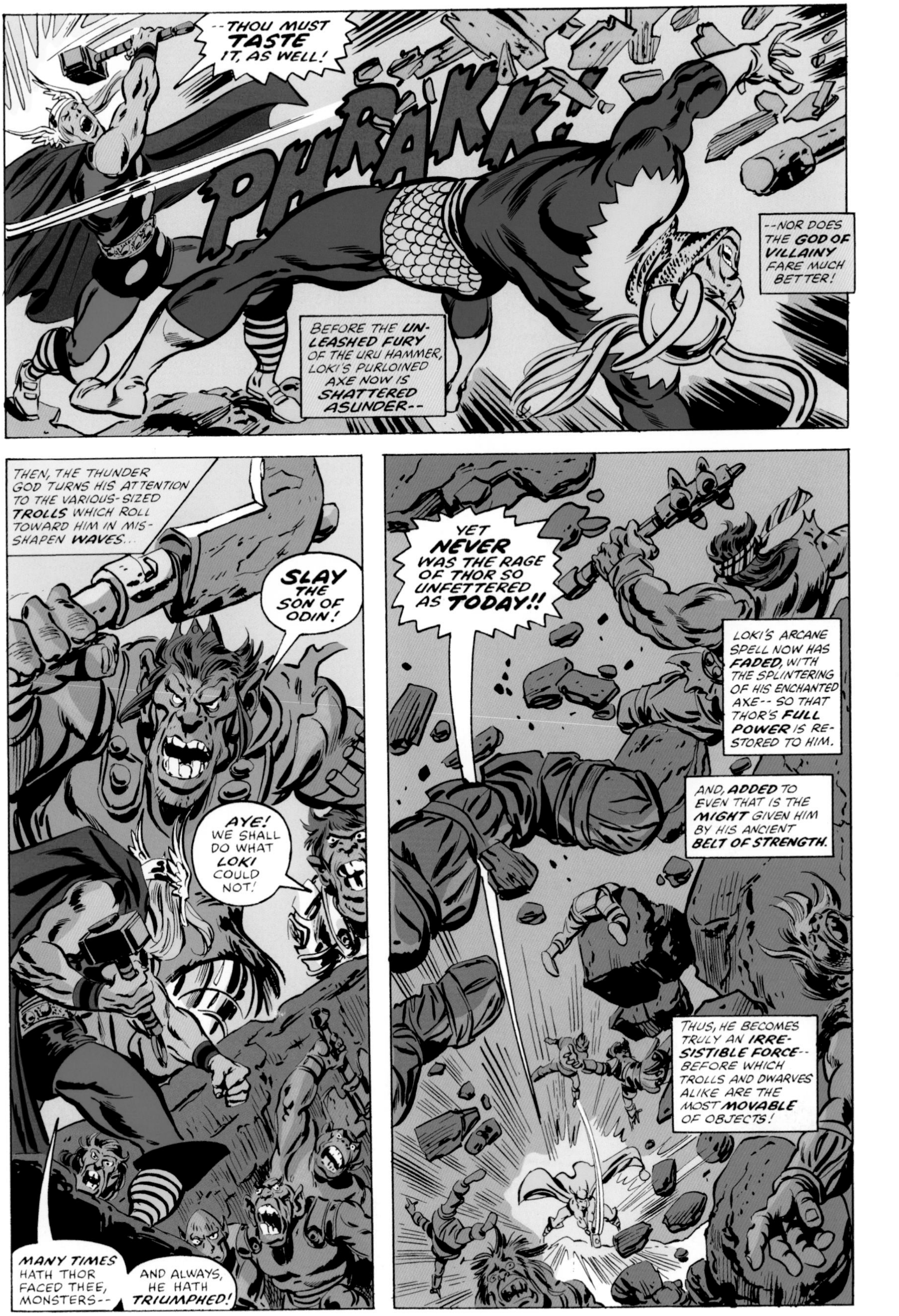
--THOU MUST TASTE IT, AS WELL!
PHRAKK!
BEFORE THE UN-LEASHED FURY OF THE URU HAMMER, LOKI'S PURLOINED AXE NOW IS SHATTERED ASUNDER--
--NOR DOES THE GOD OF VILLAINY FARE MUCH BETTER!
THEN, THE THUNDER GOD TURNS HIS ATTENTION TO THE VARIOUS-SIZED TROLLS WHICH ROLL TOWARD HIM IN MIS-SHAPEN WAVES...
SLAY THE SON OF ODIN!
AYE! WE SHALL DO WHAT LOKI COULD NOT!
MANY TIMES HATH THOR FACED THEE, MONSTERS--
AND ALWAYS, HE HATH TRIUMPHED!
YET NEVER WAS THE RAGE OF THOR SO UNFETTERED AS TODAY!!
LOKI'S ARCANE SPELL NOW HAS FADED, WITH THE SPLINTERING OF HIS ENCHANTED AXE-- SO THAT THOR'S FULL POWER IS RE-STORED TO HIM.
AND, ADDED TO EVEN THAT IS THE MIGHT GIVEN HIM BY HIS ANCIENT BELT OF STRENGTH.
THUS, HE BECOMES TRULY AN IRRE-SISTIBLE FORCE-- BEFORE WHICH TROLLS AND DWARVES ALIKE ARE THE MOST MOVABLE OF OBJECTS!

LOKI SHALL DO NO HARM-- *EVER AGAIN!*

NOW, MORTAL-- BRING HITHER THINE INFERNAL *GADGET*--

--AND I'LL HIE US ALL TO THE *GLEAMING REALM!*

AS MAGIC *MJOLNIR* BRIDGES WHAT LESSER MINDS CALL *HYPERSPACE,* THE SON OF ODIN SAYS *NOTHING*--

--HIS MIND FILLED WITH IMAGES OF *BALDER THE BRAVE,* HOVERING AT BEST BETWEEN VIBRANT *LIFE* AND ETERNAL *DEATH.*

THEN-- *ASGARD!*

THANKS, FRIEND-- BUT *LOOK,* I HOPE YOU DON'T THINK *I* WAS PART OF ANY *PLOT* TO--

NAY. BUT, THINE ILK WOULD DO ANYTHING FOR WHAT THOU WOULDST TERM-- A *SCOOP.*

HERE! HOLD MY *BELT OF STRENGTH,* UNTIL AND UNLESS I DO *ASK* FOR IT!

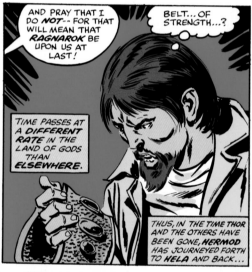

AND PRAY THAT I DO *NOT*-- FOR THAT WILL MEAN THAT *RAGNAROK* BE UPON US AT LAST!

BELT... OF STRENGTH...?

TIME PASSES AT A *DIFFERENT RATE* IN THE LAND OF GODS THAN *ELSEWHERE.*

THUS, IN THE TIME THOR AND THE OTHERS HAVE BEEN GONE, *HERMOD* HAS JOURNEYED FORTH TO *HELA* AND BACK...

...AND ALL HAS GONE, ALAS, JUST AS *HARRIS HOBBS* PREDICTED:

--BUT, BECAUSE THE GIANTESS *THOKK* WOULD NOT WEEP, BALDER IS FOR- EVER *LOST* TO US!

CAN *NOTHING,* THEN, STAVE OFF THE GATHERING TWILIGHT, SIRE?

FOR, THOUGH *I* SCATTERED THE TROLLS, THEY WILL SOON *RE- GROUP* IN NUMBERS BEYOND COUNTING.

CAN *NAUGHT* PUT OFF THE *DAY OF DOOM?*

MAYHAP... IT *CAN,* MY SON.

LONG HAVE I *DELAYED* MY NEXT ACTION, HOPING AGAINST HOPE THAT *SOME OTHER WAY* WOULD BE FOUND.

BUT NOW, I KNOW THAT WAS *NOT TO BE.*

COME THEN, YE GODS AND GODDESSES!

162

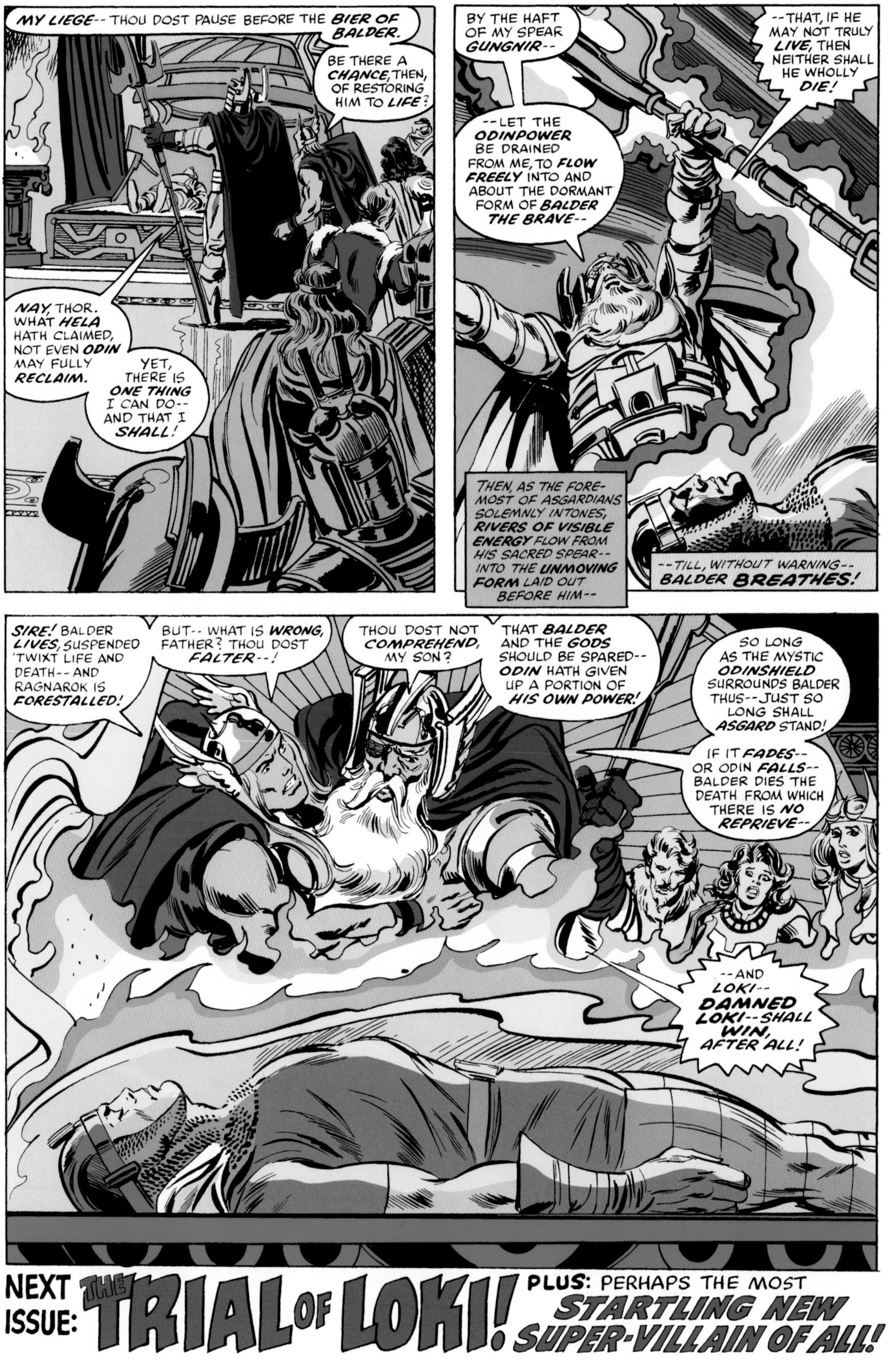
MY LIEGE-- THOU DOST PAUSE BEFORE THE BIER OF BALDER.
BE THERE A CHANCE, THEN, OF RESTORING HIM TO LIFE?
NAY, THOR. WHAT HELA HATH CLAIMED, NOT EVEN ODIN MAY FULLY RECLAIM.
YET, THERE IS ONE THING I CAN DO-- AND THAT I SHALL!
BY THE HAFT OF MY SPEAR GUNGNIR--
--THAT, IF HE MAY NOT TRULY LIVE, THEN NEITHER SHALL HE WHOLLY DIE!
--LET THE ODINPOWER BE DRAINED FROM ME, TO FLOW FREELY INTO AND ABOUT THE DORMANT FORM OF BALDER THE BRAVE--
THEN, AS THE FOREMOST OF ASGARDIANS SOLEMNLY INTONES, RIVERS OF VISIBLE ENERGY FLOW FROM HIS SACRED SPEAR-- INTO THE UNMOVING FORM LAID OUT BEFORE HIM--
--TILL, WITHOUT WARNING-- BALDER BREATHES!
SIRE! BALDER LIVES, SUSPENDED 'TWIXT LIFE AND DEATH-- AND RAGNAROK IS FORESTALLED!
BUT-- WHAT IS WRONG, FATHER? THOU DOST FALTER--!
THOU DOST NOT COMPREHEND, MY SON?
THAT BALDER AND THE GODS SHOULD BE SPARED-- ODIN HATH GIVEN UP A PORTION OF HIS OWN POWER!
SO LONG AS THE MYSTIC ODINSHIELD SURROUNDS BALDER THUS--JUST SO LONG SHALL ASGARD STAND!
IF IT FADES-- OR ODIN FALLS-- BALDER DIES THE DEATH FROM WHICH THERE IS NO REPRIEVE--
--AND LOKI-- DAMNED LOKI--SHALL WIN, AFTER ALL!

NEXT ISSUE: THE TRIAL OF LOKI! PLUS: PERHAPS THE MOST STARTLING NEW SUPER-VILLAIN OF ALL!

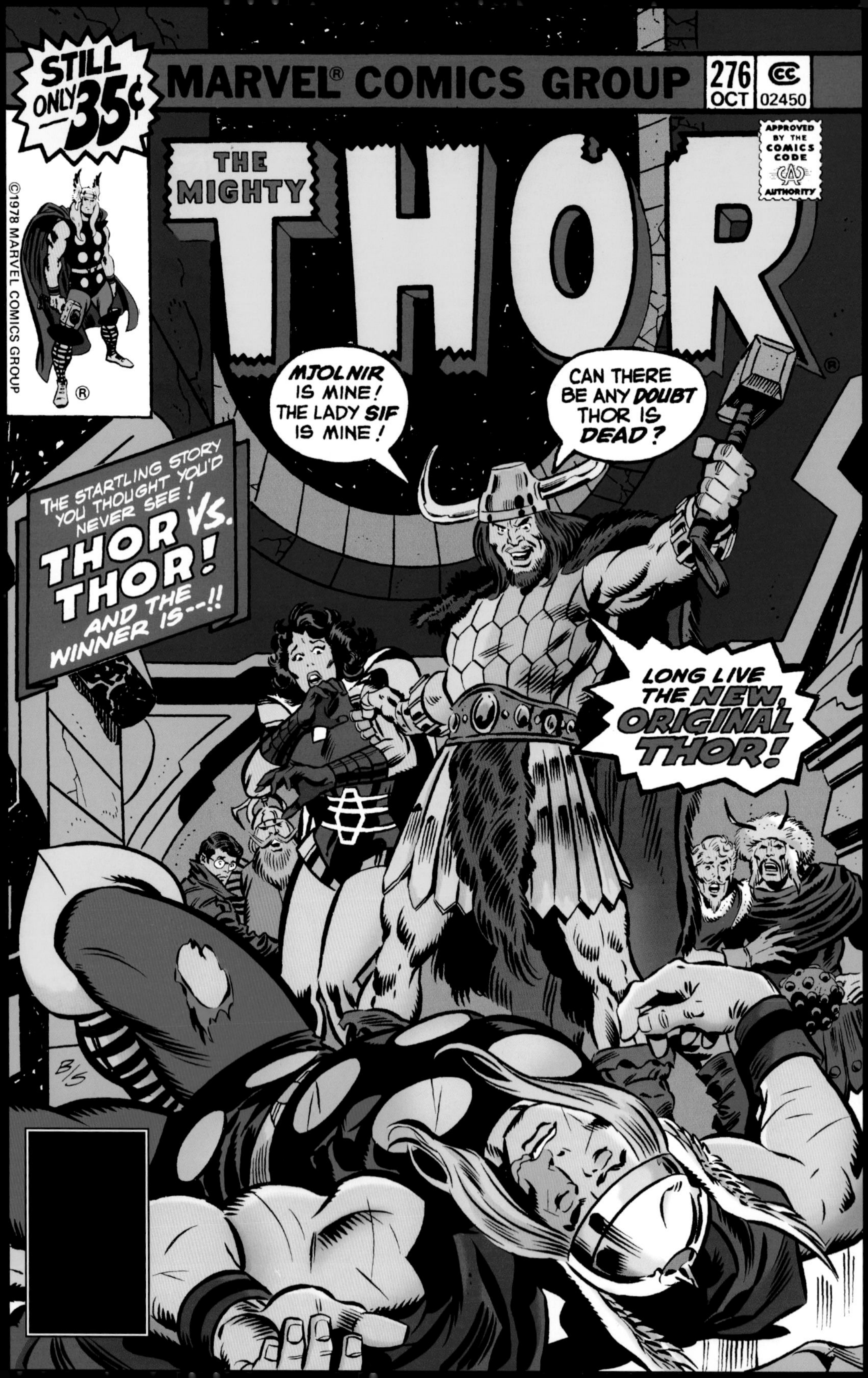

STILL ONLY 35¢
MARVEL® COMICS GROUP
276 OCT
CC 02450
APPROVED BY THE COMICS CODE AUTHORITY
©1978 MARVEL COMICS GROUP
THE MIGHTY THOR®
MJOLNIR IS MINE! THE LADY SIF IS MINE!
CAN THERE BE ANY DOUBT THOR IS DEAD?
THE STARTLING STORY YOU THOUGHT YOU'D NEVER SEE! THOR VS. THOR! AND THE WINNER IS--!!
LONG LIVE THE NEW, ORIGINAL THOR!
B/S

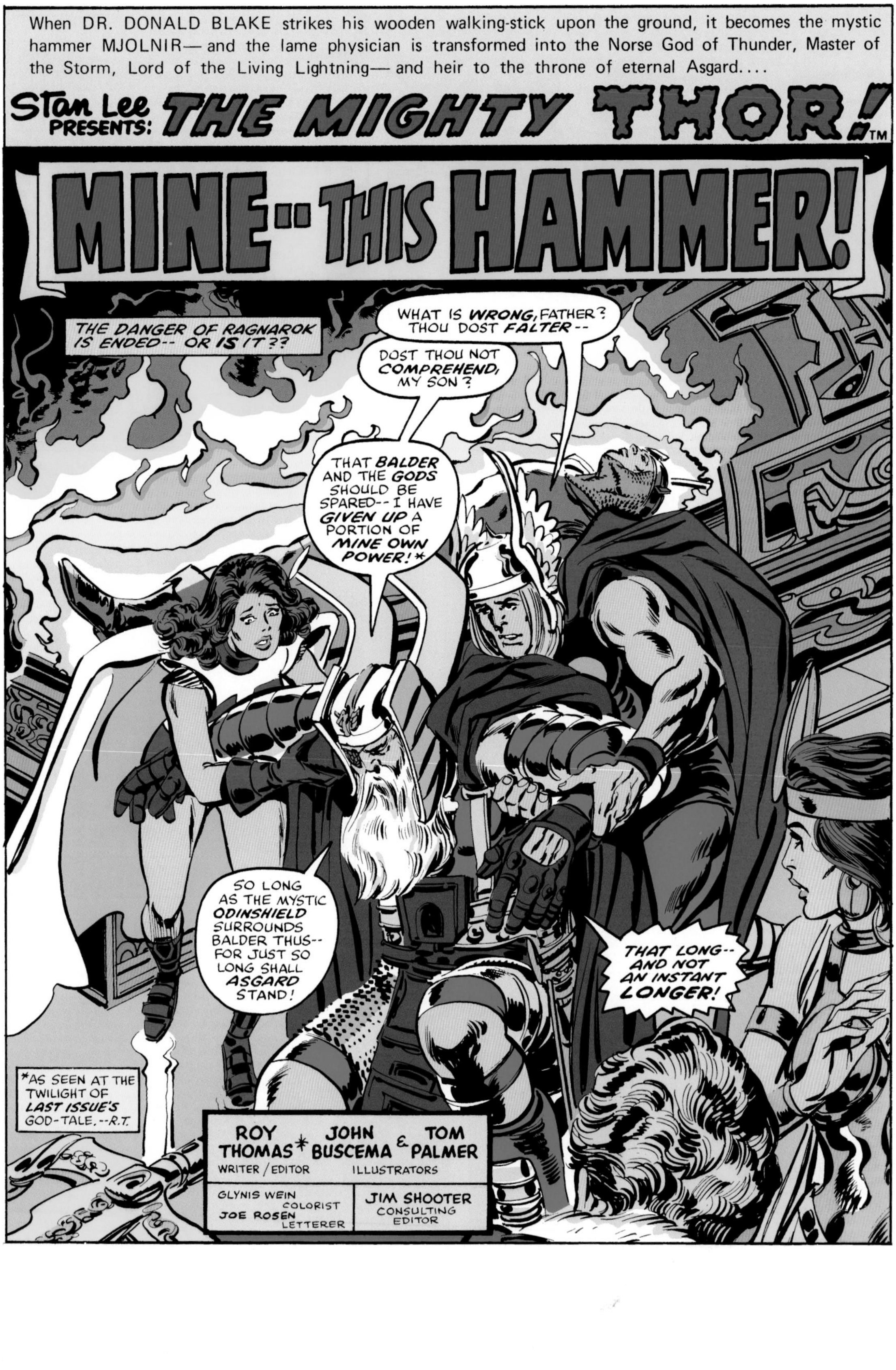
When DR. DONALD BLAKE strikes his wooden walking-stick upon the ground, it becomes the mystic hammer MJOLNIR— and the lame physician is transformed into the Norse God of Thunder, Master of the Storm, Lord of the Living Lightning— and heir to the throne of eternal Asgard....
Stan Lee PRESENTS: THE MIGHTY THOR! TM
MINE-- THIS HAMMER!
THE DANGER OF RAGNAROK IS ENDED-- OR IS IT??
WHAT IS WRONG, FATHER? THOU DOST FALTER--
DOST THOU NOT COMPREHEND, MY SON?
THAT BALDER AND THE GODS SHOULD BE SPARED-- I HAVE GIVEN UP A PORTION OF MINE OWN POWER!*
SO LONG AS THE MYSTIC ODINSHIELD SURROUNDS BALDER THUS-- FOR JUST SO LONG SHALL ASGARD STAND!
THAT LONG-- AND NOT AN INSTANT LONGER!
*AS SEEN AT THE TWILIGHT OF LAST ISSUE'S GOD-TALE. --R.T.
ROY THOMAS WRITER / EDITOR
JOHN BUSCEMA & TOM PALMER ILLUSTRATORS
GLYNIS WEIN COLORIST
JOE ROSEN LETTERER
JIM SHOOTER CONSULTING EDITOR

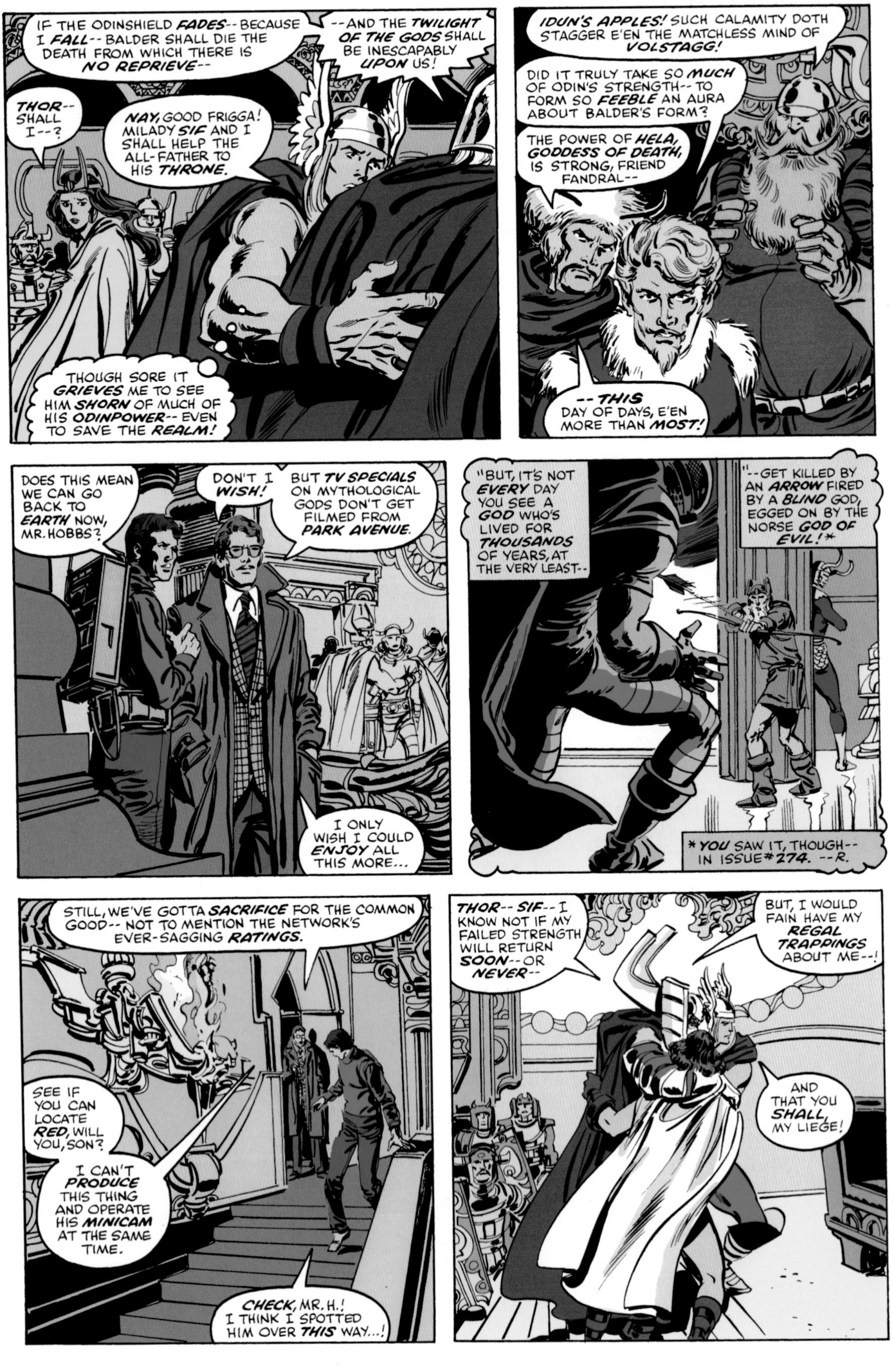

IF THE ODINSHIELD FADES-- BECAUSE I FALL-- BALDER SHALL DIE THE DEATH FROM WHICH THERE IS NO REPRIEVE--
--AND THE TWILIGHT OF THE GODS SHALL BE INESCAPABLY UPON US!
THOR-- SHALL I--?
NAY, GOOD FRIGGA! MILADY SIF AND I SHALL HELP THE ALL-FATHER TO HIS THRONE.
THOUGH SORE IT GRIEVES ME TO SEE HIM SHORN OF MUCH OF HIS ODINPOWER-- EVEN TO SAVE THE REALM!
IDUN'S APPLES! SUCH CALAMITY DOTH STAGGER E'EN THE MATCHLESS MIND OF VOLSTAGG!
DID IT TRULY TAKE SO MUCH OF ODIN'S STRENGTH-- TO FORM SO FEEBLE AN AURA ABOUT BALDER'S FORM?
THE POWER OF HELA, GODDESS OF DEATH, IS STRONG, FRIEND FANDRAL--
--THIS DAY OF DAYS, E'EN MORE THAN MOST!
DOES THIS MEAN WE CAN GO BACK TO EARTH NOW, MR. HOBBS?
DON'T I WISH!
BUT TV SPECIALS ON MYTHOLOGICAL GODS DON'T GET FILMED FROM PARK AVENUE.
I ONLY WISH I COULD ENJOY ALL THIS MORE...
"BUT, IT'S NOT EVERY DAY YOU SEE A GOD WHO'S LIVED FOR THOUSANDS OF YEARS, AT THE VERY LEAST--
"--GET KILLED BY AN ARROW FIRED BY A BLIND GOD, EGGED ON BY THE NORSE GOD OF EVIL!*
*YOU SAW IT, THOUGH-- IN ISSUE #274. --R.
STILL, WE'VE GOTTA SACRIFICE FOR THE COMMON GOOD-- NOT TO MENTION THE NETWORK'S EVER-SAGGING RATINGS.
SEE IF YOU CAN LOCATE RED, WILL YOU, SON?
I CAN'T PRODUCE THIS THING AND OPERATE HIS MINICAM AT THE SAME TIME.
CHECK, MR. H.! I THINK I SPOTTED HIM OVER THIS WAY...!
THOR-- SIF-- I KNOW NOT IF MY FAILED STRENGTH WILL RETURN SOON--OR NEVER--
BUT, I WOULD FAIN HAVE MY REGAL TRAPPINGS ABOUT ME--!
AND THAT YOU SHALL, MY LIEGE!

HERE BE THY POWER-GIVING ARM-RING *DRAUPNIR*-- FROM WHICH *EIGHT MORE* SUCH RINGS *DROP*-- EVERY NINTH NIGHT.

WHEN *THAT* HAPPENS, SIRE, WILL NOT THEIR COMBINED POWER *RESTORE* TO THEE VIRTUALLY *ALL* OF THY FORMER MIGHT?

AYE...

...BUT ONLY IN TIME, MAYHAP, TO *REVITALIZE* THE ODINSHIELD WHICH ENVELOPES THE COMATOSE *BALDER.*

YET, WE ARE *GODS* ALL, NOT MERE *MORTALS.*

LET *THEM* FEAR DEATH-- WHILE WE OF *ASGARD* RIDE FORTH, TIME AND AGAIN, TO *DO BATTLE* WITH HELA'S HORDES!

WITH MY *RAVENS* AND *WOLVES* ABOUT ME-- *DRAUPNIR* ON MY ARM, AND *GUNGNIR* IN MY HAND--

I AM ONCE MORE *ODIN, LORD OF ASGARD!*

AND NOW, LET THERE *BEGIN* AT ONCE--

--THE *TRIAL OF LOKI*-- HE WHO HATH BASELY *BETRAYED* THE GODS!

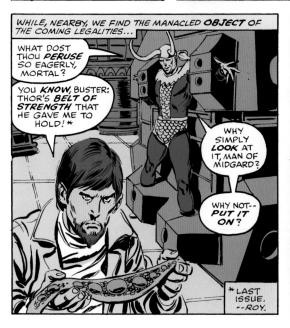

WHILE, NEARBY, WE FIND THE MANACLED *OBJECT* OF THE COMING LEGALITIES...

WHAT DOST THOU *PERUSE* SO EAGERLY, MORTAL?

YOU *KNOW,* BUSTER: *THOR'S BELT OF STRENGTH* THAT HE GAVE ME TO HOLD!*

WHY SIMPLY *LOOK* AT IT, MAN OF MIDGARD?

WHY NOT-- *PUT IT ON?*

* LAST ISSUE. --ROY.

YEAH-- *WHY NOT?*

MAYBE IT'LL GIVE *ME* POWER, LIKE IT GAVE *THOR* TO FIGHT THOSE GI[...]

A MAN WITH A WEAKER HEART THAN "*RED*" *NORVELL* MIGHT NEVER RECOVER FROM THE QUASI-ELECTRICAL *CHARGE* WHICH RACES NOW THRU HIS QUIVERING *BODY...*

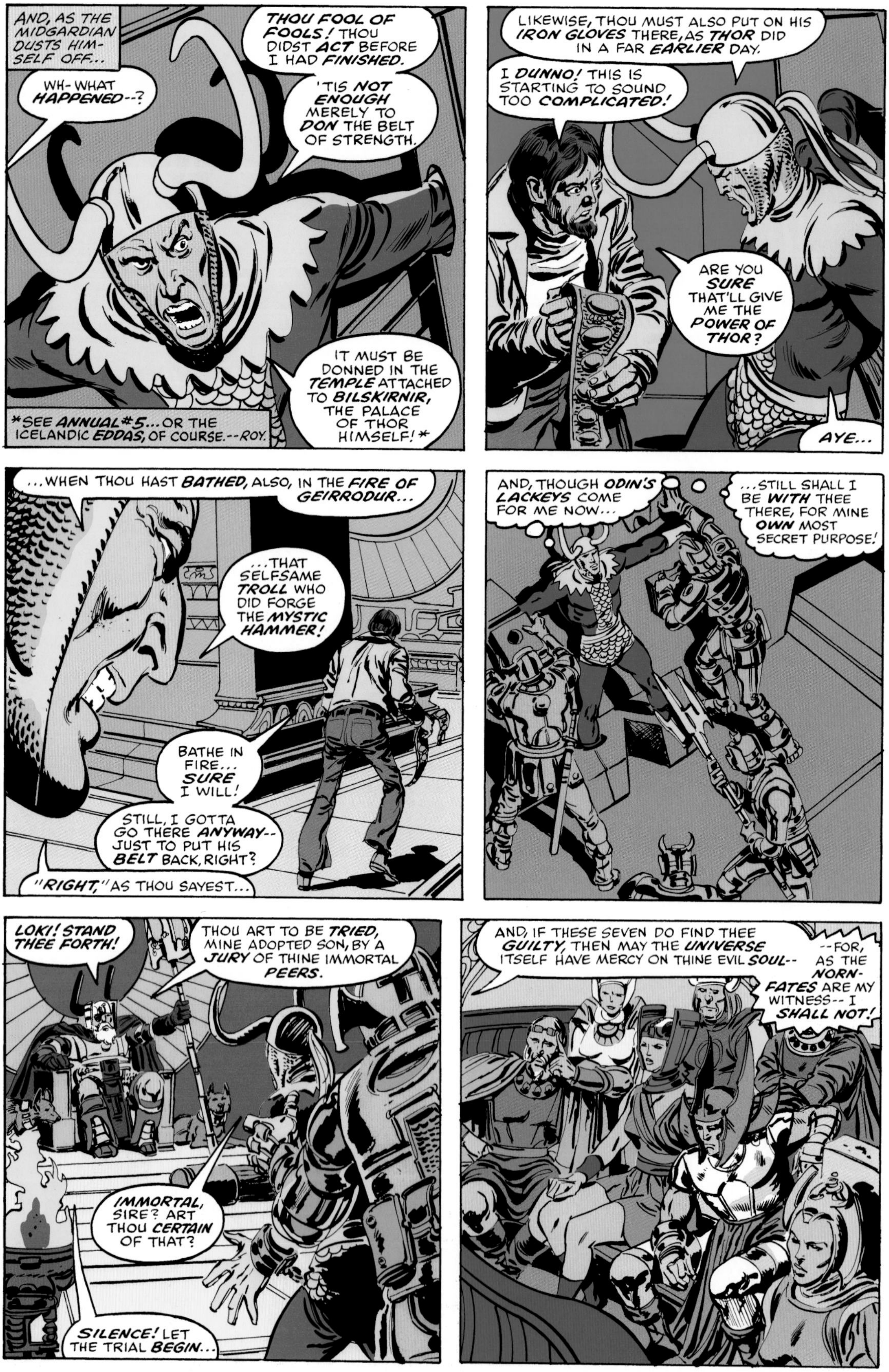
AND, AS THE MIDGARDIAN DUSTS HIMSELF OFF...
THOU FOOL OF FOOLS! THOU DIDST ACT BEFORE I HAD FINISHED.
WH-WHAT HAPPENED--?
'TIS NOT ENOUGH MERELY TO DON THE BELT OF STRENGTH.
IT MUST BE DONNED IN THE TEMPLE ATTACHED TO BILSKIRNIR, THE PALACE OF THOR HIMSELF! *
*SEE ANNUAL #5... OR THE ICELANDIC EDDAS, OF COURSE.--ROY.
LIKEWISE, THOU MUST ALSO PUT ON HIS IRON GLOVES THERE, AS THOR DID IN A FAR EARLIER DAY.
I DUNNO! THIS IS STARTING TO SOUND TOO COMPLICATED!
ARE YOU SURE THAT'LL GIVE ME THE POWER OF THOR?
AYE...
...WHEN THOU HAST BATHED, ALSO, IN THE FIRE OF GEIRRODUR...
...THAT SELFSAME TROLL WHO DID FORGE THE MYSTIC HAMMER!
BATHE IN FIRE... SURE I WILL!
STILL, I GOTTA GO THERE ANYWAY--JUST TO PUT HIS BELT BACK, RIGHT?
"RIGHT," AS THOU SAYEST...
AND, THOUGH ODIN'S LACKEYS COME FOR ME NOW...
...STILL SHALL I BE WITH THEE THERE, FOR MINE OWN MOST SECRET PURPOSE!
LOKI! STAND THEE FORTH!
THOU ART TO BE TRIED, MINE ADOPTED SON, BY A JURY OF THINE IMMORTAL PEERS.
IMMORTAL, SIRE? ART THOU CERTAIN OF THAT?
SILENCE! LET THE TRIAL BEGIN...
AND, IF THESE SEVEN DO FIND THEE GUILTY, THEN MAY THE UNIVERSE ITSELF HAVE MERCY ON THINE EVIL SOUL--
--FOR, AS THE NORN-FATES ARE MY WITNESS--I SHALL NOT!

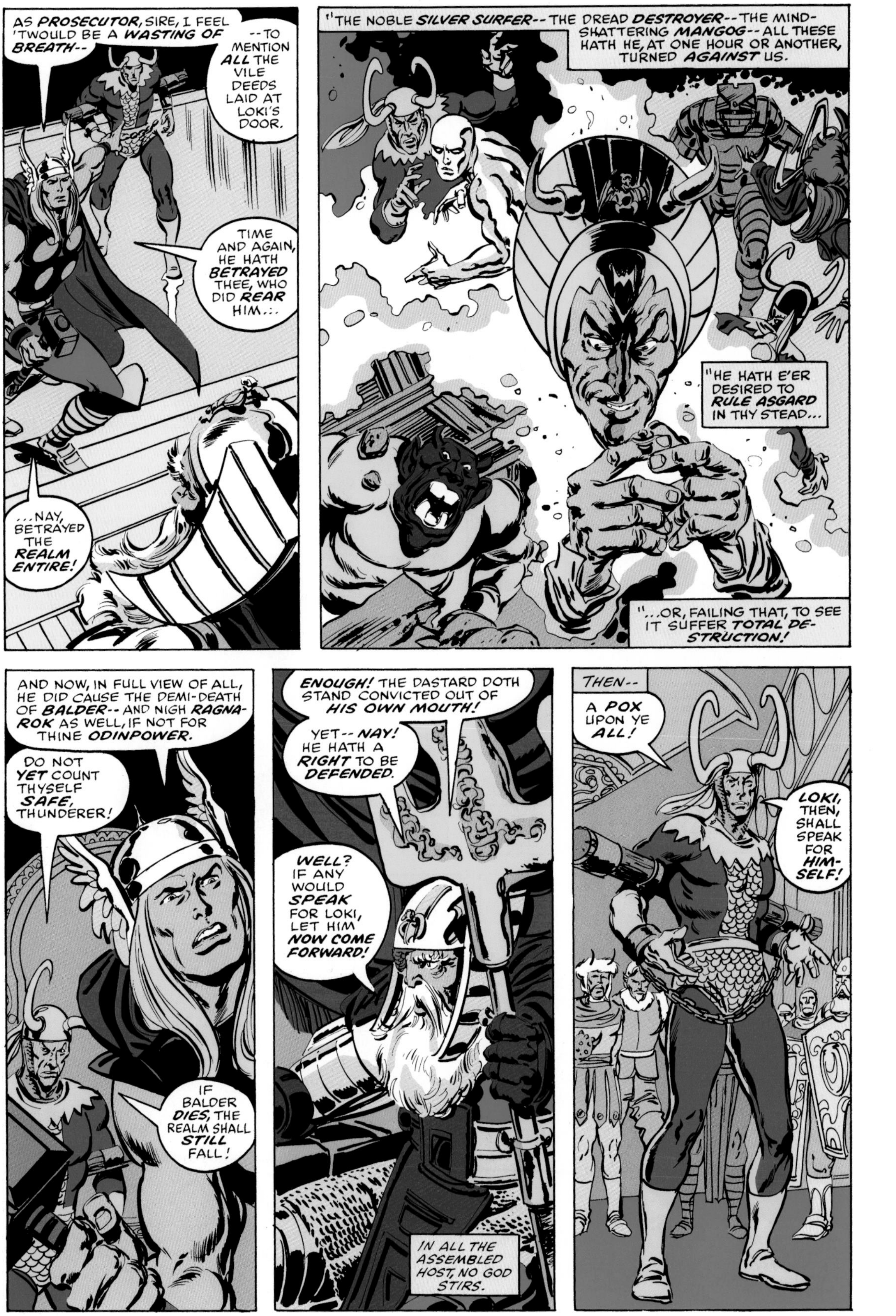
AS PROSECUTOR, SIRE, I FEEL 'TWOULD BE A WASTING OF BREATH--
--TO MENTION ALL THE VILE DEEDS LAID AT LOKI'S DOOR.
TIME AND AGAIN, HE HATH BETRAYED THEE, WHO DID REAR HIM...
...NAY, BETRAYED THE REALM ENTIRE!
"THE NOBLE SILVER SURFER-- THE DREAD DESTROYER-- THE MIND-SHATTERING MANGOG-- ALL THESE HATH HE, AT ONE HOUR OR ANOTHER, TURNED AGAINST US.
"HE HATH E'ER DESIRED TO RULE ASGARD IN THY STEAD...
"...OR, FAILING THAT, TO SEE IT SUFFER TOTAL DESTRUCTION!
AND NOW, IN FULL VIEW OF ALL, HE DID CAUSE THE DEMI-DEATH OF BALDER-- AND NIGH RAGNAROK AS WELL, IF NOT FOR THINE ODINPOWER.
DO NOT YET COUNT THYSELF SAFE, THUNDERER!
IF BALDER DIES, THE REALM SHALL STILL FALL!
ENOUGH! THE DASTARD DOTH STAND CONVICTED OUT OF HIS OWN MOUTH!
YET-- NAY! HE HATH A RIGHT TO BE DEFENDED.
WELL? IF ANY WOULD SPEAK FOR LOKI, LET HIM NOW COME FORWARD!
IN ALL THE ASSEMBLED HOST, NO GOD STIRS.
THEN--
A POX UPON YE ALL!
LOKI, THEN, SHALL SPEAK FOR HIMSELF!

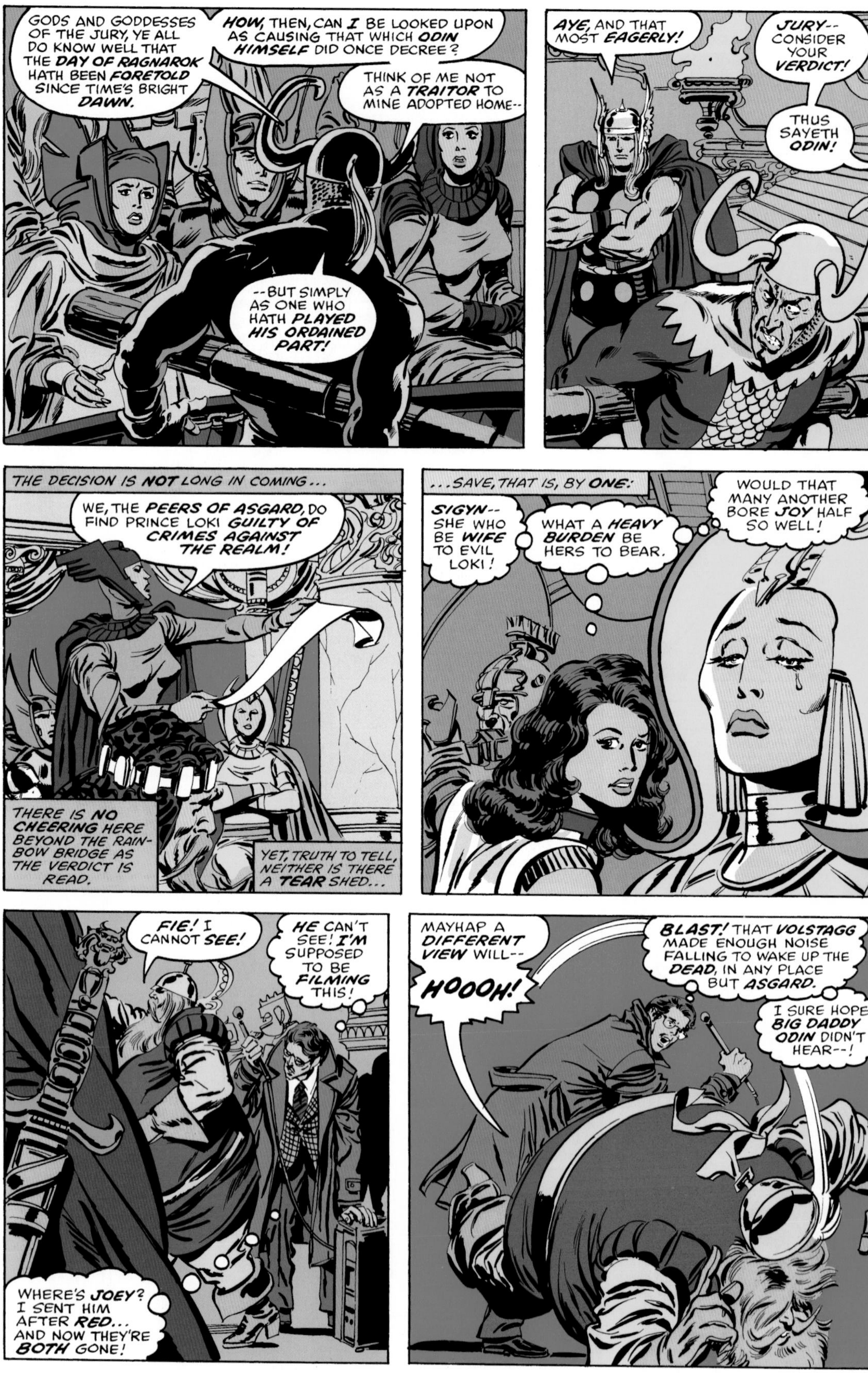
GODS AND GODDESSES OF THE JURY, YE ALL DO KNOW WELL THAT THE DAY OF RAGNAROK HATH BEEN FORETOLD SINCE TIME'S BRIGHT DAWN.
HOW, THEN, CAN I BE LOOKED UPON AS CAUSING THAT WHICH ODIN HIMSELF DID ONCE DECREE?
THINK OF ME NOT AS A TRAITOR TO MINE ADOPTED HOME--
--BUT SIMPLY AS ONE WHO HATH PLAYED HIS ORDAINED PART!
AYE, AND THAT MOST EAGERLY!
JURY-- CONSIDER YOUR VERDICT!
THUS SAYETH ODIN!
THE DECISION IS NOT LONG IN COMING...
WE, THE PEERS OF ASGARD, DO FIND PRINCE LOKI GUILTY OF CRIMES AGAINST THE REALM!
THERE IS NO CHEERING HERE BEYOND THE RAINBOW BRIDGE AS THE VERDICT IS READ.
YET, TRUTH TO TELL, NEITHER IS THERE A TEAR SHED...
...SAVE, THAT IS, BY ONE:
SIGYN-- SHE WHO BE WIFE TO EVIL LOKI!
WHAT A HEAVY BURDEN BE HERS TO BEAR.
WOULD THAT MANY ANOTHER BORE JOY HALF SO WELL!
FIE! I CANNOT SEE!
HE CAN'T SEE! I'M SUPPOSED TO BE FILMING THIS!
WHERE'S JOEY? I SENT HIM AFTER RED... AND NOW THEY'RE BOTH GONE!
MAYHAP A DIFFERENT VIEW WILL--
HOOOH!
BLAST! THAT VOLSTAGG MADE ENOUGH NOISE FALLING TO WAKE UP THE DEAD, IN ANY PLACE BUT ASGARD.
I SURE HOPE BIG DADDY ODIN DIDN'T HEAR--!

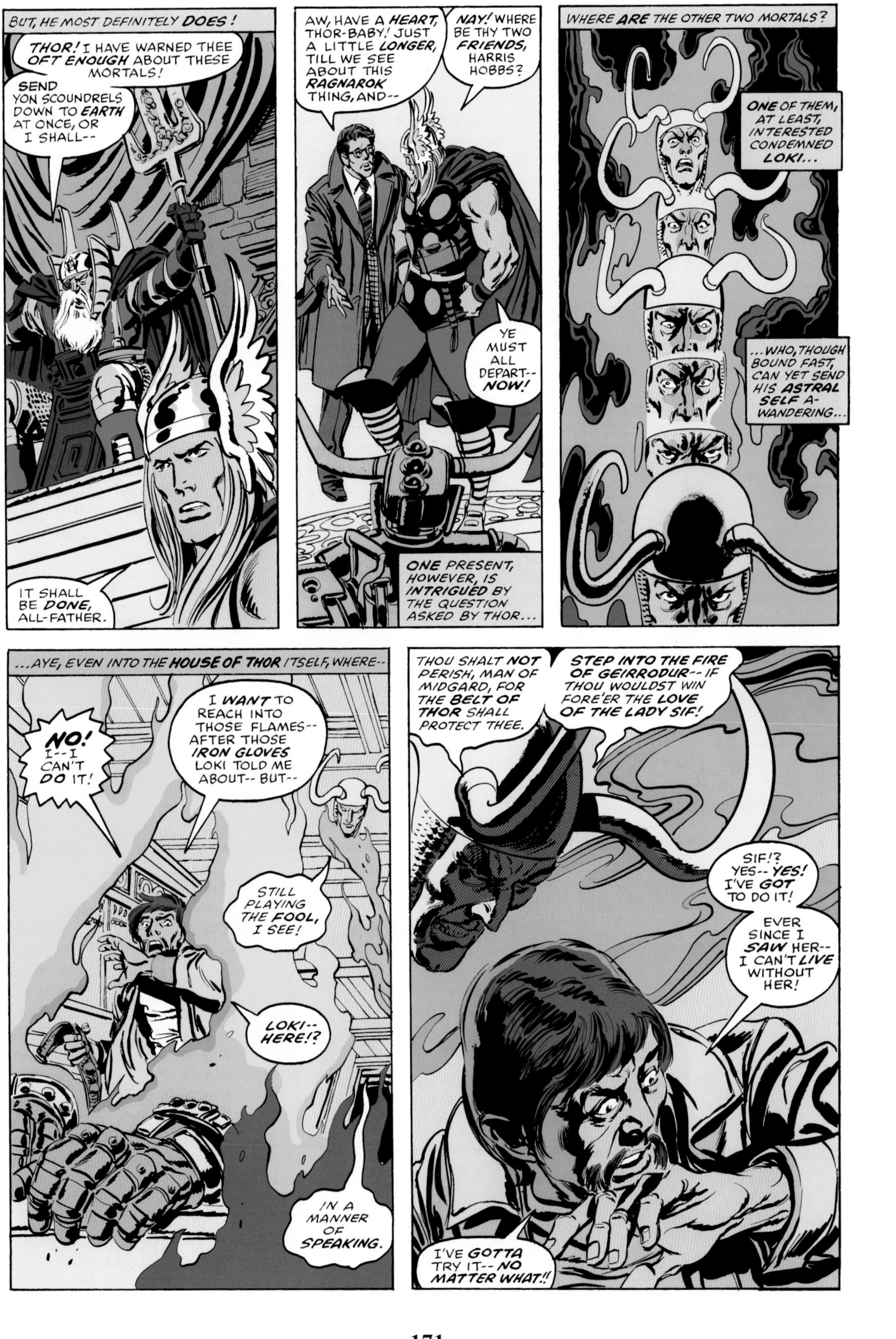
BUT, HE MOST DEFINITELY DOES!
THOR! I HAVE WARNED THEE OFT ENOUGH ABOUT THESE MORTALS!
SEND YON SCOUNDRELS DOWN TO EARTH AT ONCE, OR I SHALL--
IT SHALL BE DONE, ALL-FATHER.
AW, HAVE A HEART, THOR-BABY! JUST A LITTLE LONGER, TILL WE SEE ABOUT THIS RAGNAROK THING, AND--
NAY! WHERE BE THY TWO FRIENDS, HARRIS HOBBS?
YE MUST ALL DEPART-- NOW!
ONE PRESENT, HOWEVER, IS INTRIGUED BY THE QUESTION ASKED BY THOR...
WHERE ARE THE OTHER TWO MORTALS?
ONE OF THEM, AT LEAST, INTERESTED CONDEMNED LOKI...
...WHO, THOUGH BOUND FAST, CAN YET SEND HIS ASTRAL SELF A-WANDERING...
...AYE, EVEN INTO THE HOUSE OF THOR ITSELF, WHERE--
NO! I--I CAN'T DO IT!
I WANT TO REACH INTO THOSE FLAMES-- AFTER THOSE IRON GLOVES LOKI TOLD ME ABOUT-- BUT--
STILL PLAYING THE FOOL, I SEE!
LOKI-- HERE!?
IN A MANNER OF SPEAKING.
THOU SHALT NOT PERISH, MAN OF MIDGARD, FOR THE BELT OF THOR SHALL PROTECT THEE.
STEP INTO THE FIRE OF GEIRRODUR-- IF THOU WOULDST WIN FORE'ER THE LOVE OF THE LADY SIF!
SIF!? YES-- YES! I'VE GOT TO DO IT!
EVER SINCE I SAW HER-- I CAN'T LIVE WITHOUT HER!
I'VE GOTTA TRY IT-- NO MATTER WHAT!!

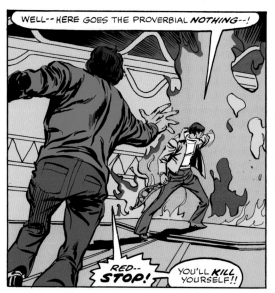

WELL-- HERE GOES THE PROVERBIAL *NOTHING*--!

RED-- *STOP!*

You'll *KILL* YOURSELF!!

HUH? GET *AWAY* FROM ME, KID! YOU DON'T *UNDERSTAND* -- I GOT *NO CHOICE!*

BESIDES, IT *DIDN'T HURT* WHEN I STUCK MY HAND IN THERE-- SO *MAYBE*--

YOU'VE GONE *CRAZY,* RED! I'VE GOTTA *STOP* YOU--!

YOU'RE STOPPIN' *NOTHING,* LITTLE MAN--

--EXCEPT MY *FIST!*

UNNH!

NOW, MORTAL! DO IT *NOW--* ERE THE MOMENT *PASSES!*

NO! IT *WON'T* PASS! I *WON'T LET* IT!!

RED-- *DON'T!*

OH MY *GOD*--!

FOR A FROZEN YET FINITE *ETERNITY,* A LOOK OF SUPREME UNMITIGATED *HORROR* GRIPS THE FEATURES OF THE YOUNG SOUND-MAN NAMED *JOEY...*

...ONLY TO BE *REPLACED,* IN THE SHADOW OF AN INSTANT, BY... *SOMETHING ELSE.*

WHILE *LOKI'S SPIRIT* VANISHES, IN A BURST OF SHEER *MALIGNANCY,* FROM THE *TEMPLE OF THOR*--

--LEAVING ONLY HIS *MOCKING,* MIRTHLESS *LAUGHTER* BEHIND!

HA HA HA HA

172

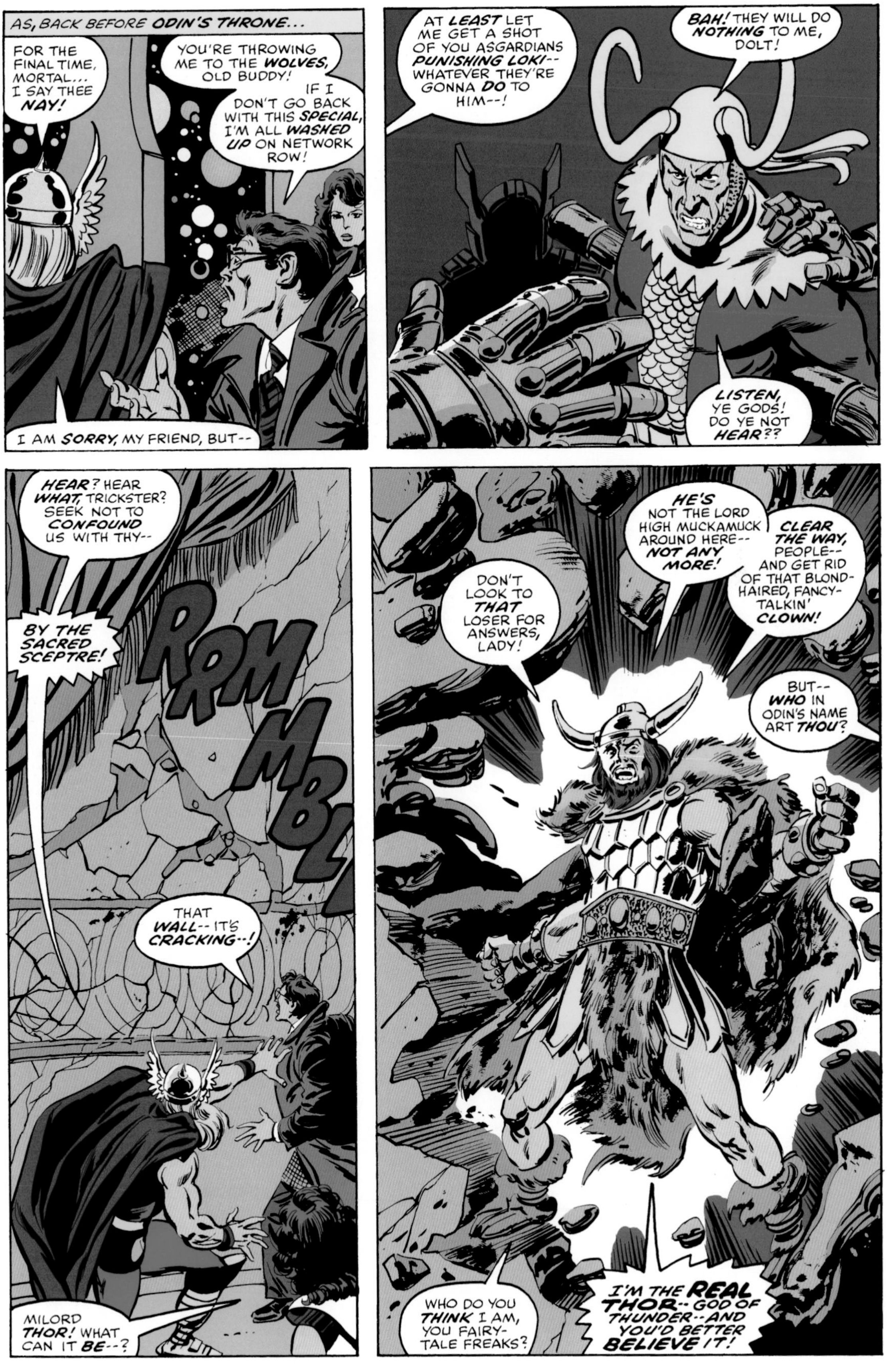
AS, BACK BEFORE ODIN'S THRONE...
FOR THE FINAL TIME, MORTAL... I SAY THEE NAY!
YOU'RE THROWING ME TO THE WOLVES, OLD BUDDY!
IF I DON'T GO BACK WITH THIS SPECIAL, I'M ALL WASHED UP ON NETWORK ROW!
I AM SORRY, MY FRIEND, BUT--
AT LEAST LET ME GET A SHOT OF YOU ASGARDIANS PUNISHING LOKI-- WHATEVER THEY'RE GONNA DO TO HIM--!
BAH! THEY WILL DO NOTHING TO ME, DOLT!
LISTEN, YE GODS! DO YE NOT HEAR??
HEAR? HEAR WHAT, TRICKSTER? SEEK NOT TO CONFOUND US WITH THY--
BY THE SACRED SCEPTRE!
RRRM MMBL
THAT WALL-- IT'S CRACKING--!
MILORD THOR! WHAT CAN IT BE--?
HE'S NOT THE LORD HIGH MUCKAMUCK AROUND HERE-- NOT ANY MORE!
DON'T LOOK TO THAT LOSER FOR ANSWERS, LADY!
CLEAR THE WAY, PEOPLE-- AND GET RID OF THAT BLOND-HAIRED, FANCY-TALKIN' CLOWN!
BUT-- WHO IN ODIN'S NAME ART THOU?
WHO DO YOU THINK I AM, YOU FAIRY-TALE FREAKS?
I'M THE REAL THOR-- GOD OF THUNDER-- AND YOU'D BETTER BELIEVE IT!

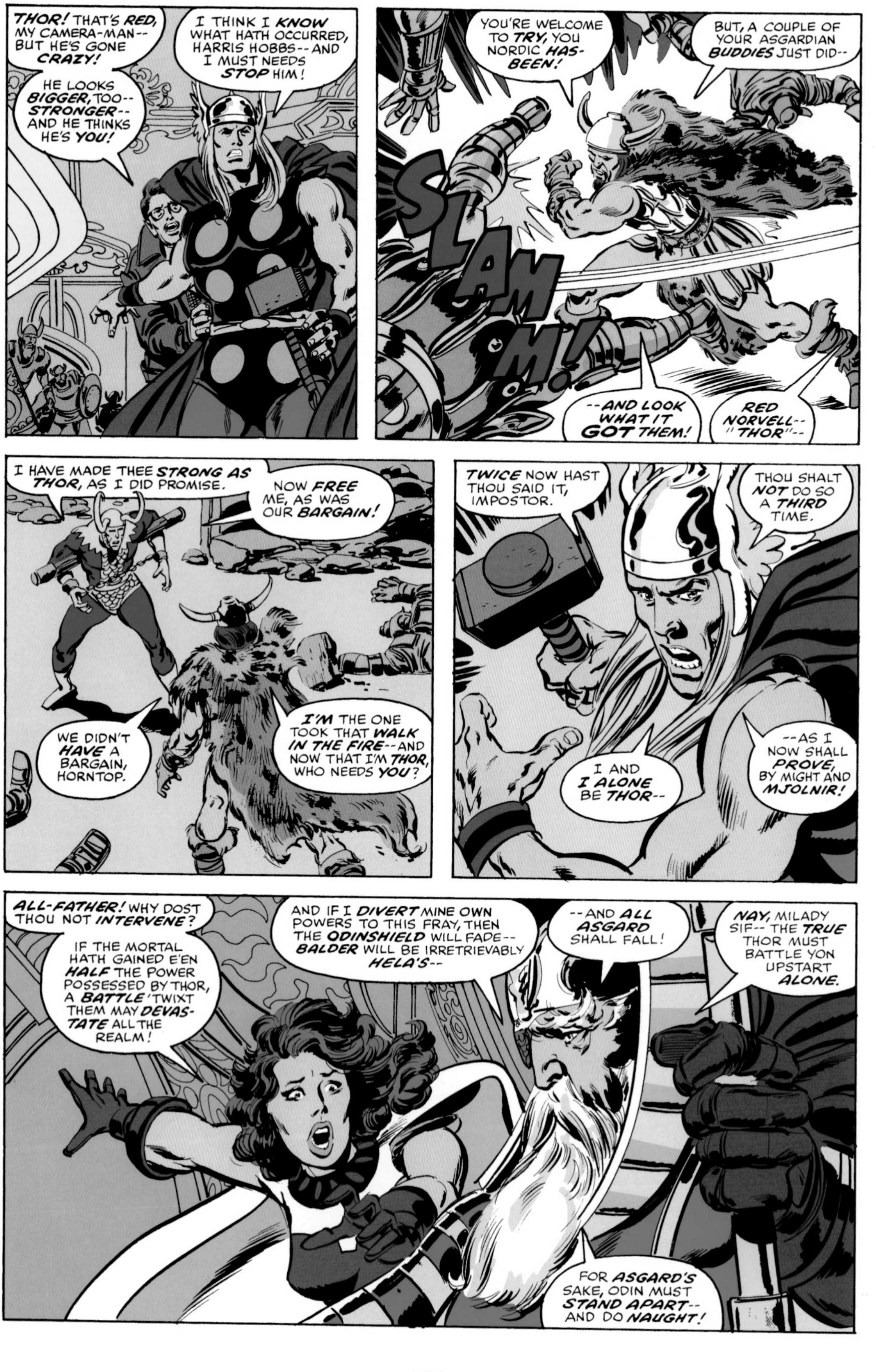
THOR! THAT'S RED, MY CAMERA-MAN-- BUT HE'S GONE CRAZY!
HE LOOKS BIGGER, TOO-- STRONGER-- AND HE THINKS HE'S YOU!
I THINK I KNOW WHAT HATH OCCURRED, HARRIS HOBBS-- AND I MUST NEEDS STOP HIM!
YOU'RE WELCOME TO TRY, YOU NORDIC HAS-BEEN!
BUT, A COUPLE OF YOUR ASGARDIAN BUDDIES JUST DID--
SLAMM!
--AND LOOK WHAT IT GOT THEM!
RED NORVELL-- "THOR"--
I HAVE MADE THEE STRONG AS THOR, AS I DID PROMISE.
NOW FREE ME, AS WAS OUR BARGAIN!
WE DIDN'T HAVE A BARGAIN, HORNTOP.
I'M THE ONE TOOK THAT WALK IN THE FIRE--AND NOW THAT I'M THOR, WHO NEEDS YOU?
TWICE NOW HAST THOU SAID IT, IMPOSTOR.
THOU SHALT NOT DO SO A THIRD TIME.
I AND I ALONE BE THOR--
--AS I NOW SHALL PROVE, BY MIGHT AND MJOLNIR!
ALL-FATHER! WHY DOST THOU NOT INTERVENE?
IF THE MORTAL HATH GAINED E'EN HALF THE POWER POSSESSED BY THOR, A BATTLE 'TWIXT THEM MAY DEVASTATE ALL THE REALM!
AND IF I DIVERT MINE OWN POWERS TO THIS FRAY, THEN THE ODINSHIELD WILL FADE-- BALDER WILL BE IRRETRIEVABLY HELA'S--
--AND ALL ASGARD SHALL FALL!
NAY, MILADY SIF-- THE TRUE THOR MUST BATTLE YON UPSTART ALONE.
FOR ASGARD'S SAKE, ODIN MUST STAND APART-- AND DO NAUGHT!

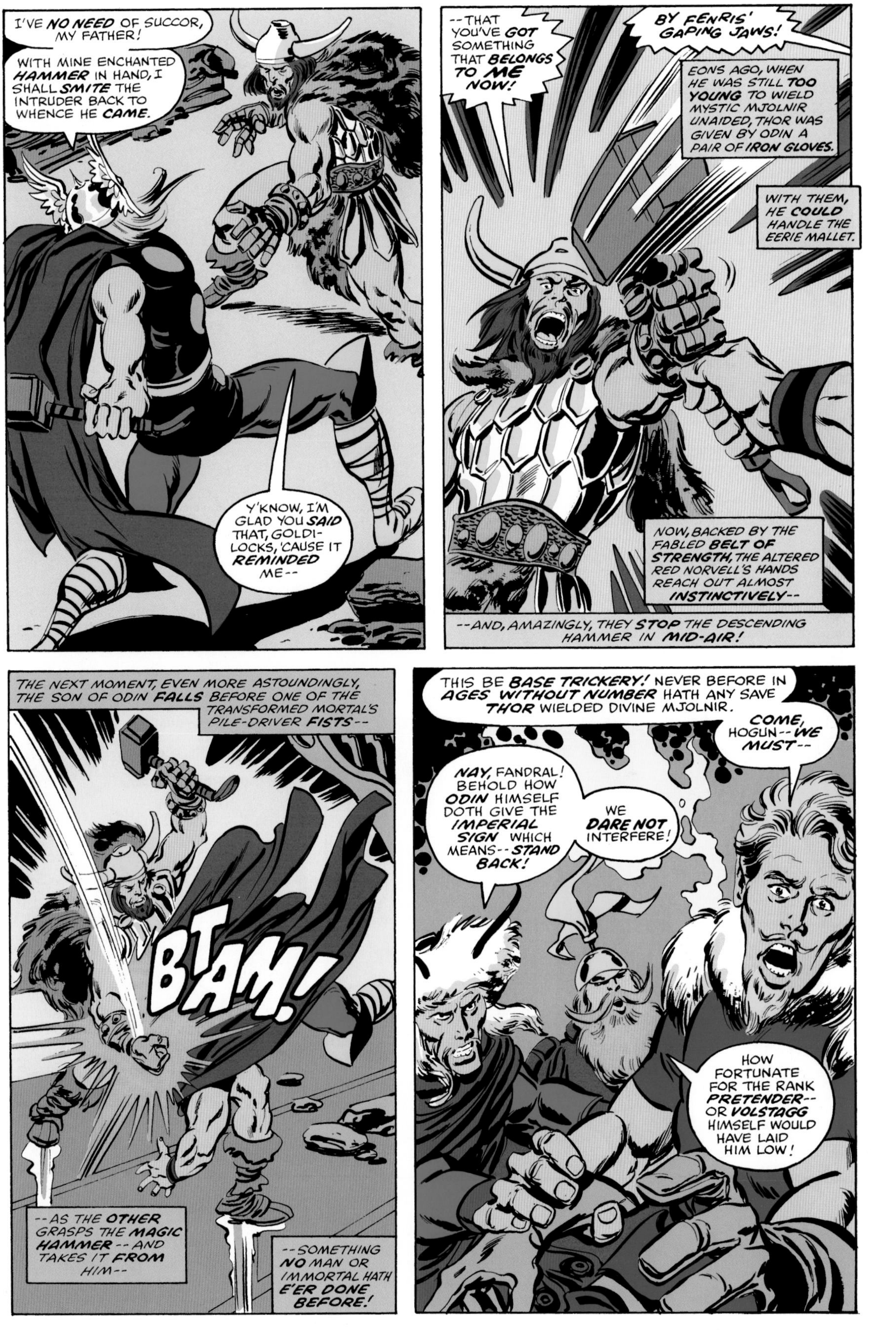
I'VE NO NEED OF SUCCOR, MY FATHER!
WITH MINE ENCHANTED HAMMER IN HAND, I SHALL SMITE THE INTRUDER BACK TO WHENCE HE CAME.
Y'KNOW, I'M GLAD YOU SAID THAT, GOLDI-LOCKS, 'CAUSE IT REMINDED ME--
--THAT YOU'VE GOT SOMETHING THAT BELONGS TO ME NOW!
BY FENRIS' GAPING JAWS!
EONS AGO, WHEN HE WAS STILL TOO YOUNG TO WIELD MYSTIC MJOLNIR UNAIDED, THOR WAS GIVEN BY ODIN A PAIR OF IRON GLOVES.
WITH THEM, HE COULD HANDLE THE EERIE MALLET.
NOW, BACKED BY THE FABLED BELT OF STRENGTH, THE ALTERED RED NORVELL'S HANDS REACH OUT ALMOST INSTINCTIVELY--
--AND, AMAZINGLY, THEY STOP THE DESCENDING HAMMER IN MID-AIR!
THE NEXT MOMENT, EVEN MORE ASTOUNDINGLY, THE SON OF ODIN FALLS BEFORE ONE OF THE TRANSFORMED MORTAL'S PILE-DRIVER FISTS--
BTAM!
--AS THE OTHER GRASPS THE MAGIC HAMMER--AND TAKES IT FROM HIM--
--SOMETHING NO MAN OR IMMORTAL HATH E'ER DONE BEFORE!
THIS BE BASE TRICKERY! NEVER BEFORE IN AGES WITHOUT NUMBER HATH ANY SAVE THOR WIELDED DIVINE MJOLNIR.
COME, HOGUN--WE MUST--
NAY, FANDRAL! BEHOLD HOW ODIN HIMSELF DOTH GIVE THE IMPERIAL SIGN WHICH MEANS--STAND BACK!
WE DARE NOT INTERFERE!
HOW FORTUNATE FOR THE RANK PRETENDER--OR VOLSTAGG HIMSELF WOULD HAVE LAID HIM LOW!

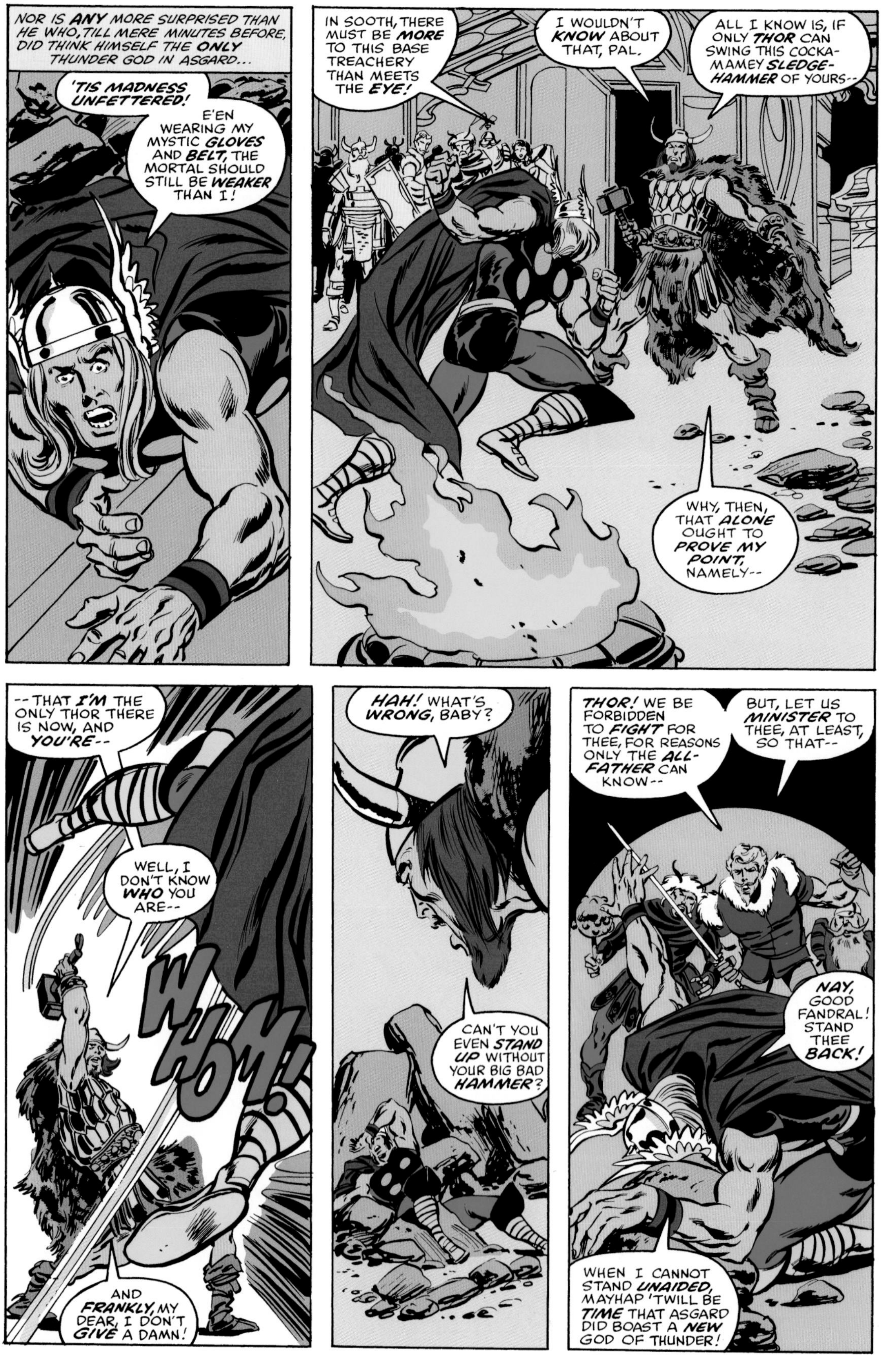
NOR IS ANY MORE SURPRISED THAN HE WHO, TILL MERE MINUTES BEFORE, DID THINK HIMSELF THE ONLY THUNDER GOD IN ASGARD...
'TIS MADNESS UNFETTERED!
E'EN WEARING MY MYSTIC GLOVES AND BELT, THE MORTAL SHOULD STILL BE WEAKER THAN I!
IN SOOTH, THERE MUST BE MORE TO THIS BASE TREACHERY THAN MEETS THE EYE!
I WOULDN'T KNOW ABOUT THAT, PAL.
ALL I KNOW IS, IF ONLY THOR CAN SWING THIS COCKAMAMEY SLEDGEHAMMER OF YOURS--
WHY, THEN, THAT ALONE OUGHT TO PROVE MY POINT, NAMELY--
--THAT I'M THE ONLY THOR THERE IS NOW, AND YOU'RE--
WELL, I DON'T KNOW WHO YOU ARE--
WHOM!
AND FRANKLY, MY DEAR, I DON'T GIVE A DAMN!
HAH! WHAT'S WRONG, BABY?
CAN'T YOU EVEN STAND UP WITHOUT YOUR BIG BAD HAMMER?
THOR! WE BE FORBIDDEN TO FIGHT FOR THEE, FOR REASONS ONLY THE ALL-FATHER CAN KNOW--
BUT, LET US MINISTER TO THEE, AT LEAST, SO THAT--
NAY, GOOD FANDRAL! STAND THEE BACK!
WHEN I CANNOT STAND UNAIDED, MAYHAP 'TWILL BE TIME THAT ASGARD DID BOAST A NEW GOD OF THUNDER!

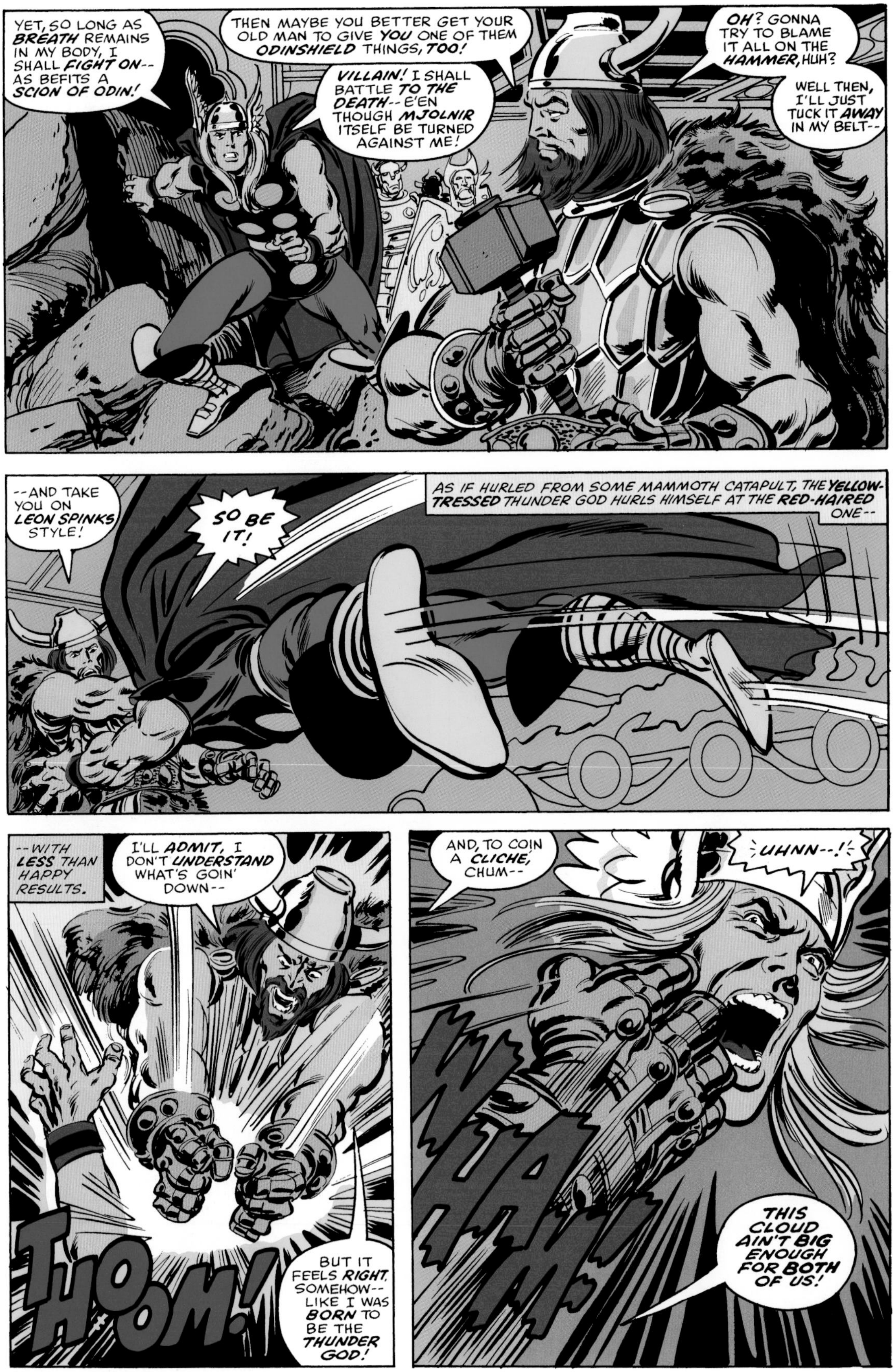
YET, SO LONG AS BREATH REMAINS IN MY BODY, I SHALL FIGHT ON-- AS BEFITS A SCION OF ODIN!
THEN MAYBE YOU BETTER GET YOUR OLD MAN TO GIVE YOU ONE OF THEM ODINSHIELD THINGS, TOO!
VILLAIN! I SHALL BATTLE TO THE DEATH-- E'EN THOUGH MJOLNIR ITSELF BE TURNED AGAINST ME!
OH? GONNA TRY TO BLAME IT ALL ON THE HAMMER, HUH?
WELL THEN, I'LL JUST TUCK IT AWAY IN MY BELT--
--AND TAKE YOU ON LEON SPINKS STYLE!
SO BE IT!
AS IF HURLED FROM SOME MAMMOTH CATAPULT, THE YELLOW-TRESSED THUNDER GOD HURLS HIMSELF AT THE RED-HAIRED ONE--
--WITH LESS THAN HAPPY RESULTS.
I'LL ADMIT, I DON'T UNDERSTAND WHAT'S GOIN' DOWN--
THOOM!
BUT IT FEELS RIGHT, SOMEHOW-- LIKE I WAS BORN TO BE THE THUNDER GOD!
AND, TO COIN A CLICHE, CHUM--
UHNN--!
THIS CLOUD AIN'T BIG ENOUGH FOR BOTH OF US!

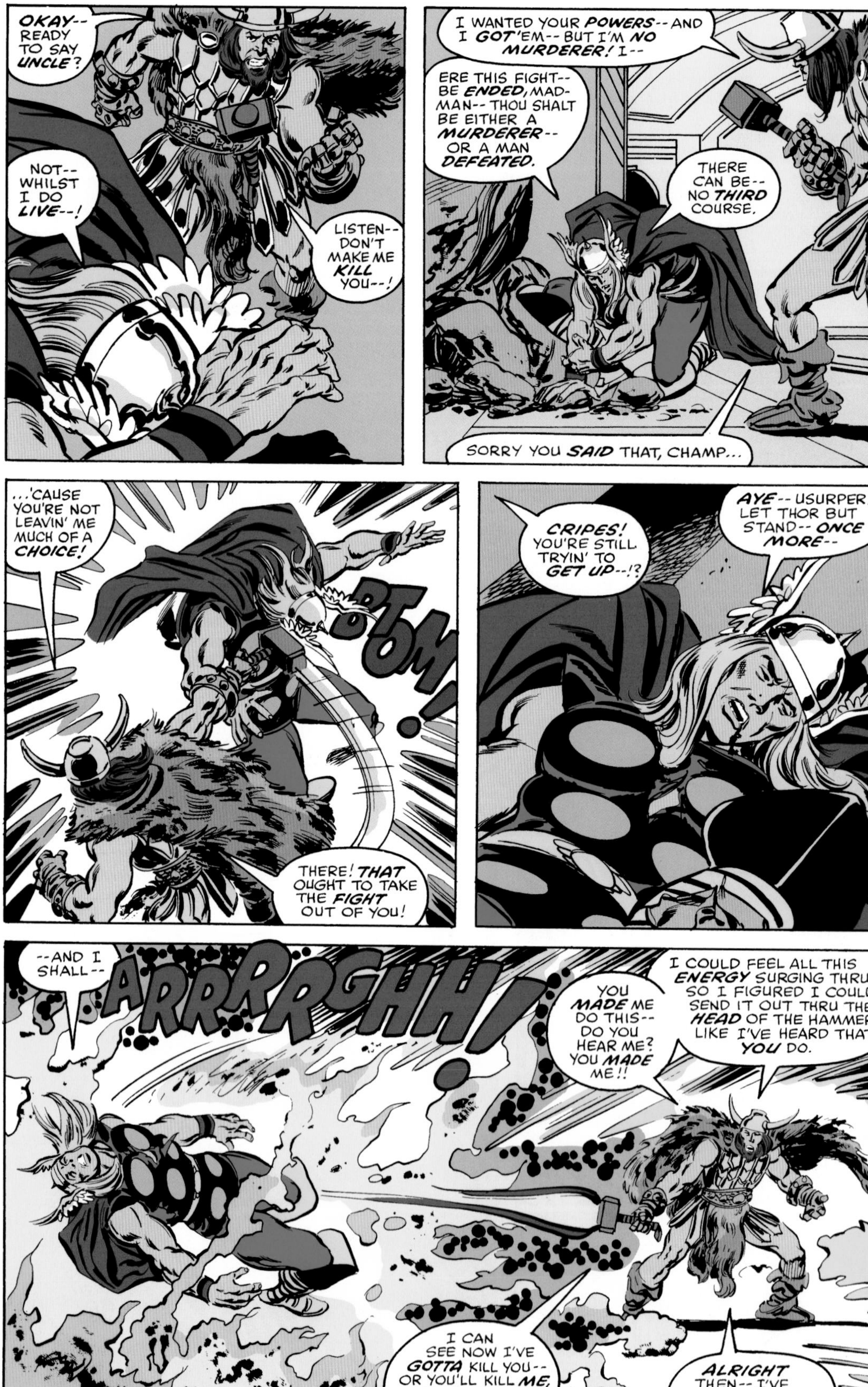
OKAY-- READY TO SAY UNCLE?
NOT-- WHILST I DO LIVE--!
LISTEN-- DON'T MAKE ME KILL YOU--!
I WANTED YOUR POWERS-- AND I GOT 'EM-- BUT I'M NO MURDERER! I--
ERE THIS FIGHT-- BE ENDED, MAD-MAN-- THOU SHALT BE EITHER A MURDERER-- OR A MAN DEFEATED.
THERE CAN BE-- NO THIRD COURSE.
SORRY YOU SAID THAT, CHAMP...
...'CAUSE YOU'RE NOT LEAVIN' ME MUCH OF A CHOICE!
BTOOM!
THERE! THAT OUGHT TO TAKE THE FIGHT OUT OF YOU!
CRIPES! YOU'RE STILL TRYIN' TO GET UP--!?
AYE-- USURPER! LET THOR BUT STAND-- ONCE MORE--
--AND I SHALL--
ARRRRGHH!
YOU MADE ME DO THIS-- DO YOU HEAR ME? YOU MADE ME!!
I COULD FEEL ALL THIS ENERGY SURGING THRU ME-- SO I FIGURED I COULD SEND IT OUT THRU THE HEAD OF THE HAMMER, LIKE I'VE HEARD THAT YOU DO.
I CAN SEE NOW I'VE GOTTA KILL YOU-- OR YOU'LL KILL ME, SOONER OR LATER!
ALRIGHT THEN-- I'VE COME THIS FAR--!

NNOOOO!

STOP HIM! HE WOULD SLAY MY BELOVED!

HASTEN, ASGARDIANS! AH, IF ONLY VALIANT VOLSTAGG COULD REACH THE FOREFRONT OF BATTLE...!

NOW I STRIKE, GRIM HOGUN-- WHETHER ODIN GIVE THE SIGN OR NAY!

AND HOGUN WITH THEE, MY FRIEND!

KEEP BACK, YOU MYTHOLOGICAL MISFITS!

MAYBE I'M JUST STARTIN' TO LEARN THIS HAMMER'S BAG OF TRICKS-- BUT I SEEM TO HAVE A REAL GIFT FOR IT--

--SO YOU MIGHT AS WELL BREAK FOR LUNCH!

HELA'S SWORD! HE HATH THROWN UP A WALL OF MYSTIC FIRE AROUND HIMSELF AND THOR!

CHECK! WHAT'S MORE, IN THE FEW SECONDS IT'LL TAKE FOR YOU GODS TO FIGHT YOUR WAY THRU IT, I'M GONNA SMASH ODIN'S LITTLE BOY CLEAR BACK INTO THE TEXTBOOKS!

G'BYE, PAL! SORRY TO DO THIS, BUT--

YET, EVEN AS THE "NEW THOR" AIMS MIGHTY MJOLNIR--

--SOMEONE ELSE ENTERS THE SCENE-- SOMEONE WHO, COMING FROM A DIFFERENT DIRECTION, WAS ALREADY WITHIN THE AREA WHEN THE FIERY RING WAS FORMED--!

RED! LISTEN TO ME! IT'S JOEY!

YOU CAN'T KILL HIM, RED! I WON'T LET YOU! I--

GET OUTTA THE WAY, KID! IT'S TOO LATE TO--

GOOD LORD!

ZRAKKK!

AAAAA!

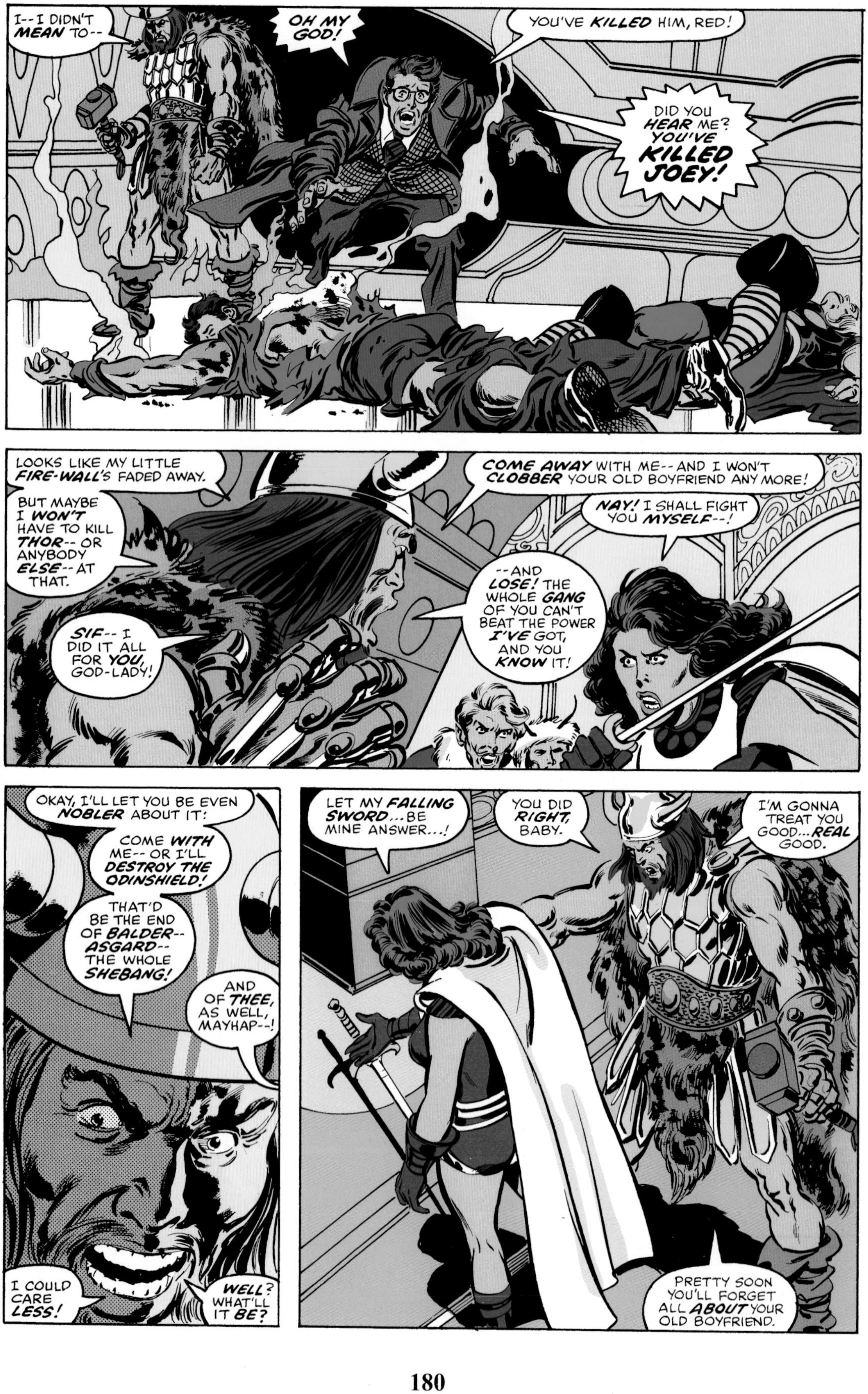
I--I DIDN'T MEAN TO--
OH MY GOD!
YOU'VE KILLED HIM, RED!
DID YOU HEAR ME? YOU'VE KILLED JOEY!
LOOKS LIKE MY LITTLE FIRE-WALL'S FADED AWAY.
BUT MAYBE I WON'T HAVE TO KILL THOR-- OR ANYBODY ELSE-- AT THAT.
COME AWAY WITH ME--AND I WON'T CLOBBER YOUR OLD BOYFRIEND ANY MORE!
NAY! I SHALL FIGHT YOU MYSELF--!
SIF-- I DID IT ALL FOR YOU, GOD-LADY!
--AND LOSE! THE WHOLE GANG OF YOU CAN'T BEAT THE POWER I'VE GOT, AND YOU KNOW IT!
OKAY, I'LL LET YOU BE EVEN NOBLER ABOUT IT:
COME WITH ME-- OR I'LL DESTROY THE ODINSHIELD!
THAT'D BE THE END OF BALDER-- ASGARD-- THE WHOLE SHEBANG!
AND OF THEE, AS WELL, MAYHAP--!
I COULD CARE LESS!
WELL? WHAT'LL IT BE?
LET MY FALLING SWORD... BE MINE ANSWER...!
YOU DID RIGHT, BABY.
I'M GONNA TREAT YOU GOOD... REAL GOOD.
PRETTY SOON YOU'LL FORGET ALL ABOUT YOUR OLD BOYFRIEND.

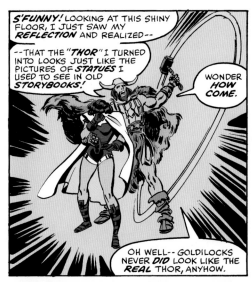

S'FUNNY! LOOKING AT THIS SHINY FLOOR, I JUST SAW MY *REFLECTION* AND REALIZED--

--THAT THE *"THOR"* I TURNED INTO LOOKS JUST LIKE THE PICTURES OF *STATUES* I USED TO SEE IN OLD *STORYBOOKS!*

WONDER *HOW* COME.

OH WELL-- GOLDILOCKS NEVER *DID* LOOK LIKE THE *REAL* THOR, ANYHOW.

I REMEMBER READIN' HOW THOR WAS SUPPOSED TO BE A *RED-HEAD*--JUST LIKE *ME!*

WONDER IF THAT'S JUST A *COINCIDENCE,* OR--

NUTS! NO SENSE TRYIN' TO FIGURE OUT JUST WHAT *HAPPENED.*

I'M JUST GONNA *ENJOY* IT-- FOR MAYBE A *MILLENNIUM* OR TWO.

BELOW, THE GATHERED GODS TURN NOW--

--TO LOOK WITH DAZED EYES AT *ODIN,* WHO HAS EVER BEEN THEIR *TOWER*... THEIR TIMELESS *PILLAR.*

AND HE SEEMS NOW NOT SO MUCH THE *LORD OF ASGARD*...AS A *FATHER* WHO KNOWS HE MAY WELL LOSE HIS *ONLY SON* TO DUSKY *DEATH.*

THE *FIRE* IS GONE NOW FROM THE ONE EYE HE HAS LEFT... AYE, AND SEEMINGLY FROM HIS VERY *SPIRIT.*

AND, IF THE FLAMES THAT BURN IN *ODIN'S SOUL* BE BANKED AND DIM...

...THEN WHAT OF THE BLAZING *ODINSHIELD* WHICH ALONE PREVENTS FALLEN *BALDER* FROM BEING FULLY POSSESSED BY THE *GODDESS OF DEATH*?

WE THINK YOU ALREADY *KNOW* THE ANSWER TO *THAT*...!

NEXT ISSUE: **TIME OF THE TROLLS!**

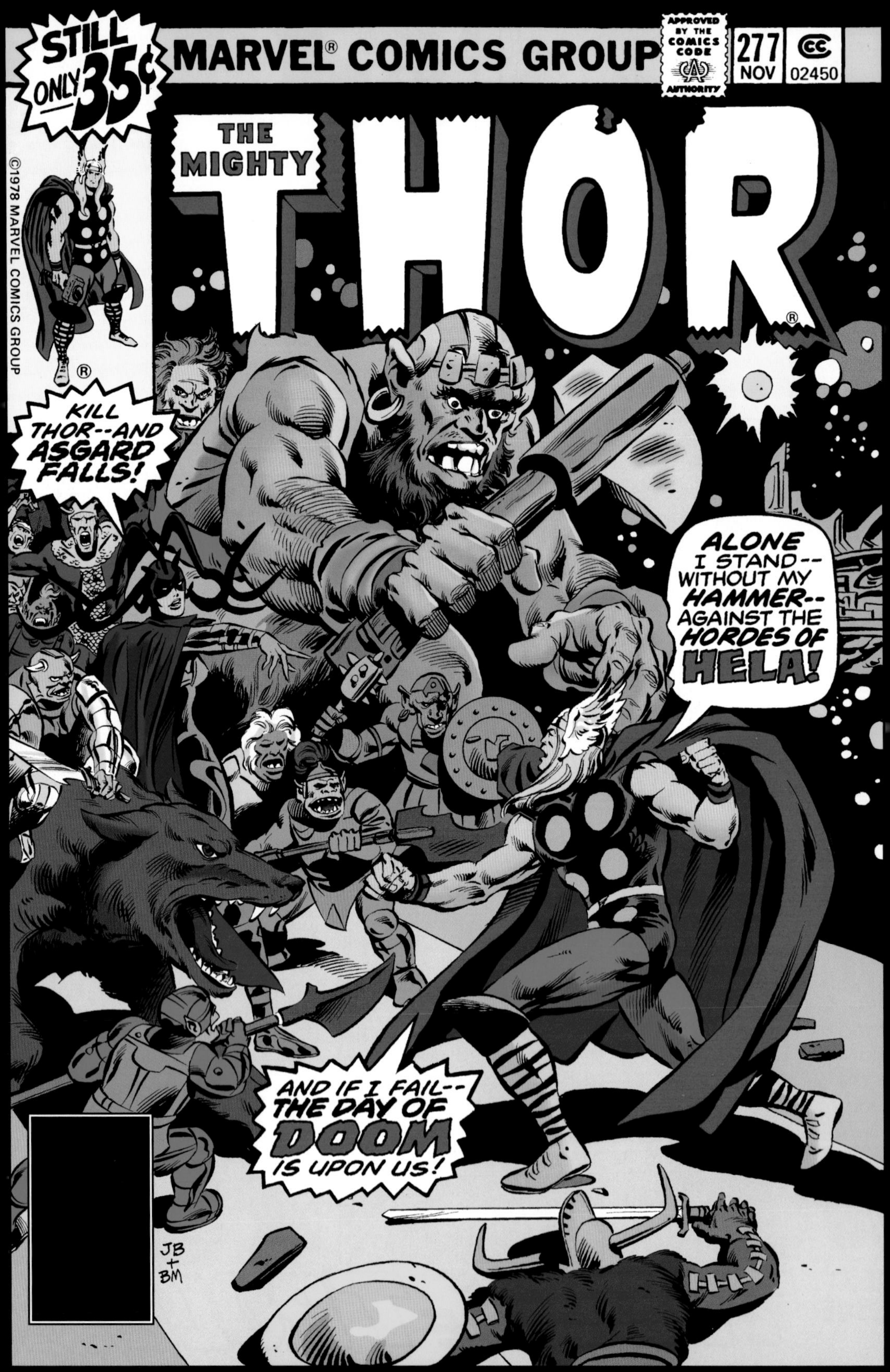

STILL ONLY 35¢
MARVEL® COMICS GROUP
APPROVED BY THE COMICS CODE AUTHORITY
277
NOV
CC
02450
THE MIGHTY
THOR®
©1978 MARVEL COMICS GROUP
KILL THOR--AND ASGARD FALLS!
ALONE I STAND-- WITHOUT MY HAMMER-- AGAINST THE HORDES OF HELA!
AND IF I FAIL-- THE DAY OF DOOM IS UPON US!
JB + BM

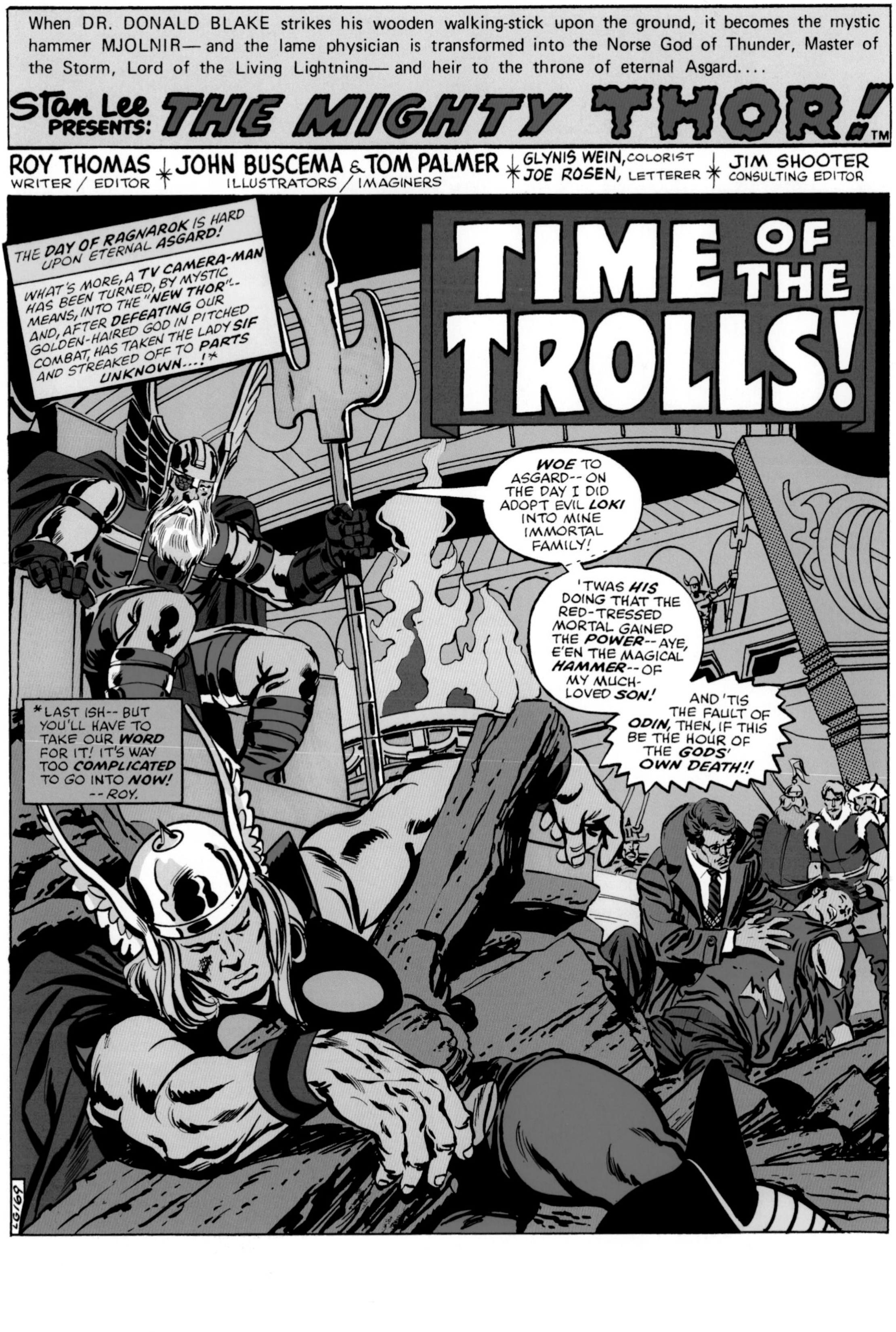

When DR. DONALD BLAKE strikes his wooden walking-stick upon the ground, it becomes the mystic hammer MJOLNIR— and the lame physician is transformed into the Norse God of Thunder, Master of the Storm, Lord of the Living Lightning— and heir to the throne of eternal Asgard....
Stan Lee PRESENTS: THE MIGHTY THOR!™
ROY THOMAS WRITER / EDITOR
JOHN BUSCEMA & TOM PALMER ILLUSTRATORS / IMAGINERS
GLYNIS WEIN, COLORIST
JOE ROSEN, LETTERER
JIM SHOOTER CONSULTING EDITOR
THE DAY OF RAGNAROK IS HARD UPON ETERNAL ASGARD!
WHAT'S MORE, A TV CAMERA-MAN HAS BEEN TURNED, BY MYSTIC MEANS, INTO THE "NEW THOR"-- AND, AFTER DEFEATING OUR GOLDEN-HAIRED GOD IN PITCHED COMBAT, HAS TAKEN THE LADY SIF AND STREAKED OFF TO PARTS UNKNOWN...!*
TIME OF THE TROLLS!
WOE TO ASGARD-- ON THE DAY I DID ADOPT EVIL LOKI INTO MINE IMMORTAL FAMILY!
'TWAS HIS DOING THAT THE RED-TRESSED MORTAL GAINED THE POWER-- AYE, E'EN THE MAGICAL HAMMER-- OF MY MUCH-LOVED SON!
AND 'TIS THE FAULT OF ODIN, THEN, IF THIS BE THE HOUR OF THE GODS' OWN DEATH!!
*LAST ISH-- BUT YOU'LL HAVE TO TAKE OUR WORD FOR IT! IT'S WAY TOO COMPLICATED TO GO INTO NOW! --ROY.

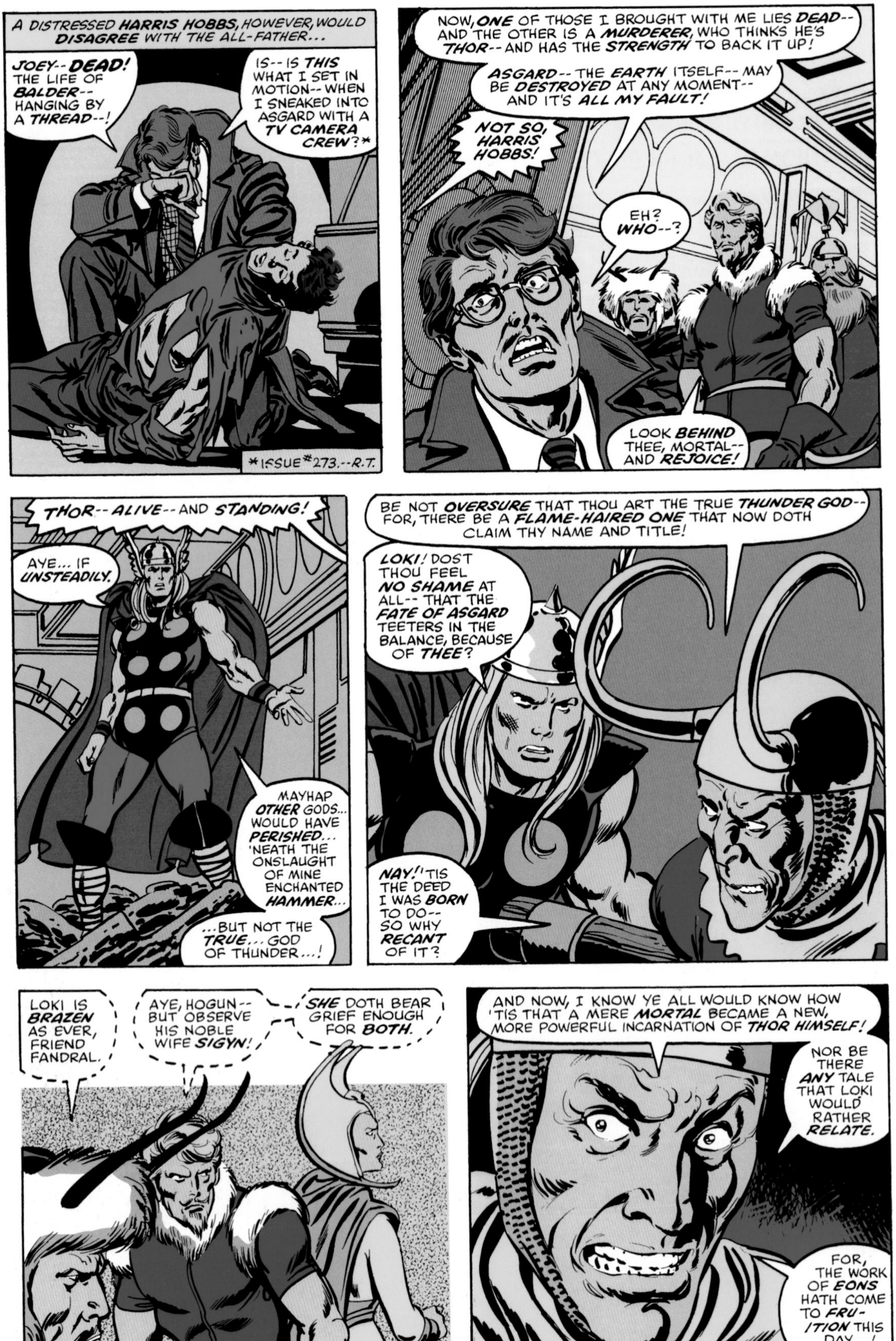
A DISTRESSED HARRIS HOBBS, HOWEVER, WOULD DISAGREE WITH THE ALL-FATHER...
JOEY-- DEAD! THE LIFE OF BALDER-- HANGING BY A THREAD--!
IS-- IS THIS WHAT I SET IN MOTION-- WHEN I SNEAKED INTO ASGARD WITH A TV CAMERA CREW?*
*ISSUE #273.--R.T.
NOW, ONE OF THOSE I BROUGHT WITH ME LIES DEAD-- AND THE OTHER IS A MURDERER, WHO THINKS HE'S THOR-- AND HAS THE STRENGTH TO BACK IT UP!
ASGARD-- THE EARTH ITSELF-- MAY BE DESTROYED AT ANY MOMENT-- AND IT'S ALL MY FAULT!
NOT SO, HARRIS HOBBS!
EH? WHO--?
LOOK BEHIND THEE, MORTAL-- AND REJOICE!
THOR-- ALIVE-- AND STANDING!
AYE... IF UNSTEADILY.
MAYHAP OTHER GODS... WOULD HAVE PERISHED... 'NEATH THE ONSLAUGHT OF MINE ENCHANTED HAMMER...
...BUT NOT THE TRUE... GOD OF THUNDER...!
BE NOT OVERSURE THAT THOU ART THE TRUE THUNDER GOD-- FOR, THERE BE A FLAME-HAIRED ONE THAT NOW DOTH CLAIM THY NAME AND TITLE!
LOKI! DOST THOU FEEL NO SHAME AT ALL-- THAT THE FATE OF ASGARD TEETERS IN THE BALANCE, BECAUSE OF THEE?
NAY! 'TIS THE DEED I WAS BORN TO DO-- SO WHY RECANT OF IT?
LOKI IS BRAZEN AS EVER, FRIEND FANDRAL.
AYE, HOGUN-- BUT OBSERVE HIS NOBLE WIFE SIGYN!
SHE DOTH BEAR GRIEF ENOUGH FOR BOTH.
AND NOW, I KNOW YE ALL WOULD KNOW HOW 'TIS THAT A MERE MORTAL BECAME A NEW, MORE POWERFUL INCARNATION OF THOR HIMSELF!
NOR BE THERE ANY TALE THAT LOKI WOULD RATHER RELATE.
FOR, THE WORK OF EONS HATH COME TO FRUITION THIS DAY...!

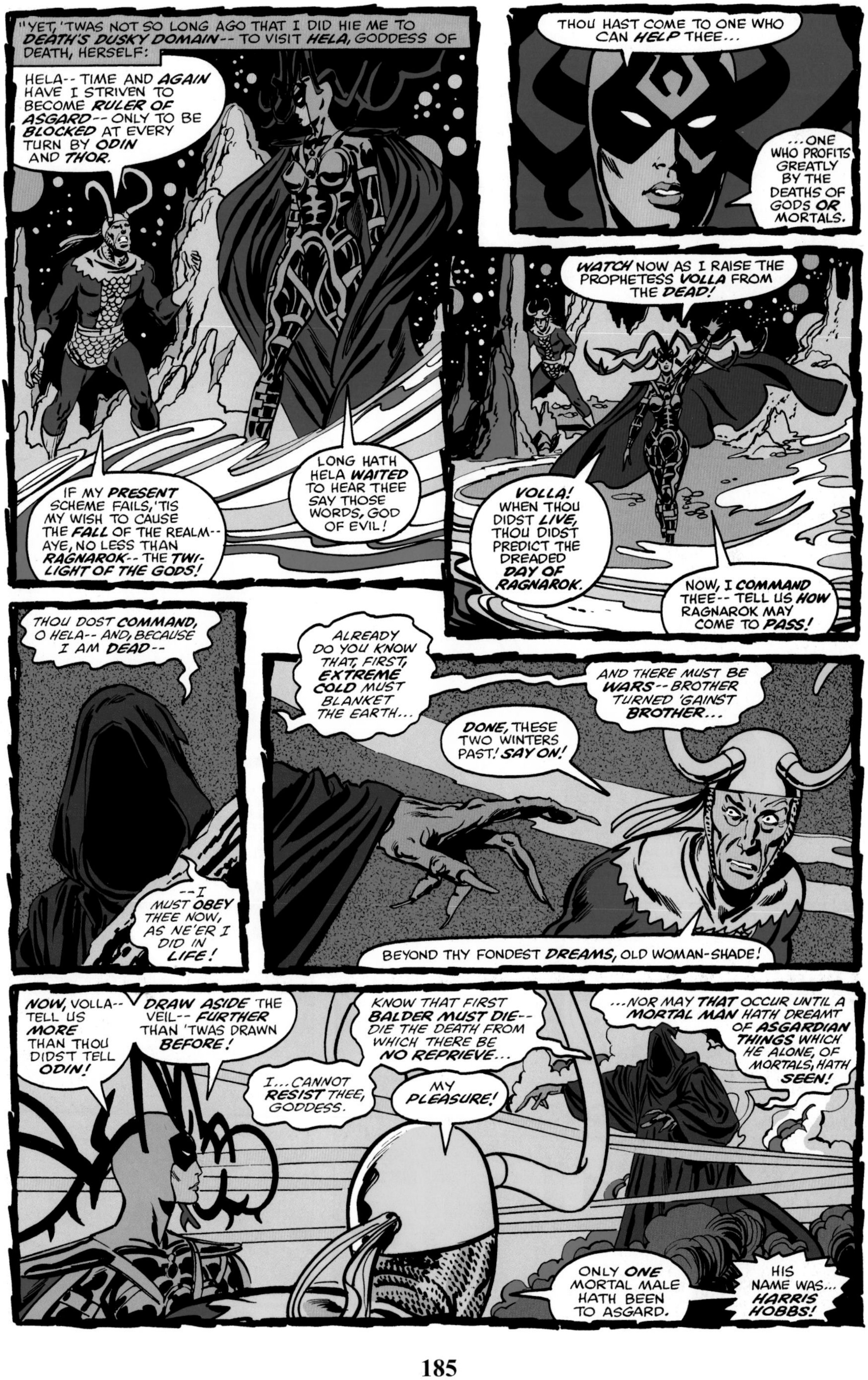
"YET, 'TWAS NOT SO LONG AGO THAT I DID HIE ME TO DEATH'S DUSKY DOMAIN-- TO VISIT HELA, GODDESS OF DEATH, HERSELF:
HELA-- TIME AND AGAIN HAVE I STRIVEN TO BECOME RULER OF ASGARD-- ONLY TO BE BLOCKED AT EVERY TURN BY ODIN AND THOR.
IF MY PRESENT SCHEME FAILS, 'TIS MY WISH TO CAUSE THE FALL OF THE REALM-- AYE, NO LESS THAN RAGNAROK-- THE TWILIGHT OF THE GODS!
LONG HATH HELA WAITED TO HEAR THEE SAY THOSE WORDS, GOD OF EVIL!
THOU HAST COME TO ONE WHO CAN HELP THEE...
...ONE WHO PROFITS GREATLY BY THE DEATHS OF GODS OR MORTALS.
WATCH NOW AS I RAISE THE PROPHETESS VOLLA FROM THE DEAD!
VOLLA! WHEN THOU DIDST LIVE, THOU DIDST PREDICT THE DREADED DAY OF RAGNAROK.
NOW, I COMMAND THEE-- TELL US HOW RAGNAROK MAY COME TO PASS!
THOU DOST COMMAND, O HELA-- AND, BECAUSE I AM DEAD--
--I MUST OBEY THEE NOW, AS NE'ER I DID IN LIFE!
ALREADY DO YOU KNOW THAT, FIRST, EXTREME COLD MUST BLANKET THE EARTH...
DONE, THESE TWO WINTERS PAST! SAY ON!
AND THERE MUST BE WARS--BROTHER TURNED 'GAINST BROTHER...
BEYOND THY FONDEST DREAMS, OLD WOMAN-SHADE!
NOW, VOLLA-- TELL US MORE THAN THOU DIDST TELL ODIN!
DRAW ASIDE THE VEIL-- FURTHER THAN 'TWAS DRAWN BEFORE!
I...CANNOT RESIST THEE, GODDESS.
KNOW THAT FIRST BALDER MUST DIE-- DIE THE DEATH FROM WHICH THERE BE NO REPRIEVE...
MY PLEASURE!
...NOR MAY THAT OCCUR UNTIL A MORTAL MAN HATH DREAMT OF ASGARDIAN THINGS WHICH HE ALONE, OF MORTALS, HATH SEEN!
ONLY ONE MORTAL MALE HATH BEEN TO ASGARD.
HIS NAME WAS... HARRIS HOBBS!

"THUS," SAYS HELA, "WE DID SEND *EERIE DREAMS* TO HARRIS HOBBS-- BOTH OF THINGS HE HAD KNOWN AND *FORGOTTEN*, AND OF THINGS HE *COULD NOT KNOW*."

"IN THAT WAY," *ADDS LOKI*, "WE *HELPED* BRING ABOUT THE *PROPHECY OF VOLLA*...

"...SO THAT, WHEN MY *LAST PLAN* FAILED, DESPITE THE AID OF THE *ENCHANTRESS* AND THE BRUTISH *EXECUTIONER*...

"...AND I WAS *BANISHED TO EARTH*, STRIPPED OF ALL GODLY POWERS..."*

**#267. --ROY.

...I HAD ALREADY *SET IN MOTION* THE EVENTS WHICH WOULD LEAD TO *RAGNAROK*!

ONLY *HELA AND I* COULD HAVE REVERSED THEM THEN.

AND NOW-- *NO ONE CAN!*

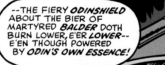

--THE FIERY *ODINSHIELD* ABOUT THE BIER OF MARTYRED *BALDER* DOTH BURN LOWER, E'ER *LOWER*-- E'EN THOUGH POWERED BY *ODIN'S OWN ESSENCE!*

LOOK THEE, FANDRAL, HOW ODIN DOTH GROW *WEARY*, WEEPING INWARDLY OF THE *EVIL* HIS ADOPTED SON HATH WROUGHT!

BUT NOT EVEN THE *ALL-FATHER* CAN ERASE WHAT THE *MOVING HAND* HATH WRIT LARGE.

AYE, NOR SHALL E'EN THE *REALM OF THE GODS* STAND FOR LONG, IT SEEMS-- FOR, *BEHOLD*--

AND, IF E'ER *IT* DOTH DIE-- BE IT *TODAY*, OR A *THOUSAND EONS* HENCE--

--THEN TOO SHALL *RAGNAROK* TRULY OCCUR, AND *ASGARD PERISH!*

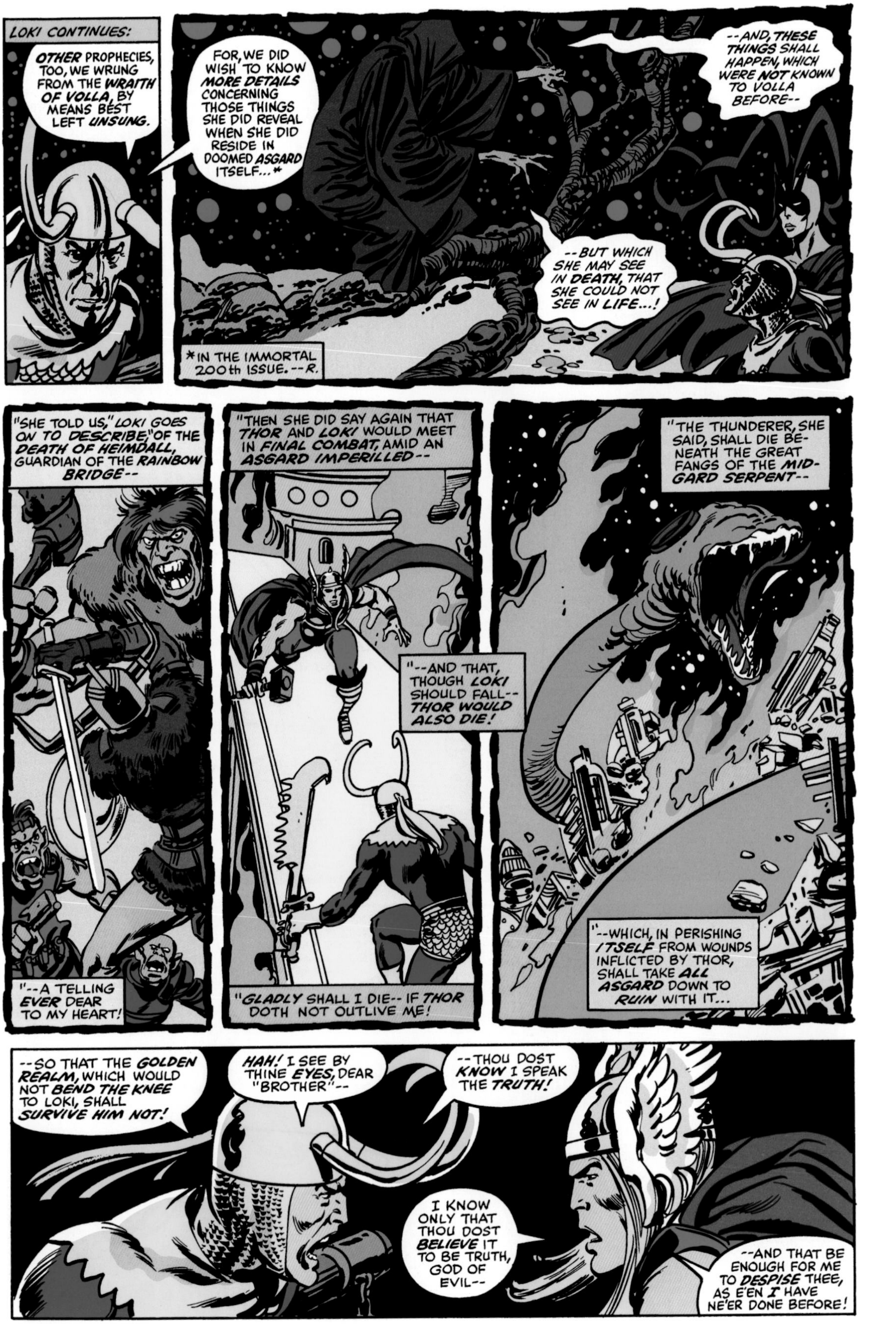

LOKI CONTINUES:
OTHER PROPHECIES, TOO, WE WRUNG FROM THE WRAITH OF VOLLA, BY MEANS BEST LEFT UNSUNG.
FOR, WE DID WISH TO KNOW MORE DETAILS CONCERNING THOSE THINGS SHE DID REVEAL WHEN SHE DID RESIDE IN DOOMED ASGARD ITSELF...*
--AND, THESE THINGS SHALL HAPPEN, WHICH WERE NOT KNOWN TO VOLLA BEFORE--
--BUT WHICH SHE MAY SEE IN DEATH, THAT SHE COULD NOT SEE IN LIFE...!
*IN THE IMMORTAL 200th ISSUE.--R.
"SHE TOLD US," LOKI GOES ON TO DESCRIBE, "OF THE DEATH OF HEIMDALL, GUARDIAN OF THE RAINBOW BRIDGE--
"--A TELLING EVER DEAR TO MY HEART!
"THEN SHE DID SAY AGAIN THAT THOR AND LOKI WOULD MEET IN FINAL COMBAT, AMID AN ASGARD IMPERILLED--
"--AND THAT, THOUGH LOKI SHOULD FALL-- THOR WOULD ALSO DIE!
"GLADLY SHALL I DIE-- IF THOR DOTH NOT OUTLIVE ME!
"THE THUNDERER, SHE SAID, SHALL DIE BENEATH THE GREAT FANGS OF THE MIDGARD SERPENT--
"--WHICH, IN PERISHING ITSELF FROM WOUNDS INFLICTED BY THOR, SHALL TAKE ALL ASGARD DOWN TO RUIN WITH IT...
--SO THAT THE GOLDEN REALM, WHICH WOULD NOT BEND THE KNEE TO LOKI, SHALL SURVIVE HIM NOT!
HAH! I SEE BY THINE EYES, DEAR "BROTHER"--
--THOU DOST KNOW I SPEAK THE TRUTH!
I KNOW ONLY THAT THOU DOST BELIEVE IT TO BE TRUTH, GOD OF EVIL--
--AND THAT BE ENOUGH FOR ME TO DESPISE THEE, AS E'EN I HAVE NE'ER DONE BEFORE!

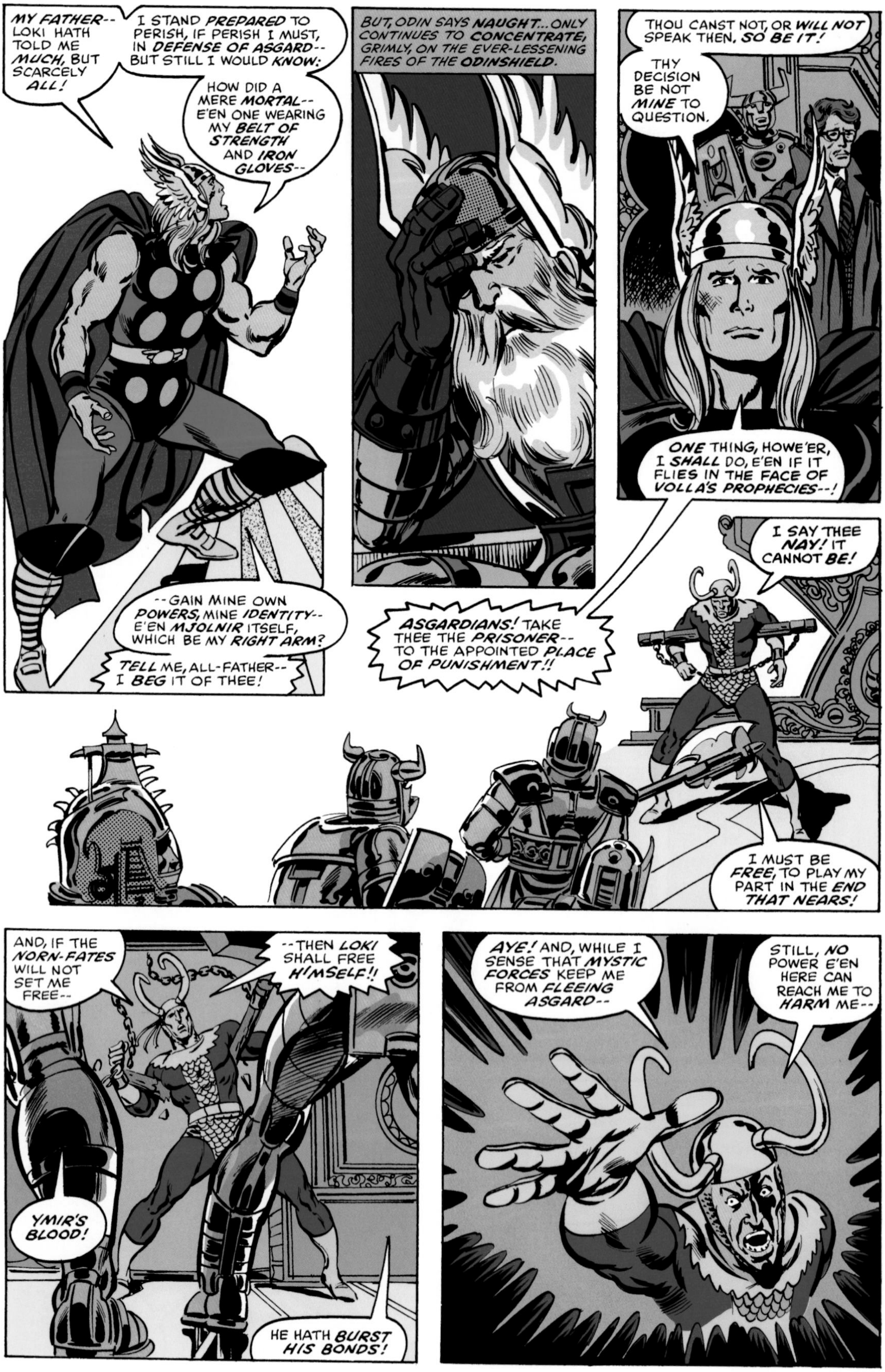

MY FATHER-- LOKI HATH TOLD ME MUCH, BUT SCARCELY ALL!
I STAND PREPARED TO PERISH, IF PERISH I MUST, IN DEFENSE OF ASGARD-- BUT STILL I WOULD KNOW:
HOW DID A MERE MORTAL-- E'EN ONE WEARING MY BELT OF STRENGTH AND IRON GLOVES--
--GAIN MINE OWN POWERS, MINE IDENTITY-- E'EN MJOLNIR ITSELF, WHICH BE MY RIGHT ARM?
TELL ME, ALL-FATHER-- I BEG IT OF THEE!
BUT, ODIN SAYS NAUGHT...ONLY CONTINUES TO CONCENTRATE, GRIMLY, ON THE EVER-LESSENING FIRES OF THE ODINSHIELD.
THOU CANST NOT, OR WILL NOT SPEAK THEN, SO BE IT!
THY DECISION BE NOT MINE TO QUESTION.
ONE THING, HOWE'ER, I SHALL DO, E'EN IF IT FLIES IN THE FACE OF VOLLA'S PROPHECIES--!
ASGARDIANS! TAKE THEE THE PRISONER-- TO THE APPOINTED PLACE OF PUNISHMENT!!
I SAY THEE NAY! IT CANNOT BE!
I MUST BE FREE, TO PLAY MY PART IN THE END THAT NEARS!
AND, IF THE NORN-FATES WILL NOT SET ME FREE--
--THEN LOKI SHALL FREE HIMSELF!!
YMIR'S BLOOD!
HE HATH BURST HIS BONDS!
AYE! AND, WHILE I SENSE THAT MYSTIC FORCES KEEP ME FROM FLEEING ASGARD--
STILL, NO POWER E'EN HERE CAN REACH ME TO HARM ME--

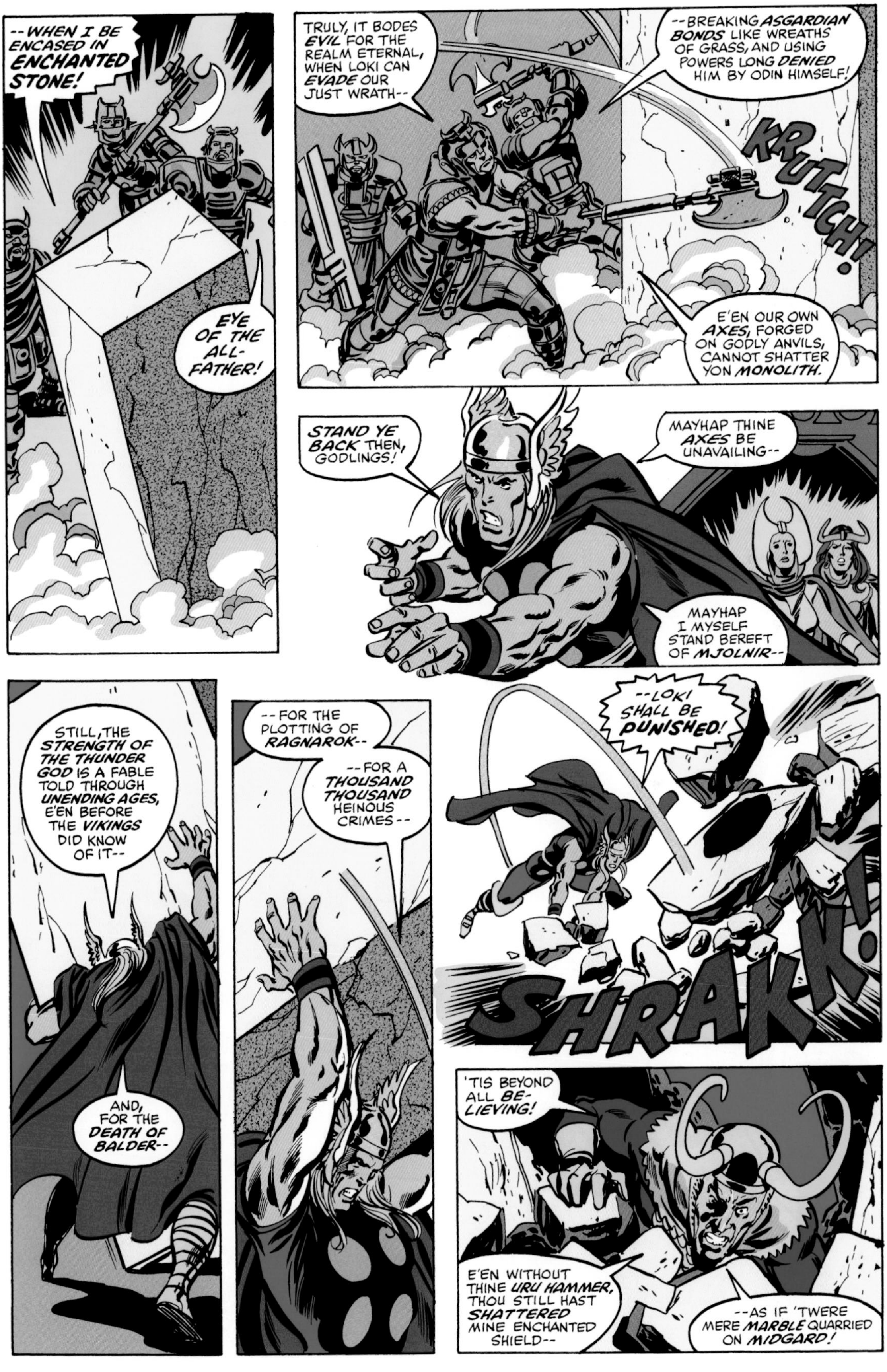
--WHEN I BE ENCASED IN ENCHANTED STONE!
EYE OF THE ALL-FATHER!
TRULY, IT BODES EVIL FOR THE REALM ETERNAL, WHEN LOKI CAN EVADE OUR JUST WRATH--
--BREAKING ASGARDIAN BONDS LIKE WREATHS OF GRASS, AND USING POWERS LONG DENIED HIM BY ODIN HIMSELF!
KRUTTCH!
E'EN OUR OWN AXES, FORGED ON GODLY ANVILS, CANNOT SHATTER YON MONOLITH.
STAND YE BACK THEN, GODLINGS!
MAYHAP THINE AXES BE UNAVAILING--
MAYHAP I MYSELF STAND BEREFT OF MJOLNIR--
STILL, THE STRENGTH OF THE THUNDER GOD IS A FABLE TOLD THROUGH UNENDING AGES, E'EN BEFORE THE VIKINGS DID KNOW OF IT--
AND, FOR THE DEATH OF BALDER--
--FOR THE PLOTTING OF RAGNAROK--
--FOR A THOUSAND THOUSAND HEINOUS CRIMES--
--LOKI SHALL BE PUNISHED!
SHRAKK!
'TIS BEYOND ALL BE-LIEVING!
E'EN WITHOUT THINE URU HAMMER, THOU STILL HAST SHATTERED MINE ENCHANTED SHIELD--
--AS IF 'TWERE MERE MARBLE QUARRIED ON MIDGARD!

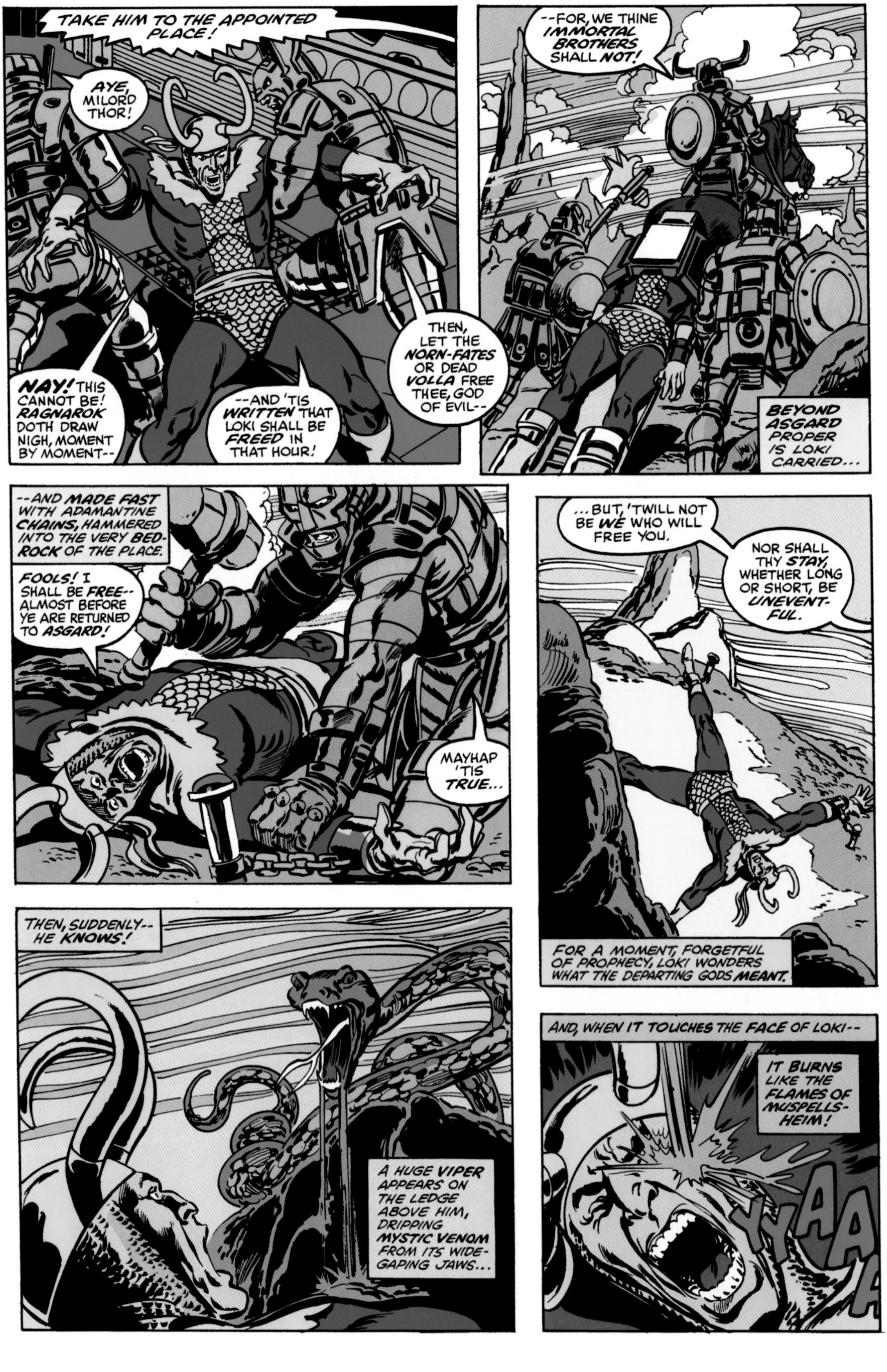
TAKE HIM TO THE APPOINTED PLACE!
AYE, MILORD THOR!
NAY! THIS CANNOT BE! RAGNAROK DOTH DRAW NIGH, MOMENT BY MOMENT--
--AND 'TIS WRITTEN THAT LOKI SHALL BE FREED IN THAT HOUR!
THEN, LET THE NORN-FATES OR DEAD VOLLA FREE THEE, GOD OF EVIL--
--FOR, WE THINE IMMORTAL BROTHERS SHALL NOT!
BEYOND ASGARD PROPER IS LOKI CARRIED...
--AND MADE FAST WITH ADAMANTINE CHAINS, HAMMERED INTO THE VERY BED-ROCK OF THE PLACE.
FOOLS! I SHALL BE FREE-- ALMOST BEFORE YE ARE RETURNED TO ASGARD!
MAYHAP 'TIS TRUE...
...BUT, 'TWILL NOT BE WE WHO WILL FREE YOU.
NOR SHALL THY STAY, WHETHER LONG OR SHORT, BE UNEVENT-FUL.
FOR A MOMENT, FORGETFUL OF PROPHECY, LOKI WONDERS WHAT THE DEPARTING GODS MEANT.
THEN, SUDDENLY-- HE KNOWS!
A HUGE VIPER APPEARS ON THE LEDGE ABOVE HIM, DRIPPING MYSTIC VENOM FROM ITS WIDE-GAPING JAWS...
AND, WHEN IT TOUCHES THE FACE OF LOKI--
IT BURNS LIKE THE FLAMES OF MUSPELLS-HEIM!
YAAA

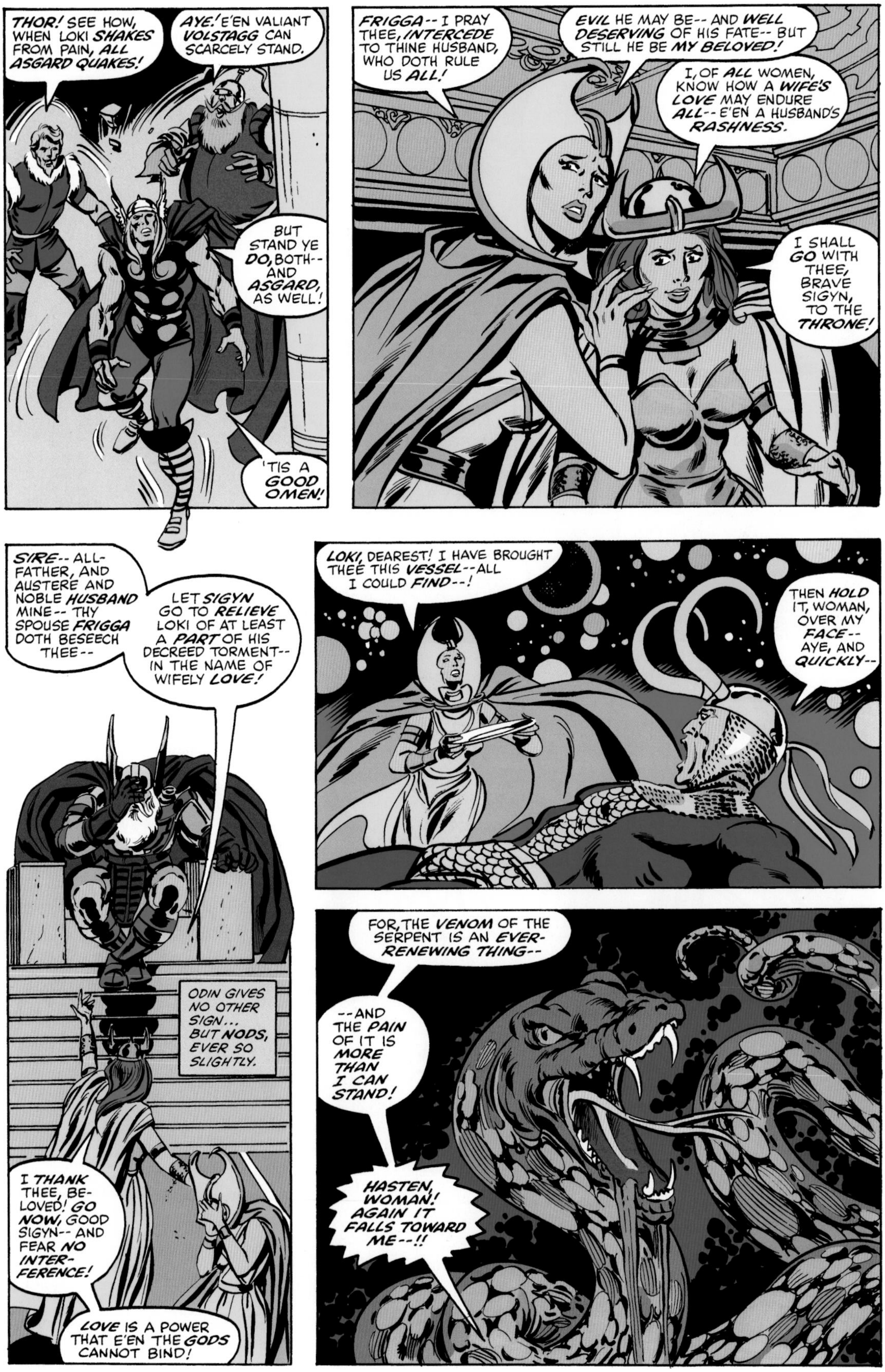
THOR! SEE HOW, WHEN LOKI SHAKES FROM PAIN, ALL ASGARD QUAKES!
AYE! E'EN VALIANT VOLSTAGG CAN SCARCELY STAND.
BUT STAND YE DO, BOTH-- AND ASGARD, AS WELL!
'TIS A GOOD OMEN!
FRIGGA-- I PRAY THEE, INTERCEDE TO THINE HUSBAND, WHO DOTH RULE US ALL!
EVIL HE MAY BE-- AND WELL DESERVING OF HIS FATE-- BUT STILL HE BE MY BELOVED!
I, OF ALL WOMEN, KNOW HOW A WIFE'S LOVE MAY ENDURE ALL-- E'EN A HUSBAND'S RASHNESS.
I SHALL GO WITH THEE, BRAVE SIGYN, TO THE THRONE!
SIRE-- ALL-FATHER, AND AUSTERE AND NOBLE HUSBAND MINE-- THY SPOUSE FRIGGA DOTH BESEECH THEE--
LET SIGYN GO TO RELIEVE LOKI OF AT LEAST A PART OF HIS DECREED TORMENT-- IN THE NAME OF WIFELY LOVE!
ODIN GIVES NO OTHER SIGN... BUT NODS, EVER SO SLIGHTLY.
I THANK THEE, BE-LOVED! GO NOW, GOOD SIGYN-- AND FEAR NO INTER-FERENCE!
LOVE IS A POWER THAT E'EN THE GODS CANNOT BIND!
LOKI, DEAREST! I HAVE BROUGHT THEE THIS VESSEL-- ALL I COULD FIND--!
THEN HOLD IT, WOMAN, OVER MY FACE-- AYE, AND QUICKLY--
FOR, THE VENOM OF THE SERPENT IS AN EVER-RENEWING THING--
--AND THE PAIN OF IT IS MORE THAN I CAN STAND!
HASTEN, WOMAN! AGAIN IT FALLS TOWARD ME--!!

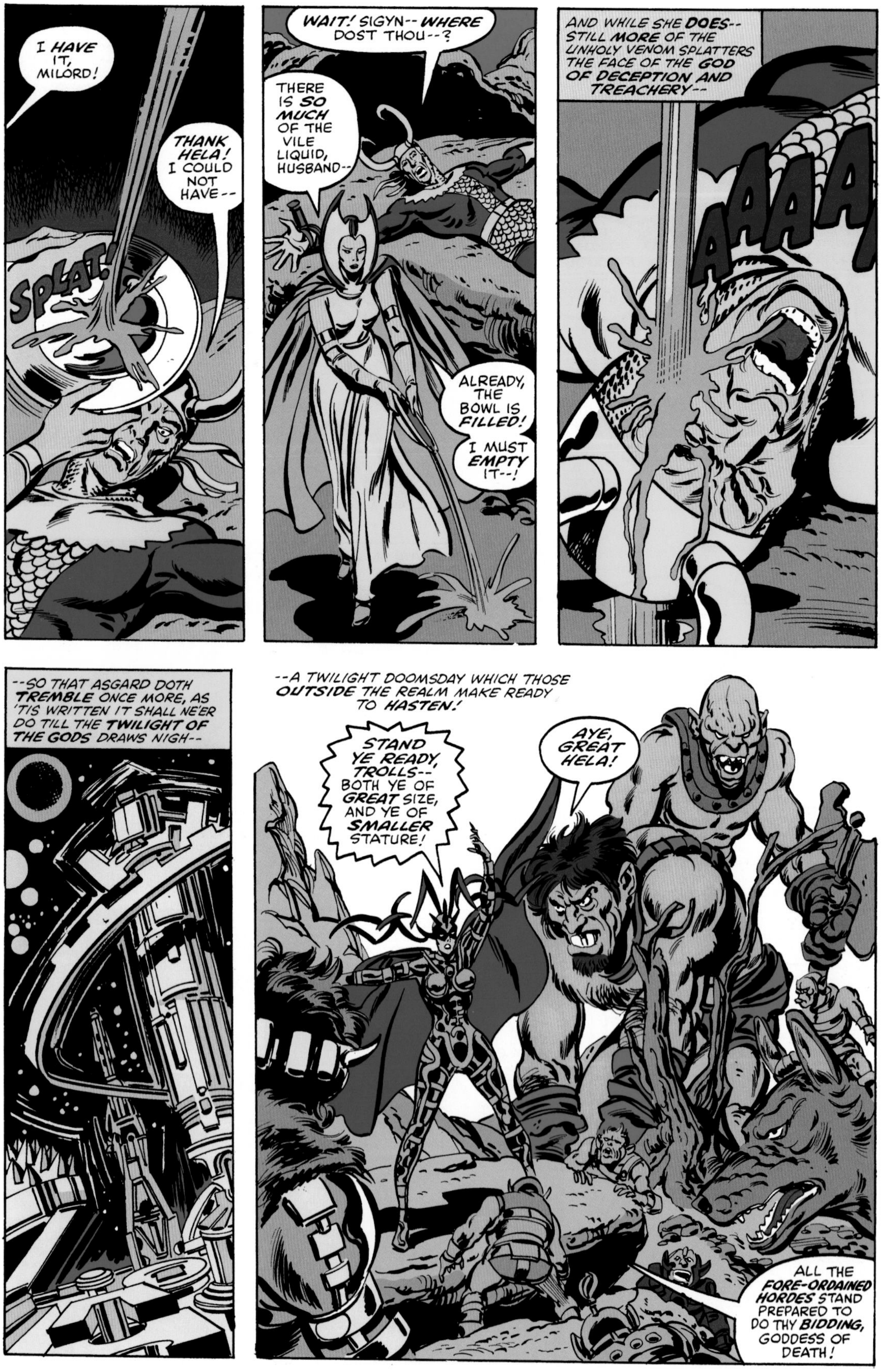
I HAVE IT, MILORD!
THANK HELA! I COULD NOT HAVE--
SPLAT!
WAIT! SIGYN-- WHERE DOST THOU--?
THERE IS SO MUCH OF THE VILE LIQUID, HUSBAND--
ALREADY, THE BOWL IS FILLED!
I MUST EMPTY IT--!
AND WHILE SHE DOES-- STILL MORE OF THE UNHOLY VENOM SPLATTERS THE FACE OF THE GOD OF DECEPTION AND TREACHERY--
AAAAA
--SO THAT ASGARD DOTH TREMBLE ONCE MORE, AS 'TIS WRITTEN IT SHALL NE'ER DO TILL THE TWILIGHT OF THE GODS DRAWS NIGH--
--A TWILIGHT DOOMSDAY WHICH THOSE OUTSIDE THE REALM MAKE READY TO HASTEN!
STAND YE READY, TROLLS-- BOTH YE OF GREAT SIZE, AND YE OF SMALLER STATURE!
AYE, GREAT HELA!
ALL THE FORE-ORDAINED HORDES STAND PREPARED TO DO THY BIDDING, GODDESS OF DEATH!

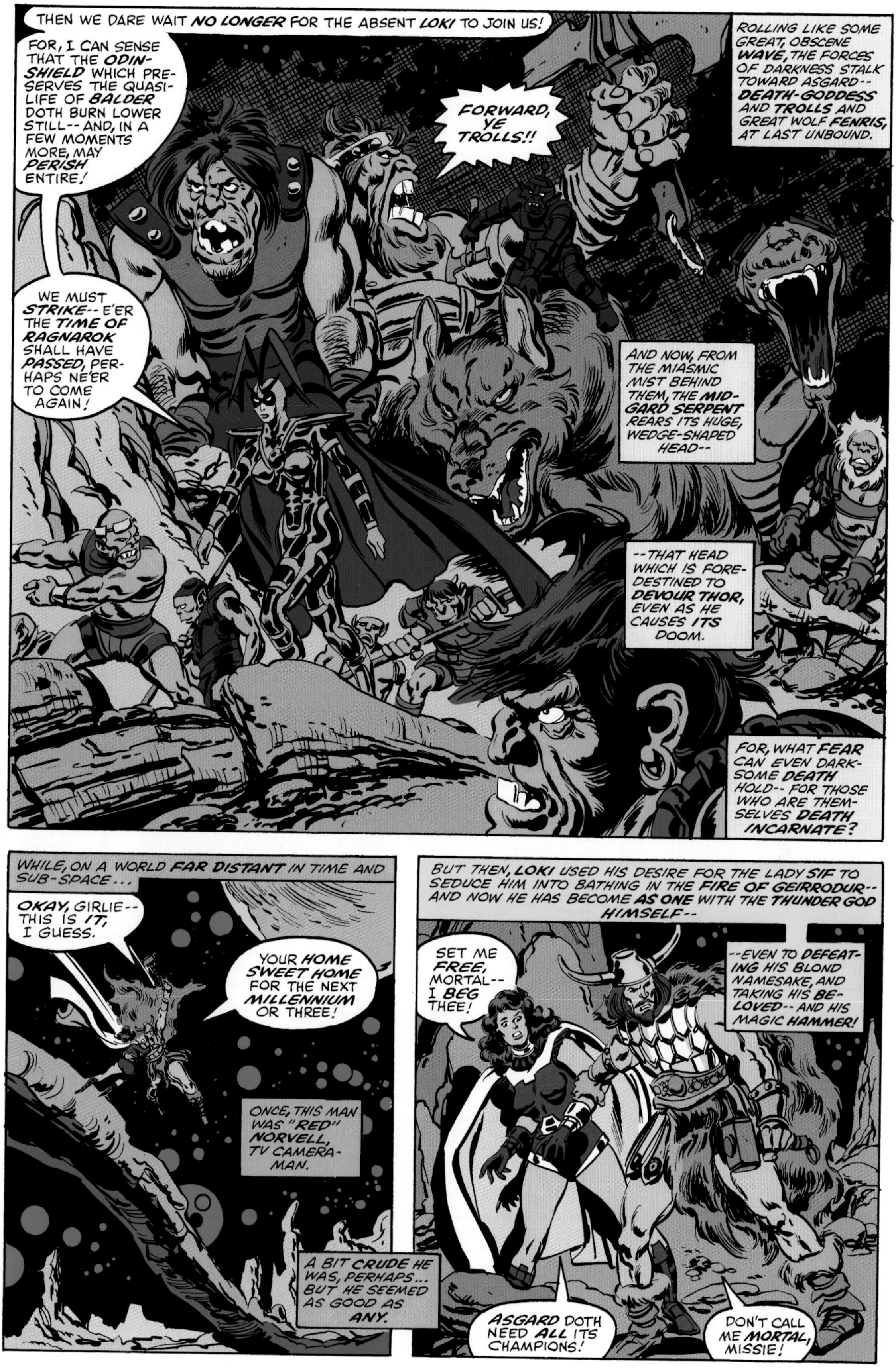
THEN WE DARE WAIT NO LONGER FOR THE ABSENT LOKI TO JOIN US!
FOR, I CAN SENSE THAT THE ODIN-SHIELD WHICH PRESERVES THE QUASI-LIFE OF BALDER DOTH BURN LOWER STILL-- AND, IN A FEW MOMENTS MORE, MAY PERISH ENTIRE!
ROLLING LIKE SOME GREAT, OBSCENE WAVE, THE FORCES OF DARKNESS STALK TOWARD ASGARD-- DEATH-GODDESS AND TROLLS AND GREAT WOLF FENRIS, AT LAST UNBOUND.
FORWARD, YE TROLLS!!
WE MUST STRIKE-- E'ER THE TIME OF RAGNAROK SHALL HAVE PASSED, PERHAPS NE'ER TO COME AGAIN!
AND NOW, FROM THE MIASMIC MIST BEHIND THEM, THE MIDGARD SERPENT REARS ITS HUGE, WEDGE-SHAPED HEAD--
--THAT HEAD WHICH IS FOREDESTINED TO DEVOUR THOR, EVEN AS HE CAUSES ITS DOOM.
FOR, WHAT FEAR CAN EVEN DARKSOME DEATH HOLD-- FOR THOSE WHO ARE THEMSELVES DEATH INCARNATE?
WHILE, ON A WORLD FAR DISTANT IN TIME AND SUB-SPACE...
OKAY, GIRLIE-- THIS IS IT, I GUESS.
YOUR HOME SWEET HOME FOR THE NEXT MILLENNIUM OR THREE!
ONCE, THIS MAN WAS "RED" NORVELL, TV CAMERAMAN.
A BIT CRUDE HE WAS, PERHAPS... BUT HE SEEMED AS GOOD AS ANY.
BUT THEN, LOKI USED HIS DESIRE FOR THE LADY SIF TO SEDUCE HIM INTO BATHING IN THE FIRE OF GEIRRODUR-- AND NOW HE HAS BECOME AS ONE WITH THE THUNDER GOD HIMSELF--
SET ME FREE, MORTAL-- I BEG THEE!
--EVEN TO DEFEATING HIS BLOND NAMESAKE, AND TAKING HIS BELOVED-- AND HIS MAGIC HAMMER!
ASGARD DOTH NEED ALL ITS CHAMPIONS!
DON'T CALL ME MORTAL, MISSIE!

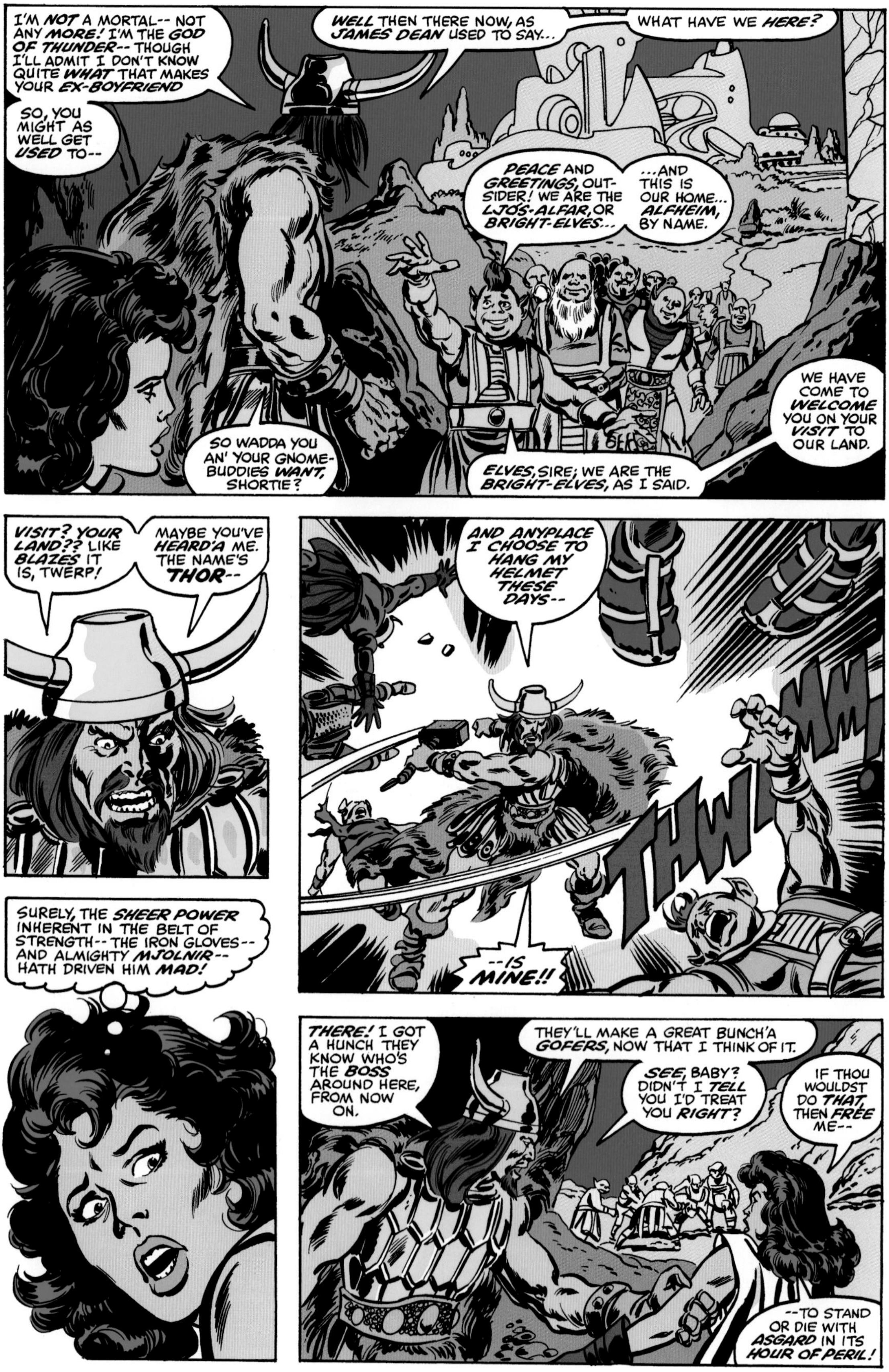
I'M NOT A MORTAL-- NOT ANY MORE! I'M THE GOD OF THUNDER-- THOUGH I'LL ADMIT I DON'T KNOW QUITE WHAT THAT MAKES YOUR EX-BOYFRIEND
SO, YOU MIGHT AS WELL GET USED TO--
WELL THEN THERE NOW, AS JAMES DEAN USED TO SAY...
WHAT HAVE WE HERE?
PEACE AND GREETINGS, OUT-SIDER! WE ARE THE LJOS-ALFAR, OR BRIGHT-ELVES...
...AND THIS IS OUR HOME... ALFHEIM, BY NAME.
WE HAVE COME TO WELCOME YOU ON YOUR VISIT TO OUR LAND.
SO WADDA YOU AN' YOUR GNOME-BUDDIES WANT, SHORTIE?
ELVES, SIRE; WE ARE THE BRIGHT-ELVES, AS I SAID.
VISIT? YOUR LAND?? LIKE BLAZES IT IS, TWERP!
MAYBE YOU'VE HEARD'A ME. THE NAME'S THOR--
AND ANYPLACE I CHOOSE TO HANG MY HELMET THESE DAYS--
THWMM!
--IS MINE!!
SURELY, THE SHEER POWER INHERENT IN THE BELT OF STRENGTH-- THE IRON GLOVES-- AND ALMIGHTY MJOLNIR-- HATH DRIVEN HIM MAD!
THERE! I GOT A HUNCH THEY KNOW WHO'S THE BOSS AROUND HERE, FROM NOW ON.
THEY'LL MAKE A GREAT BUNCH'A GOFERS, NOW THAT I THINK OF IT.
SEE, BABY? DIDN'T I TELL YOU I'D TREAT YOU RIGHT?
IF THOU WOULDST DO THAT, THEN FREE ME--
--TO STAND OR DIE WITH ASGARD IN ITS HOUR OF PERIL!

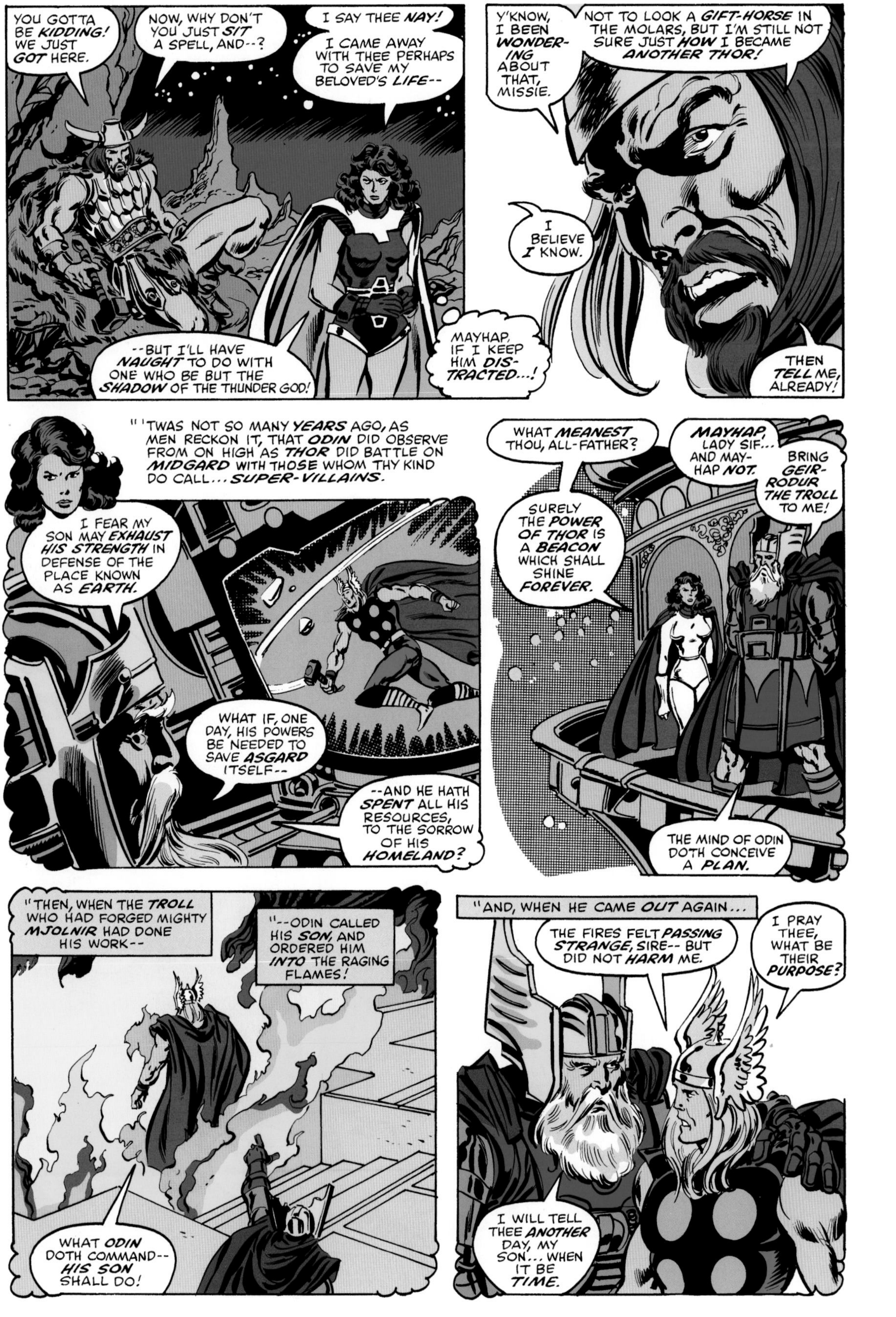
YOU GOTTA BE KIDDING! WE JUST GOT HERE.
NOW, WHY DON'T YOU JUST SIT A SPELL, AND--?
I SAY THEE NAY!
I CAME AWAY WITH THEE PERHAPS TO SAVE MY BELOVED'S LIFE--
--BUT I'LL HAVE NAUGHT TO DO WITH ONE WHO BE BUT THE SHADOW OF THE THUNDER GOD!
MAYHAP, IF I KEEP HIM DISTRACTED...!
Y'KNOW, I BEEN WONDERING ABOUT THAT, MISSIE.
NOT TO LOOK A GIFT-HORSE IN THE MOLARS, BUT I'M STILL NOT SURE JUST HOW I BECAME ANOTHER THOR!
I BELIEVE I KNOW.
THEN TELL ME, ALREADY!
"'TWAS NOT SO MANY YEARS AGO, AS MEN RECKON IT, THAT ODIN DID OBSERVE FROM ON HIGH AS THOR DID BATTLE ON MIDGARD WITH THOSE WHOM THY KIND DO CALL... SUPER-VILLAINS.
I FEAR MY SON MAY EXHAUST HIS STRENGTH IN DEFENSE OF THE PLACE KNOWN AS EARTH.
WHAT IF, ONE DAY, HIS POWERS BE NEEDED TO SAVE ASGARD ITSELF--
--AND HE HATH SPENT ALL HIS RESOURCES, TO THE SORROW OF HIS HOMELAND?
WHAT MEANEST THOU, ALL-FATHER?
SURELY THE POWER OF THOR IS A BEACON WHICH SHALL SHINE FOREVER.
MAYHAP, LADY SIF... AND MAYHAP NOT.
BRING GEIRRODUR THE TROLL TO ME!
THE MIND OF ODIN DOTH CONCEIVE A PLAN.
"THEN, WHEN THE TROLL WHO HAD FORGED MIGHTY MJOLNIR HAD DONE HIS WORK--
"--ODIN CALLED HIS SON, AND ORDERED HIM INTO THE RAGING FLAMES!
WHAT ODIN DOTH COMMAND-- HIS SON SHALL DO!
"AND, WHEN HE CAME OUT AGAIN...
THE FIRES FELT PASSING STRANGE, SIRE-- BUT DID NOT HARM ME.
I PRAY THEE, WHAT BE THEIR PURPOSE?
I WILL TELL THEE ANOTHER DAY, MY SON... WHEN IT BE TIME.

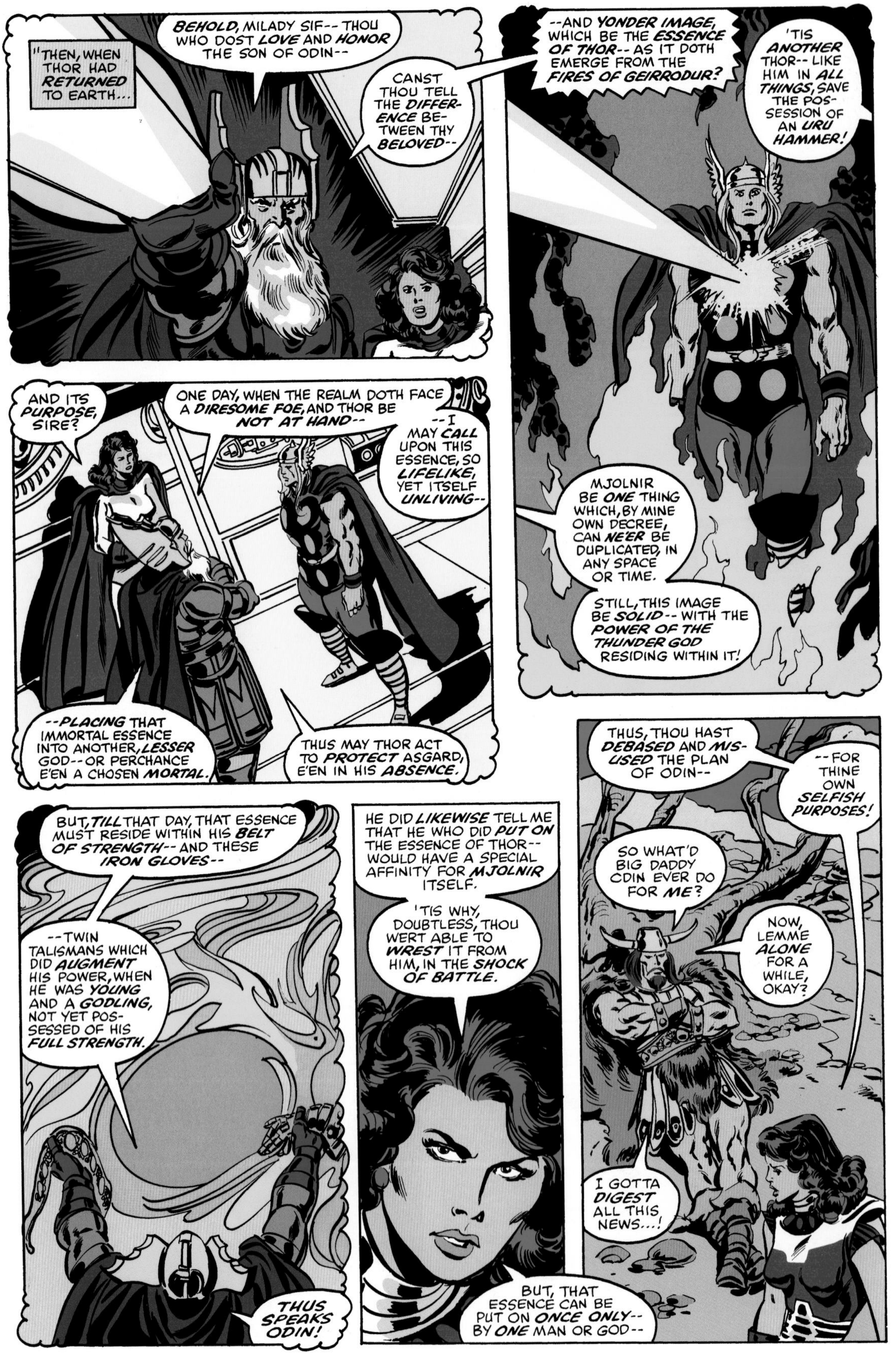
"THEN, WHEN THOR HAD RETURNED TO EARTH...
BEHOLD, MILADY SIF-- THOU WHO DOST LOVE AND HONOR THE SON OF ODIN--
CANST THOU TELL THE DIFFERENCE BETWEEN THY BELOVED--
--AND YONDER IMAGE, WHICH BE THE ESSENCE OF THOR-- AS IT DOTH EMERGE FROM THE FIRES OF GEIRRODUR?
'TIS ANOTHER THOR-- LIKE HIM IN ALL THINGS, SAVE THE POSSESSION OF AN URU HAMMER!
MJOLNIR BE ONE THING WHICH, BY MINE OWN DECREE, CAN NE'ER BE DUPLICATED, IN ANY SPACE OR TIME.
STILL, THIS IMAGE BE SOLID-- WITH THE POWER OF THE THUNDER GOD RESIDING WITHIN IT!
AND ITS PURPOSE, SIRE?
ONE DAY, WHEN THE REALM DOTH FACE A DIRESOME FOE, AND THOR BE NOT AT HAND--
--I MAY CALL UPON THIS ESSENCE, SO LIFELIKE, YET ITSELF UNLIVING--
--PLACING THAT IMMORTAL ESSENCE INTO ANOTHER, LESSER GOD-- OR PERCHANCE E'EN A CHOSEN MORTAL.
THUS MAY THOR ACT TO PROTECT ASGARD, E'EN IN HIS ABSENCE.
BUT, TILL THAT DAY, THAT ESSENCE MUST RESIDE WITHIN HIS BELT OF STRENGTH-- AND THESE IRON GLOVES--
--TWIN TALISMANS WHICH DID AUGMENT HIS POWER, WHEN HE WAS YOUNG AND A GODLING, NOT YET POSSESSED OF HIS FULL STRENGTH.
THUS SPEAKS ODIN!
HE DID LIKEWISE TELL ME THAT HE WHO DID PUT ON THE ESSENCE OF THOR-- WOULD HAVE A SPECIAL AFFINITY FOR MJOLNIR ITSELF.
'TIS WHY, DOUBTLESS, THOU WERT ABLE TO WREST IT FROM HIM, IN THE SHOCK OF BATTLE.
BUT, THAT ESSENCE CAN BE PUT ON ONCE ONLY-- BY ONE MAN OR GOD--
THUS, THOU HAST DEBASED AND MISUSED THE PLAN OF ODIN--
--FOR THINE OWN SELFISH PURPOSES!
SO WHAT'D BIG DADDY ODIN EVER DO FOR ME?
NOW, LEMME ALONE FOR A WHILE, OKAY?
I GOTTA DIGEST ALL THIS NEWS...!

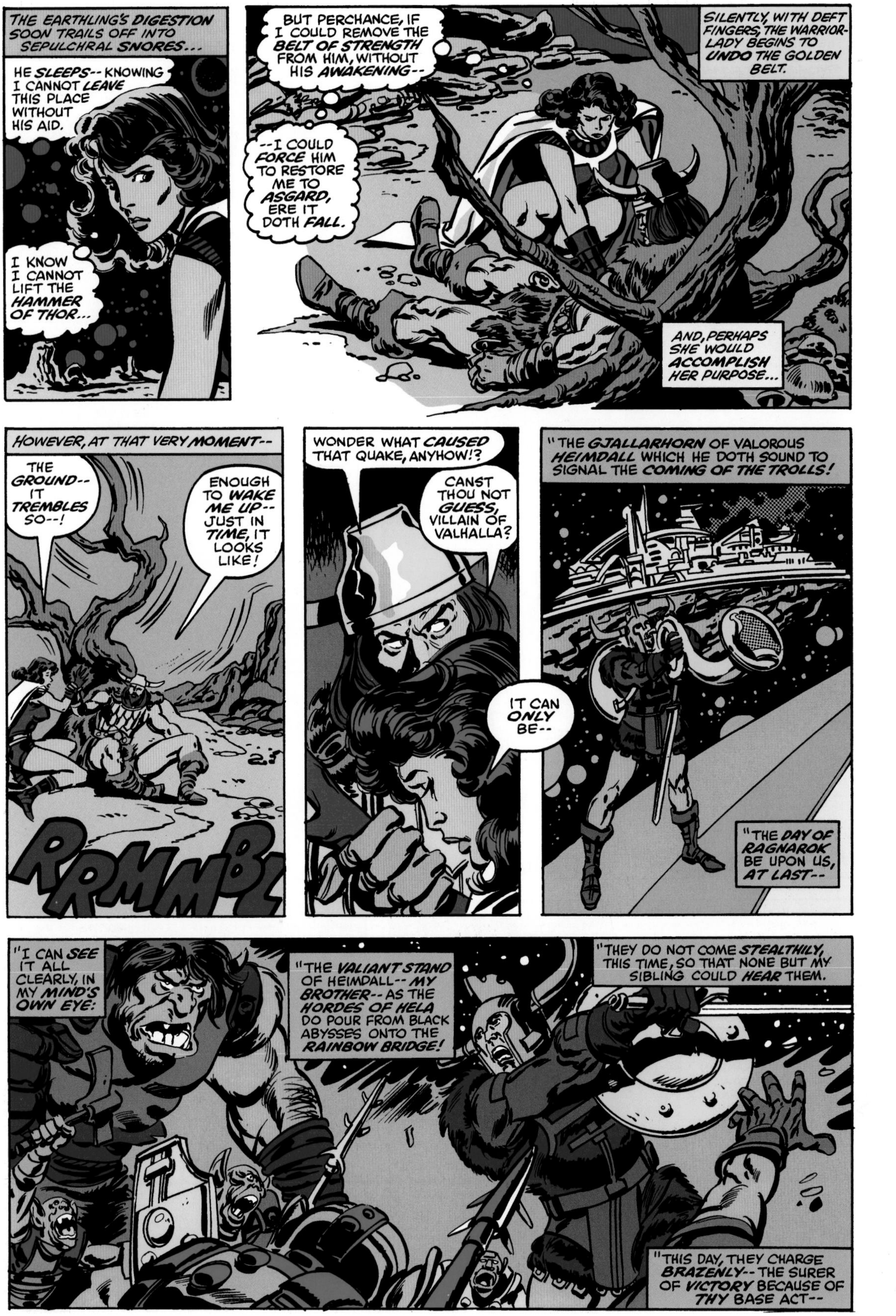
THE EARTHLING'S DIGESTION SOON TRAILS OFF INTO SEPULCHRAL SNORES...
HE SLEEPS-- KNOWING I CANNOT LEAVE THIS PLACE WITHOUT HIS AID.
I KNOW I CANNOT LIFT THE HAMMER OF THOR...
BUT PERCHANCE, IF I COULD REMOVE THE BELT OF STRENGTH FROM HIM, WITHOUT HIS AWAKENING--
--I COULD FORCE HIM TO RESTORE ME TO ASGARD, ERE IT DOTH FALL.
SILENTLY, WITH DEFT FINGERS, THE WARRIOR-LADY BEGINS TO UNDO THE GOLDEN BELT.
AND, PERHAPS SHE WOULD ACCOMPLISH HER PURPOSE...
HOWEVER, AT THAT VERY MOMENT--
THE GROUND-- IT TREMBLES SO--!
ENOUGH TO WAKE ME UP-- JUST IN TIME, IT LOOKS LIKE!
RRMMBL
WONDER WHAT CAUSED THAT QUAKE, ANYHOW!?
CANST THOU NOT GUESS, VILLAIN OF VALHALLA?
IT CAN ONLY BE--
"THE GJALLARHORN OF VALOROUS HEIMDALL WHICH HE DOTH SOUND TO SIGNAL THE COMING OF THE TROLLS!
"THE DAY OF RAGNAROK BE UPON US, AT LAST--
"I CAN SEE IT ALL CLEARLY, IN MY MIND'S OWN EYE:
"THE VALIANT STAND OF HEIMDALL-- MY BROTHER-- AS THE HORDES OF HELA DO POUR FROM BLACK ABYSSES ONTO THE RAINBOW BRIDGE!
"THEY DO NOT COME STEALTHILY, THIS TIME, SO THAT NONE BUT MY SIBLING COULD HEAR THEM.
"THIS DAY, THEY CHARGE BRAZENLY-- THE SURER OF VICTORY BECAUSE OF THY BASE ACT--

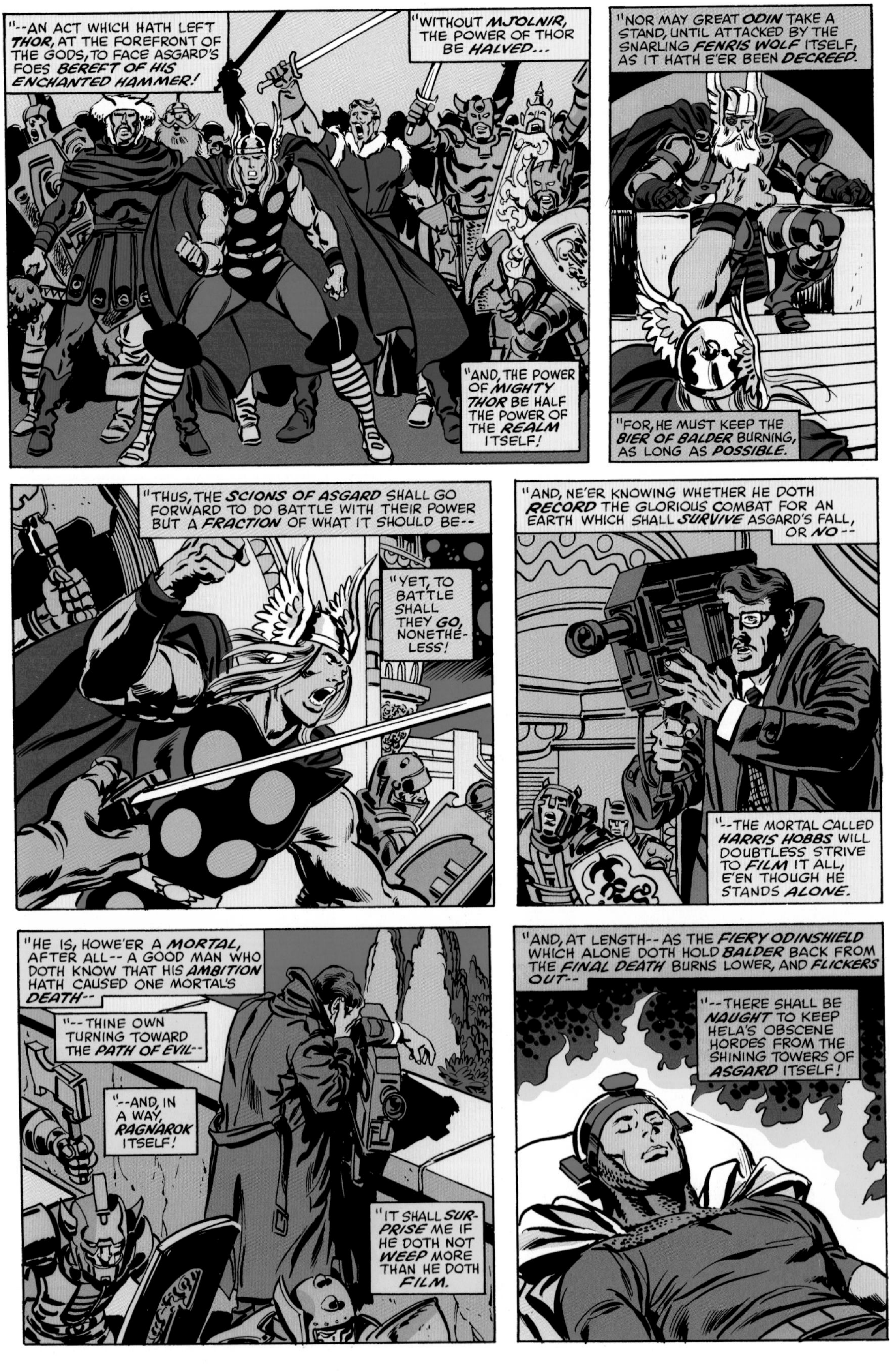
"--AN ACT WHICH HATH LEFT THOR, AT THE FOREFRONT OF THE GODS, TO FACE ASGARD'S FOES BEREFT OF HIS ENCHANTED HAMMER!
"WITHOUT MJOLNIR, THE POWER OF THOR BE HALVED...
"AND, THE POWER OF MIGHTY THOR BE HALF THE POWER OF THE REALM ITSELF!
"NOR MAY GREAT ODIN TAKE A STAND, UNTIL ATTACKED BY THE SNARLING FENRIS WOLF ITSELF, AS IT HATH E'ER BEEN DECREED.
"FOR, HE MUST KEEP THE BIER OF BALDER BURNING, AS LONG AS POSSIBLE.
"THUS, THE SCIONS OF ASGARD SHALL GO FORWARD TO DO BATTLE WITH THEIR POWER BUT A FRACTION OF WHAT IT SHOULD BE--
"YET, TO BATTLE SHALL THEY GO, NONETHELESS!
"AND, NE'ER KNOWING WHETHER HE DOTH RECORD THE GLORIOUS COMBAT FOR AN EARTH WHICH SHALL SURVIVE ASGARD'S FALL, OR NO--
"--THE MORTAL CALLED HARRIS HOBBS WILL DOUBTLESS STRIVE TO FILM IT ALL, E'EN THOUGH HE STANDS ALONE.
"HE IS, HOWE'ER A MORTAL, AFTER ALL-- A GOOD MAN WHO DOTH KNOW THAT HIS AMBITION HATH CAUSED ONE MORTAL'S DEATH--
"--THINE OWN TURNING TOWARD THE PATH OF EVIL--
"--AND, IN A WAY, RAGNAROK ITSELF!
"IT SHALL SURPRISE ME IF HE DOTH NOT WEEP MORE THAN HE DOTH FILM.
"AND, AT LENGTH-- AS THE FIERY ODINSHIELD WHICH ALONE DOTH HOLD BALDER BACK FROM THE FINAL DEATH BURNS LOWER, AND FLICKERS OUT--
"--THERE SHALL BE NAUGHT TO KEEP HELA'S OBSCENE HORDES FROM THE SHINING TOWERS OF ASGARD ITSELF!

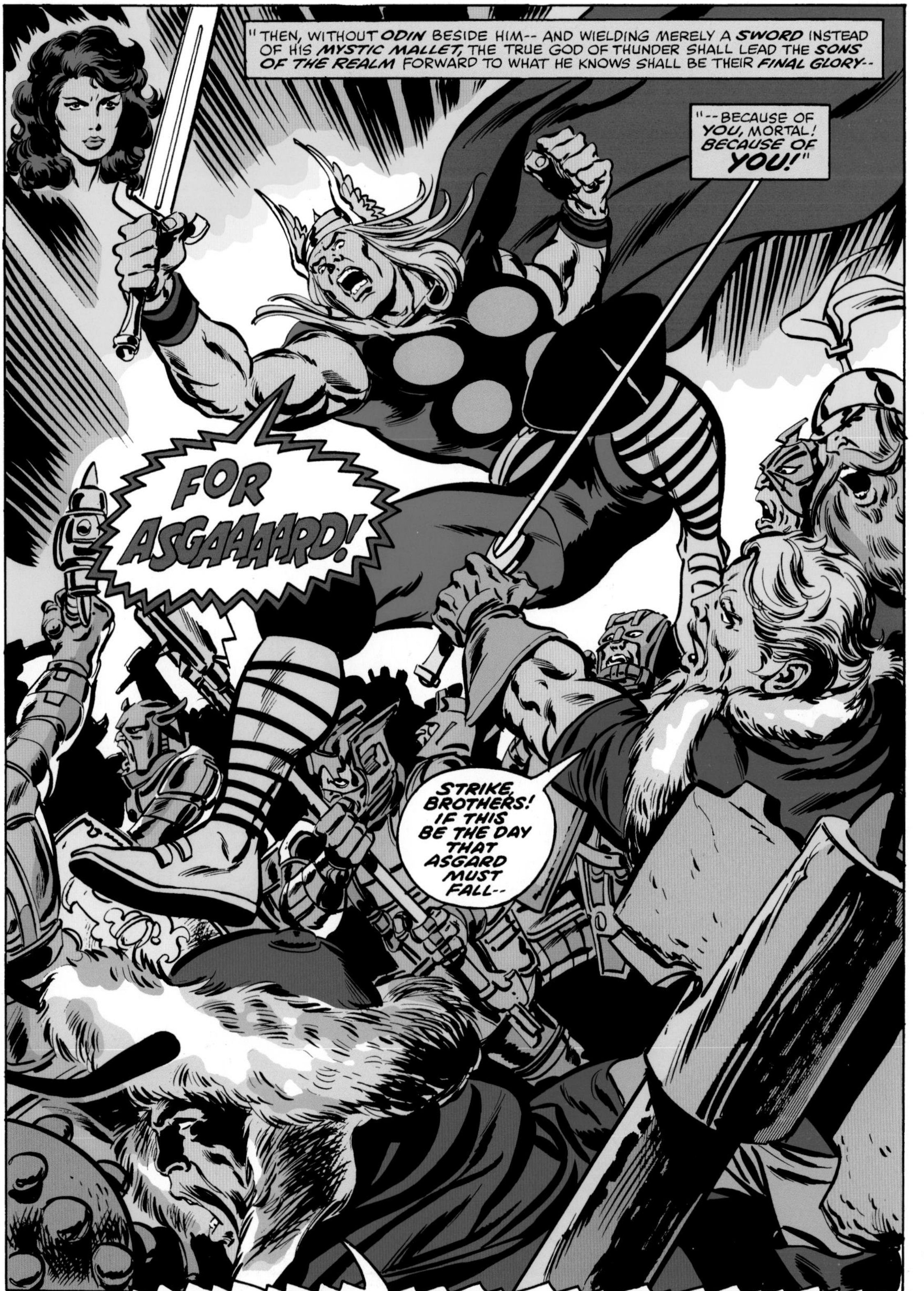
"THEN, WITHOUT ODIN BESIDE HIM-- AND WIELDING MERELY A SWORD INSTEAD OF HIS MYSTIC MALLET, THE TRUE GOD OF THUNDER SHALL LEAD THE SONS OF THE REALM FORWARD TO WHAT HE KNOWS SHALL BE THEIR FINAL GLORY--
"--BECAUSE OF YOU, MORTAL! BECAUSE OF YOU!"
FOR ASGAAAARD!
STRIKE, BROTHERS! IF THIS BE THE DAY THAT ASGARD MUST FALL--

NEXT ISSUE: --LET NONE SURVIVE THE DAY OF RAGNAROK!

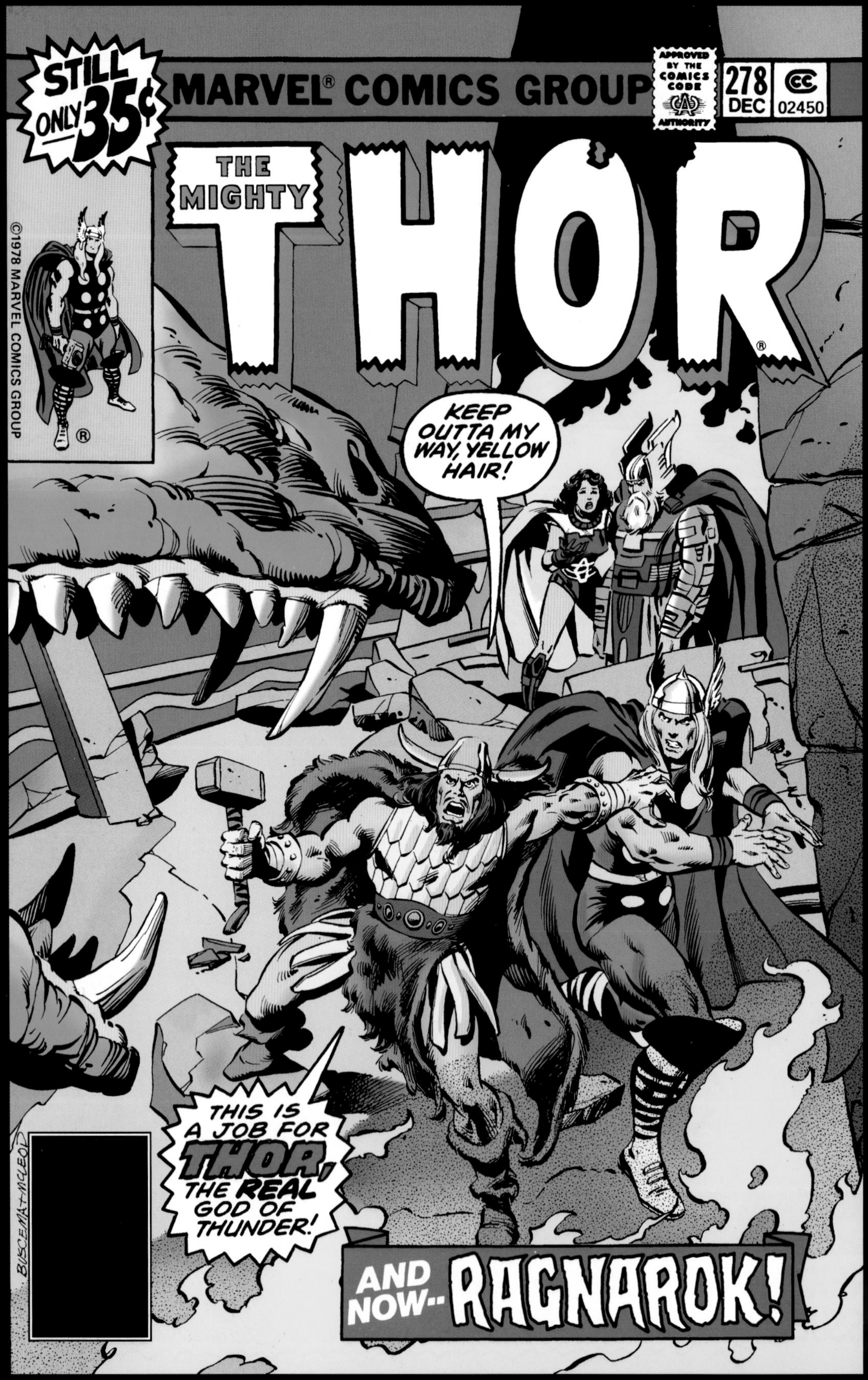
STILL ONLY 35¢
MARVEL® COMICS GROUP
APPROVED BY THE COMICS CODE AUTHORITY
278 DEC
CC 02450
THE MIGHTY THOR®
©1978 MARVEL COMICS GROUP
KEEP OUTTA MY WAY, YELLOW HAIR!
THIS IS A JOB FOR THOR, THE REAL GOD OF THUNDER!
AND NOW-- RAGNAROK!
BUSCEMA + MCLEOD

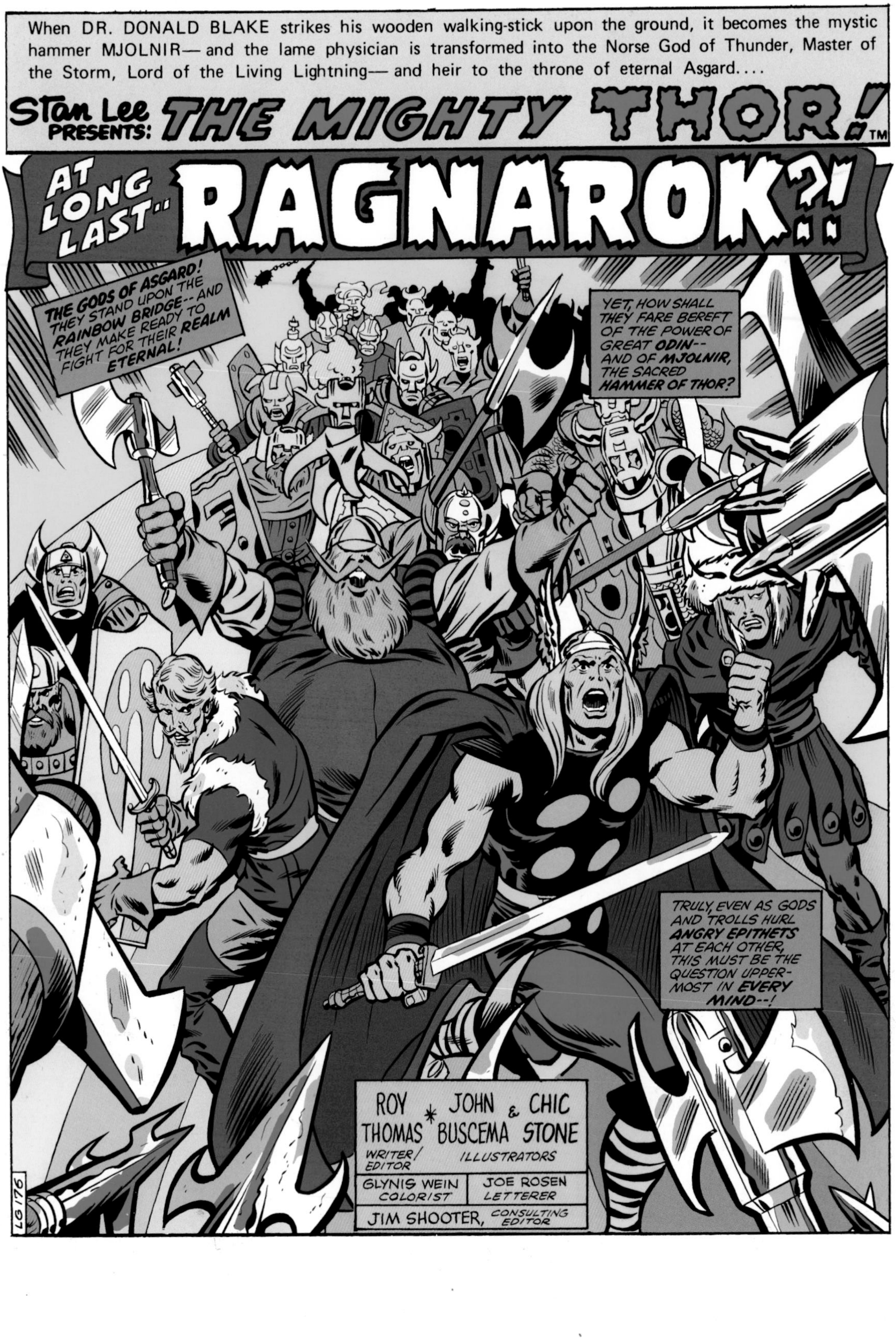
When DR. DONALD BLAKE strikes his wooden walking-stick upon the ground, it becomes the mystic hammer MJOLNIR— and the lame physician is transformed into the Norse God of Thunder, Master of the Storm, Lord of the Living Lightning— and heir to the throne of eternal Asgard....
Stan Lee PRESENTS: THE MIGHTY THOR!™
AT LONG LAST.. RAGNAROK?!
THE GODS OF ASGARD! THEY STAND UPON THE RAINBOW BRIDGE--AND THEY MAKE READY TO FIGHT FOR THEIR REALM ETERNAL!
YET, HOW SHALL THEY FARE BEREFT OF THE POWER OF GREAT ODIN-- AND OF MJOLNIR, THE SACRED HAMMER OF THOR?
TRULY, EVEN AS GODS AND TROLLS HURL ANGRY EPITHETS AT EACH OTHER, THIS MUST BE THE QUESTION UPPERMOST IN EVERY MIND--!
ROY THOMAS WRITER/EDITOR
JOHN BUSCEMA & CHIC STONE ILLUSTRATORS
GLYNIS WEIN COLORIST
JOE ROSEN LETTERER
JIM SHOOTER, CONSULTING EDITOR
LG176

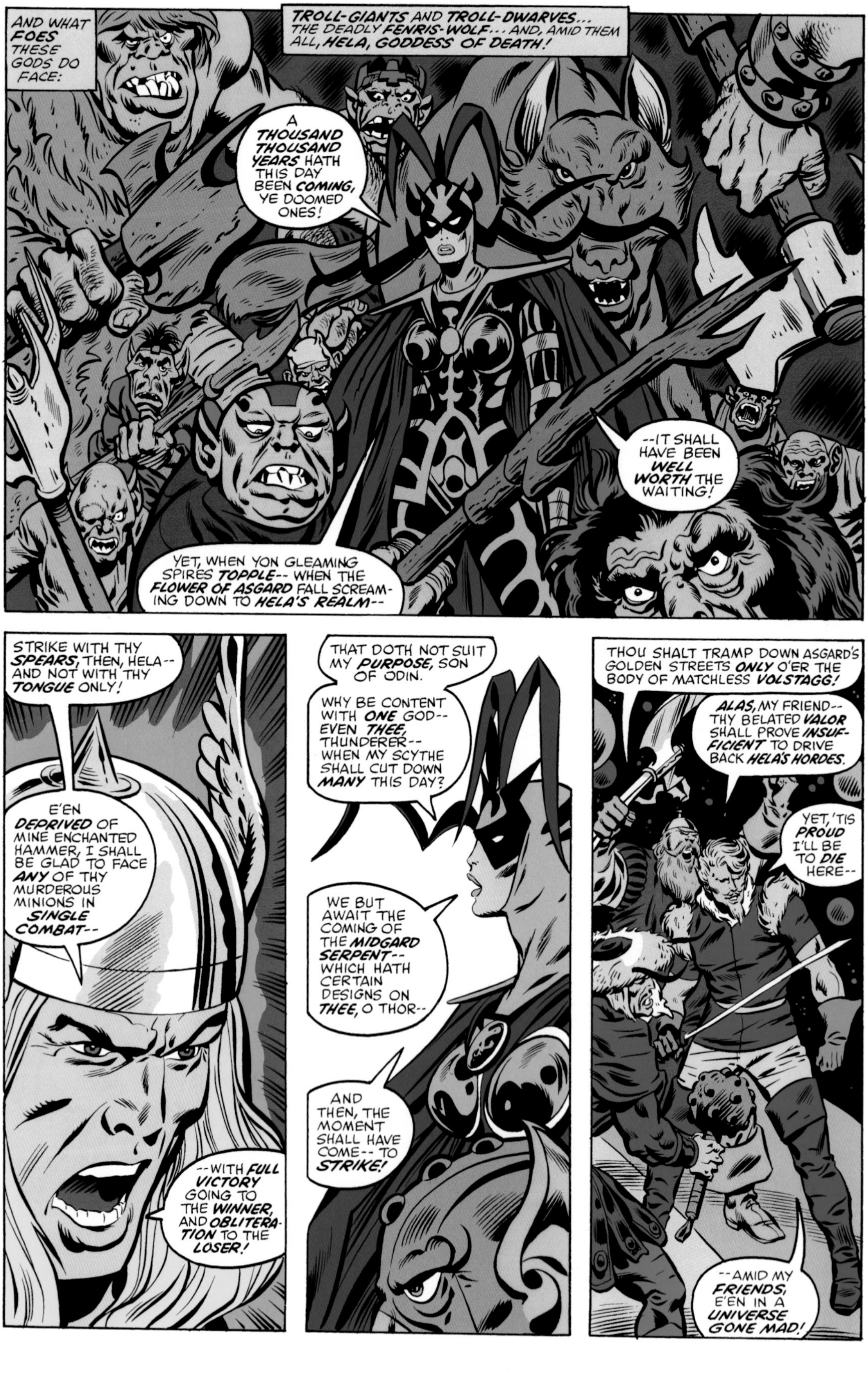
AND WHAT FOES THESE GODS DO FACE:
TROLL-GIANTS AND TROLL-DWARVES... THE DEADLY FENRIS-WOLF... AND, AMID THEM ALL, HELA, GODDESS OF DEATH!
A THOUSAND THOUSAND YEARS HATH THIS DAY BEEN COMING, YE DOOMED ONES!
YET, WHEN YON GLEAMING SPIRES TOPPLE-- WHEN THE FLOWER OF ASGARD FALL SCREAMING DOWN TO HELA'S REALM--
--IT SHALL HAVE BEEN WELL WORTH THE WAITING!
STRIKE WITH THY SPEARS, THEN, HELA-- AND NOT WITH THY TONGUE ONLY!
E'EN DEPRIVED OF MINE ENCHANTED HAMMER, I SHALL BE GLAD TO FACE ANY OF THY MURDEROUS MINIONS IN SINGLE COMBAT--
--WITH FULL VICTORY GOING TO THE WINNER, AND OBLITERATION TO THE LOSER!
THAT DOTH NOT SUIT MY PURPOSE, SON OF ODIN.
WHY BE CONTENT WITH ONE GOD-- EVEN THEE, THUNDERER-- WHEN MY SCYTHE SHALL CUT DOWN MANY THIS DAY?
WE BUT AWAIT THE COMING OF THE MIDGARD SERPENT-- WHICH HATH CERTAIN DESIGNS ON THEE, O THOR--
AND THEN, THE MOMENT SHALL HAVE COME-- TO STRIKE!
THOU SHALT TRAMP DOWN ASGARD'S GOLDEN STREETS ONLY O'ER THE BODY OF MATCHLESS VOLSTAGG!
ALAS, MY FRIEND-- THY BELATED VALOR SHALL PROVE INSUFFICIENT TO DRIVE BACK HELA'S HORDES.
YET, 'TIS PROUD I'LL BE TO DIE HERE--
--AMID MY FRIENDS, E'EN IN A UNIVERSE GONE MAD!

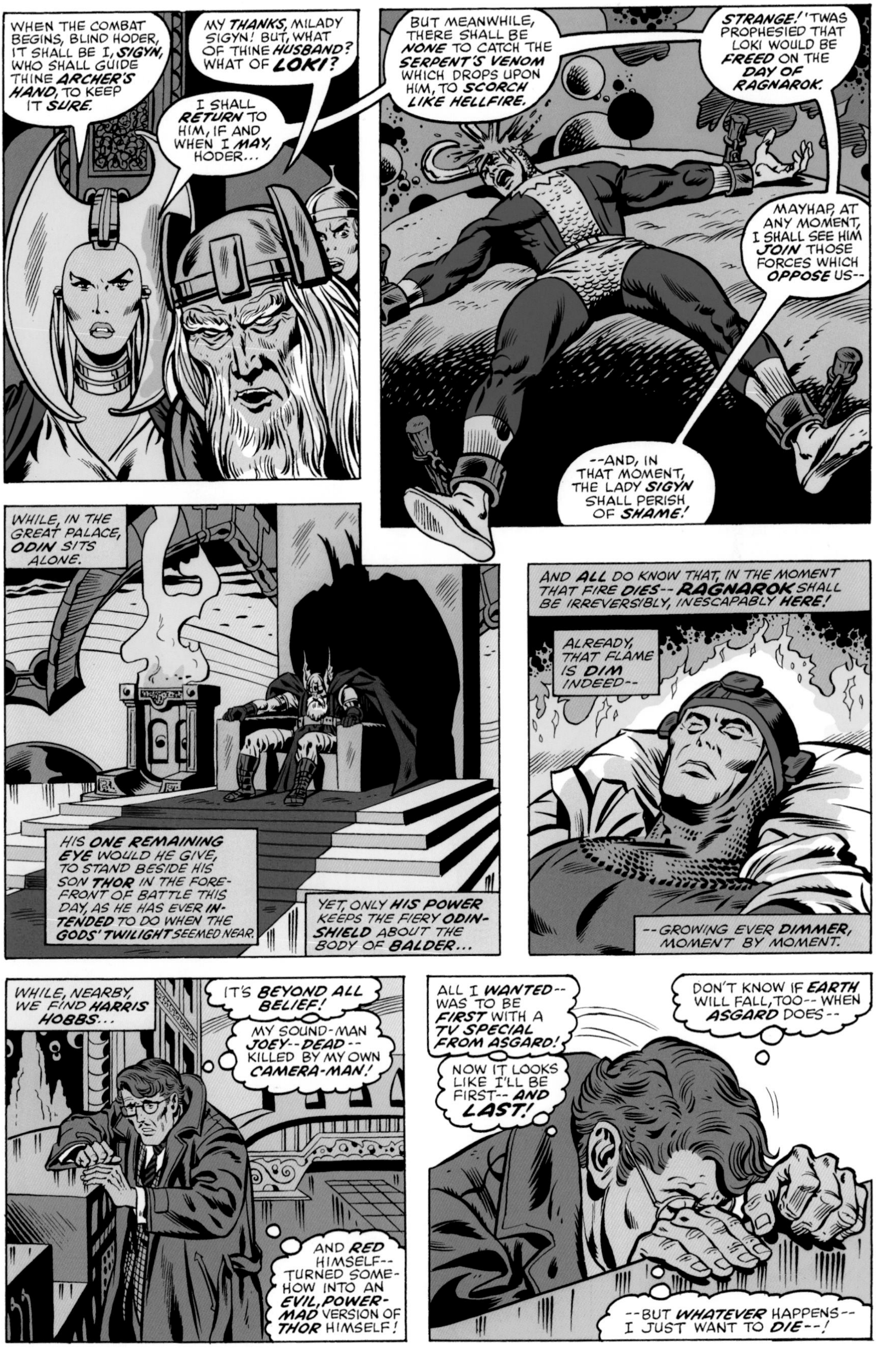
WHEN THE COMBAT BEGINS, BLIND HODER, IT SHALL BE I, SIGYN, WHO SHALL GUIDE THINE ARCHER'S HAND, TO KEEP IT SURE.
MY THANKS, MILADY SIGYN! BUT, WHAT OF THINE HUSBAND? WHAT OF LOKI?
I SHALL RETURN TO HIM, IF AND WHEN I MAY, HODER...
BUT MEANWHILE, THERE SHALL BE NONE TO CATCH THE SERPENT'S VENOM WHICH DROPS UPON HIM, TO SCORCH LIKE HELLFIRE.
STRANGE! 'TWAS PROPHESIED THAT LOKI WOULD BE FREED ON THE DAY OF RAGNAROK.
MAYHAP, AT ANY MOMENT, I SHALL SEE HIM JOIN THOSE FORCES WHICH OPPOSE US--
--AND, IN THAT MOMENT, THE LADY SIGYN SHALL PERISH OF SHAME!
WHILE, IN THE GREAT PALACE, ODIN SITS ALONE.
HIS ONE REMAINING EYE WOULD HE GIVE, TO STAND BESIDE HIS SON THOR IN THE FORE-FRONT OF BATTLE THIS DAY, AS HE HAS EVER IN-TENDED TO DO WHEN THE GODS' TWILIGHT SEEMED NEAR.
YET, ONLY HIS POWER KEEPS THE FIERY ODIN-SHIELD ABOUT THE BODY OF BALDER...
AND ALL DO KNOW THAT, IN THE MOMENT THAT FIRE DIES-- RAGNAROK SHALL BE IRREVERSIBLY, INESCAPABLY HERE!
ALREADY, THAT FLAME IS DIM INDEED--
--GROWING EVER DIMMER, MOMENT BY MOMENT.
WHILE, NEARBY, WE FIND HARRIS HOBBS...
IT'S BEYOND ALL BELIEF!
MY SOUND-MAN JOEY--DEAD-- KILLED BY MY OWN CAMERA-MAN!
AND RED HIMSELF-- TURNED SOME-HOW INTO AN EVIL, POWER-MAD VERSION OF THOR HIMSELF!
ALL I WANTED-- WAS TO BE FIRST WITH A TV SPECIAL FROM ASGARD!
NOW IT LOOKS LIKE I'LL BE FIRST-- AND LAST!
DON'T KNOW IF EARTH WILL FALL, TOO-- WHEN ASGARD DOES--
--BUT WHATEVER HAPPENS-- I JUST WANT TO DIE--!

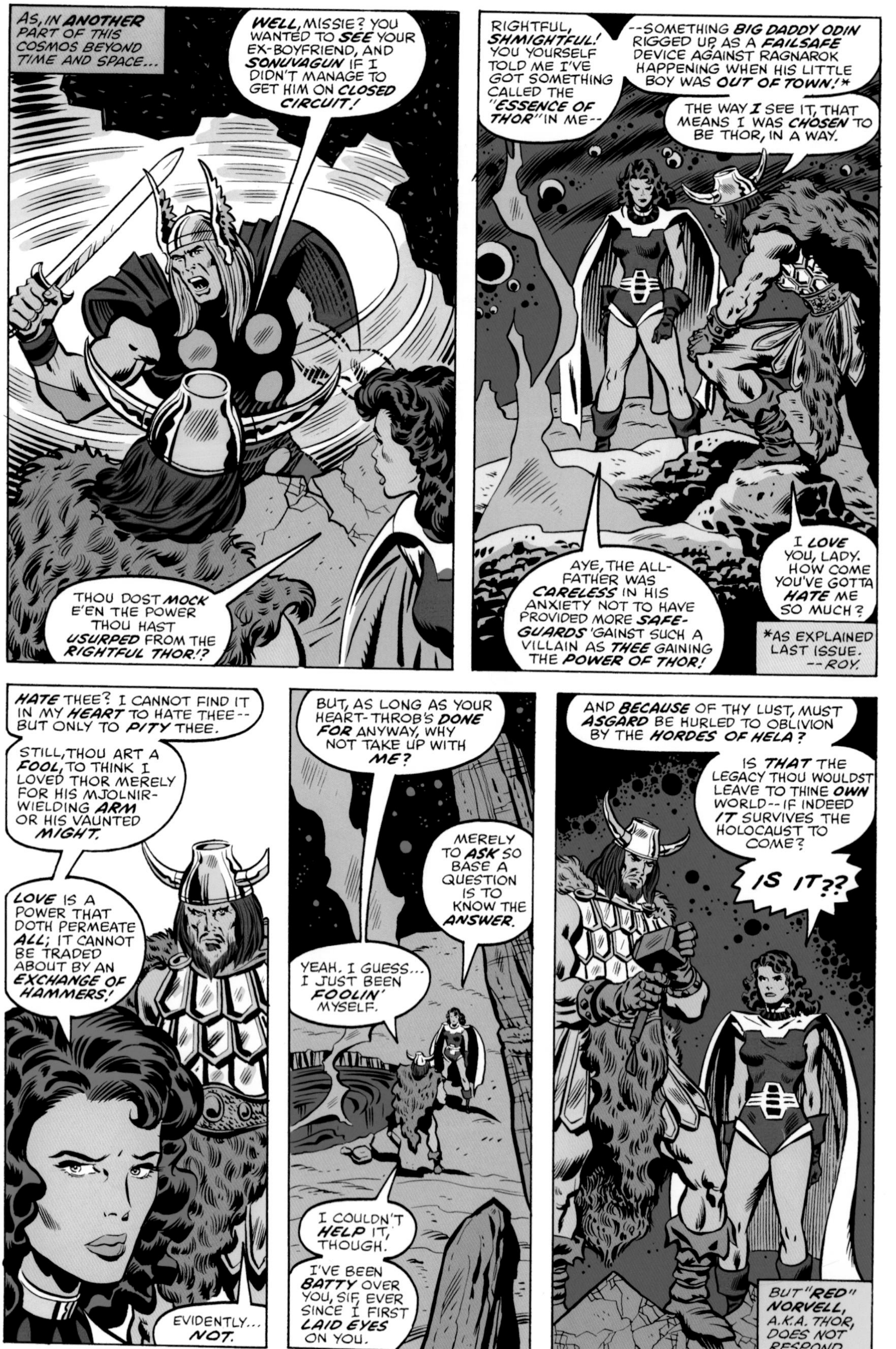

AS, IN ANOTHER PART OF THIS COSMOS BEYOND TIME AND SPACE...
WELL, MISSIE? YOU WANTED TO SEE YOUR EX-BOYFRIEND, AND SONUVAGUN IF I DIDN'T MANAGE TO GET HIM ON CLOSED CIRCUIT!
THOU DOST MOCK E'EN THE POWER THOU HAST USURPED FROM THE RIGHTFUL THOR!?
RIGHTFUL, SHMIGHTFUL! YOU YOURSELF TOLD ME I'VE GOT SOMETHING CALLED THE "ESSENCE OF THOR" IN ME--
--SOMETHING BIG DADDY ODIN RIGGED UP AS A FAILSAFE DEVICE AGAINST RAGNAROK HAPPENING WHEN HIS LITTLE BOY WAS OUT OF TOWN!*
THE WAY I SEE IT, THAT MEANS I WAS CHOSEN TO BE THOR, IN A WAY.
AYE, THE ALL-FATHER WAS CARELESS IN HIS ANXIETY NOT TO HAVE PROVIDED MORE SAFE-GUARDS 'GAINST SUCH A VILLAIN AS THEE GAINING THE POWER OF THOR!
I LOVE YOU, LADY. HOW COME YOU'VE GOTTA HATE ME SO MUCH?
*AS EXPLAINED LAST ISSUE. --ROY.
HATE THEE? I CANNOT FIND IT IN MY HEART TO HATE THEE--BUT ONLY TO PITY THEE.
STILL, THOU ART A FOOL, TO THINK I LOVED THOR MERELY FOR HIS MJOLNIR-WIELDING ARM OR HIS VAUNTED MIGHT.
LOVE IS A POWER THAT DOTH PERMEATE ALL; IT CANNOT BE TRADED ABOUT BY AN EXCHANGE OF HAMMERS!
BUT, AS LONG AS YOUR HEART-THROB'S DONE FOR ANYWAY, WHY NOT TAKE UP WITH ME?
MERELY TO ASK SO BASE A QUESTION IS TO KNOW THE ANSWER.
YEAH. I GUESS... I JUST BEEN FOOLIN' MYSELF.
I COULDN'T HELP IT, THOUGH.
I'VE BEEN BATTY OVER YOU, SIF, EVER SINCE I FIRST LAID EYES ON YOU.
EVIDENTLY... NOT.
AND BECAUSE OF THY LUST, MUST ASGARD BE HURLED TO OBLIVION BY THE HORDES OF HELA?
IS THAT THE LEGACY THOU WOULDST LEAVE TO THINE OWN WORLD--IF INDEED IT SURVIVES THE HOLOCAUST TO COME?
IS IT??
BUT "RED" NORVELL, A.K.A. THOR, DOES NOT RESPOND.

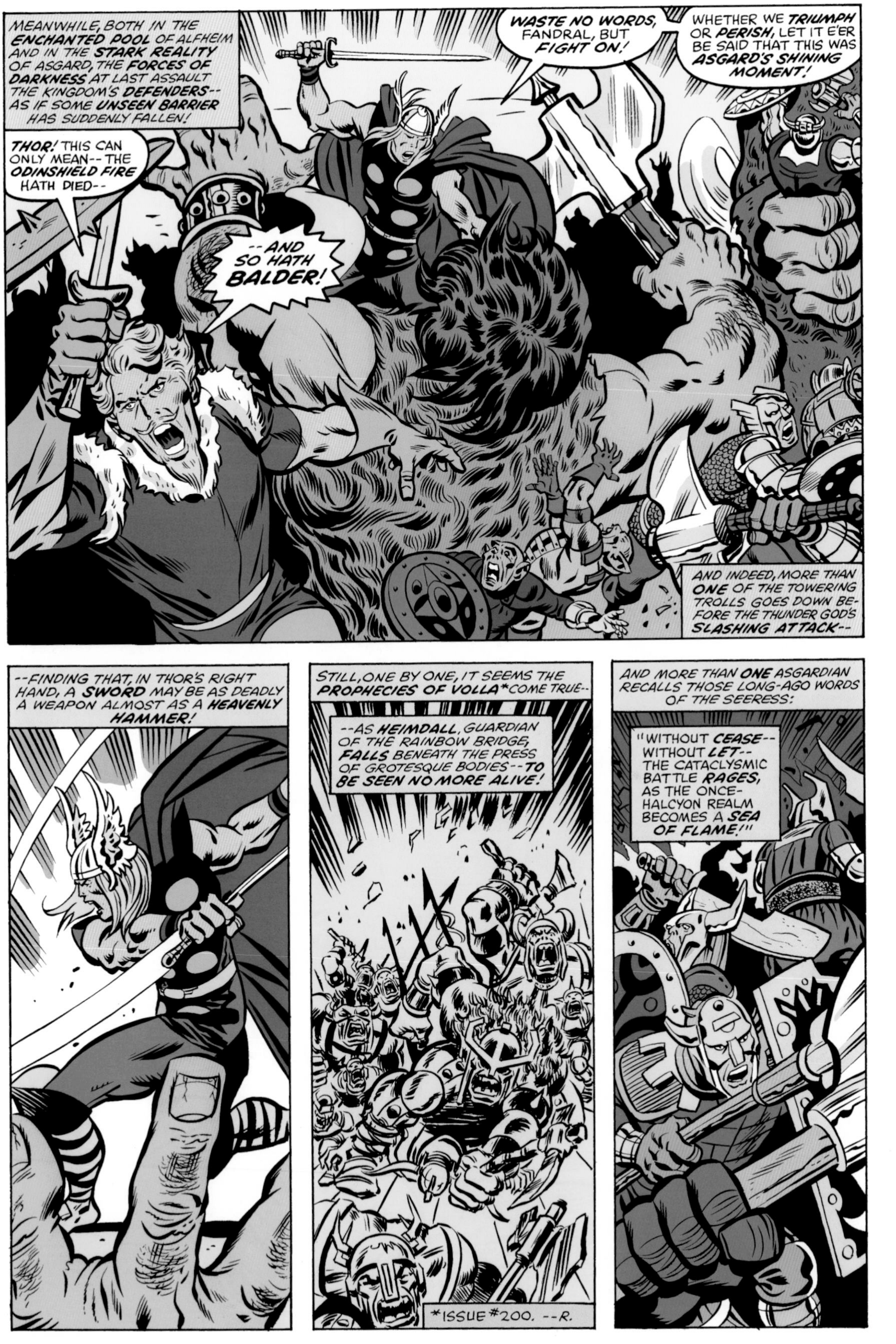

MEANWHILE, BOTH IN THE ENCHANTED POOL OF ALFHEIM AND IN THE STARK REALITY OF ASGARD, THE FORCES OF DARKNESS AT LAST ASSAULT THE KINGDOM'S DEFENDERS-- AS IF SOME UNSEEN BARRIER HAS SUDDENLY FALLEN!
WASTE NO WORDS, FANDRAL, BUT FIGHT ON!
WHETHER WE TRIUMPH OR PERISH, LET IT E'ER BE SAID THAT THIS WAS ASGARD'S SHINING MOMENT!
THOR! THIS CAN ONLY MEAN-- THE ODINSHIELD FIRE HATH DIED--
--AND SO HATH BALDER!
AND INDEED, MORE THAN ONE OF THE TOWERING TROLLS GOES DOWN BEFORE THE THUNDER GOD'S SLASHING ATTACK--
--FINDING THAT, IN THOR'S RIGHT HAND, A SWORD MAY BE AS DEADLY A WEAPON ALMOST AS A HEAVENLY HAMMER!
STILL, ONE BY ONE, IT SEEMS THE PROPHECIES OF VOLLA* COME TRUE--
--AS HEIMDALL, GUARDIAN OF THE RAINBOW BRIDGE, FALLS BENEATH THE PRESS OF GROTESQUE BODIES--TO BE SEEN NO MORE ALIVE!
*ISSUE #200. --R.
AND MORE THAN ONE ASGARDIAN RECALLS THOSE LONG-AGO WORDS OF THE SEERESS:
"WITHOUT CEASE-- WITHOUT LET-- THE CATACLYSMIC BATTLE RAGES, AS THE ONCE-HALCYON REALM BECOMES A SEA OF FLAME!"

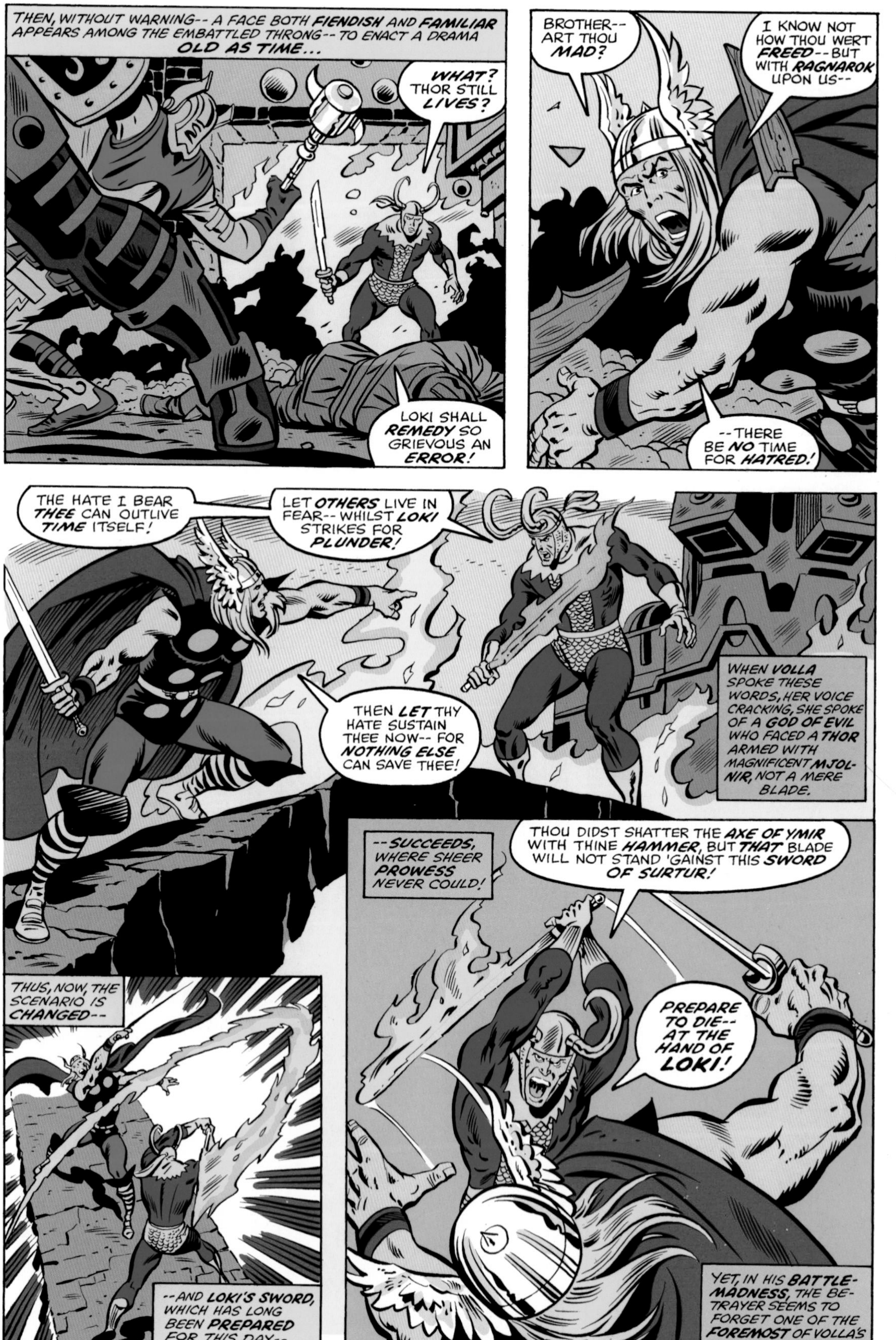
THEN, WITHOUT WARNING-- A FACE BOTH FIENDISH AND FAMILIAR APPEARS AMONG THE EMBATTLED THRONG-- TO ENACT A DRAMA OLD AS TIME...
WHAT? THOR STILL LIVES?
LOKI SHALL REMEDY SO GRIEVOUS AN ERROR!
BROTHER-- ART THOU MAD?
I KNOW NOT HOW THOU WERT FREED--BUT WITH RAGNAROK UPON US--
--THERE BE NO TIME FOR HATRED!
THE HATE I BEAR THEE CAN OUTLIVE TIME ITSELF!
LET OTHERS LIVE IN FEAR--WHILST LOKI STRIKES FOR PLUNDER!
THEN LET THY HATE SUSTAIN THEE NOW-- FOR NOTHING ELSE CAN SAVE THEE!
WHEN VOLLA SPOKE THESE WORDS, HER VOICE CRACKING, SHE SPOKE OF A GOD OF EVIL WHO FACED A THOR ARMED WITH MAGNIFICENT MJOLNIR, NOT A MERE BLADE.
THUS, NOW, THE SCENARIO IS CHANGED--
--AND LOKI'S SWORD, WHICH HAS LONG BEEN PREPARED FOR THIS DAY--
--SUCCEEDS, WHERE SHEER PROWESS NEVER COULD!
THOU DIDST SHATTER THE AXE OF YMIR WITH THINE HAMMER, BUT THAT BLADE WILL NOT STAND 'GAINST THIS SWORD OF SURTUR!
PREPARE TO DIE-- AT THE HAND OF LOKI!
YET, IN HIS BATTLE-MADNESS, THE BETRAYER SEEMS TO FORGET ONE OF THE FOREMOST OF VOLLA'S FORETELLINGS--

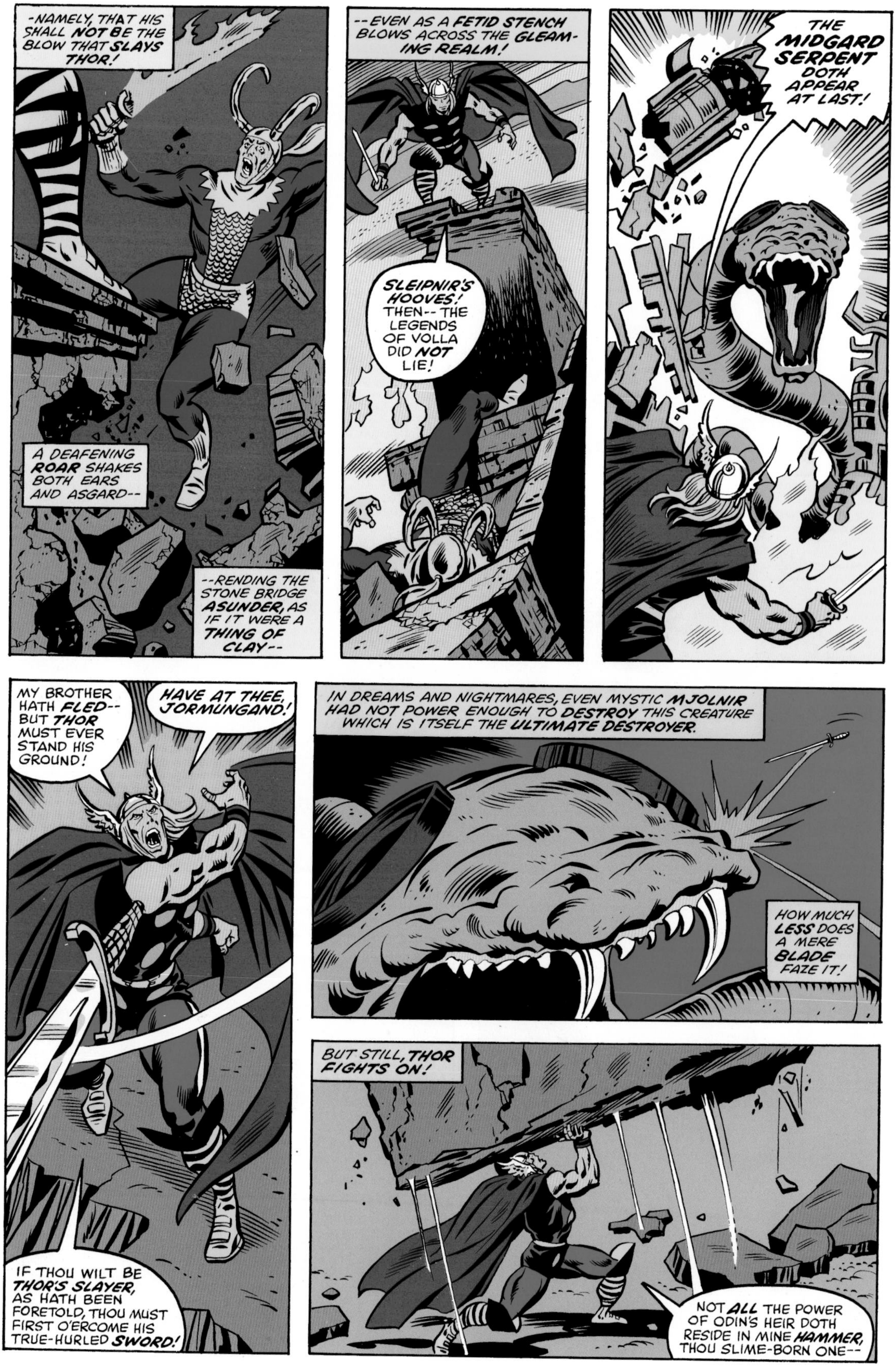
-NAMELY, THAT HIS SHALL NOT BE THE BLOW THAT SLAYS THOR!
A DEAFENING ROAR SHAKES BOTH EARS AND ASGARD--
--RENDING THE STONE BRIDGE ASUNDER, AS IF IT WERE A THING OF CLAY--
--EVEN AS A FETID STENCH BLOWS ACROSS THE GLEAMING REALM!
SLEIPNIR'S HOOVES! THEN--THE LEGENDS OF VOLLA DID NOT LIE!
THE MIDGARD SERPENT DOTH APPEAR AT LAST!
MY BROTHER HATH FLED-- BUT THOR MUST EVER STAND HIS GROUND!
HAVE AT THEE, JORMUNGAND!
IF THOU WILT BE THOR'S SLAYER, AS HATH BEEN FORETOLD, THOU MUST FIRST O'ERCOME HIS TRUE-HURLED SWORD!
IN DREAMS AND NIGHTMARES, EVEN MYSTIC MJOLNIR HAD NOT POWER ENOUGH TO DESTROY THIS CREATURE WHICH IS ITSELF THE ULTIMATE DESTROYER.
HOW MUCH LESS DOES A MERE BLADE FAZE IT!
BUT STILL, THOR FIGHTS ON!
NOT ALL THE POWER OF ODIN'S HEIR DOTH RESIDE IN MINE HAMMER, THOU SLIME-BORN ONE--

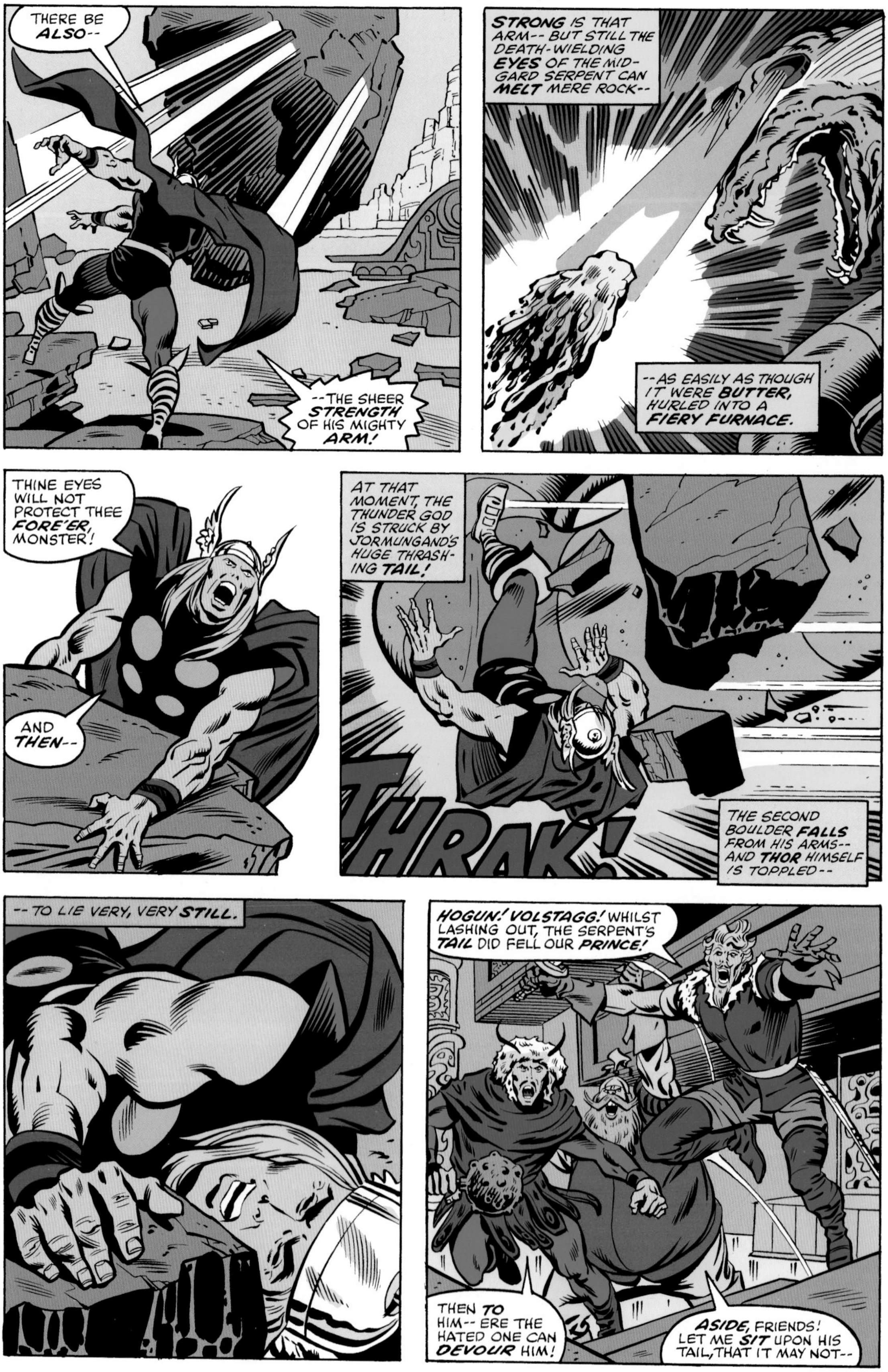

THERE BE ALSO--
--THE SHEER STRENGTH OF HIS MIGHTY ARM!
STRONG IS THAT ARM-- BUT STILL THE DEATH-WIELDING EYES OF THE MIDGARD SERPENT CAN MELT MERE ROCK--
--AS EASILY AS THOUGH IT WERE BUTTER, HURLED INTO A FIERY FURNACE.
THINE EYES WILL NOT PROTECT THEE FORE'ER, MONSTER!
AND THEN--
AT THAT MOMENT, THE THUNDER GOD IS STRUCK BY JORMUNGAND'S HUGE THRASHING TAIL!
THRAK!
THE SECOND BOULDER FALLS FROM HIS ARMS-- AND THOR HIMSELF IS TOPPLED--
--TO LIE VERY, VERY STILL.
HOGUN! VOLSTAGG! WHILST LASHING OUT, THE SERPENT'S TAIL DID FELL OUR PRINCE!
THEN TO HIM-- ERE THE HATED ONE CAN DEVOUR HIM!
ASIDE, FRIENDS! LET ME SIT UPON HIS TAIL, THAT IT MAY NOT--

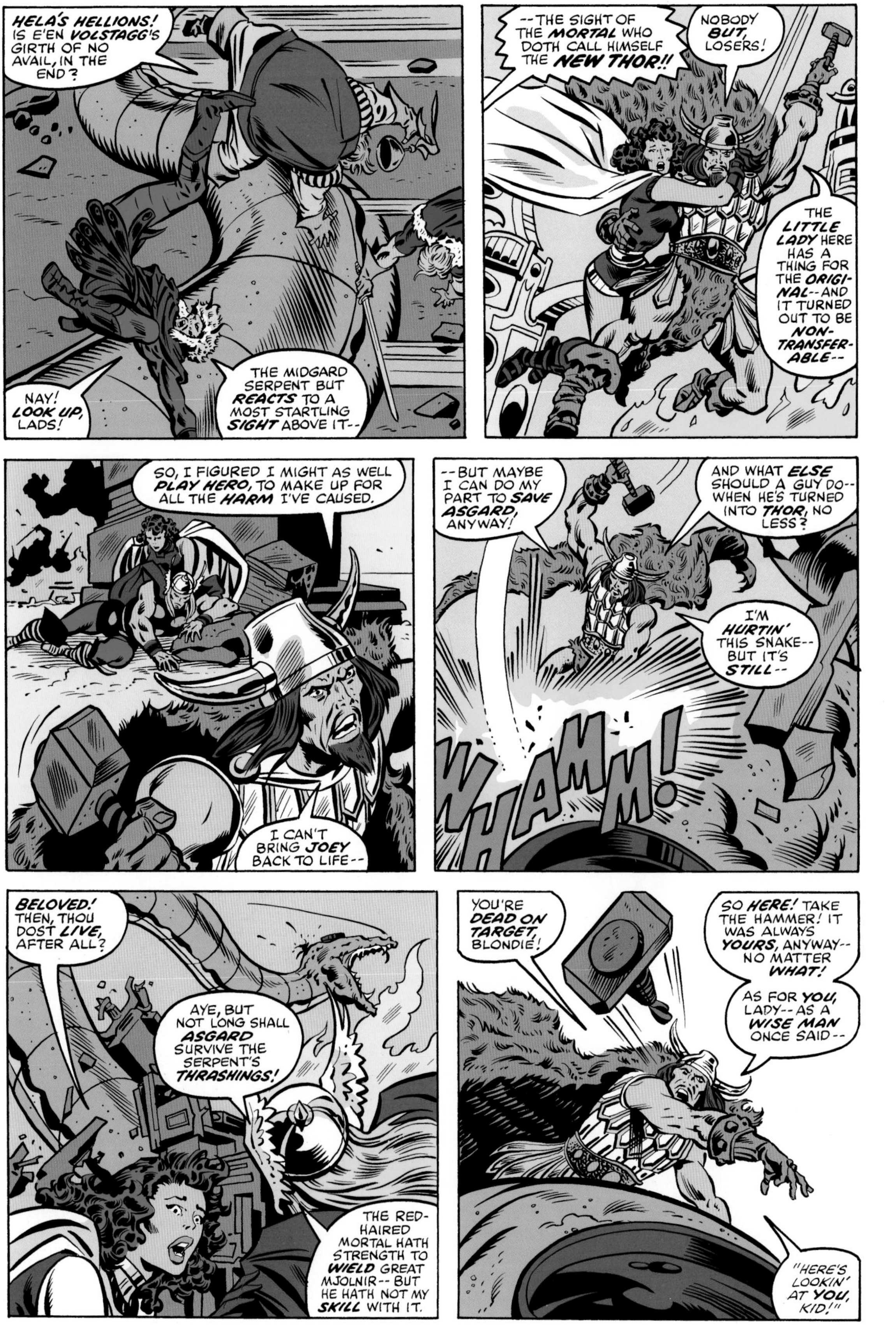
HELA'S HELLIONS! IS E'EN VOLSTAGG'S GIRTH OF NO AVAIL, IN THE END?
NAY! LOOK UP, LADS!
THE MIDGARD SERPENT BUT REACTS TO A MOST STARTLING SIGHT ABOVE IT--
--THE SIGHT OF THE MORTAL WHO DOTH CALL HIMSELF THE NEW THOR!!
NOBODY BUT, LOSERS!
THE LITTLE LADY HERE HAS A THING FOR THE ORIGINAL--AND IT TURNED OUT TO BE NON-TRANSFERABLE--
SO, I FIGURED I MIGHT AS WELL PLAY HERO, TO MAKE UP FOR ALL THE HARM I'VE CAUSED.
I CAN'T BRING JOEY BACK TO LIFE--
--BUT MAYBE I CAN DO MY PART TO SAVE ASGARD, ANYWAY!
AND WHAT ELSE SHOULD A GUY DO--WHEN HE'S TURNED INTO THOR, NO LESS?
I'M HURTIN' THIS SNAKE--BUT IT'S STILL--
WHAMM!
BELOVED! THEN, THOU DOST LIVE, AFTER ALL?
AYE, BUT NOT LONG SHALL ASGARD SURVIVE THE SERPENT'S THRASHINGS!
THE RED-HAIRED MORTAL HATH STRENGTH TO WIELD GREAT MJOLNIR--BUT HE HATH NOT MY SKILL WITH IT.
YOU'RE DEAD ON TARGET, BLONDIE!
SO HERE! TAKE THE HAMMER! IT WAS ALWAYS YOURS, ANYWAY--NO MATTER WHAT!
AS FOR YOU, LADY--AS A WISE MAN ONCE SAID--
"HERE'S LOOKIN' AT YOU, KID!"

MILORD! HE HATH RETURNED TO THEE-- *THINE HAMMER!*

'TWOULD SEEM THERE BE SOME *HUMAN SPARK* STILL LEFT WITHIN THE CREATURE THAT *"RED" NORVELL* BECAME.

YET, *WITHOUT* MJOLNIR, HE SHALL NOT HAVE THE SHEER *FIGHTING PROWESS* TO STAND 'GAINST *JORMUNGAND.*

I HAVE FOUGHT THE SERPENT *BE-FORE*-- AND HE HATH *NOT!*

WHATEVER THE REASON, THOR ARRIVES AT THE SITE JUST IN TIME TO WITNESS--

BY MIMIR'S WELL OF WISDOM!

THE MIDGARD SERPENT, *WOUNDED,* DOTH RETREAT INTO THE *DEPTH* 'NEATH ASGARD--

--BEARING THE TRANS-FORMED MORTAL *WITH* HIM!

"RED" NORVELL HATH *SACRIFICED* HIMSELF-- THAT THE *GLEAMING REALM* MIGHT PERCHANCE BE *SAVED!*

YET, I CANNOT LET HIM *DIE*-- NOT IF IT IT BE IN MY POWER TO *SAVE* HIM.

I MUST HIE ME *AFTER* THEM *WHERE'ER* THEY MAY HAVE--

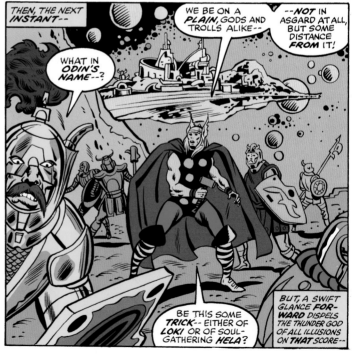

THEN, THE NEXT *INSTANT*--

WE BE ON A *PLAIN,* GODS AND TROLLS ALIKE--

--*NOT* IN ASGARD AT ALL, BUT SOME DISTANCE *FROM* IT!

WHAT IN *ODIN'S* NAME--?

BE THIS SOME *TRICK*-- EITHER OF *LOKI* OR OF SOUL-GATHERING *HELA?*

BUT, A SWIFT GLANCE *FOR-WARD* DISPELS THE THUNDER GOD OF ALL ILLUSIONS ON *THAT* SCORE--

210

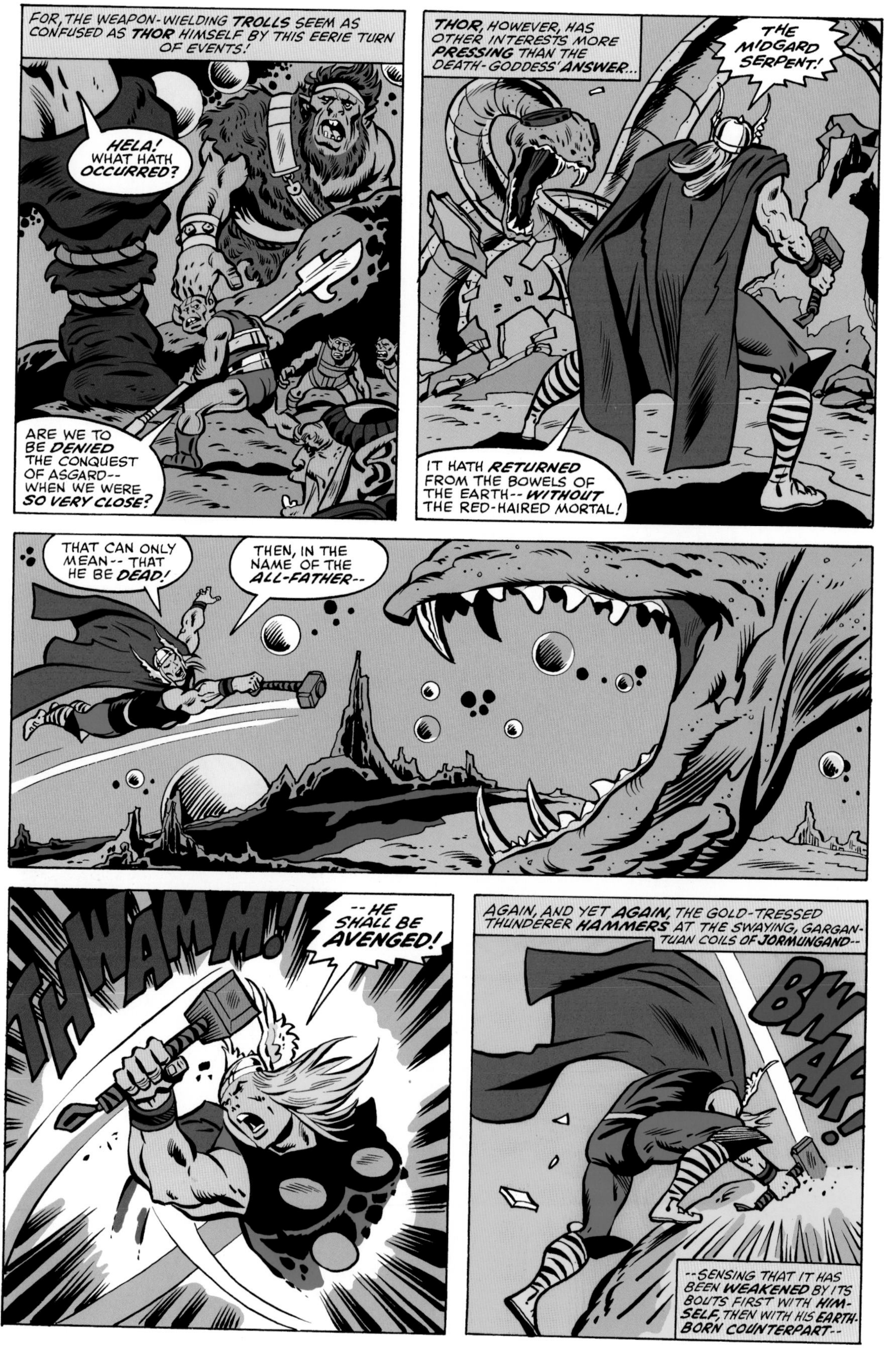
FOR, THE WEAPON-WIELDING TROLLS SEEM AS CONFUSED AS THOR HIMSELF BY THIS EERIE TURN OF EVENTS!
HELA! WHAT HATH OCCURRED?
ARE WE TO BE DENIED THE CONQUEST OF ASGARD-- WHEN WE WERE SO VERY CLOSE?
THOR, HOWEVER, HAS OTHER INTERESTS MORE PRESSING THAN THE DEATH-GODDESS' ANSWER...
THE MIDGARD SERPENT!
IT HATH RETURNED FROM THE BOWELS OF THE EARTH-- WITHOUT THE RED-HAIRED MORTAL!
THAT CAN ONLY MEAN-- THAT HE BE DEAD!
THEN, IN THE NAME OF THE ALL-FATHER--
THWAMM!
--HE SHALL BE AVENGED!
AGAIN, AND YET AGAIN, THE GOLD-TRESSED THUNDERER HAMMERS AT THE SWAYING, GARGANTUAN COILS OF JORMUNGAND--
BWAK!
--SENSING THAT IT HAS BEEN WEAKENED BY ITS BOUTS FIRST WITH HIMSELF, THEN WITH HIS EARTH-BORN COUNTERPART--

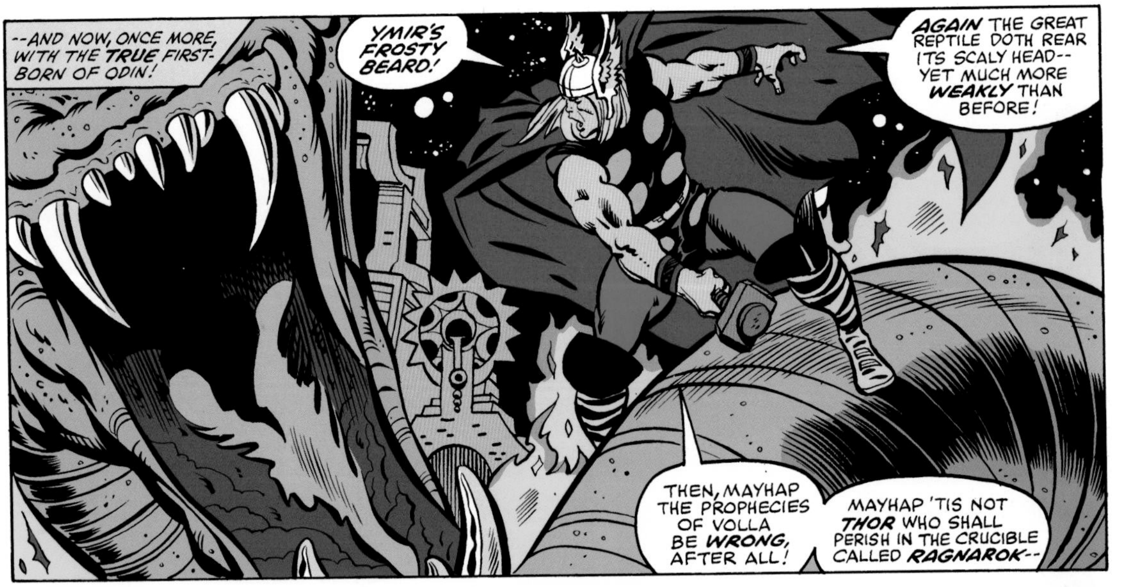
--AND NOW, ONCE MORE, WITH THE TRUE FIRST-BORN OF ODIN!
YMIR'S FROSTY BEARD!
AGAIN THE GREAT REPTILE DOTH REAR ITS SCALY HEAD--YET MUCH MORE WEAKLY THAN BEFORE!
THEN, MAYHAP THE PROPHECIES OF VOLLA BE WRONG, AFTER ALL!
MAYHAP 'TIS NOT THOR WHO SHALL PERISH IN THE CRUCIBLE CALLED RAGNAROK--

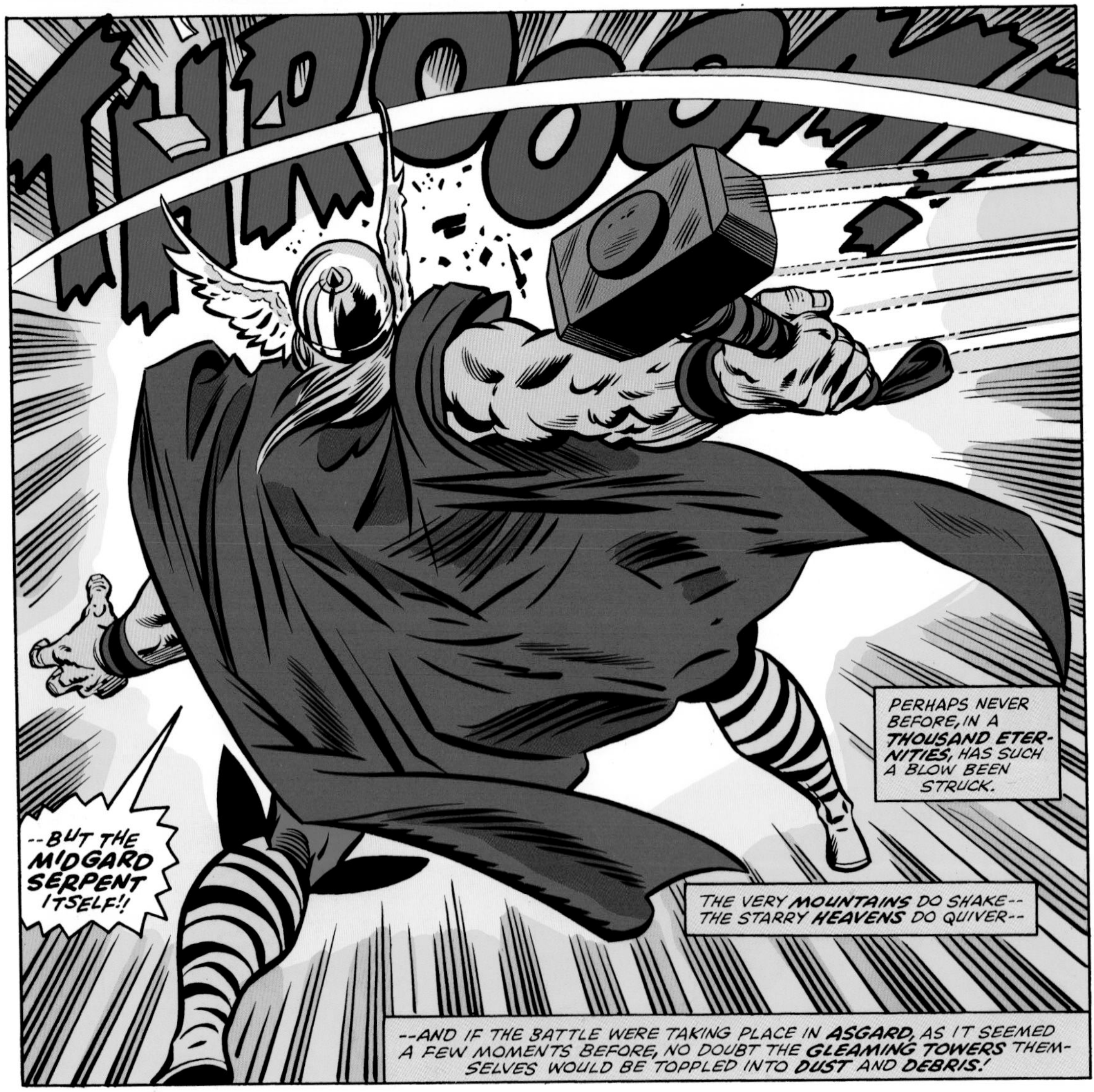
--BUT THE MIDGARD SERPENT ITSELF!!
PERHAPS NEVER BEFORE, IN A THOUSAND ETERNITIES, HAS SUCH A BLOW BEEN STRUCK.
THE VERY MOUNTAINS DO SHAKE--THE STARRY HEAVENS DO QUIVER--
--AND IF THE BATTLE WERE TAKING PLACE IN ASGARD, AS IT SEEMED A FEW MOMENTS BEFORE, NO DOUBT THE GLEAMING TOWERS THEMSELVES WOULD BE TOPPLED INTO DUST AND DEBRIS!

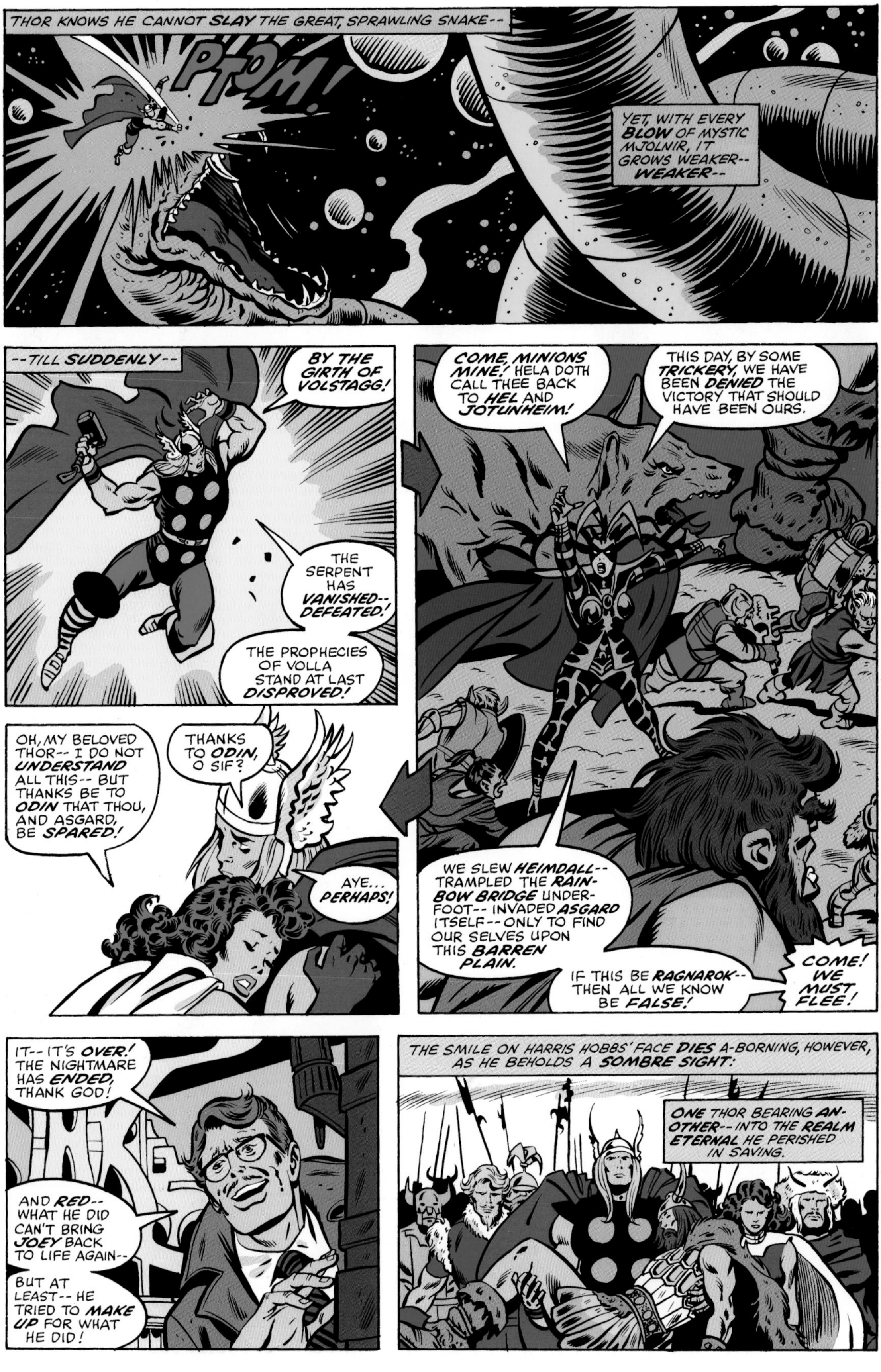
THOR KNOWS HE CANNOT SLAY THE GREAT, SPRAWLING SNAKE--
PTOOM!
YET, WITH EVERY BLOW OF MYSTIC MJOLNIR, IT GROWS WEAKER-- WEAKER--
--TILL SUDDENLY--
BY THE GIRTH OF VOLSTAGG!
THE SERPENT HAS VANISHED-- DEFEATED!
THE PROPHECIES OF VOLLA STAND AT LAST DISPROVED!
OH, MY BELOVED THOR-- I DO NOT UNDERSTAND ALL THIS-- BUT THANKS BE TO ODIN THAT THOU, AND ASGARD, BE SPARED!
THANKS TO ODIN, O SIF?
AYE... PERHAPS!
COME, MINIONS MINE! HELA DOTH CALL THEE BACK TO HEL AND JOTUNHEIM!
THIS DAY, BY SOME TRICKERY, WE HAVE BEEN DENIED THE VICTORY THAT SHOULD HAVE BEEN OURS.
WE SLEW HEIMDALL-- TRAMPLED THE RAINBOW BRIDGE UNDERFOOT-- INVADED ASGARD ITSELF-- ONLY TO FIND OUR SELVES UPON THIS BARREN PLAIN.
IF THIS BE RAGNAROK-- THEN ALL WE KNOW BE FALSE!
COME! WE MUST FLEE!
IT-- IT'S OVER! THE NIGHTMARE HAS ENDED, THANK GOD!
AND RED-- WHAT HE DID CAN'T BRING JOEY BACK TO LIFE AGAIN--
BUT AT LEAST-- HE TRIED TO MAKE UP FOR WHAT HE DID!
THE SMILE ON HARRIS HOBBS' FACE DIES A-BORNING, HOWEVER, AS HE BEHOLDS A SOMBRE SIGHT:
ONE THOR BEARING ANOTHER-- INTO THE REALM ETERNAL HE PERISHED IN SAVING.

AND, THOUGH HE WAS, FOR SO BRIEF A TIME, A **GOD** WHO WIELDED THE POWER OF THE **LIGHTNING-BOLT**, THE RUMBLING OF THE **THUNDER**...

...STILL, HE NEVER SEEMED SO **TRUE** IN ASPECT...

...AS WHEN HE NOW BECOMES AGAIN THE MAN CALLED **"RED"** NORVELL...FOR THE FINAL TIME.

AND, IN THAT SELFSAME MOMENT, A **BLAZING LIGHT** IS SEEN IN ASGARD--

--AS THE FIERY **ODINSHIELD** ABOUT THE BIER OF **BALDER** FLARES ANEW--

--SIGNIFYING THAT **ALL IS WELL** ONCE MORE IN THE **HOME OF THE GODS.**

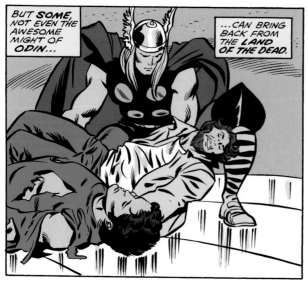

BUT **SOME,** NOT EVEN THE AWESOME MIGHT OF **ODIN**...

...CAN BRING BACK FROM THE **LAND OF THE DEAD.**

AND NOT ALL THE **TEARS** THE WORLD SHED FOR DYING **BALDER** CAN RESTORE THE BLOOM OF LIFE TO A CHEEK WHERE-FROM IT HAS FLED.

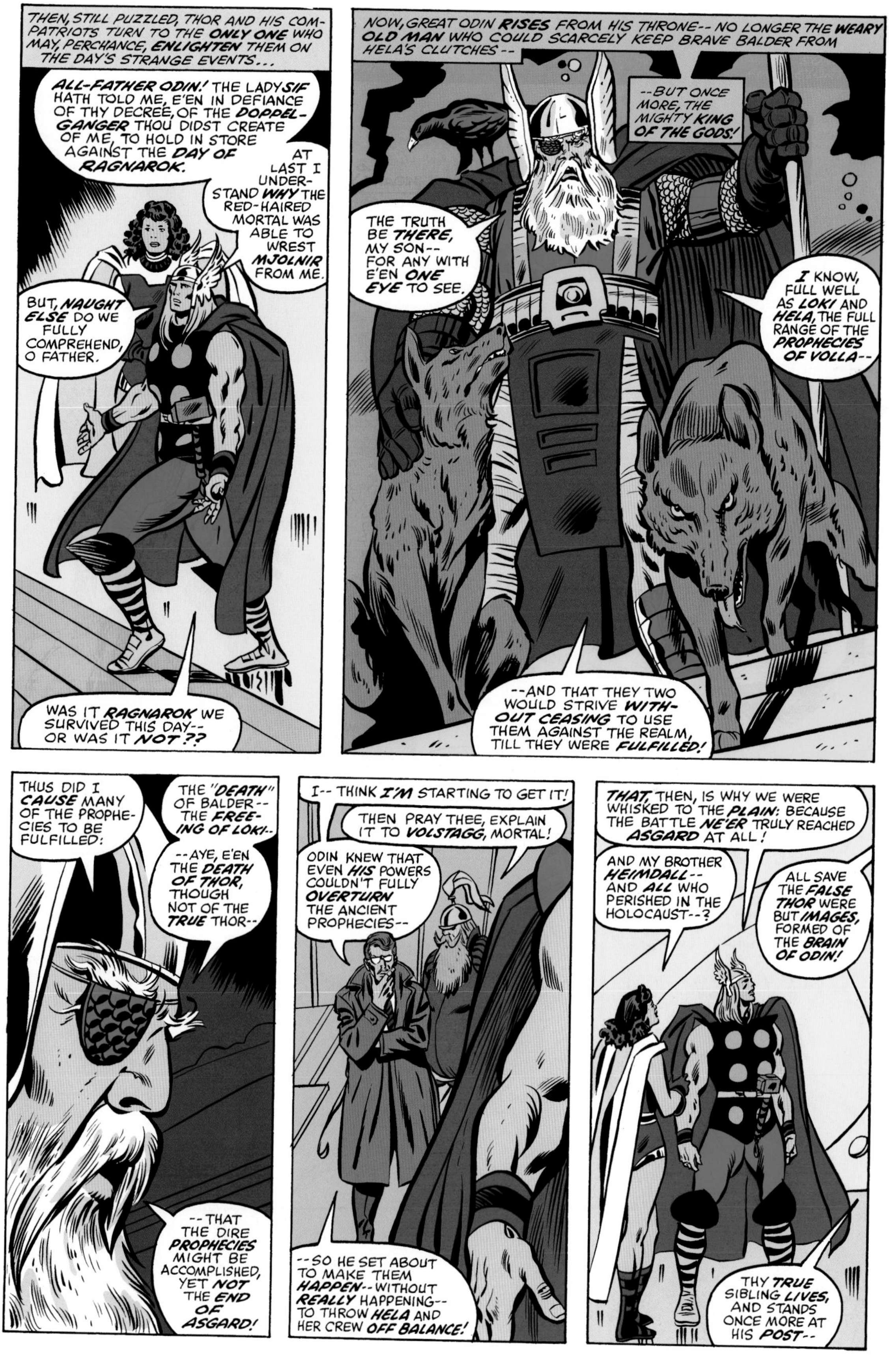
THEN, STILL PUZZLED, THOR AND HIS COMPATRIOTS TURN TO THE ONLY ONE WHO MAY, PERCHANCE, ENLIGHTEN THEM ON THE DAY'S STRANGE EVENTS...
ALL-FATHER ODIN! THE LADY SIF HATH TOLD ME, E'EN IN DEFIANCE OF THY DECREE, OF THE DOPPELGANGER THOU DIDST CREATE OF ME, TO HOLD IN STORE AGAINST THE DAY OF RAGNAROK.
AT LAST I UNDERSTAND WHY THE RED-HAIRED MORTAL WAS ABLE TO WREST MJOLNIR FROM ME.
BUT, NAUGHT ELSE DO WE FULLY COMPREHEND, O FATHER.
WAS IT RAGNAROK WE SURVIVED THIS DAY-- OR WAS IT NOT??
NOW, GREAT ODIN RISES FROM HIS THRONE-- NO LONGER THE WEARY OLD MAN WHO COULD SCARCELY KEEP BRAVE BALDER FROM HELA'S CLUTCHES--
--BUT ONCE MORE, THE MIGHTY KING OF THE GODS!
THE TRUTH BE THERE, MY SON-- FOR ANY WITH E'EN ONE EYE TO SEE.
I KNOW, FULL WELL AS LOKI AND HELA, THE FULL RANGE OF THE PROPHECIES OF VOLLA--
--AND THAT THEY TWO WOULD STRIVE WITHOUT CEASING TO USE THEM AGAINST THE REALM, TILL THEY WERE FULFILLED!
THUS DID I CAUSE MANY OF THE PROPHECIES TO BE FULFILLED:
THE "DEATH" OF BALDER-- THE FREEING OF LOKI--
--AYE, E'EN THE DEATH OF THOR, THOUGH NOT OF THE TRUE THOR--
--THAT THE DIRE PROPHECIES MIGHT BE ACCOMPLISHED, YET NOT THE END OF ASGARD!
I-- THINK I'M STARTING TO GET IT!
THEN PRAY THEE, EXPLAIN IT TO VOLSTAGG, MORTAL!
ODIN KNEW THAT EVEN HIS POWERS COULDN'T FULLY OVERTURN THE ANCIENT PROPHECIES--
--SO HE SET ABOUT TO MAKE THEM HAPPEN-- WITHOUT REALLY HAPPENING-- TO THROW HELA AND HER CREW OFF BALANCE!
THAT, THEN, IS WHY WE WERE WHISKED TO THE PLAIN: BECAUSE THE BATTLE NE'ER TRULY REACHED ASGARD AT ALL!
AND MY BROTHER HEIMDALL-- AND ALL WHO PERISHED IN THE HOLOCAUST--?
ALL SAVE THE FALSE THOR WERE BUT IMAGES, FORMED OF THE BRAIN OF ODIN!
THY TRUE SIBLING LIVES, AND STANDS ONCE MORE AT HIS POST--

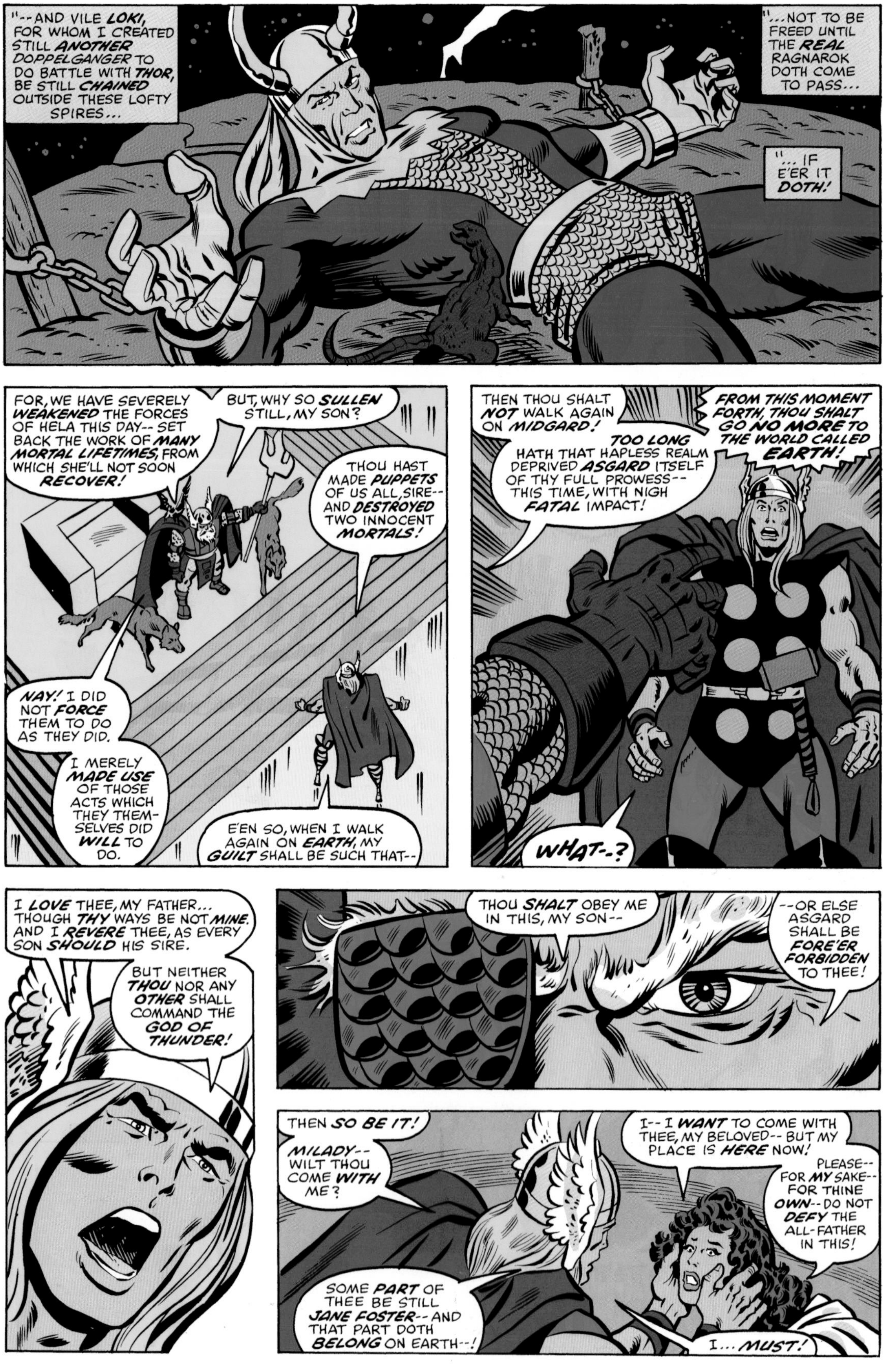

"--AND VILE LOKI, FOR WHOM I CREATED STILL ANOTHER DOPPELGANGER TO DO BATTLE WITH THOR, BE STILL CHAINED OUTSIDE THESE LOFTY SPIRES...
"...NOT TO BE FREED UNTIL THE REAL RAGNAROK DOTH COME TO PASS...
"...IF E'ER IT DOTH!
FOR, WE HAVE SEVERELY WEAKENED THE FORCES OF HELA THIS DAY-- SET BACK THE WORK OF MANY MORTAL LIFETIMES, FROM WHICH SHE'LL NOT SOON RECOVER!
BUT, WHY SO SULLEN STILL, MY SON?
THOU HAST MADE PUPPETS OF US ALL, SIRE-- AND DESTROYED TWO INNOCENT MORTALS!
NAY! I DID NOT FORCE THEM TO DO AS THEY DID.
I MERELY MADE USE OF THOSE ACTS WHICH THEY THEMSELVES DID WILL TO DO.
E'EN SO, WHEN I WALK AGAIN ON EARTH, MY GUILT SHALL BE SUCH THAT--
THEN THOU SHALT NOT WALK AGAIN ON MIDGARD!
TOO LONG HATH THAT HAPLESS REALM DEPRIVED ASGARD ITSELF OF THY FULL PROWESS-- THIS TIME, WITH NIGH FATAL IMPACT!
FROM THIS MOMENT FORTH, THOU SHALT GO NO MORE TO THE WORLD CALLED EARTH!
WHAT--?
I LOVE THEE, MY FATHER... THOUGH THY WAYS BE NOT MINE. AND I REVERE THEE, AS EVERY SON SHOULD HIS SIRE.
BUT NEITHER THOU NOR ANY OTHER SHALL COMMAND THE GOD OF THUNDER!
THOU SHALT OBEY ME IN THIS, MY SON--
--OR ELSE ASGARD SHALL BE FORE'ER FORBIDDEN TO THEE!
THEN SO BE IT!
MILADY-- WILT THOU COME WITH ME?
I-- I WANT TO COME WITH THEE, MY BELOVED-- BUT MY PLACE IS HERE NOW!
PLEASE-- FOR MY SAKE-- FOR THINE OWN-- DO NOT DEFY THE ALL-FATHER IN THIS!
SOME PART OF THEE BE STILL JANE FOSTER-- AND THAT PART DOTH BELONG ON EARTH--!
I... MUST!

GO THEN--AND *NO HAND* IN ASGARD SHALL BE RAISED *AGAINST* THEE--

--UNLESS EVER THOU DOST SEEK TO *RETURN!*

THAT SHALL I *NEVER* DO, SIRE-THAT-WAS!

FROM THIS DAY, I *RENOUNCE* MY PLACE IN THE REALM ETERNAL--

--AND *WOE* TO ANY WHO E'ER WOULD STRIVE TO BRING ME *BACK!*

THE NEXT MOMENT, WITH *HARRIS HOBBS* AND THE TWO *DEAD MORTALS* IN TOW, THOR HURLS HIS ENCHANTED *HAMMER* ABOUT HIS GOLDEN HEAD--

--TO *BRIDGE* THE GAP BETWEEN THAT WORLD AND THIS, AS IF 'TWERE BUT A *NARROW STREAM* TO BE LEAPED ACROSS.

YET, HOW *GREAT* AN EFFORT IT TAKES TO MAKE THAT LEAP--ONLY THE SILENT *THUNDER GOD* CAN KNOW.

THEN, BACK ON A ROOFTOP IN MANHATTAN...

SEE TO THY PERISHED FRIENDS, HARRIS HOBBS! I HAVE *OTHER* AFFAIRS THAT SORELY NEED TENDING.

THOR... I--I'M *SORRY* FOR CAUSING--

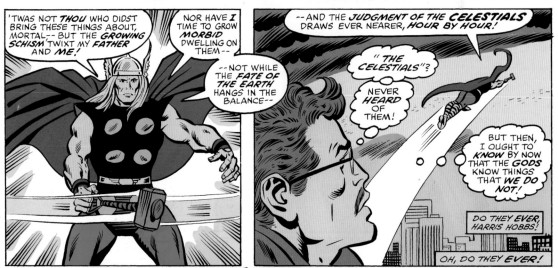

'TWAS NOT *THOU* WHO DIDST BRING THESE THINGS ABOUT, MORTAL-- BUT THE *GROWING SCHISM* 'TWIXT MY *FATHER* AND *ME!*

NOR HAVE *I* TIME TO GROW *MORBID* DWELLING ON THEM--

--NOT WHILE THE *FATE OF THE EARTH* HANGS IN THE BALANCE--

--AND THE *JUDGMENT* OF THE *CELESTIALS* DRAWS EVER NEARER, *HOUR BY HOUR!*

" *THE CELESTIALS* "? NEVER *HEARD* OF THEM!

BUT THEN, I OUGHT TO *KNOW* BY NOW THAT THE *GODS* KNOW THINGS THAT *WE DO NOT!*

DO THEY *EVER,* HARRIS HOBBS!

OH, DO THEY *EVER!*

NEXT. ISSUE· WHILE THE ETERNALS WAIT!

217

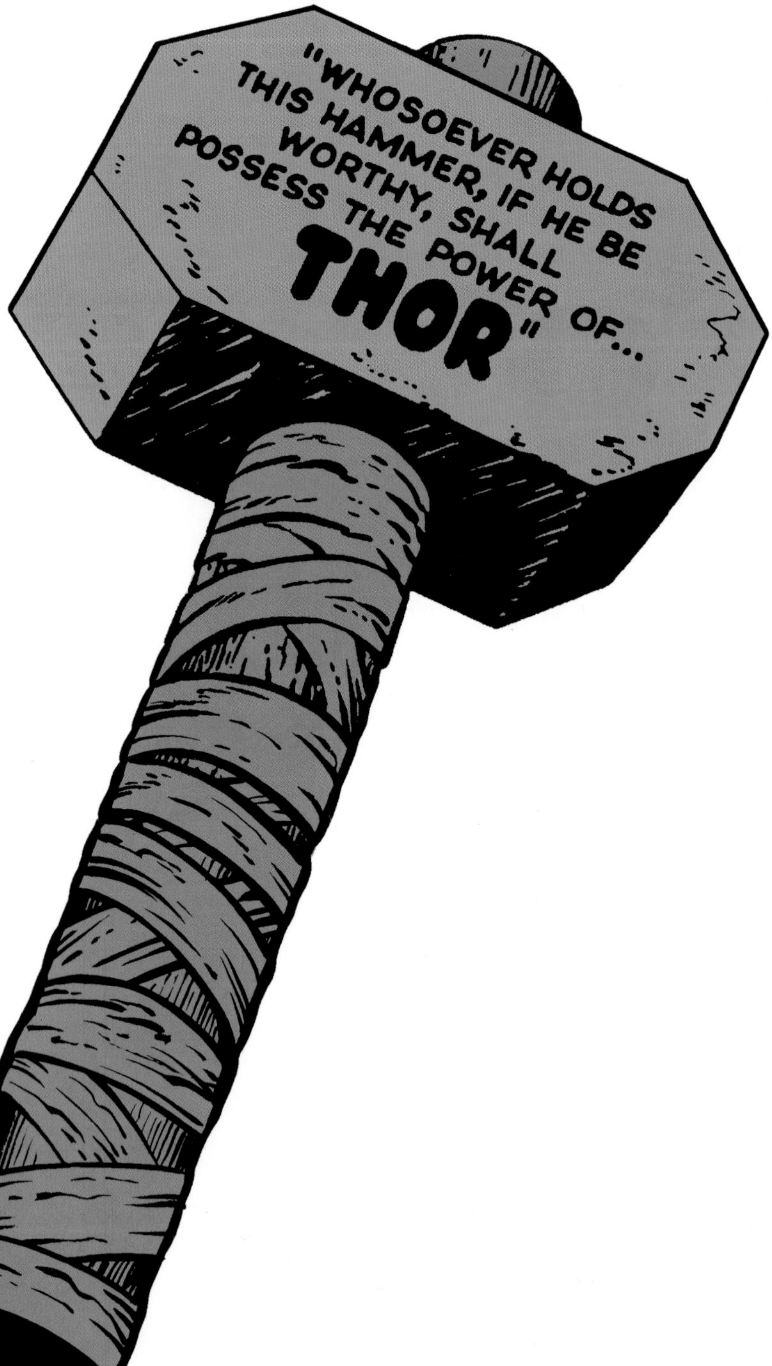
"WHOSOEVER HOLDS
THIS HAMMER, IF HE BE
WORTHY, SHALL
POSSESS THE POWER OF...
THOR"

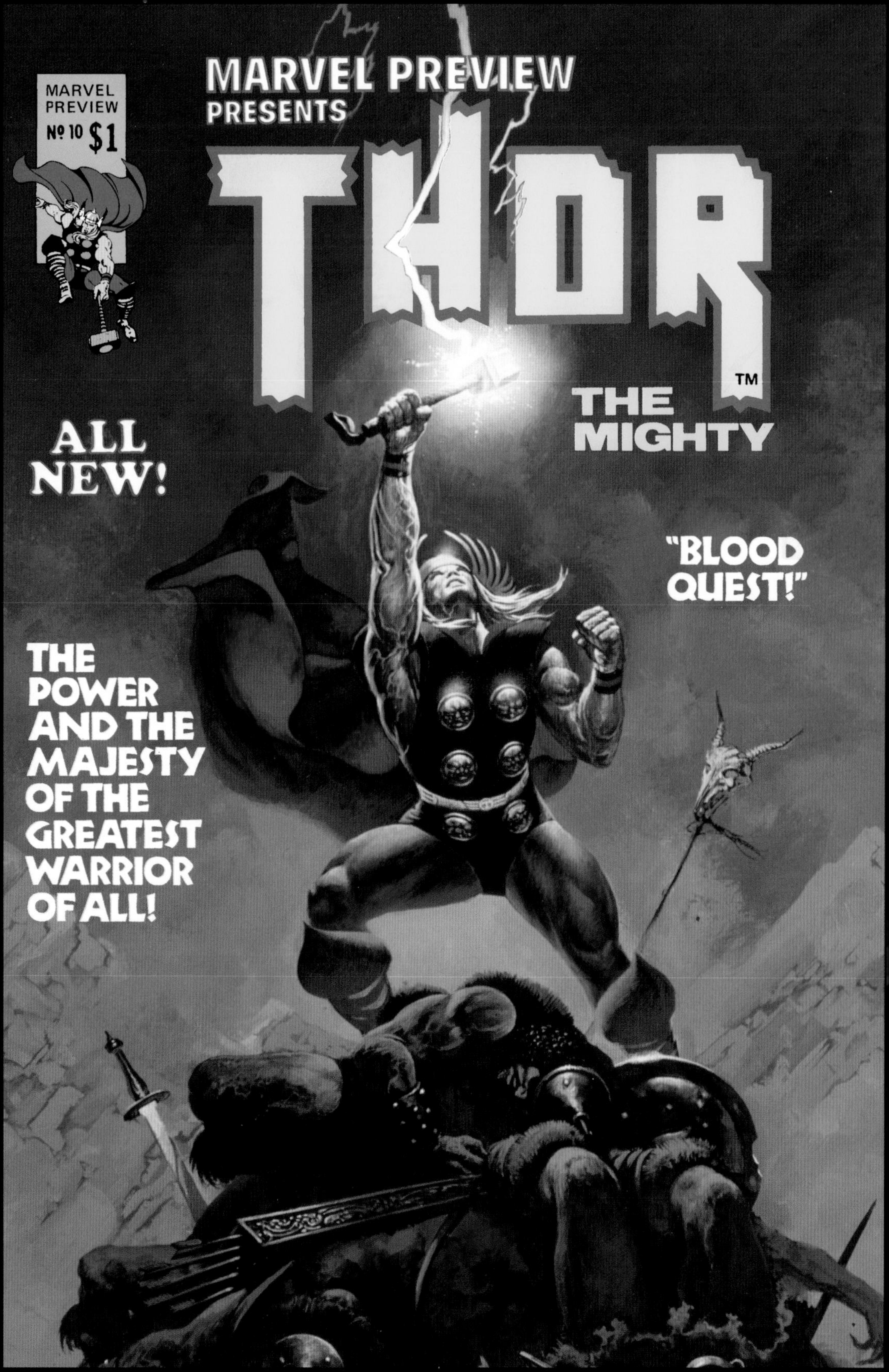
MARVEL PREVIEW
No 10 $1
MARVEL PREVIEW PRESENTS
THOR
TM
THE MIGHTY
ALL NEW!
"BLOOD QUEST!"
THE POWER AND THE MAJESTY OF THE GREATEST WARRIOR OF ALL!

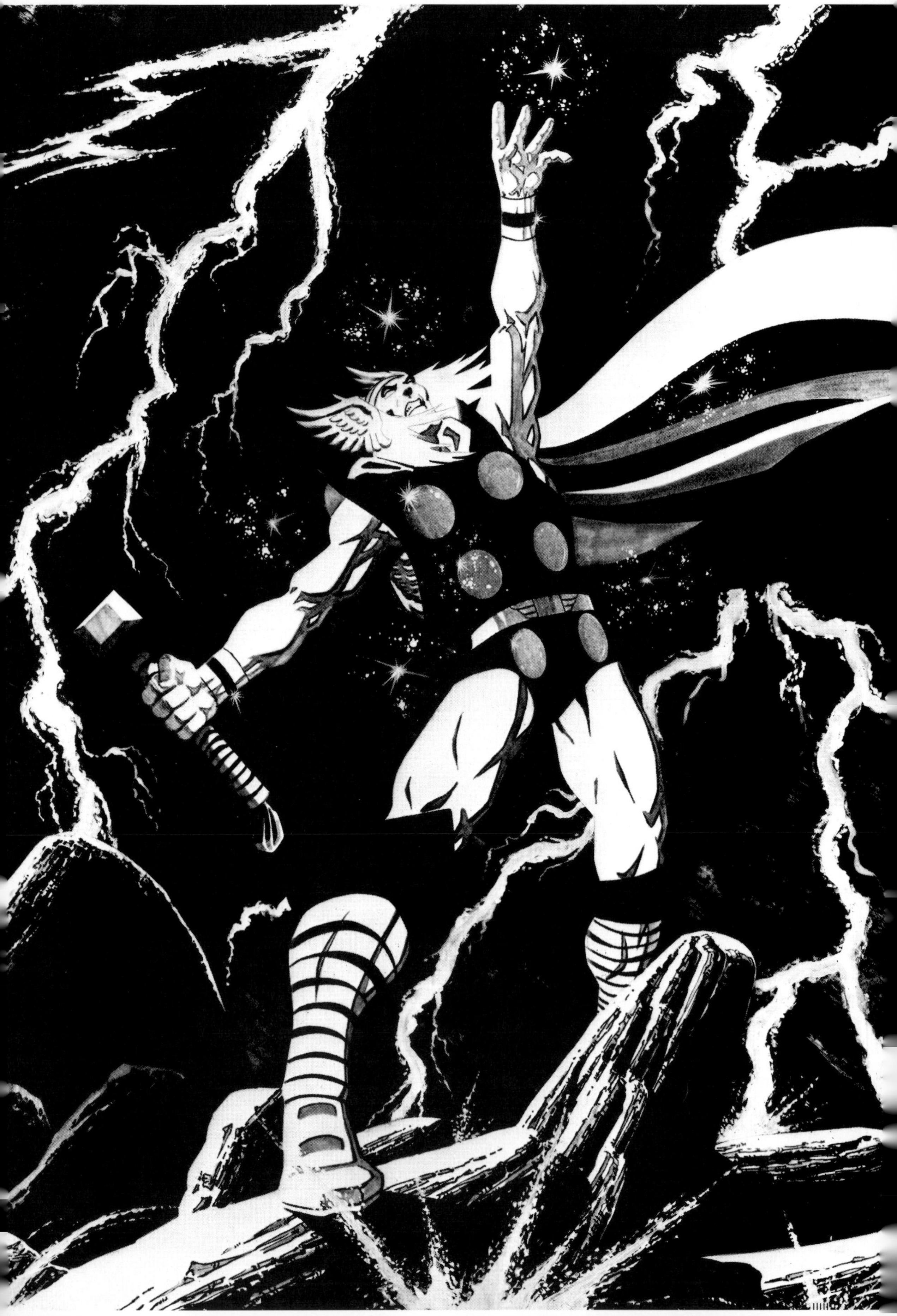

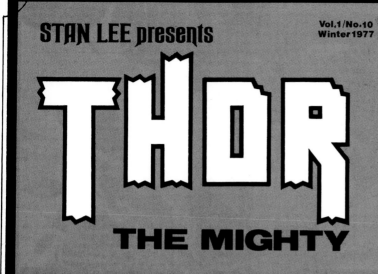

STAN LEE presents

Vol.1/No.10
Winter 1977

THOR THE MIGHTY

ARCHIE GOODWIN
Editor-in-Chief
JOHN WARNER
Editor
RALPH MACCHIO
Associate Editor
LEN WEIN
ROY THOMAS
Consulting Editors
LENNY GROW
Production
NORA MACLIN
Design
JOHN ROMITA JR.
Art Consultant
JIM NOVAK
HOWARD BENDER
DAVIDA LICHTER DALE
Staff and Such
KEN BARR
Cover
JIM STARLIN
Frontispiece

CONTENTS

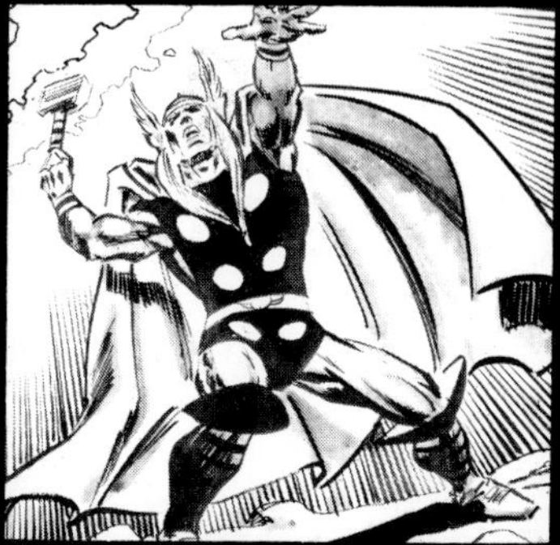

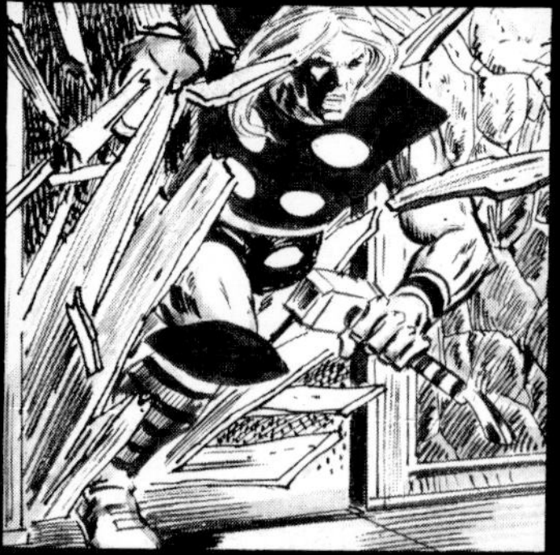

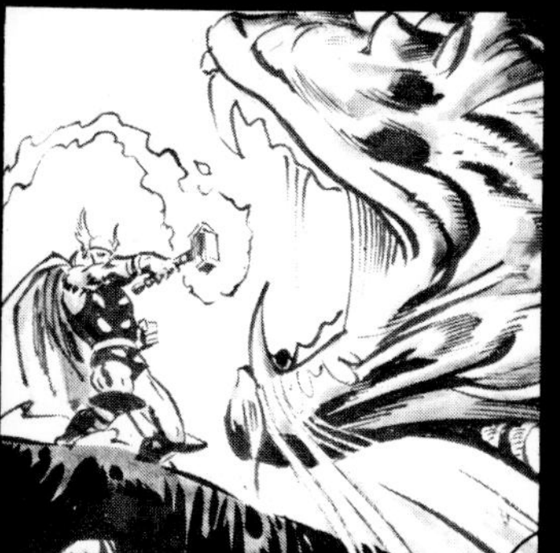

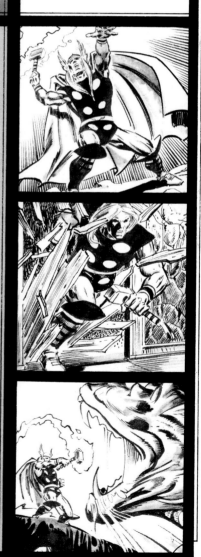

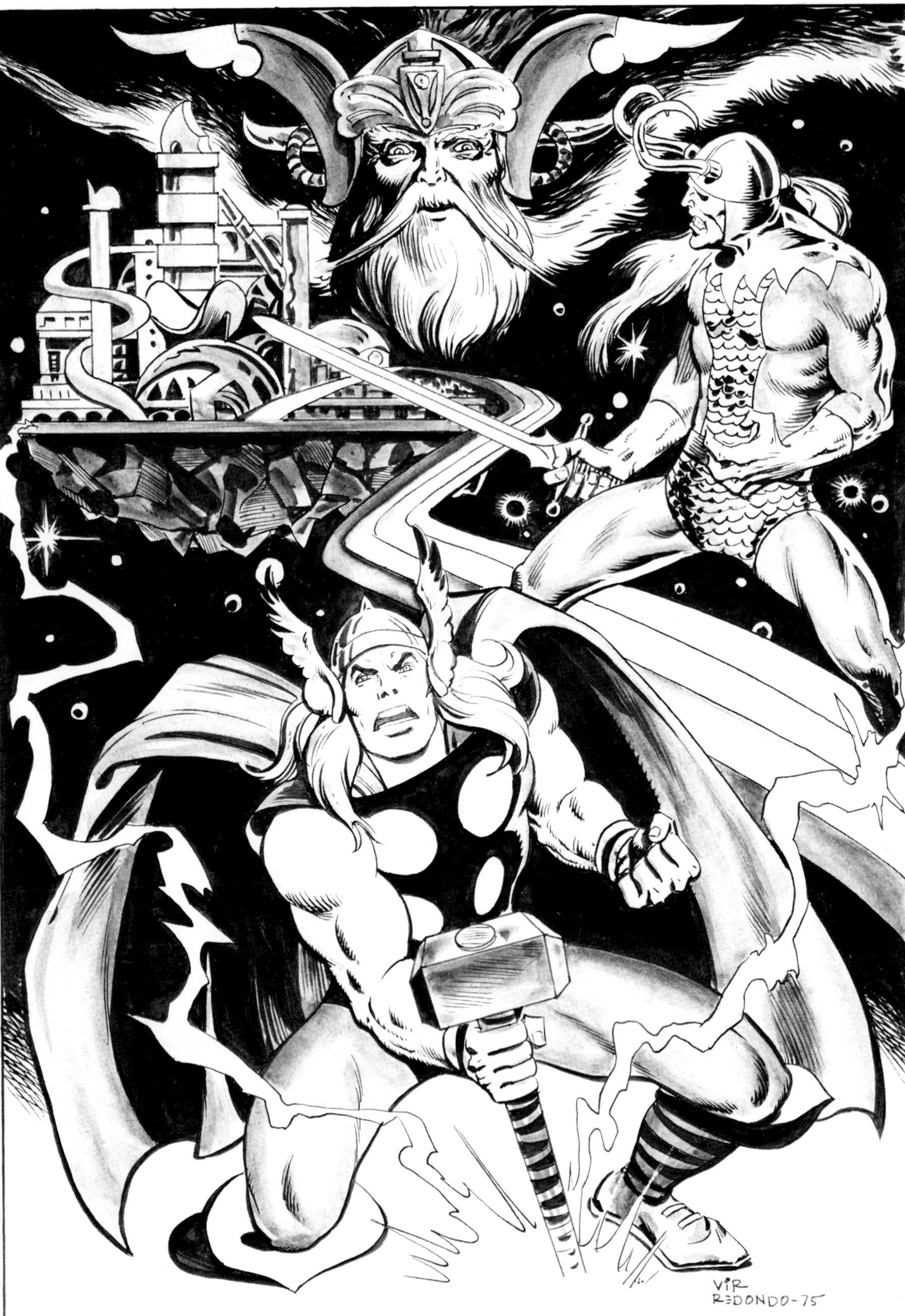
VIR
REDONDO-75

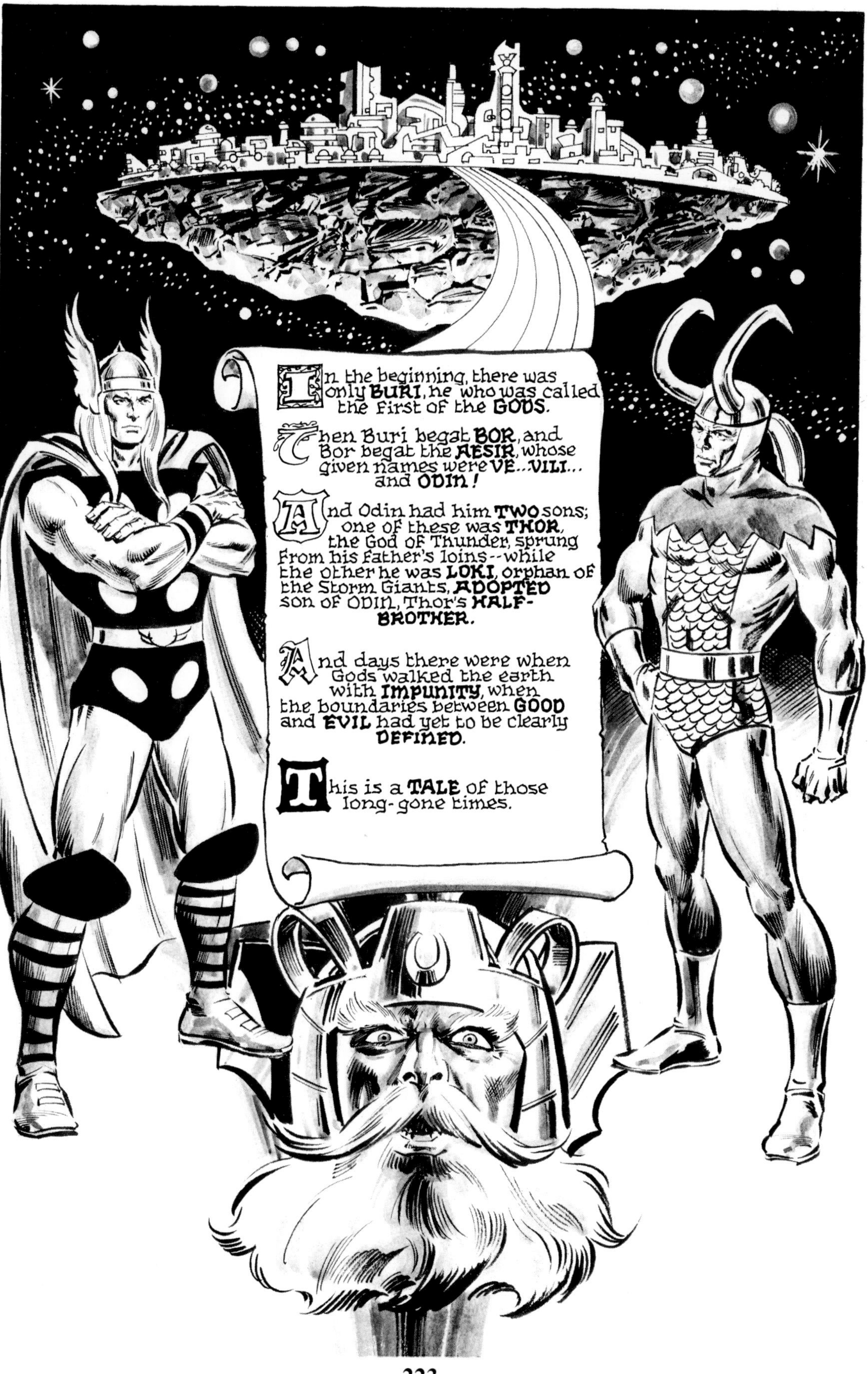
In the beginning, there was only BURI, he who was called the first of the GODS.
Then Buri begat BOR, and Bor begat the AESIR, whose given names were VE... VILI... and ODIN!
And Odin had him TWO sons; one of these was THOR, the God of Thunder, sprung from his father's loins--while the other he was LOKI, orphan of the Storm Giants, ADOPTED son of ODIN, Thor's HALF-BROTHER.
And days there were when Gods walked the earth with IMPUNITY, when the boundaries between GOOD and EVIL had yet to be clearly DEFINED.
This is a TALE of those long-gone times.

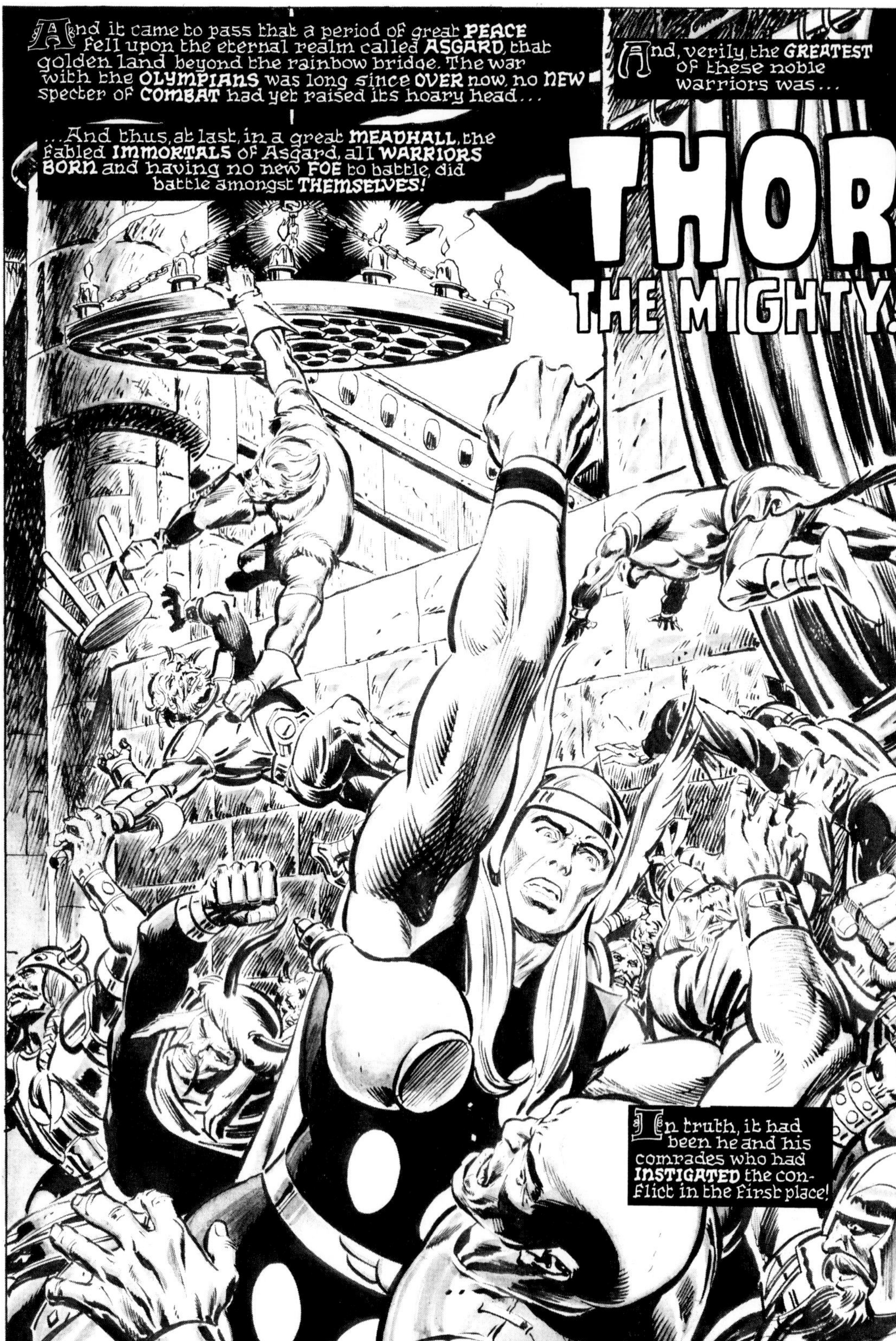
And it came to pass that a period of great PEACE fell upon the eternal realm called ASGARD, that golden land beyond the rainbow bridge. The war with the OLYMPIANS was long since OVER now, no NEW specter of COMBAT had yet raised its hoary head...
...And thus, at last, in a great MEADHALL, the fabled IMMORTALS of Asgard, all WARRIORS BORN and having no new FOE to battle, did battle amongst THEMSELVES!
And, verily, the GREATEST of these noble warriors was...
THOR
THE MIGHTY!
In truth, it had been he and his comrades who had INSTIGATED the conflict in the first place!

Story: LEN WEIN
Art: JIM STARLIN & TONY DEZUNIGA

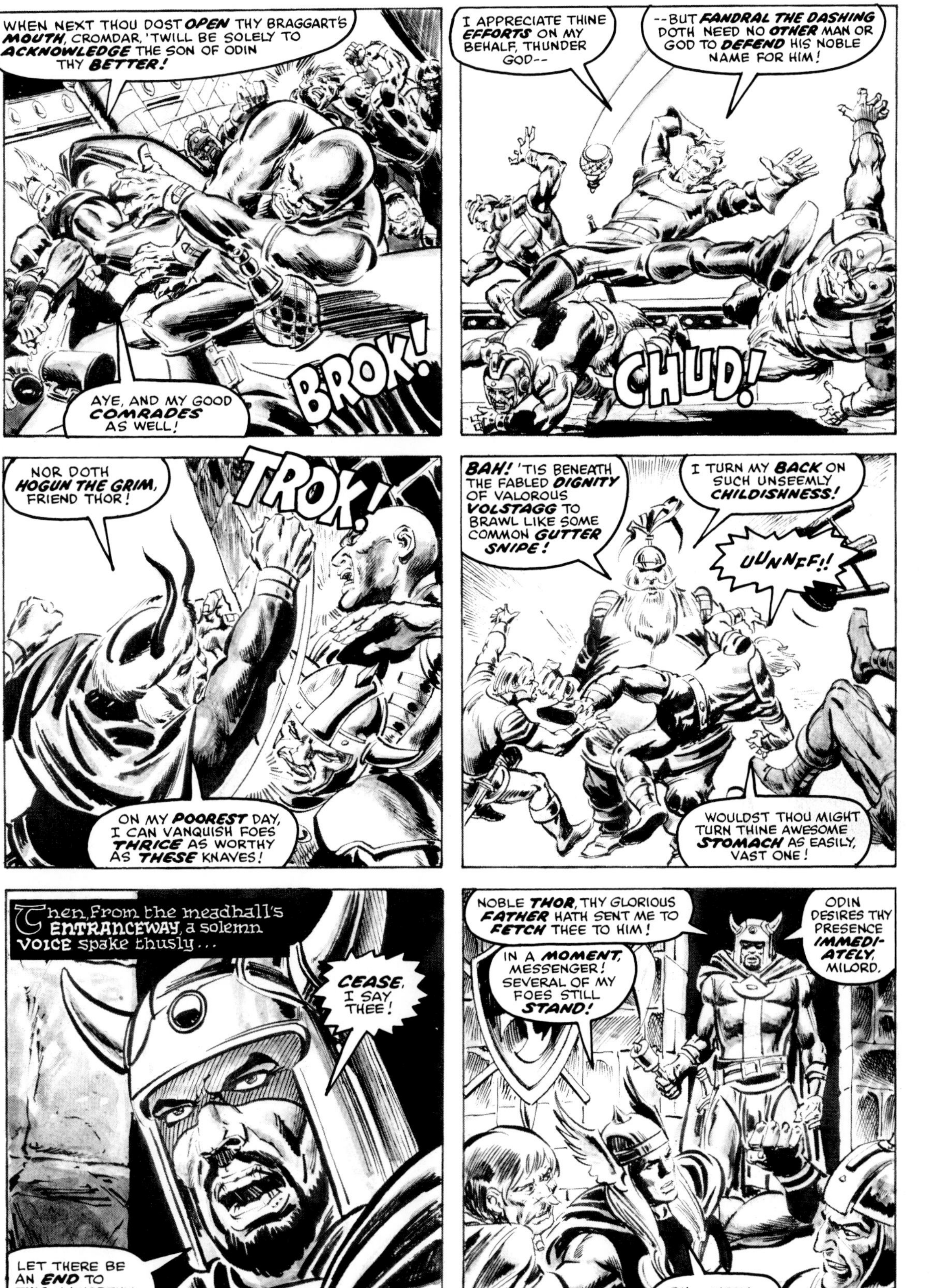

WHEN NEXT THOU DOST OPEN THY BRAGGART'S MOUTH, CROMDAR, 'TWILL BE SOLELY TO ACKNOWLEDGE THE SON OF ODIN THY BETTER!
AYE, AND MY GOOD COMRADES AS WELL!
BROK!
I APPRECIATE THINE EFFORTS ON MY BEHALF, THUNDER GOD--
--BUT FANDRAL THE DASHING DOTH NEED NO OTHER MAN OR GOD TO DEFEND HIS NOBLE NAME FOR HIM!
CHUD!
NOR DOTH HOGUN THE GRIM, FRIEND THOR!
TROK!
ON MY POOREST DAY, I CAN VANQUISH FOES THRICE AS WORTHY AS THESE KNAVES!
BAH! 'TIS BENEATH THE FABLED DIGNITY OF VALOROUS VOLSTAGG TO BRAWL LIKE SOME COMMON GUTTER SNIPE!
I TURN MY BACK ON SUCH UNSEEMLY CHILDISHNESS!
UUNNFF!!
WOULDST THOU MIGHT TURN THINE AWESOME STOMACH AS EASILY, VAST ONE!
Then, from the meadhall's ENTRANCEWAY, a solemn VOICE spake thusly...
CEASE, I SAY THEE!
LET THERE BE AN END TO THIS UNWORTHY FOOLISHNESS!
NOBLE THOR, THY GLORIOUS FATHER HATH SENT ME TO FETCH THEE TO HIM!
ODIN DESIRES THY PRESENCE IMMEDIATELY, MILORD.
IN A MOMENT, MESSENGER! SEVERAL OF MY FOES STILL STAND!
OH... VERY WELL THEN.

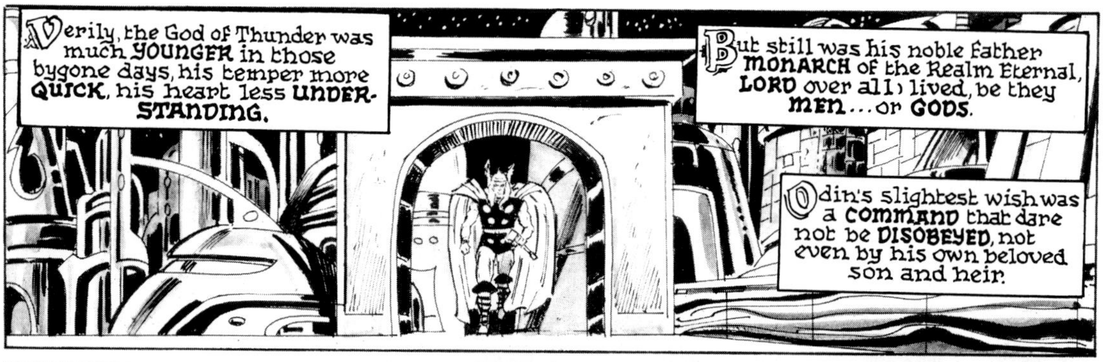
Verily, the God of Thunder was much YOUNGER in those bygone days, his temper more QUICK, his heart less UNDER-STANDING.
But still was his noble father MONARCH of the Realm Eternal, LORD over all) lived, be they MEN...or GODS.
Odin's slightest wish was a COMMAND that dare not be DISOBEYED, not even by his own beloved son and heir.

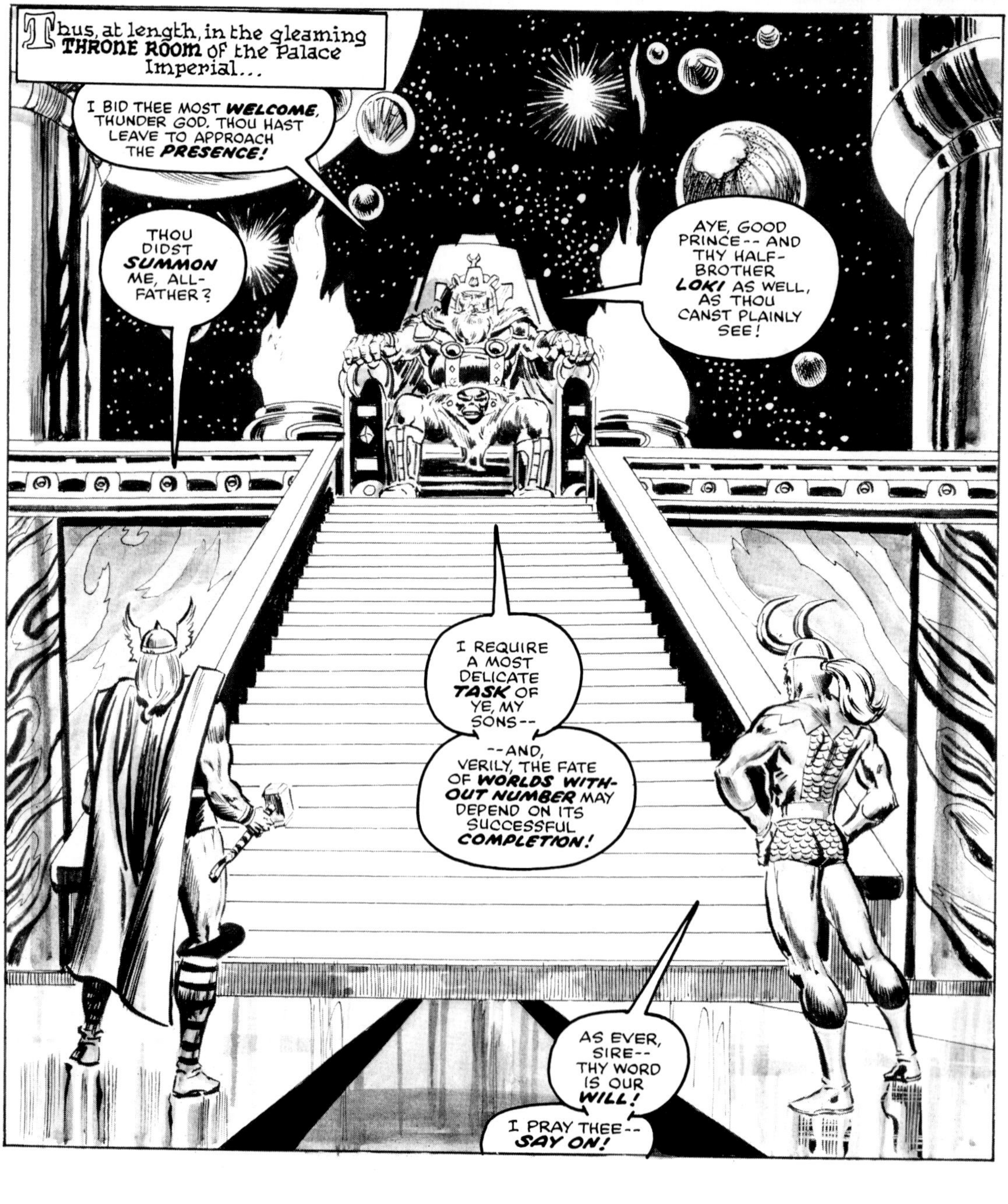
Thus, at length, in the gleaming THRONE ROOM of the Palace Imperial...
I BID THEE MOST WELCOME, THUNDER GOD. THOU HAST LEAVE TO APPROACH THE PRESENCE!
THOU DIDST SUMMON ME, ALL-FATHER?
AYE, GOOD PRINCE-- AND THY HALF-BROTHER LOKI AS WELL, AS THOU CANST PLAINLY SEE!
I REQUIRE A MOST DELICATE TASK OF YE, MY SONS--
--AND, VERILY, THE FATE OF WORLDS WITH-OUT NUMBER MAY DEPEND ON ITS SUCCESSFUL COMPLETION!
AS EVER, SIRE-- THY WORD IS OUR WILL!
I PRAY THEE-- SAY ON!

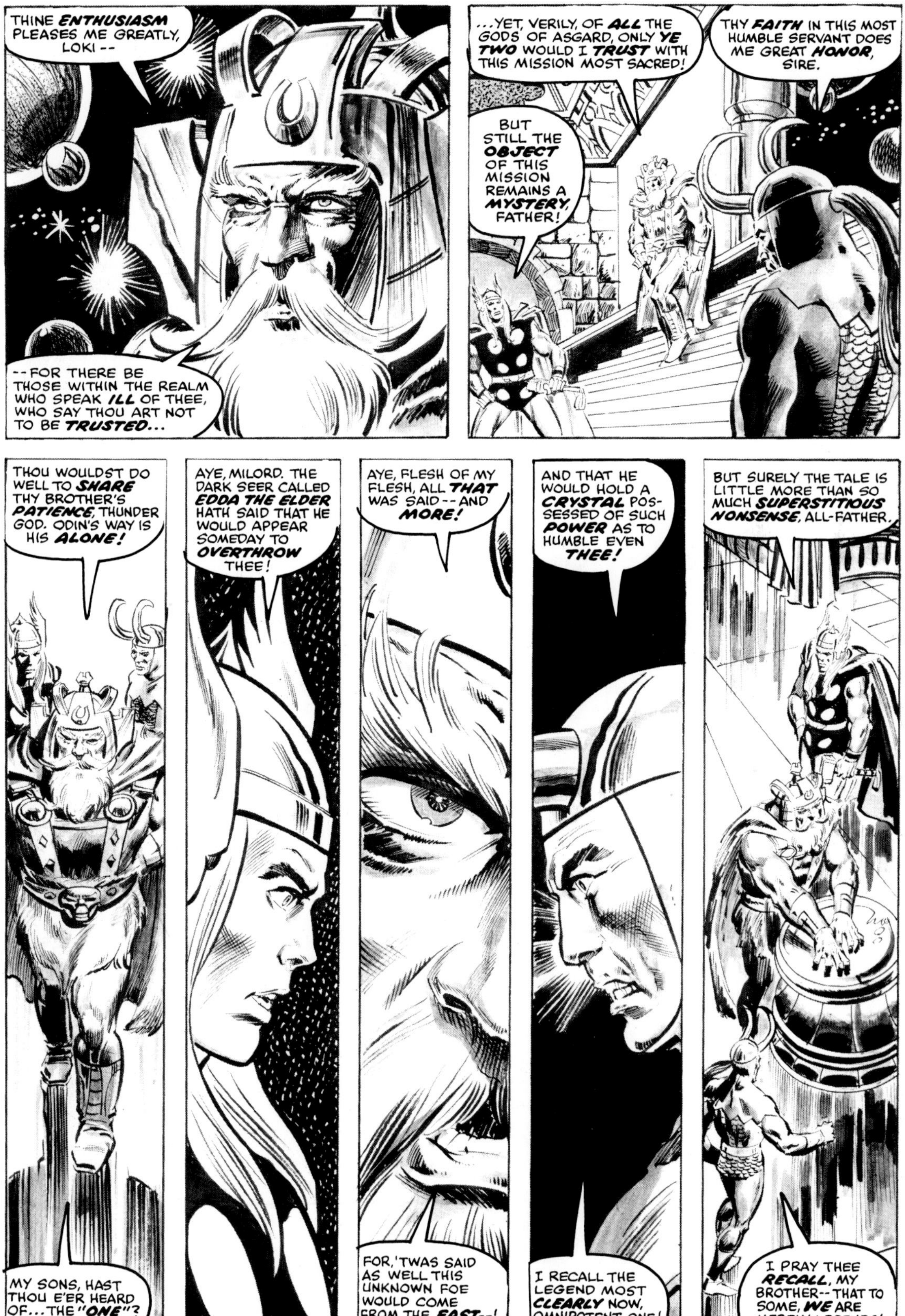
THINE ENTHUSIASM PLEASES ME GREATLY, LOKI --
--FOR THERE BE THOSE WITHIN THE REALM WHO SPEAK ILL OF THEE, WHO SAY THOU ART NOT TO BE TRUSTED...
...YET, VERILY, OF ALL THE GODS OF ASGARD, ONLY YE TWO WOULD I TRUST WITH THIS MISSION MOST SACRED!
THY FAITH IN THIS MOST HUMBLE SERVANT DOES ME GREAT HONOR, SIRE.
BUT STILL THE OBJECT OF THIS MISSION REMAINS A MYSTERY, FATHER!
THOU WOULDST DO WELL TO SHARE THY BROTHER'S PATIENCE, THUNDER GOD. ODIN'S WAY IS HIS ALONE!
MY SONS, HAST THOU E'ER HEARD OF... THE "ONE"?
AYE, MILORD. THE DARK SEER CALLED EDDA THE ELDER HATH SAID THAT HE WOULD APPEAR SOMEDAY TO OVERTHROW THEE!
AYE, FLESH OF MY FLESH, ALL THAT WAS SAID--AND MORE!
FOR, 'TWAS SAID AS WELL THIS UNKNOWN FOE WOULD COME FROM THE EAST--!
AND THAT HE WOULD HOLD A CRYSTAL POSSESSED OF SUCH POWER AS TO HUMBLE EVEN THEE!
I RECALL THE LEGEND MOST CLEARLY NOW, OMNIPOTENT ONE!
BUT SURELY THE TALE IS LITTLE MORE THAN SO MUCH SUPERSTITIOUS NONSENSE, ALL-FATHER.
I PRAY THEE RECALL, MY BROTHER--THAT TO SOME, WE ARE MERELY LEGENDS!

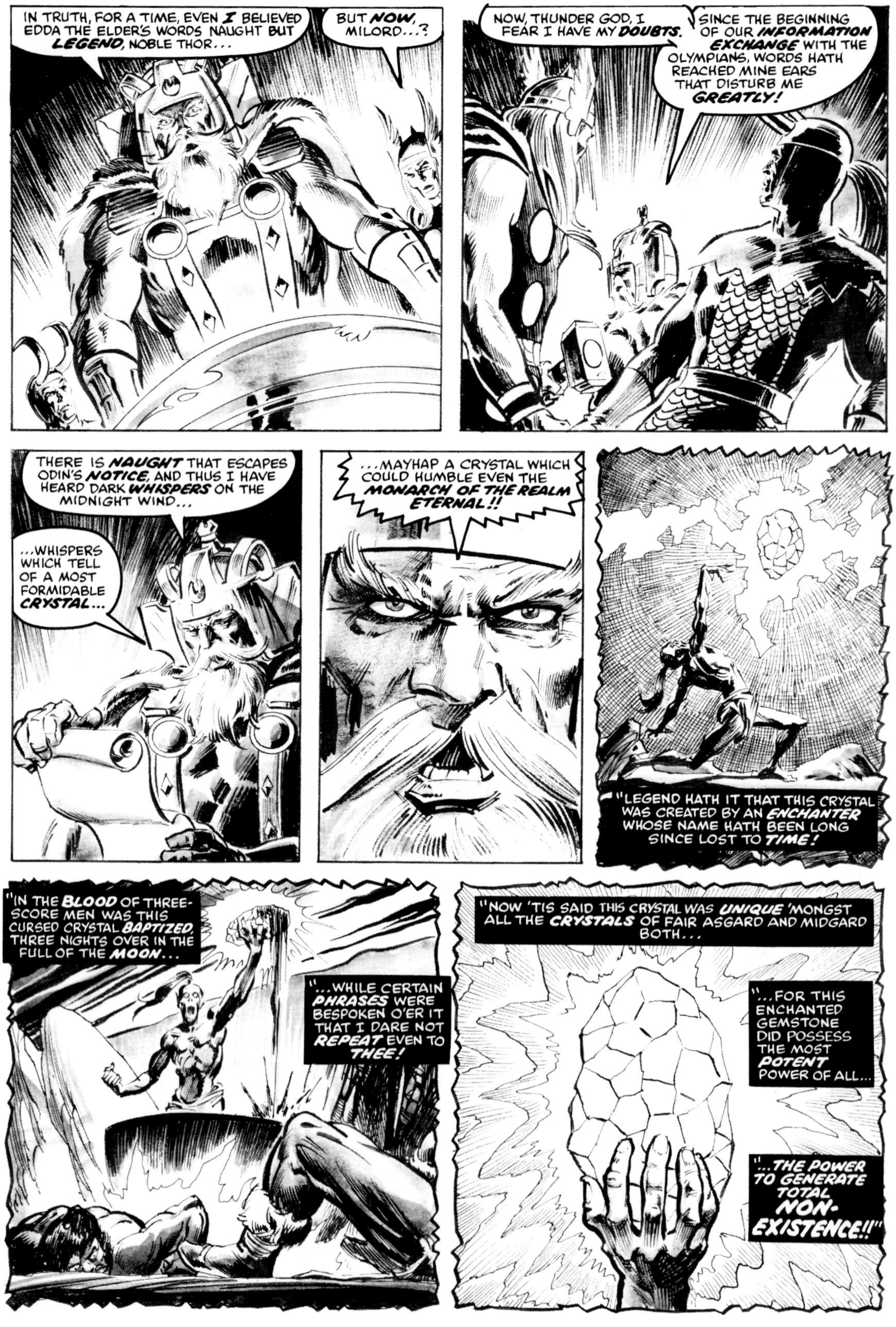
IN TRUTH, FOR A TIME, EVEN I BELIEVED EDDA THE ELDER'S WORDS NAUGHT BUT LEGEND, NOBLE THOR...
BUT NOW, MILORD...?
NOW, THUNDER GOD, I FEAR I HAVE MY DOUBTS.
SINCE THE BEGINNING OF OUR INFORMATION EXCHANGE WITH THE OLYMPIANS, WORDS HATH REACHED MINE EARS THAT DISTURB ME GREATLY!
THERE IS NAUGHT THAT ESCAPES ODIN'S NOTICE, AND THUS I HAVE HEARD DARK WHISPERS ON THE MIDNIGHT WIND...
...WHISPERS WHICH TELL OF A MOST FORMIDABLE CRYSTAL...
...MAYHAP A CRYSTAL WHICH COULD HUMBLE EVEN THE MONARCH OF THE REALM ETERNAL!!
"LEGEND HATH IT THAT THIS CRYSTAL WAS CREATED BY AN ENCHANTER WHOSE NAME HATH BEEN LONG SINCE LOST TO TIME!
"IN THE BLOOD OF THREE-SCORE MEN WAS THIS CURSED CRYSTAL BAPTIZED, THREE NIGHTS OVER IN THE FULL OF THE MOON...
"...WHILE CERTAIN PHRASES WERE BESPOKEN O'ER IT THAT I DARE NOT REPEAT EVEN TO THEE!
"NOW 'TIS SAID THIS CRYSTAL WAS UNIQUE 'MONGST ALL THE CRYSTALS OF FAIR ASGARD AND MIDGARD BOTH...
"...FOR THIS ENCHANTED GEMSTONE DID POSSESS THE MOST POTENT POWER OF ALL...
"...THE POWER TO GENERATE TOTAL NON-EXISTENCE!!"

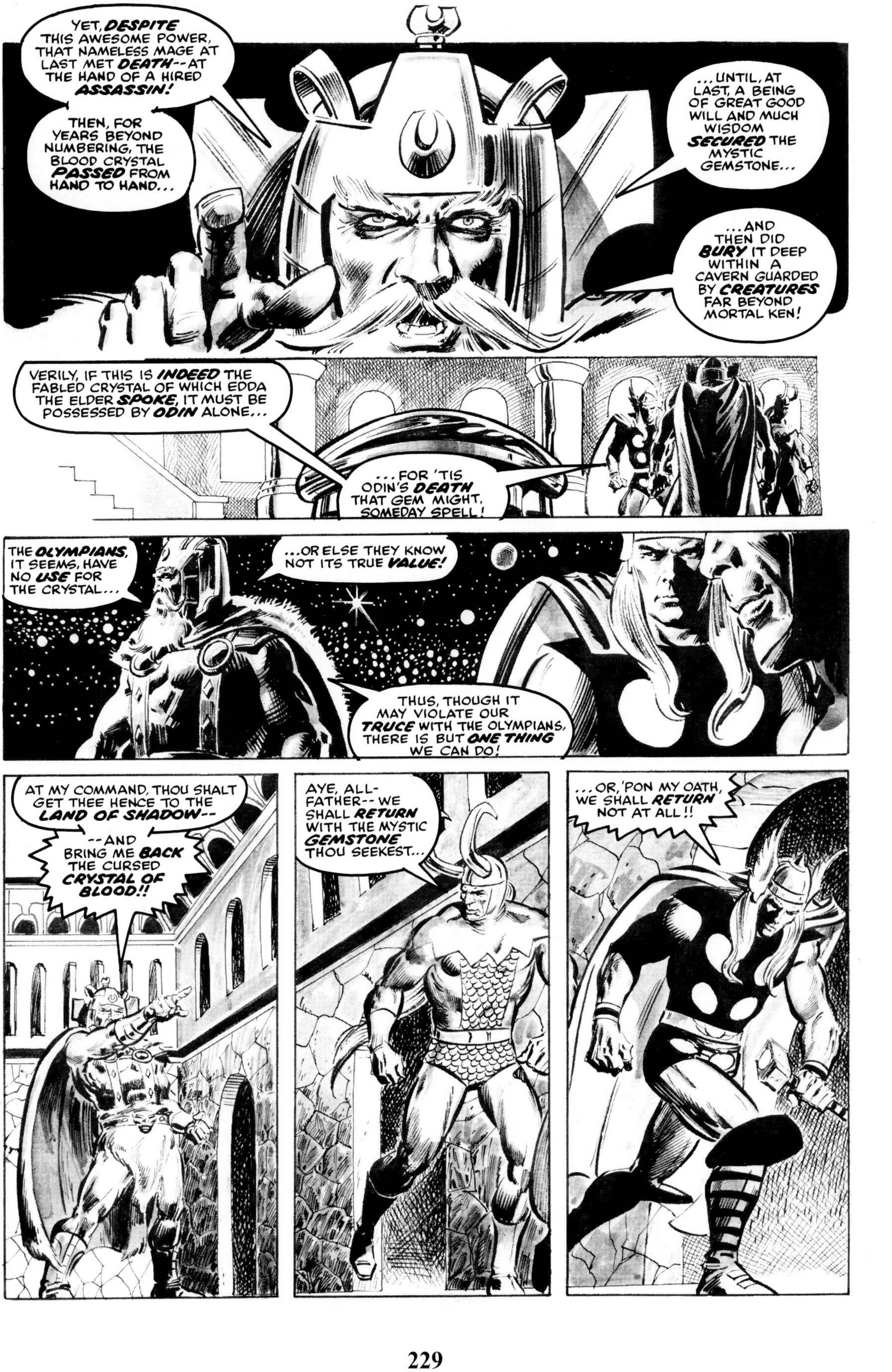

YET, DESPITE THIS AWESOME POWER, THAT NAMELESS MAGE AT LAST MET DEATH--AT THE HAND OF A HIRED ASSASSIN!
THEN, FOR YEARS BEYOND NUMBERING, THE BLOOD CRYSTAL PASSED FROM HAND TO HAND...
...UNTIL, AT LAST, A BEING OF GREAT GOOD WILL AND MUCH WISDOM SECURED THE MYSTIC GEMSTONE...
...AND THEN DID BURY IT DEEP WITHIN A CAVERN GUARDED BY CREATURES FAR BEYOND MORTAL KEN!
VERILY, IF THIS IS INDEED THE FABLED CRYSTAL OF WHICH EDDA THE ELDER SPOKE, IT MUST BE POSSESSED BY ODIN ALONE,...
...FOR 'TIS ODIN'S DEATH THAT GEM MIGHT, SOMEDAY SPELL!
THE OLYMPIANS, IT SEEMS, HAVE NO USE FOR THE CRYSTAL...
...OR ELSE THEY KNOW NOT ITS TRUE VALUE!
THUS, THOUGH IT MAY VIOLATE OUR TRUCE WITH THE OLYMPIANS, THERE IS BUT ONE THING WE CAN DO!
AT MY COMMAND, THOU SHALT GET THEE HENCE TO THE LAND OF SHADOW--
--AND BRING ME BACK THE CURSED CRYSTAL OF BLOOD!!
AYE, ALL-FATHER-- WE SHALL RETURN WITH THE MYSTIC GEMSTONE THOU SEEKEST...
...OR, 'PON MY OATH, WE SHALL RETURN NOT AT ALL!!

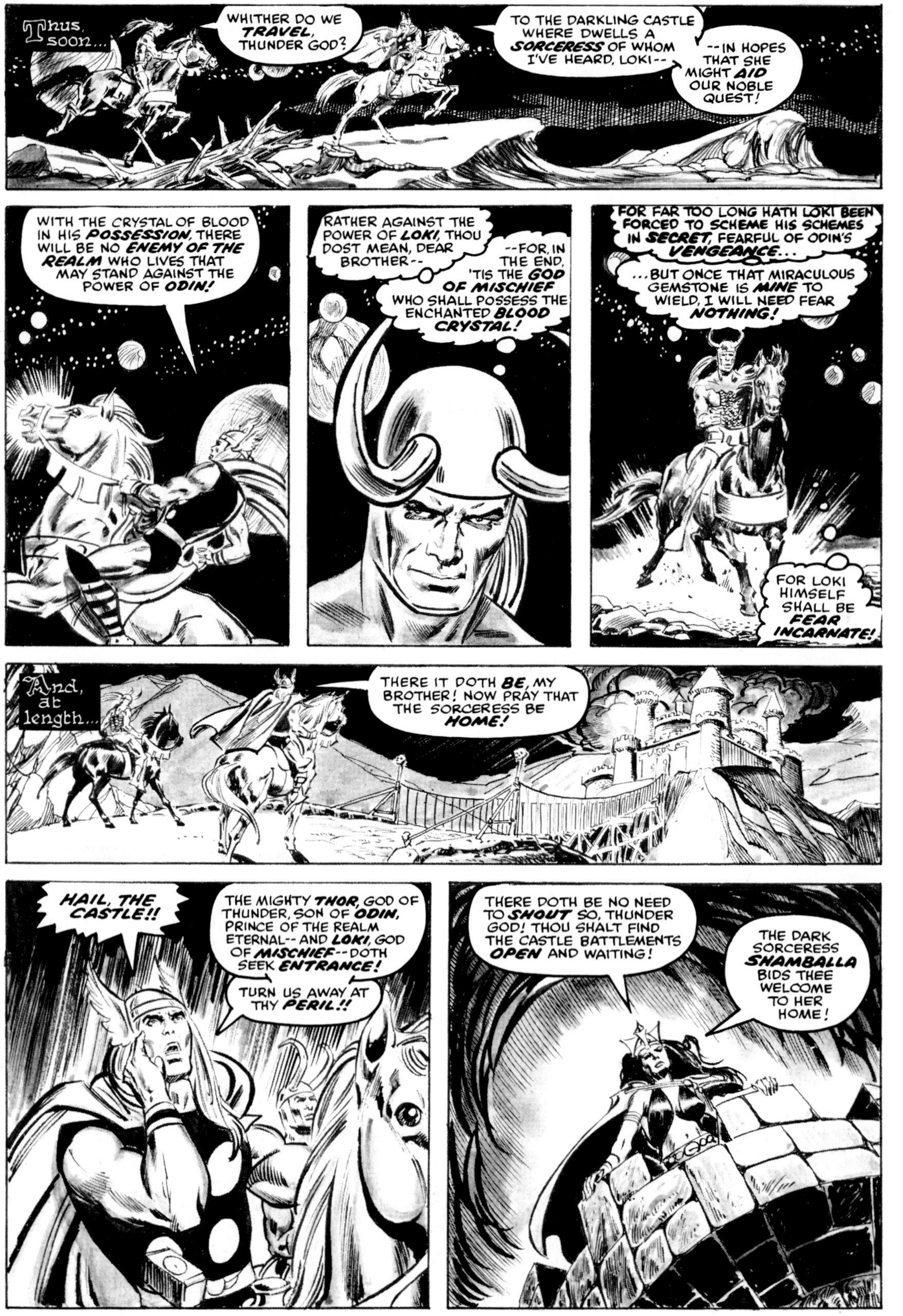
Thus, soon...
WHITHER DO WE TRAVEL, THUNDER GOD?
TO THE DARKLING CASTLE WHERE DWELLS A SORCERESS OF WHOM I'VE HEARD, LOKI--
--IN HOPES THAT SHE MIGHT AID OUR NOBLE QUEST!
WITH THE CRYSTAL OF BLOOD IN HIS POSSESSION, THERE WILL BE NO ENEMY OF THE REALM WHO LIVES THAT MAY STAND AGAINST THE POWER OF ODIN!
RATHER AGAINST THE POWER OF LOKI, THOU DOST MEAN, DEAR BROTHER--
--FOR, IN THE END, 'TIS THE GOD OF MISCHIEF WHO SHALL POSSESS THE ENCHANTED BLOOD CRYSTAL!
FOR FAR TOO LONG HATH LOKI BEEN FORCED TO SCHEME HIS SCHEMES IN SECRET, FEARFUL OF ODIN'S VENGEANCE...
...BUT ONCE THAT MIRACULOUS GEMSTONE IS MINE TO WIELD, I WILL NEED FEAR NOTHING!
FOR LOKI HIMSELF SHALL BE FEAR INCARNATE!
And, at length...
THERE IT DOTH BE, MY BROTHER! NOW PRAY THAT THE SORCERESS BE HOME!
HAIL, THE CASTLE!!
THE MIGHTY THOR, GOD OF THUNDER, SON OF ODIN, PRINCE OF THE REALM ETERNAL--AND LOKI, GOD OF MISCHIEF--DOTH SEEK ENTRANCE!
TURN US AWAY AT THY PERIL!!
THERE DOTH BE NO NEED TO SHOUT SO, THUNDER GOD! THOU SHALT FIND THE CASTLE BATTLEMENTS OPEN AND WAITING!
THE DARK SORCERESS SHAMBALLA BIDS THEE WELCOME TO HER HOME!

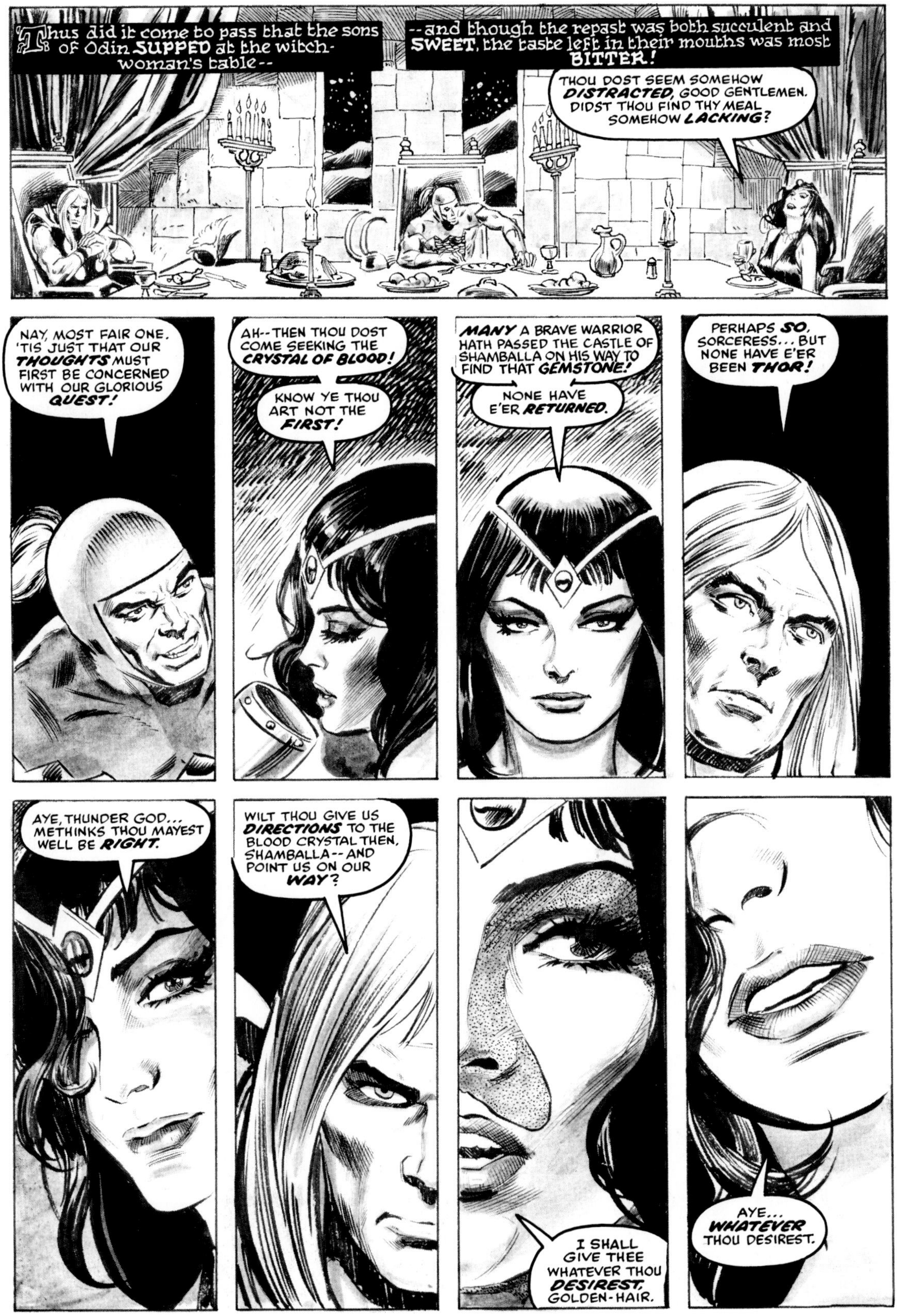
Thus did it come to pass that the sons of Odin SUPPED at the witch-woman's table--
--and though the repast was both succulent and SWEET, the taste left in their mouths was most BITTER!
THOU DOST SEEM SOMEHOW DISTRACTED, GOOD GENTLEMEN. DIDST THOU FIND THY MEAL SOMEHOW LACKING?
NAY, MOST FAIR ONE. 'TIS JUST THAT OUR THOUGHTS MUST FIRST BE CONCERNED WITH OUR GLORIOUS QUEST!
AH--THEN THOU DOST COME SEEKING THE CRYSTAL OF BLOOD!
KNOW YE THOU ART NOT THE FIRST!
MANY A BRAVE WARRIOR HATH PASSED THE CASTLE OF SHAMBALLA ON HIS WAY TO FIND THAT GEMSTONE!
NONE HAVE E'ER RETURNED.
PERHAPS SO, SORCERESS... BUT NONE HAVE E'ER BEEN THOR!
AYE, THUNDER GOD... METHINKS THOU MAYEST WELL BE RIGHT.
WILT THOU GIVE US DIRECTIONS TO THE BLOOD CRYSTAL THEN, SHAMBALLA--AND POINT US ON OUR WAY?
I SHALL GIVE THEE WHATEVER THOU DESIREST, GOLDEN-HAIR.
AYE... WHATEVER THOU DESIREST.

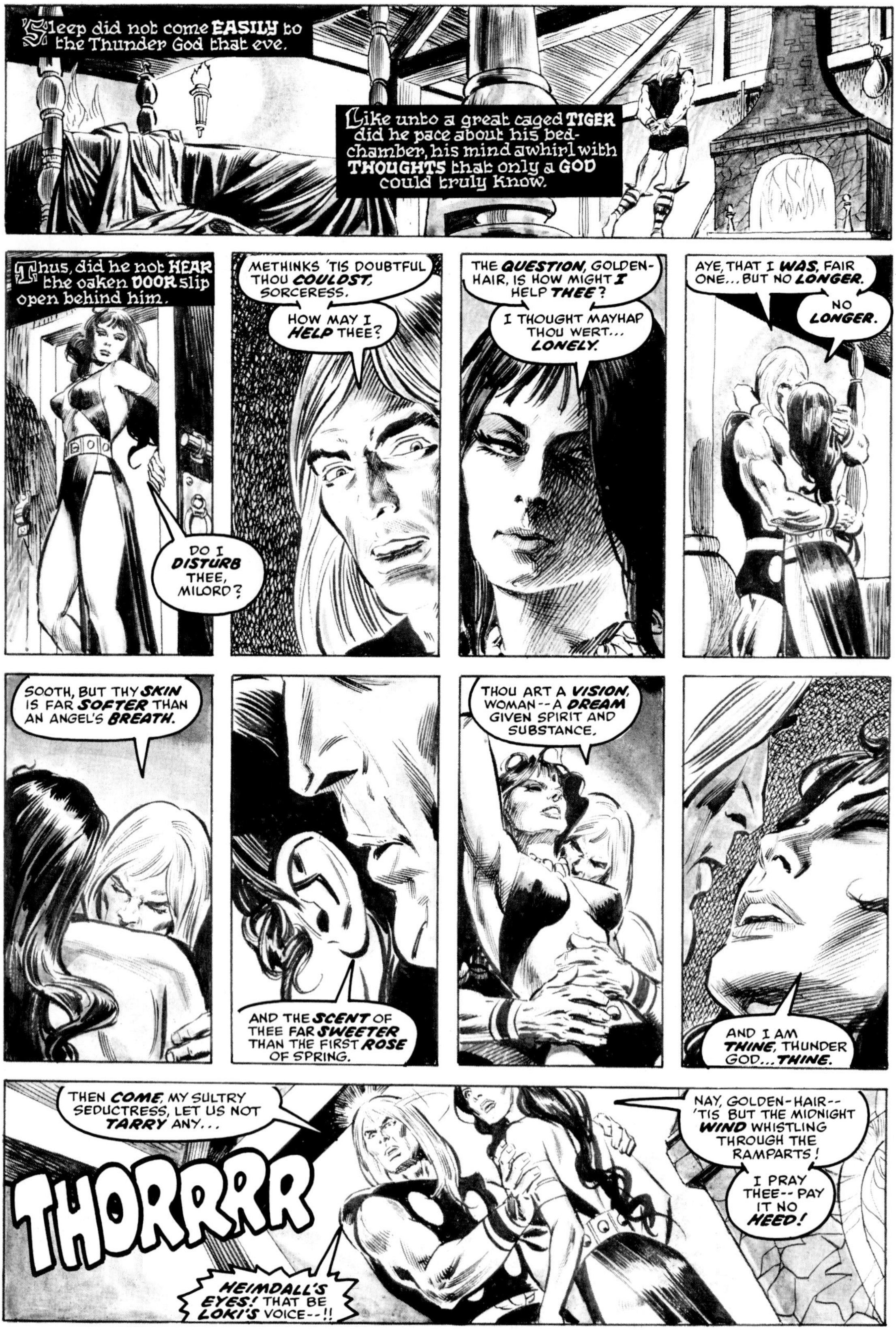
Sleep did not come EASILY to the Thunder God that eve.
Like unto a great caged TIGER did he pace about his bed-chamber, his mind awhirl with THOUGHTS that only a GOD could truly know.
Thus, did he not HEAR the oaken DOOR slip open behind him.
DO I DISTURB THEE, MILORD?
METHINKS 'TIS DOUBTFUL THOU COULDST, SORCERESS.
HOW MAY I HELP THEE?
THE QUESTION, GOLDEN-HAIR, IS HOW MIGHT I HELP THEE?
I THOUGHT MAYHAP THOU WERT... LONELY.
AYE, THAT I WAS, FAIR ONE... BUT NO LONGER.
NO LONGER.
SOOTH, BUT THY SKIN IS FAR SOFTER THAN AN ANGEL'S BREATH.
AND THE SCENT OF THEE FAR SWEETER THAN THE FIRST ROSE OF SPRING.
THOU ART A VISION, WOMAN--A DREAM GIVEN SPIRIT AND SUBSTANCE.
AND I AM THINE, THUNDER GOD... THINE.
THEN COME, MY SULTRY SEDUCTRESS, LET US NOT TARRY ANY...
THORRRR
HEIMDALL'S EYES! THAT BE LOKI'S VOICE--!!
NAY, GOLDEN-HAIR--'TIS BUT THE MIDNIGHT WIND WHISTLING THROUGH THE RAMPARTS!
I PRAY THEE--PAY IT NO HEED!

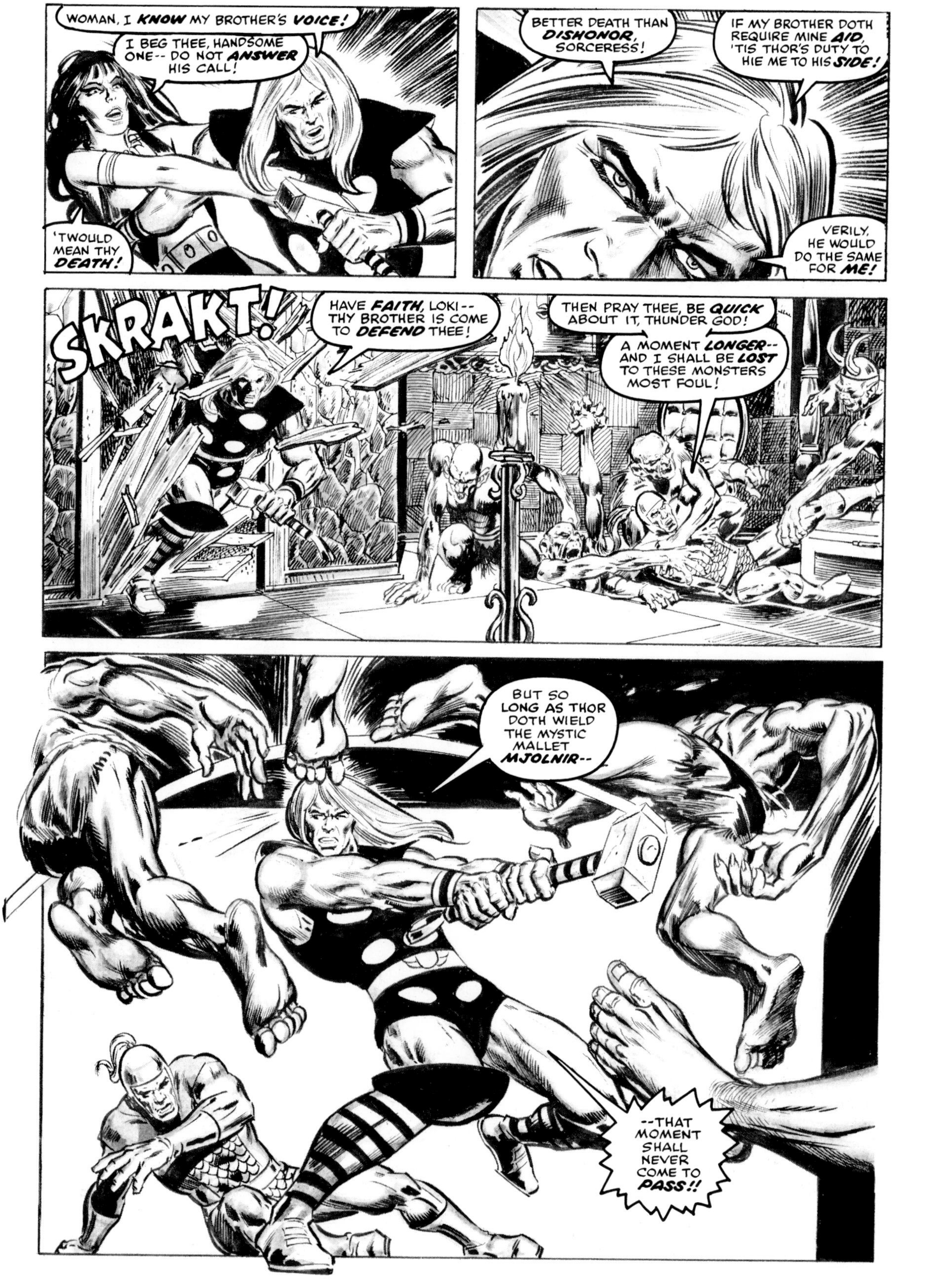
WOMAN, I KNOW MY BROTHER'S VOICE!
I BEG THEE, HANDSOME ONE-- DO NOT ANSWER HIS CALL!
'TWOULD MEAN THY DEATH!
BETTER DEATH THAN DISHONOR, SORCERESS!
IF MY BROTHER DOTH REQUIRE MINE AID, 'TIS THOR'S DUTY TO HIE ME TO HIS SIDE!
VERILY, HE WOULD DO THE SAME FOR ME!
SKRAKT!
HAVE FAITH, LOKI-- THY BROTHER IS COME TO DEFEND THEE!
THEN PRAY THEE, BE QUICK ABOUT IT, THUNDER GOD!
A MOMENT LONGER-- AND I SHALL BE LOST TO THESE MONSTERS MOST FOUL!
BUT SO LONG AS THOR DOTH WIELD THE MYSTIC MALLET MJOLNIR--
--THAT MOMENT SHALL NEVER COME TO PASS!!

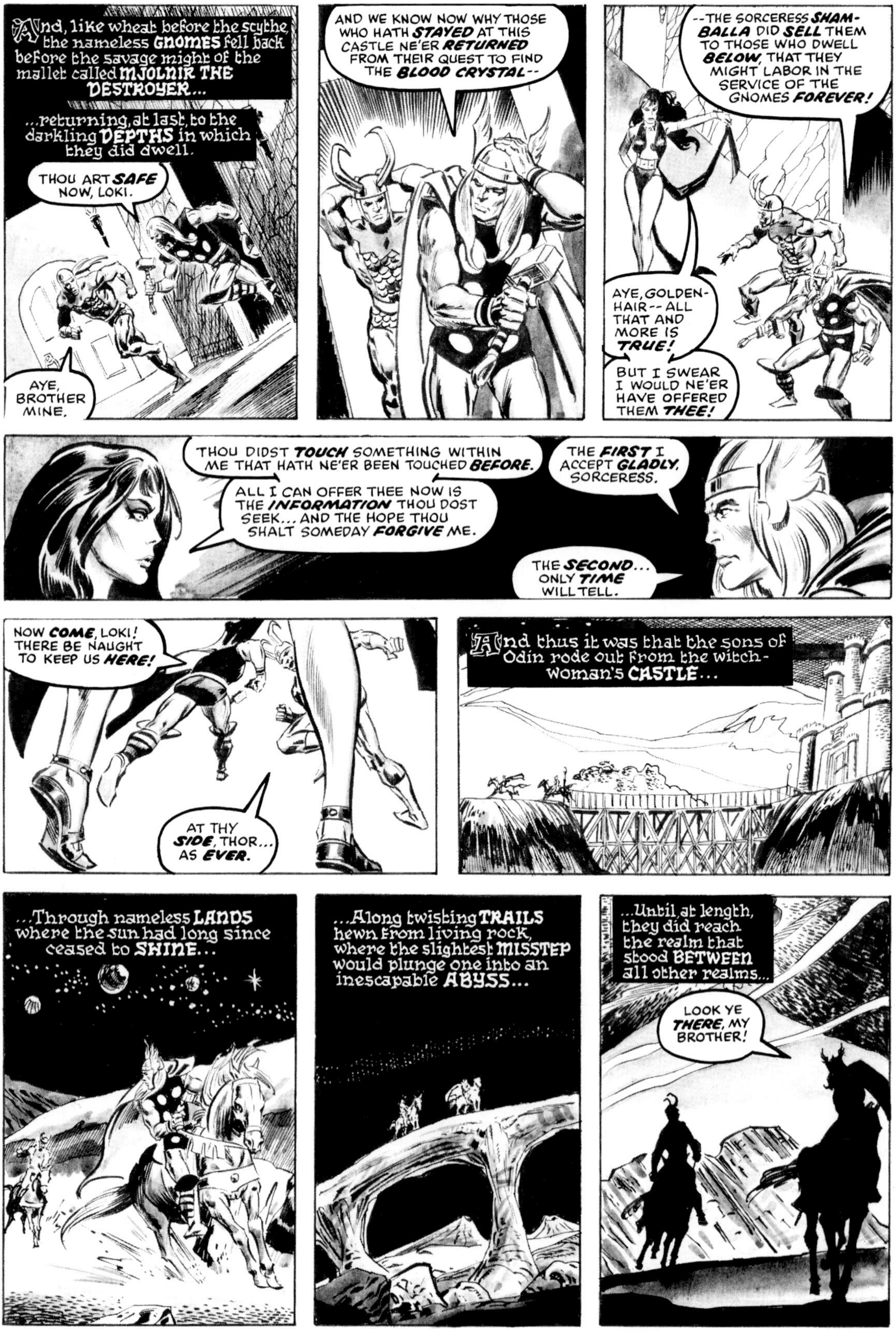
And, like wheat before the scythe, the nameless GNOMES fell back before the savage might of the mallet called MJOLNIR THE DESTROYER...
...returning, at last, to the darkling DEPTHS in which they did dwell.
THOU ART SAFE NOW, LOKI.
AYE, BROTHER MINE.
AND WE KNOW NOW WHY THOSE WHO HATH STAYED AT THIS CASTLE NE'ER RETURNED FROM THEIR QUEST TO FIND THE BLOOD CRYSTAL--
--THE SORCERESS SHAMBALLA DID SELL THEM TO THOSE WHO DWELL BELOW, THAT THEY MIGHT LABOR IN THE SERVICE OF THE GNOMES FOREVER!
AYE, GOLDEN-HAIR-- ALL THAT AND MORE IS TRUE!
BUT I SWEAR I WOULD NE'ER HAVE OFFERED THEM THEE!
THOU DIDST TOUCH SOMETHING WITHIN ME THAT HATH NE'ER BEEN TOUCHED BEFORE.
ALL I CAN OFFER THEE NOW IS THE INFORMATION THOU DOST SEEK... AND THE HOPE THOU SHALT SOMEDAY FORGIVE ME.
THE FIRST I ACCEPT GLADLY, SORCERESS.
THE SECOND... ONLY TIME WILL TELL.
NOW COME, LOKI! THERE BE NAUGHT TO KEEP US HERE!
AT THY SIDE, THOR... AS EVER.
And thus it was that the sons of Odin rode out from the witch-woman's CASTLE...
...Through nameless LANDS where the sun had long since ceased to SHINE...
...Along twisting TRAILS hewn from living rock, where the slightest MISSTEP would plunge one into an inescapable ABYSS...
...Until, at length, they did reach the realm that stood BETWEEN all other realms...
LOOK YE THERE, MY BROTHER!

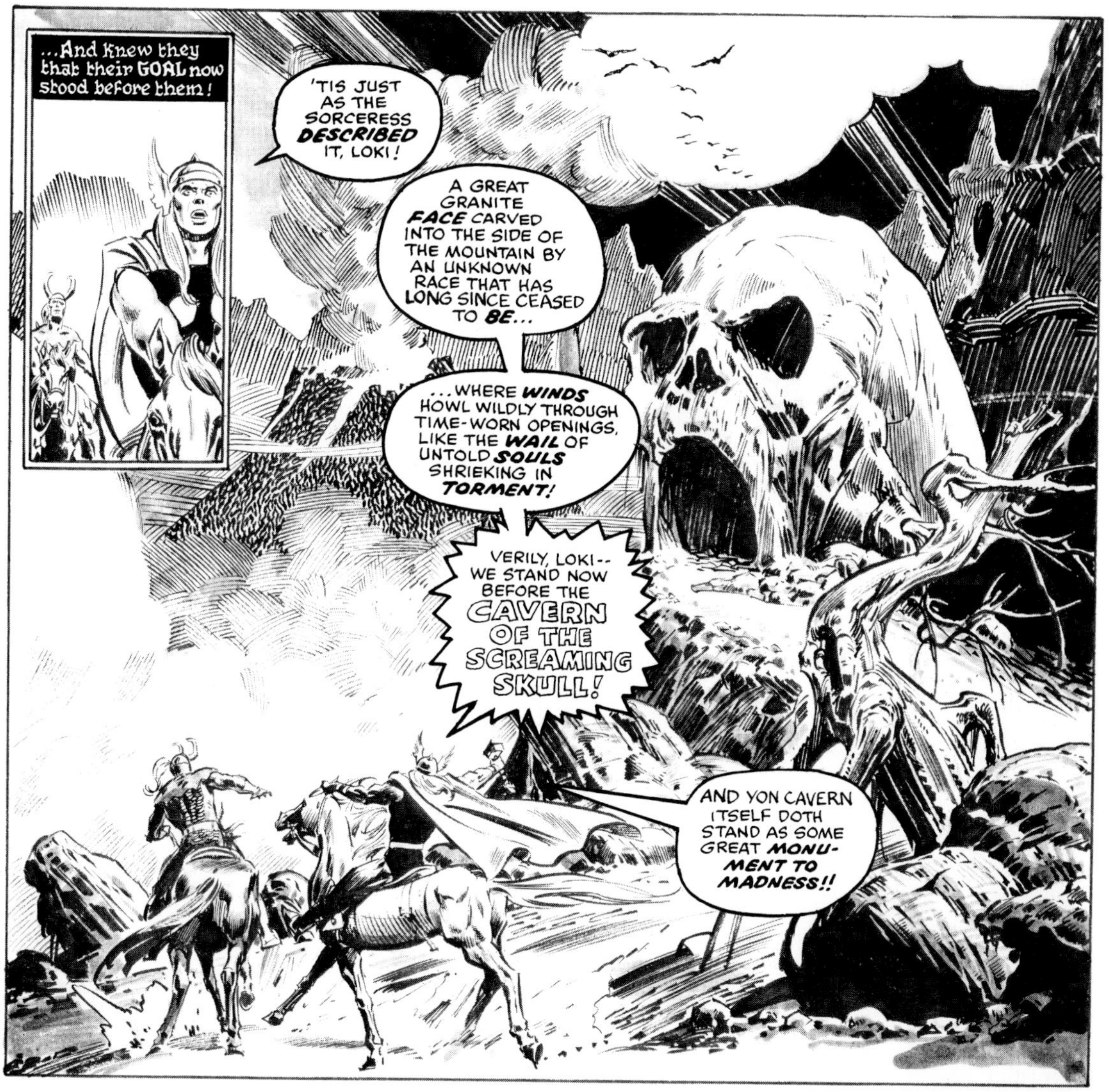
...And knew they that their GOAL now stood before them!
'TIS JUST AS THE SORCERESS DESCRIBED IT, LOKI!
A GREAT GRANITE FACE CARVED INTO THE SIDE OF THE MOUNTAIN BY AN UNKNOWN RACE THAT HAS LONG SINCE CEASED TO BE...
...WHERE WINDS HOWL WILDLY THROUGH TIME-WORN OPENINGS, LIKE THE WAIL OF UNTOLD SOULS SHRIEKING IN TORMENT!
VERILY, LOKI-- WE STAND NOW BEFORE THE CAVERN OF THE SCREAMING SKULL!
AND YON CAVERN ITSELF DOTH STAND AS SOME GREAT MONUMENT TO MADNESS!!

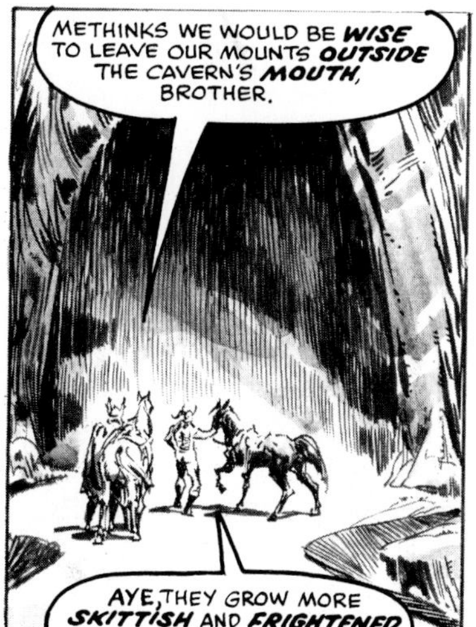
METHINKS WE WOULD BE WISE TO LEAVE OUR MOUNTS OUTSIDE THE CAVERN'S MOUTH, BROTHER.
AYE, THEY GROW MORE SKITTISH AND FRIGHTENED THE NEARER WE DRAW TO OUR GOAL!

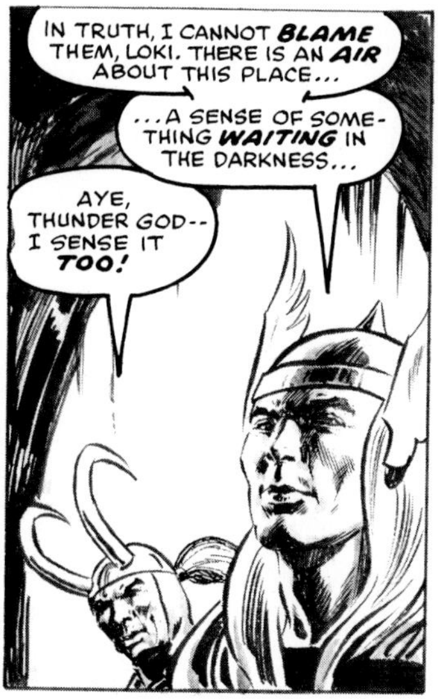
IN TRUTH, I CANNOT BLAME THEM, LOKI. THERE IS AN AIR ABOUT THIS PLACE...
...A SENSE OF SOMETHING WAITING IN THE DARKNESS...
AYE, THUNDER GOD-- I SENSE IT TOO!

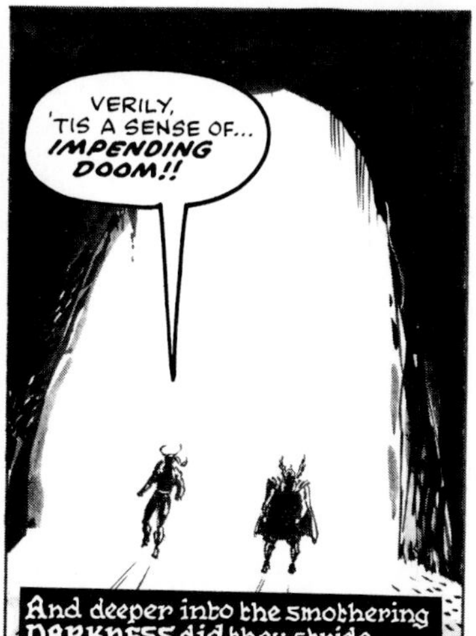
VERILY, 'TIS A SENSE OF... IMPENDING DOOM!!
And deeper into the smothering DARKNESS did they stride...

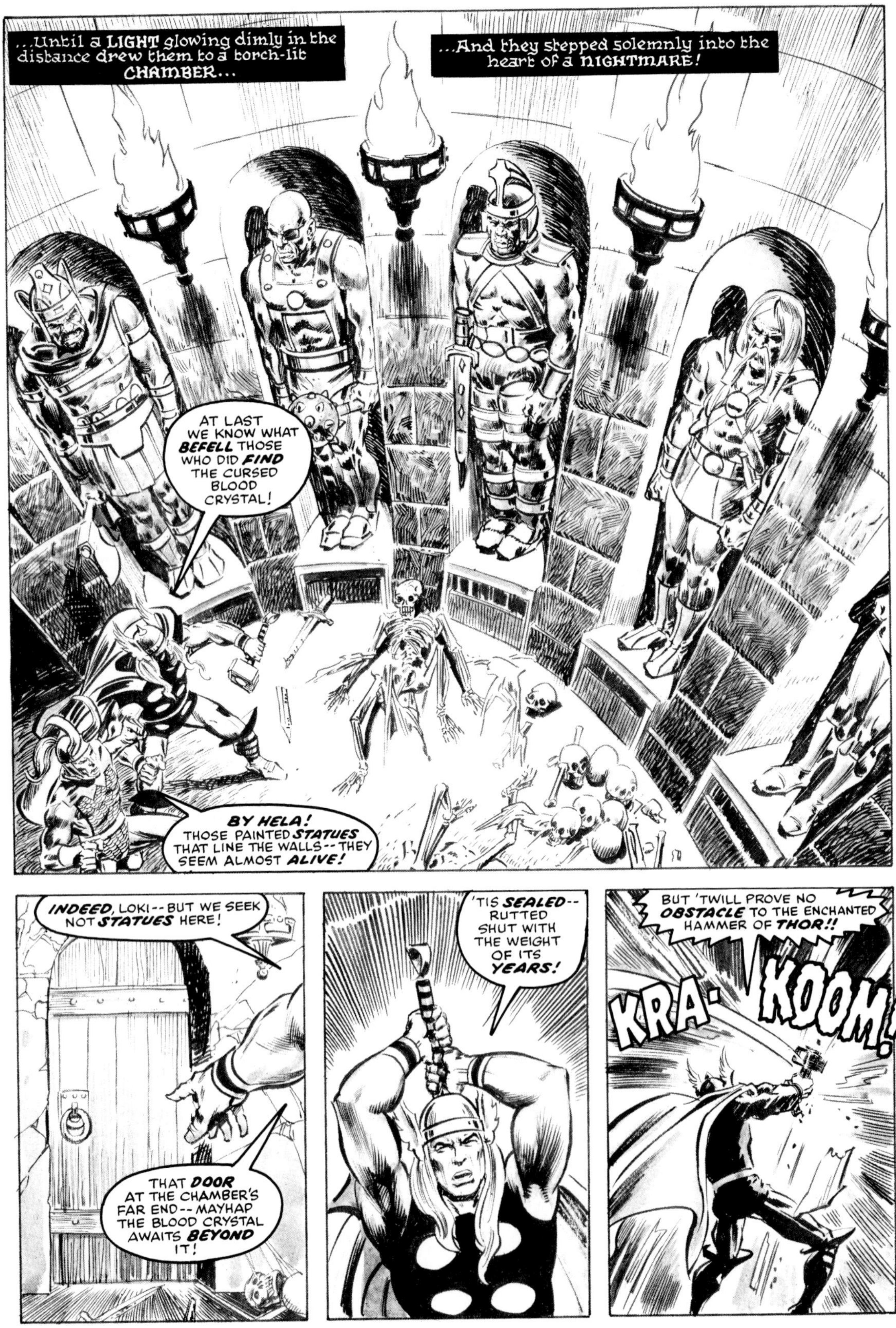
...Until a LIGHT glowing dimly in the distance drew them to a torch-lit CHAMBER...
...And they stepped solemnly into the heart of a NIGHTMARE!
AT LAST WE KNOW WHAT BEFELL THOSE WHO DID FIND THE CURSED BLOOD CRYSTAL!
BY HELA! THOSE PAINTED STATUES THAT LINE THE WALLS--THEY SEEM ALMOST ALIVE!
INDEED, LOKI--BUT WE SEEK NOT STATUES HERE!
THAT DOOR AT THE CHAMBER'S FAR END--MAYHAP THE BLOOD CRYSTAL AWAITS BEYOND IT!
'TIS SEALED--RUTTED SHUT WITH THE WEIGHT OF ITS YEARS!
BUT 'TWILL PROVE NO OBSTACLE TO THE ENCHANTED HAMMER OF THOR!!
KRA-KOOM!

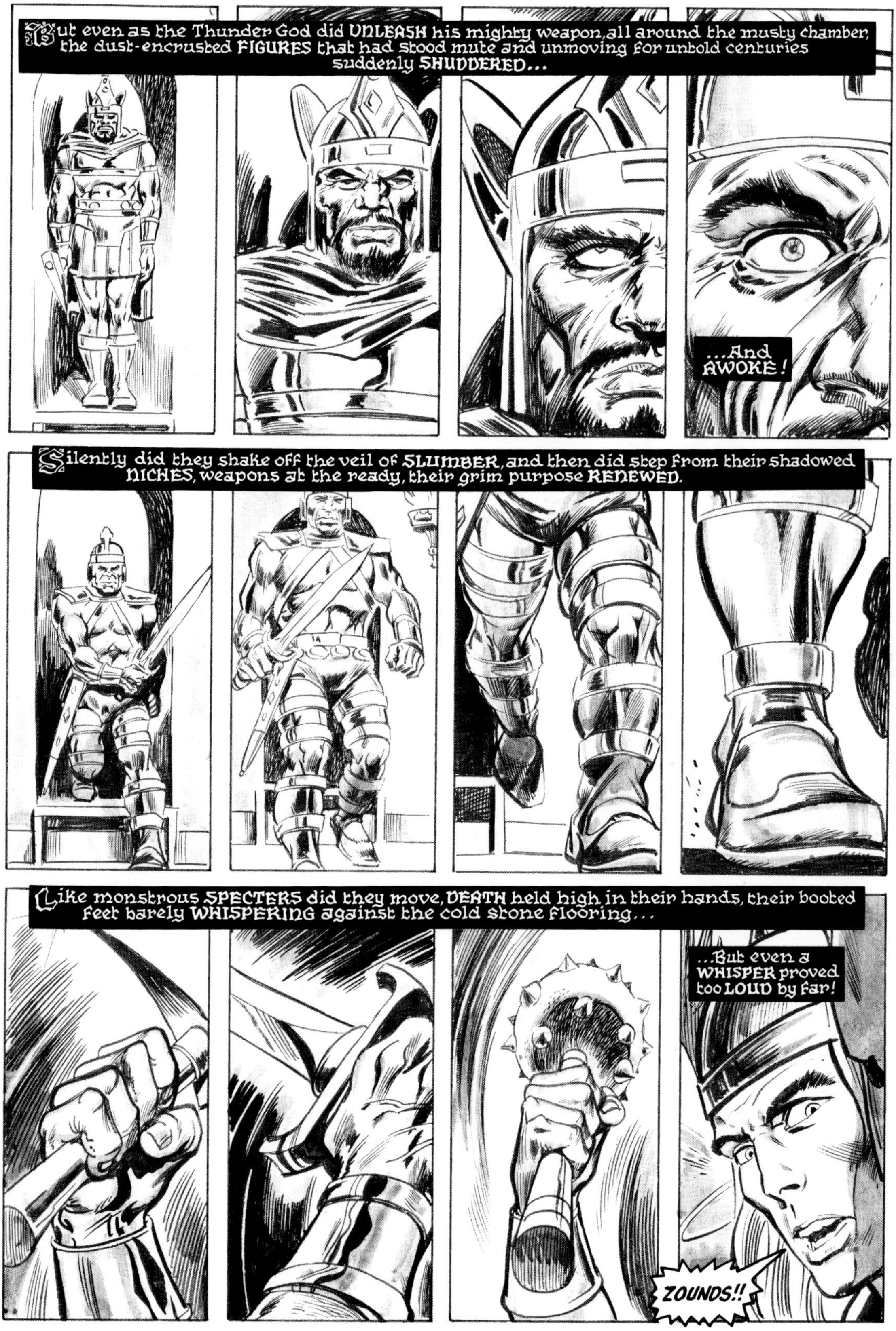
But even as the Thunder God did UNLEASH his mighty weapon, all around the musty chamber, the dust-encrusted FIGURES that had stood mute and unmoving for untold centuries suddenly SHUDDERED...
...And AWOKE!
Silently did they shake off the veil of SLUMBER, and then did step from their shadowed NICHES, weapons at the ready, their grim purpose RENEWED.
Like monstrous SPECTERS did they move, DEATH held high in their hands, their booted feet barely WHISPERING against the cold stone flooring...
...But even a WHISPER proved too LOUD by far!
ZOUNDS!!

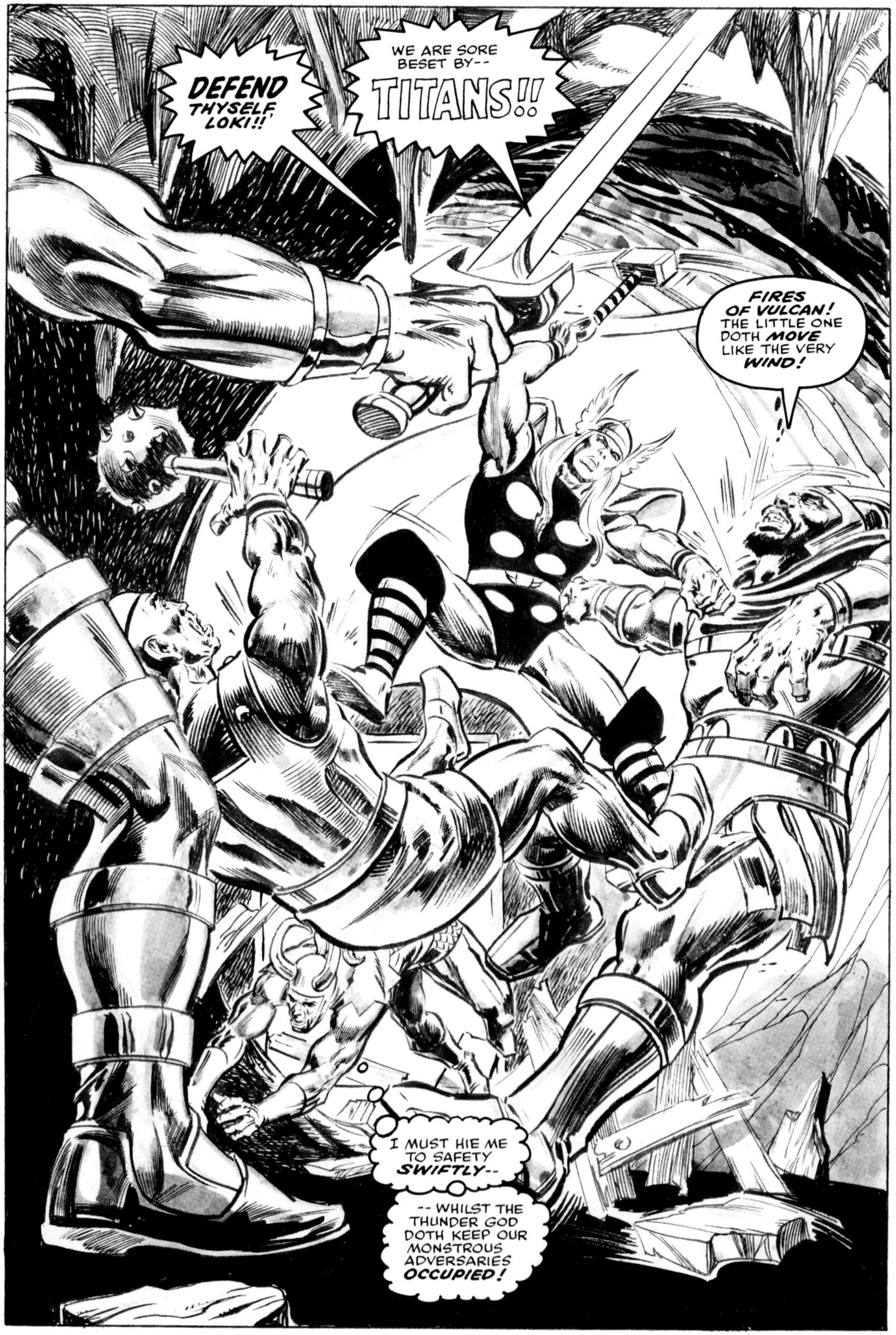
DEFEND THYSELF, LOKI!!
WE ARE SORE BESET BY-- TITANS!!
FIRES OF VULCAN! THE LITTLE ONE DOTH MOVE LIKE THE VERY WIND!
I MUST HIE ME TO SAFETY SWIFTLY--
-- WHILST THE THUNDER GOD DOTH KEEP OUR MONSTROUS ADVERSARIES OCCUPIED!

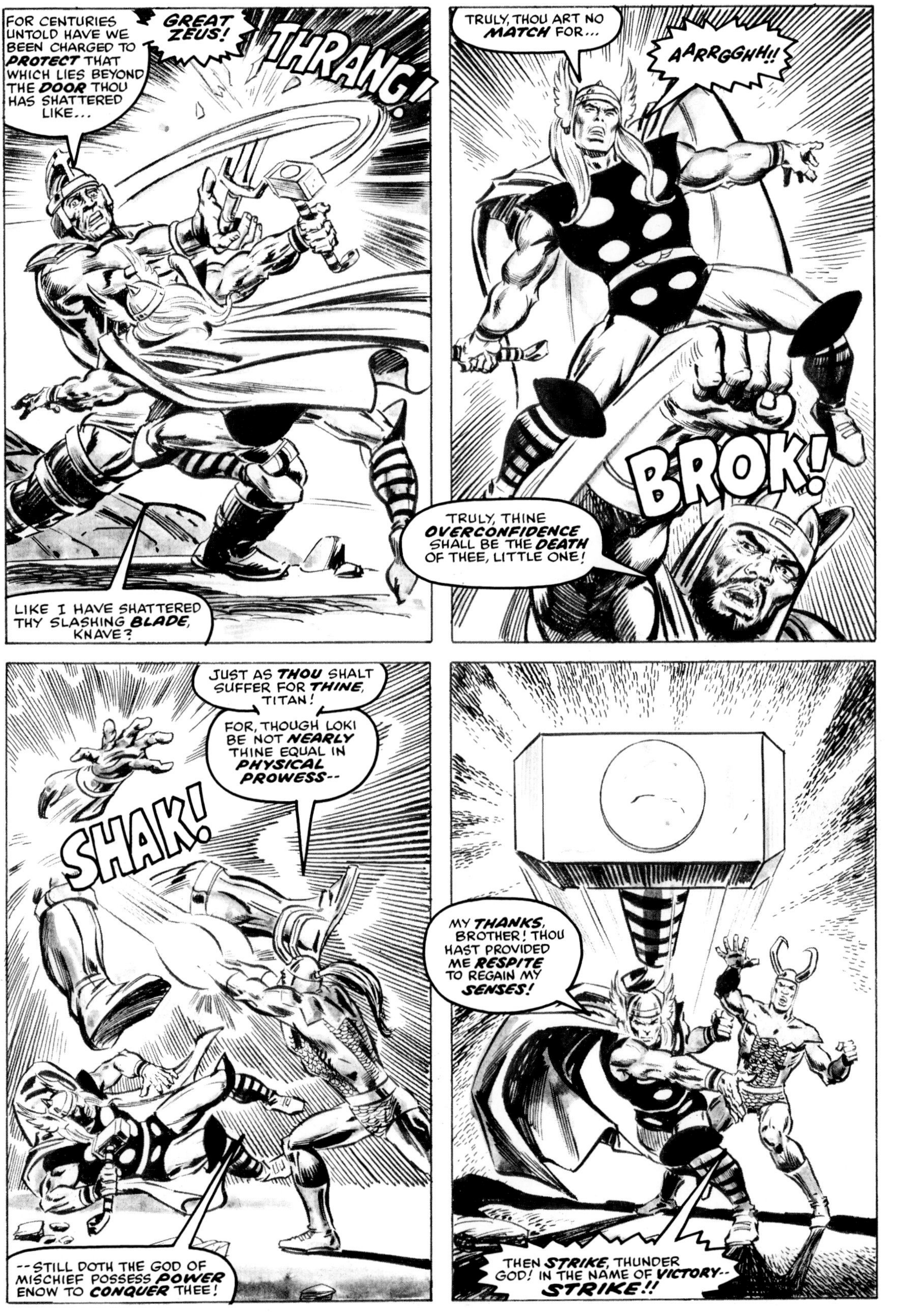
FOR CENTURIES UNTOLD HAVE WE BEEN CHARGED TO PROTECT THAT WHICH LIES BEYOND THE DOOR THOU HAS SHATTERED LIKE...
GREAT ZEUS!
THRANG!
LIKE I HAVE SHATTERED THY SLASHING BLADE, KNAVE?
TRULY, THOU ART NO MATCH FOR...
AARRGGHH!!
BROK!
TRULY, THINE OVERCONFIDENCE SHALL BE THE DEATH OF THEE, LITTLE ONE!
JUST AS THOU SHALT SUFFER FOR THINE, TITAN!
FOR, THOUGH LOKI BE NOT NEARLY THINE EQUAL IN PHYSICAL PROWESS--
SHAK!
--STILL DOTH THE GOD OF MISCHIEF POSSESS POWER ENOW TO CONQUER THEE!
MY THANKS, BROTHER! THOU HAST PROVIDED ME RESPITE TO REGAIN MY SENSES!
THEN STRIKE, THUNDER GOD! IN THE NAME OF VICTORY-- STRIKE!!

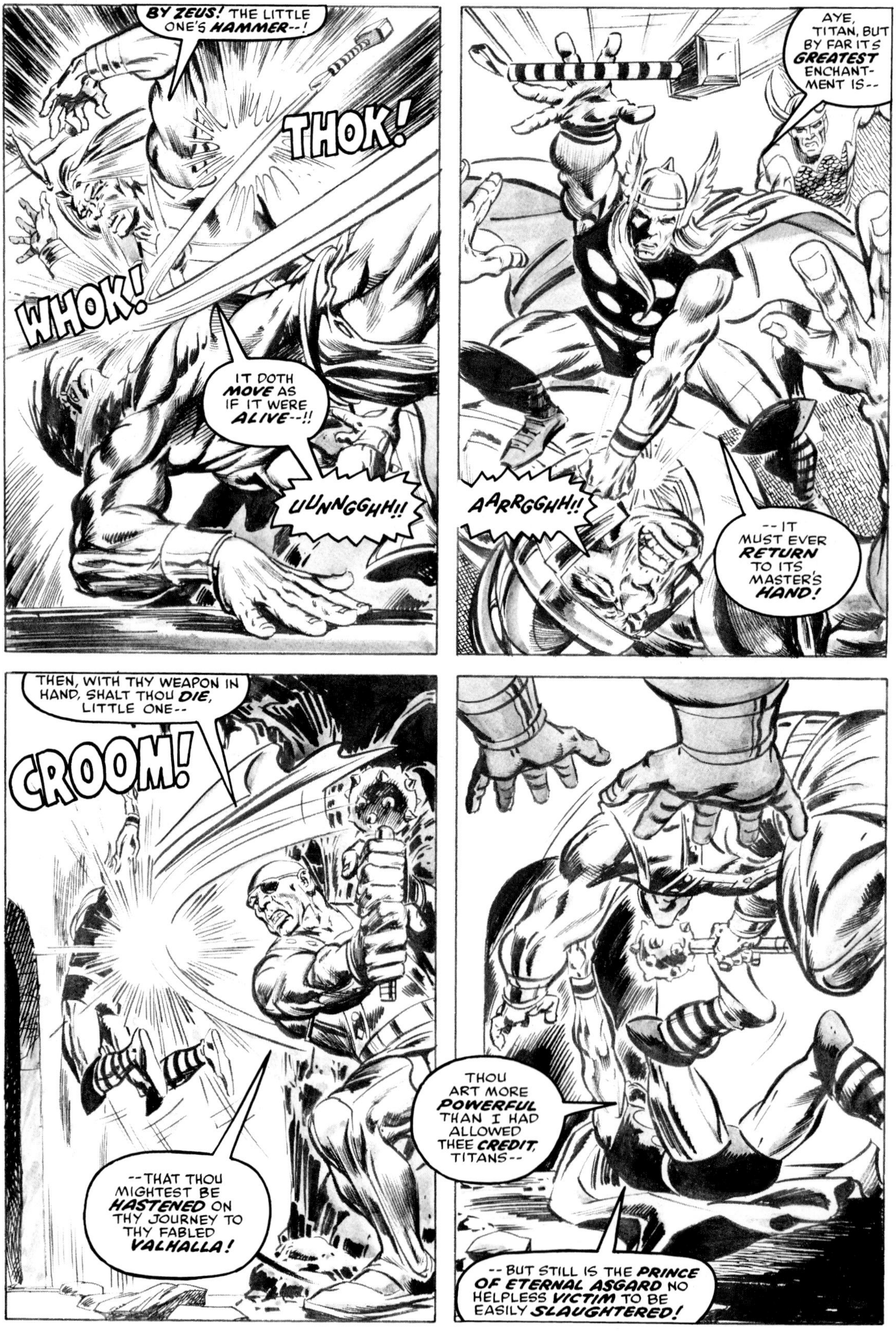
BY ZEUS! THE LITTLE ONE'S HAMMER--!
THOK!
WHOK!
IT DOTH MOVE AS IF IT WERE ALIVE--!!
UUNNGGHH!!
AYE, TITAN, BUT BY FAR ITS GREATEST ENCHANT-MENT IS--
AARRGGHH!!
--IT MUST EVER RETURN TO ITS MASTER'S HAND!
THEN, WITH THY WEAPON IN HAND, SHALT THOU DIE, LITTLE ONE--
CROOM!
--THAT THOU MIGHTEST BE HASTENED ON THY JOURNEY TO THY FABLED VALHALLA!
THOU ART MORE POWERFUL THAN I HAD ALLOWED THEE CREDIT, TITANS--
--BUT STILL IS THE PRINCE OF ETERNAL ASGARD NO HELPLESS VICTIM TO BE EASILY SLAUGHTERED!

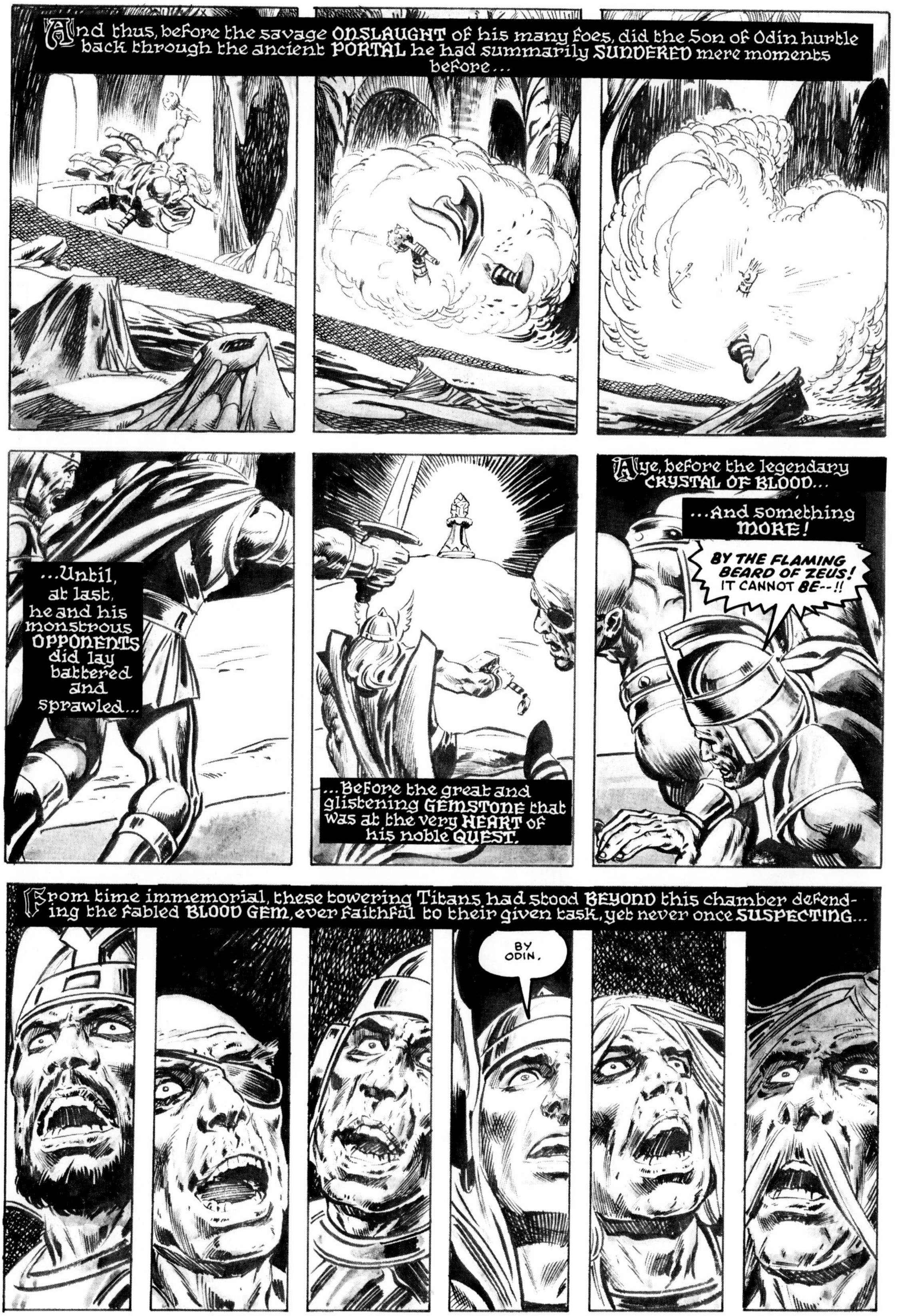
And thus, before the savage ONSLAUGHT of his many foes, did the Son of Odin hurtle back through the ancient PORTAL he had summarily SUNDERED mere moments before...
...Until, at last, he and his monstrous OPPONENTS did lay battered and sprawled...
...Before the great and glistening GEMSTONE that was at the very HEART of his noble QUEST.
Aye, before the legendary CRYSTAL OF BLOOD...
...And something MORE!
BY THE FLAMING BEARD OF ZEUS! IT CANNOT BE--!!
From time immemorial, these towering Titans had stood BEYOND this chamber defending the fabled BLOOD GEM, ever faithful to their given task, yet never once SUSPECTING...
BY ODIN,

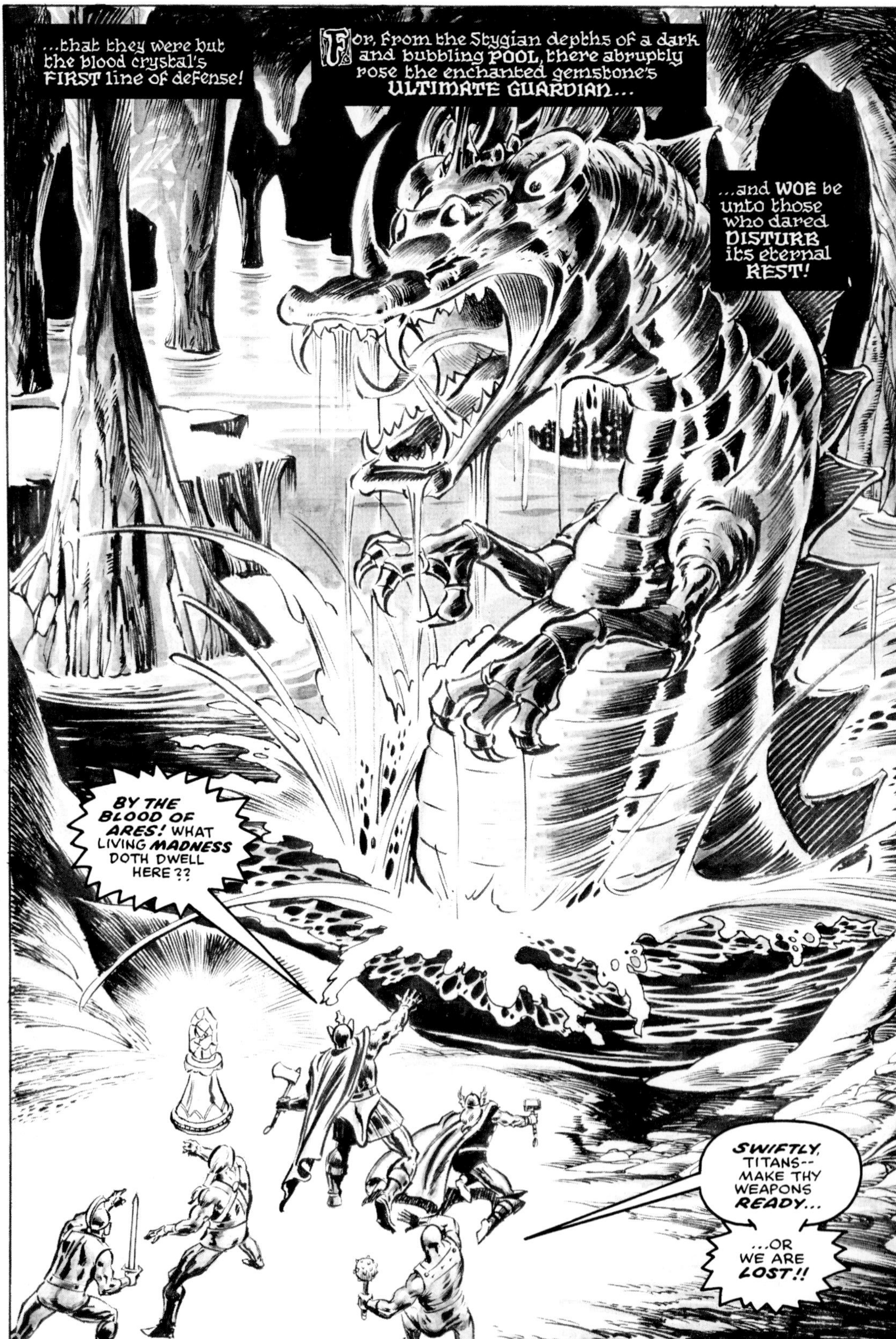
...that they were but the blood crystal's FIRST line of defense!
For, from the Stygian depths of a dark and bubbling POOL, there abruptly rose the enchanted gemstone's ULTIMATE GUARDIAN...
...and WOE be unto those who dared DISTURB its eternal REST!
BY THE BLOOD OF ARES! WHAT LIVING MADNESS DOTH DWELL HERE??
SWIFTLY, TITANS-- MAKE THY WEAPONS READY...
...OR WE ARE LOST!!

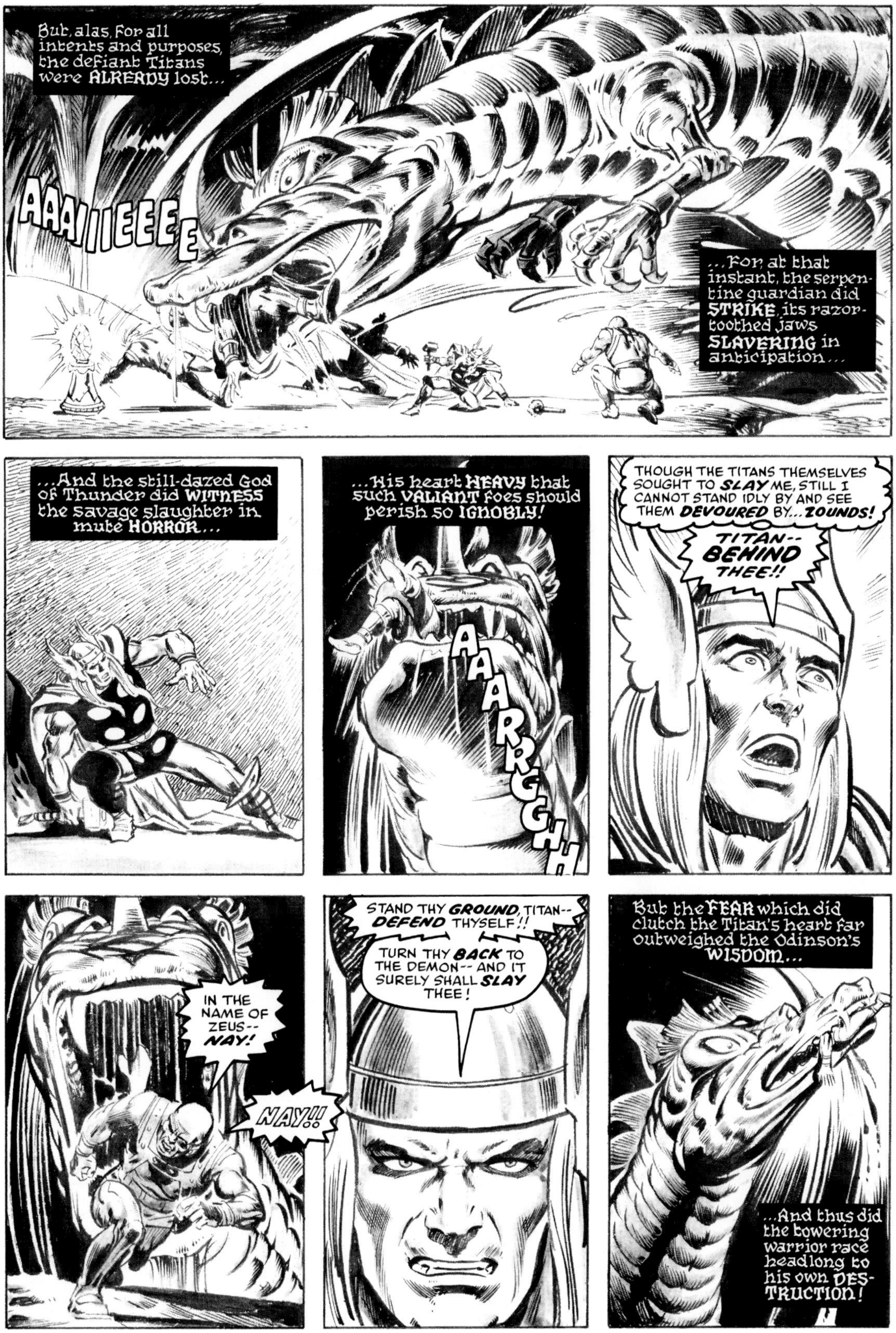
But, alas, for all intents and purposes, the defiant Titans were ALREADY lost...
AAAIIIEEEEE
...For at that instant, the serpentine guardian did STRIKE, its razor-toothed jaws SLAVERING in anticipation...
...And the still-dazed God of Thunder did WITNESS the savage slaughter in mute HORROR...
...His heart HEAVY that such VALIANT foes should perish so IGNOBLY!
AAAARRGGHH
THOUGH THE TITANS THEMSELVES SOUGHT TO SLAY ME, STILL I CANNOT STAND IDLY BY AND SEE THEM DEVOURED BY... ZOUNDS!
TITAN-- BEHIND THEE!!
IN THE NAME OF ZEUS-- NAY!
NAY!!
STAND THY GROUND, TITAN-- DEFEND THYSELF!!
TURN THY BACK TO THE DEMON-- AND IT SURELY SHALL SLAY THEE!
But the FEAR which did clutch the Titan's heart far outweighed the Odinson's WISDOM...
...And thus did the towering warrior race headlong to his own DESTRUCTION!

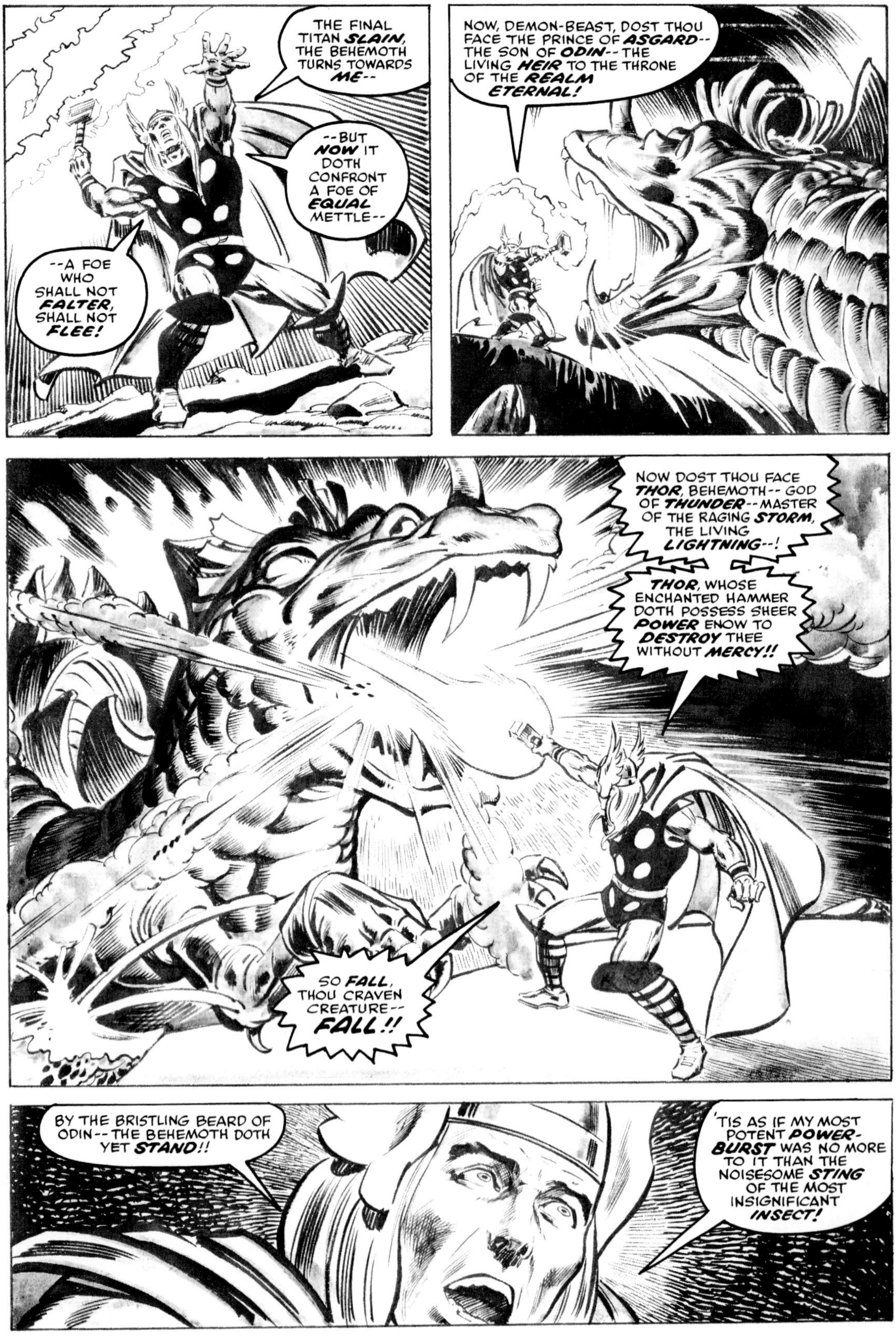
THE FINAL TITAN SLAIN, THE BEHEMOTH TURNS TOWARDS ME--
--BUT NOW IT DOTH CONFRONT A FOE OF EQUAL METTLE--
--A FOE WHO SHALL NOT FALTER, SHALL NOT FLEE!
NOW, DEMON-BEAST, DOST THOU FACE THE PRINCE OF ASGARD-- THE SON OF ODIN-- THE LIVING HEIR TO THE THRONE OF THE REALM ETERNAL!
NOW DOST THOU FACE THOR, BEHEMOTH-- GOD OF THUNDER--MASTER OF THE RAGING STORM, THE LIVING LIGHTNING--!
THOR, WHOSE ENCHANTED HAMMER DOTH POSSESS SHEER POWER ENOW TO DESTROY THEE WITHOUT MERCY!!
SO FALL, THOU CRAVEN CREATURE-- FALL!!
BY THE BRISTLING BEARD OF ODIN-- THE BEHEMOTH DOTH YET STAND!!
'TIS AS IF MY MOST POTENT POWER-BURST WAS NO MORE TO IT THAN THE NOISESOME STING OF THE MOST INSIGNIFICANT INSECT!

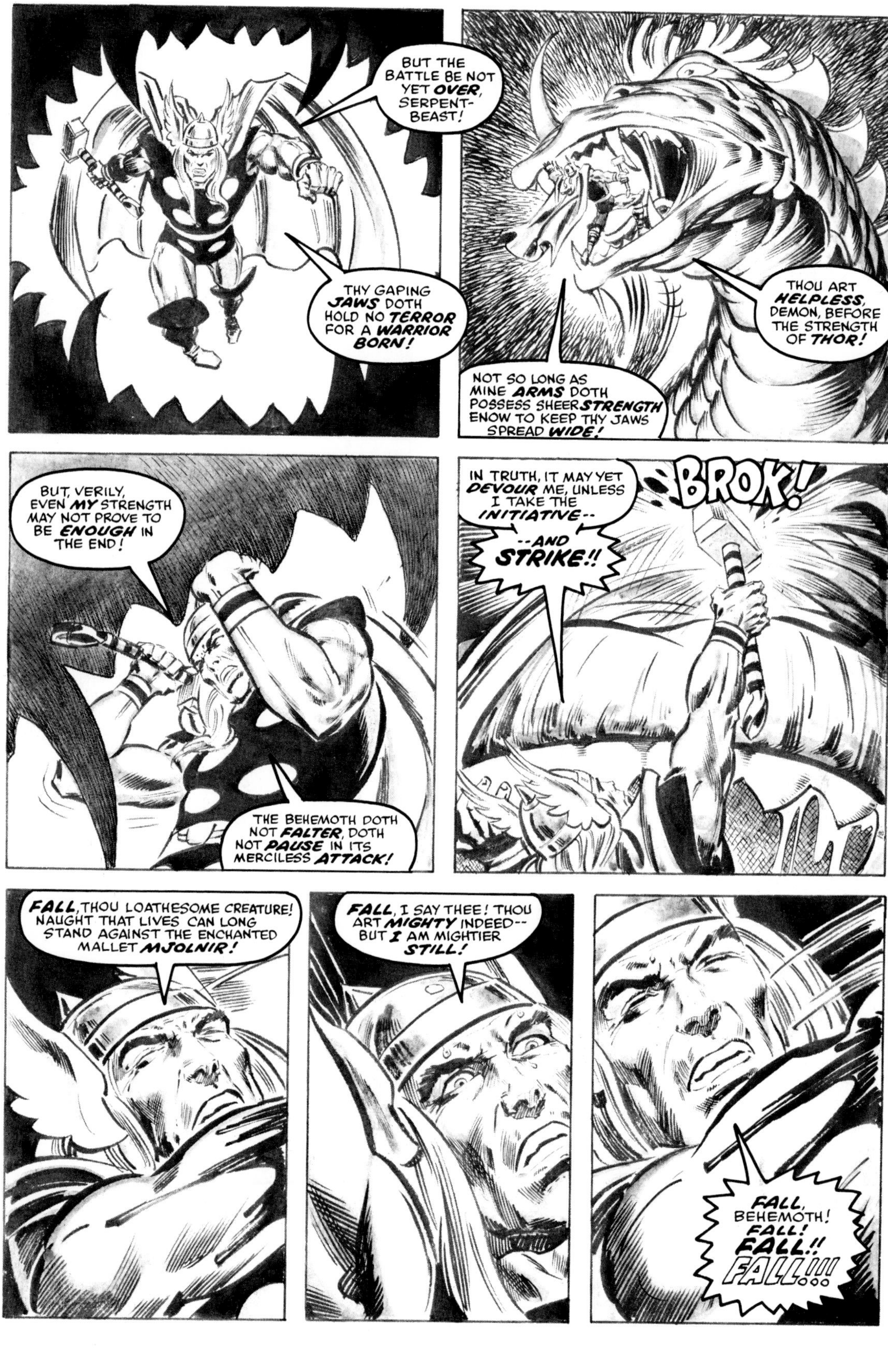
BUT THE BATTLE BE NOT YET OVER, SERPENT-BEAST!
THY GAPING JAWS DOTH HOLD NO TERROR FOR A WARRIOR BORN!
THOU ART HELPLESS, DEMON, BEFORE THE STRENGTH OF THOR!
NOT SO LONG AS MINE ARMS DOTH POSSESS SHEER STRENGTH ENOW TO KEEP THY JAWS SPREAD WIDE!
BUT, VERILY, EVEN MY STRENGTH MAY NOT PROVE TO BE ENOUGH IN THE END!
THE BEHEMOTH DOTH NOT FALTER, DOTH NOT PAUSE IN ITS MERCILESS ATTACK!
IN TRUTH, IT MAY YET DEVOUR ME, UNLESS I TAKE THE INITIATIVE--
--AND STRIKE!!
BROK!
FALL, THOU LOATHESOME CREATURE! NAUGHT THAT LIVES CAN LONG STAND AGAINST THE ENCHANTED MALLET MJOLNIR!
FALL, I SAY THEE! THOU ART MIGHTY INDEED-- BUT I AM MIGHTIER STILL!
FALL, BEHEMOTH! FALL! FALL!! FALL!!!

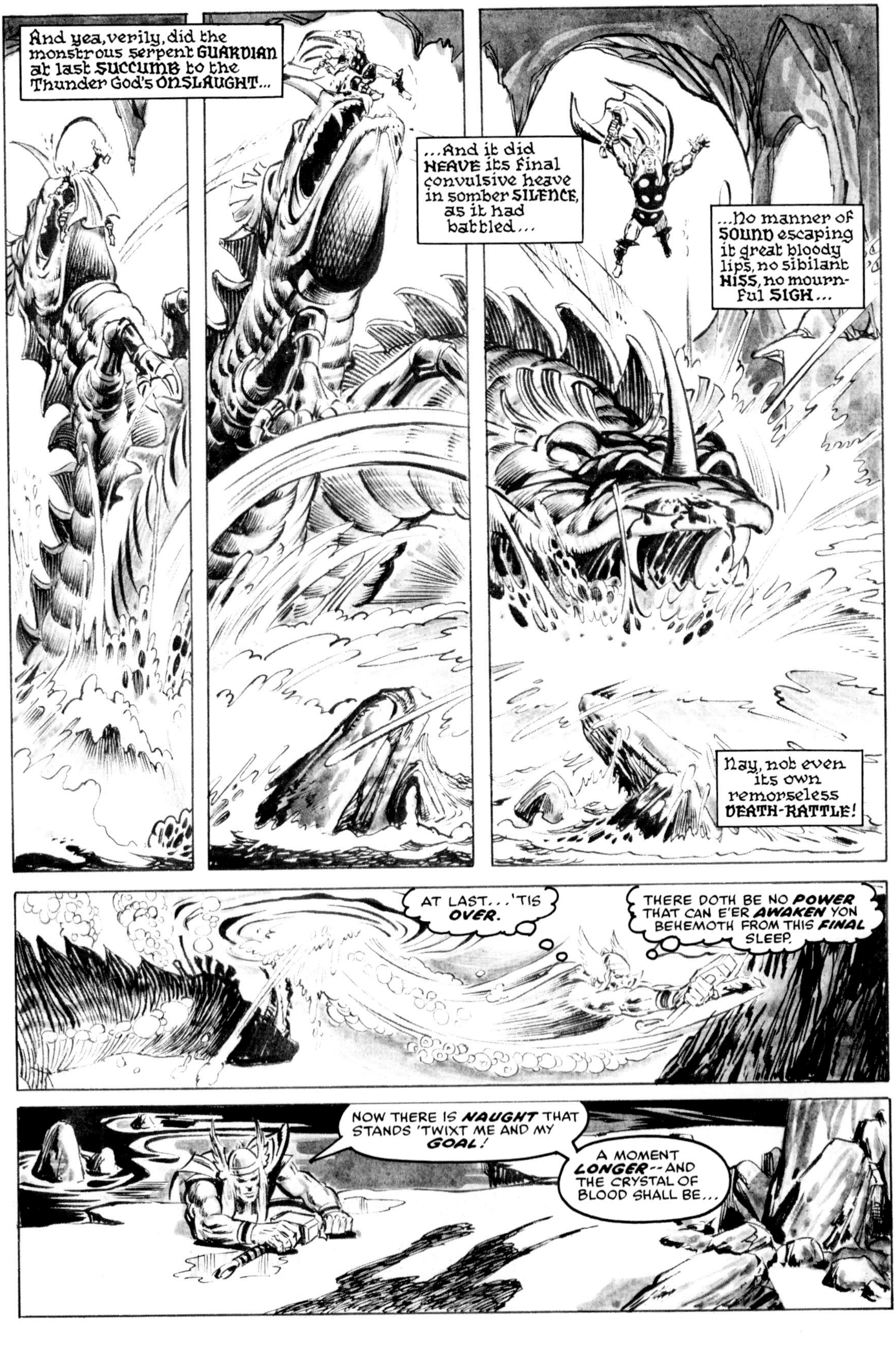
And yea, verily, did the monstrous serpent GUARDIAN at last SUCCUMB to the Thunder God's ONSLAUGHT...
...And it did HEAVE its final convulsive heave in somber SILENCE, as it had battled...
...No manner of SOUND escaping it great bloody lips, no sibilant HISS, no mournful SIGH...
Nay, not even its own remorseless DEATH-RATTLE!
AT LAST... 'TIS OVER.
THERE DOTH BE NO POWER THAT CAN E'ER AWAKEN YON BEHEMOTH FROM THIS FINAL SLEEP.
NOW THERE IS NAUGHT THAT STANDS 'TWIXT ME AND MY GOAL!
A MOMENT LONGER-- AND THE CRYSTAL OF BLOOD SHALL BE...

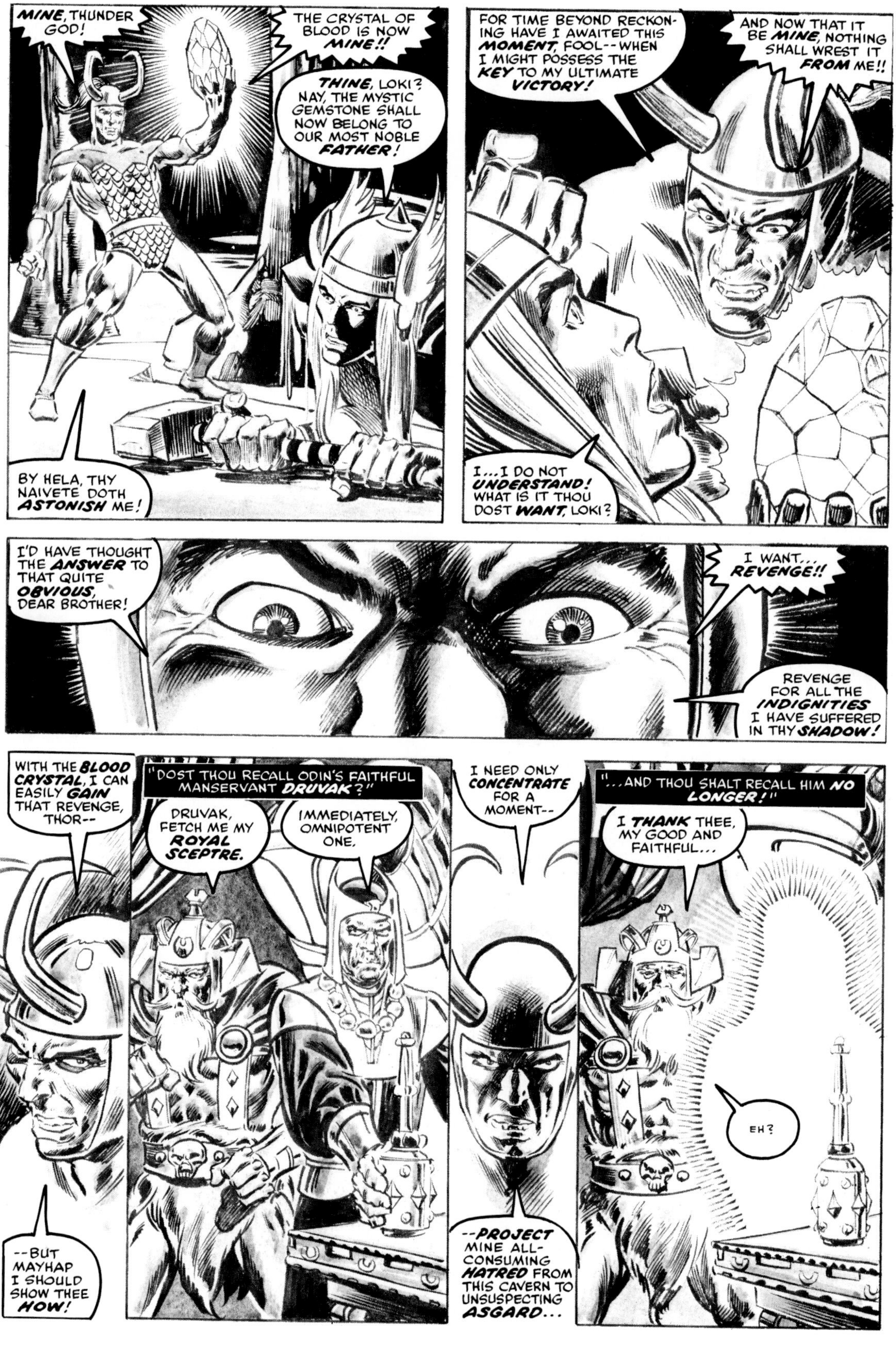
MINE, THUNDER GOD!
THE CRYSTAL OF BLOOD IS NOW MINE!!
THINE, LOKI? NAY, THE MYSTIC GEMSTONE SHALL NOW BELONG TO OUR MOST NOBLE FATHER!
BY HELA, THY NAIVETE DOTH ASTONISH ME!
FOR TIME BEYOND RECKONING HAVE I AWAITED THIS MOMENT, FOOL--WHEN I MIGHT POSSESS THE KEY TO MY ULTIMATE VICTORY!
AND NOW THAT IT BE MINE, NOTHING SHALL WREST IT FROM ME!!
I...I DO NOT UNDERSTAND! WHAT IS IT THOU DOST WANT, LOKI?
I'D HAVE THOUGHT THE ANSWER TO THAT QUITE OBVIOUS, DEAR BROTHER!
I WANT... REVENGE!!
REVENGE FOR ALL THE INDIGNITIES I HAVE SUFFERED IN THY SHADOW!
WITH THE BLOOD CRYSTAL, I CAN EASILY GAIN THAT REVENGE, THOR--
--BUT MAYHAP I SHOULD SHOW THEE HOW!
"DOST THOU RECALL ODIN'S FAITHFUL MANSERVANT DRUVAK?"
DRUVAK, FETCH ME MY ROYAL SCEPTRE.
IMMEDIATELY, OMNIPOTENT ONE.
I NEED ONLY CONCENTRATE FOR A MOMENT--
--PROJECT MINE ALL-CONSUMING HATRED FROM THIS CAVERN TO UNSUSPECTING ASGARD...
"...AND THOU SHALT RECALL HIM NO LONGER!"
I THANK THEE, MY GOOD AND FAITHFUL...
EH?

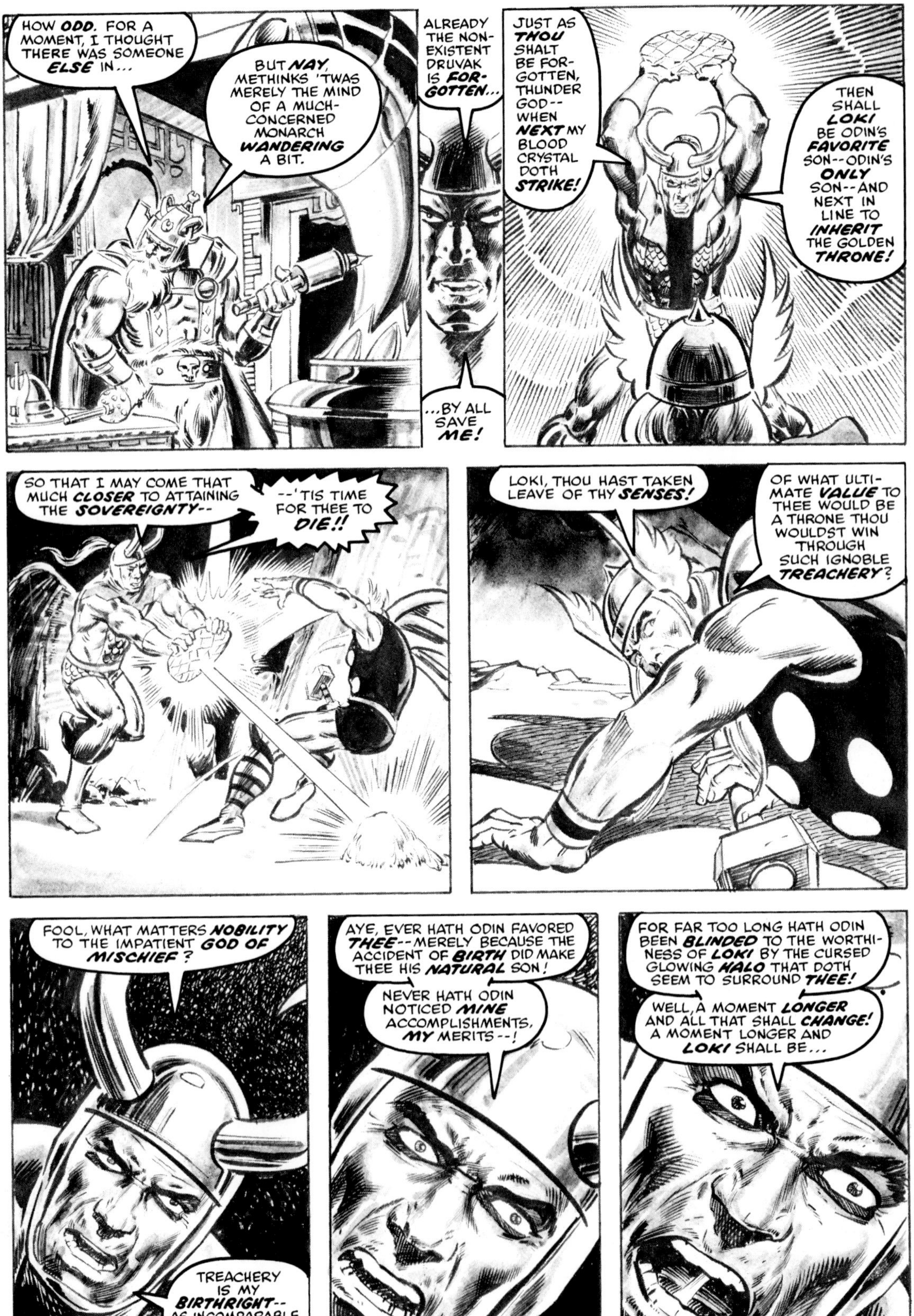

HOW ODD. FOR A MOMENT, I THOUGHT THERE WAS SOMEONE ELSE IN...
BUT NAY, METHINKS 'TWAS MERELY THE MIND OF A MUCH-CONCERNED MONARCH WANDERING A BIT.
ALREADY THE NON-EXISTENT DRUVAK IS FORGOTTEN...
...BY ALL SAVE ME!
JUST AS THOU SHALT BE FORGOTTEN, THUNDER GOD-- WHEN NEXT MY BLOOD CRYSTAL DOTH STRIKE!
THEN SHALL LOKI BE ODIN'S FAVORITE SON--ODIN'S ONLY SON--AND NEXT IN LINE TO INHERIT THE GOLDEN THRONE!
SO THAT I MAY COME THAT MUCH CLOSER TO ATTAINING THE SOVEREIGNTY--
--'TIS TIME FOR THEE TO DIE!!
LOKI, THOU HAST TAKEN LEAVE OF THY SENSES!
OF WHAT ULTIMATE VALUE TO THEE WOULD BE A THRONE THOU WOULDST WIN THROUGH SUCH IGNOBLE TREACHERY?
FOOL, WHAT MATTERS NOBILITY TO THE IMPATIENT GOD OF MISCHIEF?
TREACHERY IS MY BIRTHRIGHT-- AS INCOMPARABLE STRENGTH IS THINE!
AYE, EVER HATH ODIN FAVORED THEE--MERELY BECAUSE THE ACCIDENT OF BIRTH DID MAKE THEE HIS NATURAL SON!
NEVER HATH ODIN NOTICED MINE ACCOMPLISHMENTS, MY MERITS--!
FOR FAR TOO LONG HATH ODIN BEEN BLINDED TO THE WORTHINESS OF LOKI BY THE CURSED GLOWING HALO THAT DOTH SEEM TO SURROUND THEE!
WELL, A MOMENT LONGER AND ALL THAT SHALL CHANGE! A MOMENT LONGER AND LOKI SHALL BE...

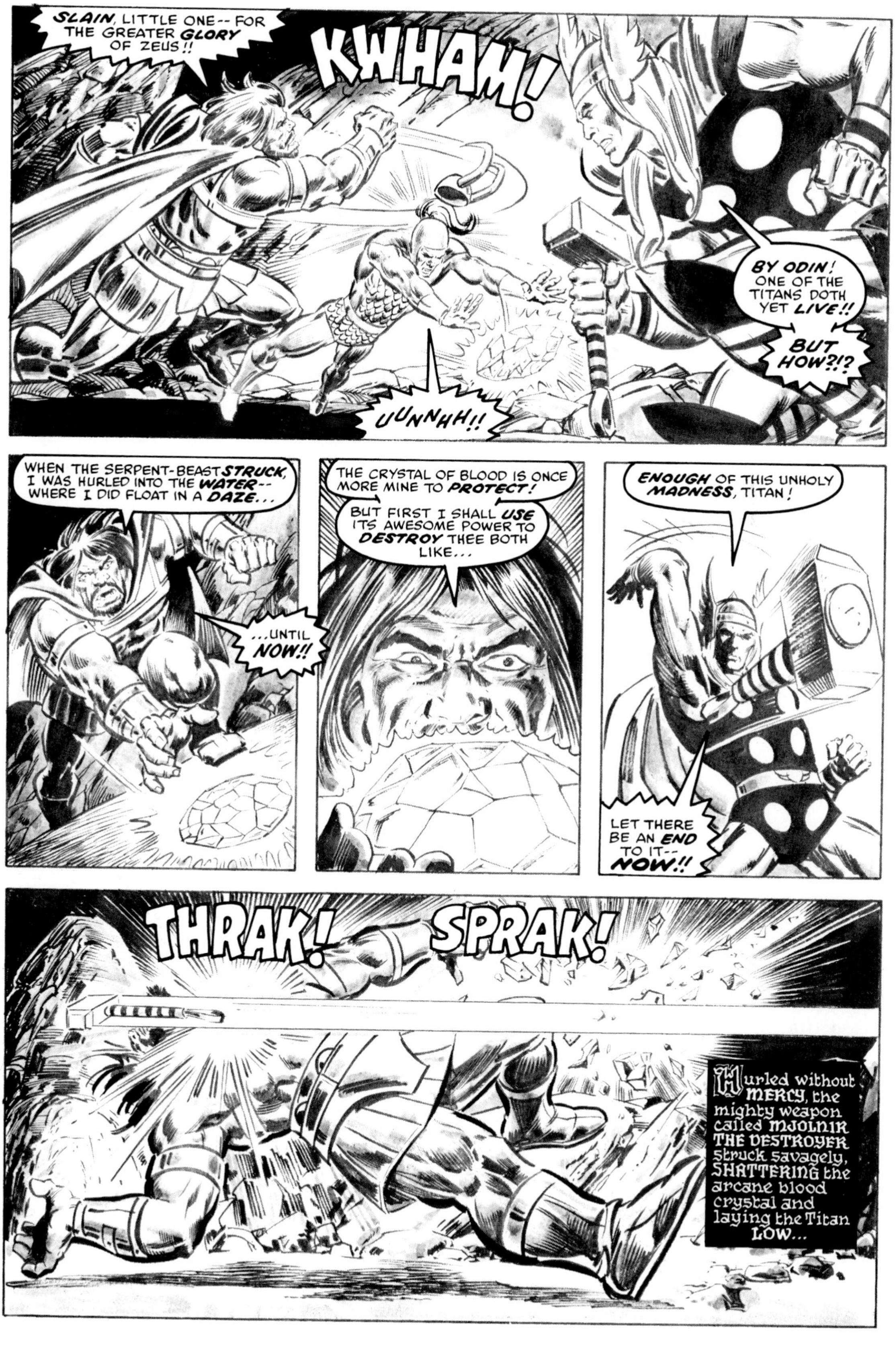
SLAIN, LITTLE ONE-- FOR THE GREATER GLORY OF ZEUS!!
KWHAM!
BY ODIN! ONE OF THE TITANS DOTH YET LIVE!!
BUT HOW?!?
UUNNHH!!
WHEN THE SERPENT-BEAST STRUCK, I WAS HURLED INTO THE WATER-- WHERE I DID FLOAT IN A DAZE...
...UNTIL NOW!!
THE CRYSTAL OF BLOOD IS ONCE MORE MINE TO PROTECT!
BUT FIRST I SHALL USE ITS AWESOME POWER TO DESTROY THEE BOTH LIKE...
ENOUGH OF THIS UNHOLY MADNESS, TITAN!
LET THERE BE AN END TO IT-- NOW!!
THRAK! SPRAK!
Hurled without MERCY, the mighty weapon called MJOLNIR THE DESTROYER struck savagely, SHATTERING the arcane blood crystal and laying the Titan LOW...

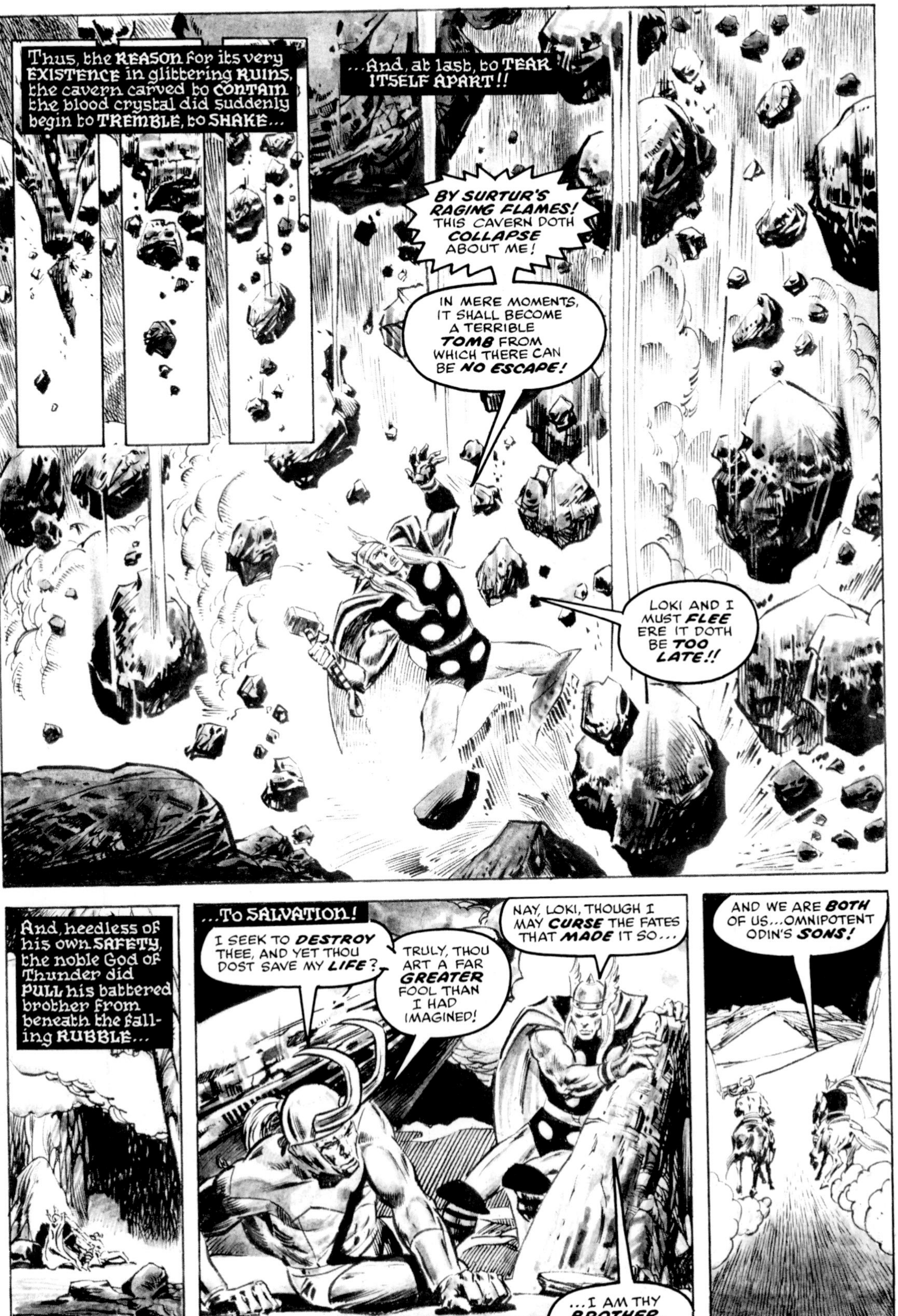
Thus, the REASON for its very EXISTENCE in glittering RUINS, the cavern carved to CONTAIN the blood crystal did suddenly begin to TREMBLE, to SHAKE...
...And, at last, to TEAR ITSELF APART!!
BY SURTUR'S RAGING FLAMES! THIS CAVERN DOTH COLLAPSE ABOUT ME!
IN MERE MOMENTS, IT SHALL BECOME A TERRIBLE TOMB FROM WHICH THERE CAN BE NO ESCAPE!
LOKI AND I MUST FLEE ERE IT DOTH BE TOO LATE!!
And, heedless of his own SAFETY, the noble God of Thunder did PULL his battered brother from beneath the falling RUBBLE...
...To SALVATION!
I SEEK TO DESTROY THEE, AND YET THOU DOST SAVE MY LIFE?
TRULY, THOU ART A FAR GREATER FOOL THAN I HAD IMAGINED!
NAY, LOKI, THOUGH I MAY CURSE THE FATES THAT MADE IT SO...
...I AM THY BROTHER.
AND WE ARE BOTH OF US...OMNIPOTENT ODIN'S SONS!

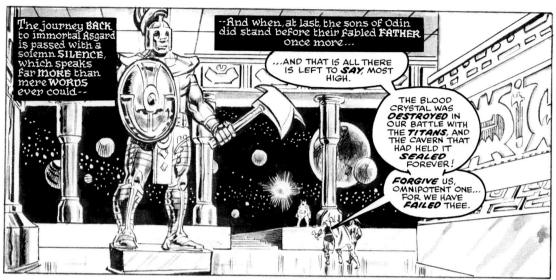

The journey BACK to immortal Asgard is passed with a solemn SILENCE, which speaks far MORE than mere WORDS ever could--

--And when, at last, the sons of Odin did stand before their fabled FATHER once more...

...AND THAT IS ALL THERE IS LEFT TO SAY, MOST HIGH.

THE BLOOD CRYSTAL WAS DESTROYED IN OUR BATTLE WITH THE TITANS, AND THE CAVERN THAT HAD HELD IT SEALED FOREVER!

FORGIVE US, OMNIPOTENT ONE... FOR WE HAVE FAILED THEE.

NAY, THOR--THOU DIDST NOT FAIL ME.

THAT ENCHANTED GEMSTONE WAS FAR TOO POWERFUL TO REMAIN IN EXISTENCE, THUNDER GOD.

BUT WE RETURNED WITHOUT THE BLOOD CRYSTAL, SIRE.

I WOULD HAVE DESTROYED IT MYSELF HADST THOU BROUGHT IT TO ME!

AYE, THOU DIDST WELL...MY GOOD AND FAITHFUL SONS.

THOU ART FREE TO DEPART THE PRESENCE.

NAY, THOR--NOT THEE. I BID THEE REMAIN.

I WOULD HAVE A WORD WITH THEE, THUNDER GOD.

I AM EVER AT THY SERVICE, MILORD.

THEN TELL ME, MY SON... HOW DIDST THY BROTHER LOKI FARE ON THY PERILOUS QUEST?

HE...HE WAS...HE WAS EVERY INCH AN ASGARDIAN, FATHER, TRUE TO HIS NOBLE HERITAGE.

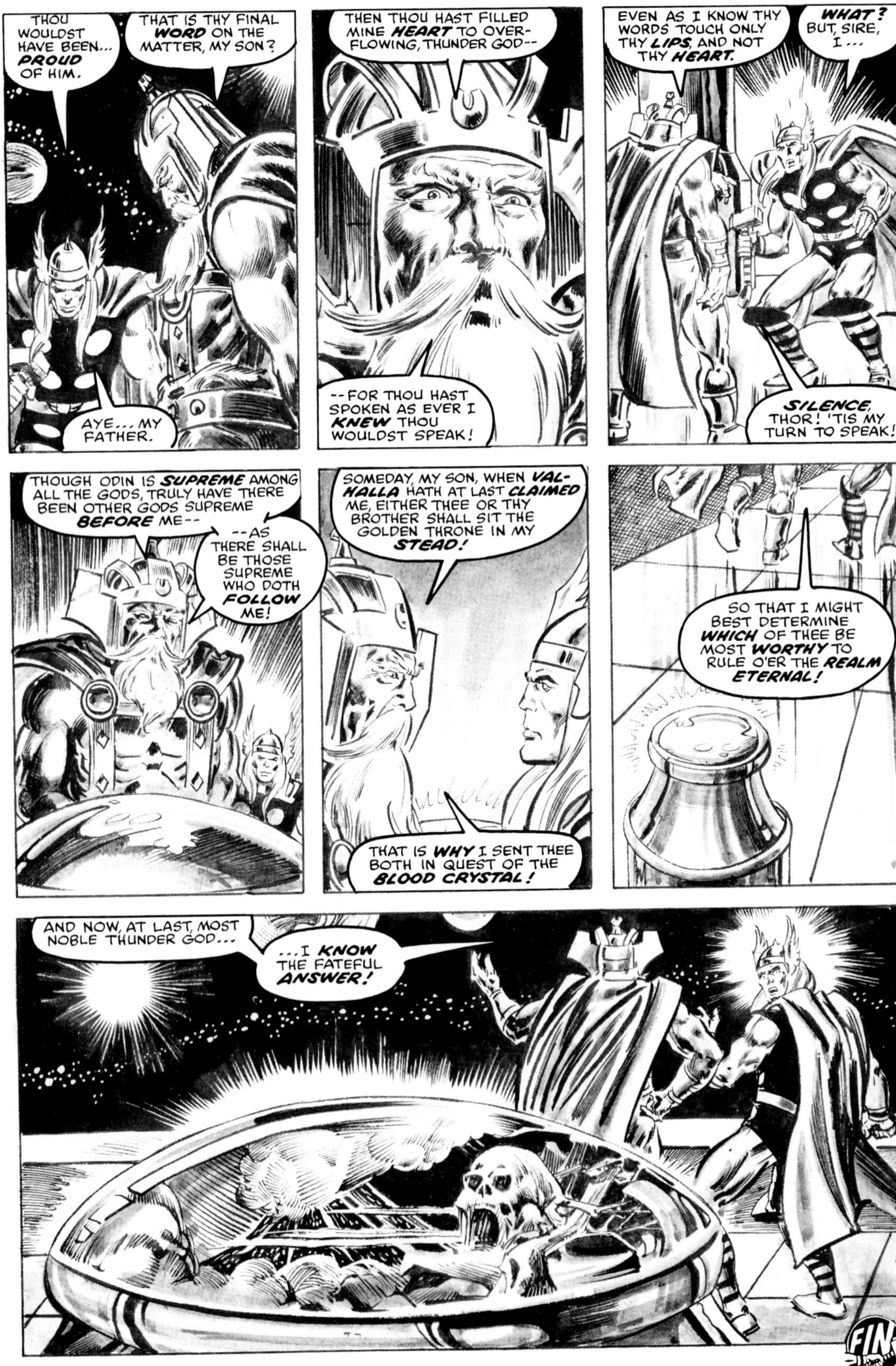
THOU WOULDST HAVE BEEN... PROUD OF HIM.
THAT IS THY FINAL WORD ON THE MATTER, MY SON?
AYE... MY FATHER.
THEN THOU HAST FILLED MINE HEART TO OVERFLOWING, THUNDER GOD--
--FOR THOU HAST SPOKEN AS EVER I KNEW THOU WOULDST SPEAK!
EVEN AS I KNOW THY WORDS TOUCH ONLY THY LIPS, AND NOT THY HEART.
WHAT? BUT, SIRE, I...
SILENCE, THOR! 'TIS MY TURN TO SPEAK!
THOUGH ODIN IS SUPREME AMONG ALL THE GODS, TRULY HAVE THERE BEEN OTHER GODS SUPREME BEFORE ME--
--AS THERE SHALL BE THOSE SUPREME WHO DOTH FOLLOW ME!
SOMEDAY, MY SON, WHEN VALHALLA HATH AT LAST CLAIMED ME, EITHER THEE OR THY BROTHER SHALL SIT THE GOLDEN THRONE IN MY STEAD!
THAT IS WHY I SENT THEE BOTH IN QUEST OF THE BLOOD CRYSTAL!
SO THAT I MIGHT BEST DETERMINE WHICH OF THEE BE MOST WORTHY TO RULE O'ER THE REALM ETERNAL!
AND NOW, AT LAST, MOST NOBLE THUNDER GOD...
...I KNOW THE FATEFUL ANSWER!
FIN

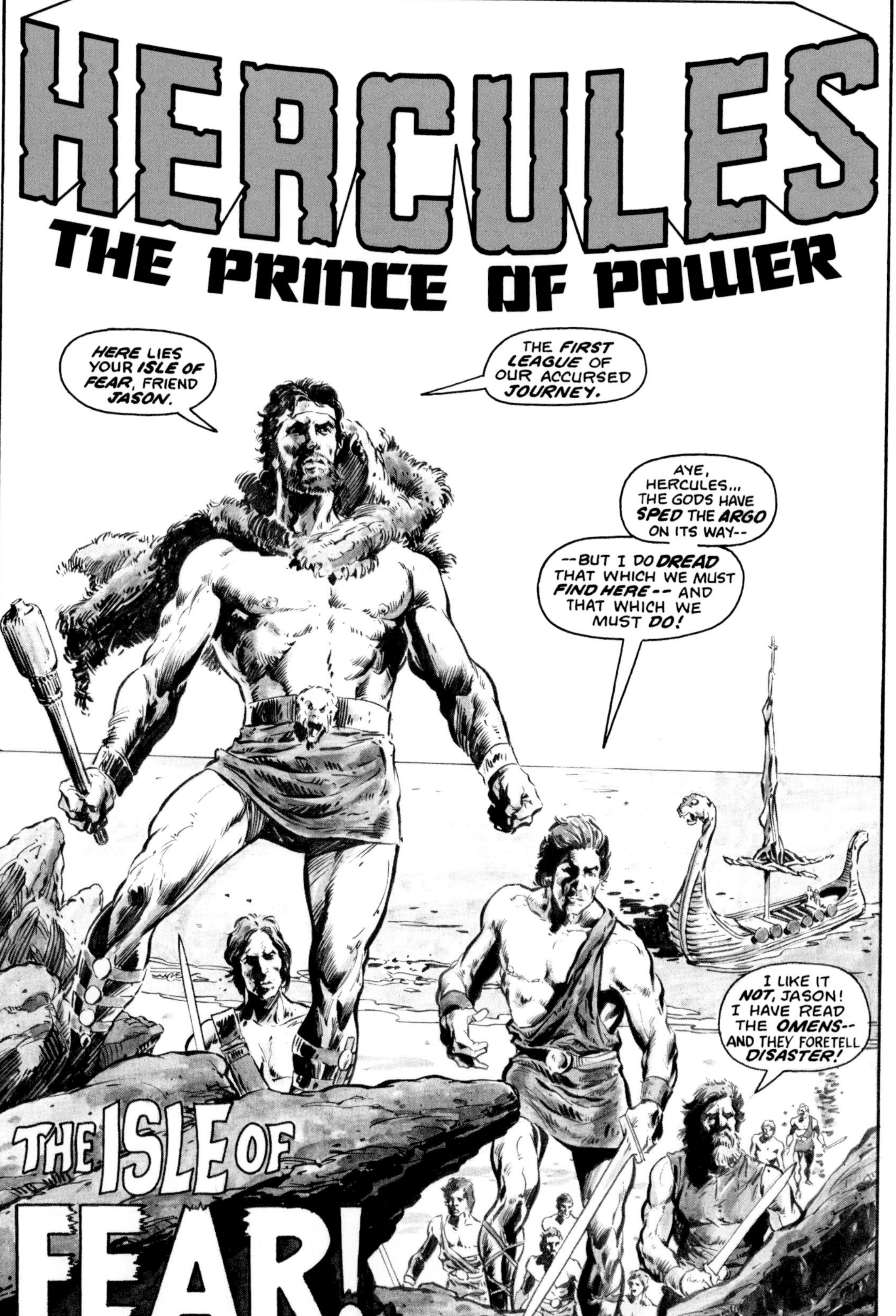
HERCULES
THE PRINCE OF POWER
HERE LIES YOUR ISLE OF FEAR, FRIEND JASON.
THE FIRST LEAGUE OF OUR ACCURSED JOURNEY.
AYE, HERCULES... THE GODS HAVE SPED THE ARGO ON ITS WAY--
--BUT I DO DREAD THAT WHICH WE MUST FIND HERE -- AND THAT WHICH WE MUST DO!
I LIKE IT NOT, JASON! I HAVE READ THE OMENS-- AND THEY FORETELL DISASTER!
THE ISLE OF FEAR!

Story: BILL MANTLO / Art: VAL MAYERIK

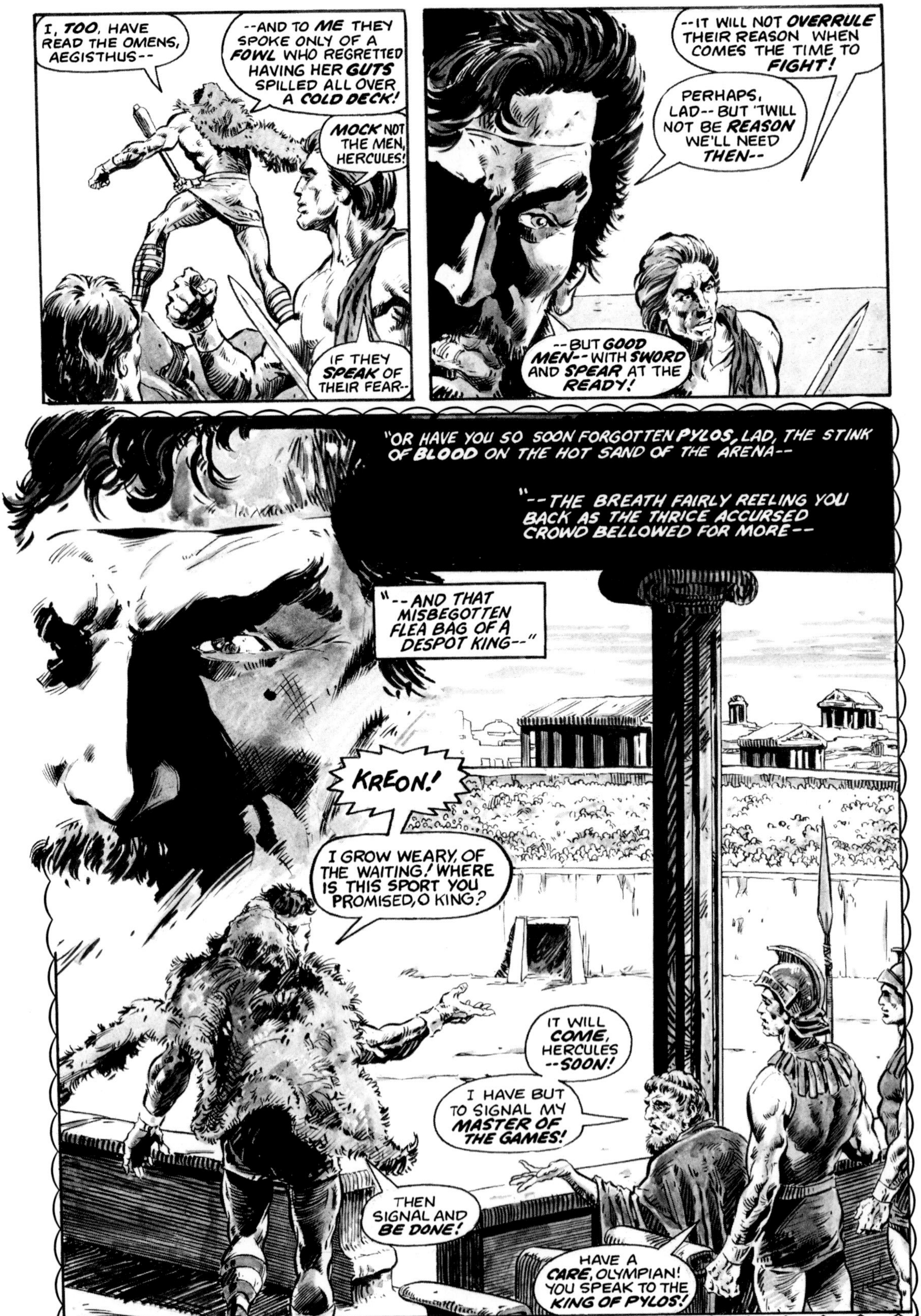
I, TOO, HAVE READ THE OMENS, AEGISTHUS--
--AND TO ME THEY SPOKE ONLY OF A FOWL WHO REGRETTED HAVING HER GUTS SPILLED ALL OVER A COLD DECK!
MOCK NOT THE MEN, HERCULES!
IF THEY SPEAK OF THEIR FEAR--
--IT WILL NOT OVERRULE THEIR REASON WHEN COMES THE TIME TO FIGHT!
PERHAPS, LAD-- BUT 'TWILL NOT BE REASON WE'LL NEED THEN--
--BUT GOOD MEN-- WITH SWORD AND SPEAR AT THE READY!
"OR HAVE YOU SO SOON FORGOTTEN PYLOS, LAD, THE STINK OF BLOOD ON THE HOT SAND OF THE ARENA--
"--THE BREATH FAIRLY REELING YOU BACK AS THE THRICE ACCURSED CROWD BELLOWED FOR MORE--
"--AND THAT MISBEGOTTEN FLEA BAG OF A DESPOT KING--"
KREON!
I GROW WEARY OF THE WAITING! WHERE IS THIS SPORT YOU PROMISED, O KING?
IT WILL COME, HERCULES --SOON!
I HAVE BUT TO SIGNAL MY MASTER OF THE GAMES!
THEN SIGNAL AND BE DONE!
HAVE A CARE, OLYMPIAN! YOU SPEAK TO THE KING OF PYLOS!

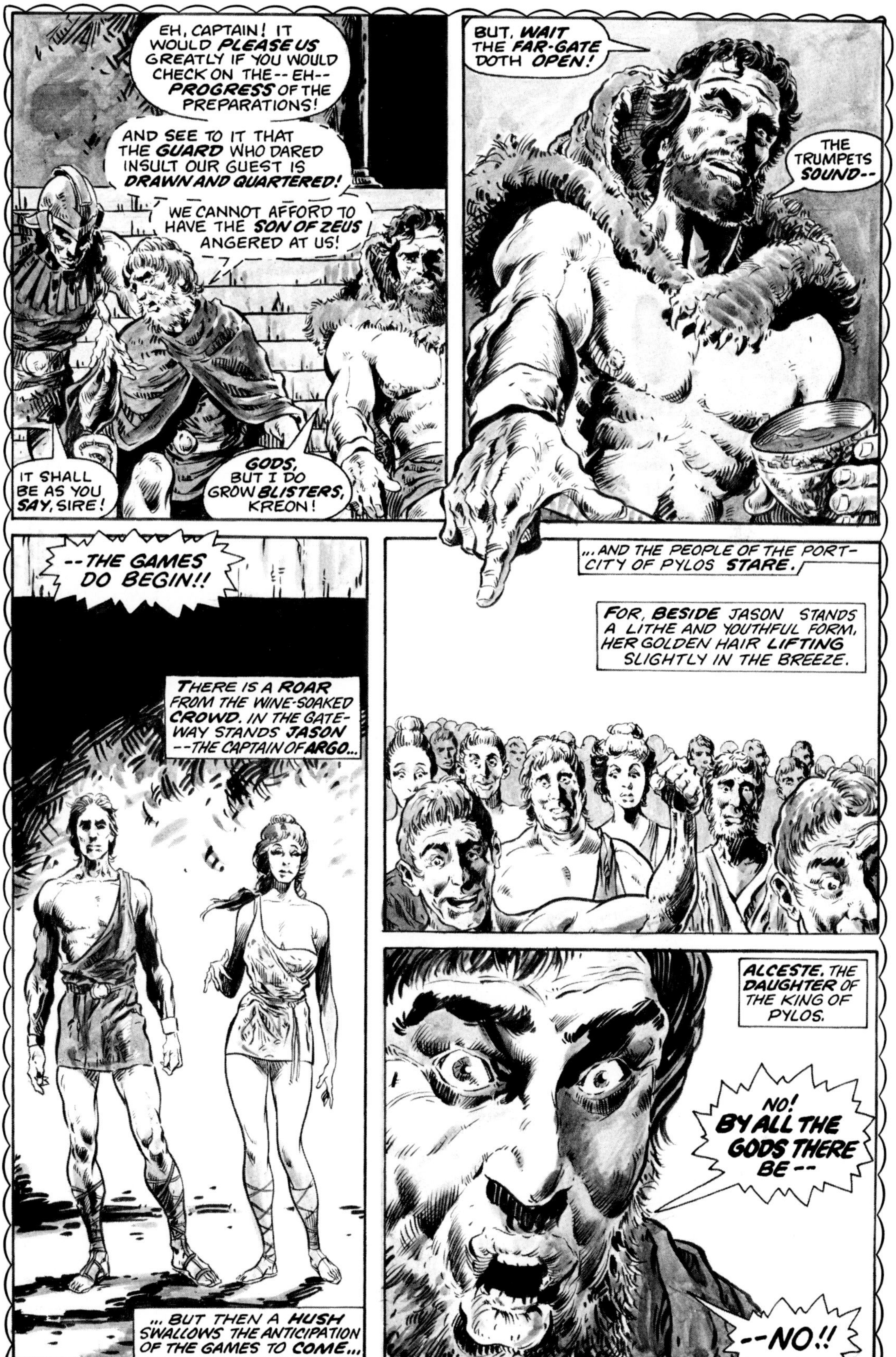
EH, CAPTAIN! IT WOULD PLEASE US GREATLY IF YOU WOULD CHECK ON THE-- EH-- PROGRESS OF THE PREPARATIONS!
AND SEE TO IT THAT THE GUARD WHO DARED INSULT OUR GUEST IS DRAWN AND QUARTERED!
WE CANNOT AFFORD TO HAVE THE SON OF ZEUS ANGERED AT US!
IT SHALL BE AS YOU SAY, SIRE!
GODS, BUT I DO GROW BLISTERS, KREON!
BUT, WAIT THE FAR-GATE DOTH OPEN!
THE TRUMPETS SOUND--
--THE GAMES DO BEGIN!!
THERE IS A ROAR FROM THE WINE-SOAKED CROWD. IN THE GATEWAY STANDS JASON --THE CAPTAIN OF ARGO...
... BUT THEN A HUSH SWALLOWS THE ANTICIPATION OF THE GAMES TO COME...
...AND THE PEOPLE OF THE PORT-CITY OF PYLOS STARE.
FOR, BESIDE JASON STANDS A LITHE AND YOUTHFUL FORM, HER GOLDEN HAIR LIFTING SLIGHTLY IN THE BREEZE.
ALCESTE, THE DAUGHTER OF THE KING OF PYLOS.
NO! BY ALL THE GODS THERE BE --
--NO!!

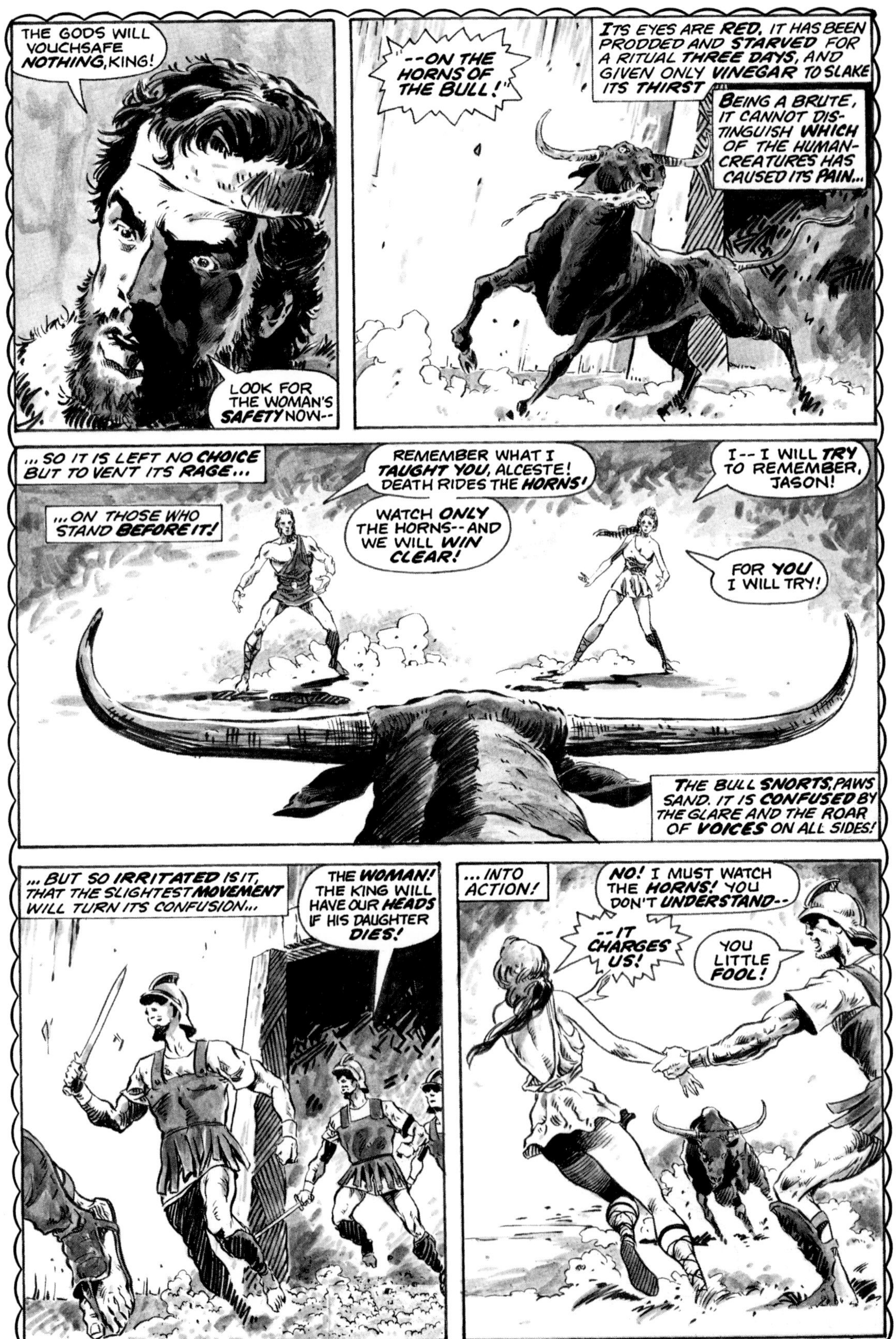
THE GODS WILL VOUCHSAFE NOTHING, KING!
LOOK FOR THE WOMAN'S SAFETY NOW--
"--ON THE HORNS OF THE BULL!"
ITS EYES ARE RED, IT HAS BEEN PRODDED AND STARVED FOR A RITUAL THREE DAYS, AND GIVEN ONLY VINEGAR TO SLAKE ITS THIRST
BEING A BRUTE, IT CANNOT DISTINGUISH WHICH OF THE HUMAN-CREATURES HAS CAUSED ITS PAIN...
...SO IT IS LEFT NO CHOICE BUT TO VENT ITS RAGE...
REMEMBER WHAT I TAUGHT YOU, ALCESTE! DEATH RIDES THE HORNS!
I-- I WILL TRY TO REMEMBER, JASON!
...ON THOSE WHO STAND BEFORE IT!
WATCH ONLY THE HORNS-- AND WE WILL WIN CLEAR!
FOR YOU I WILL TRY!
THE BULL SNORTS, PAWS SAND. IT IS CONFUSED BY THE GLARE AND THE ROAR OF VOICES ON ALL SIDES!
...BUT SO IRRITATED IS IT, THAT THE SLIGHTEST MOVEMENT WILL TURN ITS CONFUSION...
THE WOMAN! THE KING WILL HAVE OUR HEADS IF HIS DAUGHTER DIES!
...INTO ACTION!
NO! I MUST WATCH THE HORNS! YOU DON'T UNDERSTAND--
--IT CHARGES US!
YOU LITTLE FOOL!

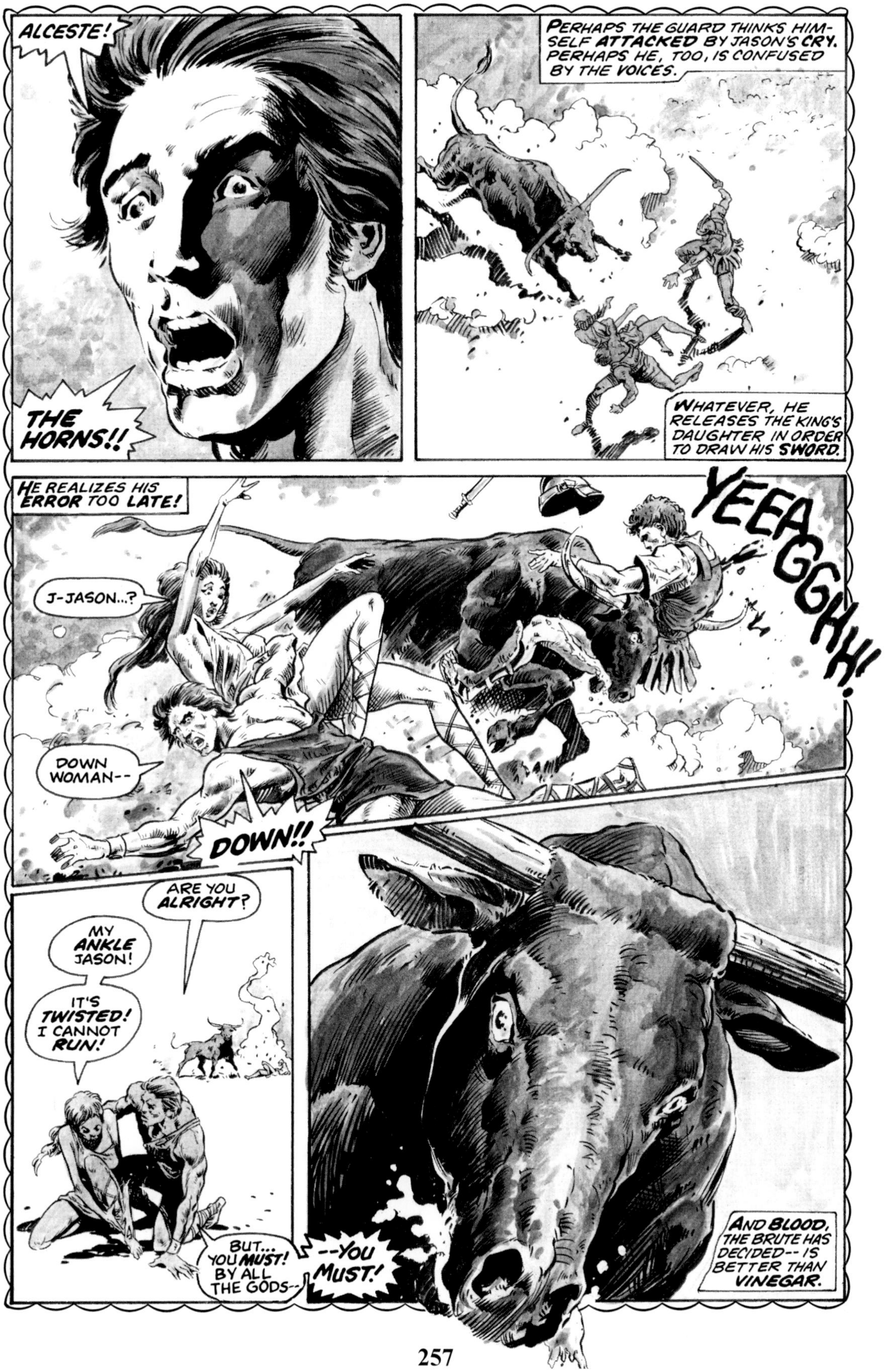
ALCESTE!
THE HORNS!!
PERHAPS THE GUARD THINKS HIMSELF ATTACKED BY JASON'S CRY. PERHAPS HE, TOO, IS CONFUSED BY THE VOICES.
WHATEVER, HE RELEASES THE KING'S DAUGHTER IN ORDER TO DRAW HIS SWORD.
HE REALIZES HIS ERROR TOO LATE!
YEEAGGHH!
J-JASON...?
DOWN WOMAN--
DOWN!!
ARE YOU ALRIGHT?
MY ANKLE JASON!
IT'S TWISTED! I CANNOT RUN!
BUT... YOU MUST! BY ALL THE GODS--
--YOU MUST!
AND BLOOD, THE BRUTE HAS DECIDED-- IS BETTER THAN VINEGAR.

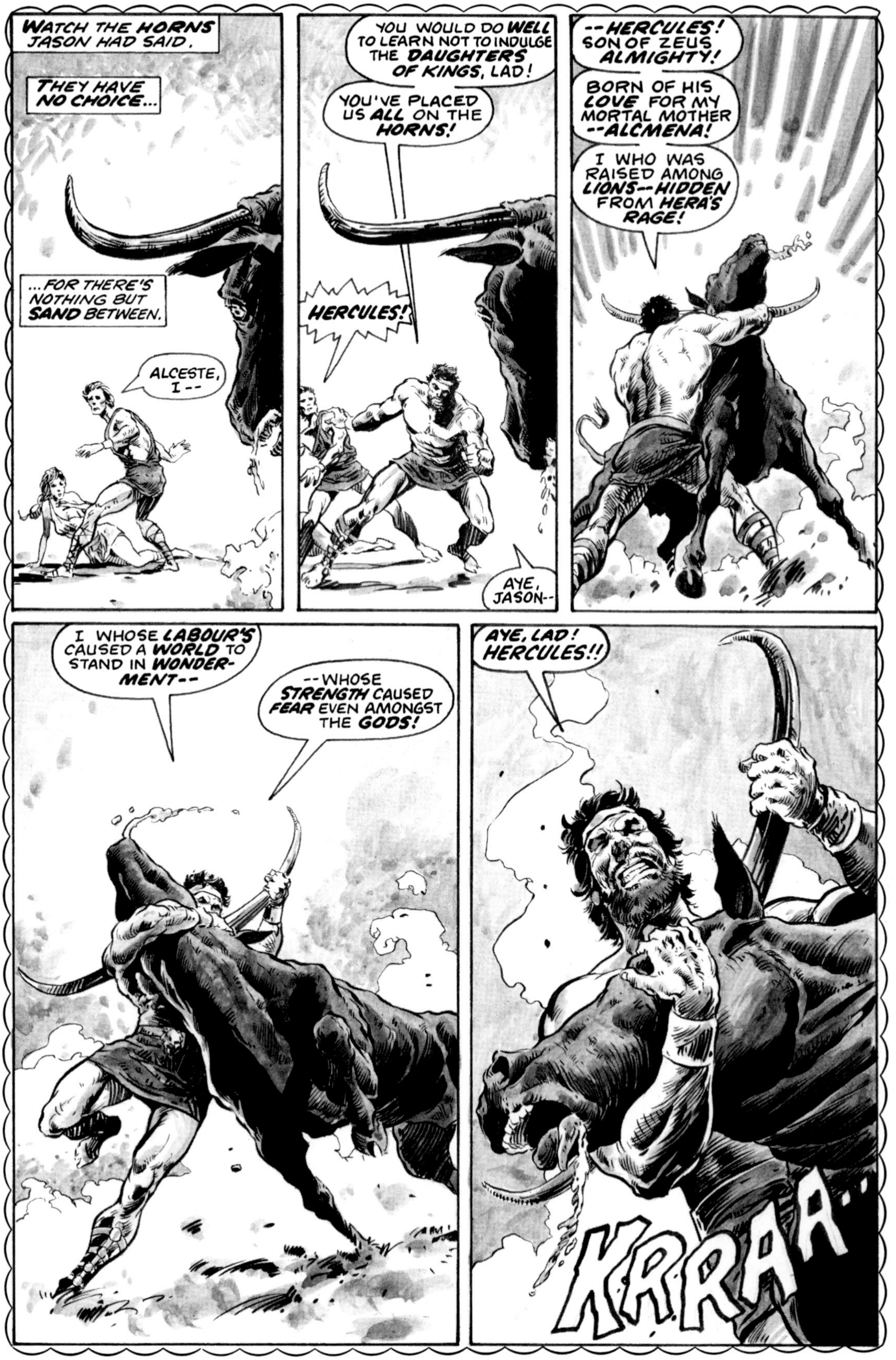
WATCH THE HORNS JASON HAD SAID.
THEY HAVE NO CHOICE...
...FOR THERE'S NOTHING BUT SAND BETWEEN.
ALCESTE, I--
YOU WOULD DO WELL TO LEARN NOT TO INDULGE THE DAUGHTERS OF KINGS, LAD!
YOU'VE PLACED US ALL ON THE HORNS!
HERCULES!
AYE, JASON--
--HERCULES! SON OF ZEUS ALMIGHTY!
BORN OF HIS LOVE FOR MY MORTAL MOTHER --ALCMENA!
I WHO WAS RAISED AMONG LIONS--HIDDEN FROM HERA'S RAGE!
I WHOSE LABOUR'S CAUSED A WORLD TO STAND IN WONDER-MENT--
--WHOSE STRENGTH CAUSED FEAR EVEN AMONGST THE GODS!
AYE, LAD! HERCULES!!
KRRAA...

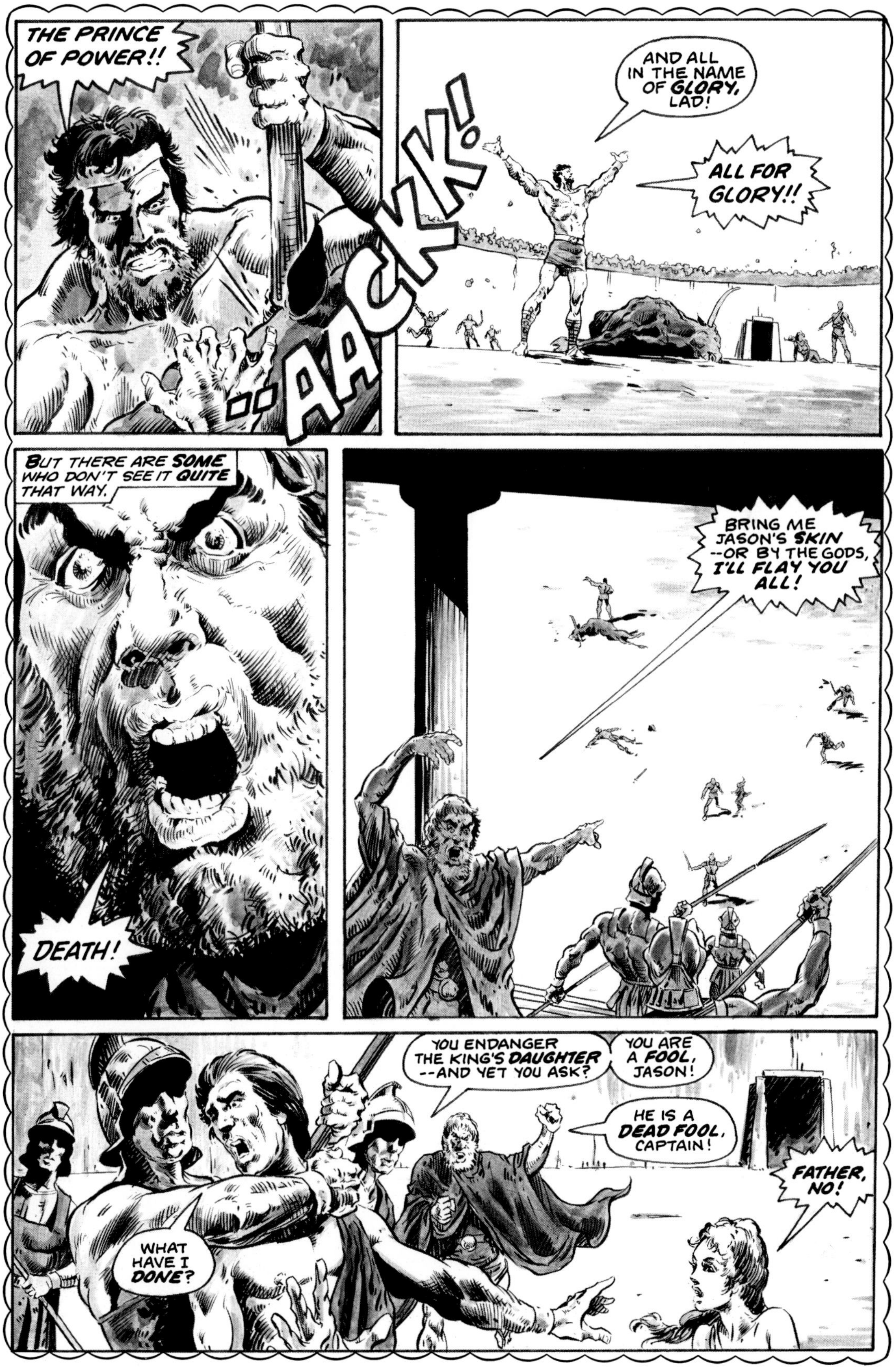
THE PRINCE OF POWER!!
..AACK!
AND ALL IN THE NAME OF GLORY, LAD!
ALL FOR GLORY!!
BUT THERE ARE SOME WHO DON'T SEE IT QUITE THAT WAY.
DEATH!
BRING ME JASON'S SKIN --OR BY THE GODS, I'LL FLAY YOU ALL!
YOU ENDANGER THE KING'S DAUGHTER --AND YET YOU ASK?
YOU ARE A FOOL, JASON!
HE IS A DEAD FOOL, CAPTAIN!
FATHER, NO!
WHAT HAVE I DONE?

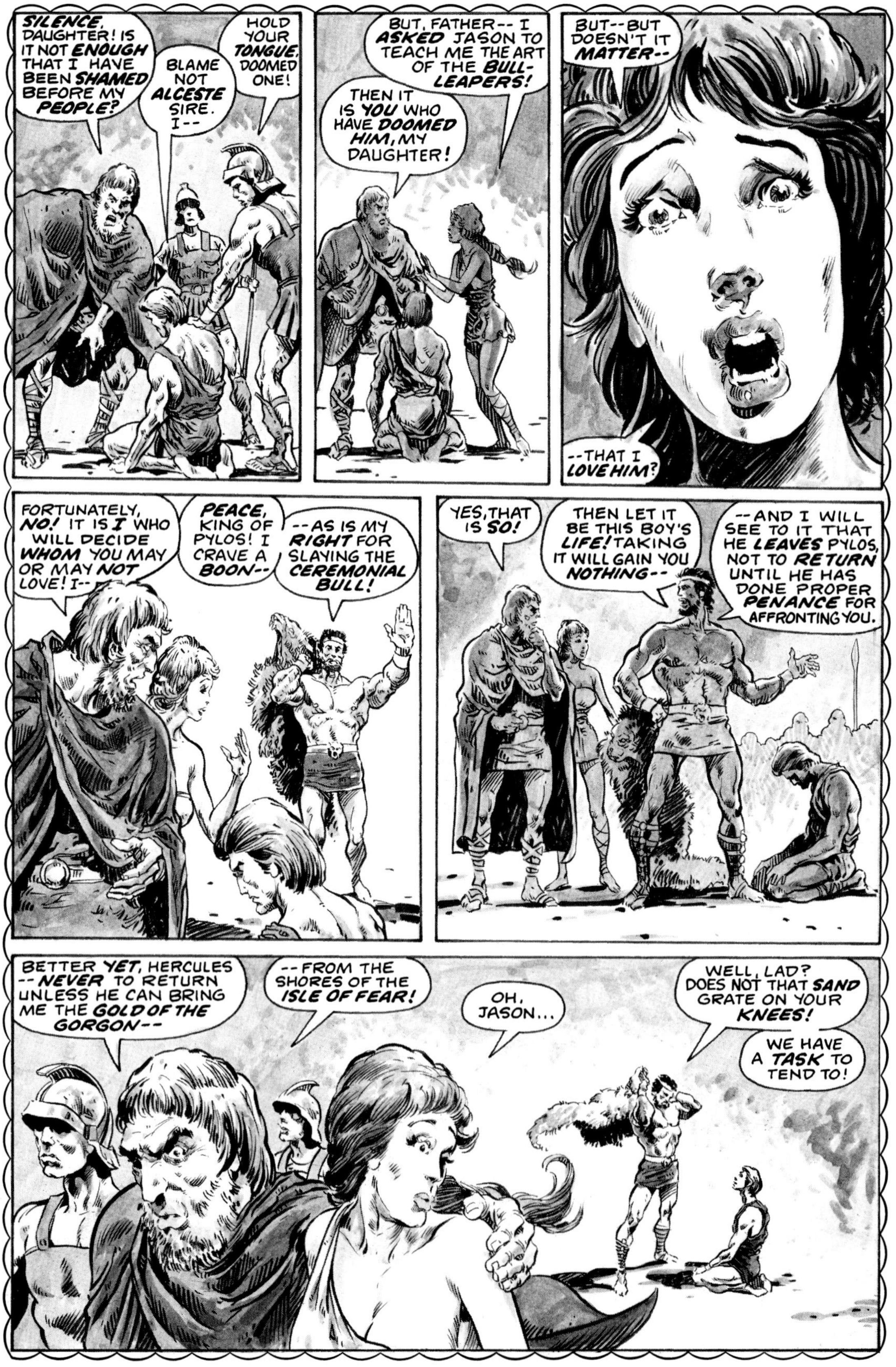
SILENCE, DAUGHTER! IS IT NOT ENOUGH THAT I HAVE BEEN SHAMED BEFORE MY PEOPLE?
BLAME NOT ALCESTE SIRE. I--
HOLD YOUR TONGUE, DOOMED ONE!
BUT, FATHER-- I ASKED JASON TO TEACH ME THE ART OF THE BULL-LEAPERS!
THEN IT IS YOU WHO HAVE DOOMED HIM, MY DAUGHTER!
BUT--BUT DOESN'T IT MATTER--
--THAT I LOVE HIM?
FORTUNATELY, NO! IT IS I WHO WILL DECIDE WHOM YOU MAY OR MAY NOT LOVE! I--
PEACE, KING OF PYLOS! I CRAVE A BOON--
--AS IS MY RIGHT FOR SLAYING THE CEREMONIAL BULL!
YES, THAT IS SO!
THEN LET IT BE THIS BOY'S LIFE! TAKING IT WILL GAIN YOU NOTHING--
--AND I WILL SEE TO IT THAT HE LEAVES PYLOS, NOT TO RETURN UNTIL HE HAS DONE PROPER PENANCE FOR AFFRONTING YOU.
BETTER YET, HERCULES --NEVER TO RETURN UNLESS HE CAN BRING ME THE GOLD OF THE GORGON--
--FROM THE SHORES OF THE ISLE OF FEAR!
OH, JASON...
WELL, LAD? DOES NOT THAT SAND GRATE ON YOUR KNEES!
WE HAVE A TASK TO TEND TO!

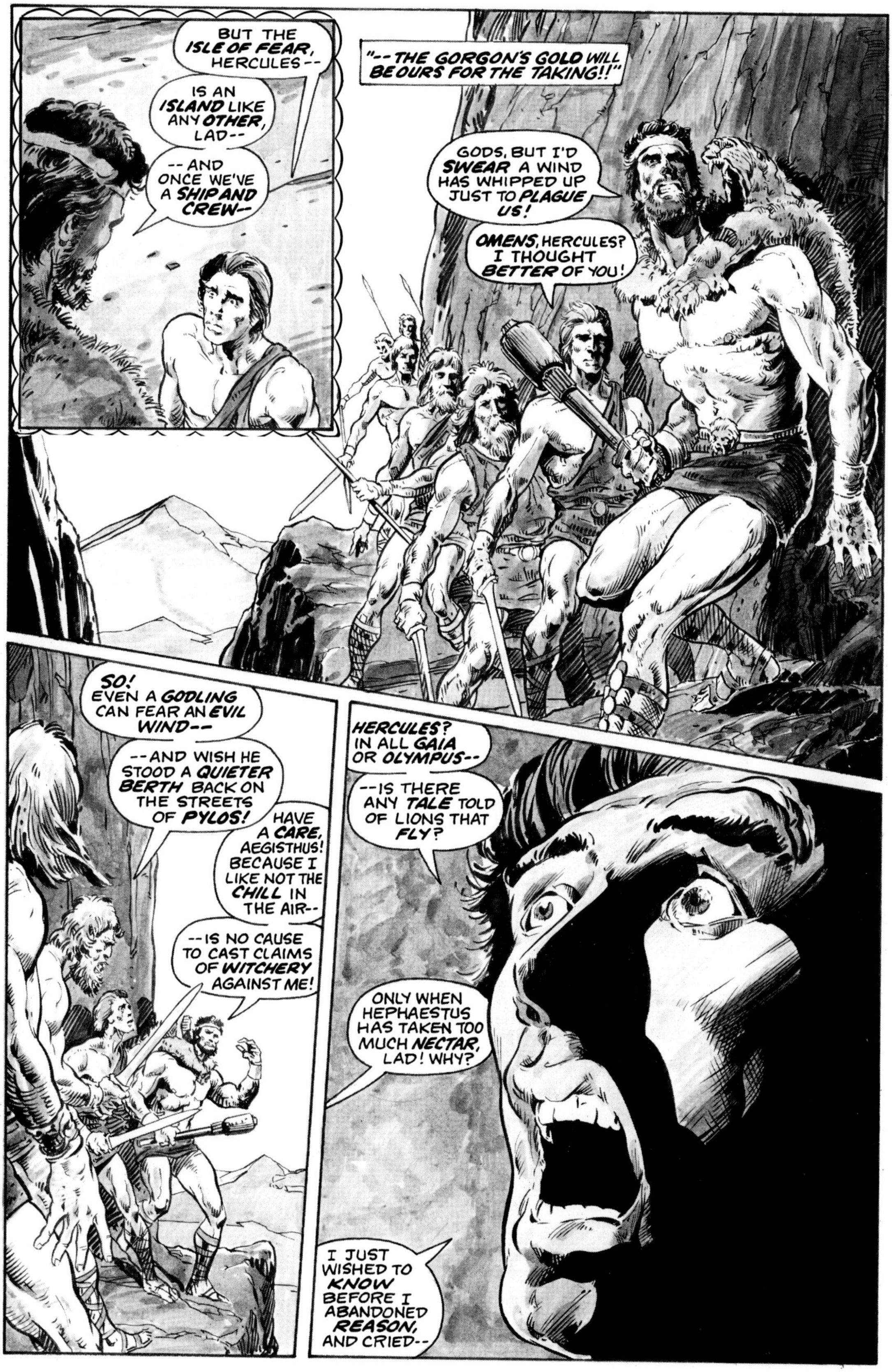

BUT THE ISLE OF FEAR, HERCULES--
IS AN ISLAND LIKE ANY OTHER, LAD--
--AND ONCE WE'VE A SHIP AND CREW--
"--THE GORGON'S GOLD WILL BE OURS FOR THE TAKING!!"
GODS, BUT I'D SWEAR A WIND HAS WHIPPED UP JUST TO PLAGUE US!
OMENS, HERCULES? I THOUGHT BETTER OF YOU!
SO! EVEN A GODLING CAN FEAR AN EVIL WIND--
--AND WISH HE STOOD A QUIETER BERTH BACK ON THE STREETS OF PYLOS!
HAVE A CARE, AEGISTHUS! BECAUSE I LIKE NOT THE CHILL IN THE AIR--
--IS NO CAUSE TO CAST CLAIMS OF WITCHERY AGAINST ME!
HERCULES? IN ALL GAIA OR OLYMPUS--
--IS THERE ANY TALE TOLD OF LIONS THAT FLY?
ONLY WHEN HEPHAESTUS HAS TAKEN TOO MUCH NECTAR, LAD! WHY?
I JUST WISHED TO KNOW BEFORE I ABANDONED REASON, AND CRIED--

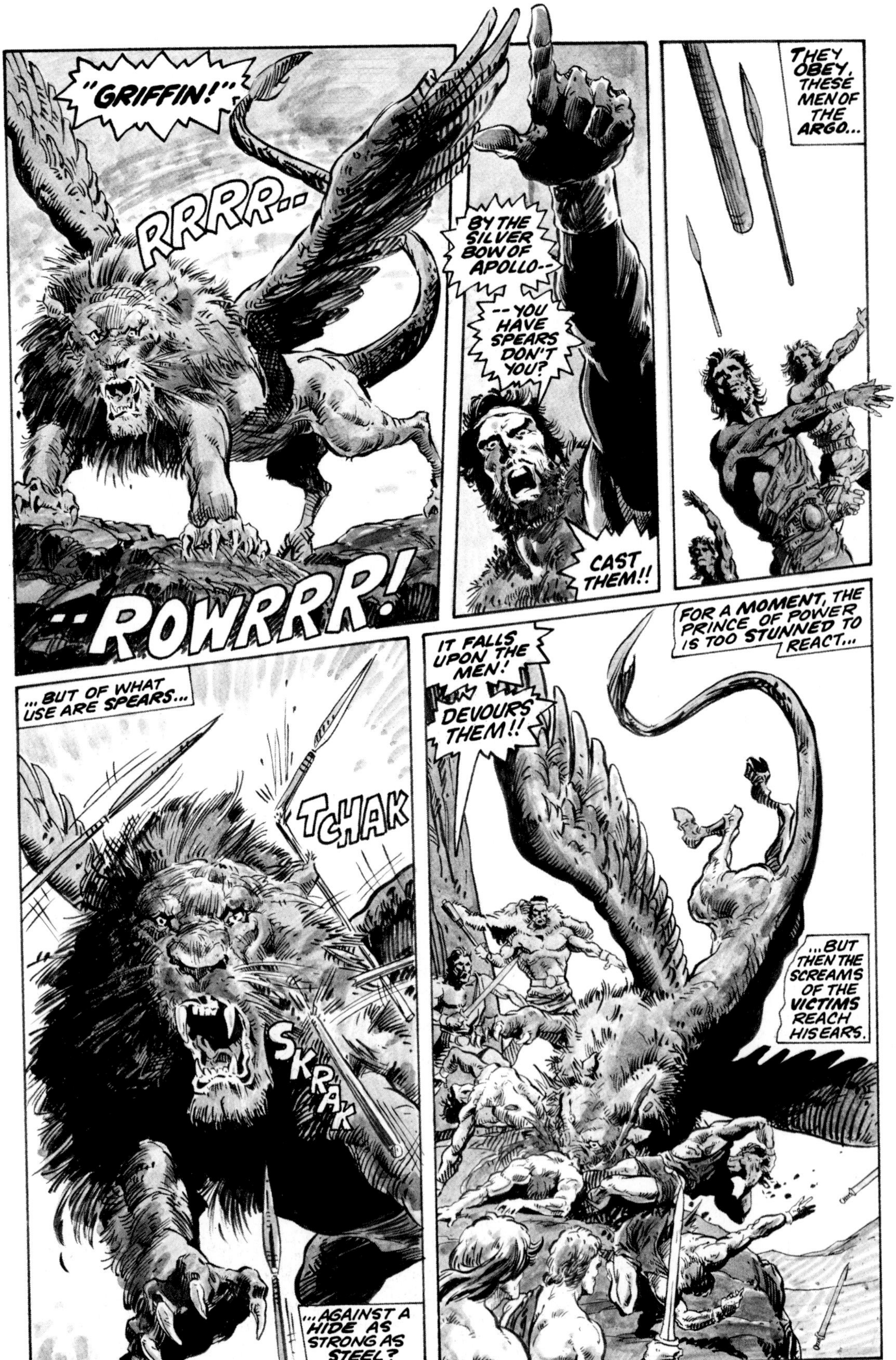
"GRIFFIN!"
RRRR..
..ROWRRR!
BY THE SILVER BOW OF APOLLO--
--YOU HAVE SPEARS DON'T YOU?
CAST THEM!!
THEY OBEY, THESE MEN OF THE ARGO...
...BUT OF WHAT USE ARE SPEARS...
TCHAK
SKRAK
...AGAINST A HIDE AS STRONG AS STEEL?
FOR A MOMENT, THE PRINCE OF POWER IS TOO STUNNED TO REACT...
IT FALLS UPON THE MEN!
DEVOURS THEM!!
...BUT THEN THE SCREAMS OF THE VICTIMS REACH HIS EARS.

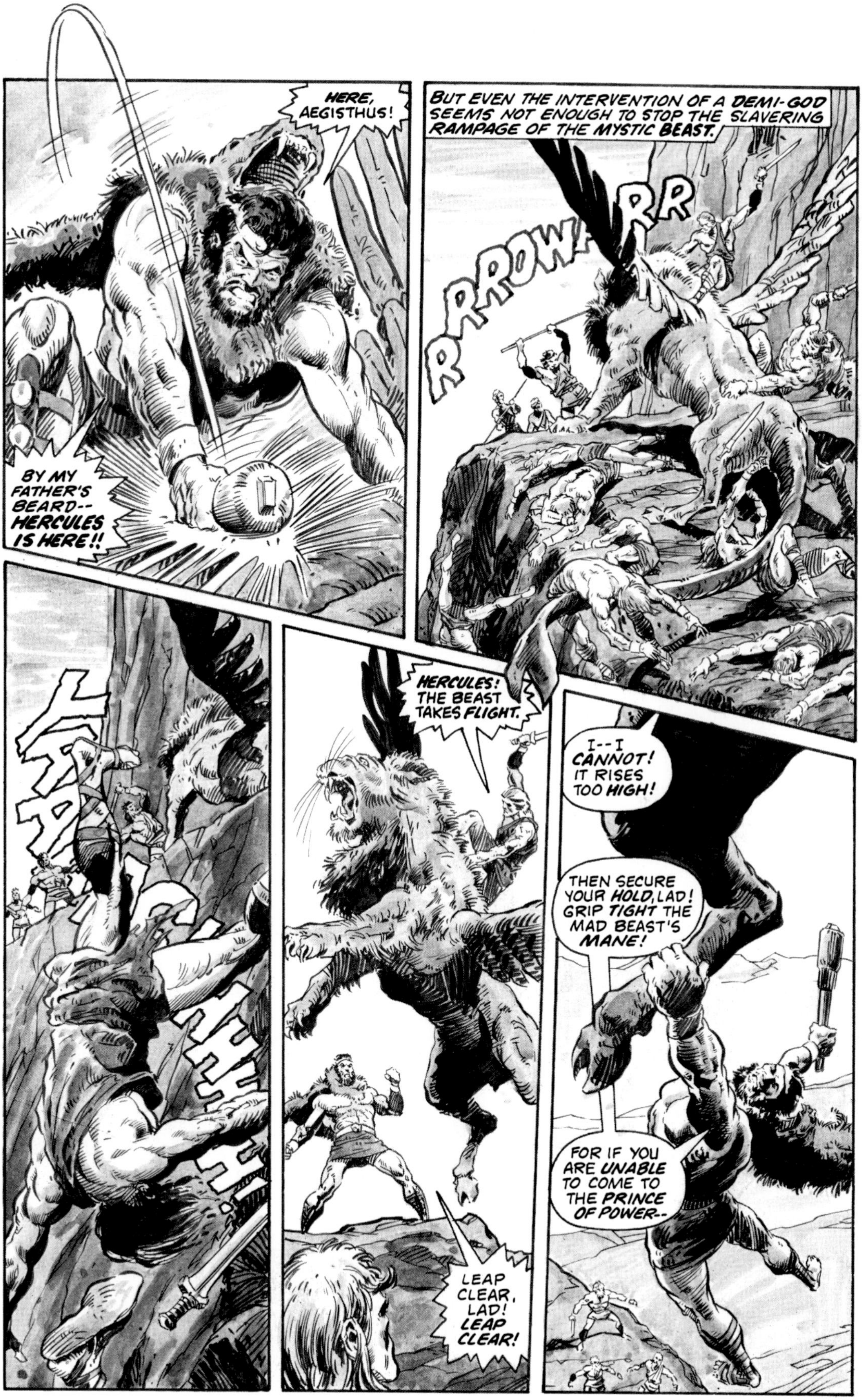
HERE, AEGISTHUS!
BY MY FATHER'S BEARD-- HERCULES IS HERE!!
BUT EVEN THE INTERVENTION OF A DEMI-GOD SEEMS NOT ENOUGH TO STOP THE SLAVERING RAMPAGE OF THE MYSTIC BEAST.
RRROWRRR
HERCULES! THE BEAST TAKES FLIGHT.
LEAP CLEAR, LAD! LEAP CLEAR!
I--I CANNOT! IT RISES TOO HIGH!
THEN SECURE YOUR HOLD, LAD! GRIP TIGHT THE MAD BEAST'S MANE!
FOR IF YOU ARE UNABLE TO COME TO THE PRINCE OF POWER--

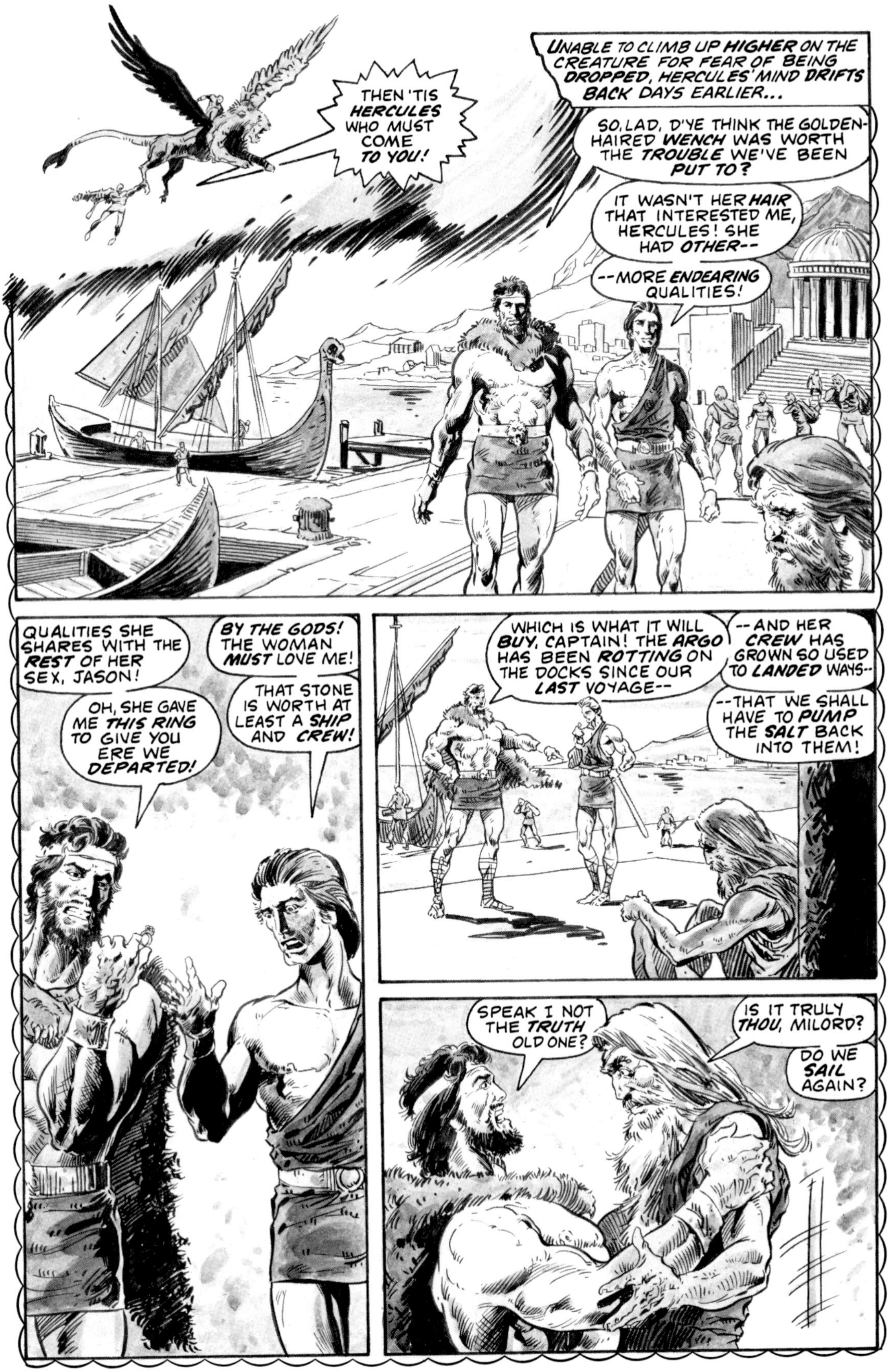

THEN 'TIS HERCULES WHO MUST COME TO YOU!
UNABLE TO CLIMB UP HIGHER ON THE CREATURE FOR FEAR OF BEING DROPPED, HERCULES' MIND DRIFTS BACK DAYS EARLIER...
SO, LAD, D'YE THINK THE GOLDEN-HAIRED WENCH WAS WORTH THE TROUBLE WE'VE BEEN PUT TO?
IT WASN'T HER HAIR THAT INTERESTED ME, HERCULES! SHE HAD OTHER--
--MORE ENDEARING QUALITIES!
QUALITIES SHE SHARES WITH THE REST OF HER SEX, JASON!
OH, SHE GAVE ME THIS RING TO GIVE YOU ERE WE DEPARTED!
BY THE GODS! THE WOMAN MUST LOVE ME!
THAT STONE IS WORTH AT LEAST A SHIP AND CREW!
WHICH IS WHAT IT WILL BUY, CAPTAIN! THE ARGO HAS BEEN ROTTING ON THE DOCKS SINCE OUR LAST VOYAGE--
--AND HER CREW HAS GROWN SO USED TO LANDED WAYS--
--THAT WE SHALL HAVE TO PUMP THE SALT BACK INTO THEM!
SPEAK I NOT THE TRUTH OLD ONE?
IS IT TRULY THOU, MILORD?
DO WE SAIL AGAIN?

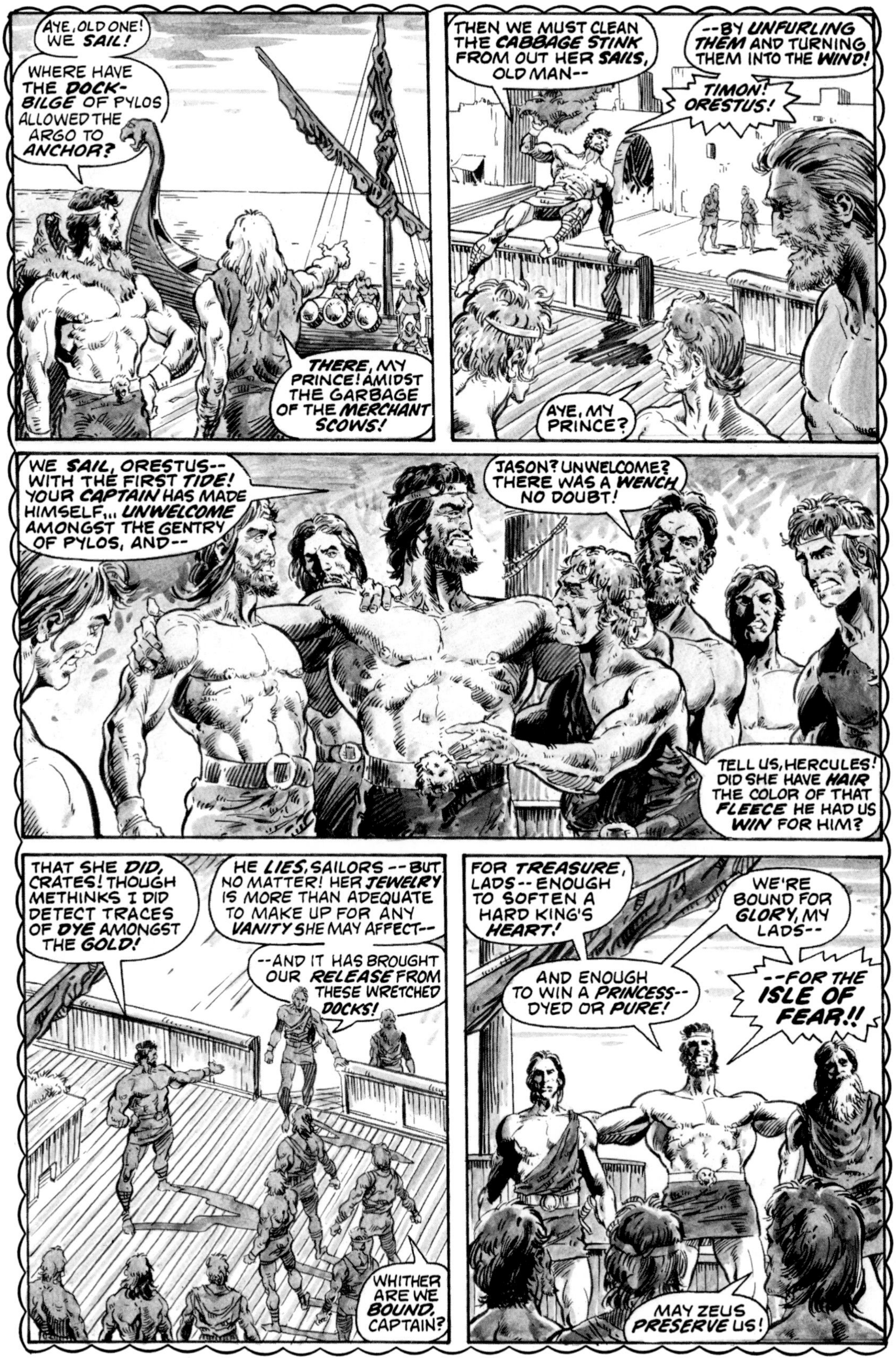

AYE, OLD ONE! WE SAIL!
WHERE HAVE THE DOCK-BILGE OF PYLOS ALLOWED THE ARGO TO ANCHOR?
THERE, MY PRINCE! AMIDST THE GARBAGE OF THE MERCHANT SCOWS!
THEN WE MUST CLEAN THE CABBAGE STINK FROM OUT HER SAILS, OLD MAN--
--BY UNFURLING THEM AND TURNING THEM INTO THE WIND!
TIMON! ORESTUS!
AYE, MY PRINCE?
WE SAIL, ORESTUS-- WITH THE FIRST TIDE! YOUR CAPTAIN HAS MADE HIMSELF... UNWELCOME AMONGST THE GENTRY OF PYLOS, AND--
JASON? UNWELCOME? THERE WAS A WENCH NO DOUBT!
TELL US, HERCULES! DID SHE HAVE HAIR THE COLOR OF THAT FLEECE HE HAD US WIN FOR HIM?
THAT SHE DID, CRATES! THOUGH METHINKS I DID DETECT TRACES OF DYE AMONGST THE GOLD!
HE LIES, SAILORS -- BUT NO MATTER! HER JEWELRY IS MORE THAN ADEQUATE TO MAKE UP FOR ANY VANITY SHE MAY AFFECT--
--AND IT HAS BROUGHT OUR RELEASE FROM THESE WRETCHED DOCKS!
WHITHER ARE WE BOUND, CAPTAIN?
FOR TREASURE, LADS-- ENOUGH TO SOFTEN A HARD KING'S HEART!
AND ENOUGH TO WIN A PRINCESS-- DYED OR PURE!
WE'RE BOUND FOR GLORY, MY LADS--
--FOR THE ISLE OF FEAR!!
MAY ZEUS PRESERVE US!

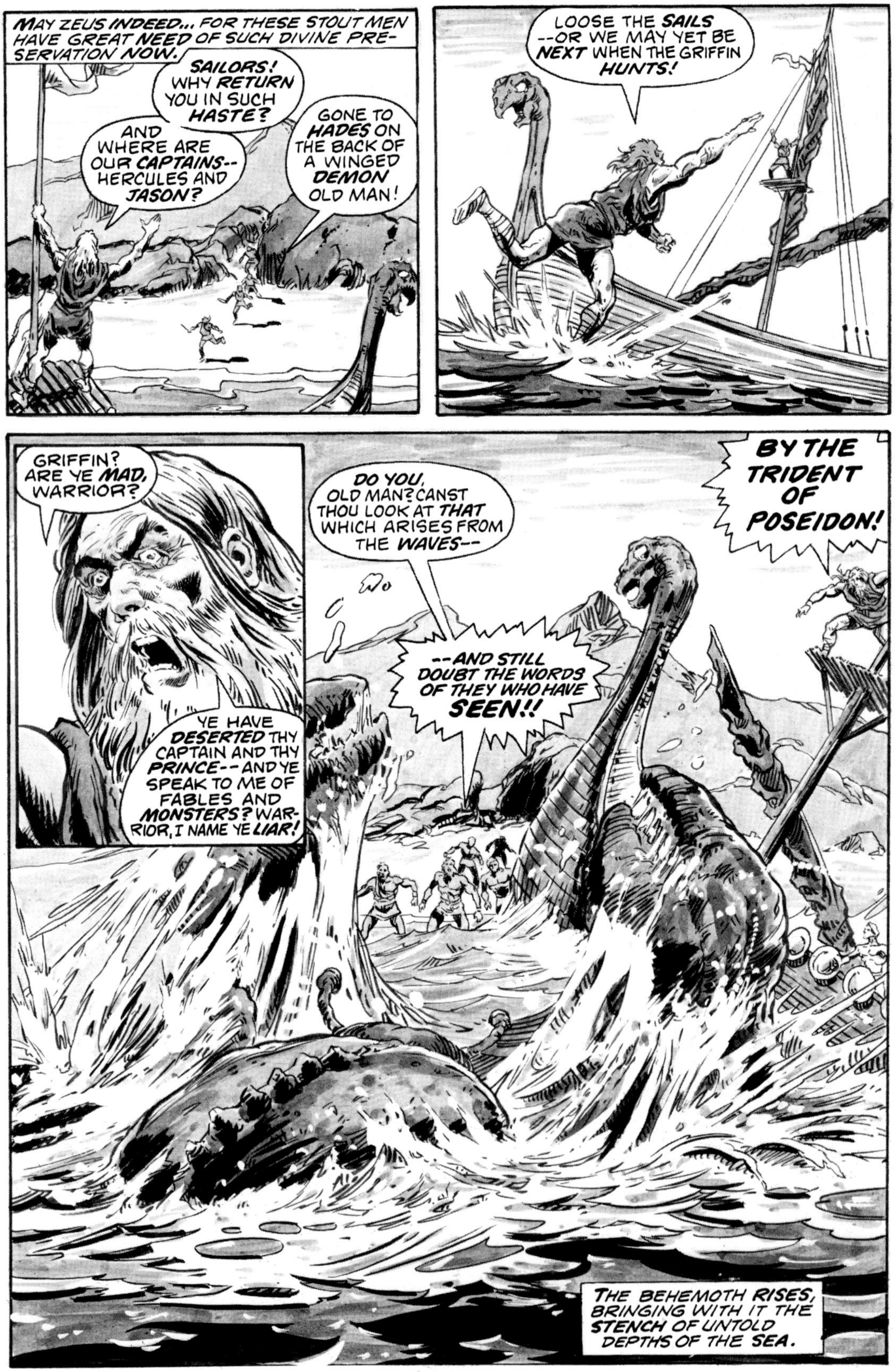
MAY ZEUS INDEED... FOR THESE STOUT MEN HAVE GREAT NEED OF SUCH DIVINE PRESERVATION NOW.
SAILORS! WHY RETURN YOU IN SUCH HASTE?
AND WHERE ARE OUR CAPTAINS-- HERCULES AND JASON?
GONE TO HADES ON THE BACK OF A WINGED DEMON OLD MAN!
LOOSE THE SAILS --OR WE MAY YET BE NEXT WHEN THE GRIFFIN HUNTS!
GRIFFIN? ARE YE MAD, WARRIOR?
DO YOU, OLD MAN? CANST THOU LOOK AT THAT WHICH ARISES FROM THE WAVES--
--AND STILL DOUBT THE WORDS OF THEY WHO HAVE SEEN!!
BY THE TRIDENT OF POSEIDON!
YE HAVE DESERTED THY CAPTAIN AND THY PRINCE--AND YE SPEAK TO ME OF FABLES AND MONSTERS? WARRIOR, I NAME YE LIAR!
THE BEHEMOTH RISES, BRINGING WITH IT THE STENCH OF UNTOLD DEPTHS OF THE SEA.

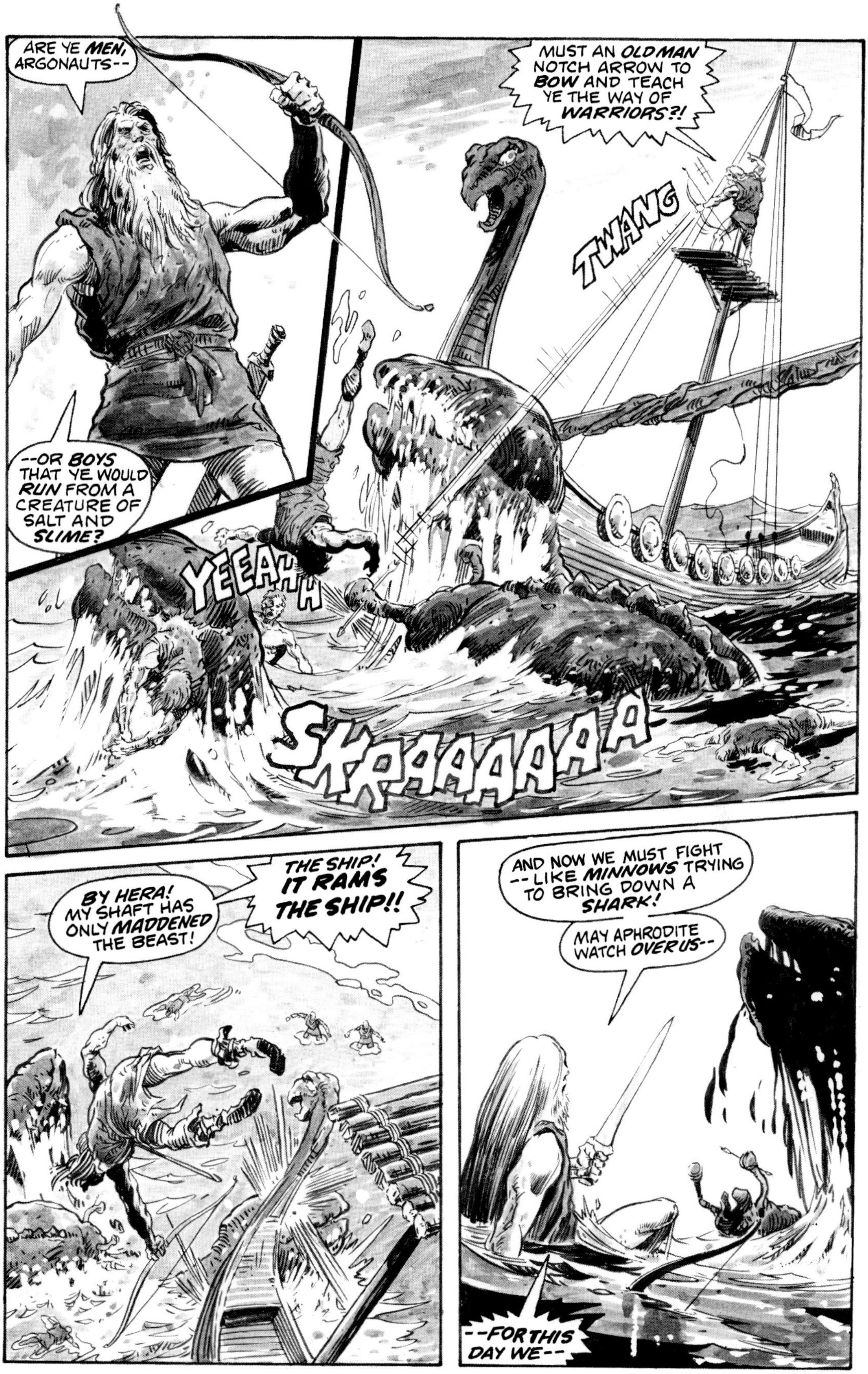
ARE YE MEN, ARGONAUTS--
MUST AN OLD MAN NOTCH ARROW TO BOW AND TEACH YE THE WAY OF WARRIORS?!
TWANG
--OR BOYS THAT YE WOULD RUN FROM A CREATURE OF SALT AND SLIME?
YEEAHH
SKRAAAAAA
BY HERA! MY SHAFT HAS ONLY MADDENED THE BEAST!
THE SHIP! IT RAMS THE SHIP!!
AND NOW WE MUST FIGHT --LIKE MINNOWS TRYING TO BRING DOWN A SHARK!
MAY APHRODITE WATCH OVER US--
--FOR THIS DAY WE--

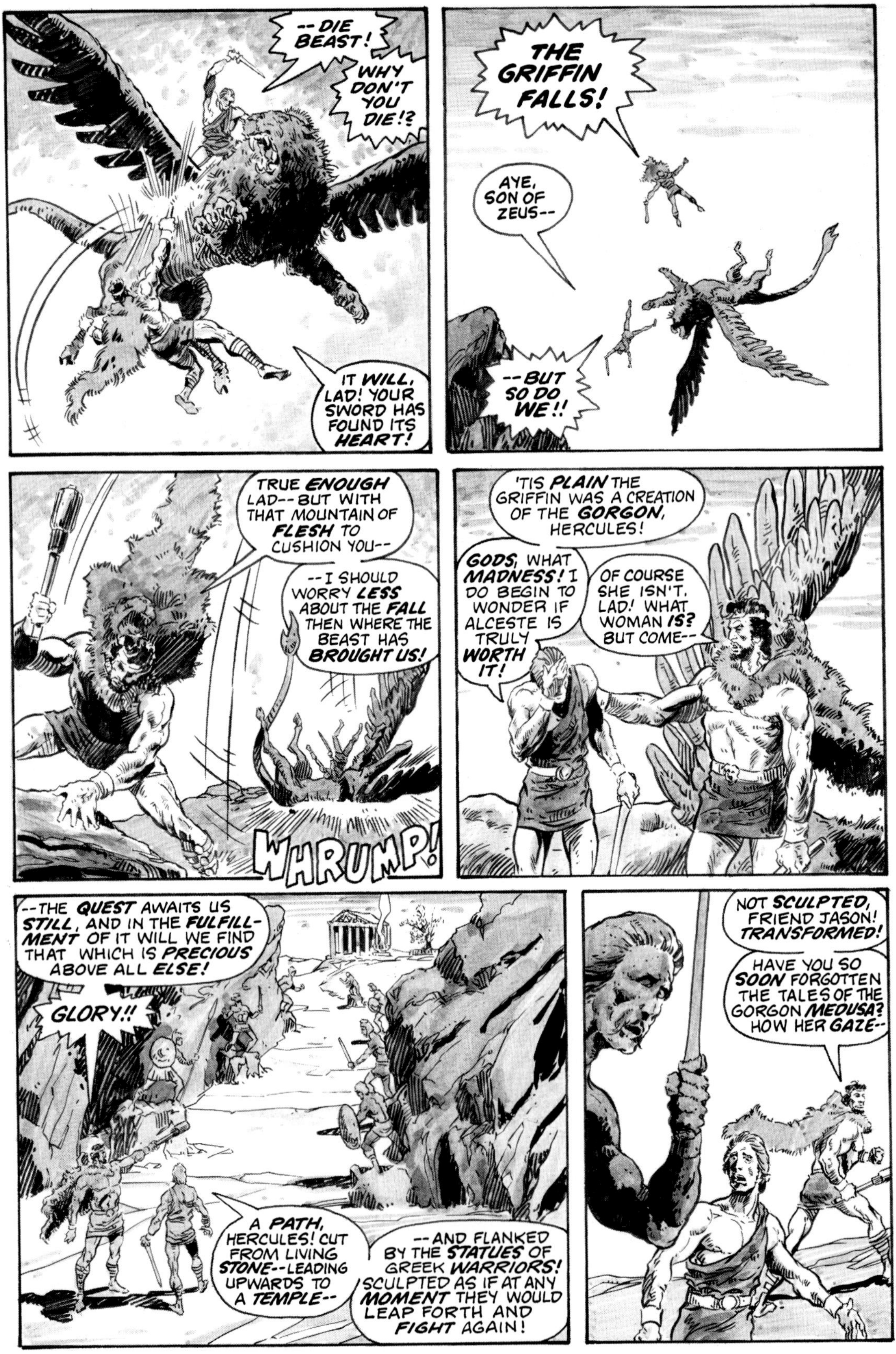
--DIE BEAST!
WHY DON'T YOU DIE!?
IT WILL, LAD! YOUR SWORD HAS FOUND ITS HEART!
THE GRIFFIN FALLS!
AYE, SON OF ZEUS--
--BUT SO DO WE!!
TRUE ENOUGH LAD--BUT WITH THAT MOUNTAIN OF FLESH TO CUSHION YOU--
--I SHOULD WORRY LESS ABOUT THE FALL THEN WHERE THE BEAST HAS BROUGHT US!
WHRUMP!
'TIS PLAIN THE GRIFFIN WAS A CREATION OF THE GORGON, HERCULES!
GODS, WHAT MADNESS! I DO BEGIN TO WONDER IF ALCESTE IS TRULY WORTH IT!
OF COURSE SHE ISN'T, LAD! WHAT WOMAN IS? BUT COME--
--THE QUEST AWAITS US STILL, AND IN THE FULFILLMENT OF IT WILL WE FIND THAT WHICH IS PRECIOUS ABOVE ALL ELSE!
GLORY!!
A PATH, HERCULES! CUT FROM LIVING STONE--LEADING UPWARDS TO A TEMPLE--
--AND FLANKED BY THE STATUES OF GREEK WARRIORS! SCULPTED AS IF AT ANY MOMENT THEY WOULD LEAP FORTH AND FIGHT AGAIN!
NOT SCULPTED, FRIEND JASON! TRANSFORMED!
HAVE YOU SO SOON FORGOTTEN THE TALES OF THE GORGON MEDUSA? HOW HER GAZE--

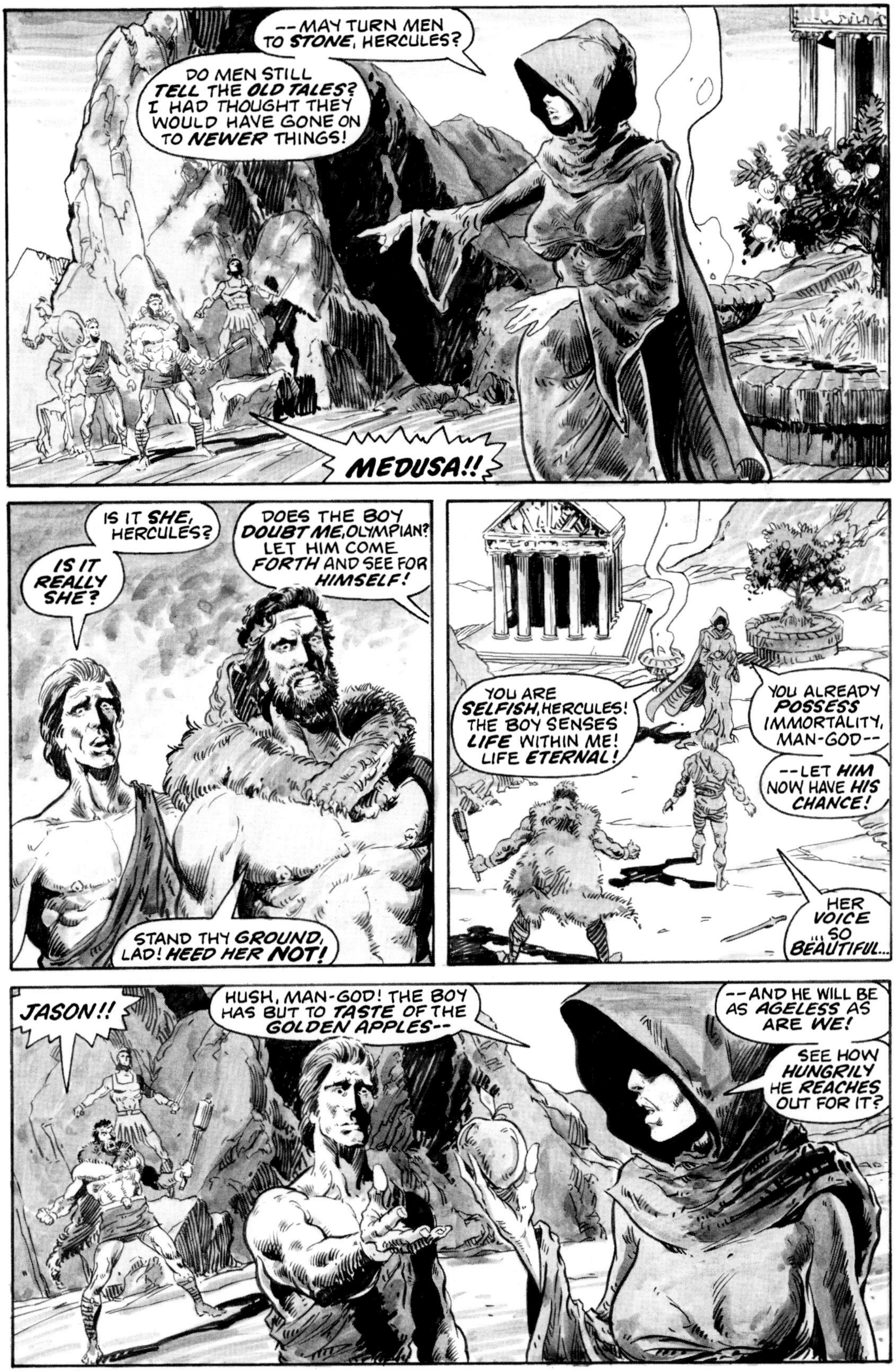
--MAY TURN MEN TO STONE, HERCULES?
DO MEN STILL TELL THE OLD TALES? I HAD THOUGHT THEY WOULD HAVE GONE ON TO NEWER THINGS!
MEDUSA!!
IS IT SHE, HERCULES?
IS IT REALLY SHE?
DOES THE BOY DOUBT ME, OLYMPIAN? LET HIM COME FORTH AND SEE FOR HIMSELF!
STAND THY GROUND, LAD! HEED HER NOT!
YOU ARE SELFISH, HERCULES! THE BOY SENSES LIFE WITHIN ME! LIFE ETERNAL!
YOU ALREADY POSSESS IMMORTALITY, MAN-GOD--
--LET HIM NOW HAVE HIS CHANCE!
HER VOICE ...SO BEAUTIFUL...
JASON!!
HUSH, MAN-GOD! THE BOY HAS BUT TO TASTE OF THE GOLDEN APPLES--
--AND HE WILL BE AS AGELESS AS ARE WE!
SEE HOW HUNGRILY HE REACHES OUT FOR IT?

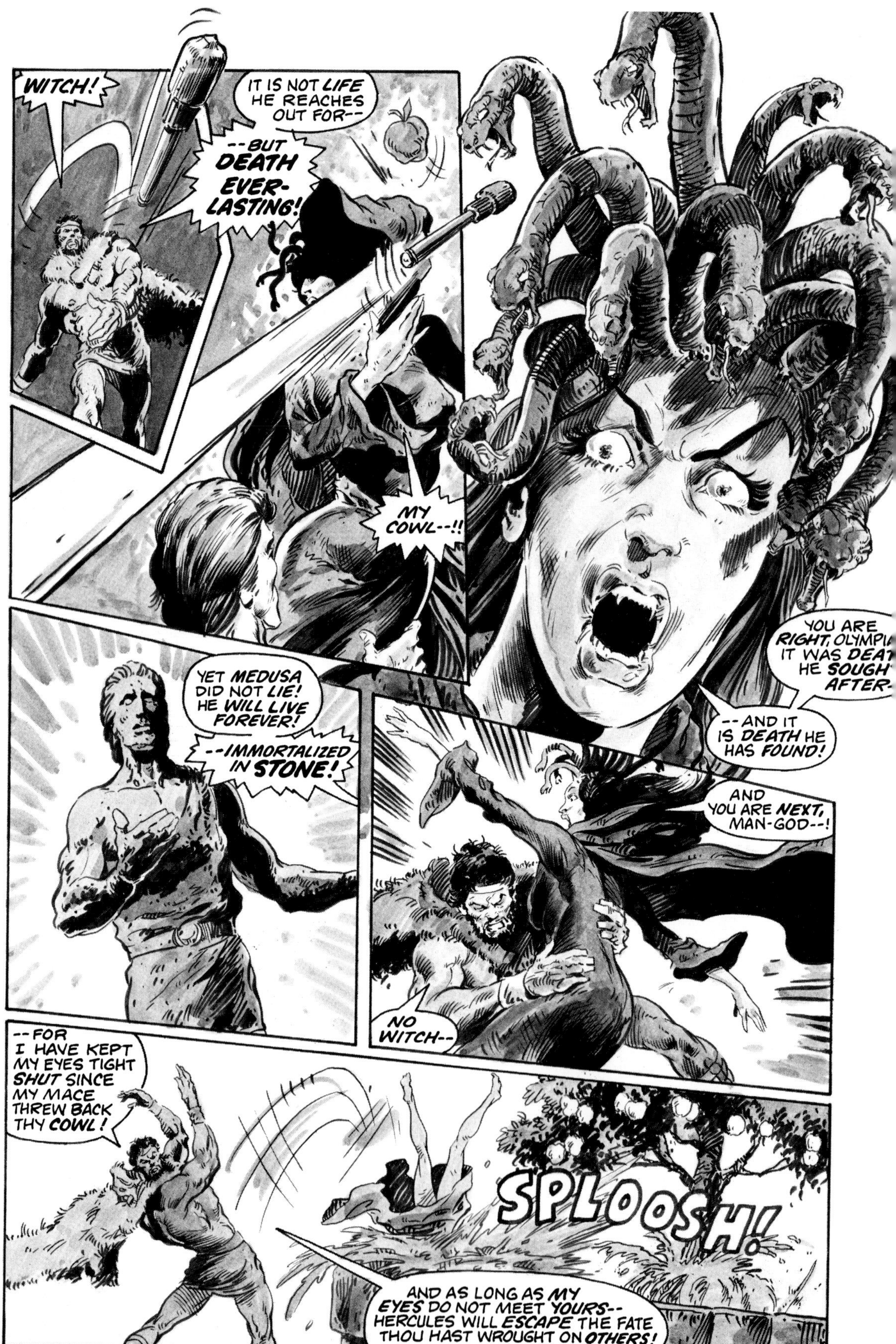
WITCH!
IT IS NOT LIFE HE REACHES OUT FOR--
--BUT DEATH EVER-LASTING!
MY COWL--!!
YOU ARE RIGHT, OLYMPIA IT WAS DEAT HE SOUGH AFTER-
YET MEDUSA DID NOT LIE! HE WILL LIVE FOREVER!
--IMMORTALIZED IN STONE!
--AND IT IS DEATH HE HAS FOUND!
AND YOU ARE NEXT, MAN-GOD--!
NO WITCH--
--FOR I HAVE KEPT MY EYES TIGHT SHUT SINCE MY MACE THREW BACK THY COWL!
SPLOOSH!
AND AS LONG AS MY EYES DO NOT MEET YOURS-- HERCULES WILL ESCAPE THE FATE THOU HAST WROUGHT ON OTHERS!

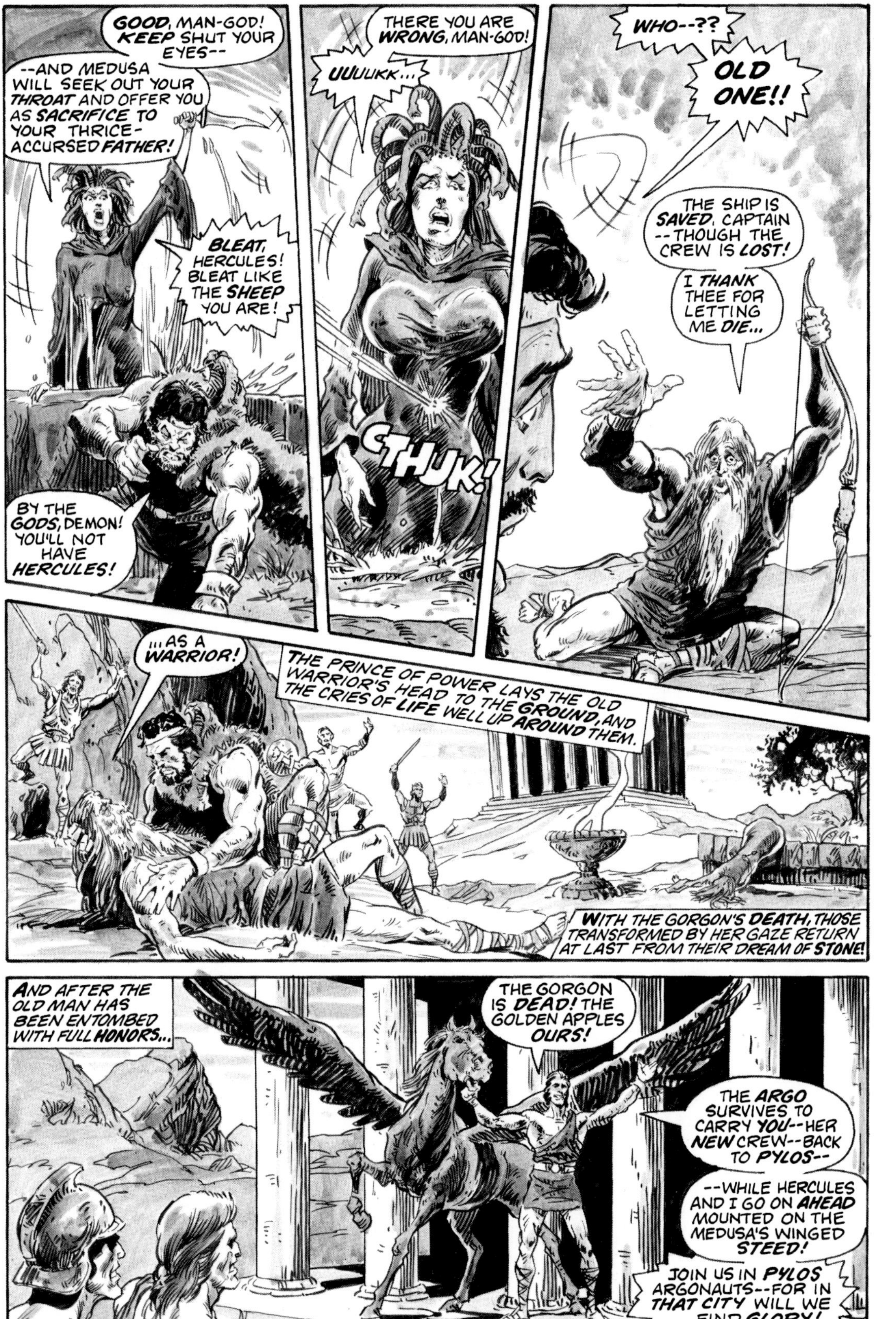
GOOD, MAN-GOD! KEEP SHUT YOUR EYES--
--AND MEDUSA WILL SEEK OUT YOUR THROAT AND OFFER YOU AS SACRIFICE TO YOUR THRICE-ACCURSED FATHER!
BLEAT, HERCULES! BLEAT LIKE THE SHEEP YOU ARE!
BY THE GODS, DEMON! YOU'LL NOT HAVE HERCULES!
THERE YOU ARE WRONG, MAN-GOD!
UUUUKK...
CTHUK!
WHO--??
OLD ONE!!
THE SHIP IS SAVED, CAPTAIN --THOUGH THE CREW IS LOST!
I THANK THEE FOR LETTING ME DIE...
...AS A WARRIOR!
THE PRINCE OF POWER LAYS THE OLD WARRIOR'S HEAD TO THE GROUND, AND THE CRIES OF LIFE WELL UP AROUND THEM.
WITH THE GORGON'S DEATH, THOSE TRANSFORMED BY HER GAZE RETURN AT LAST FROM THEIR DREAM OF STONE!
AND AFTER THE OLD MAN HAS BEEN ENTOMBED WITH FULL HONORS...
THE GORGON IS DEAD! THE GOLDEN APPLES OURS!
THE ARGO SURVIVES TO CARRY YOU--HER NEW CREW--BACK TO PYLOS--
--WHILE HERCULES AND I GO ON AHEAD MOUNTED ON THE MEDUSA'S WINGED STEED!
JOIN US IN PYLOS ARGONAUTS--FOR IN THAT CITY WILL WE FIND GLORY!

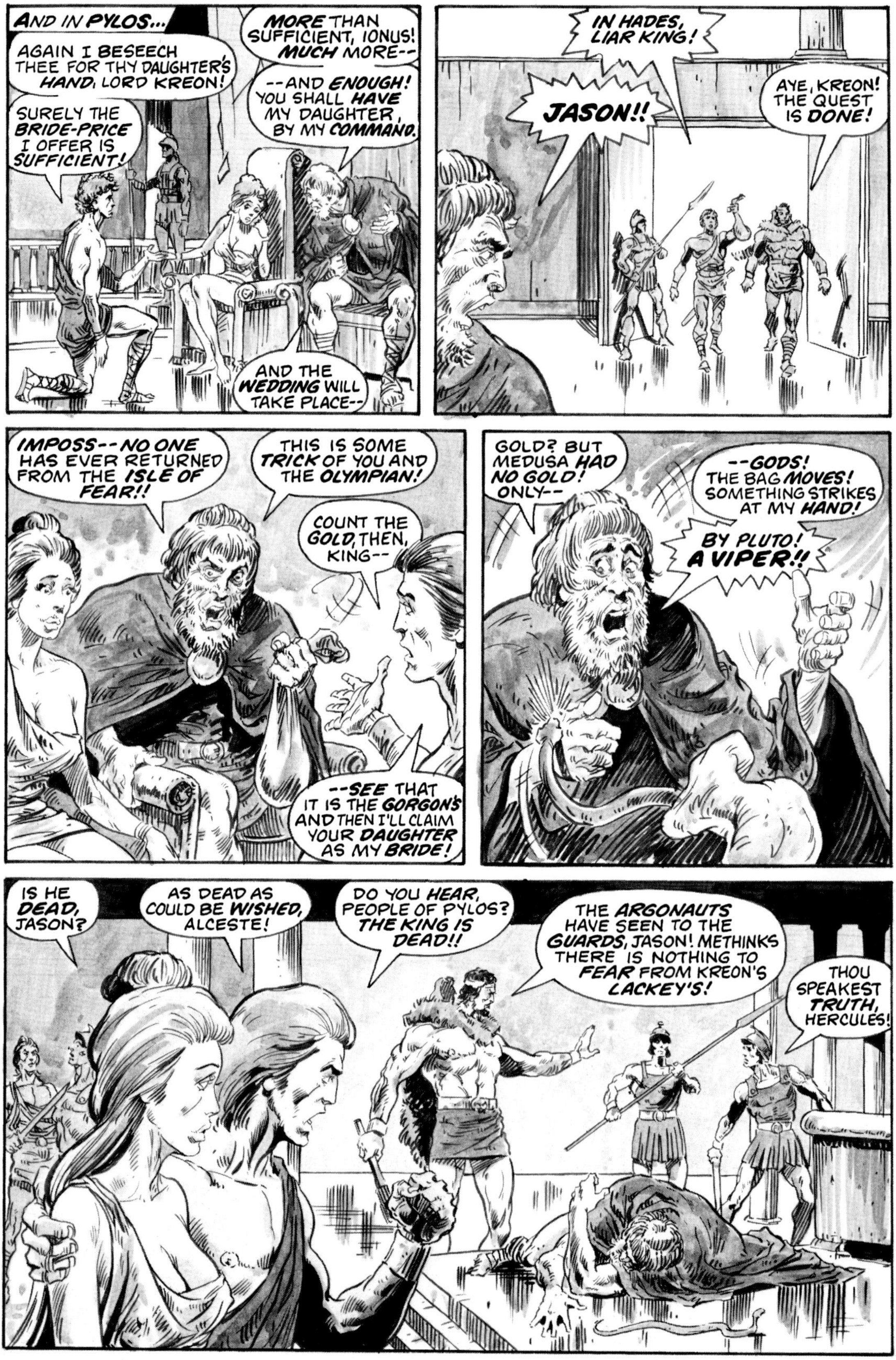
AND IN PYLOS...
AGAIN I BESEECH THEE FOR THY DAUGHTER'S HAND, LORD KREON!
SURELY THE BRIDE-PRICE I OFFER IS SUFFICIENT!
MORE THAN SUFFICIENT, IONUS! MUCH MORE--
--AND ENOUGH! YOU SHALL HAVE MY DAUGHTER, BY MY COMMAND.
AND THE WEDDING WILL TAKE PLACE--
IN HADES, LIAR KING!
JASON!!
AYE, KREON! THE QUEST IS DONE!
IMPOSS--NO ONE HAS EVER RETURNED FROM THE ISLE OF FEAR!!
THIS IS SOME TRICK OF YOU AND THE OLYMPIAN!
COUNT THE GOLD, THEN, KING--
--SEE THAT IT IS THE GORGON'S AND THEN I'LL CLAIM YOUR DAUGHTER AS MY BRIDE!
GOLD? BUT MEDUSA HAD NO GOLD! ONLY--
--GODS! THE BAG MOVES! SOMETHING STRIKES AT MY HAND!
BY PLUTO! A VIPER!!
IS HE DEAD, JASON?
AS DEAD AS COULD BE WISHED, ALCESTE!
DO YOU HEAR, PEOPLE OF PYLOS? THE KING IS DEAD!!
THE ARGONAUTS HAVE SEEN TO THE GUARDS, JASON! METHINKS THERE IS NOTHING TO FEAR FROM KREON'S LACKEY'S!
THOU SPEAKEST TRUTH, HERCULES!

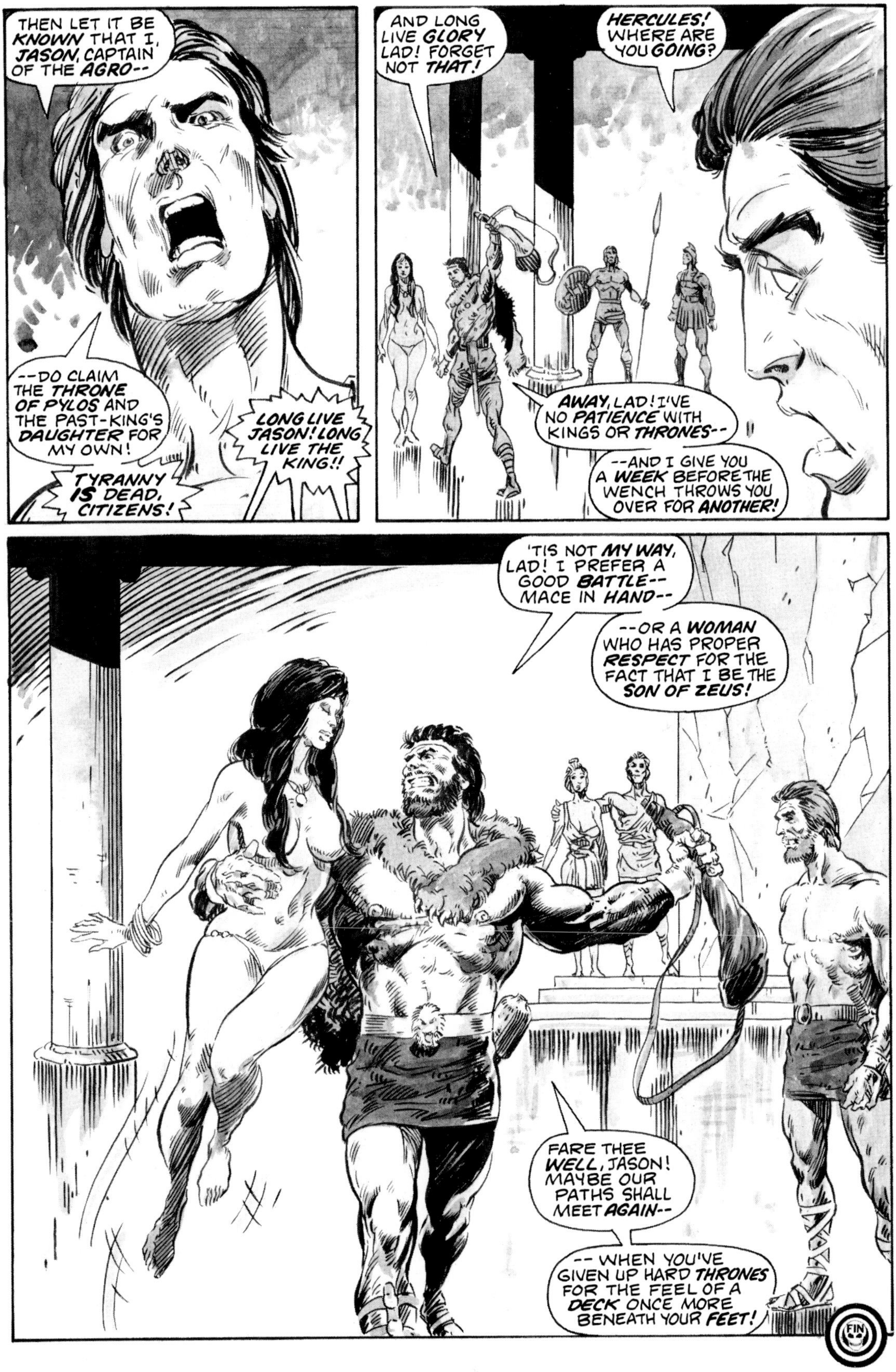
THEN LET IT BE KNOWN THAT I, JASON, CAPTAIN OF THE AGRO--
--DO CLAIM THE THRONE OF PYLOS AND THE PAST-KING'S DAUGHTER FOR MY OWN!
TYRANNY IS DEAD, CITIZENS!
LONG LIVE JASON! LONG LIVE THE KING!!
AND LONG LIVE GLORY LAD! FORGET NOT THAT!
HERCULES! WHERE ARE YOU GOING?
AWAY, LAD! I'VE NO PATIENCE WITH KINGS OR THRONES--
--AND I GIVE YOU A WEEK BEFORE THE WENCH THROWS YOU OVER FOR ANOTHER!
'TIS NOT MY WAY, LAD! I PREFER A GOOD BATTLE-- MACE IN HAND--
--OR A WOMAN WHO HAS PROPER RESPECT FOR THE FACT THAT I BE THE SON OF ZEUS!
FARE THEE WELL, JASON! MAYBE OUR PATHS SHALL MEET AGAIN--
-- WHEN YOU'VE GIVEN UP HARD THRONES FOR THE FEEL OF A DECK ONCE MORE BENEATH YOUR FEET!
FIN

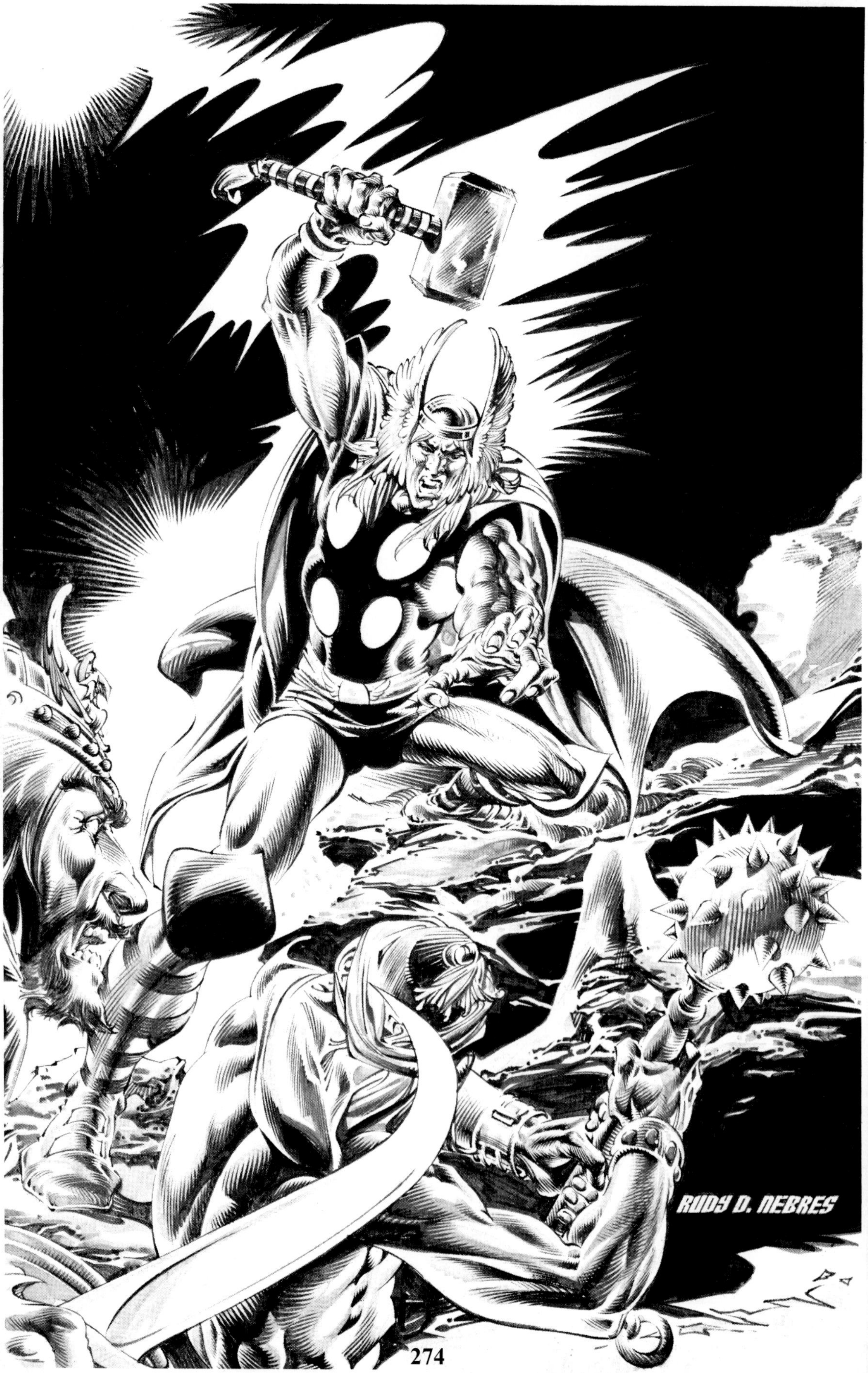
RUDY D. NEBRES

After plans for a black-and-white *Thor the Mighty* magazine were scrapped in 1975, it was some time before the stories commissioned for the magazine found homes. Steve Englehart and John Buscema's Thor/Hercules adventure saw print in *The Mighty Thor Annual* #5 (1976) while the Wein/Starlin Thor and Mantlo/Mayerik Hercules stories were slated for September 1975's *Marvel Preview* #3 (as seen in this house ad from issue #2, June 1975) before finally seeing print in issue *Marvel Preview* #10 (Winter 1977).

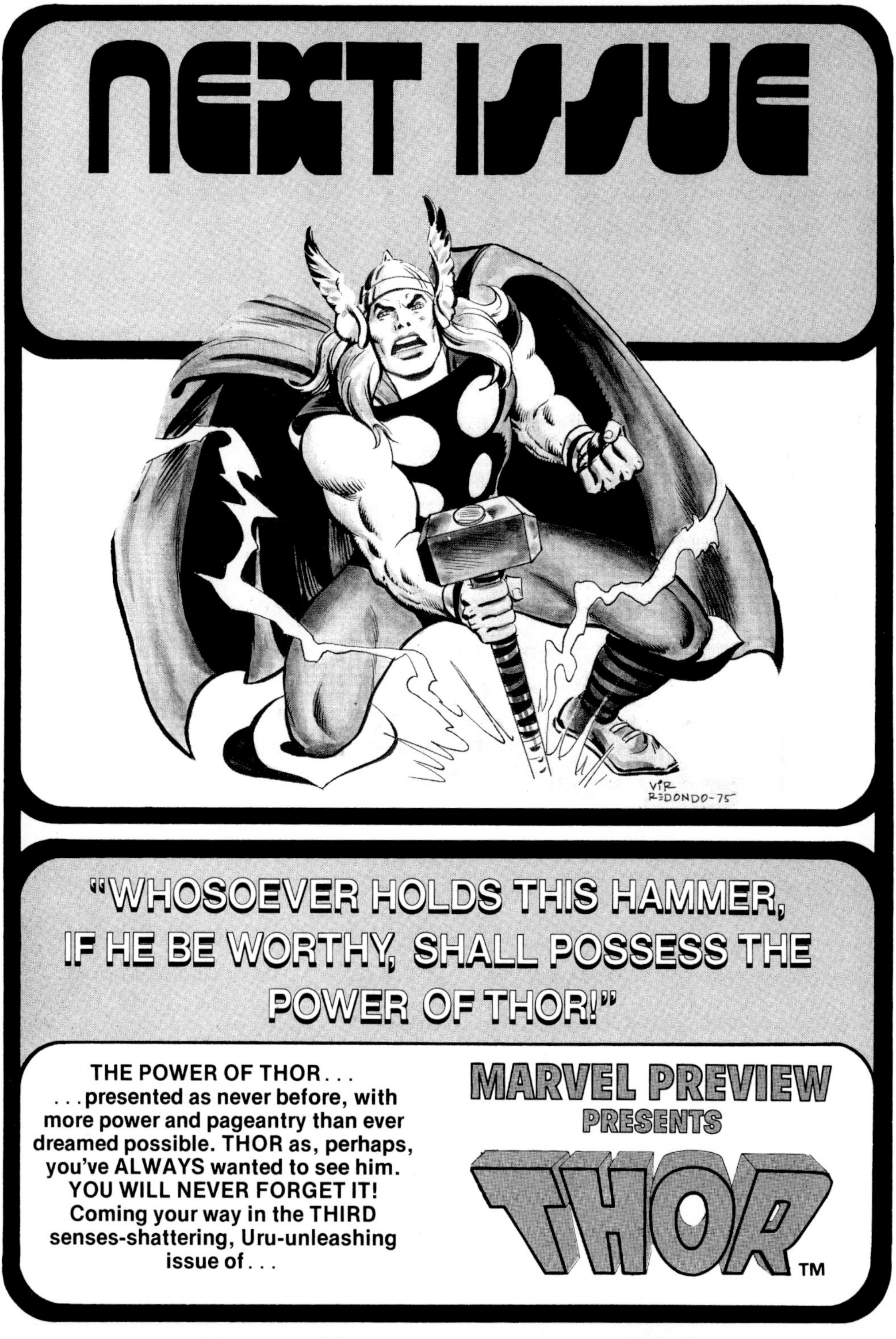

NEXT ISSUE
VIR REDONDO-75
"WHOSOEVER HOLDS THIS HAMMER, IF HE BE WORTHY, SHALL POSSESS THE POWER OF THOR!"
THE POWER OF THOR . . . . . . presented as never before, with more power and pageantry than ever dreamed possible. THOR as, perhaps, you've ALWAYS wanted to see him. YOU WILL NEVER FORGET IT! Coming your way in the THIRD senses-shattering, Uru-unleashing issue of . . .
MARVEL PREVIEW PRESENTS THOR TM

Bottom: *The Mighty Thor* #272 house ad, from May 1978 titles

THE HAMMER STRIKES

c/o MARVEL COMICS GROUP, 575 MADISON AVE. N.Y.C. 10022

A NORDIC NOTE FROM YE NEW WRITER/EDITOR:

I guess it was bound to happen.

For years now, I've toyed with the idea of scripting the awesome adventures of Thor and his fellow Asgardians. And at last, here I am—again.

For me, as a new editorial flunkie around Marvel circa 1965-66, one of the great thrills was being one of the first people on earth (or elsewhere) to see each vintage tale of Spidey, the F.F., *et al.*, as they came into Marvel's Madison Avenue offices. I was around, admiring, during the final great days of the Lee-Ditko team (even scripting a couple of Sturdy Steve's last Doc Strange stories) and for the beginning of the Lee-Romita collaboration on SPIDER-MAN which, building on what came before, lifted the ol' wall-crawler into first place among the Marvel stars. What a gas it was to see the Inhumans, Galactus, the Silver Surfer, the Black Panther months before anybody else except Fabulous Flo Steinberg, Jolly Solly Brodsky— and of course the writer and artists themselves.

And, in a way— at least for a while— THOR was up there ahead of all of them, for me.

It started, I suppose, with the tail-end of the thunder god's clash with Crusher Creel, the Absorbing Man, back in THOR #123 and thereabouts— with a blackmailing reporter named Harris Hobbs in tow, as the first mortal to visit Asgard. It continued thru the multi-part Thor-Hercules-Pluto slugfest, which is one of the highlights of the Marvel Age of Comics by *any* sane standard, as Stan Lee and Jack Kirby gave new meaning to the word "cosmic." There've been some head-trips since then between Marvel covers, and they've been fun— but for me, THOR #124-129 was *it*!

Nor did the mag taper off unduly after that— what with Tana Nile and the Colonizers from Rigel (sounds like a rock group, huh?), the rhapsodizin' Recorder, the High Evolutionary and his nefarious New-Men, Him (whom I eventually turned into Adam Warlock with a bit of help from Gil Kane)— and, last but far from least, that fateful day when Jane Foster got her one real shot at goddess-hood. . . and blew it.

From that moment on, the mag changed— irreversibly, irretrievably. It didn't necessary get better or worse; it merely. . . changed. The raven-haired Sif entered the strip (replacing both the Norse golden-tressed goddess of that name, and Marvel's own earlier edition of same in a "Tale of Asgard")— new gods like Hogun, Fandral, and Volstagg made the giant leap from "Tales of Asgard" into the main body of the mag— and what I think of as the Second Age of Thor began. In a way, THOR #136 ("To Become an Immortal!") marked a watershed between two eras.

Stan continued to turn out first-rate forays into the unknown, of course— first in connection with "King" Kirby, later with Neal Adams and, most noticeably, Big John Buscema. Interestingly, THOR has had fewer writers than probably any other of the Marvel titles spawned in the 60's— and only two of these, Gerry Conway and lately Len Wein, stuck around long enough to make any imprint on the mag. (My own earlier stint on THOR lasted just one issue of scripting and one issue of plotting; Bill Mantlo and I *together* did only three or so.)

Nor have there been many pencil-artists since the 1964-65 period when Jack Kirby took over the reins again from a host of others. Adams, briefly— then John B.— an issue here and there by his sibling Sal— and most recently and notably, Walt Simonson.

Perhaps it's this small number of writers and artists in the course of nearly 200 issues (ish #282, coming up, is the *real* #200 of the mag, since Thor debuted in JOURNEY INTO MYSTERY #83 back in summer of '62) which has given the book its fairly consistent quality, both in look and in popularity.

For myself, I've long regretted that various circumstances forced me to drop the segment I began (introducing the Egyptian pantheon of gods) in the middle. Fact is, I don't even recall offhand just *why* I left. And I wish I hadn't.

Point being: I'm back, and I plan to stick around a while.

First thing I did when Archie Goodwin asked me to take the writing and editorial chores on THOR was to make certain that, since Wondrous Walt Simonson was going to be busy on our CLOSE ENCOUNTERS OF THE THIRD KIND SPECIAL, I could re-unite the team with which I had turned out, I think, some of the more memorable issues of THE AVENGERS, a few years back. Turns out that John B. *volunteered* to pencil the mag, as a change of pace from CONAN and TARZAN— and talented Tom was only too happy to round out our new/old triumvirate. (It was originally intended to be only a two-issue thing, but since then Walt has decided to pursue other artistic directions— save hopefully for this year's THOR ANNUAL and perhaps a special issue now and then— so it looks as if the Thomas/Buscema/Palmer team is back in business!)

As to the mag itself— well, for the most part, we prefer to let you discover our plans for THOR in the pages of the comics themselves, a month at a time. Except for cleaning up a few loose ends of Asgardian dialect here and there (never again, for instance, will Thor say "Thou doth," which is the equivalent of saying "You is"— but that's hardly to fault Len Wein, since who *really* talks like that, anyway?), I prefer the changes in the mag to be more subtle, more gradual.

Suffice it to say that one of my own chief interests for some three decades has been *mythology*. As Odin or somebody used to say: " 'Nuff said."

And now, back to our previously-announced mag!

—Roy Thomas.

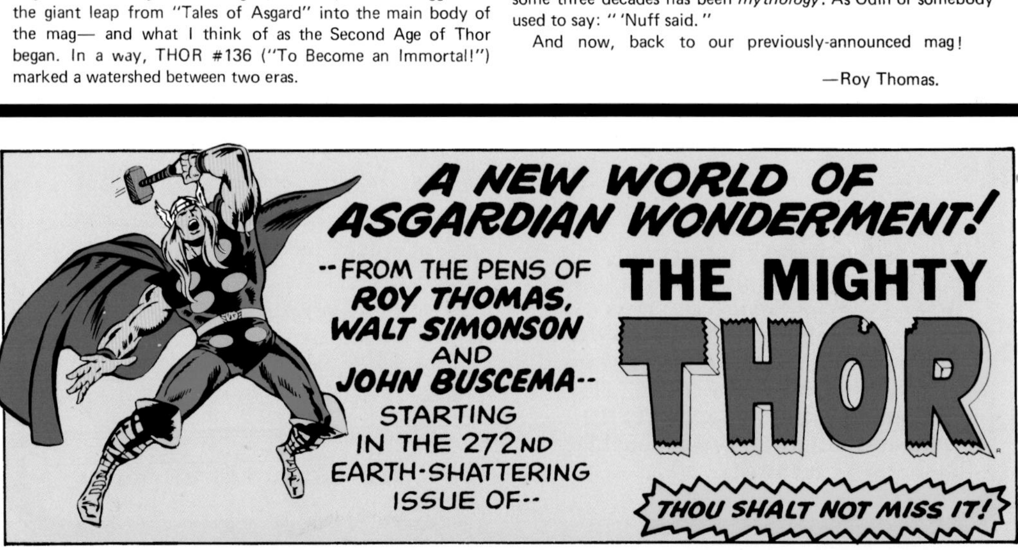
A NEW WORLD OF ASGARDIAN WONDERMENT!
--FROM THE PENS OF ROY THOMAS, WALT SIMONSON AND JOHN BUSCEMA-- STARTING IN THE 272ND EARTH-SHATTERING ISSUE OF--
THE MIGHTY THOR
THOU SHALT NOT MISS IT!

House ad promoting Marvel's solo hero titles, including *The Mighty Thor*, from July 1978 titles

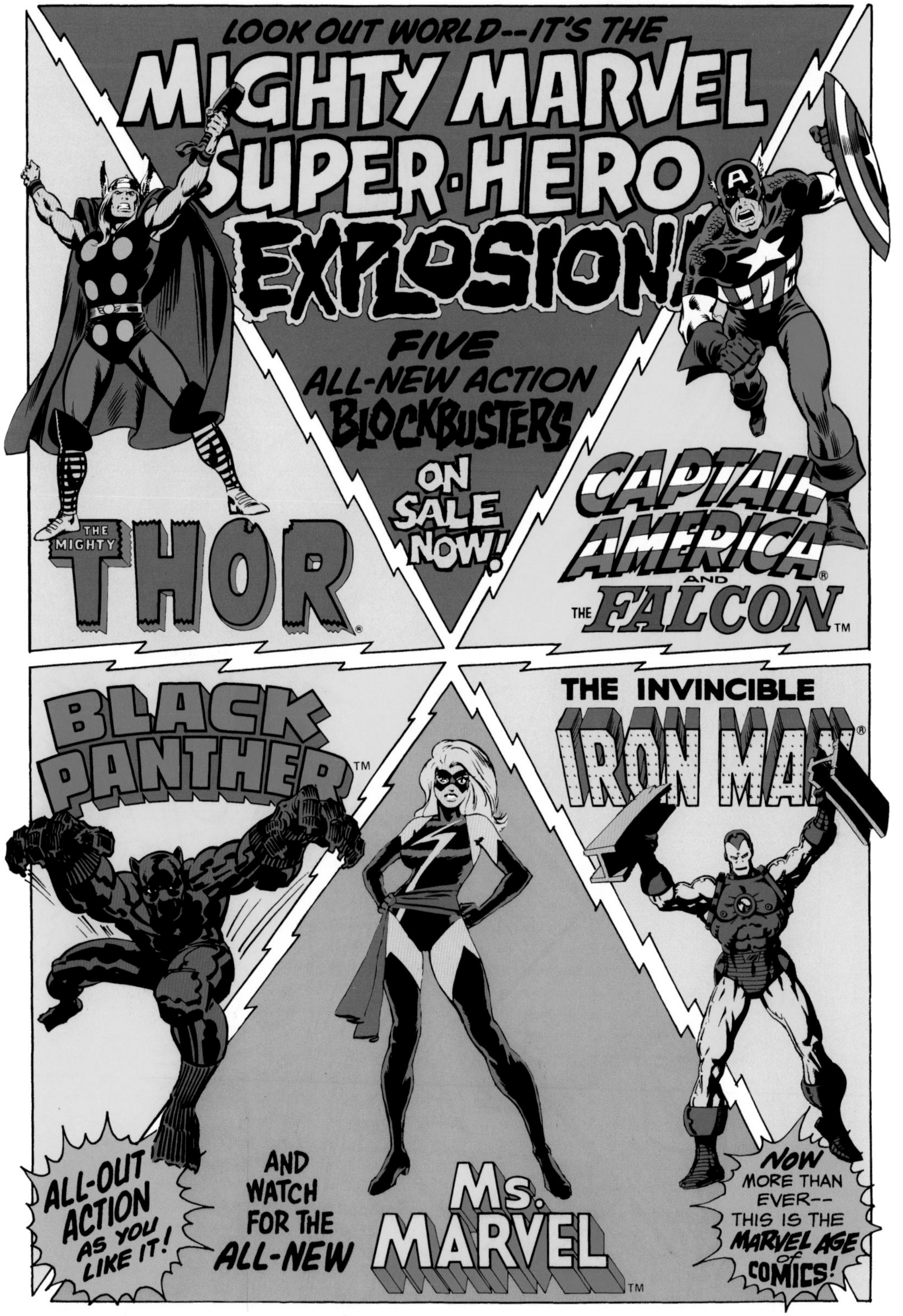
LOOK OUT WORLD--IT'S THE
MIGHTY MARVEL SUPER-HERO EXPLOSION!
FIVE ALL-NEW ACTION BLOCKBUSTERS
ON SALE NOW!
THE MIGHTY THOR®
CAPTAIN AMERICA® AND THE FALCON™
BLACK PANTHER™
THE INVINCIBLE IRON MAN®
ALL-OUT ACTION AS YOU LIKE IT!
AND WATCH FOR THE ALL-NEW
Ms. MARVEL™
NOW MORE THAN EVER-- THIS IS THE MARVEL AGE of COMICS!

by Walter Simonson & Tony DeZuniga

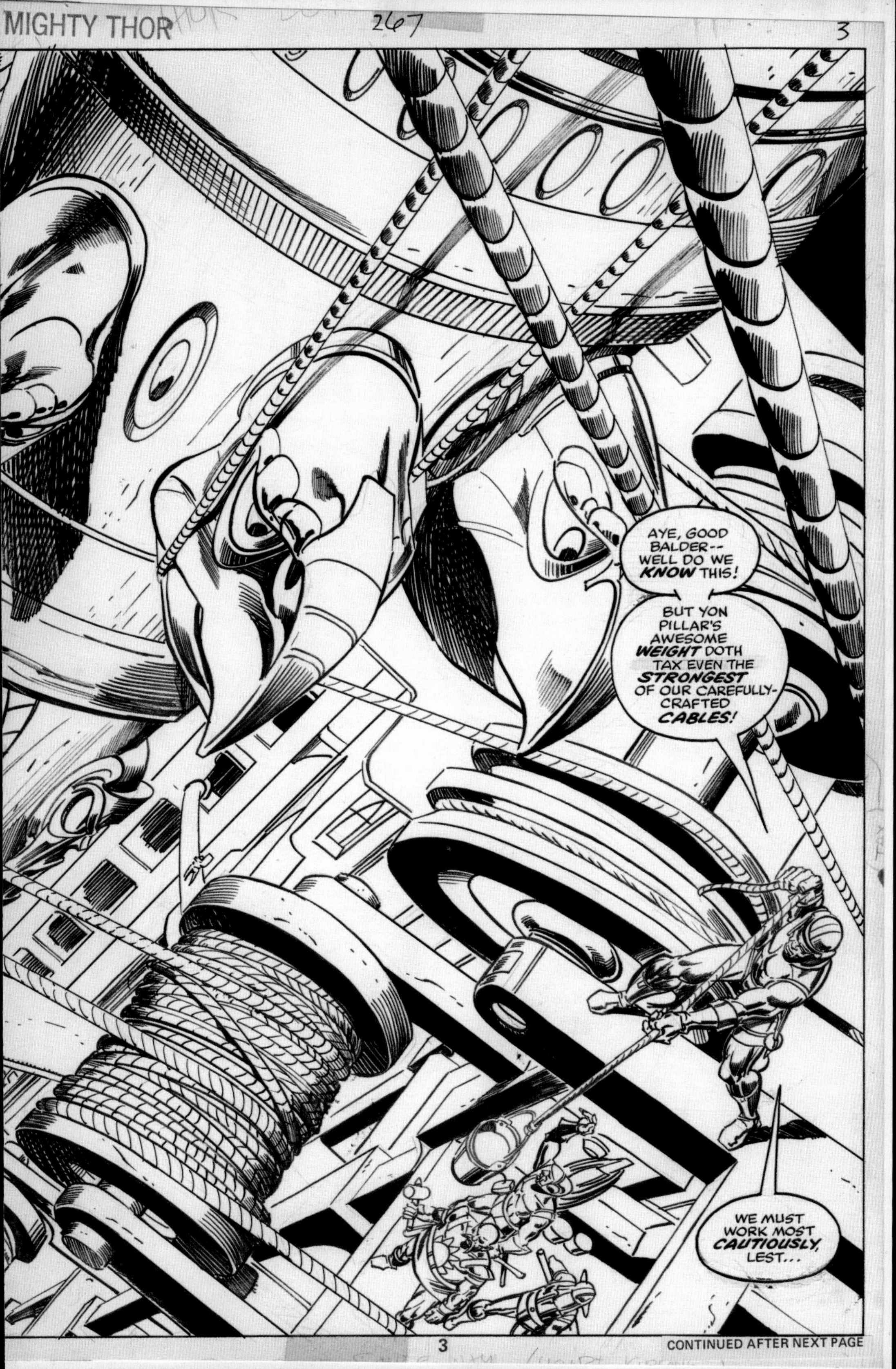
MIGHTY THOR
267
3
AYE, GOOD BALDER-- WELL DO WE KNOW THIS!
BUT YON PILLAR'S AWESOME WEIGHT DOTH TAX EVEN THE STRONGEST OF OUR CAREFULLY-CRAFTED CABLES!
WE MUST WORK MOST CAUTIOUSLY, LEST...
3
CONTINUED AFTER NEXT PAGE

Courtesy Walter Simonson

The Mighty Thor #270 cover original art
by Walter Simonson & Tony DeZuniga

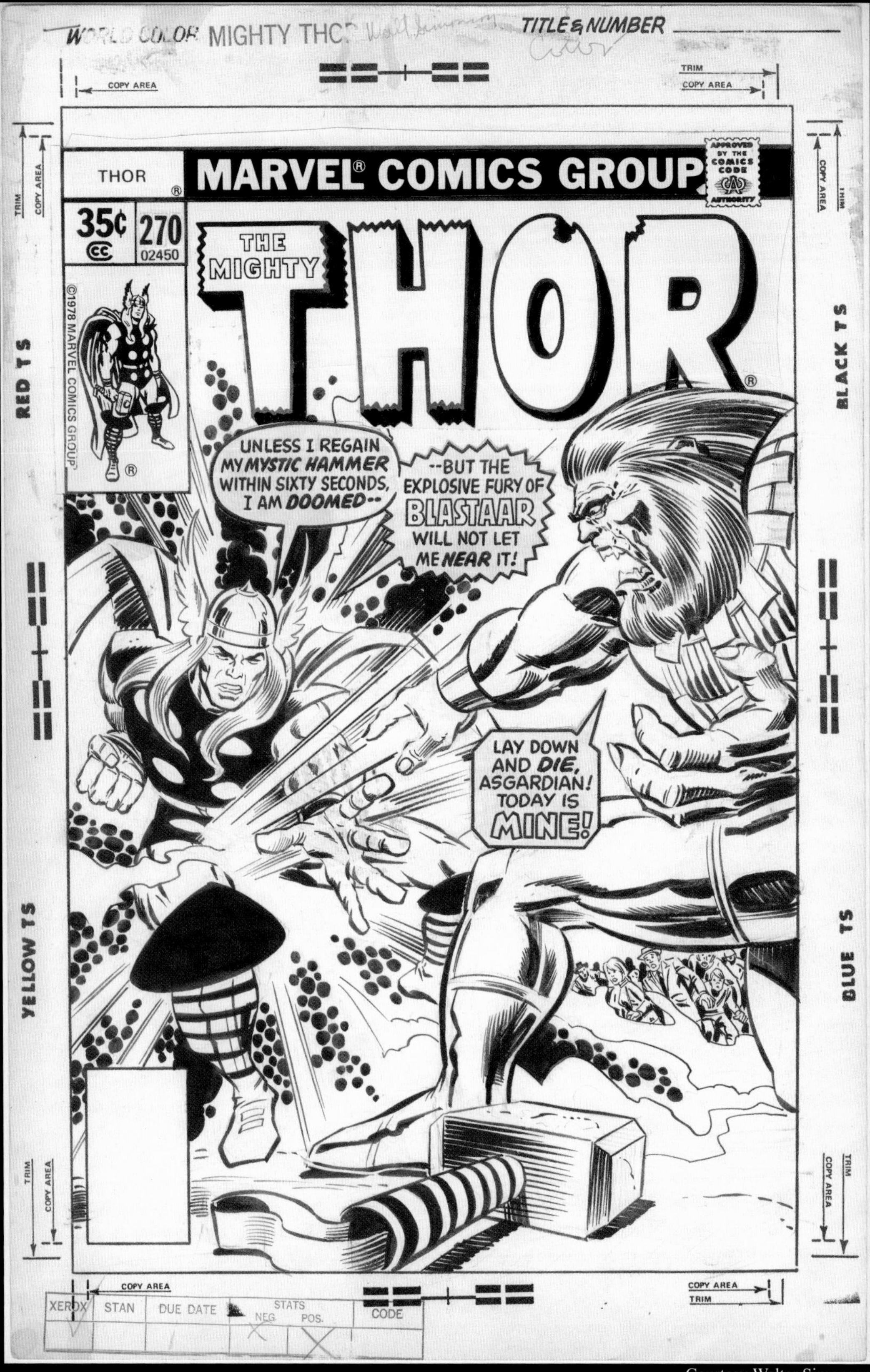
MIGHTY THOR
TITLE & NUMBER
THOR
MARVEL® COMICS GROUP
APPROVED BY THE COMICS CODE AUTHORITY
35¢
270
02450
THE MIGHTY THOR®
©1978 MARVEL COMICS GROUP
UNLESS I REGAIN MY MYSTIC HAMMER WITHIN SIXTY SECONDS, I AM DOOMED--
--BUT THE EXPLOSIVE FURY OF BLASTAAR WILL NOT LET ME NEAR IT!
LAY DOWN AND DIE, ASGARDIAN! TODAY IS MINE!
RED TS
YELLOW TS
BLACK TS
BLUE TS
XEROX
STAN
DUE DATE
STATS
NEG.
POS.
CODE

Courtesy Walter Simonson

THOR® is published by MARVEL COMICS GROUP, James E. Galton, President. Stan Lee, Publisher. OFFICE OF PUBLICATION: 575 MADISON AVENUE, NEW YORK, N.Y. 10022. SECOND CLASS POSTAGE PAID AT NEW YORK, N.Y. AND AT ADDITIONAL MAILING OFFICES. Published monthly. Copyright ©1978 by Marvel Comics Group. A Division of Cadence Industries Corporation. All rights reserved. Vol. 1, No. 270, April, 1978 issue. Price 35¢ per copy in the U.S. and Canada. Subscription rate $4.50 for 12 issues. Canada, $5.50. Foreign, $6.50. No similarity between any of the names, characters, persons, and/or institutions in this magazine with those of any living or dead person or institution is intended, and any such similarity which may exist is purely coincidental. Printed in the U.S.A. This periodical may not be sold except by authorized dealers and is sold subject to the conditions that it shall not be sold or distributed with any part of its cover or markings removed, nor in a mutilated condition. THOR (including all prominent characters featured in the issue), and the distinctive likenesses thereof, are trademarks of MARVEL COMICS GROUP.

by Walter Simonson

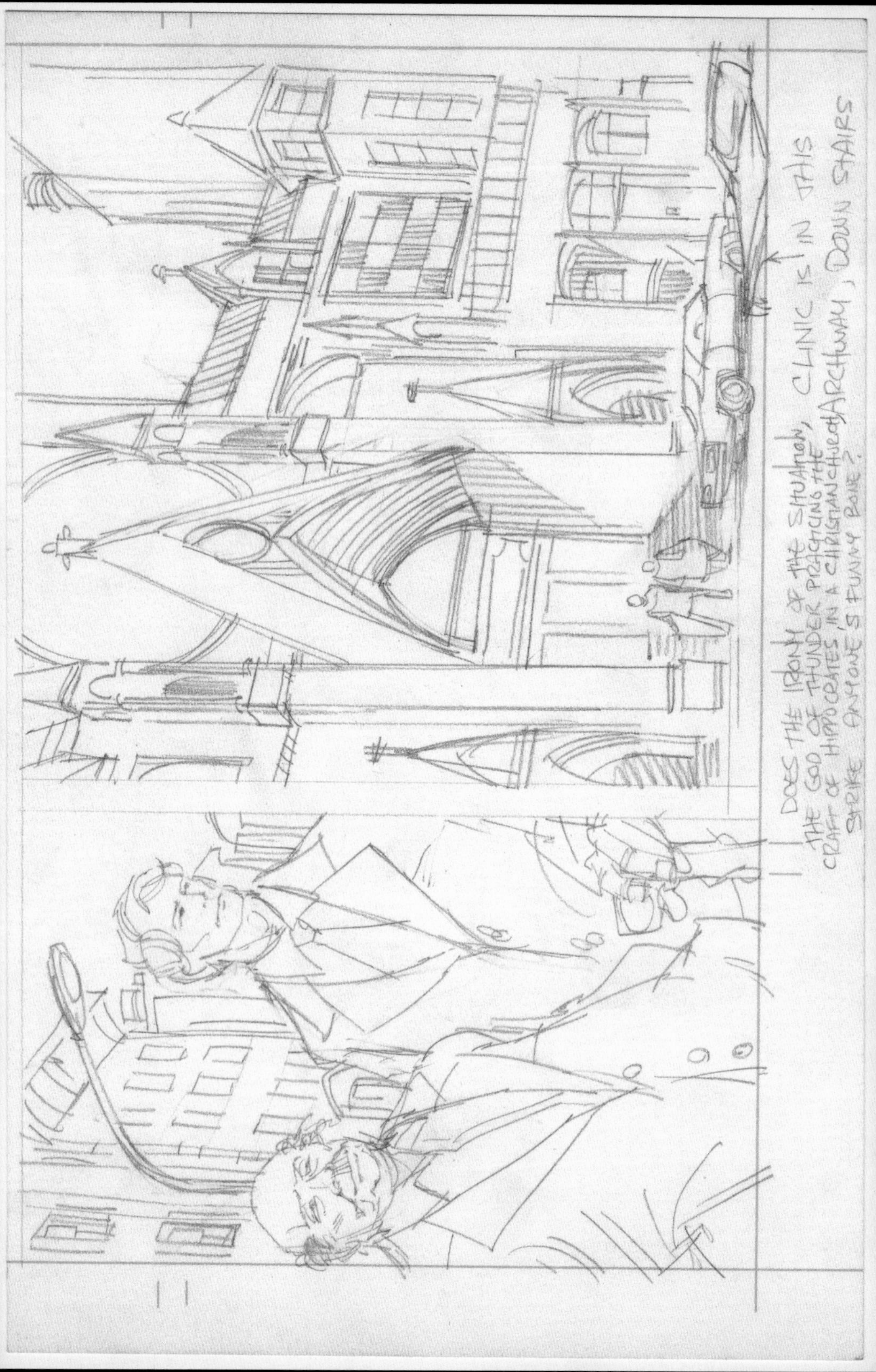
DOES THE IRONY OF THE SITUATION, THE GOD OF THUNDER PRACTICING THE CRAFT OF HIPPOCRATES, IN A CHRISTIAN CHURCH, STRIKE ANYONE'S FUNNY BONE?
CLINIC IS IN THIS ARCHWAY, DOWN STAIRS

Courtesy Walter Simonson

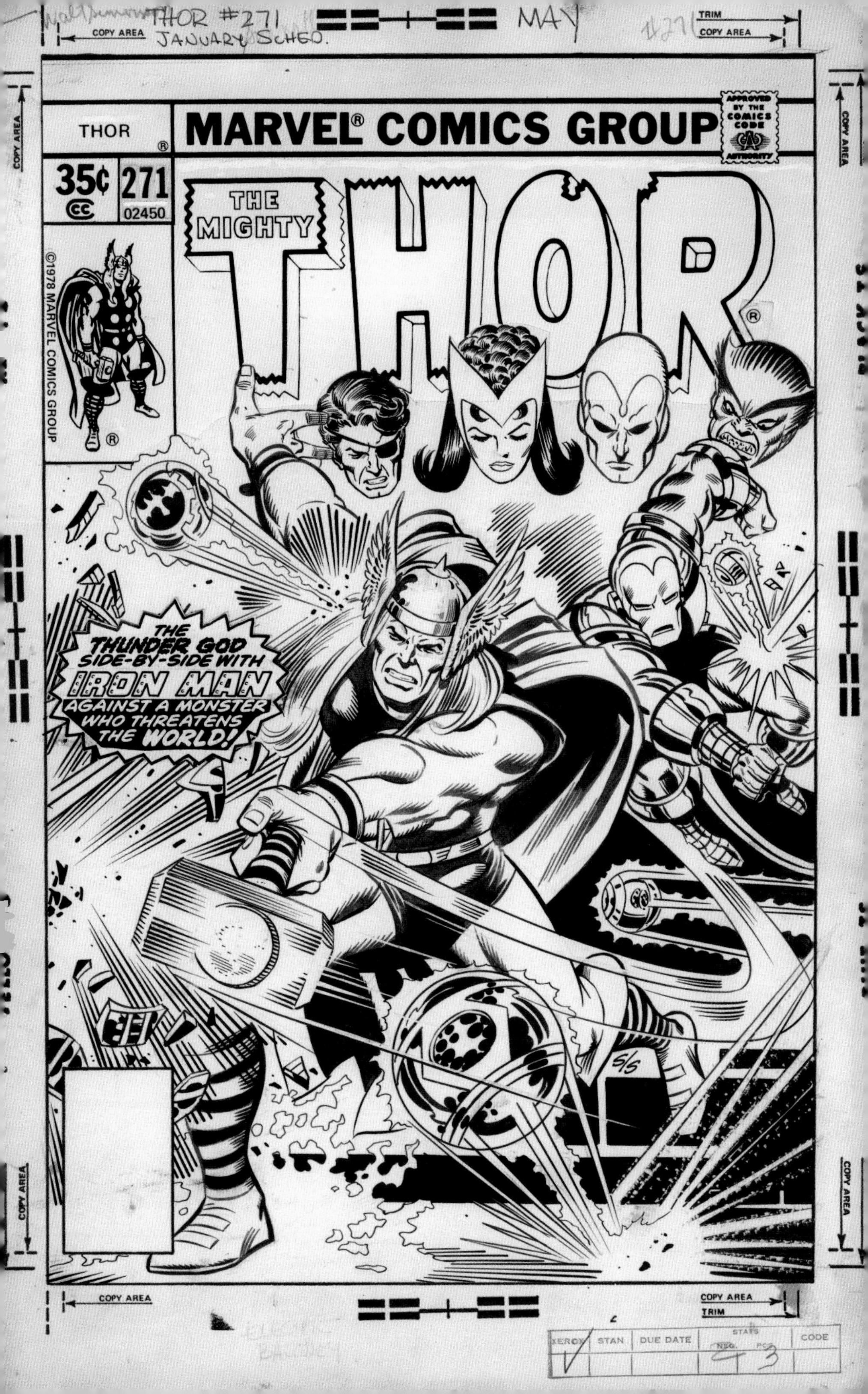
THOR #271
JANUARY SCHED.
MAY
#271
COPY AREA
TRIM
THOR
MARVEL® COMICS GROUP
APPROVED BY THE COMICS CODE AUTHORITY
35¢
271
02450
THE MIGHTY THOR
©1978 MARVEL COMICS GROUP
THE THUNDER GOD SIDE-BY-SIDE WITH IRON MAN AGAINST A MONSTER WHO THREATENS THE WORLD!
S/S
XEROX
STAN
DUE DATE
STATS
NEG.
POS.
CODE

Book Issue# pg.# 13

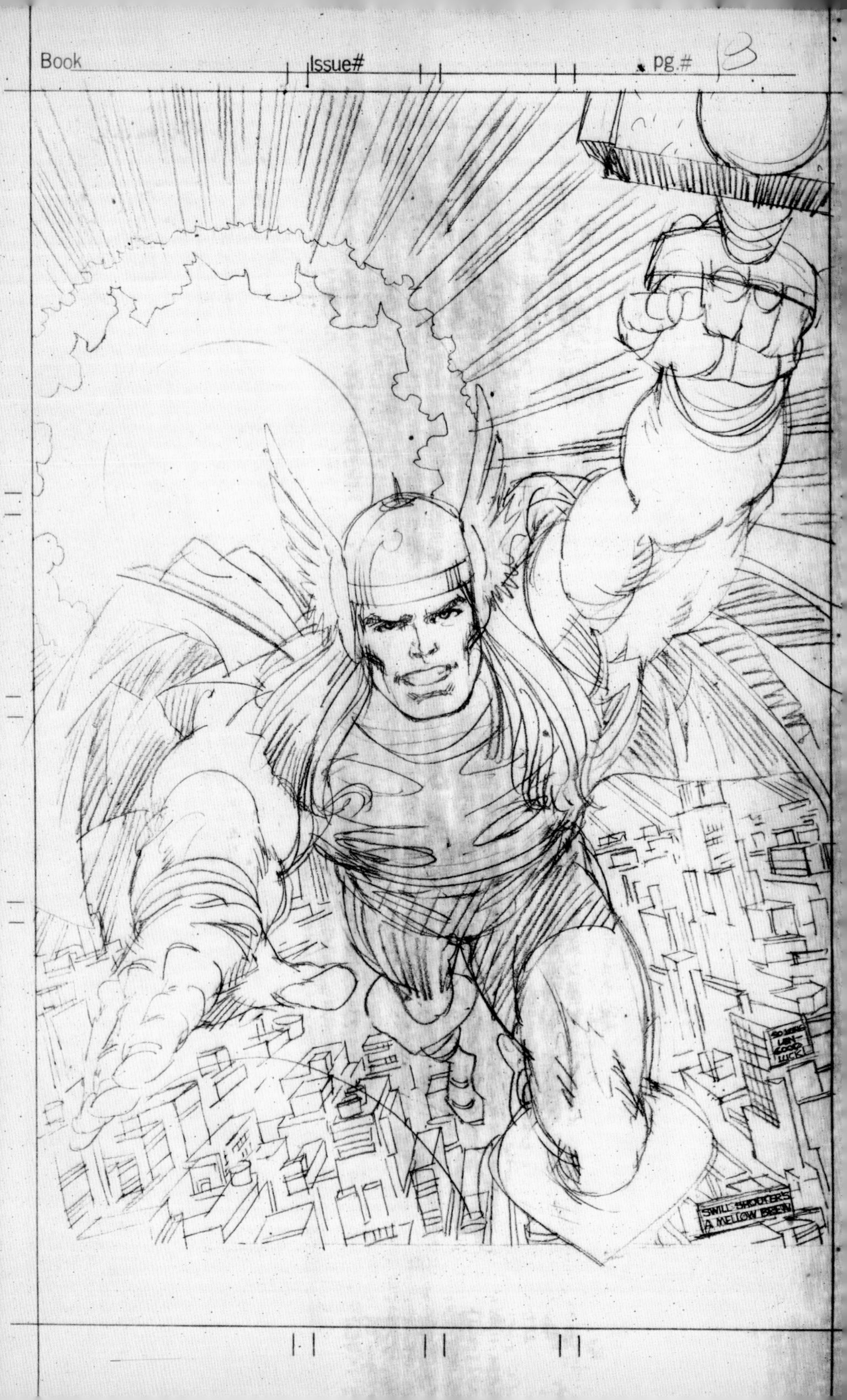
SO LONG LEN— GOOD LUCK!
SWILL SHOCKER'S A MELLOW BREW

18

Book MIGHTY THOR Issue# 271 pg.# 31

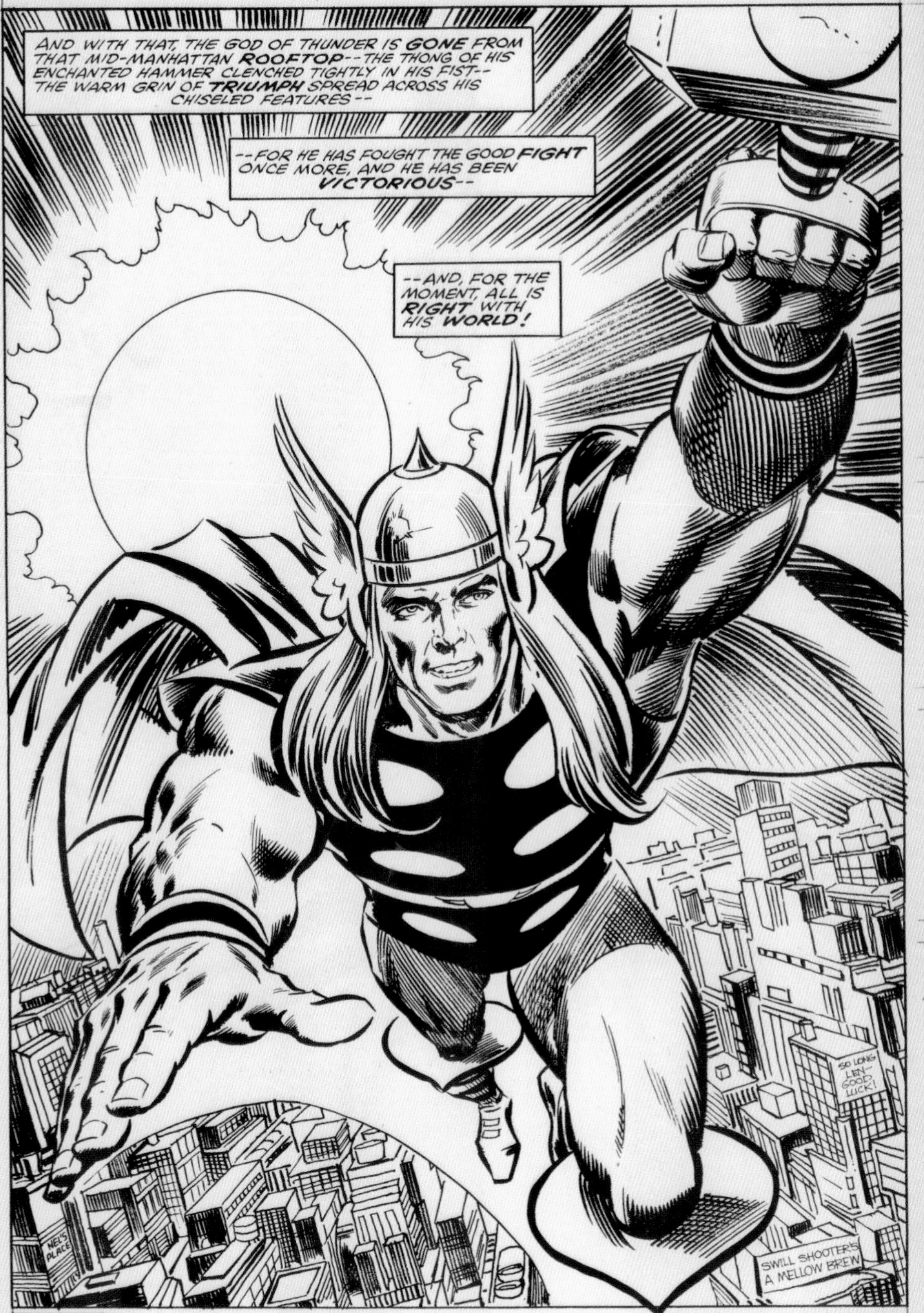
AND WITH THAT, THE GOD OF THUNDER IS GONE FROM THAT MID-MANHATTAN ROOFTOP--THE THONG OF HIS ENCHANTED HAMMER CLENCHED TIGHTLY IN HIS FIST--THE WARM GRIN OF TRIUMPH SPREAD ACROSS HIS CHISELED FEATURES--
--FOR HE HAS FOUGHT THE GOOD FIGHT ONCE MORE, AND HE HAS BEEN VICTORIOUS--
--AND, FOR THE MOMENT, ALL IS RIGHT WITH HIS WORLD!
SO LONG LEN- GOOD LUCK!
NEL'S PLACE
SWILL SHOOTER'S A MELLOW BREW
NEXT ISSUE:

XEROX	STAN	DUE DATE	STATS NTG.	CODE

CALL ROY FOR BLURB!

#272 — COVER

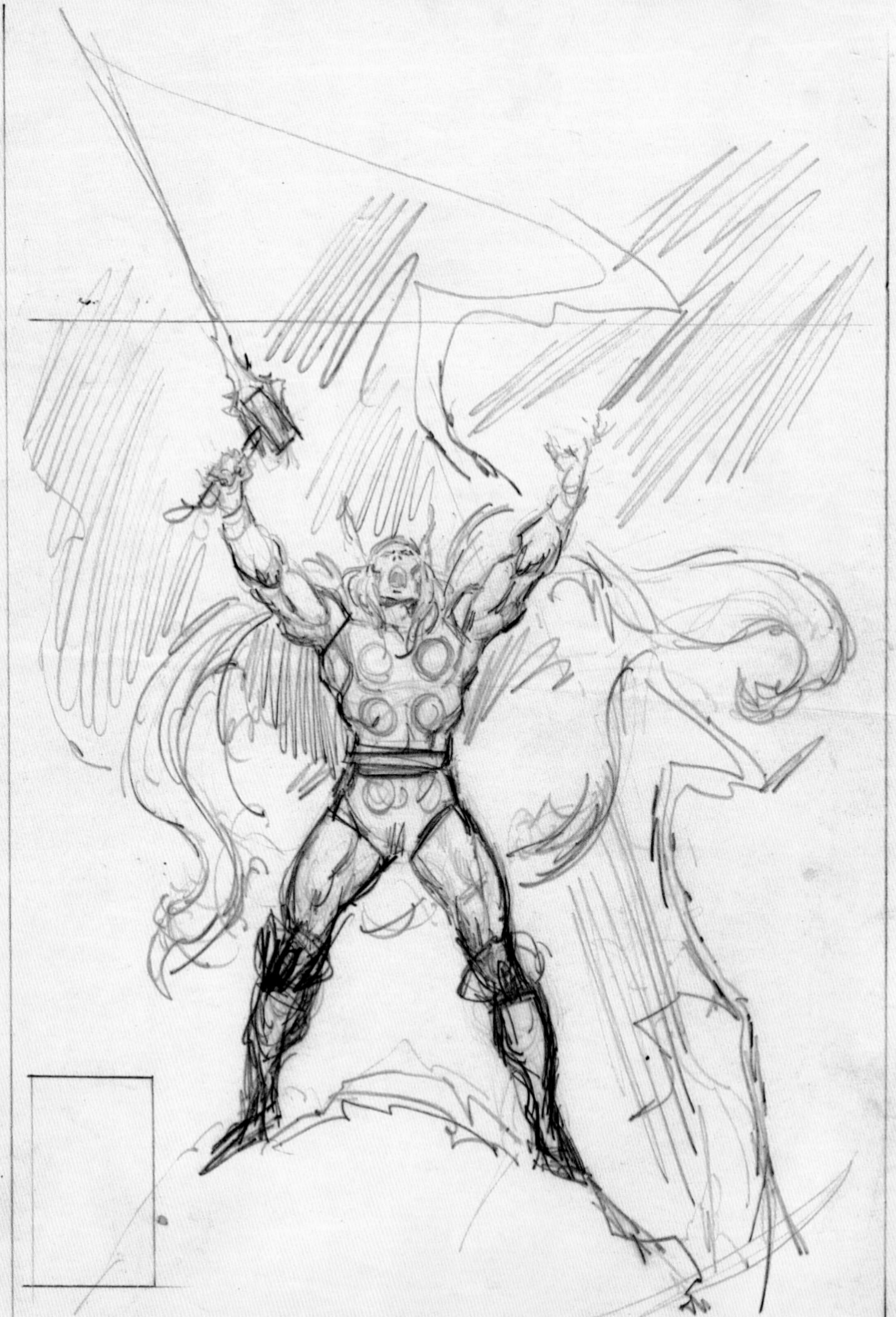

by John Buscema

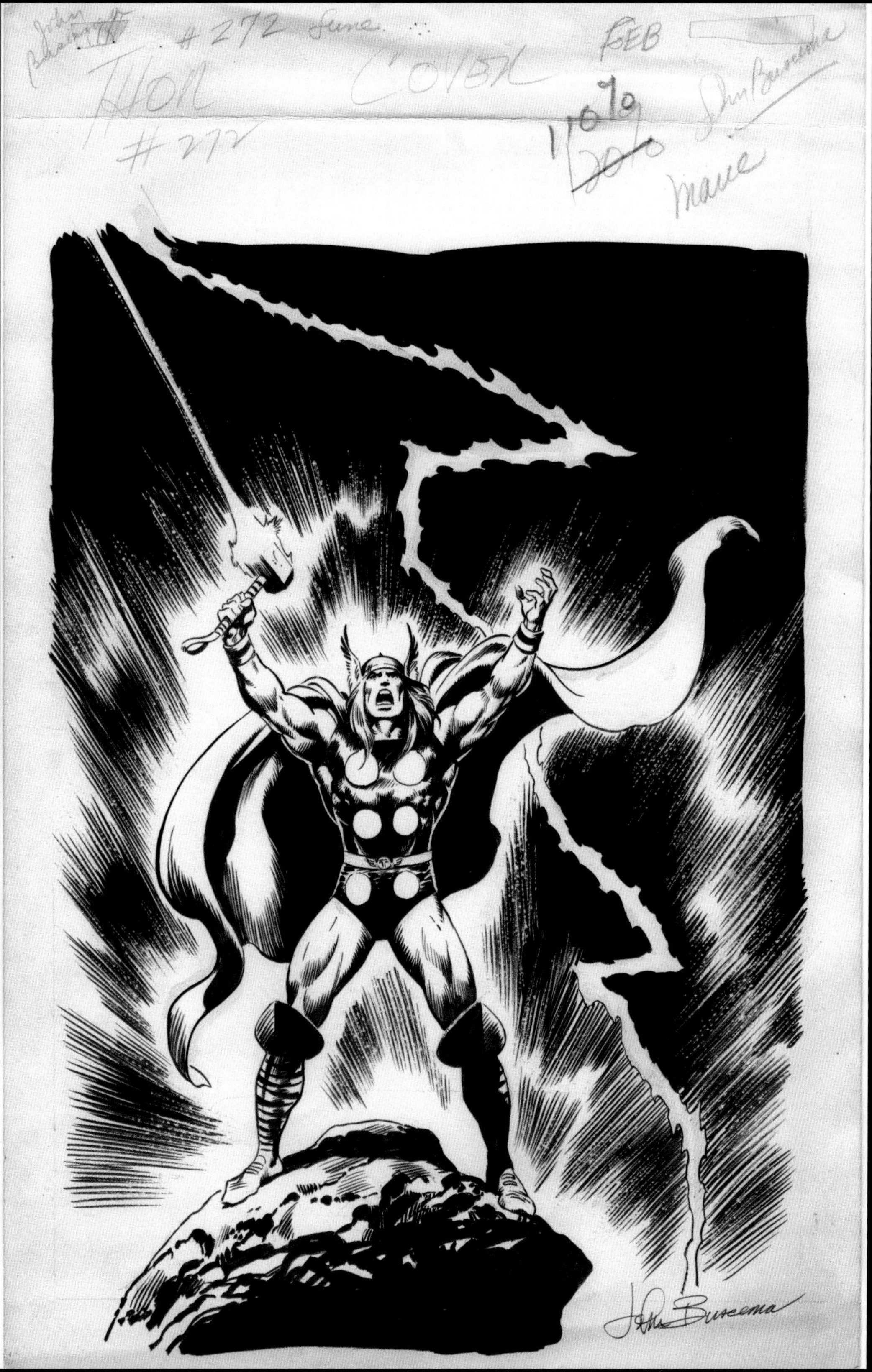

Courtesy Benny Gelillo

by John Buscema

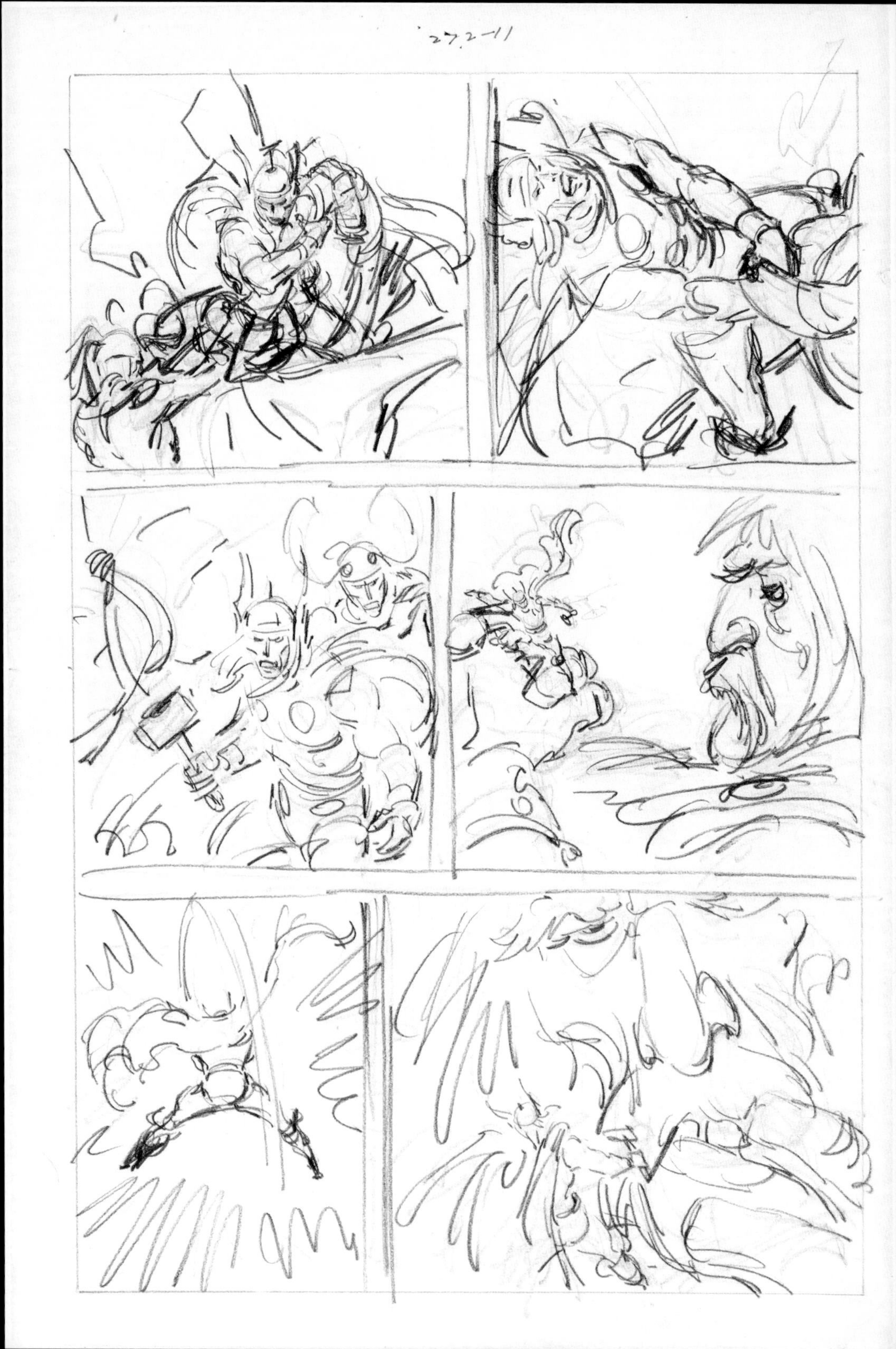

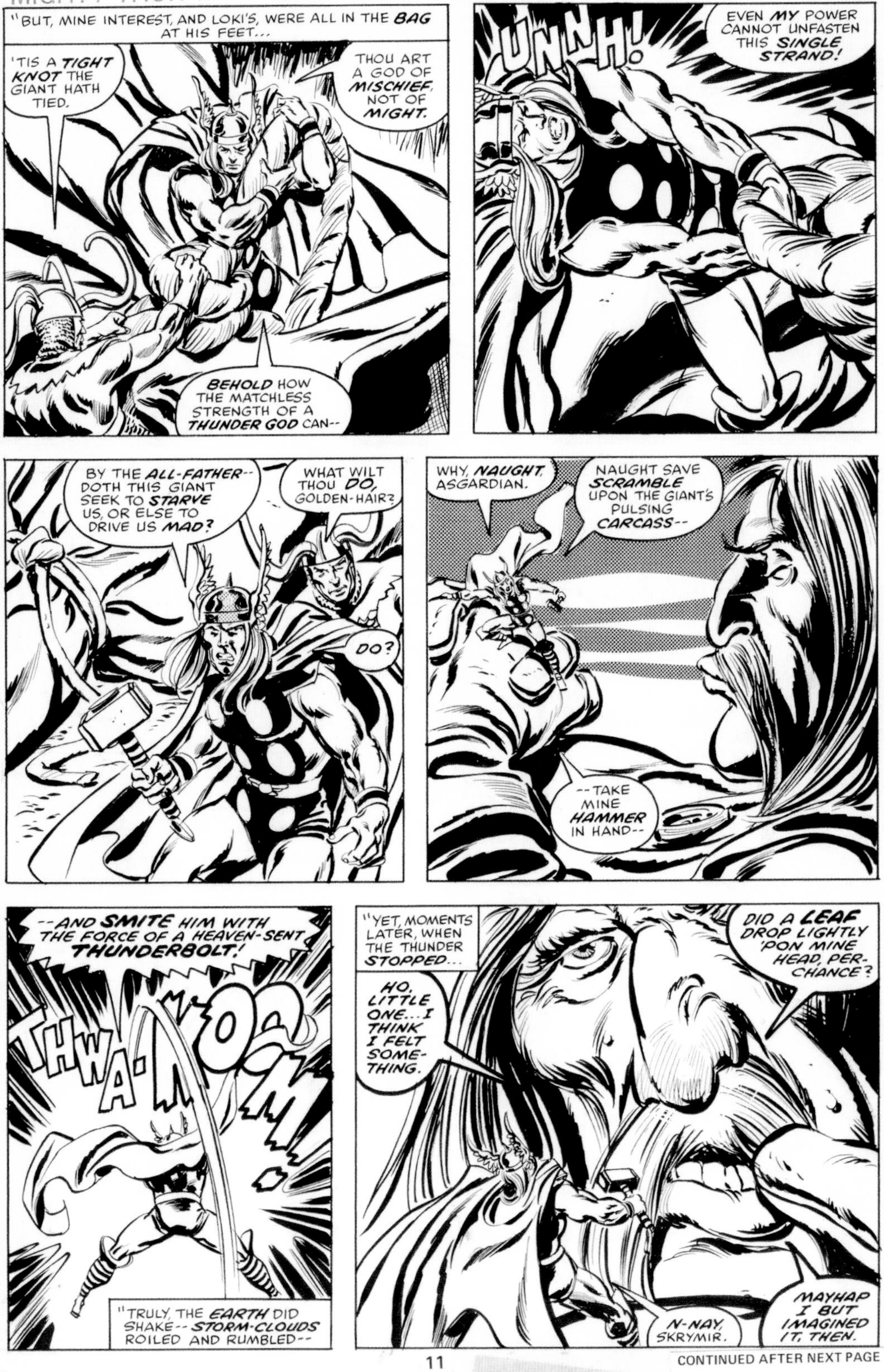
"BUT, MINE INTEREST, AND LOKI'S, WERE ALL IN THE BAG AT HIS FEET...
'TIS A TIGHT KNOT THE GIANT HATH TIED.
THOU ART A GOD OF MISCHIEF, NOT OF MIGHT.
BEHOLD HOW THE MATCHLESS STRENGTH OF A THUNDER GOD CAN--
UNNH!
EVEN MY POWER CANNOT UNFASTEN THIS SINGLE STRAND!
BY THE ALL-FATHER-- DOTH THIS GIANT SEEK TO STARVE US, OR ELSE TO DRIVE US MAD?
WHAT WILT THOU DO, GOLDEN-HAIR?
DO?
WHY, NAUGHT, ASGARDIAN.
NAUGHT SAVE SCRAMBLE UPON THE GIANT'S PULSING CARCASS--
--TAKE MINE HAMMER IN HAND--
--AND SMITE HIM WITH THE FORCE OF A HEAVEN-SENT THUNDERBOLT!
THWA-KOOM
"TRULY, THE EARTH DID SHAKE--STORM-CLOUDS ROILED AND RUMBLED--
"YET, MOMENTS LATER, WHEN THE THUNDER STOPPED...
HO, LITTLE ONE... I THINK I FELT SOME-THING.
DID A LEAF DROP LIGHTLY 'PON MINE HEAD, PER-CHANCE?
N-NAY, SKRYMIR.
MAYHAP I BUT IMAGINED IT, THEN.

CONTINUED AFTER NEXT PAGE

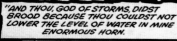

"AND THOU, GOD OF STORMS, DIDST BROOD BECAUSE THOU COULDST NOT LOWER THE LEVEL OF WATER IN MINE ENORMOUS HORN.

"LITTLE DIDST THOU SUSPECT--"

"--THAT THE HORN'S NETHER END WAS SET IN THE GREAT OCEAN ITSELF!

"IN FACT, THOU DIDST LOWER THE LEVEL OF THE WATERS DOWN TO EBB-TIDE!"

"AND THE CAT THOU DIDST STRIVE TO LIFT WAS NO CAT AT ALL--"

"--BUT THE GARGANTUAN MIDGARD SERPENT WHICH GIRDLES THE EARTH AND HOLDS THE SEA IN PLACE!

"HOW I DID INWARDLY TREMBLE WHEN THOU DIDST LIFT THE CREATURE ALL UN-KNOWING, EVEN THE SLIGHTEST BIT!"

"LOKI ASKED THEE," SAYS THOR, "AND NOW I ASK THEE: WHY DIDST THOU TRICK THUS OUR SIGHT AND SENSES?"

"WHY? BECAUSE I DESIRED TO TEST THE METTLE AND MERIT OF YE GODS!

"IF YE WERE NOT STRONG OR BRAVE ENOW TO STAND, WE GIANTS WOULD INVADE ASGARD AT ONCE--

"--AND THE DREADED DAY OF RAGNAROK WOULD OCCUR MIL-LENNIA SOONER THAN THE NORN-FATES PREDICT!"

"WHEN YE FOUGHT ON, EVEN IN THE FACE OF FOUR DEFEATS, I SENT OLD ELLI AGAINST THEE...

"ELLI, SHE WHO IS THE PERSONIFI-CATION OF OLD AGE ITSELF!

"UNKNOWN TO THEE, SHE DID AGE THEE... AND THUS WEAKEN THEE!"

CONTINUED AFTER NEXT PAGE

The Mighty Thor #273 cover original art
by John Buscema & Tom Palmer

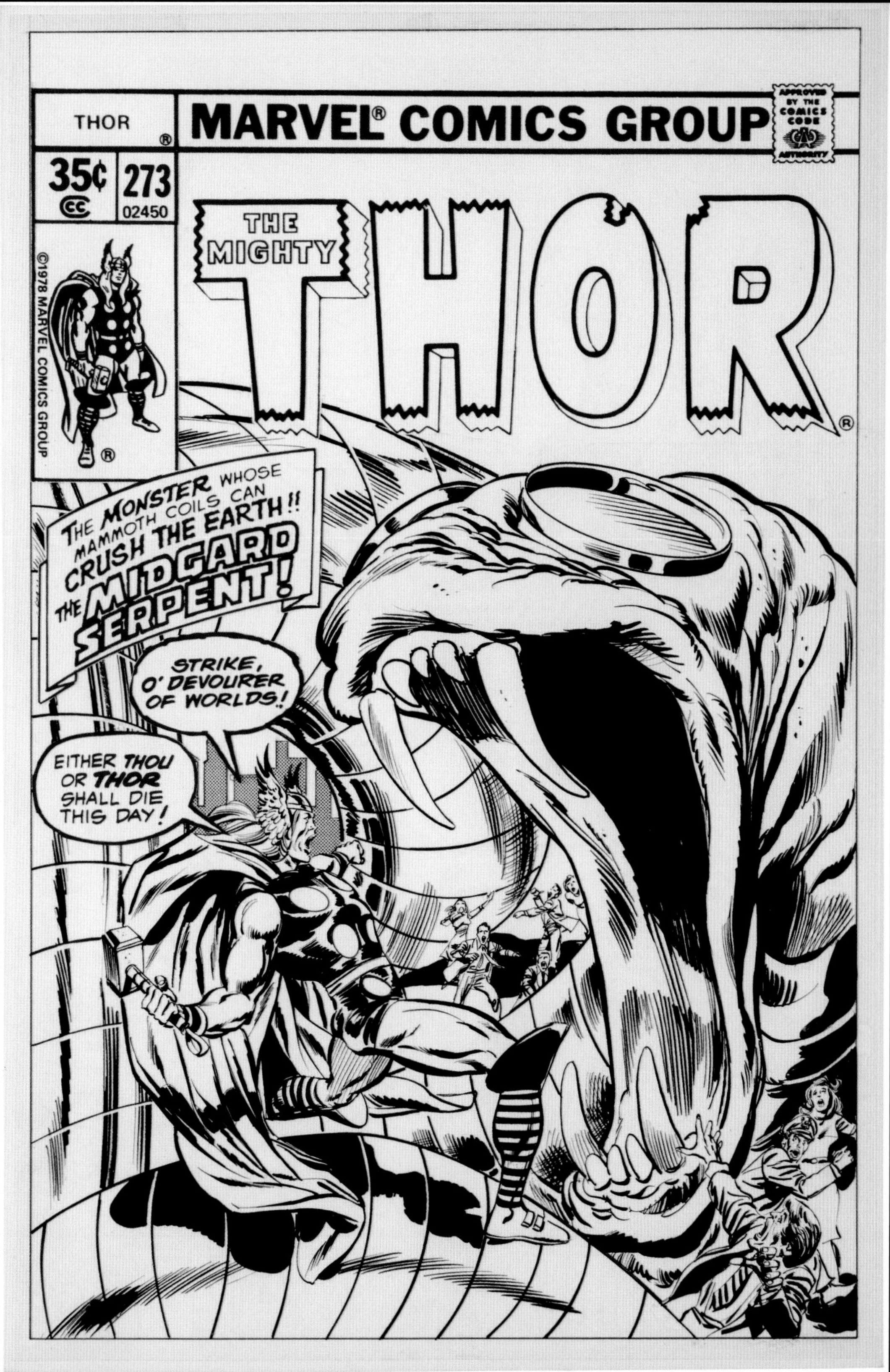
THOR
MARVEL® COMICS GROUP
APPROVED BY THE COMICS CODE AUTHORITY
35¢
273
02450
THE MIGHTY THOR®
©1978 MARVEL COMICS GROUP
THE MONSTER WHOSE MAMMOTH COILS CAN CRUSH THE EARTH!! THE MIDGARD SERPENT!
STRIKE, O' DEVOURER OF WORLDS!
EITHER THOU OR THOR SHALL DIE THIS DAY!

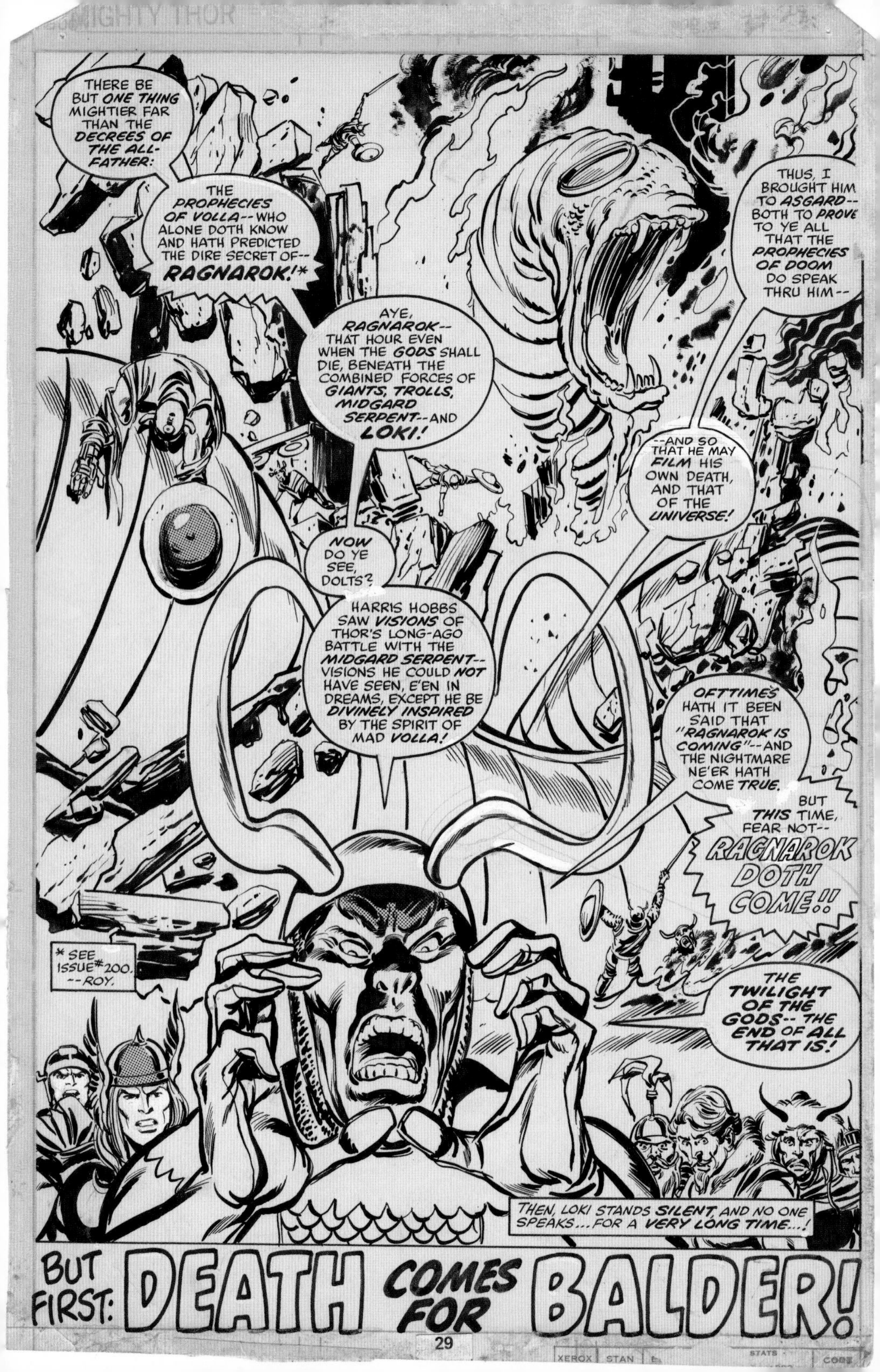
MIGHTY THOR
THERE BE BUT ONE THING MIGHTIER FAR THAN THE DECREES OF THE ALL-FATHER:
THE PROPHECIES OF VOLLA--WHO ALONE DOTH KNOW AND HATH PREDICTED THE DIRE SECRET OF--RAGNAROK!*
THUS, I BROUGHT HIM TO ASGARD--BOTH TO PROVE TO YE ALL THAT THE PROPHECIES OF DOOM DO SPEAK THRU HIM--
AYE, RAGNAROK--THAT HOUR EVEN WHEN THE GODS SHALL DIE, BENEATH THE COMBINED FORCES OF GIANTS, TROLLS, MIDGARD SERPENT--AND LOKI!
--AND SO THAT HE MAY FILM HIS OWN DEATH, AND THAT OF THE UNIVERSE!
NOW DO YE SEE, DOLTS?
HARRIS HOBBS SAW VISIONS OF THOR'S LONG-AGO BATTLE WITH THE MIDGARD SERPENT--VISIONS HE COULD NOT HAVE SEEN, E'EN IN DREAMS, EXCEPT HE BE DIVINELY INSPIRED BY THE SPIRIT OF MAD VOLLA!
OFTTIMES HATH IT BEEN SAID THAT "RAGNAROK IS COMING"--AND THE NIGHTMARE NE'ER HATH COME TRUE.
BUT THIS TIME, FEAR NOT--RAGNAROK DOTH COME!!
THE TWILIGHT OF THE GODS--THE END OF ALL THAT IS!
*SEE ISSUE #200. --ROY.
THEN, LOKI STANDS SILENT, AND NO ONE SPEAKS... FOR A VERY LONG TIME...!
BUT FIRST: DEATH COMES FOR BALDER!
29
XEROX STAN STATS CODE

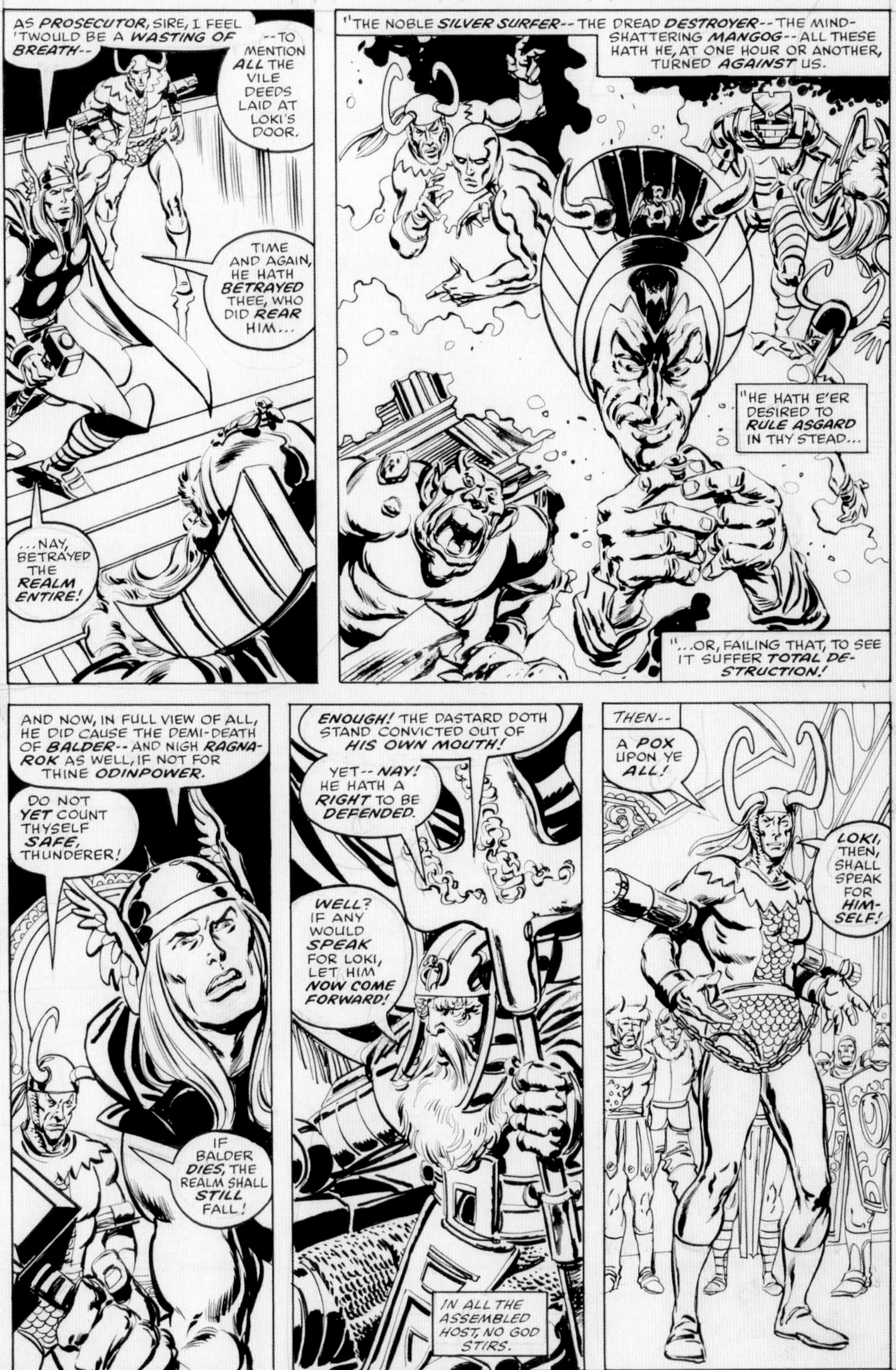
AS PROSECUTOR, SIRE, I FEEL 'TWOULD BE A WASTING OF BREATH--
--TO MENTION ALL THE VILE DEEDS LAID AT LOKI'S DOOR.
TIME AND AGAIN, HE HATH BETRAYED THEE, WHO DID REAR HIM...
...NAY, BETRAYED THE REALM ENTIRE!
"THE NOBLE SILVER SURFER-- THE DREAD DESTROYER-- THE MIND-SHATTERING MANGOG-- ALL THESE HATH HE, AT ONE HOUR OR ANOTHER, TURNED AGAINST US.
"HE HATH E'ER DESIRED TO RULE ASGARD IN THY STEAD...
"...OR, FAILING THAT, TO SEE IT SUFFER TOTAL DESTRUCTION!
AND NOW, IN FULL VIEW OF ALL, HE DID CAUSE THE DEMI-DEATH OF BALDER-- AND NIGH RAGNAROK AS WELL, IF NOT FOR THINE ODINPOWER.
DO NOT YET COUNT THYSELF SAFE, THUNDERER!
IF BALDER DIES, THE REALM SHALL STILL FALL!
ENOUGH! THE DASTARD DOTH STAND CONVICTED OUT OF HIS OWN MOUTH!
YET-- NAY! HE HATH A RIGHT TO BE DEFENDED.
WELL? IF ANY WOULD SPEAK FOR LOKI, LET HIM NOW COME FORWARD!
IN ALL THE ASSEMBLED HOST, NO GOD STIRS.
THEN--
A POX UPON YE ALL!
LOKI, THEN, SHALL SPEAK FOR HIMSELF!

CONTINUED AFTER NEXT PAGE

The Mighty Thor #276, page 9 pencil breakdown
by John Buscema

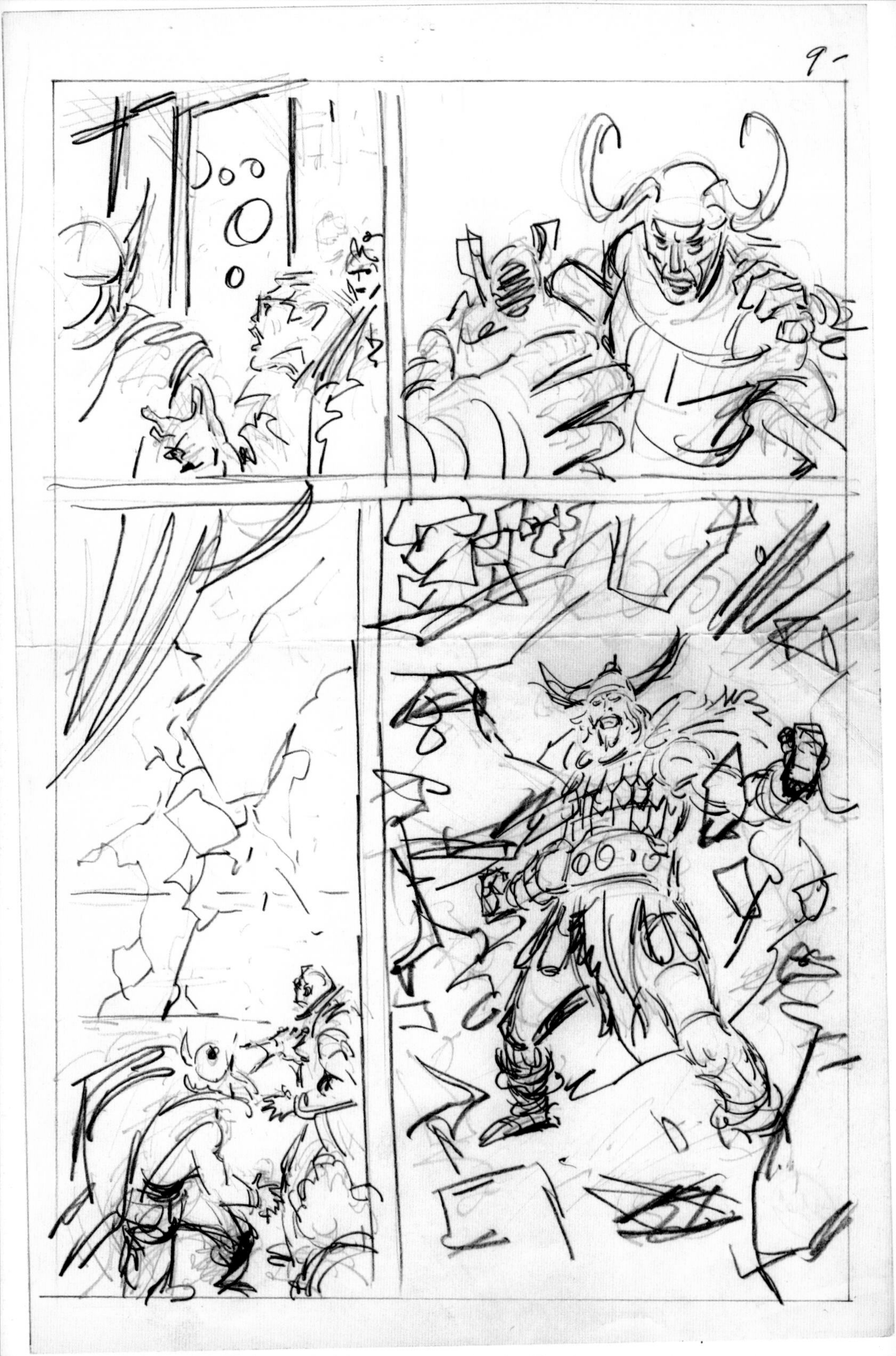
9-

Courtesy Benny Gelillo

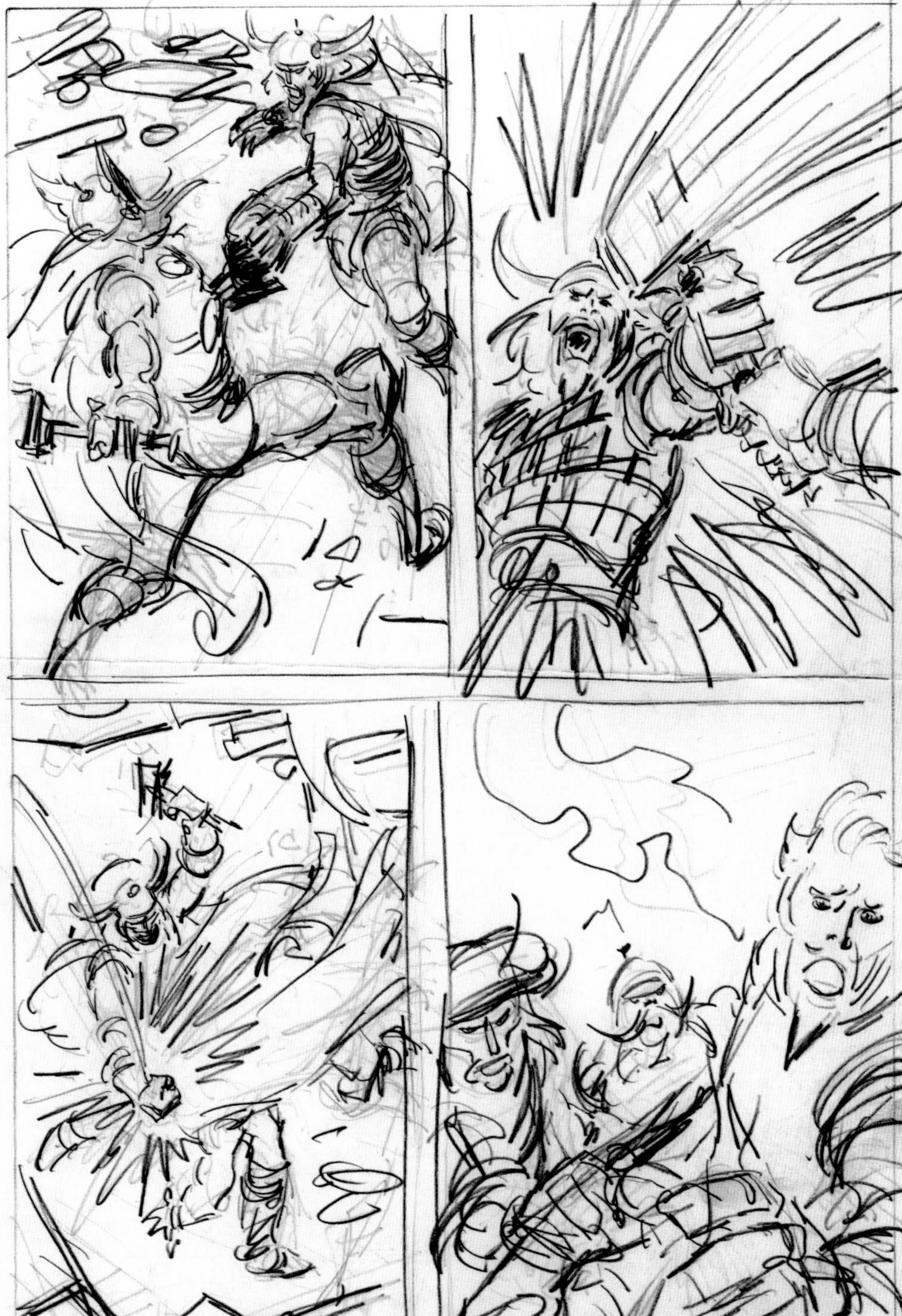

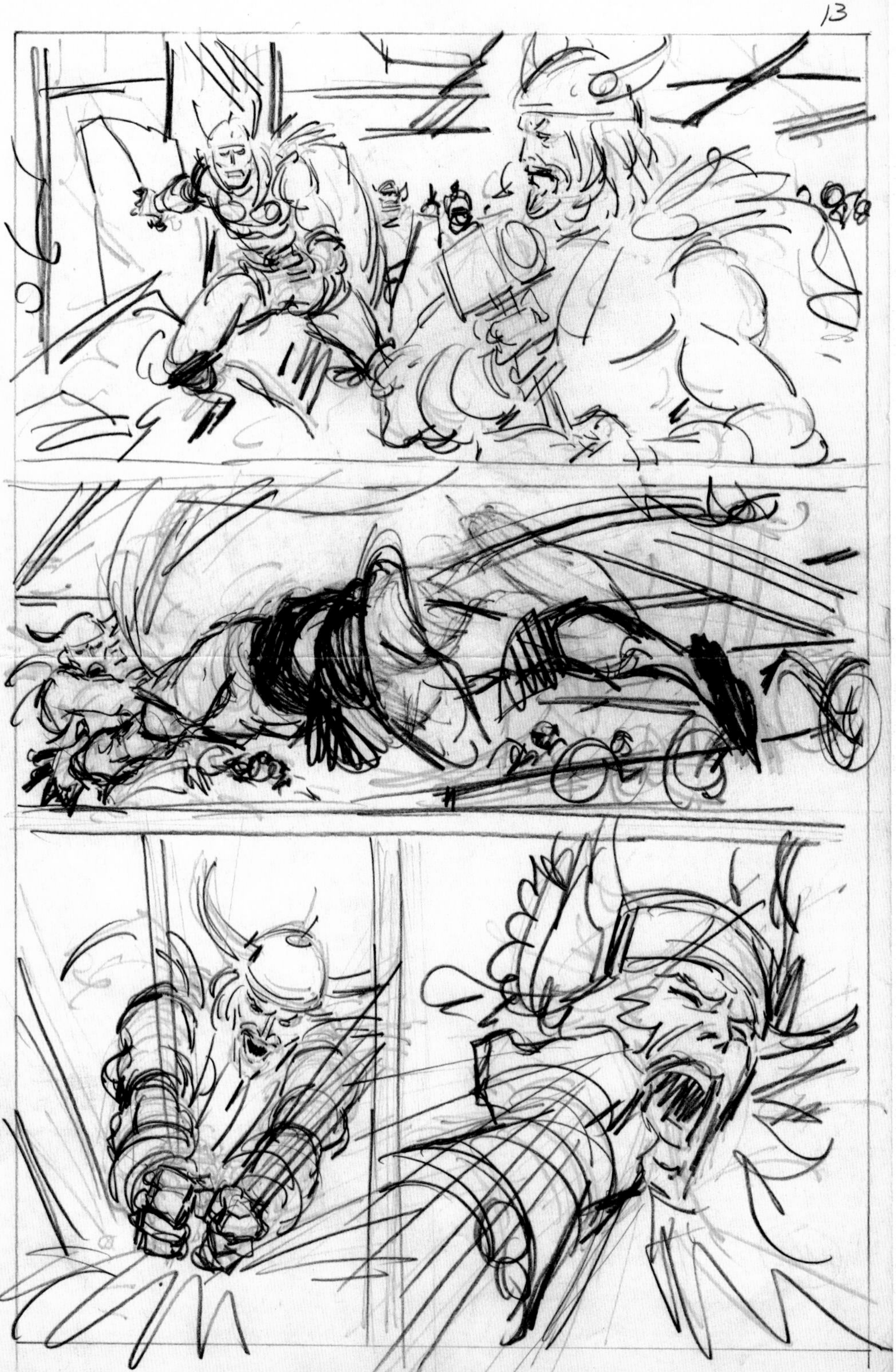
13

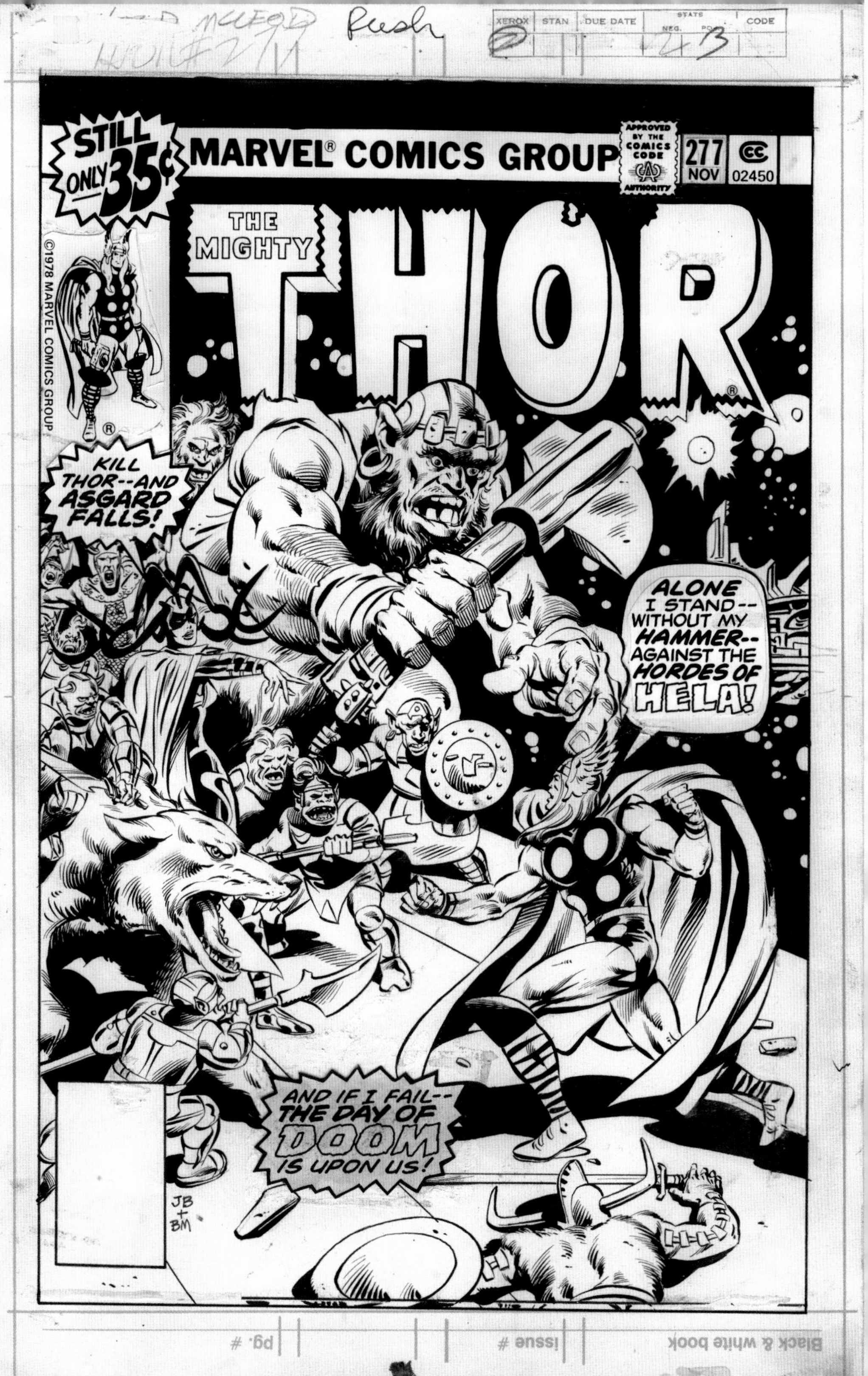
STILL ONLY 35¢
MARVEL® COMICS GROUP
APPROVED BY THE COMICS CODE AUTHORITY
277 NOV
CC 02450
THE MIGHTY THOR®
©1978 MARVEL COMICS GROUP
KILL THOR--AND ASGARD FALLS!
ALONE I STAND-- WITHOUT MY HAMMER-- AGAINST THE HORDES OF HELA!
AND IF I FAIL-- THE DAY OF DOOM IS UPON US!
JB + BM

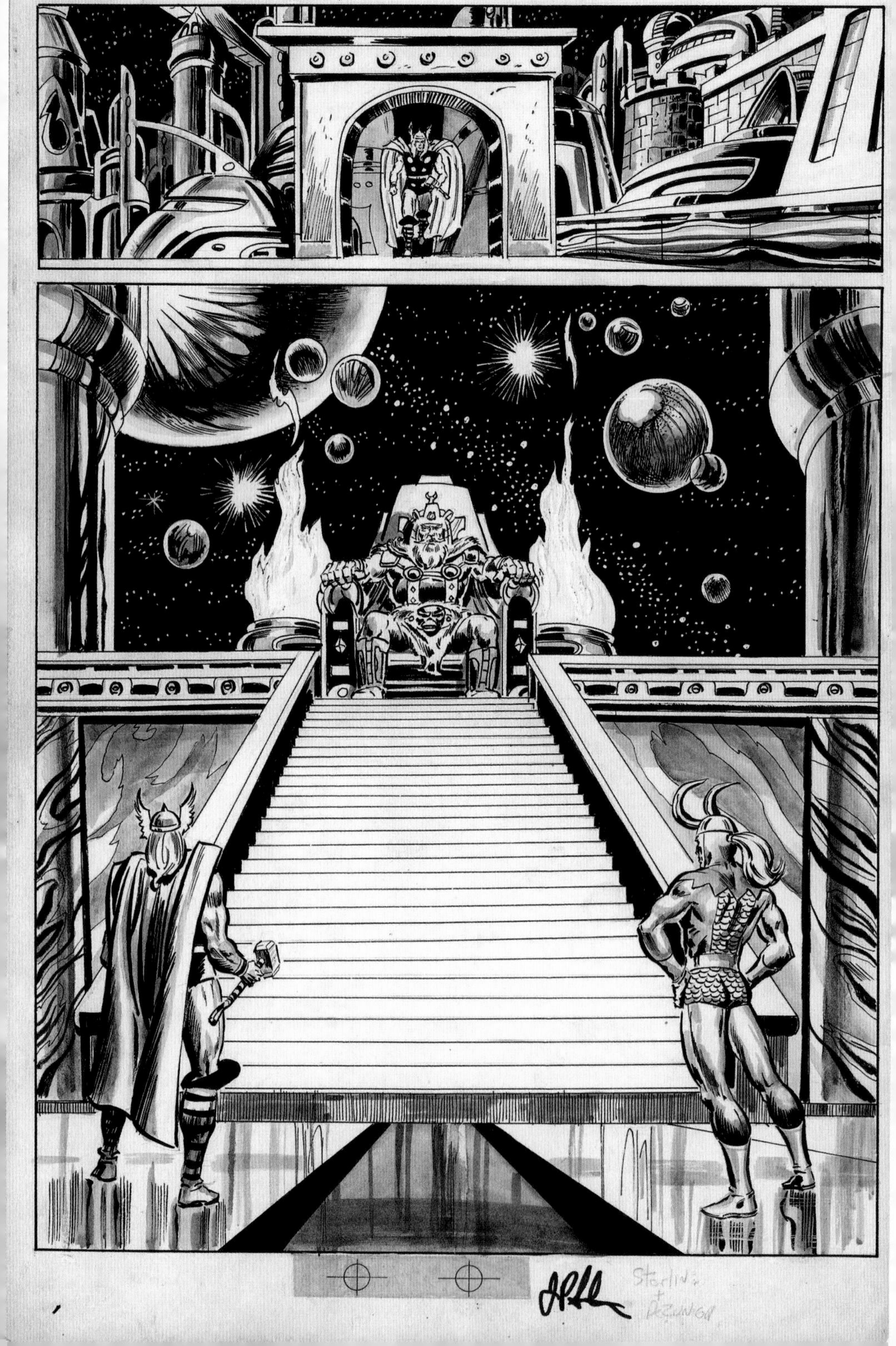

Marvel Preview #10, Thor, page 13 original art
by Jim Starlin & Tony DeZuniga

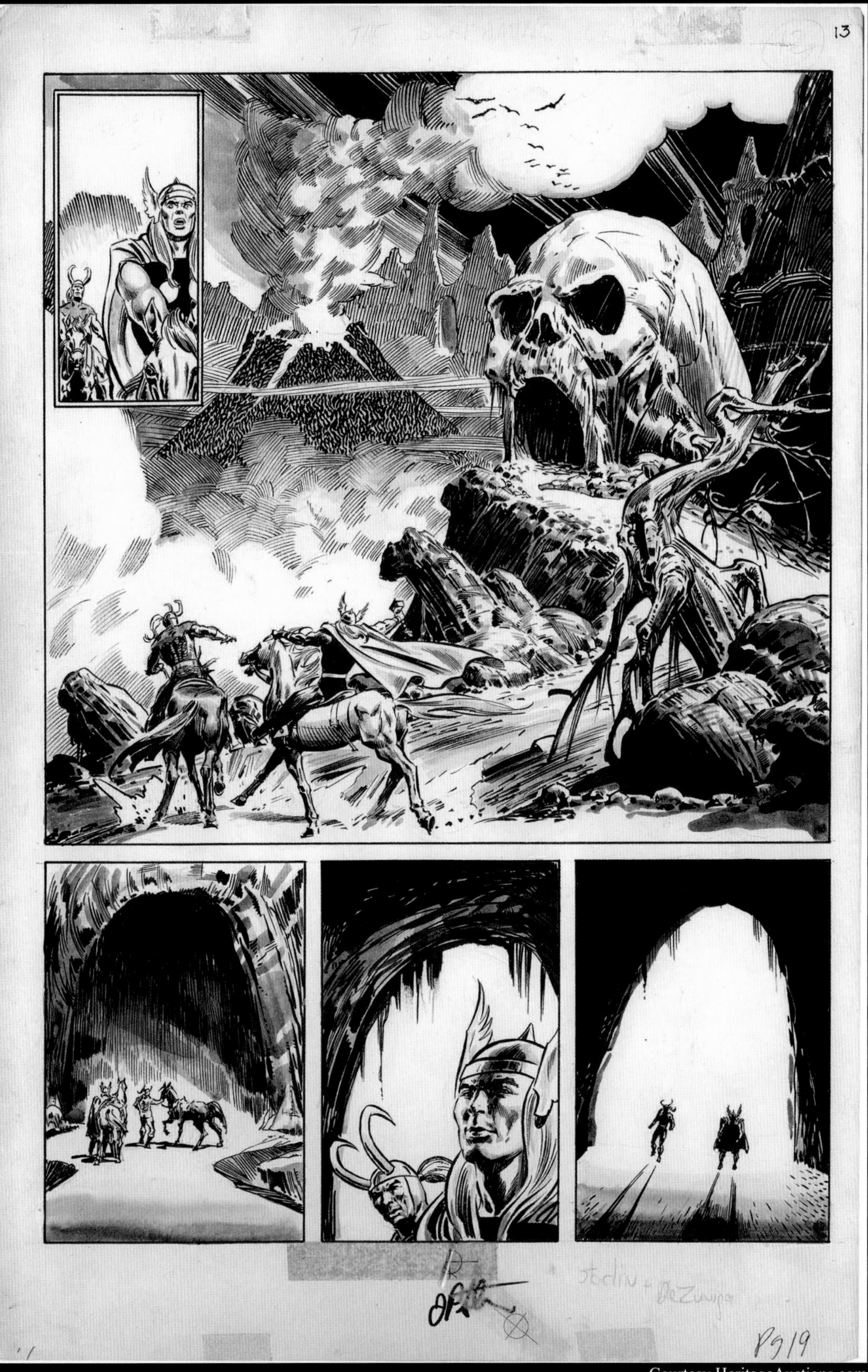
13
Starlin + DeZuniga
Pg 19

Marvel Preview #10, Hercules, page 1 original art
by Val Mayerik

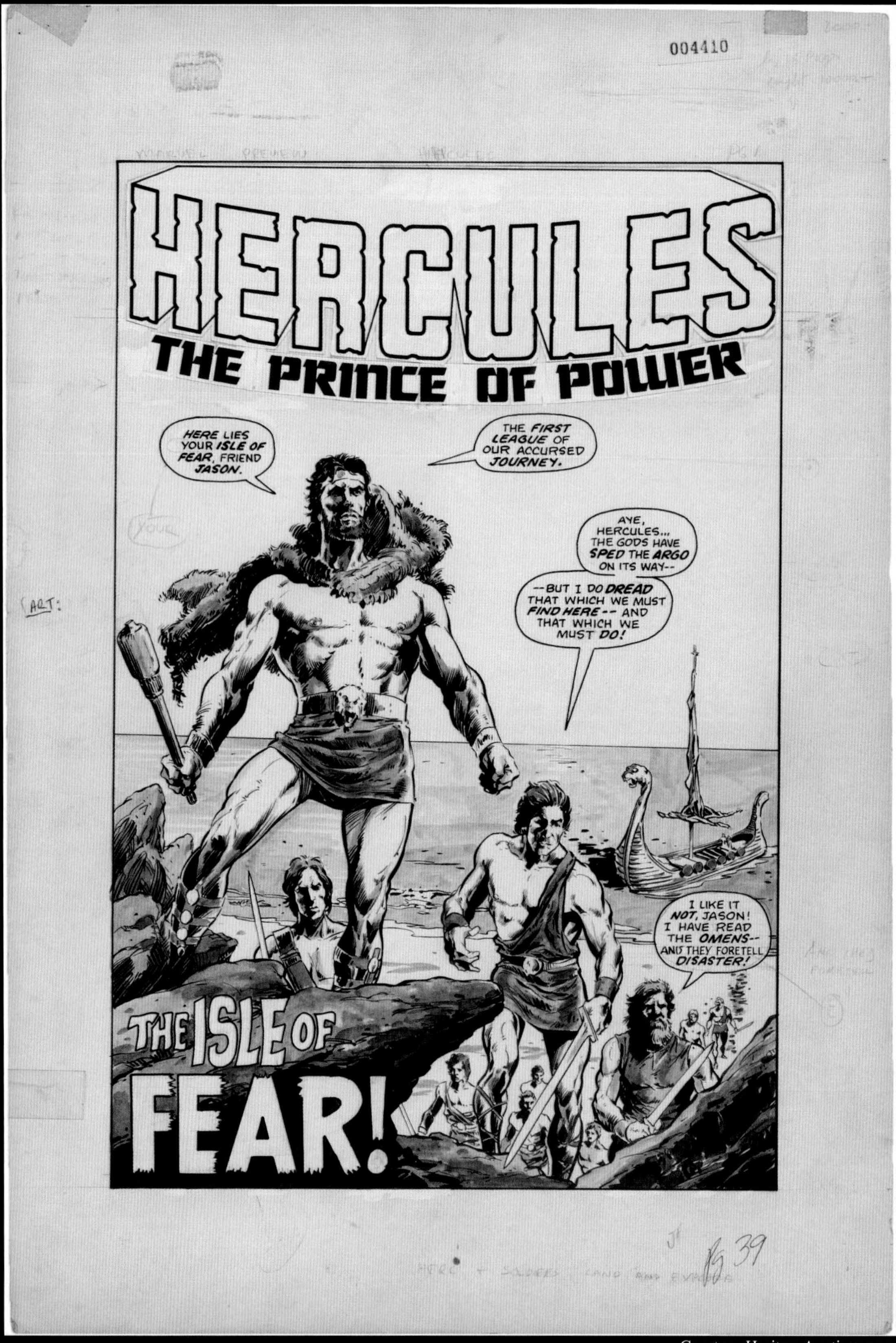
004410
HERCULES
THE PRINCE OF POWER
HERE LIES YOUR ISLE OF FEAR, FRIEND JASON.
THE FIRST LEAGUE OF OUR ACCURSED JOURNEY.
AYE, HERCULES... THE GODS HAVE SPED THE ARGO ON ITS WAY--
--BUT I DO DREAD THAT WHICH WE MUST FIND HERE-- AND THAT WHICH WE MUST DO!
I LIKE IT NOT, JASON! I HAVE READ THE OMENS-- AND THEY FORETELL DISASTER!
THE ISLE OF FEAR!
Pg 39

004425

JASON CLAIMS THRONE

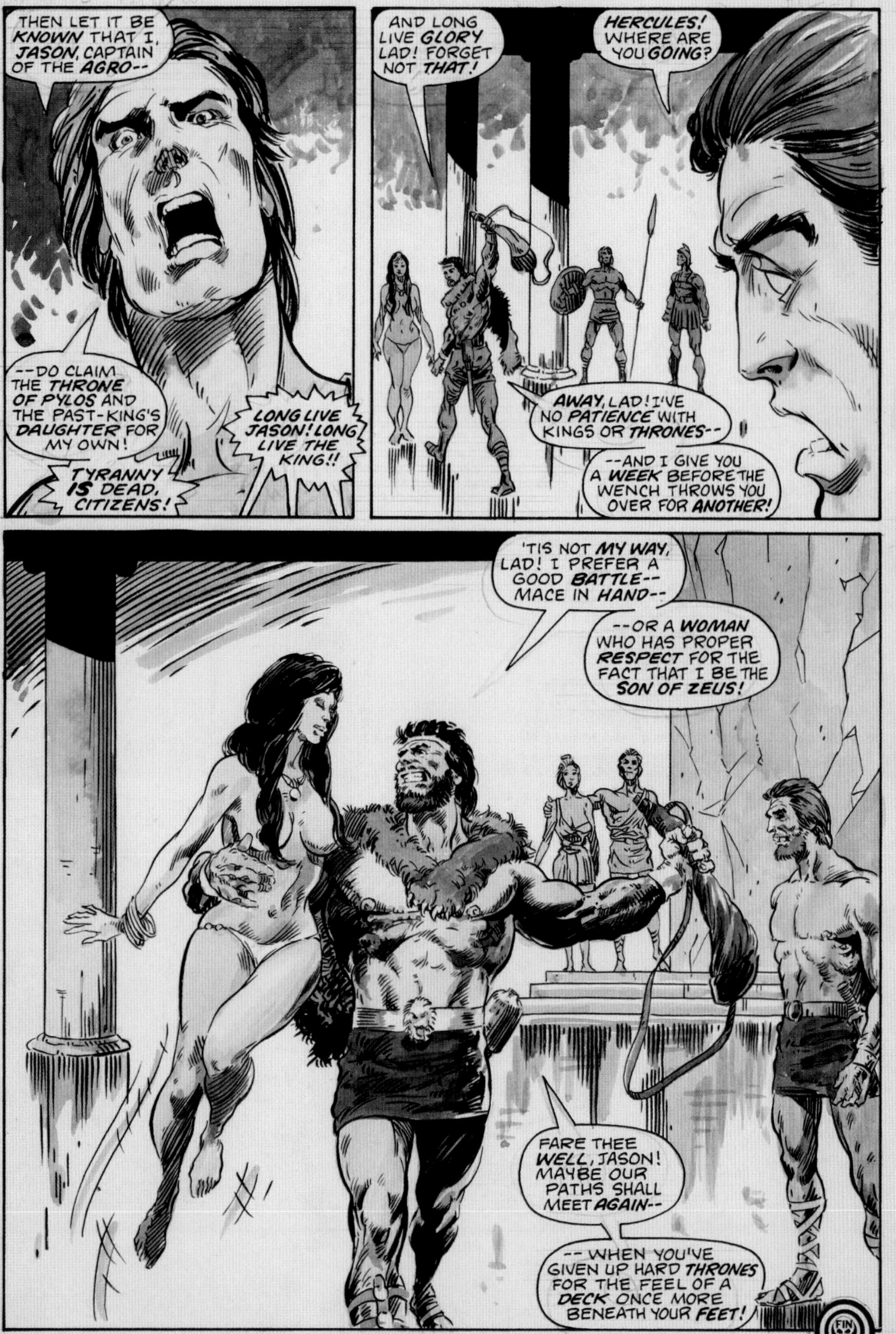
THEN LET IT BE KNOWN THAT I, JASON, CAPTAIN OF THE AGRO--
--DO CLAIM THE THRONE OF PYLOS AND THE PAST-KING'S DAUGHTER FOR MY OWN!
TYRANNY IS DEAD, CITIZENS!
LONG LIVE JASON! LONG LIVE THE KING!!
AND LONG LIVE GLORY LAD! FORGET NOT THAT!
HERCULES! WHERE ARE YOU GOING?
AWAY, LAD! I'VE NO PATIENCE WITH KINGS OR THRONES--
--AND I GIVE YOU A WEEK BEFORE THE WENCH THROWS YOU OVER FOR ANOTHER!
'TIS NOT MY WAY, LAD! I PREFER A GOOD BATTLE-- MACE IN HAND--
--OR A WOMAN WHO HAS PROPER RESPECT FOR THE FACT THAT I BE THE SON OF ZEUS!
FARE THEE WELL, JASON! MAYBE OUR PATHS SHALL MEET AGAIN--
-- WHEN YOU'VE GIVEN UP HARD THRONES FOR THE FEEL OF A DECK ONCE MORE BENEATH YOUR FEET!
FIN

59 Pg 59 HERC WANTS NO PART OF POLITICS TAKES WENCH + WINE AND SPLITS Pg 59

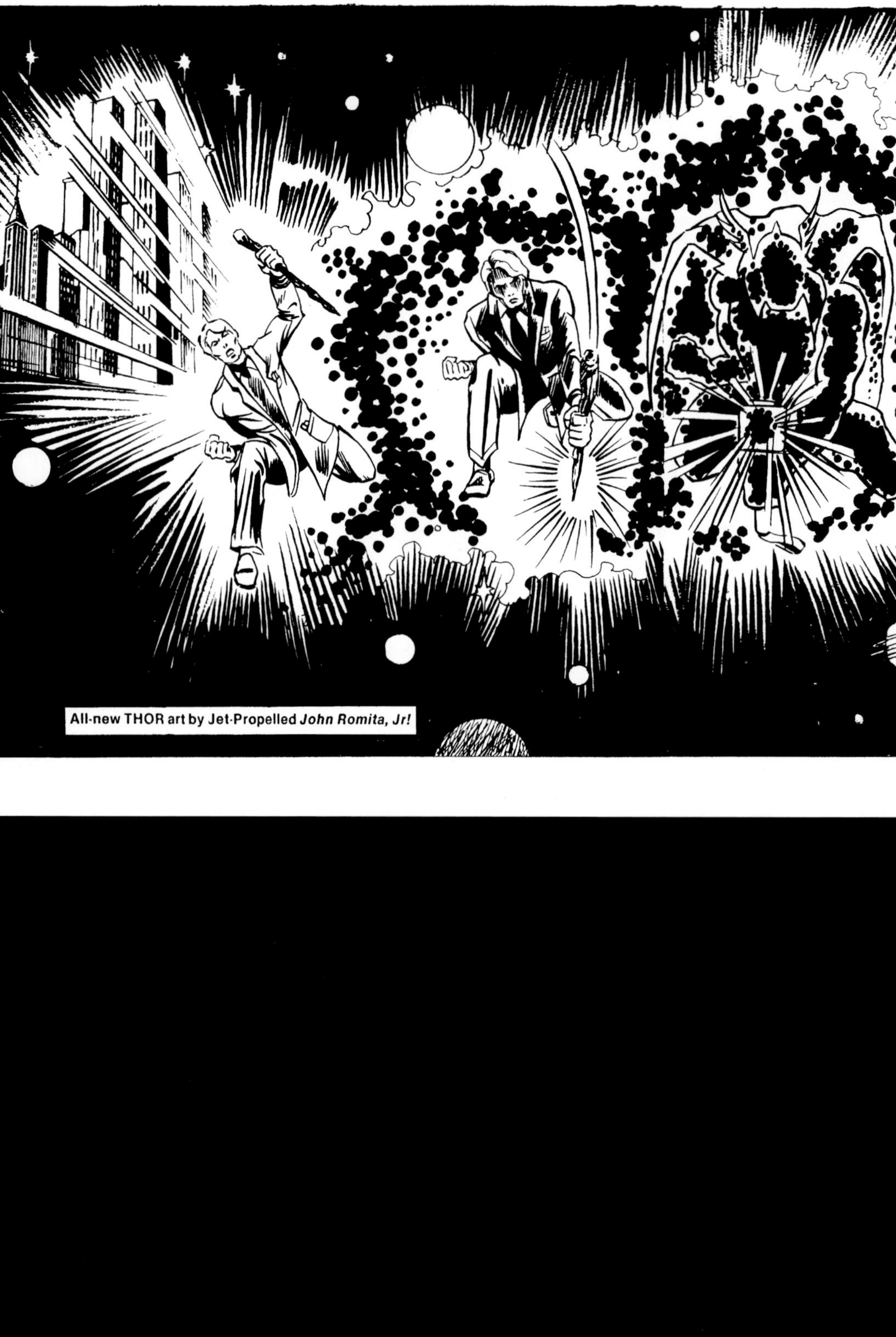
All-new THOR art by Jet-Propelled John Romita, Jr!

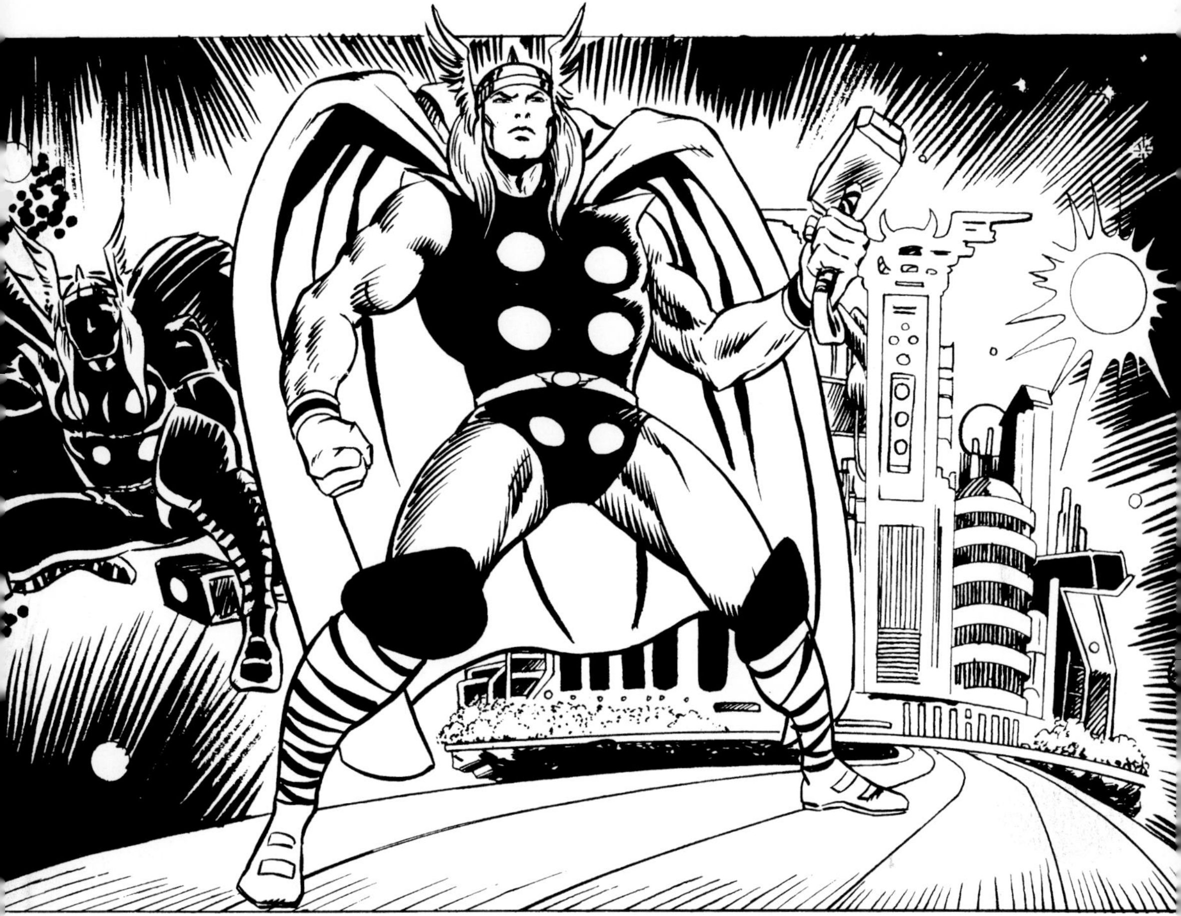

Unused Thor pencil art by Rich Buckler
featured in *F.O.O.M.* #21 (Spring 1978)

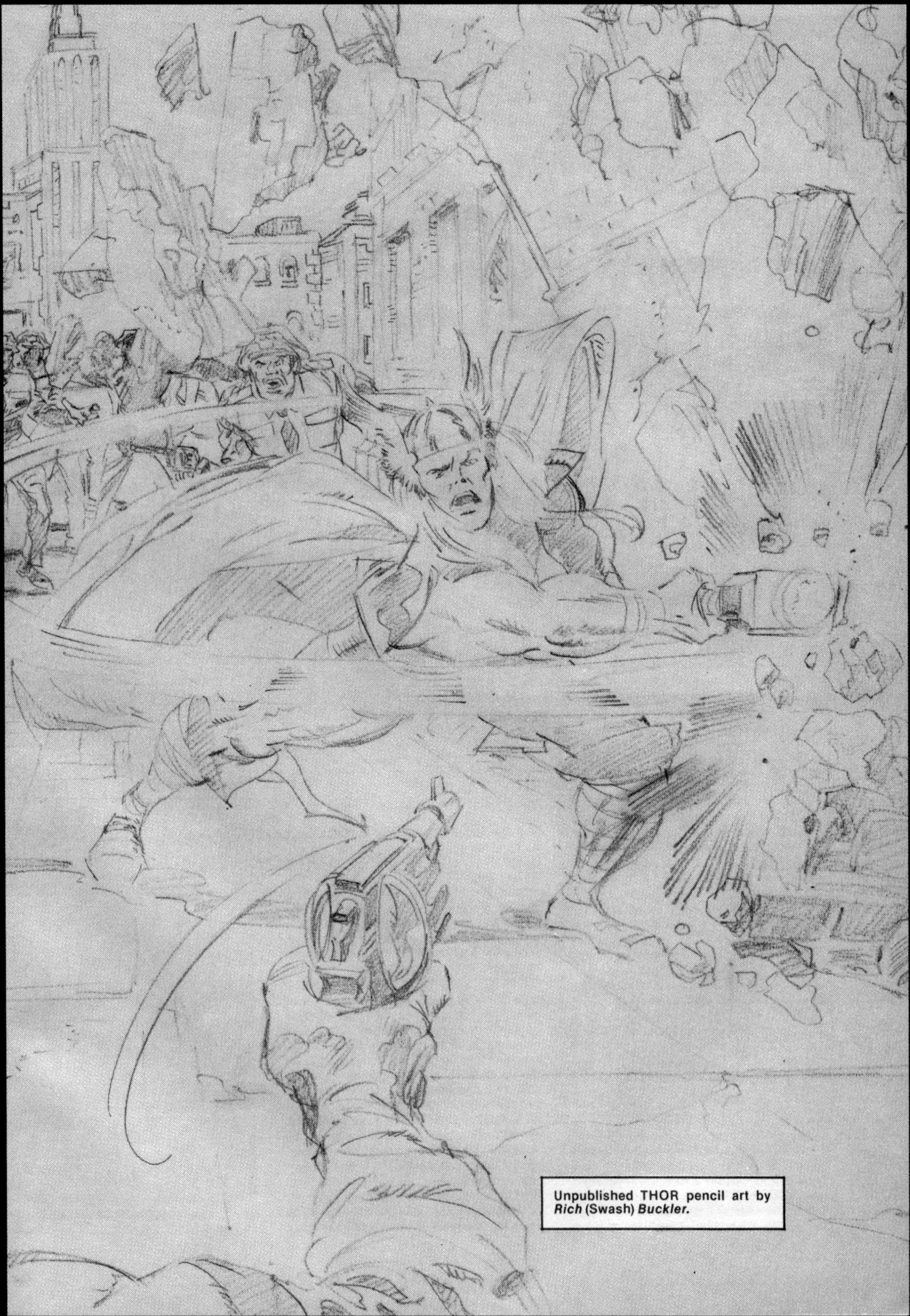

Unpublished THOR pencil art by *Rich* (Swash) ***Buckler.***

BIOGRAPHIES

LEN WEIN

Len Wein's career is highlighted by successes from Swamp Thing to the "All-New, All-Different" X-Men, but few fans know that the award-winning writer and editor started out as a comic-book artist.

As a teenager, Wein was tied to the hip with fellow fanzine writer Marv Wolfman, regularly skipping school to tour the DC Comics offices. After building a rapport with artists and execs like Dick Giordano, Carmine Infantino and Joe Orlando, Wein was able to credibly pitch to the editors. Though his artwork was politely passed upon, a script for *House of Mystery* was accepted and a career as a writer was born. Len attacked his new occupation with gusto, writing for DC, Marvel, Gold Key and Skywald, on everything from Western to horror, and licensed properties from Hot Wheels to Star Trek.

Although his desired career as an artist didn't quite pan out, it did give Wein insight into his collaborator's creative process and helped him garner acclaim as a writer that was "easy to draw." After super-hero work in the early '70s (Daredevil, Superman, Flash), he and artist Bernie Wrightson launched horror mainstay Swamp Thing in the pages of *House of Secrets* #92. Other notable achievements from his tenure at DC include a run on *Justice League of America* and the debut of the Human Target.

Hopping over to Marvel in 1974, where he followed Roy Thomas as editor in chief, Wein scripted several series, including *Incredible Hulk*, where he and artist Herb Trimpe introduced one of comics' most famous characters—Wolverine. That wasn't the end of his mutant milestones, as with artist Dave Cockrum he revived the dormant X-Men property with a new international cast. Its cadre of characters, including Storm, Nightcrawler and Colossus would shortly turn into comics' biggest phenomenon.

Returning to DC, Wein helped spur a creative revival at the company, editing *New Teen Titans*, *Camelot 3000* and *Swamp Thing*, which gave writer Alan Moore his American debut; shortly thereafter, Wein would preside over Moore and Dave Gibbon's groundbreaking *Watchmen*. Since then, Wein's credits in comics, animation and television writing have been numerous and well received. He was inducted into the Eisner Hall of Fame in 2008 and passed away in 2017, leaving behind a creative legacy celebrated worldwide.

ROY THOMAS

Along with fellow fan Jerry Bails, Roy Thomas developed the first known organized comic fandom in the pages of *Alter Ego*, a self-published fanzine. Leaving his teaching position in 1965, Roy took his deep knowledge of comics characters and their history and moved to New York City, accepting a job under DC Comics editor Mort Weisinger. His stay lasted little over a week before he opted for a position at Marvel, where under Stan Lee, his duties quickly matured from proofreading to more serious work as an editorial assistant and writer.

Titles as disparate as *Modeling With Millie*, *Kid Colt* and *Sgt. Fury* were written under his auspices before he was able to fulfill his desire to write super-hero stories on Iron Man in *Tales of Suspense* #73 and a pair of Dr. Strange stories for *Strange Tales*.

Stan must have liked what he was reading, because after this seeming trial period, Roy "The Boy" (as he was called in credits) was given both *Sgt. Fury* and *The X-Men*. Along with artist Werner Roth, Thomas took the X-Men on adventures around the world and told the characters' pre-X-Men origins. In addition to introducing Banshee, Sunfire and Havok, Thomas' X-Men credits also include his watershed collaboration with artist Neal Adams.

Proving his mettle on *X-Men* led him to *The Avengers*, and it was with this team that Roy really started crafting his legacy. Across 70 consecutive issues of Earth's Mightiest Heroes, he became perhaps the title's definitive writer, introducing characters such as the Vision and penning classic sagas including the "Kree/Skrull War." Before the '60s ended, Thomas chalked up noteworthy runs as writer of *Doctor Strange*, *Sub-Mariner*, *Captain Marvel* and more.

In the '70s, Thomas' influence at Marvel widened to include the first adaptation of Robert E. Howard's *Conan the Barbarian,* a reinvention of Adam Warlock, and a new super-team, The Defenders. By 1972 Roy was selected to succeed Stan Lee as editor in chief. His tenure as EIC lasted for over two years before he returned to his writer/editor role on *Fantastic Four*, *Thor*, *Savage Sword of Conan*, *What If...?* and *The Invaders*.

In 1980, he left the House of Ideas for DC to pursue a lifelong dream by reviving the Justice Society of America in the pages of *All-Star Squadron*. He wrote many more comics for DC and Marvel over the next two decades and is still active today, writing comics, historical studies, adaptations of classic novels and publishing his award-winning *Alter Ego*. Thomas' career contributions were acknowledged with his induction into the Eisner Hall of Fame's 2011 class. He lives in South Carolina with his wife and collaborator, Dann, and an amazing menagerie of animals that must make the neighbors nervous.

WALTER SIMONSON

Walter Simonson mixed the power of Jack Kirby comics with an experimental European influence to produce a visual style that has made him one of his generation's foremost innovators.

After achieving acclaim for DC's "Manhunter" feature in *Detective Comics*, Simonson moved to Marvel's black-and-white magazine line where he illustrated an adaptation of Robert E. Howard's "The Hyborean Age" and penciled the first three issues of *Rampaging Hulk*. Next came a yearlong stint on *Thor* that would be far from his last encounter with the Asgardian hero. Simonson soon made a decisive shift to sci-fi. Adaptations of *Close Encounters of the Third Time* for Marvel and *Alien: The Illustrated Story* in *Heavy Metal* were followed by runs on *Battlestar Galactica*, which featured Simonson's first writing credits, and *Star Wars*. Simonson continued to develop his craft as a writer on Marvel's *Raiders of the Lost Ark* adaptation and *Marvel Graphic Novel #6: Star Slammers*, a concept revived from his art school days that he wrote, penciled and inked.

In 1982, Simonson teamed with writer Chris Claremont on the DC/Marvel crossover team-up of the X-Men and New Teen Titans. Shortly thereafter, he began his epochal run scripting and penciling *Thor*, the first issue of which introduced Beta Ray Bill and became one of the most highly acclaimed titles of the period. His collaboration with his wife, Louise, on *X-Factor* included the introduction of Archangel and Apocalypse. Later, the husband and wife team would write the *Havok & Wolverine: Meltdown* prestige miniseries.

In the early '90s, Simonson had a memorable run writing and drawing *Fantastic Four*. Other credits from this era included the *Iron Man: 2020* one-shot and *Avengers*. More recent work has included *Orion* at DC, *Elric: The Making of a Sorcerer* with Michael Moorcock and *Avengers* and *Indestructible Hulk* for Marvel.

JOHN BUSCEMA

Though primarily known for his long tenure as one of Marvel Comics' most prolific pencilers, John Buscema began his celebrated career at the age of 21 with Timely Comics. After Timely closed its in-house Bullpen, Buscema pursued comics work for a time before he left comics altogether for advertising in 1958.

When he returned to comics, however, he did so with a vengeance. Stan Lee recruited him away from advertising and quickly ensconced him into the upper ranks of Marvel artists. Picking up where *Avengers* mainstay Don Heck left off, "Big John" began what would be one of the title's definitive artistic runs. The much-anticipated *Silver Surfer* series was launched with Buscema at the helm, and top-tier books like *Fantastic Four* and *Thor* were entrusted to his care after Jack Kirby left Marvel for DC Comics.

Buscema's bold, muscular artwork commanded the comic-book page with realistic figurework that represented the next evolutionary step in post-Kirby Marvel Comics style. The respect accorded him within Marvel as an artist's artist was of such renown that he literally wrote the book on drawing, composing *How To Draw Comics the Marvel Way* with Stan Lee, the classic "how to" book in comic-book illustration.

He worked from the '70s through the '90s on nearly every title in the Marvel stable, including his personal favorite, *Conan the Barbarian*, with Roy Thomas. He retired in 1996, but returned every now and then to the comics scene until he passed away after a battle with cancer in 2002, the same year he was inducted into the Eisner Hall of Fame.

BILL MANTLO

From the mid-'70s through the late-'80s, Bill Mantlo established himself as one of the most dedicated writers in the comics industry, writing hundreds of stories across dozens of titles, primarily for Marvel Comics.

Mantlo broke into comics as a colorist, but it wasn't long before he was given a crack at writing a fill-in story, a "Sons of the Tiger" story in the black-and-white *Deadly Hands of Kung Fu* magazine, and his true comics talent began to emerge. The quality of his work led to his installation as that book's regular writer, a tenure that included the notable achievement of introducing comics' first Puerto Rican hero, the White Tiger.

After achieving notoriety within the Marvel offices as a guy who could knock out credible fill-in scripts at a moment's notice, Mantlo was given more regular work. One early highlight was his 20-issue tenure on *Iron Man* that began the Golden Avenger's return to prominence. As one might expect from someone with such a volume of work, Mantlo was game to take on projects others dismissed, and he did it with an unfeigned aplomb that elevated the work.

It was on two licensed titles that Mantlo built his legacy. Inspired by a toy given to his son at Christmas, Mantlo lobbied Marvel to adapt Micronauts into an ongoing series. The award-winning epic he spun with artistic luminaries like Michael Golden and Pat Broderick is still highly revered by comics fandom as is his even longer run on *Rom*, wherein he developed a universe filled with Spaceknights, Dire Wraith monsters and outer space intrigue. Other notable credits in Mantlo's career include *Incredible Hulk*, *Alpha Flight* and *Spectacular Spider-Man*.

Just as Mantlo had begun a new career as a public defender with the New York City Legal Aid Society, he was struck by a hit-and-run driver and went into a weeks-long coma from severe head trauma. He has since been under constant medical care. The comics community has led multiple fundraisers to aid in the continuing care of a talented writer who is missed by his many fans.

VAL MAYERIK

Val Mayerik was born in the steel town of Youngstown, Ohio, and worked in the mills to earn money for college. His artist friend and mentor Dan Adkins opened the door for him at Marvel, where he quickly found work drawing Thongor the Barbarian in *Creatures on the Loose*, as well as adaptations of John Jakes' Brak the Barbarian in *Chamber of Chills* and H.G. Wells' Invisible Man in *Supernatural Thrillers*. In addition to his regular work on Thongor, Mayerik illustrated the macabre Man-Thing in *Fear*, and would carry on drawing into the character's self-titled series in 1974. Mayerik quickly became a key contributor to Marvel's early '70s horror revival, augmenting his Man-Thing work with *Frankenstein* and the Living Mummy in *Supernatural Thrillers*. It was in the 19th issue of *Fear* that Mayerik would co-create one of comics' most unusual and memorable characters, Howard the Duck. In 1976, Mayerik began a six-issue stint drawing *Ka-Zar*, a title he would return to in 1982 for the "Tales of Zabu" backup. In between penciling assignments, Mayerik inked a host of comics as well. Mayerik also had an interest in acting, starring in the low-budget horror film *The Demon Lover* in 1977 and acting off-Broadway. By the early '90s, Mayerik was drawing various Punisher series and *Bruce Lee*, a six-issue 1994 series from Malibu, but he had begun to transition to work in advertising. He returned to comics in 2015 after successfully funding a Kickstarter initiative to draw *Of Dust and Blood*, an original graphic novel about Little Big Horn.

JIM STARLIN

When Jim Starlin came along in the early '70s, super-hero comics were populated primarily by earthbound heroes, but this young writer/artist revolutionized "cosmic" comics, a genre full of space-opera drama and high-minded philosophizing that required the expansive reaches of the universe to fully flourish.

Inspired as a young man by Jack Kirby and Steve Ditko, in 1972 Starlin followed fellow Detroiter Rich Buckler to Marvel. After assisting John Romita on Spider-Man and drawing covers, Starlin spun a short stint on *Iron Man*—

where he introduced Thanos and Drax the Destroyer – into the beginnings of an epic *Captain Marvel* saga that would redefine the character.

In late 1973, Starlin and writer Steve Englehart launched the first kung fu comic in the pages of *Special Marvel Edition*, and later in *Shang-Chi, Master of Kung Fu*. Then, in perhaps his most ambitious work to date, Jim revived Roy Thomas and Gil Kane's Adam Warlock, taking the messianic hero to mind-bending new heights. The short run on the cosmic character is still regarded as a high point of '70s Marvel.

By the late '70s, Starlin headed over to DC, but in 1982 he returned to Marvel for the *Death of Captain Marvel* graphic novel. Inspired by Starlin's compulsion to work through the death of his father, the story is considered to be his masterpiece. Soon after, *Dreadstar*, the debut title of Marvel's Epic line, introduced fans to Starlin's wholly original cosmic concept. Writing and drawing the adventures of Vanth Dreadstar as he fought against the monolithic vestiges of church and state, Starlin guided the series throughout a long and successful run. At DC, Starlin penned the milestone "A Death in the Family" in *Batman*, which culminated in Robin's demise; *Batman: The Cult* and *The Weird* with Bernie Wrightson; and *Cosmic Odyssey* with Mike Mignola.

In the early '90s, he took over writing *Silver Surfer* for a 17-issue run that reintroduced Thanos and Adam Warlock. At the same time, he wrote the first chapters in what would be a sprawling epic that would play out over the next 15 years with *The Thanos Quest*, *The Infinity Gauntlet*, *Infinity War* and *Infinity Crusade*. In 2001, Starlin would return to Warlock and Thanos in the *Infinity Abyss* and *Thanos*.

Recent projects include *Kid Kosmos* for Dynamite, *Death of the New Gods* and *Mystery In Space* for DC and a series of *Thanos* original graphic novels for Marvel.

Biographies researched and written by John Rhett Thomas

THE MARVEL MASTERWORKS

THE MARVEL MASTERWORKS LIBRARY PRESENTS THE WORLD'S GREATEST COMIC BOOKS, PAINSTAKINGLY RESTORED FROM THE HIGHEST-QUALITY SOURCES AND WITH THE MOST DILIGENT ARCHIVAL METHODS.

THE GOLDEN AGE

As the Great Depression wore on and the specter of war hung over America, a new storytelling medium was born: the comic book. Within their four-color pages, larger-than-life super heroes could make short work of America's foes, giving readers of all ages hope for victory against the real-life enemies that faced the United States. At the forefront of this new medium was Timely Comics, a young company staffed by such legendary creators as Carl Burgos, Bill Everett, Joe Simon, Jack Kirby and Stan Lee. These trailblazing talents birthed a vast array of characters that would give rise to the Marvel Universe!

GOLDEN AGE ALL-WINNERS VOLS. 1-4
GOLDEN AGE CAPTAIN AMERICA VOLS. 1-6
GOLDEN AGE DARING MYSTERY VOLS. 1-2
GOLDEN AGE HUMAN TORCH VOLS. 1-3
GOLDEN AGE MARVEL COMICS VOLS. 1-7
GOLDEN AGE MYSTIC COMICS VOL. 1
GOLDEN AGE SUB-MARINER VOLS. 1-3
GOLDEN AGE U.S.A. COMICS VOLS. 1-2
GOLDEN AGE YOUNG ALLIES VOLS. 1-2

THE ATLAS ERA

Seeing super heroes waning, Timely Comics evolved into Atlas Comics and took on a vast new range of genres: science-fiction tales of outer space adventures; realistic war comics; buxom jungle heroines; horror comics that would become the center of a moral panic that rocked the industry; and romance comics for the emerging teen audience. Even the classic costumed heroes of the Golden Age retooled to take on the threat of Communism. From Western gunfighters to crime to horror, the Atlas Era had it all!

ATLAS ERA BATTLEFIELD VOL. 1
ATLAS ERA BLACK KNIGHT/YELLOW CLAW VOL. 1
ATLAS ERA HEROES VOLS. 1-3
ATLAS ERA JOURNEY INTO MYSTERY VOLS. 1-4
ATLAS ERA JUNGLE ADVENTURE VOLS. 1-3
ATLAS ERA MENACE VOL. 1
ATLAS ERA STRANGE TALES VOLS. 1-6
ATLAS ERA TALES TO ASTONISH VOLS. 1-4
ATLAS ERA TALES OF SUSPENSE VOLS. 1-4
ATLAS ERA VENUS VOL. 1

THE MARVEL AGE

In August 1961, change hit newsstands: *The Fantastic Four* #1 did not feature the squeaky-clean heroes of yesteryear. They were real characters placed in extraordinary circumstances. They lived together, they fought among themselves — and sometimes, they even lost to the bad guys. This was more than a change in attitude: It was the beginning of something entirely different — the beginning of the Marvel Age of Comics!

Thanks to the fertile imaginations of Stan Lee, Jack Kirby, Steve Ditko and others, an unending list of heroes followed the FF with ever-increasing acclaim and popularity: the Amazing Spider-Man, the Mighty Thor, the Incredible Hulk, Daredevil, Iron Man and the X-Men, to name but a few. These were the Marvel heroes, born of conflict and a continuous struggle to balance human lives with superhuman responsibilities.

THE AMAZING SPIDER-MAN VOLS. 1-19
ANT-MAN/GIANT-MAN VOLS. 1-3
THE AVENGERS VOLS. 1-18
THE BLACK PANTHER VOLS. 1-2
CAPTAIN AMERICA VOLS. 1-10
CAPTAIN MARVEL VOLS. 1-6
THE CHAMPIONS VOL. 1
DAREDEVIL VOLS. 1-12
DEATHLOK VOL. 1
THE DEFENDERS VOLS. 1-6
DOCTOR STRANGE VOLS. 1-8
THE FANTASTIC FOUR VOLS. 1-20
THE HUMAN TORCH VOLS. 1-2
THE INCREDIBLE HULK VOLS. 1-12
THE INHUMANS VOLS. 1-2
THE INVINCIBLE IRON MAN VOLS. 1-11
IRON FIST VOLS. 1-2
KA-ZAR VOLS. 1-2
KILLRAVEN VOL. 1
LUKE CAGE VOLS. 1-2
MARVEL RARITIES VOL. 1
MARVEL TEAM-UP VOLS. 1-3
MARVEL TWO-IN-ONE VOLS. 1-3
THE MIGHTY THOR VOLS. 1-17
MS. MARVEL VOLS. 1-2
NICK FURY, AGENT OF S.H.I.E.L.D. VOLS. 1-3
NOT BRAND ECHH VOL. 1
RAWHIDE KID VOLS. 1-2
THE SAVAGE SHE-HULK VOL. 1
SGT. FURY VOLS. 1-4
THE SPECTACULAR SPIDER-MAN VOL. 1
SPIDER-WOMAN VOL. 1
THE SILVER SURFER VOLS. 1-2
THE SUB-MARINER VOLS. 1-8
WARLOCK VOLS. 1-2
THE X-MEN VOLS. 1-8
THE UNCANNY X-MEN VOLS. 1-10